I0882238

Artificial Intelligence Approaches to Sustainable Accounting

Maria C. Tavares
ISCA, University of Aveiro, Portugal

Graça Azevedo
University of Aveiro, Portugal

José Vale
ISCAP, Polytechnic Institute of Porto, Portugal

Rui Marques
University of Aveiro, Portugal

Maria Anunciação Bastos
ISCA, University of Aveiro, Portugal

IGI Global
PUBLISHER of TIMELY KNOWLEDGE

A volume in the Advances in Finance, Accounting, and Economics (AFAE) Book Series

Published in the United States of America by
IGI Global
Business Science Reference (an imprint of IGI Global)
701 E. Chocolate Avenue
Hershey PA, USA 17033
Tel: 717-533-8845
Fax: 717-533-8661
E-mail: cust@igi-global.com
Web site: http://www.igi-global.com

Library of Congress Cataloging-in-Publication Data

Names: Tavares, Maria C., 1969- editor. | Azevedo, Graça Maria do Carmo, editor. | Vale, José, 1975- editor. | Marques, Rui Pedro Figueiredo, editor. | Bastos, Maria Anunciação, 1981- editor.
Title: Artificial intelligence approaches to sustainable accounting / edited by Maria Tavares, Graça Azevedo, José Vale, Rui Pedro Marques, Maria Anunciação Bastos.
Description: Hershey, PA : Business Science Reference, [2024] | Includes bibliographical references and index. | Summary: "The book analyzes the role of accounting and AI technologies in promoting sustainability"-- Provided by publisher.
Identifiers: LCCN 2023051996 (print) | LCCN 2023051997 (ebook) | ISBN 9798369308479 (hardcover) | ISBN 9798369308486 (ebook)
Subjects: LCSH: Sustainable development--Accounting. | Sustainable development reporting. | Artificial intelligence. | Accounting--Technological innovations.
Classification: LCC HD60.3 .A78 2024 (print) | LCC HD60.3 (ebook) | DDC 658.4/083--dc23/eng/20240125
LC record available at https://lccn.loc.gov/2023051996
LC ebook record available at https://lccn.loc.gov/2023051997

This book is published in the IGI Global book series Advances in Finance, Accounting, and Economics (AFAE) (ISSN: 2327-5677; eISSN: 2327-5685)

British Cataloguing in Publication Data
A Cataloguing in Publication record for this book is available from the British Library.

All work contributed to this book is new, previously-unpublished material. The views expressed in this book are those of the authors, but not necessarily of the publisher.

For electronic access to this publication, please contact: eresources@igi-global.com.

Advances in Finance, Accounting, and Economics (AFAE) Book Series

Ahmed Driouchi
Al Akhawayn University, Morocco

ISSN:2327-5677
EISSN:2327-5685

Mission

In our changing economic and business environment, it is important to consider the financial changes occurring internationally as well as within individual organizations and business environments. Understanding these changes as well as the factors that influence them is crucial in preparing for our financial future and ensuring economic sustainability and growth.

The **Advances in Finance, Accounting, and Economics (AFAE)** book series aims to publish comprehensive and informative titles in all areas of economics and economic theory, finance, and accounting to assist in advancing the available knowledge and providing for further research development in these dynamic fields.

Coverage

- Evidence-Based Studies
- International Trade
- Finance and Accounting in SMEs
- Comparative Accounting Systems
- Entrepreneurship in Accounting and Finance
- Theoretical Issues in Economics, Finance, and Accounting
- Ethics in Accounting and Finance
- Finance
- Labor Economics
- E-Finance

IGI Global is currently accepting manuscripts for publication within this series. To submit a proposal for a volume in this series, please contact our Acquisition Editors at Acquisitions@igi-global.com or visit: http://www.igi-global.com/publish/.

The Advances in Finance, Accounting, and Economics (AFAE) Book Series (ISSN 2327-5677) is published by IGI Global, 701 E. Chocolate Avenue, Hershey, PA 17033-1240, USA, www.igi-global.com. This series is composed of titles available for purchase individually; each title is edited to be contextually exclusive from any other title within the series. For pricing and ordering information please visit http://www.igi-global.com/book-series/advances-finance-accounting-economics/73685. Postmaster: Send all address changes to above address.

Titles in this Series

For a list of additional titles in this series, please visit:
http://www.igi-global.com/book-series/advances-finance-accounting-economics/73685

Financial Inclusion, Sustainability, and the Influence of Religion and Technology
Awais Ur Rehman (Faculty of Management Sciences, University of Central Punjab, Pakistan) and Arsalan Haneef Malik (College of Business Management, Department of Accounting and Finance, Institute of Business Management (IoBM), Karachi, Pakistan)
Business Science Reference • © 2024 • 324pp • H/C (ISBN: 9798369314753) • US $270.00

Recent Developments in Financial Management and Economics
Abdelkader Mohamed Sghaier Derbali (Taibah University, Saudi Arabia)
Business Science Reference • © 2024 • 436pp • H/C (ISBN: 9798369326831) • US $325.00

Issues of Sustainability in AI and New-Age Thematic Investing
Mohammad Irfan (NSB Academy, India) Khaled Hussainey (University of Portsmouth, UK) Syed Ahmad Chan Bukhari (St. John's University, USA) and Yunyoung Nam (Department of Computer Science and Engineering, Soonchunhyang University, South Korea)
Business Science Reference • © 2024 • 295pp • H/C (ISBN: 9798369332825) • US $325.00

Exploring Central Bank Digital Currencies Concepts, Frameworks, Models, and Challenges
Guneet Kaur (University of Stirling, UK) Pooja Lekhi (University Canada West, Canada) and Simriti Popli (Kaplan International College, UK)
Business Science Reference • © 2024 • 359pp • H/C (ISBN: 9798369318829) • US $325.00

Harnessing Blockchain-Digital Twin Fusion for Sustainable Investments
Syed Hasan Jafar (Woxsen University, India) Raul Villamarin Rodriguez (Woxsen University, India) Hemachandran Kannan (Woxsen University, India) Shakeb Akhtar (Woxsen University, India) and Philipp Plugmann (SRH Hochschule für Gesundheit Gera, Germany)
Business Science Reference • © 2024 • 441pp • H/C (ISBN: 9798369318782) • US $290.00

Harnessing Technology for Knowledge Transfer in Accountancy, Auditing, and Finance
Samuel Kwok (Xi'an Jiaotong-Liverpool University, China) Mohamed Omran (Xi'an Jiaotong-Liverpool University, China) and Poshan Yu (Xi'an Jiaotong-Liverpool University, China & European Business University of Luxembourg, Luxembourg)
Business Science Reference • © 2024 • 279pp • H/C (ISBN: 9798369313312) • US $275.00

IGI Global
PUBLISHER of TIMELY KNOWLEDGE

701 East Chocolate Avenue, Hershey, PA 17033, USA
Tel: 717-533-8845 x100 • Fax: 717-533-8661
E-Mail: cust@igi-global.com • www.igi-global.com

Table of Contents

Detailed Table of Contents

Through a comprehensive bibliometric analysis, this chapter aims to explore the intersection between accounting, sustainability, and artificial intelligence (AI), examining the temporal evolution of publications in the field of business, management and accounting. Trends, emerging themes, and knowledge gaps are identified, providing a panoramic view of the current research landscape. The results reveal a growing convergence between accounting, sustainability, and AI, indicating a growing interest in these domains when considered as a whole. They also show that most studies are co-authored and have an article-type nature. This chapter contributes to the knowledge and understanding of the scientific production that crosses the area of accounting for sustainability and AI, towards the Sustainable Development Goals. It offers valuable insights for academics, providing a solid understanding of research streams and promising future directions at the intersection of accounting, sustainability, and AI. It also guides practitioners in decision-making and policy formulation.

There are several problems with the use of AI within the scope of criminal law, which the authors will not address in order not to escape the core of this chapter, but which are essentially related to how to criminalize actions carried out by computer software. Is the aforementioned software eradicated, as a "capital punishment", repairing the evil it committed or could its creator be held criminally liable for the acts that resulted from its creation? Therefore, the authors analyze the use of AI in criminal investigation and the possibilities offered by its use in the analysis and detection of profiles in organized crime, such as in the prevention and investigation of terrorist events, among other situations.

The world is on the cusp of entering a new era of artificial intelligence, and it has become necessary to develop laws. Artificial intelligence is one of the most critical topics for criminal law jurists, given that there is a need to establish legal rules commensurate with the nature of this technology that is expected to prevail worldwide. The problem of the study is the lack of a legal framework that regulates the uses of artificial intelligence and shows the criminal rules that should be applied. The chapter aims to introduce the applications of artificial intelligence, its fields, advantages, and its expected impact during the next stage, highlighting the proposed rules of criminal law to regulate the use of artificial intelligence and discussing the appropriate penalties proposed to be applied. The study recommended the international community develop a global framework governing the use of artificial intelligence technologies, calling national legislators to set rules that regulate the use of artificial intelligence and determine appropriate penalties in case of misuse.

Agriculture is a backbone for the monetary situation of a country. But plant disease is the principle drawback of agriculture because it reduces the first-class and amount of agriculture products. Disease detection through guide approach is highly priced and time consuming. To reap the most yield from the agriculture area, it is required that farmers need to be provided with the excellent era and methodologies. In this case, artificial intelligence is one of the era used significantly due to its capacity to perceive the issues, developing the proper motives for that, and to establish most appropriate answers for it. Artificial intelligence can act as a useful resource in addressing the illnesses of plants. The present review offers a short compare of the software of artificial intelligence in agriculture, its available techniques for agriculture, and highlights several strategies for the detection of plant disease in plant life.

Artificial intelligence can greatly assist accounting professionals in information management, streamlining processes, and improving overall efficiency. AI-powered software can automate data entry tasks by extracting relevant information from documents, such as invoices, receipts, and bank statements. AI algorithms can analyze financial data and identify patterns or anomalies indicative of fraud or financial irregularities. AI can analyze historical financial data and market trends to provide predictive insights, helping businesses anticipate future financial challenges and opportunities. Human accountants will continue to play a vital role in interpreting AI-generated insights, making strategic decisions, and maintaining a human touch in client interactions. Based on the above, it is intended to systematically review the bibliometric literature on how artificial intelligence can help accounting in information management using the Scopus database to analyse 77 academic and/or scientific documents

This study aims to assess the impacts that cryptocurrencies and blockchain have on financial accounting and auditing through eight interviews. The results allowed the authors to conclude that cryptocurrencies are considered cryptoassets, which can be classified in different ways, but above all, as inventories and intangible assets. Respondents believe that cryptocurrencies will have an impact on auditing, triggering a dematerialization of paper in its various stages. Therefore, the auditor will spend less time collecting and verifying information, focusing on activities with greater risk and complexity. It will also be possible to carry out an audit in real time and on the entire population. Regarding audit risk, accounting and auditing standards respond indirectly to the topic, yet the risk is considered high for most auditors, as they did not deepen their knowledge on the topic. Despite limitations, such as sample size, this study contributes to understanding the impact of cryptocurrencies on financial accounting and auditing in Portugal, being a pioneer in this field.

This chapter provides a comprehensive analysis of the impact of machine learning on the specific domains of financial accounting and management accounting. By tracing the historical evolution, conceptually delineating key parameters, and systematizing various modalities of machine learning, the investigation highlights the notable advancements it engenders in financial management. The study underscores the central role of machine learning in automating processes, optimizing decision-making, and generating innovative analytical perspectives, while identifying ethical concerns inherent in its implementation, such as algorithmic transparency and data preservation. This research is based on a literature review approach using a descriptive analytical method. In conclusion, machine learning emerges as a significant driver of progress in the accounting domain, redefining professional standards and necessitating ethical management to fully capitalize on its benefits while minimizing potential risks.

The rise of cloud computing, internet of things, and information technology has made big data technology a common concern for many professionals and researchers. A financial risk control model, known as the MSHDS-RS model, was creatively suggested in response to the present state of inappropriate feature data design in big data risk control technology. The concept is built on multi source heterogeneous data structure (MSHDS) and random subspace (RS). This model is novel in that it uses a normalized sparse model for feature fusion optimization to create integrated features after extracting the hard and soft features from loan customer information sources. Subsequently, a base classifier is trained on the feature subset acquired via probability sampling, and its output is combined and refined by the application of evidence reasoning principles. The accuracy improvement rate of the MSHDS-RS method is approximately 3.0% and 3.6% higher than that of the current PMB-RS methods under the conditions of soft feature indicators and integrated feature indicators, respectively, according to an observation of the operation results of MSHDS-RS models under various feature sets. As a result, the suggested optimization fusion approach is trustworthy and workable. This study has helped to reduce financial risks associated with the internet and may be useful in helping lenders make wise judgments.

The theme of artificial intelligence has sparked significant discussion and interest across all fields, and auditing is no exception. Therefore, this study aims to assess the perceptions of auditing professionals regarding the influence of artificial intelligence in auditing. For this, interviews were conducted with 14 auditing professionals. The results demonstrate that despite the current limited presence of artificial intelligence in auditing, there is a perception that its implementation will be inevitable. It is also concluded that the primary effect of using artificial intelligence in auditing is enhancing audit process efficiency. This study allows the authors to foresee the paradigm shift in auditing, constituting an essential contribution to academia, but essentially, to professional auditing bodies, in defining their change strategy.

This chapter examines how artificial intelligence (AI) is affecting the accounting sector with a particular emphasis on Lebanon. It examines the significant shifts that brought about information and communications technology (ICT)-based technologies and automation, in addition to the historical changes in accounting. The combination of AI awareness and accounting automation has resulted in a significant revolution in the industry, which has boosted AI-powered accounting education. The chapter suggests ongoing AI advancements as well as proactive cooperation between accountants and accounting companies in order to increase the effectiveness and efficiency of accounting procedures. AI can cut expenses and free up accountants' time so they may focus on making decisions using analytics and data. However, the Middle Eastern accounting sector is confronted with a number of potential risks, such as the loss of jobs, the spread of artificial intelligence in the sector, the decline in human bias, the impact on accounting education, and the recurrence of past accounting mishaps.

The challenges that the accounting sector is facing in the modern era of globalization, digital technology, and artificial intelligence (AI) are addressed in this chapter. The authors achieve this by prioritizing social sustainability. One of the most important technological advancements that have drastically changed society is globalization. Additionally covered in this chapter are the significance of non-financial reporting and data quality, strategies for integrating sustainability within company operations, and management and governance ideals that promote sustainable development.

The sustainability of the accounting profession is starting to be questioned. Will it still exist, or will it be replaced by technology? This chapter will provide a literature review on the relationship between accounting and artificial intelligence and harmonize them to maintain the sustainability of the accounting profession in Indonesia. The authors conducted this literature review process using the bibliometric analysis method and described it by embedding several assumptions from various literature opinions. In the end, according to the authors' point of view, the accountant profession will not be completely displaced by technology, but the presence of technology will actually facilitate the work of accountants, so that all processes are carried out by system and not manually. This shorter way will produce more accurate, faster, and less workforce output. Meanwhile, the presence of technology can also reduce the need for human resources (accountants). Nevertheless, the emergence of technology also opens up opportunities for the accounting profession with new technology-related expertise, such as digital forensic accounting, environmental management accounting/green accountant, and information systems-based auditing. The green accountant is an accountant who performs green accounting practices. Therefore, the scope of accounting today is no longer limited to financial matters, but also includes social and environmental matters. This integration of financial, social, and environmental accounting is called green accounting.

This chapter aims to contribute to the understanding of how artificial intelligence (AI) technologies can promote increased business revenues, cost reductions, and enhanced customer experience, as well as society´s well-being in a sustainable way. However, these AI benefits also come with risks and challenges concerning organizations, the environment, customers, and society, which need further investigation. This chapter also examines and discusses how AI can either enable or inhibit the delivery of the goals recognized in the UN 2030 Agenda for Sustainable Business Models Development. In this chapter, the authors conduct a bibliometric review of the emerging literature on artificial intelligence (AI) technologies implications on sustainable business models (SBM), in the perspective of Sustainable Development Goals (SDGs) and investigate research spanning the areas of AI, and SDGs within the economic group. The authors examine an effective sample of 69 publications from 49 different journals, 225 different institutions, and 47 different countries. On the basis of the bibliometric analysis, this study selected the most significant published sources and examined the changes that have occurred in the conceptual framework of AI and SBM in light of SDGs research. This chapter makes some significant contributions to the literature by presenting a detailed bibliometric analysis of the research on the impacts of AI on SBM, enhancing the understanding of the knowledge structure of this research topic and helping to identify key knowledge gaps and future challenges.

Preface

In this rapidly evolving era marked by globalization and unprecedented technological advancements, the intersection of artificial intelligence (AI) and sustainable accounting emerges as a critical focal point for addressing the pressing challenges facing our planet and society. As editors of *Artificial Intelligence Approaches to Sustainable Accounting*, we are honored to present this comprehensive reference book, which reflects the collective efforts of esteemed scholars and practitioners dedicated to advancing sustainability through innovative AI-driven approaches.

Our aim in compiling this volume is to catalyze international discourse and collaboration surrounding the transition to a New Era characterized by sustainable development. We recognize the imperative for a transdisciplinary approach that transcends traditional boundaries, uniting diverse fields in pursuit of shared objectives outlined in the Sustainable Development Goals (SDGs). At the heart of this endeavor lies the pivotal role of accounting and accountability in navigating the complexities of sustainability challenges.

In the context of Era 5.0, where the synergies between AI, industry, education, and society are reshaping the landscape, it becomes increasingly evident that conventional paradigms must adapt to meet the demands of a rapidly changing world. By harnessing the power of AI technologies, organizations can enhance their capacity to promote sustainability across all facets of operation, from governance and decision-making to reporting and risk management.

The chapters contained within this volume offer a nuanced exploration of key themes, ranging from the integration of AI in sustainable accounting practices to the implications for organizational governance and the broader socio-economic landscape. Through rigorous analysis and empirical evidence, contributors shed light on the effectiveness and efficiency of sustainability initiatives, while also critically examining the theoretical underpinnings that inform our understanding of this complex domain.

In Chapter 1, the authors conduct a comprehensive bibliometric analysis to explore the dynamic intersection of accounting, sustainability, and Artificial Intelligence (AI). By tracing the temporal evolution of publications in the field of Business, Management & Accounting, trends, emerging themes, and knowledge gaps are identified, offering a panoramic view of the current research landscape. The findings reveal a growing convergence between accounting, sustainability, and AI, underscoring the increasing interest in these domains as a cohesive entity. This chapter provides valuable insights for academics, guiding future research directions, while also offering practical implications for decision-makers and policy formulation.

Chapter 2 delves into the complex terrain of criminal law and the utilization of AI, particularly in criminal investigation. By examining the potential of AI in analyzing and detecting profiles in organized crime, as well as its role in preventing and investigating terrorist events, the chapter navigates through the intricacies of AI application within the criminal justice system. While acknowledging the challenges and ethical considerations, the authors offer critical insights into the opportunities and possibilities presented by AI in enhancing law enforcement efforts.

In Chapter 3, the focus shifts to the imperative of developing legal frameworks commensurate with the rapid advancements in artificial intelligence. The authors highlight the pressing need for establishing robust regulations governing the use of AI technologies, particularly within the realm of criminal law. Through a meticulous examination of AI applications, proposed rules, and appropriate penalties, the chapter advocates for international collaboration in crafting a cohesive global framework. By addressing the gaps in current legislation, this chapter lays the groundwork for fostering responsible AI deployment while mitigating potential risks.

Chapter 4 explores the transformative potential of artificial intelligence in agriculture, particularly in disease detection and management. By harnessing AI technologies, farmers can effectively identify and address plant diseases, thereby enhancing agricultural productivity and quality. The chapter provides a comprehensive overview of AI applications in agriculture, highlighting various detection methods and technological advancements. By leveraging AI's capacity for problem-solving and decision-making, this chapter underscores its pivotal role in promoting sustainable agricultural practices.

In Chapter 5, the authors delve into the symbiotic relationship between artificial intelligence and accounting. By examining AI's capabilities in information management, process optimization, and fraud detection, the chapter illuminates the transformative impact of AI on accounting practices. Through a systematic review of bibliometric literature, the authors elucidate AI's role in enhancing accounting efficiency and decision-making processes, while also emphasizing the continued importance of human expertise in interpreting AI-generated insights.

Chapter 6 delves into the implications of cryptocurrencies and blockchain technology on financial accounting and auditing practices. Through interviews and analysis, the authors explore the classification of cryptocurrencies, their impact on auditing processes, and the potential for real-time auditing. By shedding light on these emerging technologies' influence on financial reporting and audit risk, the chapter offers valuable insights into navigating the evolving landscape of digital assets.

In Chapter 7, the focus shifts to machine learning's transformative effects on financial and management accounting domains. Through a comprehensive analysis, the authors delineate machine learning's historical evolution, its applications in automating processes, and its ethical considerations. By synthesizing existing literature, the chapter underscores machine learning's potential to revolutionize accounting practices while advocating for ethical management to harness its benefits responsibly.

Chapter 8 explores the integration of big data technologies and financial risk control, particularly in the context of cloud computing and the Internet of Things. The authors introduce the MSHDS-RS model as a novel solution for feature data design in big data risk control technology, highlighting its potential to optimize financial risk management. Through a detailed exposition of the model's architecture and functionality, the chapter offers insights into leveraging big data technologies for effective risk mitigation.

Chapter 9 delves into the perceptions of auditing professionals regarding the influence of artificial intelligence on auditing practices. Through interviews, the authors uncover insights into AI's perceived impact on audit process efficiency and its inevitability in shaping the future of auditing. By elucidating these perspectives, the chapter contributes to academia and professional auditing bodies, informing strategic approaches to incorporating AI into audit methodologies.

In Chapter 10, the authors examine the evolving landscape of the accounting sector in Lebanon amidst the rise of artificial intelligence. By analyzing the transformative effects of ICT-based technologies and automation on accounting practices, the chapter underscores the need for proactive cooperation between accountants and AI-powered solutions. Through a critical examination of potential risks and opportunities, the chapter offers strategic recommendations for navigating the evolving accounting landscape.

Chapter 11 tackles the challenges and opportunities presented by globalization, digital technology, and artificial intelligence in the accounting sector. By prioritizing social sustainability, the authors advocate for integrating sustainability principles within accounting operations and governance frameworks. Through a holistic examination of non-financial reporting, data quality, and management ideals, the chapter offers a roadmap for fostering sustainable development within the accounting profession.

In Chapter 12, the authors conduct a literature review on the harmonization of accounting and artificial intelligence to sustain the accounting profession in Indonesia. Through bibliometric analysis and theoretical synthesis, the chapter elucidates the transformative potential of technology in augmenting accounting practices. By identifying emerging expertise areas and skill sets, the chapter offers insights into future-proofing the accounting profession amidst technological advancements.

Chapter 13 offers a parallel literature review on the relationship between accounting and artificial intelligence, focusing on sustaining the accounting profession in Indonesia. By embedding various assumptions from literature opinions, the chapter outlines the evolving role of technology in facilitating accounting processes. By highlighting emerging expertise areas and opportunities, the chapter underscores the need for embracing technological advancements while ensuring professional sustainability.

In Chapter 14, the authors explore the nexus between taxation, innovation, and sustainable development goals (SDGs). Through a comprehensive literature review, the chapter examines the effects of taxation on innovation and its implications for achieving SDGs. By identifying both positive and negative impacts, the chapter underscores the pivotal role of taxation in driving technological advancements and fostering sustainable solutions to global challenges.

As editors, we extend our gratitude to the authors whose insights and expertise have enriched this compilation. We are confident that their contributions will resonate with a diverse audience, including regulators, researchers, public and private organizations, managers, educators, and students alike. Moreover, we envision this book as a catalyst for future research endeavors, inspiring a new generation of scholars to explore the dynamic intersection of AI, sustainability, and accounting.

In closing, we invite readers to embark on a journey through the pages of "Artificial Intelligence Approaches to Sustainable Accounting," recognizing the transformative potential of collaborative efforts in shaping a more equitable, resilient, and sustainable future for generations to come.

Maria C. Tavares
ISCA, University of Aveiro, Portugal

Graça Azevedo
University of Aveiro, Portugal

José Vale
ISCAP, Polytechnic Institute of Porto, Portugal

Rui Marques
University of Aveiro, Portugal

Maria Anunciação Bastos
ISCA, University of Aveiro, Portugal

Chapter 1
The Intersection Between Accounting, Sustainability, and AI:
A Bibliometric Analysis

Maria C. Tavares
https://orcid.org/0000-0002-6077-6359
University of Aveiro, Portugal

José Vale
https://orcid.org/0000-0001-8406-0462
Polytechnic Institute of Porto, Portugal

ABSTRACT

Through a comprehensive bibliometric analysis, this chapter aims to explore the intersection between accounting, sustainability, and artificial intelligence (AI), examining the temporal evolution of publications in the field of business, management and accounting. Trends, emerging themes, and knowledge gaps are identified, providing a panoramic view of the current research landscape. The results reveal a growing convergence between accounting, sustainability, and AI, indicating a growing interest in these domains when considered as a whole. They also show that most studies are co-authored and have an article-type nature. This chapter contributes to the knowledge and understanding of the scientific production that crosses the area of accounting for sustainability and AI, towards the Sustainable Development Goals. It offers valuable insights for academics, providing a solid understanding of research streams and promising future directions at the intersection of accounting, sustainability, and AI. It also guides practitioners in decision-making and policy formulation.

INTRODUCTION

In the last decade, the need for "artificial intelligence" systems, a term used by John McCarthy in 1956 in a research project at Dartmouth (McCarthy et al., 2006; Dhamija & Bag, 2020), has been increasing in organisations. As accounting is based on daily business and commercial transactions, all AI-based

DOI: 10.4018/979-8-3693-0847-9.ch001

software reduces task time, leaving humans to solve other accounting and management tasks (Khan et al., 2023). Hence, in recent years, the convergence of accounting, sustainability and artificial intelligence (AI) has stood out as a dynamic and constantly evolving field of research. Interest in this field has been driven by the need to address complex challenges, such as integrating sustainable practices into accounting operations and applying advanced technologies, such as artificial intelligence, to improve responsible and sustainable organisational decision-making.

In 2015, the United Nations Sustainable Development Summit launched the SDGs, adopting a universal approach to the Sustainable Development Agenda (Agenda 2030), ushering in a new era of global development goals to solve the world's most pressing problems. Also, since 2015, the progress of AI has been rapidly increasing, contributing to the development of accounting firms and other organisations due to less human capacity and lower chances of errors (Khan et al., 2023). Understanding the implications of AI for sustainability is key, as harnessing these technologies shapes operations and policies that can promote sustainable digitalisation and automation practices (Ghobakhloo et al., 2023). AI has a significant impact on most social and economic sectors and this effect is expected to increase in the near future (Zhao & Fariñas, 2023).

While the integration of AI in the implementation of the SDGs represents a modern and effective approach to tackling the complex challenges of sustainable development, accounting plays a fundamental and comprehensive role in implementing the SDGs. Accounting can play a crucial role in the SDG agenda, namely by helping to measure the impact of organisational activities, monitoring the progress and effectiveness of sustainable initiatives, transparently reporting the impact of activities, integrating sustainability criteria into decision-making, and promoting sustainable organisational practices.

Using AI capabilities in accounting practices makes it possible to strengthen efforts to achieve the goals outlined by the international community at the United Nations Sustainable Development Summit through innovative approaches and advanced technologies. AI enables accounting to transform the way organisations measure, monitor, report and manage their performance. AI facilitates and enables efficient data analysis and sharing between organisations and countries, which promotes global collaboration to achieve the SDGs through accounting for sustainability. Sustainability accounting can help organisations achieve the SDGs (Scarpellini, 2022). IA can be applied to increase the effectiveness and efficiency of corporate social responsibility (CSR) programmes (Zhao & Fariñas, 2023). However, as technology and new techniques become increasingly popular in the field of accounting, successful application will require different skills from those taught in business schools (Agustí & Orta-Pérez, 2023).

In the literature, there is research into accounting with different disciplines. For accounting researchers, knowledge of potential new areas or areas that have lost importance becomes crucial. Major key questions in the literature are still awaiting answers (Aluísta, 2023). On the one hand, companies' technological, organisational, environmental and human resource contexts impact the implementation of AI (Ghobakhloo et al., 2023). On the other hand, IA has contributed positively to poverty reduction and has helped social protection and the accumulation of benefits. However, at the current rate of AI growth, in some cases in both emerging and developing countries, economic and social inequalities have increased due to the proliferation of digital technologies. AI disrupts the markets of emerging and developing countries but creates wealth for developed countries (Meitei et al., 2023).When defining the focus of this study, we found the confluence of three themes: accounting, sustainability, and AI, associated with our line of research. Over time, we have observed a change in research priorities in the field of accounting. Specifically, research has been reflecting the growing global awareness of environmental, social and sustainability issues, well leveraged by the SDGs and technological advances, particularly

AI. Through a comprehensive cross-bibliometric, this chapter aims to provide a panoramic view of the current research landscape regarding the intersection between accounting, sustainability, and AI. In so doing, the scientific output published between 2009 and 2023 in the relevant academic database Scopus and filtered by subject area Business, Management and Accounting, is analysed. Scientific production, represented by the number of publications, serves as a quantitative indicator of this evolution.

Several studies in these areas use bibliometric analysis (see Agustí & Orta-Pérez, 2023; Aliusta, 2023; Jannah et al., 2023; Merigó & Yang, 2017; Mishra et al., 2023; Khan et al., 2023), but few have crossed these three themes. Khan et al. (2023) conclude that AI will not replace accountants, but these professionals should identify areas where financial performance could be improved, resulting in better decision-making. The various technologies offer the opportunity to drive success and accelerate progress in achieving many SDGs (Teh & Rana, 2023). Future studies should diagnose what creates problems in AI's progress in business and accounting, which should increasingly be seen as a cross-cutting area. Tavares et al. (2023) referred to the need for educational institutions and different communities to interact in the process of change, creating synergies that guarantee the successful retraining of professionals in the field, who are essential for sustainable organisations and a sustainable society. In addition, Ghobakhloo et al. (2023) point out that the organisational implementation and sustainability performance of this emerging technological innovation - AI - has been little studied despite AI representing the future of business automation. Our study seeks to fill this gap.

The first article published regarding the three domains, indexed in the Scopus database, dates back to 2000. Since then, the number has been growing, particularly since 2015, accelerating from 2019 to 2023.

Research based on crossing these three domains leads to a significant number of papers but to very poor results when we cross the three complete words. Still, very few references cross this field. Given the role of sustainability accounting in this new era of digital transformation and AI, it is increasingly relevant and important to know what is being researched. Given the global objectives and challenges organisations and society want to achieve, the conclusions and contributions of this chapter are significant for academics, organisations, policymakers and citizens in general. To do so, the current state of research in the field is depicted, and a framework that can guide the state of the art and future studies is provided.

The rest of the chapter is organised as follows: the research design is described in section two, section three presents the results and analysis, and finally, in section four, the discussion is depicted and some concluding remarks are offered.

RESEARCH DESIGN

Sources

This study is based on a quantitative and statistical approach that takes as a reference bibliometric indicator of scientific production according to their impact in the Scopus database. In addition to exposing unlikely perspectives for quantitative research methods and the research environment, bibliometric tools and procedures also help to distinguish their categories in published reviews (Khan et al., 2023). In this sense, bibliometric review studies use the main articles, authors, journals, institutions, countries/regions and keywords as their main indicators (Llanos-Herrera & Merigo, 2019).

Bibliometric techniques have been used mainly by information scientists to study the growth and distribution of scientific literature. Pritchard (1969) defined bibliometrics as the application of mathematical and statistical methods to books and other media (Lievrouw, 1989). Bibliometrics is a set of methods for measuring the academic impact of research publications. It can be easily scaled from the micro level (author, article, journal) to the macro level (subject area, country, world) (Chung et al., 2015). In order to achieve the objective of this study, a bibliometric analysis was carried out using the Scopus database. There is a growing tendency to use this database for this type of analysis, which makes it possible to explore, organise and evaluate a research topic by identifying the subjects that have received the most attention and evaluating the characteristics and impact of the articles published. It allows for a better understanding of the topic of study, as well as identifying trends and gaps in academic research (Baker et al. 2020; Rajan et al. 2020). Although this type of analysis cuts across all scientific fields, bibliometric studies predominate in the social sciences. The main objective of this methodology is to identify, organise and analyse the main components of a specific field of research (Lievrouw, 1989) in order to evaluate and measure different aspects related to publications.

This analysis allows us to get to know the scientific production published in a recognised database and analyse its contributions, conclusions and directions for future research developments. From then until now, the number of this type of work has been constantly on the rise, surpassing 3,000 references in 2021 alone. There is a growing trend towards using this database for this type of analysis. Although this type of analysis cuts across all scientific fields, bibliometric studies predominate in the social sciences.

Data Collection

Based on the SCOPUS database, the bibliometric analysis was carried out at the beginning of 27 January 2024. In the first instance, the search was conducted by using the terms "accounting" and "sustainability" and "artificial intelligence" or "ai" in the articles, title, abstract and keywords. Without applying any filter, 66 documents were obtained in a wide variety of areas, with only 21 in the "Business, Management & Accounting" area, followed by Engineering, with 26 documents. This fact shows the transversality of research in the field of AI and accounting for sustainability. Then, considering that relevant documents could be left out, it was decided to broaden the field of terminology. To do so, two search strategies were followed (see Table 1). The criteria used in the first search strategy was the adoption of the following terms: "account*" and "sustainab*" or "sdg" and "artificial intelligence" or "ai", in the articles, title, abstract and keywords (see Table 1 – 1st survey). This first strategy only aimed to map the scientific field (see section 3.1). In the second search strategy, the same keywords were adopted and only. However, a filter for the subject area "Business, Management & Accounting" was applied in this case (see Table 1 – 2nd survey). This second strategy, which led to a final sample of 102 articles, was used in this chapter.

During the period under analysis (2000-2023), it is also possible to assess whether research has increased since 2015, the year of the publication of the United Nations 2030 Agenda and the progress of AI.

BIBLIOMETRIC ANALYSIS OF THE RESEARCH

Bibliometric analysis is a valuable approach for researchers, academics and professionals and plays a crucial role in scientific research. It offers several significant contributions and benefits to the academic and scientific community since it provides an objective and quantifiable understanding of the state of research in a given area by examining the temporal evolution of publications in this field, identifying trends, emerging themes, knowledge gaps and future research directions.

Table 1. Scopus search strategy

Source	Scopus: TITLE-ABS-KEY 1st Survey
Keywords	(TITLE-ABS-KEY (account*) AND TITLE-ABS-KEY (sustainab*) OR TITLE-ABS-KEY (sdg) AND TITLE-ABS-KEY (artificial AND intelligence) OR TITLE-ABS-KEY (ai)) AND PUBYEAR > 1999 AND PUBYEAR < 2024
Results	702 documents
Source	Scopus: TITLE-ABS-KEY 2nd survey
Keywords (with filter for the area "Business, Management & Accounting")	(TITLE-ABS-KEY (account*) AND TITLE-ABS-KEY (sustainab*) OR TITLE-ABS-KEY (sdg) AND TITLE-ABS-KEY (artificial AND intelligence) OR TITLE-ABS-KEY (ai)) AND PUBYEAR > 1999 AND PUBYEAR < 2024 AND (LIMIT-TO (SUBJAREA, "BUSI"))
Results	102 documents

Source: Own elaboration

Mapping the Scientific Field

Bibliometric analysis makes it possible to map and visualise the evolution of a field of research over time. This is essential for understanding emerging trends, identifying areas of rapid growth and noticing paradigmatic shifts at the intersection of Accounting, Sustainability and Artificial Intelligence. For this study, analysing the convergence of AI in sustainability accounting (the first survey strategy) using the keywords presented and without any filter, 702 documents were produced. The first published article, with a reference in the title to the research strategy presented, dates from 2000 (Figure 1), from a Conference Paper, with the title "A decision support system for holistic technology assessment" and 1 citation. The most cited article (298) dates from 2018, with the title "Agriculture 4.0: Broadening Responsible Innovation in an Era of Smart Farming", from Frontiers in Sustainable Food Systems.

An increase in this field of research was observed from 2014 onwards, with an acceleration from 2019 onwards, considering that the entire field of research does not include any filter other than keywords.

The journal in the "Business, Management & Accounting" area came in 6th place, with 102 documents found (6.8%) (Figure 2).

It is interesting to note that the areas with the highest number of documents in these domains are: Computer Science (19.9%), Engineering, Environmental Science, Social Sciences and Energy. Considering that bibliometrics helps to identify trends and emerging themes in a specific area of research and that our primary purpose was to identify the core area of "Accounting", we chose to use only the "Business, Management & Accounting" filter to analyse publication and citation patterns, aiming to compare the 1st and 2nd surveys, namely the contribution of the "Business, Management and Accounting" field for our study. Hence, and considering a large time period, looking at publications by subject area, the findings show that the Business, Management and Accounting, has seen an increase in its role, namely since 2009 with a global weight of 36.2% (Figure 3).

Furthermore, the findings show that other cross-cutting and similar areas of knowledge are exploring these topics. These are Engineering, with 38; Economics, Econometrics and Finance, with 31; Decision Sciences, with 27; Computer Science, with 21; and Environmental Science, with 19 documents. Mathematics and Psychology have a small number of papers on this cross-cutting theme, which can be deemed acceptable.

Figure 1. Documents by year: 1st survey
Source: Scopus

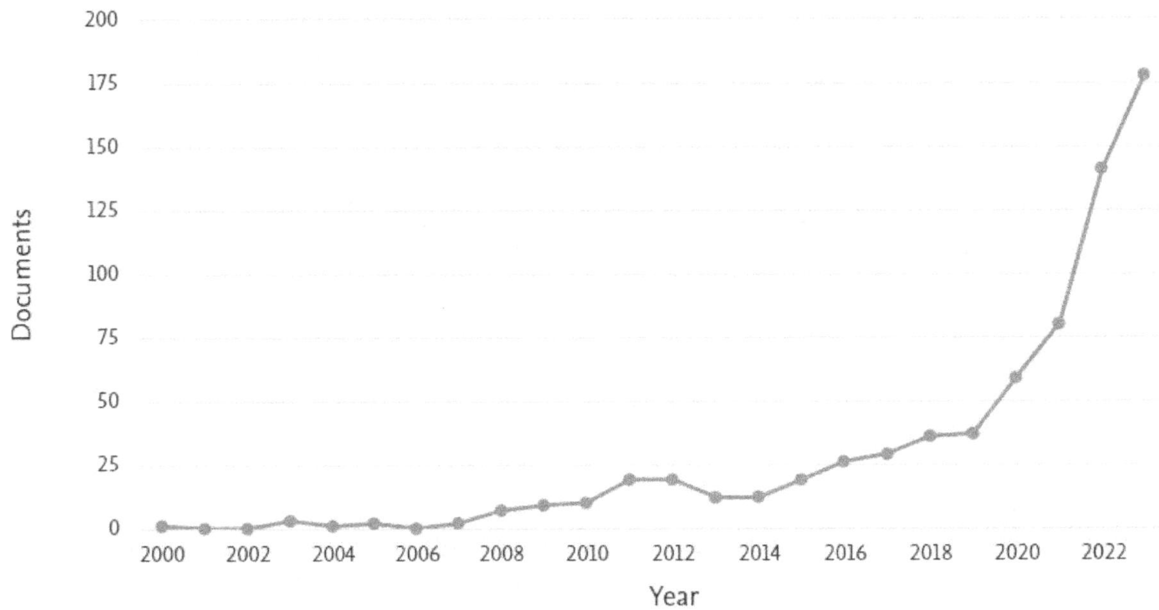

Figure 2. Analysis of documents by subject area: 1st survey
Source: Scopus

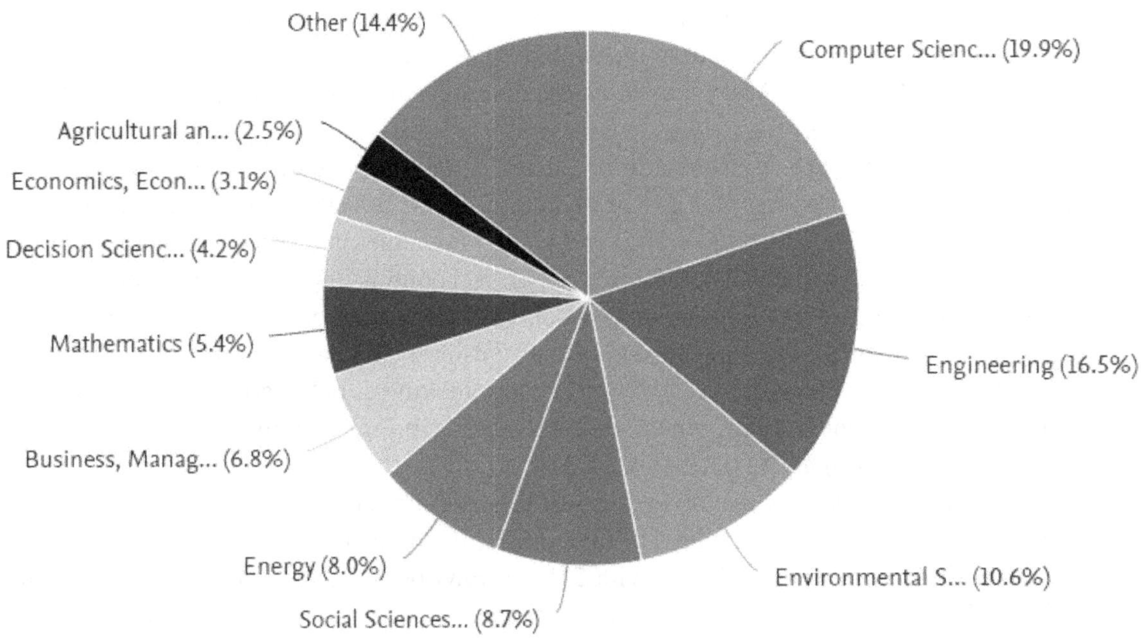

Figure 3. Published documents by subject area
Source: Scopus

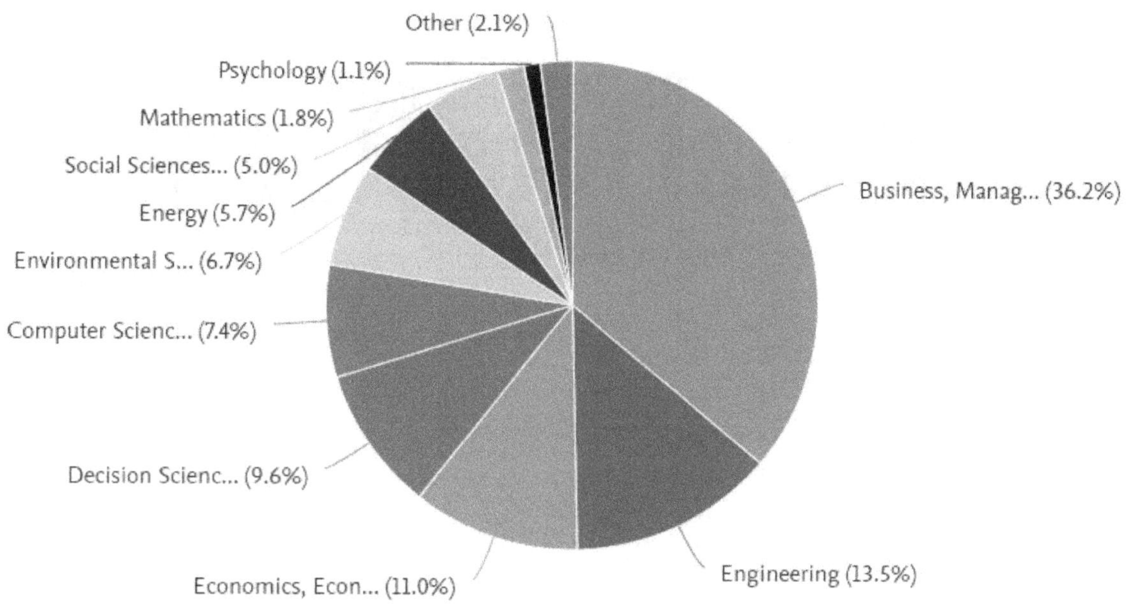

Main Themes

As portrayed in a word cloud, the results suggest that the main themes are namely related to AI and sustainability. In fact, and through a keywords' occurrence analysis, it is possible to confirm such a claim and to observe that "Artificial Intelligence" is the most addressed theme (see Figure 4).

Furthermore, in the last few years, research in AI has increased significantly. According to Figure 5, since 2019 there has been a growth in articles adopting the term "Artificial Intelligence" in their keywords and surpassing the Sustainability theme in 2020.

Finally, besides AI and sustainability being two trending themes, as it is possible to observe in Figure 6, AI pertains to the same cluster (green) of sustainability, sustainable development, big data, machine learning, and the internet of things. In fact, it has a strong connection with sustainability.

Analysis of Search Results per Year and per Year by Source

The results of the bibliometric analysis were refined to the journal area "Business, Management & Accounting", leading us to a total database of 102 documents. Figures 7 and 8 show the evolution of the documents collected by year, between 2009 and 2023, and by source title, after applying the parameters defined in the Scopus database.

There has been an almost constant increase in publications, except during 2012-2014. The growing interest in publishing in this area is noteworthy, as is the increase in the number of publications from 2017 (4) to 2023 (28) (Figure 7). Of the 102 documents collected, Figure 8 shows journal articles to which the main publication sources correspond.

Figure 4. Word cloud
Source: Own elaboration

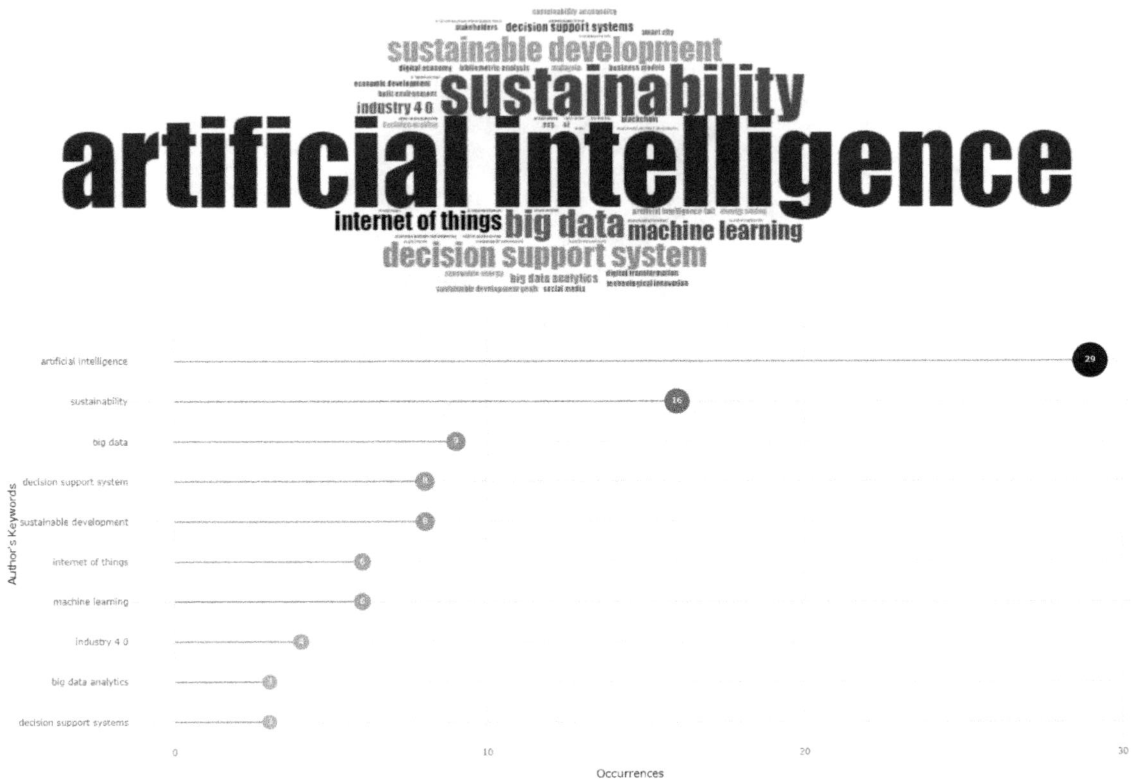

Figure 5. Words' frequency over time
Source: Own elaboration

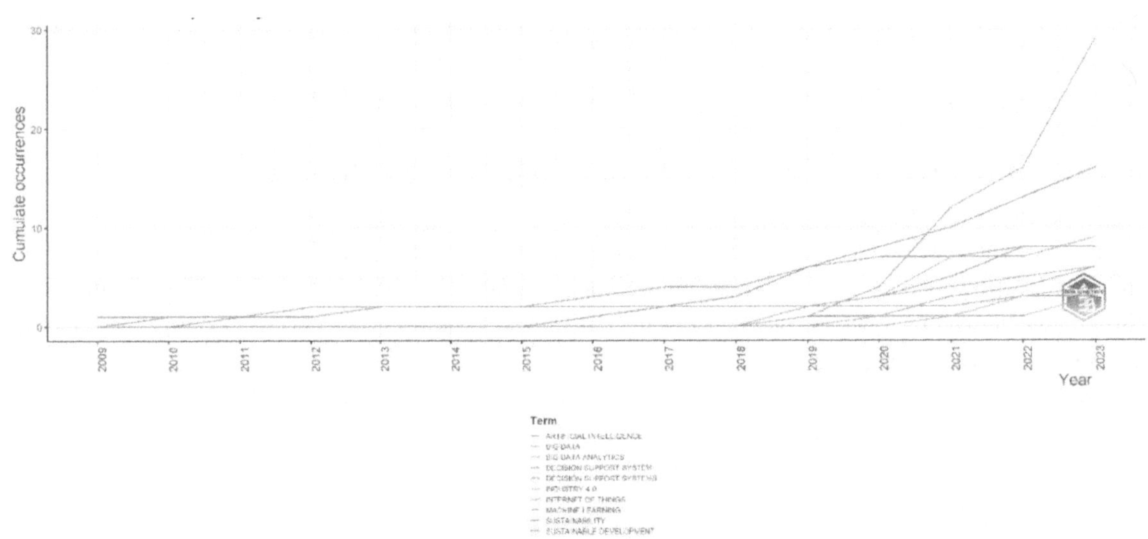

Figure 6. Thematic map
Source: Own elaboration

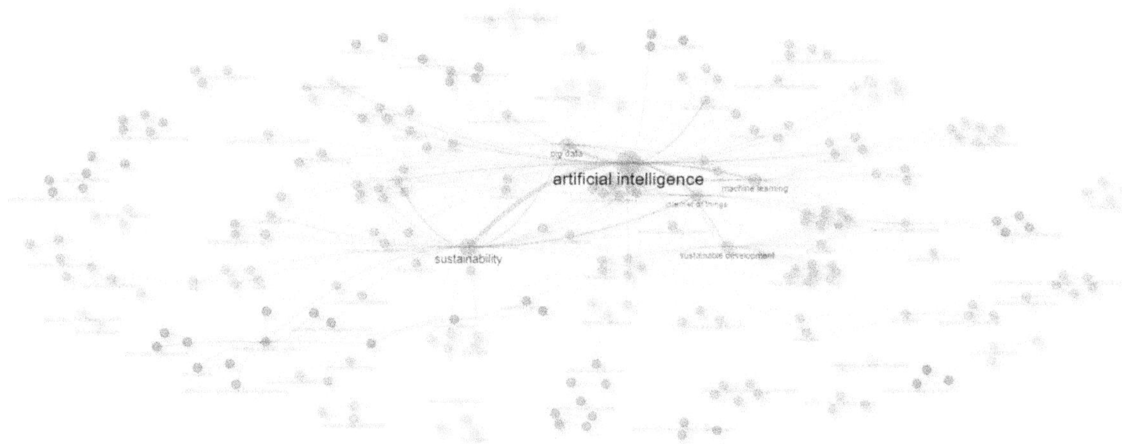

The findings show that the Journal Of Cleaner Production has published thirteen articles, while the other four have published three. This journal, published by Elsevier, has: CiteScore 2022 -18.5; SJR 2022 - 1.981; SNIP 2022 - 2.379.

Searching for journals that include the word "Accounting": Accounting Finance Sustainability Governance And Fraud; Australian Accounting Review; Contributions To Finance And Accounting; Revista De Contabilidad Spanish Accounting Review, it can be seen that each of these presents only

Figure 7. Number of documents published
Source: Scopus

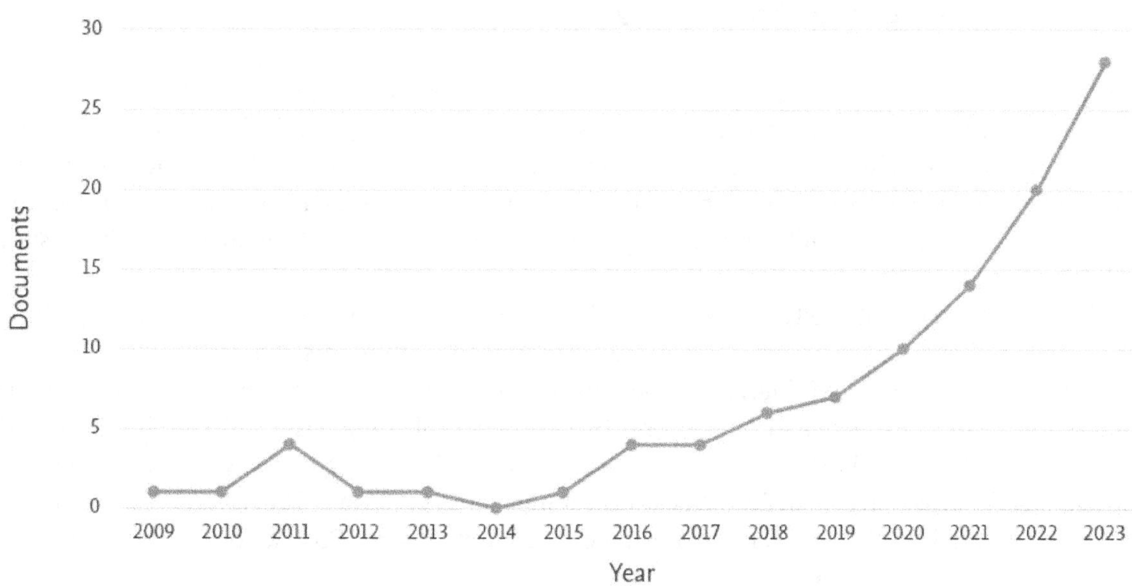

Figure 8. Published documents by source title
Source: Scopus

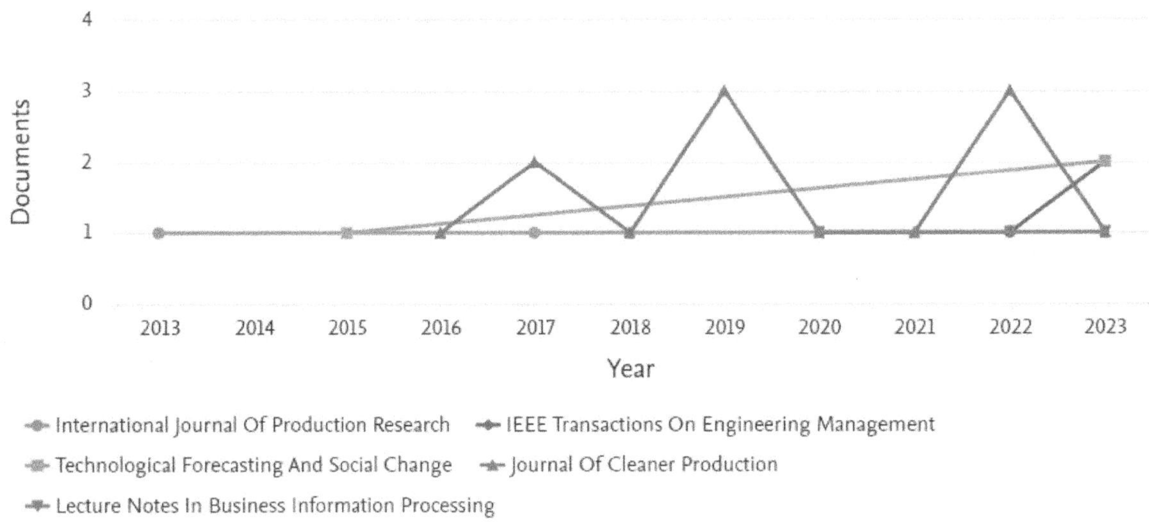

one publication, all in 2023. As mentioned, this situation may demonstrate a new path in accounting research (Khan et al., 2023).

Authors' Information

Over 15 years, 281 authors have published 102 articles on the theme under study, most under co-authorship (see Table 2).

Analysis of Search Results per Citation and Research Network per Author per Year

Through citation analysis, bibliometrics helps to evaluate the scientific impact of specific publications, journals, and researchers. This contributes to the assessment of quality and influence in the scientific community. The impact of research on the scientific community is one of the main indicators to consider and is assessed by the number of citations a given work has. The year 2015 was taken as a reference, the year in which the 2030 Agenda was published, and the importance of AI increased. Table 3 shows the articles in citation order.

The table shows the most cited articles, the first being a review and bibliometric analysis, by Dhamija and Bag, with 144 citations, from the year 2020, at the time of writing this chapter (27 January 2024). This article, published in TQM Journal in the subject area Business, Management and Accounting: General Business, Management and Accounting, by Emerald Publishing has: CiteScore 2022 - 6.7; SJR 2022 - 0.734; SNIP 2022 - 1.407. This work aimed to review significant work by eminent researchers in AI. Since 2015 there have been 25 articles with ten or more citations. The second, by Karakaya et al. (2018), is an article with 102 citations, from the Journal of Cleaner Production, as well as the third

Table 2. Main information

Main Information About the Data		Results
Timespan		2009:2023
Sources Documents		71 102
Author's information		
Authors single-authored documents multi-authored documents Co-Authors per document		281 18 263 2.8

Source: Own elaboration

most cited article (fourth on the total list), with the title "Sustainability accounting and reporting in the industry 4.0", from 2020, with 88 citations, is by Tiwari and Khan (2020). This research delves into the contribution of Industry 4.0 to sustainability objectives with sustainability accounting and reporting. There is also a paper from 2023 (July) among the most cited: Dwivedi et al., with 17 citations, 17th in the Scopus order.

Bibliometric analysis can highlight or reveal gaps in scientific literature, indicating areas that need more research. This understanding helps researchers to direct their efforts towards filling these gaps. In addition, it was decided to include the articles (7) in the table that include the word "Accounting" in the document's title and/or source, despite not having 10 citations. However, five of these papers are from 2023, which may justify the low number of citations. It can be seen that there is still little significance in these cross-cutting areas in the field of accounting.

By analysing co-authorship networks, bibliometrics helps to identify patterns of collaboration between researchers, institutions and countries, which facilitates the promotion of effective partnerships and collaborations. When we take a closer look at the collaborations among the papers with ten or more publications and with the words "artificial intelligence" / "AI" and/or "Accountability" and/or "Sustainability", it is easy to see that most of the articles are written by more than one author. Table 4 shows 1 article with six authors, 2 with five authors, 4 with three authors and 3 with two composite authors.

Continuing our analysis and taking into account the number of contributors to the articles as co-authors, we also present in Table 4 the number of documents created by each one, the total number of citations considering each author, the h-index of each author and the number of co-authors that each author added to the documents explored and identified. Dwivedi, Y.K. is the author with the highest number of published articles, citations, h-index and co-authors. However, we found that this author appears first in the publication. This author is the 17th most cited, with 20 citations, but from the year 2023, as we found. It is an article published in Technological Forecasting and Social Change, titled "Evolution of artificial intelligence research in Technological Forecasting and Social Change: Research topics, trends, and future directions". The second most published author, Rana, N.P., is part of the same paper.

It should also be noted that the author with the lowest numbers in these components is Anvari, S., with two documents, despite being in 10th place of the most cited, with the article: The facility location problem from the perspective of triple bottom line accounting of sustainability, co-authored.

Table 3. Articles cited

Order Scopus	Document Title	Authors	Year	Source	Cited by
1	Role of artificial intelligence in operations environment: a review and bibliometric analysi	Dhamija, P., Bag, S.	2020	TQM Journal, 32(4), pp. 869–896	144
2	Potential transitions in the iron and steel industry in Sweden: Towards a hydrogen-based future?	Karakaya, E., Nuur, C., Assbring, L.	2018	Journal of Cleaner Production, 195, pp. 651–663	102
4	Sustainability accounting and reporting in the industry 4.0	Tiwari, K., Khan, M.S.	2020	Journal of Cleaner Production, 258, 120783	88
5	Urban energy planning procedure for sustainable development in the built environment: A review of available spatial approaches	Torabi Moghadam, S., Delmastro, C., Corgnati, S.P., Lombardi, P.	2017	Journal of Cleaner Production, 165, pp. 811–827	88
7	A multi-objective optimisation-based pavement management decision-support system for enhancing pavement sustainability	Santos, J., Ferreira, A., Flintsch, G.	2017	Journal of Cleaner Production, 164, pp. 1380–1393	74
8	Technological Forecasting and Social Change, 90(PA), pp. 318–330	Tigabu, A.D., Berkhout, F., van Beukering, P.	2015	Technological Forecasting and Social Change, 90(PA), pp. 318–330	74
9	Machine learning-based approach: Global trends, research directions, and regulatory standpoints	Pugliese, R., Regondi, S., Marini, R.	2021	Data Science and Management, 4, pp. 19–29	61
10	The facility location problem from the perspective of triple bottom line accounting of sustainability	Anvari, S., Turkay, M.	2017	International Journal of Production Research, 55(21), pp. 6266–6287	47
11	Big data: A game changer for insurance industry	Sood, K., Dhanaraj, R.K., Balamurugan, B., Grima, S., Maheshwari, R.	2022	Big Data: A Game Changer for Insurance Industry, pp. 1–335	34
12	Carbon accounting framework for decarbonisation of European city neighbourhoods	Pulselli, R.M., Marchi, M., Neri, E., Marchettini, N., Bastianoni, S.	2019	Journal of Cleaner Production, 208, pp. 850–868	34
13	Appraisal of infrastructure sustainability by graduate students using an active-learning method	Pellicer, E., Sierra, L.A., Yepes, V.	2016	Journal of Cleaner Production, 113, pp. 884–896	34
14	Systems-based approach to contemporary business management: An enabler of business sustainability in a context of industry 4.0, circular economy, competitiveness and diverse stakeholders	Hallioui, A., Herrou, B., Santos, R.S., Katina, P.F., Egbue, O.	2022	Journal of Cleaner Production, 373, 133819	25
15	Sustainable AI: An integrated model to guide public sector decision-making	Wilson, C., van der Velden, M.	2022	Technology in Society, 68, 101926	24
16	Islamic FinTech: The digital transformation bringing sustainability to islamic finance	Atif, M., Hassan, M.K., Rabbani, M.R., Khan, S.	2021	COVID-19 and Islamic Social Finance, pp. 91–103	23

continued on following page

Table 3. Continued

Order Scopus	Document Title	Authors	Year	Source	Cited by
17	Evolution of artificial intelligence research in Technological Forecasting and Social Change: Research topics, trends, and future directions	Dwivedi, Y.K., Harma, A., Rana, N.P., ...Goel, P., Dutot, V.	2023	Technological Forecasting and Social Change, 192, 122579	17
18	Building sustainable free legal advisory systems: Experiences from the history of AI & law	Greenleaf, G., Mowbray, A., Chung, P.	2018	Computer Law and Security Review, 34(2), pp. 314–326	20
19	How machine learning activates data network effects in business models: Theory advancement through an industrial case of promoting ecological sustainability	Haftor, D.M., Costa Climent, R., Lundström, J.E.	2021	Journal of Business Research, 131, pp. 196–205	19
21	Implementation of digital technologies in financial management	Chernov, V.A.	2020	Economy of Regions, 16(1), pp. 283–297	14
22	Increasing resource efficiency with an engineering decision support system for comparison of product design variants	Buchert, T., Ko, N., Graf, R., Vollmer, T., Alkhayat, M., Brandenburg, E., Stark, R., Klocke, F., Leistner, P., Schleifenbaum, J.H.	2019	Journal of Cleaner Production, 210, pp. 1051–1062	14
23	Integrated reconfigurable manufacturing systems and smart value chain: Sustainable infrastructure for the factory of the future	Abdi, M.R., Labib, A., Edalat, F.D., Abdi, A.	2018	Integrated Reconfigurable Manufacturing Systems and Smart Value Chain: Sustainable Infrastructure for the Factory of the Future, pp. 1–279	13
24	Decision model to integrate community preferences and nudges into the selection of alternatives in infrastructure development	Yoon, S., Naderpajouh, N., Hastak, M.	2019	Journal of Cleaner Production, 228, pp. 1413–1424	12
25	Industry Commons: an ecosystem approach to horizontal enablers for sustainable cross-domain industrial innovation (a positioning paper)	Magas, M., Kiritsis, D.	2022	International Journal of Production Research, 60(2), pp. 479–492	10
26	Roles of geospatial technology in eco-industrial park site selection: State–of–the-art review	Nuhu, S.K., Manan, Z.A., Wan Alwi, S.R., Md Reba, M.N.	2021	Journal of Cleaner Production, 309, 127361	10
27	Project Management, Planning and Control: Managing Engineering, Construction and Manufacturing Projects to PMI, APM and BSI Standards (BOOK)	Lester, A.	2021	Project Management, Planning and Control: Managing Engineering, Construction and Manufacturing Projects to PMI, APM and BSI Standards, pp. 1–696	10
...	...	...	...	...	...

continued on following page

Table 3. Continued

Order Scopus	Document Title	Authors	Year	Source	Cited by
41	The Use of Internet of Things, Big Data Analytics and Artificial Intelligence for Attaining UN's SDGs	Teh, D., Rana, T.	2023	Handbook of Big Data and Analytics in Accounting and Auditing, pp. 235–253	4
43	Management accounting practices among small and medium enterprises	Ahmad, K., Zabri, S.M.	2016	Proceedings of the 28th International Business Information Management Association Conference - Vision 2020: Innovation Management, Development Sustainability, and Competitive Economic Growth, pp. 3627–3637	4
44	A circularity accounting network: CO2 measurement along supply chains using machine learning | Una red de contabilidad de la circularidad: Medición del CO2 a lo largo de las cadenas de suministro mediante aprendizaje automático	Jesse, F.F., Antonini, C., Luque-Vilchez, M.	2023	Revista de Contabilidad-Spanish Accounting Review, 26(Special Issue), pp. 21–33	3
49	Environmental Management Accounting – Developments Over the Last 20 years from a Framework Perspective	Burritt, R.L., Schaltegger, S., Khrist, K.L.	2023	Australian Accounting Review, 33(4), pp. 336–351	2
50	Challenges of education in the accounting profession in the Era 5.0: A systematic review	Tavares, M.C., Azevedo, G., Marques, R.P., Bastos, M.A.	2023	Cogent Business and Management, 10(2), 2220198	2
51	The intellectual structure of sustainability accounting in the corporate environment: A literature review	Kalbouneh, A., Aburisheh, K., Shaheen, L., Aldabbas, Q.	2023	Cogent Business and Management, 10(2), 2211370	2
53	Digital Corporate Governance: Inevitable Transformation	Varoglu, A., Gokten, S., Ozdogan, B.	2021	Contributions to Finance and Accounting, Part F212, pp. 219–236	2

Source: Own elaboration

Analysis by Author, Affiliation, and Country

The analysis goes on to identify and characterise the reference authors in this cross-cutting area of research. However, the results do not point to the existence of reference authors, although we did see four authors with 2 published articles: Greenleaf, G.; Mowbray, A., Chung, P. (18th and 67th) and Pan, C.-L. (42nd and 61st) (Figure 9).

Regarding the affiliation of these authors, Figure 10 shows that each author belongs to a different university. Specifically, we have the United Nations Office for Project Services (UNOPS), the Department of Financial and Accounting Economics at the University of Essex, Arizona State University, the University of Leipzig, the University of Zagreb, The Australian National University, the Technical

Table 4. Research activity and facts for the authors of the articles published during

Order Scopus	Authors	Documents per Author	Citations by Documents	h-Index	Co-Authors
1	Dhamija, P.,	30	1,085	13	34
	Bag, S.	116	3,179	34	121
4	Tiwari, K.,	8	98	3	12
	Khan, M.S.	3	95	2	1
7	Santos, J.,	61	983	22	89
	Ferreira, A.,	83	1,051	23	63
	Flintsch, G.	176	2,090	29	148
10	Anvari, S.,	2	89	2	3
	Turkay, M.	85	1,736	24	127
12	Pulselli, R.M.,	83	2,032	25	100
	Marchi, M.,	34	381	12	53
	Neri, E.,	17	258	7	48
	Marchettini, N.,	199	3,085	33	251
	Bastianoni, S.	180	4,611	43	247
13	Pellicer, E.,	144	1,935	30	150
	Sierra, L.A.,	11	324	7	11
	Yepes, V.	198	2,269	40	117
14	Hallioui, A.,	10	32	3	12
	Herrou, B.,	37	73	5	25
	Santos, R.S.,	27	101	7	26
	Katina, P.F.,	112	502	18	71
	Egbue, O.	50	1,479	9	43
17	Dwivedi, Y.K.,	669	23,418	99	787
	Sharma, A.,	37	722	16	61
	Rana, N.P.,	301	13,246	68	435
	Giannakis, M.	62	3,840	26	163
	Goel, P.,	24	266	9	33
	Dutot, V.	38	1,370	17	123
18	Greenleaf, G.,	66	360	12	33
	Mowbray, A.,	21	69	5	14
	Chung, P.	13	39	3	6
19	Haftor, D.M.,	65	385	11	33
	Costa Climent, R.,	11	164	7	11
	Lundström, J.E.	19	125	5	36

Source: Own elaboration

University of Denmark, the Christian-Albrechts-University of Kiel, and the University of Almería. This indicates that this topic is recent and of interest in various parts of the world.

When analysing the research carried out by affiliation, Uppsala University, the University of Aveiro, and UNSW Sydney are in the lead with three papers. In general, the number of publications is small and more research is needed in this field. In this respect, bibliometric analysis offers valuable guidance and information for strategic decision-makers, such as policymakers, research funders and institutional leaders. This information helps with the efficient allocation of resources and the development of strategies to advance certain areas of research. Figure 11 shows the documents by country or territory during the period under analysis.

We can see that research on this topic is focused on the United States, which presents 14 documents, followed by Germany and the United Kingdom with 9 documents and China with 8 documents. France

Figure 9. Published documents by author
Source: Scopus

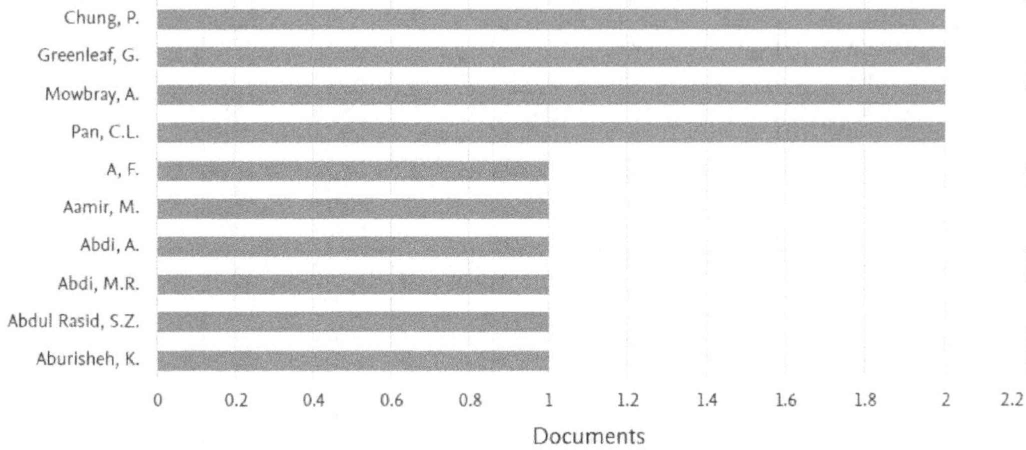

Figure 10. Published documents by affiliation
Source: Scopus

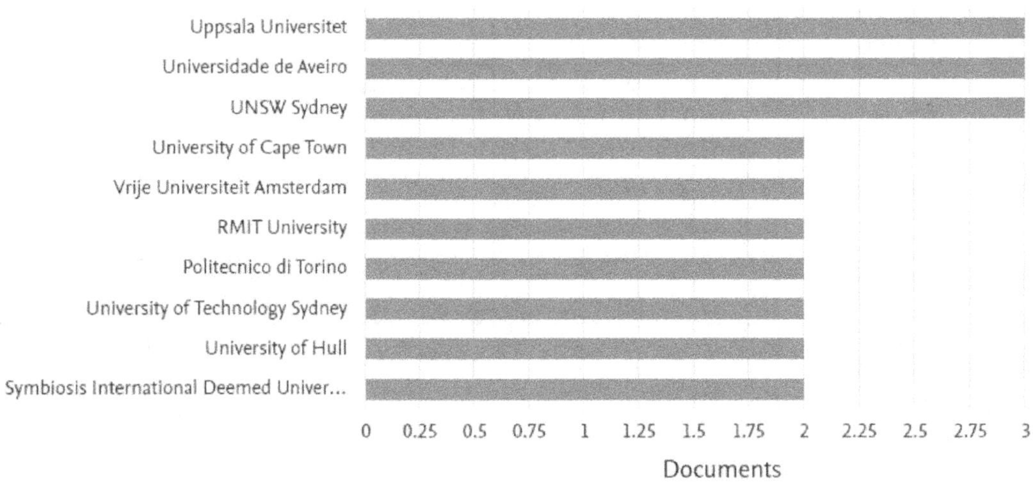

has the fewest documents, 5 out of the 10 presented. This would mean that much more research is needed, as is the case in European countries where there is a lack of research on the subject.

Analysis by Type and Funding Sponsor

The analysis of the type of work, the theme of the work and the source of funding also contributes to a better understanding of the research being published. We should point out that we are considering all types of documents published under the research keywords for the period of analysis, whether they are full articles or not, as shown in Figure 12.

Figure 11. Published documents by country or territory
Source: Scopus

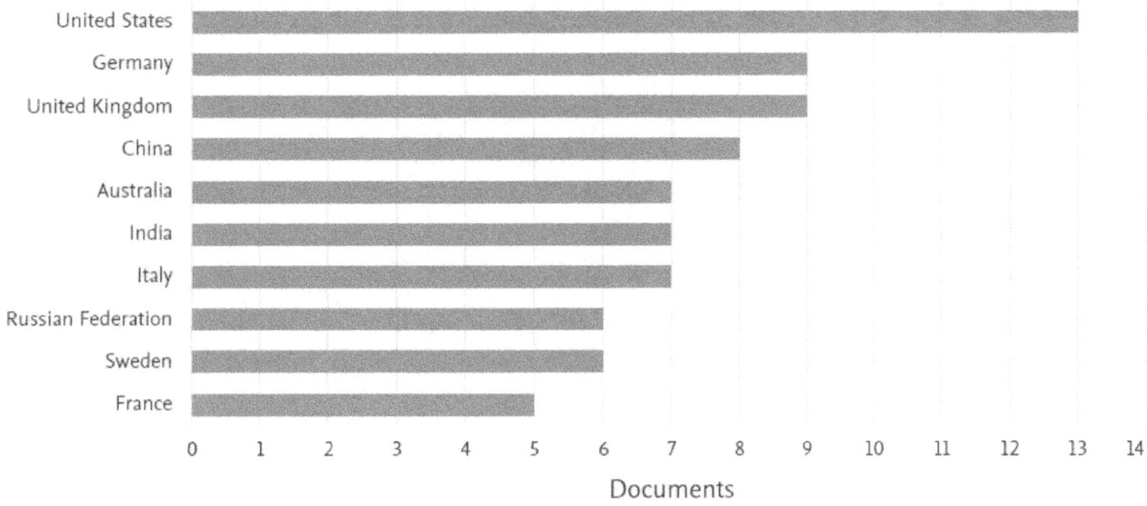

Figure 12. Published documents by type
Source: Scopus

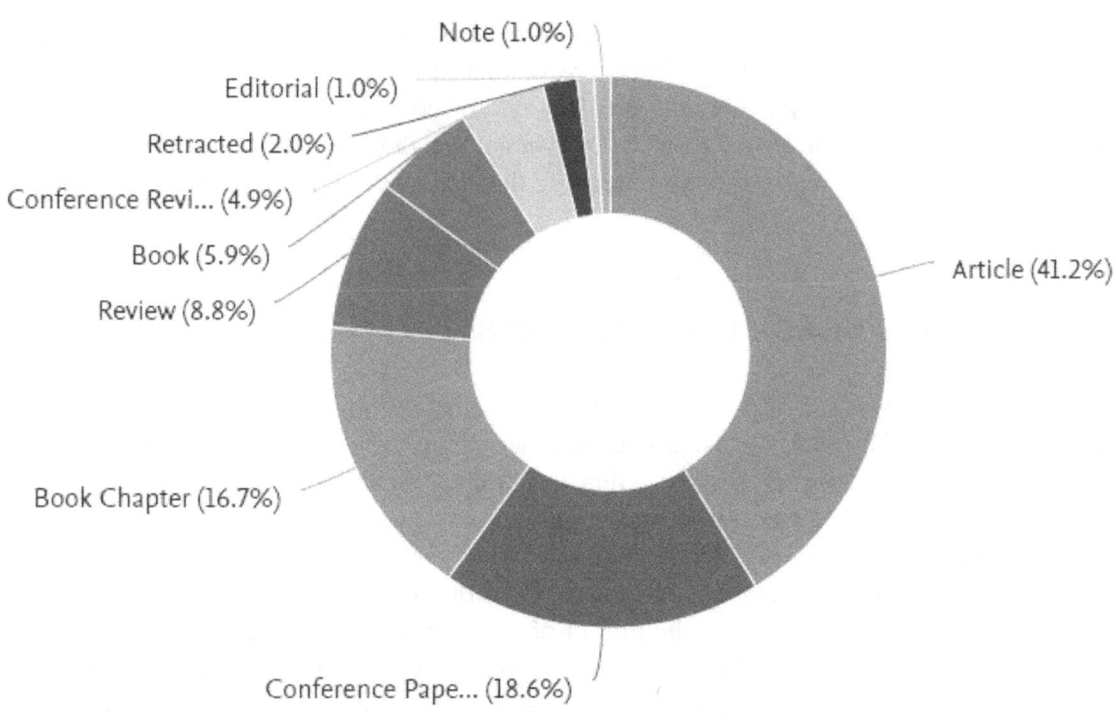

Figure 13. Documents published by funding sponsor
Source: Scopus

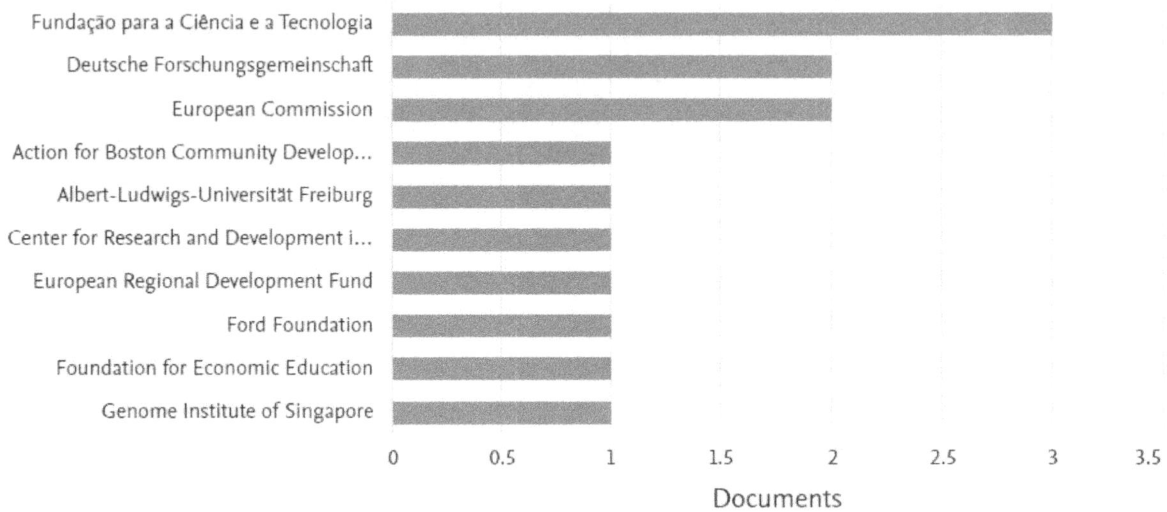

The most published documents in this period were mainly in the form of scientific articles (41.2%), conference papers (18.6%) and book chapters (16.7%).

As for the sponsor of the funding for these documents, we can see in Figure 13 that the Foundation for Science and Technology stands out with 3 documents.

Deutsche Forschungsgemeinschaft, European Commission and Action for Boston Community Development have submitted 2 documents. There are another 26 funding sponsors with 1 document.

In short, bibliometric analysis not only provides an objective and quantitative view of the current state of scientific research, but also plays a vital role in guiding the decisions of researchers, institutions, and policymakers. It is a valuable tool for improving the efficiency, quality, and relevance of scientific research.

DISCUSSION AND CONCLUDING REMARKS

By exploring the intersection between accounting, sustainability and AI, we have identified trends, emerging themes and knowledge gaps, providing a panoramic view of the current research landscape. This multidisciplinary approach is key to tackling the complex challenges we currently face in relation to accounting, sustainability and AI, and this study highlights how this intersection can enrich understanding and drive innovation in these areas. Researchers can identify important trends, such as the growing use of AI in sustainable accounting, emerging themes, such as the ethics of AI in accounting, and knowledge gaps, such as the lack of research into the impact of AI on transparency and corporate responsibility. Meitei et al (2023) show that AI (& ML techniques) is promising, but there is excessive exuberance about its positive outcome. They show the need to impose regulatory requirements and enforce regular checks to ensure that AI remains under constant scrutiny in terms of trust, safety, transparency and adherence to universal principles and ethical standards to achieve the SDGs.

Such as Zhao and Fariñas (2023), we found that AI applications for sustainability are at an early stage. However, this trend is already beginning to impact the application of AI to achieve the SDGs in corporate sustainability. The literature on sustainable accounting discusses the importance of measuring and reporting profits and the environmental and social impacts of business activities, as well as the Triple Bottom Line and good governance. We thus corroborate with Ghobakhloo et al. (2023) that AI can be associated with a company's triple bottom line, offer valuable opportunities to boost a company's economic and environmental sustainability performance, and accounting for the moderating role of corporate social responsibility strategy.

On the other hand, companies with a formal corporate social sustainability strategy have a significantly greater opportunity to transform the value of IA into social sustainability performance. Furthermore, the study by Villiers et al. (2024) highlights the implications of generative AI for accounting, reporting, assurance and the use of sustainability reports. It also includes the risk of AI facilitating greenwashing and the importance of more research into the use of AI for these issues.

AI also influences accounting, especially in automating routine tasks, analysing large data sets and detecting fraud. The literature discusses how AI is transforming accounting and the challenges and opportunities associated with this transformation. Alíusta (2023) points out that the rapid development of information systems or technologies has also led to the development of Accounting Information Systems, resulting in processes becoming faster and simpler. AI has been applied to various sustainability-related contexts, from optimising industrial processes to reduce energy consumption to analysing large data sets to identify unsustainable consumption patterns. The literature in this area not only examines how AI can be used to address environmental and social challenges but also as a tool for publicising, promoting and supporting sustainability and accounting for sustainability. As Zhao and Fariñas (2023) point out, AI can make significant progress on the most complicated environmental and social problems humans face. Responsible and sustainable AI can be achieved through a proactive regulatory framework supported by rigorous corporate policies and reporting.

Companies and governments must collectively address the sustainability challenges and risks AI brings. They must ensure that corporate decisions are well-informed and based on reliable information, which will optimise the decision-making process and increase the success rate of sustainability policies (Zhao & Fariñas, 2023). The ethical conduct of AI is becoming an increasingly pressing issue, given the inevitable integration of these technologies into our lives (Klarin et al., 2024). Unregulated AI would be a threat to sustainability, as it would not be possible to monitor its effects on the economy, society, and the environment effectively (Zhao & Fariñas, 2023). Klarin et al. (2024), therefore, propose that AI designers and operators should be professionalised to avoid unethical results. Tavares et al. (2023) also consider it urgent for the different entities to interact in the change process towards a sustainable Society 5.0, creating synergies that guarantee the success of retraining human resources, particularly accountants, as players in the sustainable development of organisations and society. AI offers interesting professional and employment opportunities. However, AI software developers must guarantee trust in ethical decision-making with a continuous auditing process to avoid a "black box" situation (Meitei et al., 2023).

When employees share similar visions and ambitions regarding digital organisational transformation and can collaborate internally and externally to drive innovation, the organisation would have greater capabilities to progress in integrating AI and extensively use this technology in all business operations (Ghobakhloo et al., 2023). Ghobakhloo et al. (2023) hope their findings will help managers and decision-makers simplify an unbiased and sustainable transition of organisations towards automation.

The aim of this article was to analyse the patterns of production, dissemination, and impact of research within the area of study of AI in accounting for sustainability, through a comprehensive bibliometric analysis of scientific and academic literature to evaluate and measure different aspects related to publications. This analysis allows us to know the scientific production published in a recognised database and analyse its contributions, conclusions, and directions for future research developments.

Overall, the first article published with reference to the three domains, indexed in the Scopus database, dates back to 2000. Since then, the number has been growing, particularly since 2015, accelerating from 2019, with 37 documents, to 2023, with 178 documents (see 1st survey). The results of this study describe the current state of research in this field and provide a framework that can guide researchers regarding the state of the art and future studies. We will contribute to the knowledge and understanding of the scientific production that crosses the area of accounting for sustainability and AI, towards the SDGs of the UN 2030 Agenda.

From the analysis of the results obtained from the bibliometric review, it is possible to draw some conclusions about the evolution of research in the field of AI and accounting for sustainability. When examining the temporal evolution of publications, it can be seen that since 2015, following the 2030 Agenda and the growth in the dissemination of AI, interest in publishing at the intersection of this field has increased significantly. In the last year, 2023, there has been clear exposure and inclusion of the integral term "accounting" in this area of research, which will contribute to developing the SDGs in society, in collaboration between AI and accounting for sustainability. This evidence may result from different reasons, from the current global challenges or the different world crises, contributing to greater investment in academic research in accounting and related areas.

It was noted that Elsevier's Journal Of Cleaner Production, pertaining to the field of "Business, Management and Accounting: Strategy and Management", leads the publications. However, it is the article in the TQM Journal from the subject area Business, Management and Accounting: General Business, Management and Accounting, from Emerald Publishing by Dhamija and Bag (2020), which has the most citations in this area, followed by the most cited publications in the Journal of Cleaner Production. The papers that lead this area of research are co-authored, as is the case with Chung, Greenleaf and Mowbray, who lead the papers published by author. By affiliation, Uppsala University, the University of Aveiro and UNSW Sydney lead the way, with the United States being the country that publishes the most and the funding sponsor being the Foundation for Science and Technology. It is the article-type documents that stand out and the Business, Management and Accounting area.

Through the identification of trends, emerging themes, and knowledge gaps, this study provides a panoramic view of the current research landscape. The results show a growing convergence between accounting, sustainability, and AI, indicating an increasing interest in integrating these domains. The analyses highlight the main areas of AI application in accounting to improve business sustainability, such as process automation, predictive analysis, and sustainable data-based decision-making. As Dhamija and Bag (2020) point out, AI and sustainable development are emerging themes.

This bibliometric approach offers valuable insights for academics, practitioners, and policymakers, providing a solid understanding of research streams and promising future directions at the intersection of accounting, sustainability and AI. This analysis not only contributes to the existing literature, but also guides strategic decision-making and policy formulation in an increasingly sustainability-oriented and technologically advanced business world.

This study, which covered the entire period of articles published in the field of Business, Management and Accounting (between 2009 and 2023) can provide an important guide for academics working in the area of AI, similar to Kahan et al.' (2023) study. With the help of bibliometric research, we could explain the difference in top authors, top sources/journals, top organisations, leading universities, and finally, the top-ranked countries, charting and illustrating the growth of the field. This study uses data from a broad period, making it more meaningful and useful for different actors such as researchers, entrepreneurs, professional bodies, accountants, IT professionals, investors, or organisations.

It is believed that the research will provide a broad perspective on the literature on AI and sustainability accounting, reveal research gaps and opportunities, and contribute to determining the direction of the literature. We know this study has gaps that can be filled by further research. Firstly, Scopus was the only document source we used for our analysis. Different sources like Web of Sciences (WoS) can also be used for research purposes for future perspectives in these domains, something which can bias the perception of the literature.

REFERENCES

Abdi, M. R., Labib, A., Edalat, F. D., & Abdi, A. (2018). *Integrated reconfigurable manufacturing systems and smart value chain: Sustainable infrastructure for the factory of the future*. Springer International Pu. doi:10.1007/978-3-319-76846-5

Agustí, M. A., & Orta-Pérez, M. (2023). Big data and artificial intelligence in the fields of accounting and auditing: A bibliometric analysis. *Spanish Journal of Finance and Accounting. Revista Española de Financiación y Contabilidad, 52*(3), 412–438. doi:10.1080/02102412.2022.2099675

Ahmad, K., & Zabri, S. M. (2016). Management accounting practices among small and medium enterprises. *Proceedings of the 28th International Business Information Management Association Conference - Vision 2020: Innovation Management, Development Sustainability, and Competitive Economic Growth*. 10.4018/979-8-3693-0044-2.ch024

Aliusta, H. (2023). Bibliometric Analysis of Research on The Relationship of Accounting and Information Systems/Technologies. *İşletme Araştırmaları Dergisi, 15*(2), 797-815.

Anvari, S., & Turkay, M. (2017). The facility location problem from the perspective of triple bottom line accounting of sustainability. *International Journal of Production Research, 55*(21), 6266–6287. doi:10.1080/00207543.2017.1341064

Atif, M., Hassan, M. K., Rabbani, M. R., & Khan, S. (2021). Islamic FinTech: The digital transformation bringing sustainability to islamic finance. In COVID-19 and Islamic Social Finance (pp. 91-103). doi:10.4324/9781003121718-9

Baker, H. K., Pandey, N., Kumar, S., & Haldar, A. (2020). A bibliometric analysis of board diversity: Current status, development, and future research directions. *Journal of Business Research, 108*, 232–246. doi:10.1016/j.jbusres.2019.11.025

Buchert, T., Ko, N., Graf, R., Vollmer, T., Alkhayat, M., Brandenburg, E., Stark, R., Klocke, F., Leistner, P., & Schleifenbaum, J. H. (2019). Increasing resource efficiency with an engineering decision support system for comparison of product design variants. *Journal of Cleaner Production, 210*, 1051–1062. doi:10.1016/j.jclepro.2018.11.104

Burritt, R. L., Schaltegger, S., & Christ, K. L. (2023). Environmental Management Accounting – Developments Over the Last 20 years from a Framework Perspective. *Australian Accounting Review*, *33*(4), 336–351. doi:10.1111/auar.12407

Chernov, V. A. (2020). Implementation of digital technologies in financial management. *Economy of Regions*, *16*(1), 283–297. doi:10.17059/2020-1-21

Chung, J., & Tsay, M. Y. (2017). A bibliometric analysis of the literature on open access in Scopus. *Qualitative and Quantitative Methods in Libraries*, *4*(4), 821–841.

de Villiers, C., Dimes, R., & Molinari, M. (2024). How will AI text generation and processing impact sustainability reporting? Critical analysis, a conceptual framework and avenues for future research. *Sustainability Accounting. Management and Policy Journal*, *15*(1), 96–118. doi:10.1108/SAMPJ-02-2023-0097

Dhamija, P., & Bag, S. (2020). Role of artificial intelligence in operations environment: A review and bibliometric analysis. *The TQM Journal*, *32*(4), 869–896. doi:10.1108/TQM-10-2019-0243

Dwivedi, Y. K., Sharma, A., Rana, N. P., Giannakis, M., Goel, P., & Dutot, V. (2023). Evolution of artificial intelligence research in Technological Forecasting and Social Change: Research topics, trends, and future directions. *Technological Forecasting and Social Change*, *192*, 122579. Advance online publication. doi:10.1016/j.techfore.2023.122579

Ghobakhloo, M., Asadi, S., Iranmanesh, M., Foroughi, B., Mubarak, M. F., & Yadegaridehkordi, E. (2023). Intelligent automation implementation and corporate sustainability performance: The enabling role of corporate social responsibility strategy. *Technology in Society*, *102301*, 102301. Advance online publication. doi:10.1016/j.techsoc.2023.102301

Greenleaf, G., Mowbray, A., & Chung, P. (2018). Building sustainable free legal advisory systems: Experiences from the history of AI & law. *Computer Law & Security Report*, *34*(2), 314–326. doi:10.1016/j.clsr.2018.02.007

Haftor, D. M., Costa Climent, R., & Lundström, J. E. (2021). How machine learning activates data network effects in business models: Theory advancement through an industrial case of promoting ecological sustainability. *Journal of Business Research*, *131*, 196–205. doi:10.1016/j.jbusres.2021.04.015

Hallioui, A., Herrou, B., Santos, R. S., Katina, P. F., & Egbue, O. (2022). Systems-based approach to contemporary business management: An enabler of business sustainability in a context of industry 4.0, circular economy, competitiveness and diverse stakeholders. *Journal of Cleaner Production*, *373*, 133819. Advance online publication. doi:10.1016/j.jclepro.2022.133819

Hermann, E., Hermann, G., & Tremblay, J. C. (2021). Ethical Artificial Intelligence in Chemical Research and Development: A Dual Advantage for Sustainability. *Science and Engineering Ethics*, *27*(4), 45. Advance online publication. doi:10.1007/s11948-021-00325-6 PMID:34231042

Jannah, R., Sari, M. P., Utaminingsih, N. S., Halimah, W. N., Pradana, P. T., & Rahmawati, D. A. (2023). Environmental Accounting System Model in the Era Artificial Intelligence and Blockchain Technology: A Bibliometric Analysis. *Economic Education Analysis Journal*, *1*(1), 182–197.

Jesse, F. F., Antonini, C., & Luque-Vilchez, M. (2023). A circularity accounting network: CO2 measurement along supply chains using machine learning. *Revista de Contabilidad*, *26*(Special Issue), 21–33. doi:10.6018/rcsar.564901

Jiang, N. (2011). Economic analysis of the energy saving and emission reduction. *2011 2nd International Conference on Artificial Intelligence, Management Science and Electronic Commerce, AIMSEC 2011 – Proceedings.*

Kalbouneh, A., Aburisheh, K., Shaheen, L., & Aldabbas, Q. (2023). The intellectual structure of sustainability accounting in the corporate environment: A literature review. *Cogent Business and Management*, *10*(2), 2211370. Advance online publication. doi:10.1080/23311975.2023.2211370

Karakaya, E., Nuur, C., & Assbring, L. (2018). Potential transitions in the iron and steel industry in Sweden: Towards a hydrogen-based future? *Journal of Cleaner Production*, *195*, 651–663. doi:10.1016/j.jclepro.2018.05.142

Khan, H. M. R., Ahmad, S., Javed, R., & Nasir, N. (2023). The Significance of Artificial Intelligence in Business and Accounting: A Bibliometric Analysis. *Pakistan Journal of Humanities and Social Sciences*, *11*(2), 1088–1110. doi:10.52131/pjhss.2023.1102.0417

Klarin, A., Ali Abadi, H., & Sharmelly, R. (2024). Professionalism in artificial intelligence: The link between technology and ethics. *Systems Research and Behavioral Science*, sres.2994. Advance online publication. doi:10.1002/sres.2994

Leistner, P., & Schleifenbaum, J. H. (2019). Increasing resource efficiency with an engineering decision support system for comparison of product design variants. *Journal of Cleaner Production*, *210*, 1051–1062. doi:10.1016/j.jclepro.2018.11.104

Lester, A. (2021). *Project Management, Planning and Control: Managing Engineering*. Construction and Manufacturing Projects to PMI, APM and BSI Standards. doi:10.1016/B978-0-12-824339-8.01001-4

Lievrouw, L. A. (1989). The invisible college reconsidered: Bibliometrics and the development of scientific communication theory. *Communication Research*, *16*(5), 615–628. doi:10.1177/009365089016005004

Llanos-Herrera, G., & Merigo, J. M. (2018). Overview of brand personality research with bibliometric indicators. *Kybernetes*, *48*(3), 546–569. doi:10.1108/K-02-2018-0051

Magas, M., & Kiritsis, D. (2022). Industry Commons: An ecosystem approach to horizontal enablers for sustainable cross-domain industrial innovation (a positioning paper). *International Journal of Production Research*, *60*(2), 479–492. doi:10.1080/00207543.2021.1989514

McCarthy, J., Minsky, M. L., Rochester, N., & Shannon, C. E. (2006). A proposal for the dartmouth summer research project on artificial intelligence, 31 August, 1955. *AI Magazine*, *27*(4), 12–12.

Meitei, A. J., Rai, P., & Rajkishan, S. S. (2023). Application of AI/ML techniques in achieving SDGs: A bibliometric study. *Environment, Development and Sustainability*, 1–37. doi:10.1007/s10668-023-03935-1

Merigó, J. M., & Yang, J. B. (2017). Accounting research: A bibliometric analysis. *Australian Accounting Review*, *27*(1), 71–100. doi:10.1111/auar.12109

Mishra, M., Desul, S., Santos, C. A. G., Mishra, S. K., Kamal, A. H. M., Goswami, S., Kalumba, A. M., Biswal, R., da Silva, R. M., dos Santos, C. A. C., & Baral, K. (2023). A bibliometric analysis of sustainable development goals (SDGs): A review of progress, challenges, and opportunities. *Environment, Development and Sustainability*, 1–43. doi:10.1007/s10668-023-03225-w PMID:37362966

Mowbray, A., Chung, P., & Greenleaf, G. (2023). Explainable AI (XAI) in Rules as Code (RaC): The DataLex approach. *Computer Law & Security Report*, *48*, 105771. Advance online publication. doi:10.1016/j.clsr.2022.105771

Nuhu, S. K., Manan, Z. A., Wan Alwi, S. R., & Md Reba, M. N. (2021). Roles of geospatial technology in eco-industrial park site selection: State–of–the-art review. *Journal of Cleaner Production*, *309*, 127361. Advance online publication. doi:10.1016/j.jclepro.2021.127361

Pan, C. L., Chen, H. E., Ou, Z. Q., & Chen, Y. (2022). ESG Report Intelligent Writing Assistant - Assist Chinese Enterprises in ESG Information Disclosure. *2022 IEEE Technology and Engineering Management Society Conference - Asia Pacific, TEMSCON-ASPAC.*

Pellicer, E., Sierra, L. A., & Yepes, V. (2016). Appraisal of infrastructure sustainability by graduate students using an active-learning method. *Journal of Cleaner Production*, *113*, 884–896. doi:10.1016/j.jclepro.2015.11.010

Pugliese, R., Regondi, S., & Marini, R. (2021). Machine learning-based approach: Global trends, research directions, and regulatory standpoints. *Data Science and Management*, *4*, 19–29. doi:10.1016/j.dsm.2021.12.002

Pulselli, R. M., Marchi, M., Neri, E., Marchettini, N., & Bastianoni, S. (2019). Carbon accounting framework for decarbonisation of European city neighbourhoods. *Journal of Cleaner Production*, *208*, 850–868. doi:10.1016/j.jclepro.2018.10.102

Rajan, R., Dhir, S., & Sushil. (2020). Alliance termination research: A bibliometric review and research agenda. *Journal of Strategy and Management*, *13*(3), 351–375. doi:10.1108/JSMA-10-2019-0184

Santos, J., Ferreira, A., & Flintsch, G. (2017). A multi-objective optimisation-based pavement management decision-support system for enhancing pavement sustainability. *Journal of Cleaner Production*, *164*, 1380–1393. doi:10.1016/j.jclepro.2017.07.027

Scarpellini, S. (2022). Social impacts of a circular business model: An approach from a sustainability accounting and reporting perspective. *Corporate Social Responsibility and Environmental Management*, *29*(3), 646–656. doi:10.1002/csr.2226

Sood, K., Dhanaraj, R. K., Balamurugan, B., Grima, S., & Uma Maheshwari, R. (2022). *Big data: A game changer for insurance industry*. https://doi.org/ doi:10.1108/978-1-80262-605-62022100

Tavares, M. C., Azevedo, G., Marques, R. P., & Bastos, M. A. (2023). Challenges of education in the accounting profession in the Era 5.0: A systematic review. *Cogent Business and Management*, *10*(2), 2220198. Advance online publication. doi:10.1080/23311975.2023.2220198

Teh, D., & Rana, T. (2023). The Use of Internet of Things, Big Data Analytics and Artificial Intelligence for Attaining UN's SDGs. In Handbook of Big Data and Analytics in Accounting and Auditing (pp. 235-253). doi:10.1007/978-981-19-4460-4_11

Tigabu, A. D., Berkhout, F., & van Beukering, P. (2015). Technology innovation systems and technology diffusion: Adoption of bio-digestion in an emerging innovation system in Rwanda. *Technological Forecasting and Social Change, 90*(PA), 318-330. doi:10.1016/j.techfore.2013.10.011

Tiwari, K., & Khan, M. S. (2020). Sustainability accounting and reporting in the industry 4.0. *Journal of Cleaner Production, 258*, 120783. Advance online publication. doi:10.1016/j.jclepro.2020.120783

Torabi Moghadam, S., Delmastro, C., Corgnati, S. P., & Lombardi, P. (2017). Urban energy planning procedure for sustainable development in the built environment: A review of available spatial approaches. *Journal of Cleaner Production, 165*, 811–827. doi:10.1016/j.jclepro.2017.07.142

van Schalkwyk, M. A., & Grobbelaar, S. S. (2020). A decision support system (DSS) framework for leveraging idle resources as a sustainable socio-economic enterprise: The case of a house in Velddrif. *26th International Association for Management of Technology Conference, IAMOT 2017*. 10.1007/978-3-030-72624-9_10

Wang, J., Sun, W., Zhang, Y., Ma, W., & Wang, L. (2011). Notice of Retraction: Case study: Rainwater utilisation and water saving design of a village [Retracted]. *2011 2nd International Conference on Artificial Intelligence, Management Science and Electronic Commerce, AIMSEC 2011 - Proceedings*, 6172-6175. 10.1109/AIMSEC.2011.6009626

Wang, X., Wang, H., Bhandari, B., & Cheng, L. (2023). *AI-Empowered Methods for Smart Energy Consumption: A Review of Load Forecasting, Anomaly Detection and Demand Response*. International Journal of Precision Engineering and Manufacturing - Green Technology., doi:10.1007/s40684-023-00537-0

Wilson, C., & van der Velden, M. (2022). Sustainable AI: An integrated model to guide public sector decision-making. *Technology in Society, 68*, 101926. Advance online publication. doi:10.1016/j.techsoc.2022.101926

Yoon, S., Naderpajouh, N., & Hastak, M. (2019). Decision model to integrate community preferences and nudges into the selection of alternatives in infrastructure development. *Journal of Cleaner Production, 228*, 1413–1424. doi:10.1016/j.jclepro.2019.04.243

Zhang, F., & Han, Y. (2011). Notice of Retraction: Climate change on forestry development in Heilongjiang Province and countermeasures [Retracted]. *2011 2nd International Conference on Artificial Intelligence, Management Science and Electronic Commerce, AIMSEC 2011 - Proceedings*, 7001-7003. 10.1109/AIMSEC.2011.6011455

Zhao, J., & Gómez Fariñas, B. (2023). Artificial intelligence and sustainable decisions. *European Business Organization Law Review, 24*(1), 1–39. doi:10.1007/s40804-022-00262-2

Chapter 2
AI and Its Application in Criminal Investigation:
Contribution to Identifying Profiles in Organized

Armando Ramos
ISCAL, Portugal

ABSTRACT

There are several problems with the use of AI within the scope of criminal law, which the authors will not address in order not to escape the core of this chapter, but which are essentially related to how to criminalize actions carried out by computer software. Is the aforementioned software eradicated, as a "capital punishment", repairing the evil it committed or could its creator be held criminally liable for the acts that resulted from its creation? Therefore, the authors analyze the use of AI in criminal investigation and the possibilities offered by its use in the analysis and detection of profiles in organized crime, such as in the prevention and investigation of terrorist events, among other situations.

I. INTRODUCTION

Intelligence is something that has managed to individualize and separate us from other animals, due to the fact that we are rational, we are called *Homo Sapiens*. The ability to learn, develop and adapt to different realities has brought us to the world we live in, immersed in the most cutting-edge technology that promises to continue to surprise and develop beyond what is imaginable. This profusely technological world, in which today it is possible to carry out multitasking activities, also leads us to new unprecedented challenges, in terms of technology, and gives us problems that we will not be sufficiently prepared to deal with immediately. (AAVV, 2006). Problems that may relate to the autonomy of AI when it comes to axiology, ethics and deontology, for example.

Artificial intelligence (AI) can be defined as "*the study of ideas that, when implemented in a computer, allow them to achieve the same goals that make people appear inteligent*" (Patrick Henry Windston,

DOI: 10.4018/979-8-3693-0847-9.ch002

2014). In other words, as the same author states, "*AI attempts to make computers more useful and at the same time studies the principles that make intelligence possible*". In short, AI is "*the imitation of something that is not natural, that has been modeled, manufactured or created according to natural models, through technical means*" (Ricther, 2019:145). We cannot forget that since the beginning, philosophers and mathematicians have tried to create mathematical models to interpret data more intelligibl. (Oliveira, 2019; Berberich, 2018).

The implementation of AI is increasingly being implemented. Roughly speaking, this is due to the high number of databases that allow us to massively collect terabytes of information and the consequent need to process this information and analyze it, so that results can be extracted for the most diverse purposes depending on the purpose it is intended for. It is in this field that AI comes into play as it has the ability to analyze and interpret these databases and achieve, depending on the complexity of the information processing, a reliable, fast and accepted result according to the parameterization carried out, that is, the algorithm used. It facilitates and replaces human work because "it is completely irrelevant (...) who (or what) "perceives" or "thinks" – man or computer. This is an implementation detail..." (Nilsson, 2009). The need to obtain results remains in an era in which the "thirst" for information, for obtaining answers, is considered a categorical imperative.

Today's LEAs are modern organizations that use digital tools to carry out the functions assigned to them, whether from a preventive perspective or in the reactive and investigative phase. Therefore, it is not surprising that in the technological field the Police are also quick to reap the benefits of using AI, especially its usefulness in collecting evidence, within the scope of the criminal investigations they carry out or in assisting the holder of the criminal action – Public Prosecutor's Office. The large number of Databases[1], with the information that exists there, could result in an amalgamation of meaningless and unconnected information per se.

The most complex criminal investigations lack the use of data collected and entered into Databases, whether these are public data, that is, the so-called OSINT data, or those that the investigation itself acquires and analyzes in the specific case[2].The use of AI could prove to be

an ally, but to what extent can AI select the data that it deems relevant or, through its own learning, understands to be the most suitable for the ongoing investigation?

The use of AI does not just stop at the previous statement, it can be used to use surveillance, image and voice recognition, the use of drones to recognize locations, people and objects, among many other aspects. For reasons of systematization, we will focus our object of study on databases and the use of AI in the fight against terrorism, from a preventive and reactive point of view with regard to criminal investigation.

II. THE DEVELOPMENT OF AI AND THE PROLIFERATION OF DATABASES

The development of software and hardware has boosted the appetite for creating, collecting and maintaining databases of different types. As data collection is an undeniable reality, it is urgent to understand, in addition to the purpose of its collection, what treatment and destination the data obtained in a criminal investigation will have.

To these huge databases, calledbig data, are characterized by the large volume of data they aggregate, their variety and the speed with which they are processed, as well as their format and structure (Moses, 2014: 643–678).

The vast majority of data collected, especially in OSINT, is unstructured data, i.e. images, reports, Excel sheets, web pages, etc.. Either because of its heterogeneity or because of its diversity of formats, unstructured data needs to be organized to be intelligible and to be able to be used in the most diverse aspects depending on the structuring model and its purpose. Thus, structured data emerges which, in contrast to the former, are perceptible, accessible and translate the information that is intended to be obtained.

Structured data is obtained through algorithms, and its structuring is carried out through AI, reasoning, instructions and/or highly standardized mathematical operations, for executing systematic and automatic tasks/processes based on rules (Schwab, 2016:140). It is at this crucial point that it is necessary to understand the impact of algorithms and AI, whether by those who create the program or by those who use it on a daily basis. Currently, a computer program, in addition to performing tasks assigned to it through algorithm programming, has the ability to evolve and learn on its own. This, according to Philip Boucher (2020), is what distinguishes the capacity of AI, "machine learning, referring to second generation techniques, in which the algorithm is programmed to find its own solution to the problem, instead of follow set rules".

Increasingly, criminal investigations tend to make use of more complex databases in criminal investigations, since, without being aware of this, we generate and transmit data that can later be compiled in databases. As an example: let's focus our reasoning on a normal day. A person who gets up, leaves the house, walks along the greenway on the highway, has breakfast and pays for it with their bank card. Go online and buy a book and a ticket to a concert. Have lunch with friends and split the lunch bill using banking apps. Return home, without going to the supermarket first, and buy products x, y or z, which are also stored informationally in the customer account on the card at the commercial area. Among these generated data, billing, market analysis, advertising, among others, and which could be extremely useful in a criminal investigation to reconstruct the day of the suspect or victim.

III. THE USE OF AI IN CRIMINAL INVESTIGATION, ESPECIALLY IN TERRORISM.

Terrorism is one of humanity's most heinous crimes. Its practice leads to harmful and devastating effects that could last for decades in people's memories (Amaral, 2002). The difficulty in conceptualizing terrorism can be seen due to the numerous definitions existing ones, which exceed six hundred (Ramos, 2015: 110-135)[3]

Let us consider focusing on Nuno Rogeiro (2004:525) words, who tells us: "[L]iterally, "terrorism" means the system, or regime, based on fear, that is, on the negative psychological impact (suffered by individuals, groups, masses) caused by acts of calculated violence. Additions to the initial core definition denote that it is "political" violence (to separate it from "common" delinquency), generally indiscriminate (in the sense of not privileging police or military targets), or progressively directed at the weak points of the social organization, starting with the civilian population."Also João Paulo Ventura *(*2023: 42) states that "terrorist acts can translate into several simultaneous attacks in singular or dispersed locations (...) causing massive destruction or limited human casualties, depending equally on the type and nature of the means and operational methods used (...). In a word, it means chaos".

Modern-day terrorism goes further and also involves the dissemination of information actions/co-optation of extremist ideologies and radicalization (Ventura, et al, 2020) through the internet, especially social networks, a phenomenon that experts call "new terrorism" or "fifth wave of terrorism" and also "cybercaliphate" (Whuy, 2018:14).

Considering the use of information and communication technologies as central platforms for propaganda, recruitment, financing, etc., it is urgent to combat this phenomenon in order to avoid the actual terrorist occurrence. It is in this field that AI comes into play as an instrument for analyzing thousands of data circulating on the Internet.

Be in surface web or in dark web AI is an ally of police forces because the algorithms developed can simplify the detection of terrorist phenomena on the Internet, regardless of the area used for this purpose. Thus, AI will be able to collect, process and present to those responsible for criminal investigation information related to terrorism actions, from places of incitement, conversion of believers (radicalism), identification of potential perpetrators of future terrorist actions, financing of terrorist cells, indication of who made the publications on the internet, etc.

At the same time, through AI, it is possible to use algorithms that identify the faces of potential suspects and locate their passage through public places, through surveillance cameras installed there or drones in public places, leading to a rapid analysis of thousands of data in a fraction of minutes or seconds.

Certainly, legal problems arise with the use of current technologies, such as the use of AI that we described previously, in relation to the capture of images and theiranalysis of public places because they violated the Rights and Freedoms of other citizens who, not being connoted with the terrorism may or may not appear in police databases. Are we all suspects? Are we all terrorists? We cannot forget that Law No. 5/2002, of January 11, provides for the possibility of collecting voice and image recordings, by any means, without the consent of the target in cases of crimes mentioned in art. 1 of the aforementioned diploma, which includes terrorist offenses, offenses related to a terrorist group, offenses related to terrorist activities and terrorist financing [art. 1, no.1, subparagraph b)].

AI is currently well developed to automatically select only people found in a suspect database and combine them with the images it collects and analyzes in real time. In addition to this biometric data, it is possible for AI to count people in a given space, perform biometric characterizations, as well as recognize human actions (Liciotti, 2014:1-6) being predictive of future terrorist events.

IV. THE CONTRIBUTION OF THE EUROPEAN UNION TO THE FIGHT AGAINST TERRORISM AND THE DEVELOPMENT OF AI

The European Union (EU) has made efforts to create and regulate AI, through the digital agenda for Europe, although the Treaties do not contain specific provisions relating to information and communication technologies (ICT). It was in 2010 that the first communication from the Commission to the European Parliament, the Council, the European Economic and Social Committee and the Committee of the Regions on "A Digital Agenda for Europe" (COM/2010/0245 final) appeared[4].

In this Communication you can read that "*[The] objective of this agenda is to define a roadmap that maximizes the social and economic potential of ICT, with emphasis on the Internet, a fundamental resource of economic and social activity: for business, for work, for leisure, for communication and the free expression of our ideas. If it produces the expected results, this agenda will spur innovation and economic growth and improve the daily lives of citizens and businesses. The generalization and more effective use of digital technologies will therefore enable Europe to respond to its main challenges and will offer Europeans a better quality of life, translated, for example, into better healthcare, safer and more effective transport solutions, a cleaner environment, new communication opportunities and easier access to public services and cultural content.*[5]"

The fight against terrorism is also one of the great and main priorities of the EU Member States work closely together to prevent terrorist attacks and ensure the safety of citizens.

In 2015, the EU adopted several measures to combat terrorism following attacks in previous years. A communication[6] was issued by EU leaders joint effort designed to guide the work of the EU and the Member States, which called for specific measures to be taken focusing on three areas: 1) guaranteeing the safety of citizens; 2) prevent radicalization and protect our values and 3) cooperate with international partners.

In November 2020, a new communication was issued regarding the attacks that occurred in Germany, France and Austria. In this statement, dated November 13, 2020, the focus was on radicalizationonlineof terrorism, since "*Online communication technologies have facilitated terrorists' cross-border communication and amplified terrorist propaganda and the spread of extremism.*[7]"

The work carried out resulted in Regulation EU 2021/784 of the European Parliament and the Council, of April 29, 2021, regarding combating the dissemination of terrorista content online[8]. The object and scope of this Regulation aims to establish uniform rules to combat the abusive use of virtual hosting services for the purpose of disseminating terrorist online content to the public.

On the other hand, the EU has been financing projects within the scope of AI, which will have applicability in the fight against Terrorism. So, the project *CounteR*[9]*- Countering Radicalisation* for a saferworld, aims to provide a tool for joint use by police forces, internet providers and entities responsible for social media platforms, allowing complete monitoring in the detection of radical contentonline. At the same time, the solution CounteR will preserve the protection of the privacy of content and the anonymization of data. In this sense, the proposed system aims to support the fight against organized crime and corresponding possible threats of terrorism, promoting the sharing of information and advanced collaboration between the various European entities with responsibility for combating different forms of associated crime to thetopic of radicalization.

Ongoing since October 2021, lasting 48 months, financed through the Horizon 2020 Research and Innovation Framework Program (H2020), the STARLIGHT project[10]– *Sustainable Autonomy and Resilience for LEAs using AI against Hight Priority Threats*, will allow a general improvement in the understanding of AI by police forces, contributing to a significant reinforcement of their investigative capabilities, as well as increasing their cybersecurity and supporting the preservation of values ethical, legal and social. Thus, the project will allow the involvement of police forces in the testing and validation of AI technologies that allow them to increase the protection of their own systems and, at the same time, increase their capabilities and capabilities in combating crimes and terrorist acts supported by AI.

We also have, within the scope of H2020, the *AIDA* project[11] – *Artificial Intelligence and advanced Data Analysis.cs for Law Enforcement Agencies*, which translates into the development of an analysis framework – specifically Big Data analysis, equipped with a complete set of effective and efficient tools and automated data analysis solutions, standardized research workflows, acquisition of content, extraction and fusion of information, management and enrichment of knowledge through new Big Data processing applications, Machine Learning, Artificial Intelligence and Predictive and Visual Analysis within the scope of prevention and criminal investigation of cybercrime and terrorism.

Still included in Horizonte 2020 (H2020), the *INFINITY*[12] project–*Immerse, Interact, Investigate*, aims to provide an intuitive collaborative analysis and research tool for LEAs, such as the use of new forms of visualization such as augmented reality (AR) and computer and synthetic vision in three dimensions (VR). The tool will merge large amounts of data and

information into a standardized and simple interpretation format based on entities that can be analyzed autonomously to discover trends and, in this process, assist criminal investigators in analyzing the information they usually have to treat.

In progress since January 2022, *Anti-FinTer*[13] is a European project that brings together a panel of professionals and national authorities from the EU aiming to improve law enforcement capabilities, increase capacity and develop knowledge in the area of terrorist financing associated with activities inDark Web, cryptographic assets, new payment systems and marketsdarknet. Portugal, through Polícia Judiciária – Ministry of Justice, is a partner of this consortium within the scope of this project. These and other AI programs have a single objective: to assist criminal investigation, profile possible suspects and identify perpetrators of illegal criminal practices.

V. FINAL CONSIDERATIONS

Future times will be progressive in the application of AI to the service of criminal investigation. The projects in research and development, together with the improvement of information technology, and others that may be implemented, will catapult science to the servisse of citizens and society, in the incessant search for a more egalitarian and fair society. Mass criminal phenomena can be studied and investigated using tools that accelerate the analysis of available data, its correlation with other data and obtain results with a minimum margin of error. AI in the future will be able to learn and perform tasks that will replace the criminal investigator, such as analyzing extensive data lists, carrying out surveillance, identifying suspects, analyzing crime scenes, etc. However, it will always be up to the human being, ultima racio, have a say inrail designed for the criminal investigation of a case. Even so, predictive AI, speed and analysis capacity, as well as the performance of actions that are humanly considered impossible to perform, cannot be ignored.

In the future, the emphasis on the use of AI should focus on the axiology of values that it should have (or not) in relation to the actions it will develop. We cannot, nor should we, let AI prevail over human beings, as this will lead to the domination of the machine and, at an extreme point, the exclusion of humans or their subjugation *ad aeternum*.

REFERENCES

AA.VV. (2006). *The History of Artificial Intelligence*. University of Washington.

Amaral. (2002). Reflexão sobre alguns aspectos jurídicos do 11 de Setembro e suas séquelas. In Estudos em Homenagem à Professora Doutora Isabel de Magalhães Collaço (vol. 2). Almedina.

Berberich & Diepold. (2018). The virtuous machine - Old ethics for new technology? Cornell University.

Boucher, P. (2020). Artificial intelligence: How does it work, why does it macer, and what can we do about it? EPRS, European Parliamentary Research Service, Scienfic Foresight Unit (STOA).

Chuy. (2018). *Operação Hastag, A primeira condenação de terroristas islâmicos na América La.na.* Novo Século.

Liciotti, Zingaretti, & Placidi. (2014). An automa`c analysis of shoppers behaviour using a distributed rgb-d cameras system. *Mechatronic and Embedded Systems and Applica.ons (MESA), 2014 IEEE/ASME 10th International Conference.*

Moses & Chan. (2014). Using Big Data for legal and law enforcement decisions: Tes`ng the new tools. *UNSW Law Journal, 37*(2).

Nilsson. (2009). The Quest for artificial intelligence, A History of ideias and Achievements. Cambridge University Press.

Oliveira. (2019). Inteligência Artificial. Fundação Francisco Manuel dos Santos.

Ramos. (2015). A prova digital na inves`gação do (ciber)terrorismo. In *Inves.gação Criminal.* ASFIC.

Ricther. (2019). A Review of Fundamentals and Influencial Factors of Artificial Intelligence. *International Journal of Computer and Informa.on Technology, 8*, 145.

Rogeiro. (2004). O Novo terrorismo internacional como desafio emergente de segurança, Novas e velhas dimensões de um conceito problemá`co. In Terrorismo – coordenação de Adriano Moreira (2nd ed.). Almedina.

Schwab. (2016). A quarta revolução industrial. Edipro.

Ventura & Carvalho. (2020). *Da Radicalização ideológica ao terrorismo: uma digressão.* Diário de Bordo.

Ventura. (2023). *Os "lobos solitários".* Terrorismo e (in)Sanidade Mental, Diário de Bordo.

Viana. (2010). Acerca de "Terrorismo" e de "Terrorismos." *Nação e Defesa.*

Windston. (2014). *The Genesis Story Understanding and Story Telling System A 21st Century Step toward Artificial Intelligence.* Center of Brains, Minds & Machines (CBMM).

ENDNOTES

1 Databases from Law Enforcement Agencies (LEAs), among others the Polícia Judiciária, PSP, GNR, Tax Authority, SEF, ASAE, etc... To get an idea of this reality, each LEA has a Database with criminal record, investigated processes, relevant criminal information, etc., and in Portugal there aremore than 18 LEAs. Furthermore, a more complex investigation may result in several Databases relating to the facts investigated.

2 OSINT (Open Source Intelligence) data is data obtained from open sources and freely available for universal access. Differently if, during the course of a criminal investigation, collected access logs to a server, such as IPs, date-time groups, time zone, devices that connected to the server, etc., among others, are called "closed" and restricted access data.

3 From this great diversity, two conclusions can already be drawn. From the outset, it will be useful, if not indispensable, to distinguish between three closely associated but not entirely coinciding

designations: "terrorist action", "terrorism", and "terrorist group". The first refers to the act that can be carried out, either systematically or sporadically, by any agent, political or not, when using violence. The second refers to a particular form of violence, which is aimed at the practice of "terrorist actions" with an expressly political aim. The third designates that group, allegedly political, that chooses terrorist action as the only or, at least, largely predominant form of its practice of violence." (VIANA, 2010: 10).

4 Available in https://eur-lex.europa.eu/legal-content/PT/ALL/?uri=CELEX:52010DC0245 [*accessed February 15, 2023*].

5 *Idem*

6 Available in https://www.consilium.europa.eu/pt/press/press-releases/2015/02/12/european-councilstatement-fight-against-terrorism/[*accessed February 15, 2023*].

7 The statement further states: "[A] *considerable number of the perpetrators of terrorist acts in recent years were individuals already known to the competent authorities of the affected Member States before committing such acts and already classified as a threat of terrorista violence or other acts of extremist violence. In a Europe of open internal borders and a borderless Internet, we need to take into account the danger that these individuals also pose to other Member States. Therefore, taking into account the competences of Member States, as well as national legal systems and European Union law, we must take full advantage of the tools we have for sharing information and quickly implement the regulation on interoperability of EU information systems, with the aim of detecting identity fraud. We must ensure that information* ***about such individuals are entered into relevant EU databases and information systems****, in accordance with applicable legislation. In addition, we must continually improve our level of mutual understanding of what it means in practice for a Member State to classify an individual as a threat of terrorist or extremist violence.*" (our bold), available at https://www.consilium.europa.eu/pt/press/press-releases/2020/11/13/joint-statement-by-theeu-home-affairs-ministers-on-the-recent-terrorist-attacks-in-europe/ [*accessed February 15, 2023*].

8 Published in the Official Journal of the European Union on May 17, 2021, available at https://eurlex.europa.eu/legal-content/PT/TXT/PDF/?uri=CELEX:32021R0784&qid=1681137206047&from=EN [*accessed February 11, 2023*].

9 https://counter-project.eu Portugal is partner of the consortia of this project, through Polícia Judiciária - Justice ministry, [*accessed on March 2, 2023*].

10 https://www.starlight-h2020.eu [*accessed on March 4, 2023*].

11 https://www.project-aida.eu/[accessed on March 4, 2023].

12 https://h2020-infinity.eu/ [accessed on March 4, 2023].

13 https://anti-finter.eu[*accessed on March 4, 2023*].

Chapter 3
Artificial Intelligence and Criminal Law

Ramy El-Kady
https://orcid.org/0000-0003-2208-7576
Police Academy, Egypt

ABSTRACT

The world is on the cusp of entering a new era of artificial intelligence, and it has become necessary to develop laws. Artificial intelligence is one of the most critical topics for criminal law jurists, given that there is a need to establish legal rules commensurate with the nature of this technology that is expected to prevail worldwide. The problem of the study is the lack of a legal framework that regulates the uses of artificial intelligence and shows the criminal rules that should be applied. The chapter aims to introduce the applications of artificial intelligence, its fields, advantages, and its expected impact during the next stage, highlighting the proposed rules of criminal law to regulate the use of artificial intelligence and discussing the appropriate penalties proposed to be applied. The study recommended the international community develop a global framework governing the use of artificial intelligence technologies, calling national legislators to set rules that regulate the use of artificial intelligence and determine appropriate penalties in case of misuse.

INTRODUCTION

There is no doubt that the whole world, due to successive technological developments, is on the cusp of entering a new era, which is the era of the fourth industrial revolution and digital transformation, which will change the details of human life by relying on applications of artificial intelligence, the Internet of things, and the blockchain (Ghaitas, 2017).

The name "Fourth Industrial Revolution" was launched during the World Economic Forum in Davos, Switzerland, in 2016, on the last episode of the current Industrial Revolution series. Prof. Dr. Klaus Schwab, Professor of Comparative Economics and President of the Davos Economic Forum, points out, "There are three reasons that support the belief in the emergence of a fourth industrial revolution, which is the development of the current revolution at an extremely rapid rate, and its reliance on a digital

DOI: 10.4018/979-8-3693-0847-9.ch003

revolution that combines multiple technologies that lead to unprecedented transformations at the level of economy and business, as well as the transformation it entails in various systems. Across all countries, institutions, fields, and societies (Schwab, 2017).

In light of these developments, it becomes necessary to develop most of the laws and legislations to keep pace with this new reality, as the fourth industrial revolution today opens the doors to unlimited possibilities through the significant breakthroughs of emerging technologies in the field of artificial intelligence (El-Behairy, 2019), robots and massive databases, the Internet of Things, self-driving vehicles, 3D printing, nanotechnology, biotechnology, materials science, government computing, Blockchain and others, which will lead to humanity entering a new phase (Mayer-Schönberger & Cukier, 2013).

This requires the need to develop a governing legal framework for these new uses, and there is no doubt that the existence of this legal framework requires a realistic perception of the uses of artificial intelligence and their effects on human and social behavior and the various legal interests that deserve legal protection.

Significance of the Study

Artificial intelligence techniques are one of the most critical topics for criminal law jurists, given that it is a science that focuses on designing machines that engage humans in behaviors that are described as intelligent. Then, the need arises to establish legal rules commensurate with the nature of this technology that is expected to prevail worldwide. For example, some called for the need to work on amending the European Convention on Cybercrime to establish legal rules that regulate developments in the field of information technology (Khalifa, 2018).

The Study Objectives

The study aims to address the issue of the rules of liability and punishment for artificial intelligence applications, as several sub-goals emerge from this primary objective, which can be summarized as follows:

A- Introducing artificial intelligence applications, their fields, advantages, and expected impact during the next stage.
B- Highlighting the proposed rules of criminal law to regulate the use of artificial intelligence.
C- Examining the appropriate penalties proposed to be applied against artificial intelligence entities.

Problem Formulations or Methodology

The difficulty of the study is that it deals with very modern topics, and some of these topics do not have legal regulations that deal with them. Instead, some subjects are still subject to jurisprudence, which seeks to establish new legal rules commensurate with the nature of these new tools (LEEMANS & JACQUEMIN, 2017), in addition to the lack of references that deal with this subject.

Hence, the research problems arise in the lack of legal regulation of artificial intelligence applications. This prompted the researcher to address this issue and shed light on the criminal rules suitable for dealing with it. The chapter will use the comparative analytical approach that seeks to describe, analyze, and diagnose the research topic from its various aspects and dimensions to reach a clear view of criminal responsibility for crimes resulting from the use of artificial intelligence and monitoring and to analyze it from all aspects, taking the comparative approach in dealing with the subject of the study.

Chapter Plan

The chapter will address the study by defining artificial intelligence, its characteristics, advantages, images, its relationship to criminal law, and the ideas advocated by jurisprudence to establish rules for criminal liability for crimes of artificial intelligence by addressing the responsibility of the artificial intelligence program itself, and the responsibility of each of the operator, manufacturer, programmer, and third parties. Interfering in the artificial intelligence program and punishment for crimes of artificial intelligence in two parts as follows:

PART 1: INTRODUCTION TO ARTIFICIAL INTELLIGENCE

Multiple Definitions of Artificial Intelligence

The term artificial intelligence was used for the first time during a conference in Dartmouth by John McCarthy in 1956, and artificial intelligence is a branch of computer science and new technology that makes it simulate human mental capabilities and modes of work". Some define it as the ability of digital machines and computers to perform tasks that mimic and resemble those performed by intelligent beings, such as thinking or learning from previous experiences or other operations requiring mental operations (Mohamed, 2020).

Some define it as a software system capable of imitating human ways of thinking with the help of a computer or other device (Russell & Norving, 2009) or as a simulation of human behavior and cognitive processes on a computer (Ibrahim, 2020). Hence, it becomes clear that artificial intelligence is intended to provide the computer with programs and capabilities similar to human intelligence, enabling it to perform intelligent operations (Pham et al., 2020). With many definitions of artificial intelligence, the researcher sees the importance of concerted international efforts to develop a unified definition.

Characteristics and Fields of Artificial Intelligence

Artificial intelligence applications are characterized by many characteristics, the most prominent of which are the ability to learn, infer, and react to situations that were not programmed into the machine. The areas of using artificial intelligence have multiplied in the commercial, economic, and industrial fields. Such as the use of industrial robots in many industrial projects and the health field, such as the use of medical robots in performing delicate surgeries, where the applications of artificial intelligence indicate the expansion of its use in performing surgeries, as the available evidence of artificial intelligence tools was not found, due to its speed in surgical operations, but the matter is not without a cause on the part of the robot in one of the surgeries (Poirot-Mazeresdu, 2013).

In the fields of education, transportation, communications, and traffic, the environment, the security and military fields, and in all aspects of social life, even on social networking sites, in a way that is expected to predominate in applications of artificial intelligence in human life (Weng et al., 2015).

One of the most prominent fields of artificial intelligence in Egypt is in the societal field of searching for missing persons by comparing images of missing children with pictures of homeless children through face recognition technology, and in the field of tourism and antiquities in the Grand Egyptian Museum, through face recognition technology as well and displaying antiquities according to the characteristics of the interested public, and in the field of security to determine the personality of the suspects, through the use of crime data, their timing and geographical location in addition to the database of accused, wanted and convicted persons, which facilitates the speedy detection of crimes, and in the field of agriculture, through the use of satellites to determine the quality of crops and estimate the amount of water needed by those crops (IDSC, 2020).

Advantages of Artificial Intelligence

Some enumerate the advantages of a robot or robot as being able to produce more, use equipment efficiently, have lower labor costs, improved flexibility, shorter work completion, flexibility and ease of programming, ability to work in hazardous conditions, and improved quality of workplace and production, and achieve good investment returns, in addition to having the freedom to move in the third dimensions of space (Khalifa, 2018).

Types of Artificial Intelligence

Three types of artificial intelligence can be distinguished: Specialized Artificial Intelligence, General Artificial Intelligence, and Super Artificial Intelligence.

- *Specialized artificial intelligence* means artificial intelligence systems that can perform specific tasks, such as self-driving cars, speech or image recognition programs, or the game of chess on smart devices, and this type of artificial intelligence is considered the most common and available type today.
- *General artificial intelligence* is the type that can operate with a capacity similar to human ability. In terms of thinking, it focuses on making the machine think and plan on its own, like human thinking, but there are no practical examples of this type. Everything that exists so far is just research studies that need much effort to develop and turn them into reality.
- *Super artificial intelligence*, which may exceed the level of human intelligence, can perform tasks better than a specialized and knowledgeable person does, and this type has many characteristics that it must contain, such as the ability to learn, plan, communicate automatically, and issue judgments. Superior artificial intelligence is a hypothetical concept that does not exist in our current era (Mohamed, 2020).

The importance of dealing with these types of artificial intelligence highlights the possibilities that artificial intelligence applications may reach in the future and the extent to which the rules of criminal law are perceived to apply. The reference is highlighted to the tendency of many countries to take steps to enhance the uses of artificial intelligence, among which we mention, for example, Egypt, which established a national council for artificial intelligence, and several fake intelligence colleges. There are even some countries, such as the United Arab Emirates.

The United Nations has worked to establish a Ministry of Artificial Intelligence to achieve the UAE's strategy for artificial intelligence and its inclusion in all fields in the country (Dahshan, 2020). At the same time, the report of the Science and Technology Committee of the English Parliament in 2016 recommended the establishment of a permanent committee for artificial intelligence. Its mission is to study its effects, establish principles governing its development, and establish a legal framework (UK Parliament, 2016). The United Nations Interregional Institute for Crime and Justice Research established a center on artificial intelligence and robotics in The Hague to be an international reference point in matters related to artificial intelligence (UNCCPCJ, 2020).

The Dangers of Artificial Intelligence

Some estimates indicate that in contrast to the bright aspects of artificial intelligence, a dark side makes it a fertile field for new types of crimes. Artificial intelligence will make malware and viruses aware of the context in which they move, which prompted the Executive Director of the European Police to say that: "It is necessary to be able to predict the impact of any emerging technologies that criminals will resort to so that the safety of European Union citizens can be preserved."

The European police also warned that artificial intelligence could help provide criminals, hackers, and attackers with new attack vectors to carry out malicious activities that were unfamiliar before, such as improving the success of phishing attacks by designing deceptive emails and negative responses. Artificial intelligence may make crime. Cyber security is more straightforward for criminal actors with limited experience and enables them to launch sophisticated and dangerous attacks.

One of the most prominent potential areas in this field is profound falsification, whether of video or audio, to carry out large-scale disinformation campaigns, and some criminals have already started using video and audio files to impersonate CEOs to defraud institutions and organizations.

Darktrace experts believe that artificial intelligence will make malicious programs aware of the context in which they are operating, such as whether it knows whether this is a Windows operating environment, a Linux application, a mobile application, or a network, and then make its decisions independently according to that understanding. Then, it can self-propagate and use every security vulnerability exposed to exploit networks on a network. It can also decide to postpone the attack for more learning and understanding, or it can activate the attack, which is done quietly and slowly and makes it unnoticed as if copying several straightforward files and data and transferring it to those who operate it.

According to the warnings issued by the European Police and the "Dark Trace" company, law enforcement needs more innovation, creativity, dynamism, and modernization at an accelerated pace, and for those in charge of it to work from now on to keep pace with criminal threats shortly, which are expected to benefit significantly from emerging technologies to become More dangerous than ever (Europol, 2019).

The Nexus Between Artificial Intelligence and Criminal Law

There is no doubt that the widespread use of artificial intelligence applications will raise many questions about the legal rules that these applications will be subject to, the extent to which the rules of criminal law will apply to them, and the extent to which these applications may be subject to the rules of criminal liability.

Moreover, is it possible to talk about criminal liability for the machine that is operated through artificial intelligence applications in light of recent scientific developments and the use of many robots in the implementation of many different tasks, as advanced programming has given some machines that operate with artificial intelligence capabilities that reach them to build Self-experiences that enable them to make individual decisions in any situations they face, like a human, so is it possible to say that it is acceptable to grant these machines a legal person?, and then to determine their criminal responsibility (Dahshan, 2020).

There is talk among legal circles about the expansion of the use of artificial intelligence applications in many aspects of life, which leads to questions about criminal responsibility for the activities of these applications and who bears criminal responsibility. If these activities result in an act that constitutes a crime, many questions have been raised about the validity of the prevailing ideas in criminal law.

Its applicability to artificial intelligence applications, and the extent to which a machine driven by artificial intelligence systems can be held accountable, Such as self-driving or self-driving cars in the event of traffic accidents that lead to injuries and victims, and the extent of the responsibility of each of the manufacturer of artificial intelligence systems and the operator and user of these systems, and whether he is criminally liable for crimes resulting from the use of these systems of artificial intelligence (Hallevy, 2013).

The truth is that these issues are still the subject of great controversy among jurists. This controversy is due to the recent use of these systems in practice, but instead, these uses are still subject to continuous development and modernization. Therefore, the discussion of these issues is still in the stage of speculation and assumptions unless there are some applications. The first and most important of these issues is the issue of criminal responsibility arising from crimes of artificial intelligence, so the issue of researching criminal rules that deal with applications of artificial intelligence has become an urgent matter in light of the results of reality related to some accidents, which researchers, specialists, and experts worked on analyzing and dealing with research and study.

Among the most prominent incidents that the researchers dealt with related to the uses of artificial intelligence was the incident in which an Uber self-driving car collided with a woman on the road in March 2018, resulting in her death from her injuries, and another incident represented by a robot in a Japanese bicycle factory killing a worker, by He pushed him using his hydraulic arm towards one of the machines, which led to his death, in addition to the incident of a medical robot during an operation displaying error messages. The medical team was not allowed to manually adjust his arm, which affected the patient after that with complications and severe bleeding because of what happened during the surgical operation.

PART 2: RULES OF CRIMINAL LIABILITY AND PUNISHMENT ON ARTIFICIAL INTELLIGENCE CRIMES

Criminal Liability and Its Forms

There are many jurisprudential definitions of criminal responsibility, and it can be approved as: "the obligation to bear the responsibility for criminal acts and to submit to the penalties prescribed by law" (Ali, 1980). There are only two forms of criminal liability: the first is the criminal liability of a natural person, and the second form is the new form, which is the liability of the legal person.

Then, the question arises about the possibility of criminal law defining a third form of criminal responsibility: the responsibility of the machine controlled by artificial intelligence systems. Talking about this form of criminal liability is premature as long as legalists and legislators do not decide to create this form of criminal liability.

Credit goes to the researcher called Gabriel Halevy for establishing criminal liability rules for artificial intelligence crimes, who worked on establishing criminal liability rules for artificial intelligence entities using three possible models of responsibility: models (responsibility by committing through the other - responsibility for potential corollary results - direct liability).

When we talk about the responsibility of artificial intelligence, we should speak of AI programs and the human being user, the programmer, the owner, and the manufacturing company, as follows:

Liability of the AI Program Itself

The question arises about the extent to which artificial intelligence systems can be held legally liable for their actions, and to take the matter in some detail, it should be noted the importance of distinguishing between forms of artificial intelligence, such as specialized artificial intelligence, which means artificial intelligence systems that can perform specific and clear tasks; Such as self-driving cars, and general artificial intelligence, which can work with a capacity similar to human ability in terms of thinking, as it focuses on making the machine able to think and plan on its own and like human thinking.

Super artificial intelligence, which may exceed the level of human intelligence and can perform tasks better than a specialized and knowledgeable person, is considered a hypothetical concept that does not exist in our current era.

As for specialized artificial intelligence, jurisprudence agrees that it is not currently possible to determine criminal liability for a robot or an artificial intelligence program if it commits a crime. The criminal responsibility defined by the criminal law is the responsibility of the natural person and the responsibility of the moral person in some cases if the crime is committed for his benefit and account. At the same time, for artificial intelligence, it is not possible to say it is criminal responsibility as long as it cannot perceive and distinguish, which is considered the basis for the responsibility of the natural person (Ibrahim, 2020).

A part of German criminal jurisprudence considers adherence to traditional rules related to artificial intelligence crimes, which limit criminal responsibility to humans exclusively, as most experts do not prefer to introduce fundamental changes to criminal law to deal with these new technical developments, so Dr. Susan Beck, "Professor of Law Criminal Law and Philosophy of Law at the German University of Hannover" that: "The criminal law that was developed to deal with individuals faces difficulties in keeping pace with the development of machines that are independent of humans at work, as well as dealing with the developments of artificial intelligence," and it was expressly decided that: "The criminal law naturally provides for tolerance The operator of the machine is responsible, for example, if Google gives you with false information and you make a decision based on it, you will be the one who bears the responsibility (Beck, 2019).

The Program of Artificial Intelligence as an Innocent Mediator

Some tended to examine the hypothesis of using the artificial intelligence program as a mediator to commit the crime, by analogy with the moral actor theory, when the crime is committed by a mentally minor person or an animal. Then, the artificial intelligence program can be considered an innocent mediator. The criminal liability report for everyone who programmed the artificial intelligence program

Or whoever operates or uses it, apart from discussing the issue of criminal liability for this program or application, and some cite the example regarding the responsibility of artificial intelligence as the responsibility of a person who has a mental illness or a natural mental disability that deprives him of the ability to understand what he is doing or his ability to control his actions, or the ability To know whether he is doing or refraining from doing so (Kingston, 2016).

In this case, the assumption is that the artificial intelligence entity does not attribute any mental ability to it. Therefore, there is no legal difference between it and the machine used in the crime, while about general or superior artificial intelligence, it is expected in the future to develop the rules of legal responsibility for its actions in light of its characteristics that bring it closer to the characteristics of human beings, the most prominent of which are: the availability of the two properties of perception and discrimination, and then the availability of freedom of perception, which is the basis for achieving criminal responsibility for a person's act, and then it can also be said that criminal punishment can be imposed on him (GLESS et al., 2016).

Hence, the assumption in this case is that the artificial intelligence entity is not dependent on a specific programmer or user. Therefore, three conditions are required for the responsibility of the artificial intelligence entity for the crime:

1- It must be proven that the crime occurred as a result of the behavior of the AI entity itself.
2- It proves that the AI entity committed the crime without relying on a programmer or user.
3- It proves that the entity committed the crime with knowledge or intent.

Suppose the artificial intelligence program or system controls a mechanical or other machine to move its moving parts. In that case, any positive or negative action performed by this machine can be considered implemented by the artificial intelligence entity (Ibrahim, 2020) in light of the characteristics of artificial intelligence techniques. Self-learning, as well as its use of advanced algorithms that enable it to make and implement decisions without human intervention, in addition to the feature of learning from the situations it is exposed to and the presence of giant and advanced databases inside it that enable it to do the right thing in most situations (Dahshan, 2020).

Determining the intent is the most challenging matter; some give an example of a speeding violation by self-driving cars. Speeding is a strict liability crime. Suppose a self-driving car is found to have exceeded the speed limits on the road it is running on. In that case, the law may refer criminal responsibility to the intelligence program, who was driving the car at the time," without questioning the car's owner.

Some believe that for AI entities to have criminal liability, they should be treated as legal persons, such as commercial companies, and the previous opinion adds to this the possibility of granting AI entities some legal rights in line with those given to commercial companies as moral persons (Ibrahim, 2020).

In sum, we conclude that the criminal liability for crimes of artificial intelligence is to talk about the criminal responsibility of each of the designers or manufacturers of artificial intelligence systems and its users without addressing the issue of criminal responsibility of the self-driving machine that lacks the elements of the availability of criminal liability towards it as previously mentioned. Suppose the matter may witness a development in the rules of criminal responsibility commensurate with the developments in this field. In that case, we discuss some hypotheses that regulate how to hold accountable those who cause crimes due to the misuse of artificial intelligence systems according to the established rules in the criminal law, as the person is not responsible for the crime. Its punishment is not imposed on him except as a perpetrator or accomplice.

Liability of the Natural Person for Crimes of Artificial Intelligence

Criminal responsibility is only achieved by the person responsible for this crime, which depends on attributing the material and moral pillars to him. According to the honest attribution of the act, responsibility does not occur unless the will of the perpetrator to whom the act is attributed is materially directed towards its commission.

Hence, the rules of traditional criminal liability do not apply to artificial intelligence systems or self-driving machines, which lack awareness and discrimination, which is the basis for realizing the will constituting the criminal intent carried out by criminal responsibility. A person cannot be considered criminally responsible except for his act or abstention.

The first condition is the existence of a material relationship between the crime and the behavior of the person responsible for it, which assumes the person's contribution to the crime by his act, the availability of a causal relationship between the act of contribution and the criminal result that the legislator relies on in criminalization and punishment.

On the other hand, reference is made to the importance of the role of natural persons in artificial intelligence crimes, as they play an essential role as the people behind these devices. Then, they ask about the circumstances in which the artificial intelligence entities acted, the programs they designed and implemented in the artificial intelligence program, and the machine or device running this software (Nedbálek, 2018).

Significance of Establishing a Causal Nexus in the Availability of Personal Liability

The idea of criminal activity is inseparable from the illegal result, as both are two intimate ideas that are indispensable for any of them to carry out the criminal act that constitutes the material element of the crime causal (Bilal, 2010).

The physical link between the act and the result is something that is required by the idea of material attribution, just as the moral link between the two also requires the conscious free will that must be available in the right of the criminal as a condition for his responsibility (Sorour, 2003), the most prominent of which is: the theory of sufficient causation, and then the criminal responsibility of the manufactured person may be achieved or the user of artificial intelligence systems for crimes committed by self-driving machines, as long as the error on the part of artificial intelligence systems, in which the crime was realized, should have been expected by the average person at the time of the activity that caused the crime.

In the scope of artificial intelligence, a distinction can be made between the responsibility of each programmer, manufacturer, and operator on the one hand, the responsibility of the user or owner on the other hand, and the responsibility of third parties, as follows:

Liability of the Programmer, Manufacturer, and Operator

In the framework of manufacturing and innovating artificial intelligence systems, a distinction can be made between the programmer, who means the person who sets the codes that run the work of the artificial intelligence system, which is prepared using machine language. He asks about the crimes committed by the artificial intelligence system if the crime was committed due to his fault, Feeding the system with the steps to be taken to deal with possible situations during its operation, according to the theory of probabilistic intent.

The factory means the person responsible for manufacturing the physical devices managed by the artificial intelligence system, and the programmer and the manufacturer may be one person (Dahshan, 2020). There may be more than one person, and the robot maker is asked about the machine's defects resulting from poor manufacturing, which may lead to the robot's failure and actions out of its ordinary course (Nevejans, 2016). For example, a defect in the medical care robot leads to the wrong movement of the patient, which worsens his health condition (Goeldner et al., 2016), and as another example, harming the patient due to the medical robot's miscommunication with the analysis lab or neglecting the robot's maintenance from the manufacturer (Cristiano Almonte vs. Averna Vision & Robotics, 2015).

In any case, the owner of the factory cannot refer to the worker who does not understand anything about robots and has forced him to enter the manufacturing process (Joshua Drexler vs. Tel Nexx, 2015), while the operator means the professional person who is based on exploiting the robot; Such as: managing the virtual commercial bank, which operates an intelligent application that relies on a robot in managing some banking operations, as an error may occur in managing customer accounts (Al-Qusi, 2018).

Owner and User Liability

The owner means the person who operates the robot personally to serve him or his clients, such as the doctor who owns a hospital that owns and operates a medical robot to carry out surgical operations if the robot poses a threat to the safety of patients, with the knowledge of the doctor who owns the hospital about that, and his willingness to harness the robot as he works without pay for its implementation (Al-Qusi, 2018).

The user means the affiliated person who is based on the use of the robot other than the owner or operator and who is responsible for the behavior of the robot that has caused harm to people, and the user may be a beneficiary of the robot; the self-driving robot bus may use a group of people traveling through an electronic board and one of them sends a wrong command to the bus, which causes a traffic accident, or the professional operator may take a human user to use the robot so that he is an assistant to him; The user, who is affiliated with the company operating the robot, may be sued for negligence in its maintenance (Cristiano Almonte vs. Averna Vision & Robotics, 2015).

LIABILITY OF THE OWNER OR THE USER AS THE ORIGINAL PERPETRATOR OF THE CRIME

We address the following hypotheses.

The First Hypothesis Is the Use of Artificial Intelligence as a Means of Committing a Crime

The assumption, in this case, is that the offender harnesses a machine driven by artificial intelligence systems to use it in committing crimes, which requires that a causal link be established between the behavior of the offender and the criminal outcome achieved using artificial intelligence systems so that it can be said that he has criminal responsibility for crimes committed with the knowledge of the driven machine. Artificial intelligence systems and the basis for this is that the criminal legislator has the same means of committing the crime, as the perpetrator may use a stick or a firearm to assault the victim. He may use an animal that cannot think and perceive and direct a machine driven by artificial intelligence to achieve the same result.

Jurisprudence requires that evidence be established that the robot or the artificial intelligence system is subject to the offender's will, its use of the robot with prior knowledge, and the direction of its intention to achieve the crime through this robot (GLESS et al., 2016).

In this context, researchers address the hypothesis that programmers or users program or use the artificial system entity knowingly and intentionally to commit a particular crime, but the artificial intelligence entity deviates from the plan and commits some other crime in addition to or instead of the planned crime (Ibrahim, 2020). In this case, it can be said that the intentional criminal liability of the programmer or user is available based on the general rules established in this regard regarding deviation from the goal or mistake in personality (Wazir, 2008) and the criminal liability for them does not negate.

The Second Hypothesis Is the Idea of Probabilistic Intent

Some address the hypothesis that the artificial intelligence system commits a crime if the standard procedures of the artificial intelligence system are misused to perform a criminal act, as analysts refer to the case of an artificial intelligence robot in a Japanese bicycle factory killing a human worker, the robot wrongly identified the employee and considered him a threat to its mission, and he thought that the most effective way to eliminate this threat was to push it into the neighboring operating machine, so the working robot moved the worker using the hydraulic arm towards the machine, killing him (Kingston, 2016).

Then, the previous opinion calls for holding the machine programmer accountable if he knew about the possibility of this criminal result before its occurrence. Here, the perpetrator has committed a behavior and expected that this behavior might result in a particular result. Still, despite this expectation, it occurred before the result was achieved as a possibility of his behavior or as a possible natural consequence, which is what performs his responsibility for the crime due to his probabilistic intent (Wazir, 2008).

The Third Hypothesis Is Negligence in the Manufacture, Programming, or Use of Artificial Intelligence

In this case, the assumption is that the perpetrator, as a user, manufacturer, or programmer of artificial intelligence, did not want to use it in committing the crime. Still, the crime occurred due to his negligence or negligence, or his failure to observe the rules of caution and precaution. In this case, this user, manufacturer, or programmer will be criminally responsible for the illegal intentional crime, which requires that the relationship between the occurrence of the crime be proven through the artificial intelligence system and the unintentional mistake against the perpetrator (Al-Qusi, 2018).

In this case, the assumption is pure negligence by the programmers or users, who may have acted negligently or failed to act. Therefore, nothing can prevent them from determining their criminal responsibility for unintentional crimes based on negligence and failure to perform their duties, which led to the commission of the intelligence system for a specific crime or crimes.

Some distinguish artificial intelligence crimes between two forms of crimes. The first is the crimes that occur due to a software error or a loophole in the artificial intelligence system, resulting from the fact that the machine code was insufficient to anticipate all possibilities or that the crime that was committed occurred. Through the misbehavior of the owner or the intervention of an outside party to penetrate the machine and use it as a tool in the commission of his crime, in these cases, the responsibility is achieved towards the natural persons causing the occurrence of the crime (Dahshan, 2020).

This system can learn and develop itself and make individual self-decisions outside the software system set for it. In this case, criminal behavior stems from free will without software intervention from the factory, and it is unfair to hold the programmer accountable for a mistake made by the artificial intelligence system.

A question about the nature of the criminal responsibility of the user of artificial intelligence systems: Is it direct or assumed responsibility? Can the responsibility of the person using the artificial intelligence systems be attached to the responsibility of the autonomous machine for the act? The perception of this is not valid given that the assumed responsibility assumes the realization of the criminal responsibility of another person, which is an assumption that is not available given the lack of determination of the criminal responsibility of such machines. Therefore, it cannot be said that the human criminal responsibility for the crimes of artificial intelligence is an assumed responsibility, or Responsibility is transferred automatically from the machine to the human being to realize his responsibility for the crime committed from these systems or applications.

Contrary to this opinion, some believe criminal responsibility based on error should be transformed into responsibility based on taking risks. The previous opinion believes that establishing the responsibility of the owner or user on the idea of assumed responsibility for crimes committed through artificial intelligence that falls into his possession. Consequently, the onus falls on him to prove his lack of responsibility. Some proponents of the previous opinion establish this assumed responsibility according to the responsibility model of the natural possibility, which was dealt with by Gabriel Halevy, which went to the possibility of holding the programmer or user accountable if the crime committed was a wild and probable result of the behavior of the artificial intelligence entity, and this is assumed Opinion is the ability of programmers or users to anticipate potential wrongdoing by an AI entity (Hallevy, 2010).

Hence, the possibility of any person being held accountable for the crime of artificial intelligence if it is a natural and possible consequence of this behavior, and this model for establishing responsibility based on realistic possibility requires that the programmer or user be in a neglected mental state and nothing more. Then, the programmers or users are not required to know any commission Coming to a crime due to their activity. Still, they must understand that this crime is a possible result of their actions, as they are responsible for the possible future crime even though they were unaware of it.

Liability of Third Parties for Crimes of Artificial Intelligence

As previously mentioned, a third party means anyone other than those associated with the artificial intelligence system. This third party may be a partner of one of the persons related to the artificial intelligence systems, such as the programmer or the user, and may be an independent actor from them, which we will address as follows:

Third-Party Liability as an Accomplice to the Crime

Criminal jurisprudence defines the theory of the moral perpetrator of the crime, which is meant by the person who uses others to carry out the crime, so he is like a tool or a tool that this person uses to investigate the elements of which the crime entity is based. His body, but he used the help of someone else who was more like a machine directed by the moral actor (Hosni, 1992). Examples of moral actors are those who incite crime, a person who is not qualified for criminal responsibility, such as the insane, or a person who is not discerning, such as a child, or a person with good intentions.

The basis for determining this theory is that the legislator has equated the means that the offender imagines using to commit the crime. The law does not distinguish between the tools used by the offender in committing his crime. Criminal or good faith does not have its independence of character (Hosni, 1992).

Liability of Others as Principal Perpetrators of the Crime

The researchers address the hypothesis that someone obtains in some way the codes for the operation of the artificial intelligence entity or exploits a vulnerability in the artificial intelligence system, whether by negligence on the part of the owner, user, or manufacturer or without that and through the use of these codes he enters his program or Its system and directing it to commit a crime, beyond the control of the owner or user, in which case this third party is responsible as a principal actor for the crime committed by the AI entity (Dahshan, 2020).

Liability for the Actions of Others

The Egyptian legislator has known some cases that raise the problem of responsibility for the actions of others, such as the successive liability in publishing crimes in the French legislation, which is one of the forms of responsibility for the actions of others. It should be noted that the criminal judiciary and legislation abandoned the idea of responsibility for the acts of others and the person's criminal responsibility for the actions of his subordinates, as the general rules of criminal law decide that it is not sufficient for the availability of criminal responsibility for a specific person to establish the attribution of a particular act or omission to him unless this act is the result of a free will sent This verb into existence.

This free will emanates from criminal intent or unintentional error associated with the act. The will is not free unless it results from a criminal capacity recognized by the law, awareness, or discrimination. This capacity expresses its owner's ability to legally direct his will to what violates the Penal Code. This matter is not available to the self-driving machine; therefore, the criminal responsibility prescribed for the natural person is not fulfilled. The self-driving machine using artificial intelligence lacks the criminal capacity that depends on the availability of awareness and discrimination (Hosni, 1992).

The Responsibility of the Manufacturer of the Artificial Intelligence System for Its Crimes

In light of the criminal law's recognition of the responsibility of the legal person in some cases, it can be said that it is permissible to hold the manufacturer of the artificial intelligence system accountable for its crimes, and two conditions are required for the responsibility of the legal person to be established:

1. That the crime was committed by a member of the legal person or one of its representatives.
2. The commission of the crime must be for the benefit and account of the legal person.

Among the forms of criminal penalties that may be imposed on legal persons, we mention, for example, a financial fine, suspension of the legal person's license to practice the activity for a specified period, revocation of the permit, or dissolution of the legal person, and publication of the judgment at the expense of the legal person.

Hence, it can be said that the manufacturer can be held criminally liable for AI crimes provided that it is proved that the crime occurred due to the manufacturer's fault.

The Right of Defense in Artificial Intelligence Crimes

Some raised some questions about how to exercise the right of defense in the event of an artificial intelligence system committing a crime and whether the defense can plead excluding criminal liability for these crimes, so can a program that works in error claim a defense similar to the human defense under the pretext of insanity? Could an artificial intelligence affected by a cyber-virus claim defenses similar to coercion or involuntary intoxication? These types of defenses are not theoretical at all, and the previous opinion is based on a case in the United Kingdom in which defendants who committed information crimes pleaded not responsible because their devices were infected with malicious software (viruses) that were responsible for the crime (Hallevy, 2010).

In one of the other cases, a denial-of-service defendant pleaded that the Trojan program was responsible and that the program had erased itself before being forensically analyzed, and the defense persuaded the jury to verify this possibility beyond a reasonable doubt. (Hallevy, 2010), Moreover, some support the previous view, suggesting that a robot be given the right to be exempted from punishment if interference from an external source affects its behavior, such as undergoing a hacking process in its system, which may cause it to lose the ability to control his actions and actions that resulted in the behavior (Dahshan, 2020).

Some have questioned the extent to which it is possible to rely on the availability of a state of legitimate defense for a robot or an artificial intelligence entity in the event of an attack by an individual (El-Kady, 2021) and then claim the absence of its responsibility as a reason for permissibility, as the current legal texts do not allow that, due to the limitation of the right of defense The legal right of a person to defend himself and his money and the life and money of others without others, this right is limited to humans. It does not extend to machines and animals. Therefore, it is not permissible for the artificial intelligence entity to rely on the state of legitimate defense of itself or others in the event of its assault on any human being.

Also, it is not permissible for any person to program a robot or any entity that works with artificial intelligence to defend it when it is subjected to an attack, given that this entity does not have the right to protect the life and money of others legally, as this right is limited to humans only, to the exclusion of other entities, and contrary to this opinion, Some see the possibility of this; Provided that the programming of this robot is advanced, and can balance between the act of attacking its owner and its behavior represented in the legitimate defense of its owner, but if the programming of the robot does not reach this development. The person has no right to program a robot to defend it, and its capabilities can be recognized. Robots and the extent of development of their programming systems through the producing companies and their manufacturing profile (Dahshan, 2020).

Punishment for AI Systems

If the artificial intelligence system commits a crime, who will be punished for the crime, and what form will this punishment take? Punishing individuals, even if it does not raise any problems, punishing artificial intelligence systems and robots raises a problem in the application, as it is a machine even if She had artificial intelligence (El-Kady, 2022).

It is noteworthy that this issue is still a matter of disagreement among jurisprudence, as some have argued that the future may witness a revolution in criminal law with the emergence of robots and artificial intelligence systems, as the previous opinion believes that technological development in this field may result in the manufacture of super-intelligent robots that can take decisions without relying on human beings, and then the previous opinion expects a growth in the rules of criminal responsibility to allow for the determination of penalties for such systems; Among the most prominent penalties proposed to be applied to artificial intelligence entities:

1. Confiscation of the AI machine.
2. Destroying it in whole or in part.
3. Stop operating it entirely or partially.
4. Cessation of the program or system that operates with artificial intelligence, in whole or in part.
5. reprogram it (Ibrahim, 2020).

Hence, we are expected to see penalties for artificial intelligence entities similar to those imposed on legal persons.

While some rightly argue that there are no answers to these questions, criminal liability may not apply, so the matter should be settled by civil law.

In summary, regarding the issue of punishment for crimes of artificial intelligence, determining penalties for these crimes requires the issuance of criminal legislation that criminalizes these acts and discriminates specific penalties for them in the application of the principle of illegal legality (there is no crime or punishment except by text), and therefore the separation between the two previous opinions is in the hands of criminal legislators, We can only wait for the legislators to have the final say on this particular issue.

CONCLUSION

1. The evolution of lifestyle and human behavior towards digital transformation and the use of modern technologies in all aspects of life prompts us to say that humanity has entered the era of the Fourth Industrial Revolution, which is based on applications of artificial intelligence.
2. The spread of the uses of artificial intelligence in all areas of life and the occurrence of some incidents that raise issues related to the rules of criminal liability resulting from the uses of artificial intelligence.
3. The inadequacy of the rules of criminal liability to establish a legal framework governing abuses related to the uses of artificial intelligence.

Recommendations

1. Inviting national research centers to adopt a study of the uses of artificial intelligence, establish a legal and economic framework for its use, and organize many scientific and research events to delve deeper into its studies.

2. Directing the attention of the international community towards the necessity of developing a global framework governing the use of artificial intelligence technologies similar to the Budapest Convention on Combating Information Crimes, or at the very least amending the agreement above, to ensure the existence of such rules that regulate the use of artificial intelligence applications, provided that they include a unified international definition of intelligence artificial.
3. Calling on the Egyptian legislator to set rules that regulate the use of artificial intelligence applications and determine appropriate penalties in case of misuse, or at least amend the provisions of the Information Technology Crime Law to allow for the development of an integrated framework to confront the abuse of the data of the Fourth Industrial Revolution, including artificial intelligence technologies.
4. Looking towards creating a department specialized in the use of artificial intelligence systems and digital transformation, primarily criminal justice agencies (judicial and security), to achieve an effective confrontation in dealing with all forms of misuse of these new technologies by criminal and terrorist groups, as well as a department to combat cryptocurrency crimes via the Internet In coordination with the concerned national and international authorities, within the framework of strengthening international judicial and security cooperation.
5. Considering the creation of a unit for studies of digital transformation and artificial intelligence in scientific and research entities and national research centers to research activating the policy of digital transformation and developing technological infrastructure, preparing studies related to applications of artificial intelligence in security work and discussing ways to apply them in practice in coordination with the concerned authorities, and conducting in-depth studies On various issues and topics related to information technology crimes, topics of cyber security and insurance against cyber-attacks, the development of massive databases and the expansion of their applications in the areas of security work, and conducting research in the areas of technological development related to police work to keep pace with scientific progress using modern technical and scientific devices and means.
6. Consider teaching courses for university students that deal with applications of artificial intelligence to familiarize students with the successive developments in this field.
7. Creating a department for technological training in state institutions concerned with developing individuals' technical behavior by organizing several specialized training courses based on technological developments and introducing artificial intelligence applications.
8. Expanding the establishment of specialized departments in the field of securing information networks and government websites and providing them with technical cadres to counter information penetration operations, securing these networks from the risks and repercussions of penetration, and keeping abreast of successive developments in this field, similar to developed countries.

REFERENCES

Al-Qusi, H. (2018). The Problem of the Person Responsible for Operating the Robot - A Prospective Analytical Study in the European Civil Law Rules for Robots. Generation Journal of In-Depth Legal Research, 89-93.

Ali, Y. A. (1980). *Explanation of the General Principles of the Penal Code, Part 1*. Dar Al-Nahda Al-Arabiya.

Ashley. (2017). Artificial Intelligence and Legal Analytics, new tools for law practice in the digital age, University of Pittsburgh School of Law. Cambridge University Press.

Beck, S. (2019). *Autonomous Systems and Criminal Law – new impulses for the concept of responsibility?* https://www.inf.uni-hamburg.de/en/inst/ab/eit/about/newsfeed/2019/ 20190703-beck.html

Bilal, A. A. (2010). *Principles of the Egyptian Penal Code - General Section*. Dar Al-Nahda Al-Arabiya.

Calo, R., Froomkin, A. M., & Kerr, I. (2016). *Robot Law*. Edward Elgar Publishing Limited. doi:10.4337/9781783476732

Corrales, M., Fenwick, M., & Forgó, N. (2018). *Robotics, AI and the Future of Law, Perspectives in Law, Business, and Innovation*. Kyushu University, Springer International Publishing AG.

Cristiano Almonte vs. Averna Vision & Robotics, Inc.; United States District Court, W.D. New York. No. 11-CV-1088 EAW, 128 F.Supp.3d 729 (2015), Signed August 31, 2015.

Cristiano Almonte vs. Averna Vision & Robotics, Inc.; United States District Court, W.D. New York. No. 11-CV-1088 EAW, 128 F.Supp.3d 729 (2015), Signed August 31, 2015.

Dahshan, Y. I. (2020). *Criminal Responsibility for Artificial Intelligence Crimes. Sharia and Law Journal, (82).*

El-Behairy, A. S. G. (2019). *The Impact of Artificial Intelligence Applications on Raising the Efficiency of Security Performance by Application to Road Securing* [Doctoral dissertation]. Police Academy.

El-Kady, R. (2021). Towards approving rules for criminal liability and punishment for misuse of artificial intelligence applications. *Journal of Legal and Economic Research (Mansoura)*, *11*(1), 875–924. doi:10.21608/mjle.2022.217213

El-Kady, R. (2022). Criminal confrontation of encrypted digital currencies and artificial intelligence crimes Analytical study in Egyptian and comparative legislation. *Journal Sharia and Law*, (89). Available at: https://scholarworks.uaeu.ac.ae/sharia_and_law/vol2022/iss89/6

European Police & Darktrace. (2019). *How Technology Will Shape the Future of Cybercrime?* https://www.emaratalyoum.com/

Ghaitas, G. M. (2017). Internet and Digital Transformation Department. International Policy Journal, (180).

Gless, Silverman, & Weigend. (2016). If Robots Cause Harm, who is to Blame? Self-Driving Cars and Criminal Liability. *New Criminal Law Review*, 1-12.

Goeldner. (2015, March). The emergence of care robotics – A patent and publication analysis. *Technological Forecasting and Social Change*, *92*.

Hallevy, G. (2010). The Criminal Liability of Artificial Intelligence Entities – from Science Fictions to Legal Social Control. Akron Law Journal, 4(2), 132.

Hallevy, G. (2013). *When robots kill: Artificial intelligence under criminal law*. Northeastern University Press.

Hosni, M. N. (1992). *Criminal Contribution to Arab Legislation*. Dar Al-Nahda Al-Arabi.

Ibrahim, A. I. M. (2020). *Criminal Liability Resulting from Artificial Intelligence Errors in UAE Legislation - A Comparative Study* [Doctoral dissertation]. Ain Shams University.

Information and Decision Support Center of the Egyptian Cabinet (IDSC). (2020). Artificial intelligence is the most essential element of the Fourth Industrial Revolution. *Bulletin of Future Directions, 1*(1).

Joshua Drexler vs. Tel Nexx, Inc., etc.; United States District Court, D. Massachusetts, Civil Action No. 13-cv-13009-DPW, 125 F.Supp.3d 361 (2015), Signed August 28, 2015.

Khalifa, M. M. T. (2018). Artificial Intelligence in the Balance of Legislation. Dubai Legal Journal, (28).

Khalifa, M. M. T. (2018). *Artificial Intelligence in the Balance of Legislation*. Academic Press.

Kingston, J. (2016). Artificial Intelligence and Legal Liability. *International Conference on Innovative Techniques and Applications of Artificial Intelligence*.

Kurki, V. A. J., & Pietrzykowski, T. (2017). *Legal Personhood: Animals, Artificial Intelligence and the Unborn*. Springer International Publishing AG. doi:10.1007/978-3-319-53462-6

Leemans, T. & Jacquemin, H. (2017). *La Responsabilité Extracontractuelle de l'Intelligence Artificielle*. Master en droit, Faculté de droit et de criminologie (DRT), Université Catholique de Louvain.

Mayer-Schönberger, V., & Cukier, K. (2013). *Big Data: A Revolution that Will Transform How We Live, Work and Think*. John Murray.

Mohamed, S. T. (2020). *Legal Aspects of Artificial Intelligence and Robotics*. https://democraticac.de/?p=64965

Naguib Hosni, H. (1992). *Criminal Contribution to Arab Legislation*. Dar Al-Nahda Al-Arabiya.

Nedbálek, K. (2018). *The Future Inclusion of Criminal Liability of the Robots and Artificial Intelligence in the Czech Republic*. Paradigm of Law and Public Administration, Interregional Academy for Personnel Management. Available at https://maup.com.ua/assets/files/expert/1/the-future-inclusion-of-criminal.pdf

Nevejans, N. (2016). Directorate-General for Internal Policies, Policy Department C: Citizens' Rights and Constitutional Affairs, Legal Affairs. *European Civil Law Rules in Robotics*, No. EA n° 2471.

Parliament, UK. (2016). *Robotics and artificial intelligence*. Report of the Committee on Science and Technology.

Pham, Q. V., Nguyen, D. C., Hwang, W. J., & Pathirana, P. N. (2020). *Artificial Intelligence (AI) and Big Data for Coronavirus (COVID-19) Pandemic: A Survey on the State-of-the-Arts*. Academic Press.

Poirot-Mazeresdu. (2015). Robotique et médecine: Quelle(s) responsabilité(s)? *Journal International de Bioéthique, 24*(4).

Russell, S., & Norving, P. (2009). *Artificial Intelligence - A Modern Approach* (3rd ed.). Prentice-Hall.

Schwab, K. (2017). The Fourth Industrial Revolution - A Book in Minutes. In Summaries of international books. Mohammed bin Zayed Knowledge Foundation.

Sorour, A. F. (2003). *Constitutional Criminal Law*. Dar Al Shorouk.

United Nations Congress on Crime Prevention and Criminal Justice. (2020). *Current Crime Trends, Recent Developments, and Emerging Solutions, especially New Technologies as Means of Committing Crime and Tools for Combating Crime*. Workshop at the Fourteenth Congress held in Kyoto, Japan.

Wazir, A. M. (2008). *Explanation of the Penal Code - General Section, The General Theory of Crime*. Dar Al-Nahda Al-Arabiya.

Weng. (2015, February). Intersection of "Tokku" Special Zone, Robots, and the Law: A Case Study on Legal Impacts to Humanoid Robots. *International Journal of Social Robotics*.

Chapter 4
New Era Plant Disease Detection Techniques and Methodologies Using Artificial Intelligence

Sangita Devi Sharma
Government Naveen College Bori, Durg, India

Aditi Sharma
Bhilai Institute of Technology, Durg, India

ABSTRACT

Agriculture is a backbone for the monetary situation of a country. But plant disease is the principle drawback of agriculture because it reduces the first-class and amount of agriculture products. Disease detection through guide approach is highly priced and time consuming. To reap the most yield from the agriculture area, it is required that farmers need to be provided with the excellent era and methodologies. In this case, artificial intelligence is one of the era used significantly due to its capacity to perceive the issues, developing the proper motives for that, and to establish most appropriate answers for it. Artificial intelligence can act as a useful resource in addressing the illnesses of plants. The present review offers a short compare of the software of artificial intelligence in agriculture, its available techniques for agriculture, and highlights several strategies for the detection of plant disease in plant life.

INTRODUCTION

Artificial intelligence (AI) is a branch of computer technological know-how concerned with constructing clever machines capable of acting responsibilities that generally require human intelligence. Again in 1956 on the Dartmouth conference, an American pc scientist John McCarthy coined "artificial intelligence (AI)" term. The term AI composed of phrase "artificial" which means made or produced by human being instead of occurring evidently and "intelligence" which is stands for the ability to acquire and apply understanding and competencies. AI makes it possible for machines to analyze from past enjoy, modify to new inputs and have the potential to execute obligations evidently associated with human

DOI: 10.4018/979-8-3693-0847-9.ch004

intelligence, like speech popularity, choice making, visible belief and translating languages. AI is not a "guy versus gadget saga" however it's far a "guy with system synergy". It makes a revolution in agriculture via changing conventional techniques via using extra green techniques. (Talaviya et al., 2020). Intervening of AI in Agriculture is serving farmers to get better their farming efficiency and decrease environmental hostile impacts (Suxena et al., 2020). Because of disorder infection is the fine and quantity of agriculture products are degraded (Ganatra and Patel, 2018). For identification and detection of plant sickness in agriculture subject, the AI method is delivered because of its without problems adaptability, speedy overall performance, precision, and price-viability (Eli-Chukwu, 2019). The fundamental idea of AI in agriculture is artificial Intelligence in Agriculture no longer simplest enables farmers to apply their farming competencies but also shifts to direct farming to get better yields and better pleasant with fewer resources (Khandelwal and Chavhan, 2019).

HAZARDOUS PLANT DISEASE REPORTED IN AGRICULTURE FIELD

There are types of diseases (as a result of fungi, bacteria, mycoplasma, virus, nematodes and so forth) suggested in agriculture fields, which have a tendency to resemble every other and can without difficulty be burdened with one another by using green people. False impression one spot for every other may be pretty catastrophic as utility of the wrong fungicide will bring about lack of cash without the plant being dealt with and permitting greater time for the ailment to spread further and reason intensive lack of agriculture merchandise. Some common examples are:

a. **Red rot of sugarcane:** The disorder first seems as red bright lesions on mid rib of leaves and indicates itself as drooping and converting of coloration of upper leaves. Withering of the leaves continue downwards. Commonly 0.33 or the fourth leaf from the pinnacle is affected and indicates drying at the tip. The pith becomes red and in a while brown (Fig-A).
b. **Leaf spot:** The disorder can be characterized itself on leaves as small lesions, which steadily make bigger alongside mid rib and guarantee dark crimson to brown colour. In intense infection, the leaves come to be dry affecting photosynthesis (Fig-B).
c. **Mosaic Virus Disease:** Mottling of young crown leaves displaying a exact pattern of alternating dark and mild inexperienced colored patches of varying length and run parallel to the midrib of leaf (Fig-C).
d. **Yellow Spot:** There exist two kinds of Yellow Spot. The first type of spot is yellow in colour. But, in positive varieties of sugarcane with crimson stalks, the spots appear as pink. In spite of the color, each kind has the same bodily traits. They are irregular in form and size. They can vary from minute dots to spots attaining 1 cm in diameter (Fig-D).
e. **Brown Spot:** Brown spot reasons reddish-brown to dark-brown spots on sugarcane leaves. The spots are oval in form, regularly surrounded via a yellow halo and are similarly seen on both facets of the leaf. The long axis of the spot is commonly parallel to the midrib. This spot frequently tends to be confused with the ring Spot (Fig-E).

Figure 1. Hazardous plant disease reported in agriculture field: a) red rot, b) leaf spot, c) mosoic disease, d) yellow spot, e) brown spot

BASIC METHODOLOGY USED FOR DISEASE DETECTION THROUGH ARTIFICIAL INTELLIGENCE

Artificial Intelligence (AI) is one of the mainstream of research in software engineering with its rapid scientific advancement and the tremendous region of application including agriculture. The basic methodologies utilized for disease detection are followed by flow chart:

(a) **Image Acquisition**: Image of the diseased leaves are received. This database has specific styles of plant diseases, and the photographs are stored in JPEG layout. Those images are then read in MATLAB the use of the read command.

(b) **Image Pre-processing:** Photograph pre-processing is used to erase noise from the image or other item exclusion, by specific pre-processing techniques. Image scaling is used to transform the authentic image into thumbnails because the pixel size of the unique picture is massive and it calls for extra time for the general technique therefore after changing the photo into thumbnails the pixel size gets decreases and it'll require less time.

Figure 2. Basic methodology used for disease detection and classification (Tripathi & Maktedar, 2016)

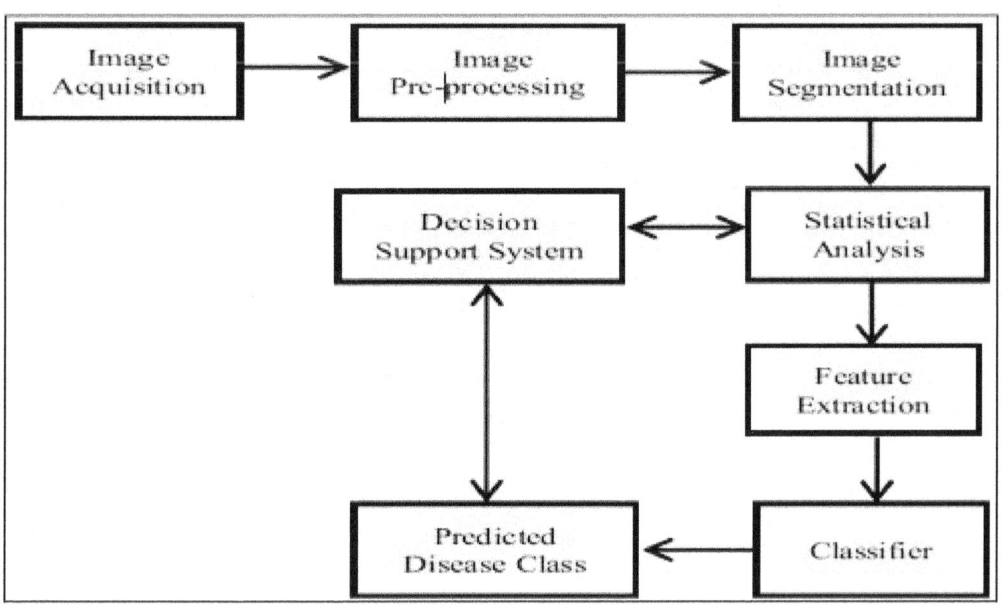

Review of literature

Name of the Researchers	Proposed Work	Result	Significance
Yan-cheng zanget al. 2007	Proposed the fuzzy feature selection approach -fuzzy curves (FC) and surfaces (FS) for cotton leaves disease image feature selection.	This research is done in two steps. Firstly to automatically and quickly isolate a small set of significant features from a set of original features according to their significance and to eliminate spurious features they make use of FC. Secondly to isolate the features dependent on the significant features, utilize FS.	This approach is useful for practical classification applications which reduce the dimensionality of the feature space. The feature selection technique has faster execution speed and higher classification success rate because it does not suffer from the local minima problems inherent in the nonlinear modeling techniques typically used in forward selection and backward elimination.
Libo Liu, Guomin Zhou 2009	Proposed a system for classifying the healthy and diseased part of rice leaves using BP neural network as classifier.	In this study rice brown spot was select as a research object. The images of rice leaves were acquired from the northern part of Ningxia Hui autonomous region. Here the color features of diseases and healthy region were served as input values to BP neural network.	The result shows that this method is also suitable to identify the other diseases.
Patil and Bodhe 2011	Proposed triangle threshold method to segment the lesion region instead of using simple thresholding method.	The average accuracy of the experiment is 98.60%.	
Revathi and Hemalatha 2012	Proposed a system for Classification of Cotton Leaf Spot Diseases Using Image Processing Edge Detection Techniques.	In this paper consists of two phases to identify the affected part of the disease.	Initially Edge detection based Image segmentation is done, and finally image analysis and classification of diseases is performed using our proposed Homogeneous Pixel Counting Technique for Cotton Diseases Detection (HPCCDD) Algorithm.
Sungkur et al. 2013	Implemented a reliable and efficient automated system to recognize fungi-caused disease spots on sugarcane leaves. Pictures of the latter have been taken in a controlled environment using a digital camera	Several descriptors such as Aspect Ratio, Eccentricity, Circularity and Moments Analysis have been analyzed to assess their suitability to recognize the spots.	Moments Analysis has proved to be the most useful. A combination of descriptors that gave the best performance has been used to develop the automated system. The system for detection of Leaf diseases. with help of the feature extracted by the machine learning approach. They have developed based on computer image processing for grading of plant diseases. The result gives the technique for detection of plant diseases. K means clustering and OTSU thresholding methods are used for segment the image
Tian, et al. 2013	Proposed system is composed of three main steps.	In first step, segmentation to divide the image into foreground and background. In the second step, support vector machine (SVM) is applied to predict the class of each pixel belonging to the foreground. And finally, further refinement by neighborhood-check to omit all falsely-classified pixels from second step	The proposed method is compared to the existing method and it is concluded that higher accuracy can be achieved with this method
Kothari J.D. 2018	Investigates the manners by which machine learning models can be applied to improve the cycle of plant disease detection in beginning phases to improve grain security and manageability of the agro-biological system.	Applications of machine learning and deep learning in the field of agriculture are picking up energy. Strategies of image preparing are utilized for precise discovery and grouping of harvest disease and the exact location and order of the plant disease's significant for the productive development of the crop	Several industrially available items are turning out to be well-known step by step to distinguish plant diseases and recognize recuperation arrangements and help farmers in improving their yield profitability and like these benefits.
Reddy and Rekha 2022	Plant Disease Detection using Advanced Convolutional Neural Networks with Region of Interest Awareness	Proposed a framework that considers extraction of ROI using deep CNN prior to prediction of pre-trained deep learning models such as VGG13, ResNet34, DenseNet19, AlexNet, Sqeezenet1_1 and Inception_v3. An algorithm named ROI Feature Map Creation (ROI-FMC) is defined to extract ROI for given input image. This will be given as input to another algorithm proposed namely ROI based Deep CNN with Transfer Learning for Leaf Disease Prediction (ROIDCNN-LDP).	deep CNN models with transfer learning and ROI awareness are found to be suitable for leaf disease detection

continued on following page

Review of literature (continued)

Name of the Researchers	Proposed Work	Result	Significance
Bansal et al. 2023	A Deep Learning Approach to Detect and Classify Wheat Leaf Spot Using Faster R-CNN and Support Vector Machine. In the proposed work, a hybrid model using faster region based convolutional neural networks (R-CNN) has been developed and support vector machine (SVM) for the detection and classification of wheat leaf spot disease.	A dataset of 10,000 images and performed binary classification to distinguish between healthy and diseased wheat leaves, achieving an accuracy of 96.63%. We also conducted multi-classification to categorize the disease severity of the wheat leaves into five different levels, achieving an accuracy of 96.33%. The results of our study demonstrate the effectiveness of the hybrid model in accurately detecting and classifying wheat leaf spot disease. The high accuracy achieved in both binary and multi-class classification indicates that the model is robust and reliable.	The agricultural industry can benefit significantly from our findings since the precise classification and timely identification of plant diseases can prevent substantial crop damage. We believe that a hybrid Faster R-CNN and SVM model offers a promising method for identifying and categorizing wheat leaf spot disease. The findings open up new avenues for agricultural study and demonstrate the potential of machine and deep learning (DL) techniques.

Table 1. Different segmentation techniques (Cheng et al. 2001)

Segmentation Technique	Description	Benefits	Drawbacks
Thresholding Method	It is the simplest method approach of image segmentation by dividing the image pixels based on their intensity level. The threshold value can be computed depending on the peak of the image histogram.	Any prior information about image is not required Fast, simple and computationally inexpensive. Can be easily applicable and suitable for real life applications	It does not work well for image with broad and flat valleys and does not have any peak. Spatial information may be ignored and resultant image cannot guarantee that the segmented regions are contiguous. Threshold selection is very crucial. Extremely noise sensitive.
Region Based Method	In this method construction of segmentation region is based on association and dissociating neighbor pixels. It works on the principle of homogeneity, with the fact the adjacent pixels inside specific region flocks related characteristics and unrelated to the pixel in the other region	It is flexible enough to choose between interactive and automatic technique for image segmentation. More clear object boundaries by the flow from the inner point to outer region. Gives more accurate result compare to other methods	Required more computation time and memory and sequential in nature. Noisy seed selection by user leads to faulty segmentation. Because of splitting scheme in region splitting segments seem square.
Clustering Method	In this method pixels having similar characteristics in image are segmented into same clusters. Cluster an image into different parts based on the features of the image. The k-means algorithm is commonly used for this method	Homogeneous regions can be easily obtained. Computationally faster. K-means works faster for the smaller value of K.	Poor worst-case behaviour. It requires similar size clusters, so the assignment of the adjacent cluster center is the correct assignment.
Edge Based Method	In this method all edges are detected first and then to segment the required region, edges are connected to form the object boundaries. It is based on discontinuity detection in edges.	Works well for the images with better contrast between regions.	Work not well for the image having more edges. Selection of right object edge is difficult
Partial Differential Equation Based Segmentation Method	These are fast and appropriate for time critical applications. It is based on the differential equation working.	Fastest Method	Computational Complexity is more

(c) **Image segmentation**: Image segmentation is one of the most extensively used strategies to distinguish pixels of photo properly in a targeted app. It distributes an picture into several discrete states such that the pixels have super similarity in each place and high dissimilarity between areas.

(d) **Statistical evaluation:** Artificial Intelligence can provide a powerful and sensible solution for the problem and brought device studying (ML) and Deep getting to know (DL) (Murugesan et al. 2019). Gadgets mastering to educate the massive facts units available publicly give us a clear manner to discover the disorder found in flora in a giant scale (Ramesh et al. 2018). The machine mastering-primarily based a process, which allows you to be used for detecting and classifying the sicknesses on agricultural merchandise including numerous plants, culmination and vegetables (Tripathi and Maktedar 2016). A robotic that identifies the leaf ailment making use of picture processing and device learning is conveyed (Kumar and Vani 2018). The survey of CNN-based research efforts applied in the agricultural area (Kamilaris and Prenafeta-Boldú 2018).

Machine Learning: Machine getting to know AI utility and were efficiently made in the gift global for the diagnosis of diseases. System gaining knowledge of algorithms are speedy and correct to discover any illnesses. The paper employed to increase the recognition fee and the accuracy of the results through the use of device learning and deep gaining knowledge of algorithm and detect the plant sickness (Ramesh et al. 2018).The support Vector gadget (device mastering algorithm) is a higher alternative for detection of illnesses (Tripathi and Maktedar 2016).

Deep Learning: Deep studying facilitates in locating out a critical relationship inside the information as well as it also records the records concerning current customers that could help sufferers having similarities in symptom or sicknesses. Plant disease identification model based on deep mastering proposed in this paper can overcome the complexity of the environment and improve the accuracy of identification (Khandelwal and Chavhan, 2019)

(e) **Feature characteristic Extraction:** Function extraction is a critical part of disorder detection. It plays a vital role within the identification of an object. Function extraction is applied in numerous packages in image processing. Shade, texture edges, morphology are the capabilities, which can be applied in ailment detection (Table-2).

(f) **Detection and classification of plant disease by classifiers:** The very last levels are the detection of the disease with the help of different classifiers (Table-3). Classifiers are used to classify the images according to their features..

ADVANCED TECHNIQUES BY USING CONVOLUTIONAL NEURAL NETWORKS (CNN)

To carry out plant disease detection and diagnosis the use of simple leaves photos of wholesome and diseased plants Convolutional Neural network (CNN) models had been created, through deep studying methodologies. First person has to capture the plant leaf photo from app. The utility will send this picture to our AI system. The image is going thru wide variety of processing steps like preprocessing, characteristic extraction, choice of function and many others. A novel technique of creating a visible database that has been effectively used to teach CNN that is a deep residue with 97.8% accuracy in detecting four species of bugs (Liu and Chahl 2021).Convolutional neural networks can receive any form of records

Table 2. Summary of different texture feature extraction techniques (Solanki et al. 2015)

Method	Description	Merits	Demerits
Grey Level Co-occurrence Matrices	a) It is statistical method used to examine the texture which considers the spatial relationship of pixels is the grey level co-occurrences matrix.	a) Feature vector length is small b) Can be applied for the different colour space for colour co-occurrence matrix	a) Many matrices is required to be computed b) It's not invariant with rotation and scaling
Wavelets Transform	a) It works better on the frequency domain rather than the spatial domain	a) Best features with the higher accuracy can be produced	a) It is quite complex and slower
Independent Component Analysis	a) It is computational method for splitting a multivariate signal into additive small subcomponents	a) Higher order statistics can be easily obtained b) It separates mixed signal into a set of independent signals.	a) It is rarely used method.
Gabor filter	a) It is used to analyses specific frequency content in the image in specific directions in a localized region around the region of interest	a) It is multi resolution and multi-scale filter b) It is used for orientation, spectral bandwidth and spatial extent	a) So many filters are used in application so overall computational cost is high.

Table 3. Summary of different classifiers (Solanki et al. 2015)

Classifier	Description	Merits	Demerits
Naive Bayes Classifier	a) It is Probabilistic classifier b) Strong independence assumption theorem c) value of the particular feature is independent of the value of any other feature	a)Small amount of training data is required for classification	a)Interaction between features can't be learnt because of independency among the feature
K-nearest neighbor	a) It is statistical and nonparametric classifier b) Weight can be assigned to the contributions of the neighbors, so nearer neighbor donate more in the average than the distance neighbor c) Distance metric has been calculated for samples and classify based on this distance d) It uses Euclidean distance to calculate distance	a) Implementation is simple b) Don't required classes to be linearly separable	a) Very Sensitive to noisy or irrelevant data b) More time consuming testing process because requires calculation of distance to all known instances
Support Vector Machine	a) It is based on the decision planes that define decision boundaries. b) There are two stages of its working 1) off-line process 2) online process c) Multi-class support vector machine as a set of binary vector machine is used for training and classification	a) It is effective in high dimensional spaces b) In comparison with other classification techniques classification accuracy is high. c) SVM is robust enough, even though training samples have some distortion.	a) Training time is very high with large data set b) For mapping original data into high dimension data selection of kernel function and kernel parameters is difficult
Decision Tree	a) It repetitively divides the working area into small sub parts by identifying its attributes. b) Leaves present the class labels and branches present features that lead to those classes.	a) Small sized trees can be easily interpreted b) For many simple data sets accuracy is comparable with other classifications	a) For some datasets it is observed to over fit with noisy classification tasks.
Artificial Neural Network	a) It is derived from the concept of the human biological neurons system b) It consist of two datasets one for training and one for testing	a) It is robust and can handle noisy data b) Well suited to analyse complex numbers	a) Requires more training time b) Requires large training samples c) Requires more processing time

as enter, inclusive of audio, video, pics, speech and herbal language (Abdel-Hamid et al. 2014). CNN constitutes a class of deep, feed forward ANN that has been implemented correctly to computer imaginative and prescient applications (Le Cun and Bengio 1995). CNN reached excessive precision within the

Figure 3. Block diagram of convolutional neural networks (CNN) (Pawar et al., 2020)

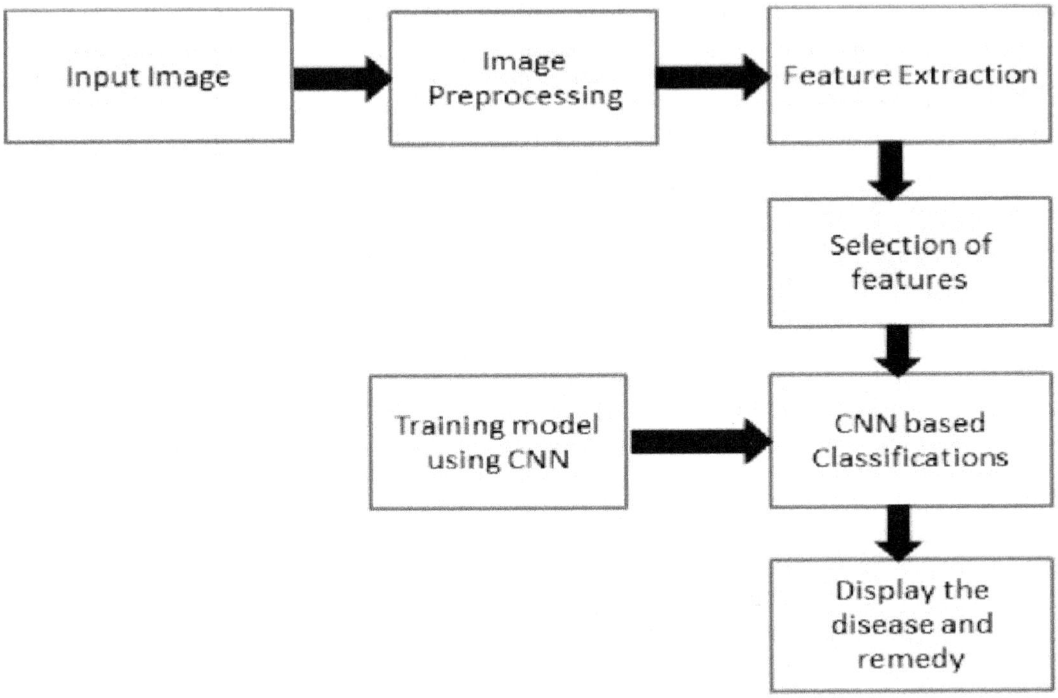

large majority of the problems where they have been used, scoring higher precision than other famous picture-processing strategies (Kamilaris and Prenafeta-Boldú 2018).

VARIOUS FIELDS OF ARTIFICIAL INTELLIGENCE TECHNIQUES USED FOR MONITORING OF PANT HEALTH IN AGRICULTURAL SECTOR (SUJAWAT & CHAUHAN, 2021)

Artificial Intelligence is a rising revolution inside the discipline of plant disease detection in agriculture quarter and has accelerate the satisfactory and manufacturing of crop by means of the usage of following techniques (Khandelwal and Chavhan 2019)

(a) **The Internet of things (IoT) driven development:** The net-of-matters (IoT) is a foundation to affect a big range of sectors and industries, ranging from production, fitness, communications, and power to the agriculture industry. The software of IoT in agriculture is ready empowering farmers with the selection tools and automation technologies that seamlessly integrate products, know-how and services for good performance, high-quality, and income.

(b) **Image-based insight technology:** Drone-based photographs can help in crop tracking, scanning of fields and so on. Farmers can be a part of them with pc vision innovation and IOT to guarantee short activities. Those feeds can produce ongoing weather alarms for farmers.

(c) **Disease detection:** The picture sensing and evaluation make certain that the plant leaf images are segmented into floor regions like heritage, diseased location and non-diseased location of the leaf. The inflamed or diseased vicinity is then harvested and sent to the laboratory for additional diagnosis.

(d) **Expert system:** The need for professional systems for the switch of technical statistics in agriculture may be diagnosed by means of figuring out troubles via the traditional technology transfer system, and by means of demonstrating that professional systems can assist to triumph over the issues recognized, and are probable to be advanced.

(e) **Field management:** Employing snap shots of high description from the drone and copters structures, actual-time estimations can be accomplished for the duration of the period of cultivation by means of building an area map and discovering areas in which the vegetation require water, fertilizer and insecticides.

(f) **Robotics in Agriculture**: Agribot or Agbot is an Agriculture robot. It helps the farmer to boom the crop's efficiency and also reduces the need for manual labour to the farmer. In the approaching generations, we are able to expect that those agricultural robots will do the tilling, sowing, harvesting and lots of other farm works personally. Certainly, even the weeding, control of pests and illnesses might be treated with the aid of these agricultural robots.

(g) **Automation techniques in irrigation and permitting farmers:** AI carried out machines alert of ancient climate outline, fine of soil and sort of plants to be grown, can automate irrigation and decorate the whole yield. Almost 70% of the sector's freshwater useful resource is applied for irrigation; such automation can preserve water and benefit farmers in handling their water probs.

(h) **Crop fitness tracking**: Remote sensing (RS) strategies at the side of hyperspectral imaging and 3-d laser scanning are essential to constructing crop metrics over thousands of acres of cultivable land.

CONCLUSION

The present review summarizes the exclusive applications of artificial intelligence in agriculture sector. The primary motive of this review from researchers to makes strategies of artificial intelligence to resolve the problems of farmers in getting the specific yield. The paper additionally highlights the different literatures, which displays numerous methodologies to discover the illnesses in vegetation, but problem here is to understand the terminology by the farmers or non-biological persons. For resolving this problem one of the suggestions by authors are that the government organized some training program and trained agriculture students/ peoples. These trained persons visit into the field and display the methods to the farmer. Additionally researchers may develop some app where we easily demonstrate how to use these methods. Once this program is result oriented then farmers are easy to use these techniques and apply to prevent their crops as early as possible from hazardous disease and enhance their yield. From the literature, it is concluded that artificial intelligence is a tremendous device for a kingdom's agronomics. Subsequently, researchers need to arrange a right dataset overlaying all area of agriculture and enhance the technology to boom the productivity of number one sectors. By means of the use of proper equipment of artificial intelligence and with the proper dataset, farming may be made greener for farmers. These techniques may be considered because the major implementations to clear up the destiny crisis.

REFERENCES

Abdel-Hamid, O., Mohamed, A. R., Jiang, H., Deng, L., Penn, G., & Yu, D. (2014). Convolutional neural networks for speech recognition. *IEEE/ACM Transactions on Audio, Speech, and Language Processing, 22*(10), 1533–1545. doi:10.1109/TASLP.2014.2339736

Bansal, A., Sharma, R., Sharma, V., & Jain, A. K. 2023. A Deep Learning Approach to Detect and Classify Wheat Leaf Spot Using Faster R-CNN and Support Vector Machine. *IEEE 8th International Conference for Convergence in Technology (I2CT).* 10.1109/I2CT57861.2023.10126124

Cheng, H. D., Jiang, X. H., Sun, Y., & Wang, J. (2001). Color image segmentation: Advances and prospects. *Pattern Recognition, 34*(12), 2259–2281. doi:10.1016/S0031-3203(00)00149-7

Chowdhury, R. R., Arko, P. S., Ali, M. E., Khan, M. A. I., & Apon, S. H. (2020). Nowrin, F. and Wasif, A. "Identification and recognition of rice diseases and pests using convolutional neural networks". *Biosystems Engineering, 194*, 112–120. doi:10.1016/j.biosystemseng.2020.03.020

Eli-Chukwu, N. C. (2019). Applications of Artificial Intelligence in Agriculture: A Review. *Engineering, Technology & Applied Science Research, 9*(4), 4377-4383. https://orcid.org/0000-0002-3995-9118

Ganatra, N., & Patel, A. (2018). A Survey on Diseases Detection and Classification of Agriculture Products using Image Processing and Machine Learning. *International Journal of Computer Applications, 180*(13), 7–12. doi:10.5120/ijca2018916249

Halder, M., Sarkar, A., & Bahar, H. (2019). Plant Disease Detection By Image Processing: A Literature Review. *SDRP Journal of Food Science & Technology, 3*(6), 534–538. doi:10.25177/JFST.3.6.6

Hu, X., Zou, Y., Xue, Z., & Wang, W. (2020). Plant Disease Identification Based on Deep Learning Algorithm in Smart Farming. Hindawi Discrete Dynamics in Nature and Society. doi:10.1155/2020/2479172

Kamble, P. L., & Pise, A. C. (2016). Review on Agricultural Plant Disease Detection by using Image Processing. *International Journal of Latest Trends in Engineering & Technology, 7*(1), 335–339. doi:10.21172/1.71.048

Kamilaris, A., & Prenafeta-Boldú, F. X. (2018). A review of the use of convolutional neural networks in agriculture. *Journal of Agricultural Science, 156*(3), 312–322. doi:10.1017/S0021859618000436

Khandelwal, P. M., & Chavhan, H. (2019). Artificial Intelligence in Agriculture: An Emerging Era of Research. *Journal of Green Engineering, 10*(11), 1–12.

Kothari, J. D. (2018). Plant Disease Identification using Artificial Intelligence: Machine Learning Approach. *International Journal of Innovative Research in Computer and Communication Engineering, 7*(11), 11082–11085.

Kumar, V., & Vani, K. (2018). Agricultural Robot: Leaf Disease Detection and Monitoring the Field Condition Using Machine Learning and Image Processing. *International Journal of Computational Intelligence Research, 14*(7), 551–561.

Le Cun, Y., & Bengio, Y. (1995). Convolutional networks for images, speech, and time series. In M. A. Arbib (Ed.), *The Handbook of Brain Theory and Neural Networks* (pp. 255–258). MIT Press.

Liu, H., & Chahl, J. S. (2021). Proximal detecting invertebrate pestson crops using a deep residual convolutional neural network trained by virtual images. *Artificial Intelligence in Agriculture*, *5*, 13–23. doi:10.1016/j.aiia.2021.01.003

Liu, L., & Zhou, G. (2009). Extraction of the Rice Leaf Disease Image Based on BP Neural Network. *International Conference on Computational Intelligence and Software Engineering 2009*. 10.1109/CISE.2009.5363225

Murugesan, R., Sudarsanam, S.K., & Malathi, G.V., Vijayakumar, Neelanarayanan, V., Venugopal, R., Rekha, D., Saha, S., Baja' R., Miral, A., & Malolan, V. (2019). Artificial Intelligence and Agriculture 5. 0. *International Journal of Recent Technology and Engineering*, *8*(2), 2277–3878.

Patil, S. B., & Bodhe, S. K. (2011). Leaf disease severity measurement using image processing. *IACSIT International Journal of Engineering and Technology*, *3*(5), 297–301.

Pawar, A., Pawaskar, M., & Ghodke, S. (2020). Review of Plant Disease Detection and Diagnosis Using Deep Learning Model. *IJFGCN*, *13*(2), 456–460.

Ramesh, S., Hebber, R., Niveditha, M., Pooja, R., Prasad, B. N., Shashank, N., & Vinod, P. V. (2018). Plant Disease Detection Using Machine Learning. *International Conference on Design Innovations for 3Cs Compute Communicate Control (ICDI3C)*, 41-45. 10.1109/ICDI3C.2018.00017

Reddy, V., & Rekha, S. K. (2022). Plant Disease Detection using Advanced Convolutional Neural Networks with Region of Interest Awareness. *Journal of Immunology Research & Reports*, *2*(4), 1–7.

Revathi, P., & Hemlatha, M. (2012). Classification of cotton leaf spot diseases using image processing edge detection technique. *International Conference on Emerging Trends in Science, Engineering and Technology (INCOSET)*. 10.1109/INCOSET.2012.6513900

Sambasivam, G., & Opiyo, G. D. (2021). A predictive machine learning application in agriculture: Cassava disease detection and classification with imbalanced dataset using convolutional neural networks. *Egyptian Informatics Journal*, *22*(1), 27–34. doi:10.1016/j.eij.2020.02.007

Saxena, A., Suna, T., & Regi, D. S. (2020). Application of Artificial Intelligence in Indian Agriculture. In *Souvenir: 19 National Convention*. RCA Alumni Association.

Singh, G. S., & Chouhanb, J.S. (n.d.). Application of Artificial Intelligence in detection of diseases in plants:. A Survey. *Turkish Journal of Computer and Mathematics Education, 12*(3), 3301-3330.

Solanki, U., Jaliya, U. K., & Thakore, D. G. (2015). A survey on detection of disease and fruit grading. *International Journal of Innovative and Emerging Research in Engineering, 2*(2), 109-114.

Sujawata, G. S., & Chouhan, J. S. (2021). Application of Artificial Intelligence in detection of diseases in plants: A Survey. *Turkish Journal of Computer and Mathematics Education*, *12*(3), 3301–3305.

Sungkur, R. K., Baichoo, S., & Poligadu, A. (2013). An Automated System to Recognise Fungi caused Diseases on Sugarcane Leaves. *Proceedings of Global Engineering, Science and Technology Conference Singapore*.

Talaviya, T., Shah, D., Patel, N., & Shah, M. (2020). Implementation of artificial intelligence in agriculture for optimization of irrigation and application of pesticides and herbicides. *Artificial Intelligence in Agriculture*, *4*, 58–73. doi:10.1016/j.aiia.2020.04.002

Tian, Y., Zhao, C., Lu, S., & Guo, X. (2011). Multiple Classifier Combination For Recognition Of Wheat Leaf Diseases. *Intelligent Automation & Soft Computing, 17*(5). 10.1109/ICCUBEA.2016.7860043

Zhang, Y. C., Mao, H. P., Hu, B., & Li, M. X. (2007). Features selection of cotton disease leaves image based on fuzzy feature selection techniques. *International conference on Wavelet Analysis and Pattern Recognition*. 10.1109/ICWAPR.2007.4420649

Chapter 5
How Artificial Intelligence Can Help Accounting in Information Management

Albérico Travassos Rosário
https://orcid.org/0000-0003-4793-4110
GOVCOPP, IADE, Universidade Europeia, Portugal

ABSTRACT

Artificial intelligence can greatly assist accounting professionals in information management, streamlining processes, and improving overall efficiency. AI-powered software can automate data entry tasks by extracting relevant information from documents, such as invoices, receipts, and bank statements. AI algorithms can analyze financial data and identify patterns or anomalies indicative of fraud or financial irregularities. AI can analyze historical financial data and market trends to provide predictive insights, helping businesses anticipate future financial challenges and opportunities. Human accountants will continue to play a vital role in interpreting AI-generated insights, making strategic decisions, and maintaining a human touch in client interactions. Based on the above, it is intended to systematically review the bibliometric literature on how artificial intelligence can help accounting in information management using the Scopus database to analyse 77 academic and/or scientific documents

INTRODUCTION

Modern enterprises understand that using traditional systems to manage and process the massive data generated in today's digital era limits their efficiency and competitiveness. As a result, they are committed to integrated advanced technologies that can potentially help them process and manage the data to enhance decision-making and operational efficiency. Artificial intelligence (AI) has emerged as one of these cutting-edge innovations, presenting multiple opportunities that can be leveraged in accounting to enhance information management. For instance, Zhao et al. (2022) indicate that integrating AI-based accounting systems improves accounting efficiency and accuracy of accounting information. In addition, these systems boost accounting informatization, which helps enhance organizational performance

DOI: 10.4018/979-8-3693-0847-9.ch005

and growth. Qiu (2021) explains that AI's capability to revolutionize information management within accounting processes is based on its capability to emulate human intelligence and perform complex tasks. AI systems leverage advanced algorithms and machine learning techniques to ingest, process, and analyze vast datasets with unparalleled speed and precision (Li, 2020). This helps mitigate the risk of human errors that often plague manual data handling, enhances the reliability of financial information, and frees up valuable human resources for more strategic and value-added tasks, such as financial analysis and decision-making.

Furthermore, AI's transformative potential extends beyond mere data processing. For instance, applying natural language processing (NLP) and sentiment analysis in AI helps extract valuable insights from unstructured textual data, such as financial reports, emails, and social media interactions (Ionescu, 2020). This capability enables accountants to comprehensively understand the broader financial landscape, including market trends, customer sentiment, and potential risks. In addition, AI-powered predictive analytics can forecast financial trends, identify anomalies, and even facilitate early fraud detection, bolstering accounting professionals' proactive risk management capabilities (Han et al., 2023). Therefore, this systematic bibliometric literature review (LRSB) explores the multifaceted ways in which AI is reshaping the information management landscape within accounting, explaining its potential to redefine industry practices and elevate financial decision-making.

METHODOLOGICAL APPROACH

The systematic bibliometric literature review (LRSB) methodology was used to collect and synthesize data. The researcher used this methodology since it provides a rigorous and structured approach to assessing the existing scholarly work on the specific study topic (Linnenluecke et al., 2019). LRSB provides a comprehensive overview of the academic landscape by systematically identifying, collecting, and analyzing relevant academic publications, thereby allowing the researcher to identify key trends, emerging research themes, and gaps in the literature. Unlike traditional literature review, LRSB adopts a replicable, scientific, and transparent process that helps minimize bias by exhaustively searching for published and unpublished literature regarding the study topic (Rosário, & Dias, 2023; Rosário, et al.,2023; Raimundo & Rosário, 2022). Moreover, the researcher provides an audit trail that helps readers assess the quality of the studies synthesized in the research and the procedures and conclusions.

Therefore, the LRSB involves the screening and selection of information sources to ensure the validity and accuracy of the data presented, in a process consisting of 3 phases and 6 steps (Rosário & Dias, 2023; Rosário, et al., 2023; Raimundo & Rosário, 2022), (Table 1).

The researchers utilized the Scopus database to locate and identify suitable sources that are highly regarded in the scientific and academic community. However, it is worth noting that this study is limited in that it only considered the Scopus database while excluding other scientific and academic databases. The literature search should encompass peer-reviewed scientific and/or academic publications until September 2023.

The Scopus data was used to search for appropriate and relevant studies. The keyword "artificial intelligence" was used for the initial search, generating 504,377 document results. Since the study focuses on the use of AI in accounting, the researcher then narrowed the search to more relevant studies by adding the keyword "accounting." This action reduced the search documents in 1,966, which were

Table 1. Process of systematic LRSB

Fase	Step	Description
Exploration	Step 1	formulating the research problem
	Step 2	searching for appropriate literature
	Step 3	critical appraisal of the selected studies
	Step 4	data synthesis from individual sources
Interpretation	Step 5	reporting findings and recommendations
Communication	Step 6	Presentation of the LRSB report

Source: adapted Rosário and Dias (2023), Rosário, et al. (2023), Raimundo and Rosário (2022).

then narrowed down using the exact keyword "information management," resulting in 77 studies that were synthesized in the final reporting (N=77). The search process is summarized in Figure 2 below.

We utilized content and theme analysis methods to identify, examine, and present the diverse documents as suggested by Rosário and Dias (2023), Rosário, et al. (2023), Raimundo and Rosário (2022).

The 77 scientific and/or academic documents indexed in Scopus are later analyzed in a narrative and bibliometric way to deepen the content and possible derivation of common themes that directly respond to the research question (Rosário & Dias, 2023; Rosário, et al., 2023; Raimundo & Rosário, 2022).

Of the 77 selected documents, 49 are Conference Proceeding; 16 Article; and 12 Book Series.

PUBLICATION DISTRIBUTION

Peer-reviewed articles on artificial intelligence can help accounting in Information management until September 2023. The year 2021 had the highest number of peer-reviewed publications on the subject, reaching 15.

Figure 2 summarizes the peer-reviewed literature published until September 2023.

The publications were sorted out as follows: 2011 2nd International Conference On Artificial Intelligence Management Science And Electronic Commerce Aimsec 2011 Proceedings (7); ACM International Conference Proceeding Series (7); Journal Of Physics Conference Series (5); Lecture Notes In Computer Science Including Subseries Lecture Notes In Artificial Intelligence And Lecture Notes In Bioinformatics (4); Computational Intelligence And Neuroscience (3); and with 2 publications (Frontiers

Table 2. Screening methodology

Database Scopus	Screening	Publications
Meta-search	Keyword: Artificial Intelligence	504,377
First Inclusion Criterion	Keyword: Artificial Intelligence, Accounting Exactkeyword:	1,966
Screening	Keyword: Artificial Intelligence, Accounting Exactkeyword: Information Management Published until September 2023	77

Source: own elaboration

Figure 1. Documents by year
Source: own elaboration

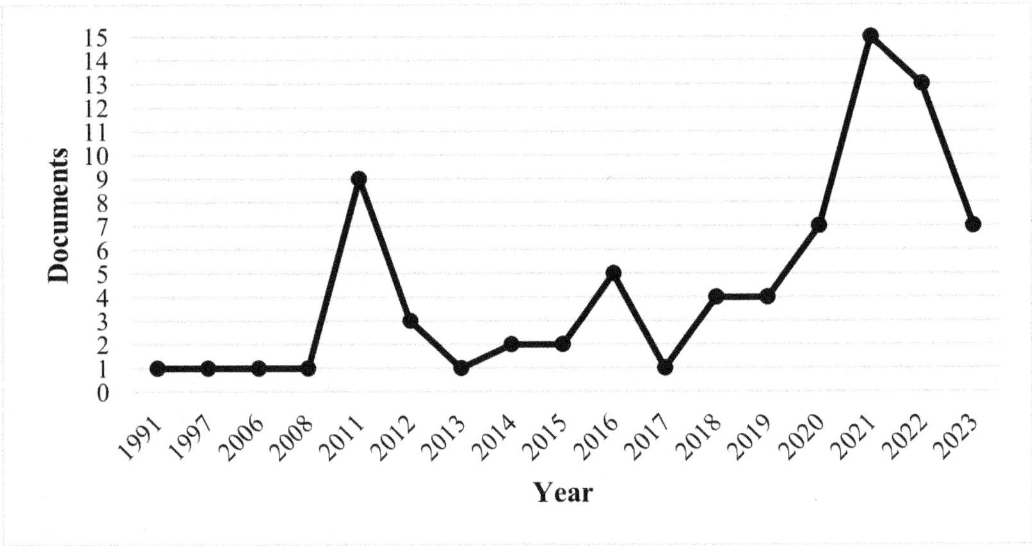

In Artificial Intelligence And Applications; Lecture Notes On Data Engineering And Communications Technologies); and the remaining publications with 1 document.

In Table 3, we analyze the Scimago Journal & Country Rank (SJR), the best quartile, and the H index by Automation In Construction is the most quoted publication with 2,440 (SJR), Q1 and H index 157.

There is a total of 6 publications in Q1, 3 publications in Q2, 3 publications Q3 and 6 publications in Q4. Publications from best quartile Q1 represent 11% of the 77 publications titles; best quartile Q2 represents 6%, best Q3 represents 6% and best Q4 represents 11% of each of the titles of 77 publications. Finally, 36 publications without indexing data represent 67% of publications.

As shown in Table 3, the expressive majority of publications are Q1 and Q4.

The subject areas covered by the 77 scientific and/or academic documents were: Computer Science (56); Engineering (19); Decision Sciences (16); Mathematics (15); Business, Management and Accounting (12); Economics, Econometrics and Finance (7); Physics and Astronomy (5); Energy (4); Neuroscience (3); Social Sciences (3); Medicine (2); Chemical Engineering (1); Earth and Planetary Sciences (1); Environmental Science (1); Materials Science (1); and Multidisciplinary (1).

The most quoted article was "Role of artificial intelligence in operations environment: a review and bibliometric analysis" from Dhamija and Bag (2020) with 110 quotes published TQM Journal 0,730 (SJR), the best quartile (Q1) and with H index (74), "article aims to review significant work by eminent researchers towards artificial intelligence...".

In Figure 2 we can analyze the evolution of citations of the documents published until 2023. The number of citations shows a positive net growth with R2 of 33% for the period ≤2013-2023, with 2023 reaching 105 citations.

The h-index was used to ascertain the productivity and impact of the published work based on the largest number of articles included that had at least the same number of citations. Of the documents considered for the h-index, 9 have been cited at least 9 times.

Table 3. Scimago journal and country rank impact factor

Title	SJR	Best Quartile	H index
Automation In Construction	2.440	Q1	157
Sustainable Energy Technologies And Assessments	1,380	Q1	61
Neural Computing And Applications	1,170	Q1	111
Enterprise Information Systems	1,040	Q1	54
TQM Journal	0,730	Q1	74
Construction Innovation	0,720	Q1	48
Procedia Computer Science	0,510	-*	109
Wireless Communications And Mobile Computing	0,450	Q2	73
Journal Of Intelligent And Fuzzy Systems	0,370	Q2	73
International Journal Of Computers And Applications	0,360	Q3	19
Mobile Information Systems	0,360	Q3	42
IFAC Papersonline	0,350	-*	86
Frontiers In Artificial Intelligence And Applications	0,250	Q4	61
International Journal Of Data Warehousing And Mining	0,250	Q4	24
Journal Of Applied Science And Engineering Taiwan	0,230	Q2	30
ACM International Conference Proceeding Series	0,210	-*	137
Communications In Computer And Information Science	0,190	Q4	62
Journal Of Physics Conference Series	0,180	-*	91
Smart Innovation Systems And Technologies	0,170	Q4	31
Lecture Notes In Electrical Engineering	0,150	Q4	40
International Journal Of Intelligent Information Technologies	0,140	Q4	12
Lecture Notes On Data Engineering And Communications Technologies	0,130	Q3	23
2011 2nd International Conference On Artificial Intelligence Management Science And Electronic Commerce Aimsec 2011 Proceedings	0	-*	13
Computational Intelligence And Neuroscience	0	-*	70
1997 Modeling And Simulation Technologies Conference	0	-*	5
2016 IEEE International Conference On Fuzzy Systems Fuzz IEEE 2016	0	-*	18
62nd IIE Annual Conference And Expo 2012	0	-*	7
Advanced Materials Research	0	-*	47
Climatic Effects On Pavement And Geotechnical Infrastructure Proceedings Of The International Symposium Of Climatic Effects On Pavement And Geotechnical Infrastructure 2013	0	-*	3
International Conference On Self Adaptive And Self Organizing Systems Saso	0	-*	16
Iop Conference Series Materials Science And Engineering	0	-*	54
Mipro 2008 31st International Convention Proceedings Computers In Education	0	-*	2
Proceedings 2011 6th IEEE Joint International Information Technology And Artificial Intelligence Conference Itaic 2011	0	-*	12
Proceedings 2014 International Symposium On Big Data Computing Bdc 2014	0	-*	6
Proceedings 2016 5th IEEE International Conference On Cloud Networking Cloudnet 2016	0	-*	12

continued on following page

Table 3. Continued

Title	SJR	Best Quartile	H index
Proceedings Of 2018 11th International Conference Quot Management Of Large Scale System Development Quot Mlsd 2018	0	-*	9
Proceedings Of The 31st International Business Information Management Association Conference Ibima 2018 Innovation Management And Education Excellence Through Vision 2020	0	-*	15
Proceedings Of The European And Mediterranean Conference On Information Systems Emcis 2006	0	-*	9
Lecture Notes In Computer Science Including Subseries Lecture Notes In Artificial Intelligence And Lecture Notes In Bioinformatics	-*	-*	-*
2022 International Conference On Business Analytics For Technology And Security Icbats 2022	-*	-*	-*
2022 International Conference On Decision Aid Sciences And Applications Dasa 2022	-*	-*	-*
2023 IEEE 3rd International Conference On Power Electronics And Computer Applications Icpeca 2023	-*	-*	-*
3rd International Conference On Cybernetics And Intelligent Systems Icoris 2021	-*	-*	-*
Atit 2020 Proceedings 2020 2nd IEEE International Conference On Advanced Trends In Information Theory	-*	-*	-*
Proceedings 2021 International Conference On Big Data Engineering And Education Bdee 2021	-*	-*	-*
Proceedings 2021 International Conference On Computers Information Processing And Advanced Education Cipae 2021	-*	-*	-*
Proceedings 2022 6th International Conference On Intelligent Computing And Control Systems Iciccs 2022	-*	-*	-*
Proceedings 20th IEEE Acis International Summer Conference On Computer And Information Science Icis 2021 Summer	-*	-*	-*
Proceedings 2nd International Conference On E Commerce And Internet Technology Ecit 2021	-*	-*	-*
Proceedings Of The 12th Iadis International Conference Information Systems 2019 Is 2019	-*	-*	-*
Proceedings Of The 27th International Business Information Management Association Conference Innovation Management And Education Excellence Vision 2020 From Regional Development Sustainability To Global Economic Growth Ibima 2016	-*	-*	-*
Proceedings Of The 28th International Business Information Management Association Conference Vision 2020 Innovation Management Development Sustainability And Competitive Economic Growth	-*	-*	-*
Proceedings Of The 5th International Conference On Electronics Communication And Aerospace Technology Iceca 2021	-*	-*	-*
Proceedings SPE Annual Technical Conference And Exhibition	-*	-*	-*

Note: *data not available.
Source: own elaboration

Citations of all scientific and/or academic documents from the period ≤2013 to April 2023, with a total of 336 citations, of the 77 documents, 33 were not cited. The self-citation of documents in the period ≤2013 to September 2023 was self-cited 285 times.

Based on the main keywords, the bibliometric study investigated and identified indicators of the dynamics and evolution of scientific and/or academic information in documents (Figure 4). The results were extracted from the scientific software VOSviewer, which aims to identify the main search keywords "Artificial Intelligence, Accounting, and Information Management".

Figure 2. Evolution of citations between ≤2013 and 2023
Source: own elaboration

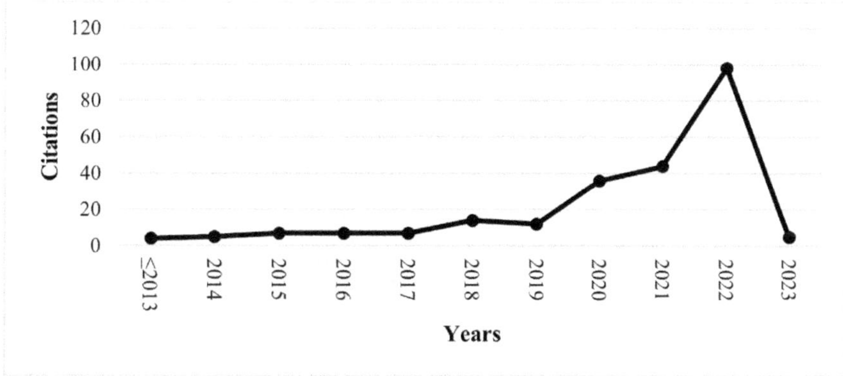

Figure 3. Network of all keywords

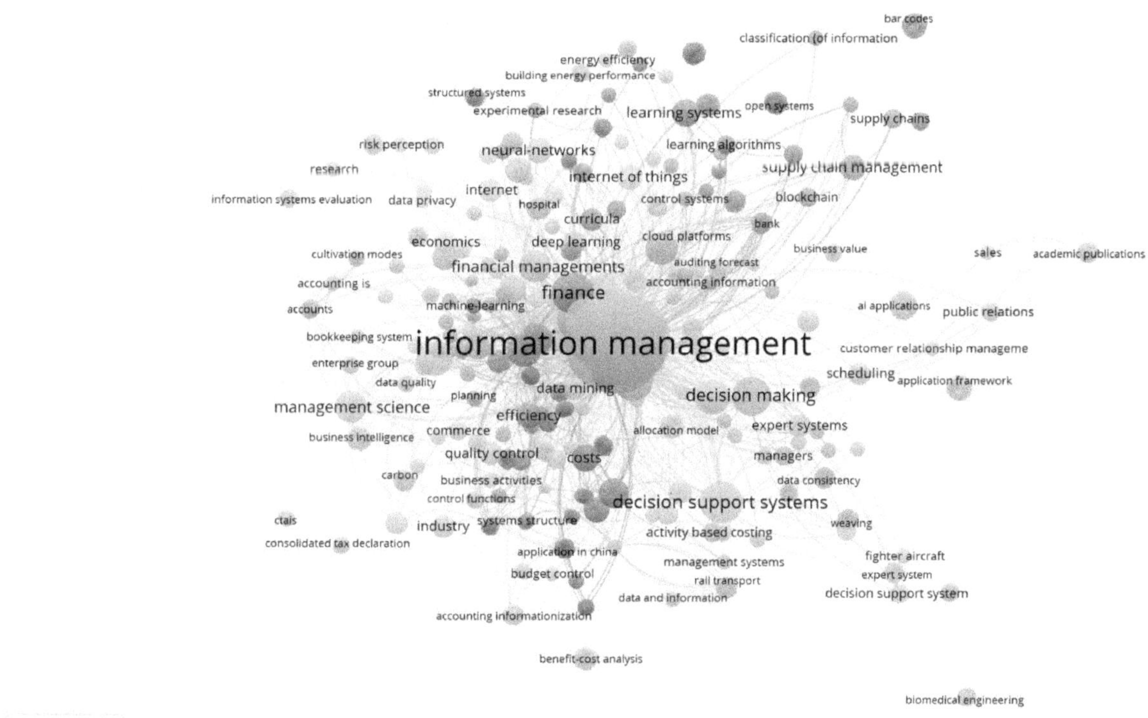

The research was based on scientific and/or academic documents on how Artificial Intelligence can help accounting in Information Management. In Figure 5, we can examine the linked keywords, and thus, it is possible to highlight the network of keywords that appear together/linked in each scientific article, allowing us to identify the topics studied by research and identify trends in future research. Finally, Figure 6 presents a profusion of co-citation with a unit of analysis of the cited references.

Figure 4. Network of linked keywords

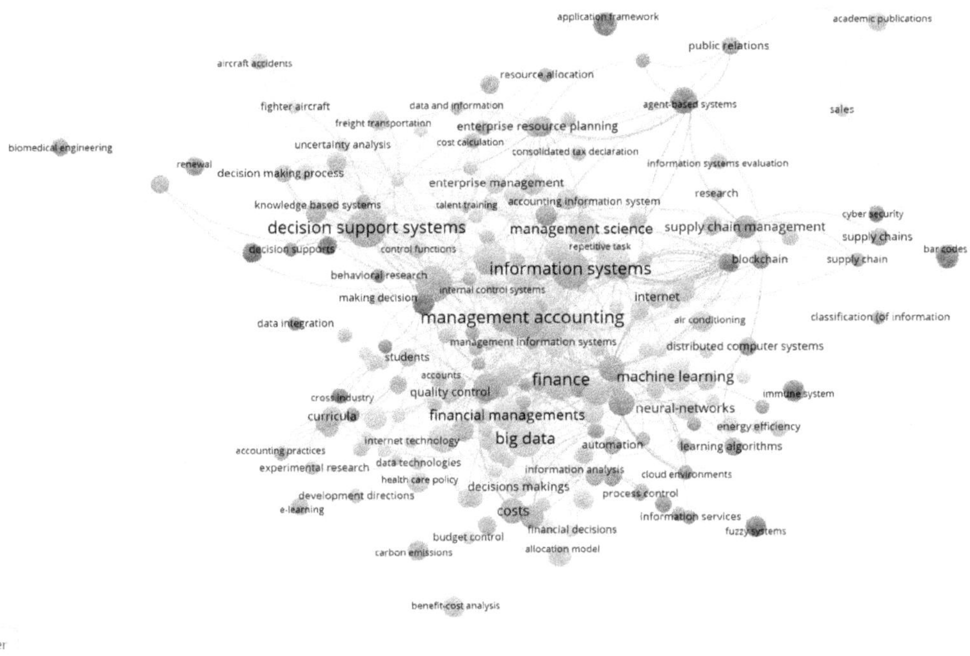

Figure 5. Network of co-citation

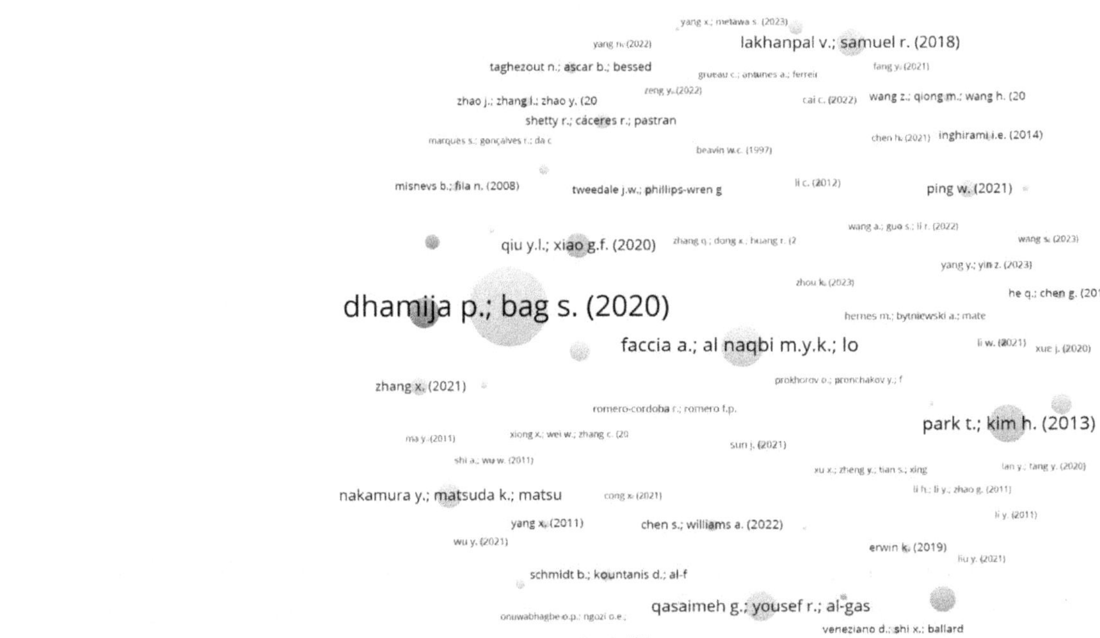

Figure 6. The general AI framework
Source : Adapted from Xu et al. (2021)

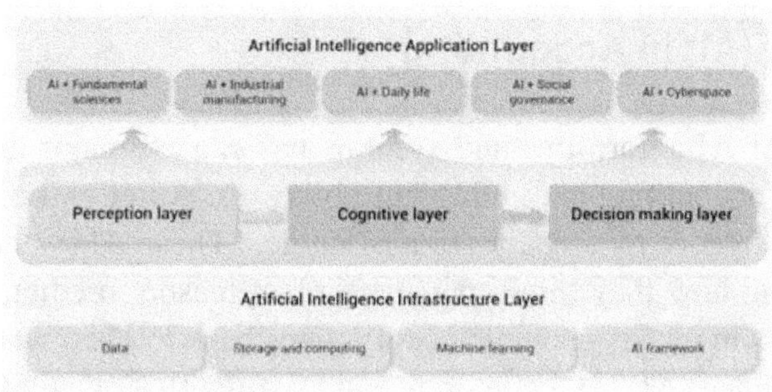

THEORETICAL PERSPECTIVES

Integrating AI tools into modern accounting practice has made it easier, more accurate, and reliable. Accounting professionals are embracing these tech tools to automate tasks and increase efficiency. For instance, AI can help accountants analyze financial data, generate reports, create invoices, and identify patterns and anomalies that suggest accounting fraud (Erwin, 2019). In addition, AI algorithms facilitate advanced data analysis and prediction, which can help accountants and firm managers identify trends and areas of improvement and analyze transactions, cash flows, and budgets more efficiently. These aspects reflect the significant AI impact on accounting, which is further explored in detail in the subsequent sections.

Information Management in Accounting

Information management in accounting constitutes a pivotal component in ensuring the integrity, accuracy, and utility of financial data for decision-making purposes. At its core, information management involves systematically collecting, storing, processing, retrieving, and disseminating financial and non-financial data within an organization (Wang, 2023). Accounting research describes information management as a multidisciplinary practice that draws upon principles of data science, information systems, and accounting standards. Its overarching objective is to provide internal and external stakeholders with reliable and timely information to inform strategic, operational, and compliance-related decisions.

Moreover, information management in accounting encompasses several critical functions. For instance, it involves establishing robust data collection mechanisms, including automating data entry processes to minimize errors and enhance efficiency (Wang et al., 2023; Yang, 2022). In addition, it necessitates the careful organization and storage of financial data in structured databases or accounting systems, ensuring data integrity and security. Ahmad and Zabri (2016) explain that information management in accounting encompasses data processing through activities such as reconciliations, journal entries, and financial statement preparation. In the modern business world, firms are integrating AI and machine learning in these data processing activities, thus transforming the practice by enhancing the speed and accuracy of data processing tasks (Xiong et al., 2022). Other crucial aspects of information management include data retrieval and dissemination, enabling users to access relevant information promptly. Advanced search functionalities and data visualization tools often facilitate this practice. Understanding these multifaceted functions of accounting information management, their interplay, and alignment with accounting principles is paramount for businesses integrating AI systems.

Artificial Intelligence (AI) in Accounting

The significant adoption of AI algorithms and systems has caused major disruptions in various professional fields, including accounting and industrial processes. Xu et al. (2021, p.1) define AI as the "simulation of human intelligence by a system or a machine." These AI systems are designed to mimic human behaviors, including how they think, perceive, plan, reason, predict, and learn. While AI has gained astonishing progress in recent years, its history dates back to 1956 when John McCarthy coined the term "artificial intelligence (AI)" at a conference at Dartmouth College (Collins et al., 2021). Over the years, scientists have developed various AI-related innovations, including expert systems, search algorithms, natural language processing, machine learning (ML), knowledge graphs, and deep learning (DL) (Zdravković et al., 2022). These innovations have continued to make machines more intelligent, thus enhancing their applications in various industries and professional fields.

The general AI framework includes three key developmental stages: perceptual intelligence, cognitive intelligence, and decision-making intelligence. According to Xu et al. (2021), perceptual intelligence equips machines with basic human-like abilities such as vision, hearing, and touch. Cognitive intelligence, inspired by cognitive and brain sciences, aims to imbue machines with advanced skills in induction, reasoning, and knowledge acquisition, mirroring human thinking and cognitive capabilities. The decision intelligence component aims to enhance data-driven decision-making by leveraging applied data science, decision theory, and social and managerial sciences (Figure 6). The AI framework acquires these intelligence components through various infrastructural layers supported by powerful computing and storage systems, data, and ML algorithms (Zeng, 2022). In addition, training models are used to train AI systems to support and realize multiple applications, including industrial manufacturing, sciences, human life, cyberspace, and social governance.

In accounting, firms and professionals leverage AI innovations to analyze the massive data generated through advanced data technologies and obtain useful insights for evidence-based decision-making. For instance, AI-powered natural language processing (NLP) techniques enable accountants to extract valuable information from unstructured textual data sources, such as financial reports, emails, and social media interactions (Li, 2012). This capability is instrumental in understanding market trends, customer sentiment, and emerging risks, empowering accountants to make informed recommendations and strategic decisions (Misnevs & Fila, 2008; Onuwabhagbe et al., 2018). In addition, AI applications in accounting streamline traditional processes and enable accountants to focus on more value-added tasks, such as financial analysis and strategic planning, ultimately contributing to the organization's growth and sustainable competitiveness.

The Role of AI in Accounting Data Processing

AI is revolutionizing how companies manage and analyze financial information. For instance, they are leveraging AI to automate labor-intensive data entry and bookkeeping tasks, reducing human errors and improving efficiency (Ma, 2022). Moreover, AI's ability to analyze vast datasets in real-time enables accountants to make informed, data-driven decisions, elevating the profession from traditional data handling to strategic financial management. This section of the literature review synthesizes research findings on the various roles of AI in managing accounting information.

Automation of Data Entry and Bookkeeping

Accounting firms and professionals use AI tools and systems to automate data entry and bookkeeping. AI technologies have machine learning algorithms, optical character recognition (OCR), and data extraction capabilities (Yang, 2011; Park & Kim, 2013). These tools can automatically ingest and process vast amounts of financial data, such as invoices, receipts, and transaction records, with exceptional accuracy and speed (Li et al., 2011). As a result, accountants using these innovations have managed to mitigate the laborious and error-prone task of manual data entry, freeing up valuable time and resources to focus on more strategic and analytical aspects of their work.

Moreover, AI-driven data entry and bookkeeping automation goes beyond mere data capturing. These systems can categorize and classify transactions, assign appropriate general ledger codes, and reconcile accounts, ensuring that financial records are accurate, organized, and compliant with accounting standards (Yang, 2011). In addition, AI can learn from historical data patterns, becoming increasingly efficient and adept at handling complex financial transactions over time (Prokhorov et al., 2020). These capabilities reduce the risk of data entry errors and enhance the overall efficiency of the accounting processes (Ping, 2021). Therefore, automating data entry and bookkeeping through AI empowers accountants with enhanced accuracy and efficiency and contributes to better financial data management.

These practices are crucial for informed decision-making and regulatory compliance in the accounting profession.

Invoice Processing and Reconciliation

AI tools are significantly improving invoice processing and reconciliation. In traditional accounting practices, accountants and bookkeepers manually extracted data from paper or electronic invoices, matched them with purchase orders and receipts, and reconciled discrepancies. This process was time-consuming and prone to human errors, leading to delayed payments, missed discounts, and reconciliation challenges (Yang & Metawa, 2023; Purnomo et al., 2021).

As a result, AI solutions powered by machine learning and OCR technologies have emerged as a game-changer in this domain. For instance, AI-driven invoice processing systems can automatically extract essential data from invoices, such as vendor details, invoice amounts, due dates, and line-item information, with remarkable accuracy. This automated process accelerates the invoice processing cycle and reduces the risk of errors associated with manual data entry (Qiu & Xiao, 2020). In addition, these AI systems can match invoices with corresponding purchase orders and receipts, flagging discrepancies for review by accounting professionals. By streamlining this reconciliation process, AI helps organizations ensure they only pay for legitimate, accurate invoices, preventing overpayments and enhancing cost control (Romero-Cordoba et al., 2016; Sharif, 2006).

Moreover, AI's ability to learn from historical data patterns means that these systems become more proficient at recognizing and handling complex invoice scenarios. As a result, this continuous progress further improves the accuracy and efficiency of the reconciliation process. Integrating AI in accounting information management ultimately contributes to better financial management and organizational decision-making.

Budgeting and Forecasting

Budgeting and forecasting are essential aspects of financial management in organizations. The integration of AI has significantly impacted these processes by enhancing efficiency and precision (Shetty et al., 2012). Unlike traditional budgeting and forecasting methods that rely on historical data and human judgment, AI's data-driven and predictive capabilities leverage historical financial data and external factors to generate more accurate and dynamic projections (Schmidt et al., 2015; Wu, 2021). Moreover, ML algorithms can analyze large datasets to identify trends, seasonality, and patterns humans might overlook, leading to more realistic and data-driven budget estimates. These systems can also incorporate real-time data, such as market conditions, economic indicators, and even social media sentiment analysis, allowing organizations to quickly adapt their budgets and forecasts in response to changing circumstances. Askary et al. (2018) further explain that AI enhances the efficiency of the budgeting process by automating tasks like data entry, consolidation, and variance analysis. As a result, this automation reduces the risks associated with manual data manipulation. Finally, using scenario modeling capabilities in AI allows organizations to simulate the impact of various financial decisions and strategies on their budgets and forecasts.

Tax Compliance and Preparation

Integrating AI into the accounting practice has ushered in a new era of efficiency and accuracy in managing the complexities of tax regulations and filings. Accounting professionals leverage AI's advanced data analysis and processing capabilities to ensure tax compliance and preparation (Wang et al., 2020). For instance, accounting can use AI-driven tax software to automatically extract and categorize relevant financial data needed to file tax returns. This can ensure compliance with tax regulations while minimizing the risk of errors (Sharma et al., 2022; Shen & Wang, 2021). In addition, ML algorithms can identify tax-saving opportunities and deductions by analyzing historical tax filings and financial transactions, thus providing businesses and individuals with valuable insights to optimize their tax strategies. Cai et al. (2011) note that companies can use AI technologies to stay updated with ever-changing tax laws and regulations, thus automatically adapting tax calculations and forms accordingly. This feature ensures that organizations remain compliant with the latest tax codes, reducing the risk of penalties and audits.

Reduction of Human Errors in Data Handling

Integrating AI into accounting information management reduces human errors in financial data handling. AI-driven data handling systems equipped with machine learning algorithms and advanced data validation techniques can automatically capture and process vast volumes of financial data with unprecedented precision (Zhao et al., 2022). This process helps eliminate the need for manual data entry, which is a common source of errors. For example, AI minimizes the chances of typographical mistakes and ensures accurate data recording. Additionally, AI systems can perform real-time data validation checks, flagging discrepancies and inconsistencies for human review (Yang & Yin, 2023). This enhances the accuracy of financial data and allows accountants and financial professionals to correct errors promptly, preventing potential financial misstatements. AI tools utilize historical data to learn patterns and trends, thus enabling

Figure 7. AI accounting information system for DSS
Source: Adapted from Qiu (2021).

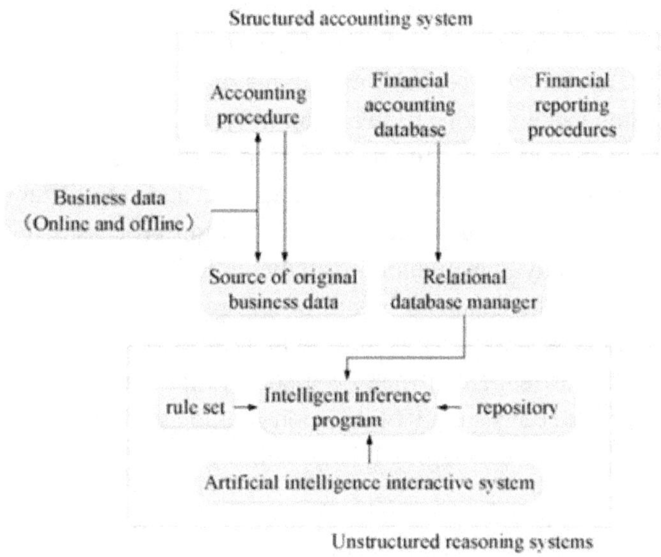

them to recognize anomalies and irregularities in financial data (Zhao & Yuan, 2019). By constantly improving its error-detection capabilities, AI maintains data integrity and ensures that financial reports and statements are reliable for decision-making and compliance purposes.

AI Tools Used in Information Management in Accounting

AI tools present technologies, such as machine learning, natural language processing, and data analytics, to facilitate the efficient processing of financial information. These innovations enable accountants to extract valuable insights from large datasets, automate routine tasks, and enhance decision-making processes, ultimately elevating the accounting field into a more sophisticated and data-driven discipline.

Machine Learning Algorithms

Machine learning (ML) algorithms have emerged as a potent tool in helping accountants handle data analysis tasks. These algorithms can identify intricate patterns, trends, and anomalies within financial data that may escape traditional analysis techniques (Zhang, 2021; Qiu, 2021). For instance, machine learning models can automatically classify and categorize financial transactions when applied to large datasets, making it easier for accountants to discern between various incomes and expenses. Moreover, machine learning can uncover hidden correlations within financial data that can inform strategic financial decisions (Zhou, 2023). By employing regression analysis, decision trees, or clustering algorithms, accountants can identify relationships between variables, such as the impact of different cost drivers on profitability or customer segmentation based on transaction histories.

Expert Systems

Expert systems (ES) are a prominent application of AI in accounting, designed to emulate the decision-making abilities of human experts in specific domains. Hasan (2021) defines expert systems as "computer programs that store an expert's knowledge and simulate his reasoning processes when solving issues in a certain topic." They leverage a knowledge base and an inference engine to provide accounting professionals with expert-level advice and recommendations. Expert systems can assist in various accounting tasks, including financial statement analysis, tax planning, and auditing (Zhang et al., 2011). They are particularly useful for complex and rule-based decision-making processes. For instance, accountants can use expert systems when analyzing financial statements to identify anomalies, calculate financial ratios, and provide insights into the financial health of an organization (Dhamija & Bag, 2020; Fang, 2021). One significant advantage of expert systems is their ability to capture and store the expertise of seasoned accountants. This knowledge can then be made available to less-experienced professionals, enhancing the overall quality and consistency of decision-making within an accounting firm. Moreover, expert systems are also valuable for working with large volumes of data quickly and accurately, reducing the risk of human error.

Decision Support Systems

Decision support systems (DSS) are a pivotal AI application in accounting to assist professionals in making well-informed decisions by processing and analyzing data. Hasan (2021) describes DSS as computer-based systems created to solve non-structured management problems to improve decision-making. DSS in accounting encompasses various functionalities and tools that aid accountants in decision-making (Grueau et al., 2019; Park & Kim, 2013). For example, accountants use DSS for financial forecasting and budgeting. DSS can process historical financial data and utilize advanced forecasting algorithms to project future financial performance (Taghezout et al., 2012). This capability helps organizations plan and allocate resources effectively, optimize budgets, and make informed financial decisions.

Accounting professionals also apply DSS to conduct risk assessment and management. By analyzing vast datasets and applying predictive analytics, DSS can identify potential risks, such as fraud or non-compliance, in real time (Qiu, 2021). Accountants can then take proactive measures to mitigate these risks, ensuring the integrity of financial data and adherence to regulatory requirements. In addition, DSS aids in investment analysis and portfolio management (Park & Kim, 2013). It helps professionals analyze market data, economic indicators, and financial statements to provide insights into investment opportunities and portfolio optimization (Tweedale et al., 2016). As a result, accountants and financial professionals utilize its insights to make data-driven investment decisions that align with their organizations' financial goals and risk tolerance (Grueau et al., 2019; Hasan, 2021). The versatility of DSS extends to other accounting areas, such as tax planning and management reporting (Tweedale et al., 2016). By integrating with various data sources and providing interactive dashboards, DSS empowers accountants to explore financial data comprehensively and extract valuable insights for strategic decision-making.

Predictive Analytics

As an AI subset, predictive analytics is revolutionizing the accounting field by offering a data-driven approach to foreseeing future financial scenarios and making proactive decisions. Accountants can use predictive analytics for financial forecasting, where predictive models leverage historical financial data, market trends, and relevant variables to generate accurate projections (Jin et al., 2022; Mahamedi et al., 2023). For instance, predictive analytics enables them to precisely anticipate revenue, expenses, and cash flow in budgeting and financial planning. This process empowers these professionals and organizations to make informed resource allocation decisions and align their financial goals more effectively (Lakhanpal & Samuel, 2018). Therefore, predictive analytics equips businesses with the ability to develop strategic plans and optimize their financial strategies based on data-driven insights. In addition to financial planning, predictive analytics is pivotal in risk assessment and management within accounting (Liu, 2021; Marques et al., 2023). These tools can be used to scrutinize historical data for patterns of fraudulent activities, unusual financial transactions, or market fluctuations, helping accountants identify potential risks and take proactive measures to mitigate them. This proactive approach enhances an organization's financial security, bolsters regulatory compliance efforts, and minimizes the likelihood of financial irregularities going unnoticed.

Natural Language Processing (NLP) for Unstructured Data Analysis

Natural Language Processing (NLP) has emerged as a transformative tool for accountants in their quest to analyze unstructured textual data. This data is often found in financial reports, emails, contracts, and social media interactions. NLP technologies enable accountants to extract valuable insights from this vast repository of information, providing a deeper understanding of the financial landscape (Mayer et al., 2020; Nakamura et al., 2016). For instance, NLP algorithms can automatically categorize financial news articles or social media discussions, helping accountants stay informed about market trends and sentiments that could impact investment decisions, risk assessments, or financial strategies. In addition, NLP can be used in financial statement analysis by automatically extracting relevant information from financial reports and disclosures (Hasan, 2021). As a result, it can identify key financial metrics, such as revenue growth or debt levels, and compare them to industry benchmarks or historical data to assess financial performance (Collins et al., 2021). Moreover, accountants leverage NLP technologies to streamline communication by automating routine tasks, such as responding to customer inquiries or managing email correspondence (Mayer et al., 2020). This practice saves time and ensures consistency and accuracy in communication, which is crucial for maintaining client relations and adhering to regulatory compliance standards.

Real-time Data Analysis for Informed Decision-Making

Real-time data analysis is crucial in accounting because it enables informed decision-making within a rapidly changing financial landscape. AI technologies present tools that facilitate continuous monitoring and analysis of financial data as it becomes available (Sun, 2021; Veneziano et al., 2014). This provides immediate insights and actionable information for accounting professionals. AI-based real-time data analysis aids financial reporting by ensuring that financial statements reflect the most up-to-date information, enhancing the accuracy and timeliness of financial disclosures (Shi & Wu, 2011; Wang et al., 2022). This is especially crucial for publicly traded companies subject to stringent reporting requirements. Additionally, real-time data analysis aids in cash flow management by continuously tracking receivables, payables, and liquidity, enabling accountants to make quick decisions to optimize cash flow, address liquidity challenges, and capitalize on favorable financial scenarios.

AI is Transforming Accounting Roles

Other than revolutionizing information management practices in accounting, AI technologies are also transforming the profession. For instance, automation replaces specific jobs such as data entry and audits previously done by accountants (Faccia et al., 2019). However, AI also creates new value-addition opportunities, such as financial consulting. This section provides a synthesized summary of the various ways in which AI is transforming the accounting profession.

Use of AI in Accountants Training and Upskilling

AI is profoundly transforming the roles and responsibilities of accountants, encouraging them to embrace innovation and efficiency. One significant aspect is using AI in accountant training (Liu, 2021). As accounting professionals prepare to adapt to the AI-driven landscape, educational institutions and training programs incorporate AI technologies into their curricula (Chen, 2021; Cong, 2021). This approach allows aspiring accountants to gain hands-on experience with AI-powered tools and understand how these technologies can enhance their analytical, auditing, and financial management skills. Cai (2022) proposes establishing intelligent classrooms for students majoring in financial management and accounting, where the teaching processes adopted cultivate skills and knowledge that meet the requirements for accounting roles in the AI context. This perspective indicates the significance of creating accounting training models that help ensure that the future workforce is better equipped to harness the full potential of AI in their roles.

Integrating AI in accounting offers accountants ample opportunities for upskilling and specialization. As data-centric tasks become automated through AI, accountants will be encouraged to diversify their skill sets and focus on higher-level functions (Cai, 2022; Dhamija & Bag, 2020). This includes delving into advanced financial analysis, forensic accounting, and advisory roles. AI-driven tools can provide accountants with valuable insights and recommendations, enabling them to offer more strategic financial guidance to their clients or organizations (Chen & Williams, 2022). This shift towards specialization empowers accountants to become trusted advisors, leveraging AI as a tool to provide more value-added services to their clients and organizations.

The Evolving Role of Accountants in Information Management

With the increased adoption of AI tools and systems, accountants are transitioning into the role of information stewards, responsible for managing and interpreting vast volumes of financial data. For instance, AI automation streamlines data entry and processing, while AI-driven analytics tools enhance data interpretation and reporting (Chen & Williams, 2022; Lin et al., 2021). In this regard, accountants are now uniquely positioned to extract meaningful insights from complex datasets, identify financial trends, and predict future scenarios. This transformation positions them as strategic decision-makers who utilize AI-generated insights to inform financial strategies, risk management, and compliance efforts, thus contributing to the overall success of organizations (Fang, 2021; Inghirami, 2014). Moreover, AI-driven automation shifts accountants from routine data entry tasks to more strategic responsibilities. For instance, AI can handle mundane, repetitive tasks like data input and transaction reconciliation, freeing accountants' time to focus on critical thinking, problem-solving, and financial analysis (Hernes et al., 2020). This shift allows accountants to focus more on understanding the broader financial landscape, identifying risks and opportunities, and providing strategic recommendations to drive organizational growth and financial success. Therefore, AI is not replacing accountants but augmenting their capabilities and redefining their roles, enabling them to deliver more value to clients and organizations in the ever-evolving accounting profession.

Challenges of Integrating AI Into Information Management in Accounting

Despite the opportunities AI presents in accounting information management, its adoption is associated with multiple challenges. For example, as the technologies become more complex, consumers have raised various concerns, such as data privacy issues and cybersecurity (Iancu & Cioban, 2016). These problems can lead to trust issues, consequently affecting brand loyalty. As a result, businesses and professionals must identify and address these challenges.

Accountability and Responsibility

Accountability and responsibility are central ethical considerations as AI systems assume a more autonomous role in financial decision-making. For instance, questions surrounding who should be held accountable for the outcomes of AI-generated financial decisions have become increasingly complex and significant (Li, 2021). When an AI system makes a significant financial error, such as a miscalculation or an incorrect prediction, the attribution of responsibility may not always be straightforward (Lan & Tang, 2020). This complexity arises because AI systems often use hybrid systems that combine automated algorithms and human oversight (Fuller & Deane, 2015). In some instances, AI processes may be initiated or guided by human instructions, while in others, they may operate independently based on historical data and machine learning algorithms. Determining whether the responsibility lies with the individuals who designed, implemented, or supervised the AI system or whether the AI should be considered accountable can be challenging (Li, 2011; Ma, 2011). Establishing clear lines of accountability for AI-generated decisions is crucial for maintaining ethical standards and ensuring errors are addressed effectively (Medennikov, 2021). This involves defining the roles and responsibilities of all stakeholders involved in the AI decision-making process, from data scientists and developers to accountants and managers. It may also necessitate the development of specific protocols and guidelines outlining how errors or discrepancies should be reported, investigated, and rectified.

Data Privacy

Data privacy is a significant challenge when integrating AI into accounting. It encompasses several complex ethical, legal, and practical considerations that must be carefully addressed to protect sensitive financial information and maintain trust in AI-driven accounting processes (He & Chen, 2011). For instance, one of the foremost concerns in AI-driven accounting is safeguarding sensitive financial data. Accounting professionals handle confidential financial information from clients and organizations, including income statements, balance sheets, and tax records (Ismailov & Kononov, 2018; Leach et al., 2017). AI systems require access to this data for analysis and decision-making, creating potential vulnerabilities if not adequately protected. Another data privacy challenge is legal and regulatory compliance (Liu, 2022). In many jurisdictions, strict data privacy laws impose stringent requirements for the handling and processing personal and financial data. As a result, accountants must ensure that AI-driven processes adhere to these regulations, including obtaining proper consent for data usage, implementing data encryption and anonymization measures, and complying with data retention policies.

Data breaches and cyberattacks pose a significant risk to financial data when AI systems are employed in accounting. AI processes require robust cybersecurity measures to protect financial information from unauthorized access, hacking, or data breaches (Leach et al., 2017). The security of AI algorithms, data storage facilities, and communication channels must be a top priority to mitigate these risks. However, some cases require accounting firms to share financial data with third-party AI service providers or cloud-based AI platforms (Liu, 2022). This introduces additional data privacy challenges related to data sharing agreements, ownership, and access control. Accountants must have clear contractual agreements stipulating how third parties handle financial data and ensure that these practices align with data privacy regulations (O'Leary, 1991; Pielawa et al., 2011). These practices are essential in maintaining client and stakeholder trust, which is paramount in accounting. Accounting professionals understand that any perception that financial data is not adequately protected can erode trust (Qasaimeh et al., 2020). Therefore, they must be transparent about their data privacy practices and reassure clients and stakeholders that sensitive financial information is handled with the utmost care and security.

Data Manipulation

Data manipulation can emerge as a major challenge when AI systems access financial data. The AI system can be designed to manipulate or prioritize insights or recommendations that benefit specific parties. This manipulation can undermine the integrity of financial reporting and decision-making (Zhou, 2023). For example, in investment analysis, selective data presentation may be used to artificially inflate the attractiveness of a particular investment option, potentially leading to financial decisions that do not align with the true risk and return profiles of investments. The ethical dilemma intensifies when AI is employed in financial audits or regulatory compliance, where unbiased and accurate data representation is critical. For instance, if data manipulation occurs to mask financial irregularities or non-compliance with regulations, it not only compromises the ethical standards of the accounting profession but also poses significant legal and reputational risks for organizations.

Discrimination and Biases in AI Algorithms

Discrimination and biases in AI algorithms represent a critical challenge in integrating AI into accounting information management. These issues raise concerns about fairness, equity, and ethical implications in financial decision-making processes. AI algorithms can inherit biases in the data used to train them (Askary et al., 2018; Xue, 2020). For example, historical financial data may contain biases related to factors like race, gender, or socioeconomic status. When AI systems analyze this data, they may inadvertently perpetuate or even exacerbate these biases in financial decision-making (Xu et al., 2021). As a result, the biased algorithms may unfairly impact certain demographic groups when assessing creditworthiness or making investment recommendations.

The presence of biases in AI algorithms poses significant ethical concerns. For instance, discriminatory outcomes in financial decisions can result in unfair treatment, worsen societal inequalities, and violate ethical principles of fairness and equity (Ouchchy et al., 2020). It is ethically problematic when AI-driven financial decisions discriminate against individuals or groups based on non-financial attributes (Coeckelbergh, 2019). Therefore, AI bias can have legal and regulatory implications since most jurisdictions have anti-discrimination laws and regulations prohibiting unfair treatment based on protected attributes such as race or gender. In this case, organizations may face legal consequences and damage to their reputation if AI algorithms lead to discriminatory financial outcomes.

CONCLUSION

With the rapid technological developments happening worldwide, it has become crucial for companies to adopt and leverage AI technologies in various professional fields, including accounting. For instance, the research findings indicate that AI plays a pivotal role in automating data processing tasks, reducing human errors, and empowering accountants with advanced financial analysis and decision-making tools. In addition, utilizing AI tools in accounting has resulted in more accurate financial reporting, improved compliance, and enhanced risk management. These tools include expert systems, decision support systems, machine learning algorithms, predictive analytics, and natural language processing. For example, decision support systems have empowered accountants with advanced forecasting capabilities, enabling organizations to make informed budgeting and investment decisions. On the other hand, machine learning algorithms have been instrumental in identifying fraudulent activities and minimizing financial risks. Moreover, natural language processing has enabled accountants to extract insights from unstructured data sources, such as textual financial reports, facilitating more comprehensive and insightful analyses. AI's real-time capacity to process vast datasets has facilitated data-driven decision-making, enhancing the value accountants bring to their organizations and clients. Therefore, these tools have streamlined processes and elevated the accounting profession, enabling accountants to shift from routine data handling to more strategic roles.

However, as AI continues to reshape the accounting profession, it presents unique challenges that demand attention. For instance, ethical concerns, including transparency, accountability, and data privacy, must be carefully navigated to ensure that AI-driven financial processes maintain trust and integrity. In addition, the risk of biases in AI algorithms, particularly in decision-making, requires vigilant monitoring and mitigation to protect fairness and equity. As a result, accountants must understand their ethical responsibilities in protecting customer and organization data and misrepresenting insights and recommendations in favor of particular parties. Addressing these challenges is imperative to harness the full potential of AI in accounting, ensuring that it continues to enhance decision-making, reduce errors, and drive efficiencies while adhering to the highest ethical and regulatory standards. As the accounting landscape evolves, the synergy between AI and human expertise promises to redefine the profession, elevating it to new heights of data-driven excellence and strategic insight.

Organizational innovation in AI can have significant implications for the field of accounting in terms of information management: (i) AI can process vast amounts of financial data quickly and accurately, providing accountants with valuable insights for decision-making. This challenges traditional accounting theories that rely on manual data analysis and opens up new possibilities for data-driven decision-support models; (ii) as AI systems can introduce complexities in financial reporting and auditing, theoretical discussions around accounting standards and principles may evolve to address the challenges and opportunities presented by AI-driven financial processes; (iii) theoretical discussions about ethics in accounting may expand to encompass AI ethics, focusing on issues like bias, transparency, and accountability in AI-driven decision-making processes.

Practical Implications: (i) AI can automate routine accounting tasks, such as data entry and reconciliation, significantly increasing the efficiency of accounting processes. This leads to cost savings and allows accountants to focus on higher-value tasks; (ii) AI enables advanced data analytics and predictive modelling, allowing accountants to identify trends, anomalies, and opportunities in financial data. This supports better financial planning and risk management; (iii) AI can play a critical role in fraud detection by continuously monitoring transactions and identifying suspicious patterns, contributing to a more robust control environment.

The integration of AI-driven organizational innovation into accounting has the potential to revolutionize information management and decision-making processes. This transformation will necessitate theoretical adaptations to accounting principles and practices while offering practical benefits such as increased efficiency, data accuracy, and improved financial insights. However, it also presents challenges, particularly related to ethical considerations and the need for ongoing skill development in the accounting profession.

The intersection of organizational innovation, artificial intelligence, and accounting in information management is a dynamic and promising field with numerous opportunities for future research: (i) Investigate the development of ethical guidelines and regulatory frameworks for the use of AI in accounting and information management. This could include exploring the ethical implications of AI-driven decision-making and how to ensure transparency and accountability in AI systems; (ii) AI technologies can enhance financial reporting processes. Research might focus on automating financial statement preparation, improving accuracy in financial data analysis, and exploring the implications of AI-generated financial reports for stakeholders; (iii) examine the role of AI in detecting and preventing financial fraud. Research could explore the effectiveness of AI-based fraud detection algorithms, the challenges in implementing them, and their impact on reducing fraud in organizations; (iv) explore how AI can provide decision support for accounting professionals; (v) Investigate the use of AI for predictive analytics in accounting. This could involve forecasting financial trends, predicting cash flow, or identifying potential financial risks using AI-driven models.

Future research in these areas can help organizations leverage AI to improve their accounting and information management practices while addressing emerging challenges and ethical considerations. Moreover, interdisciplinary collaboration between accounting, AI, and organizational innovation experts will be crucial in advancing knowledge in this field.

ACKNOWLEDGMENT

I would like to express gratitude to the Editor and the Arbitrators. They offered extremely valuable suggestions or improvements. The GOVCOPP Research Center of the University of Aveiro supported the author.

REFERENCES

Ahmad, K., & Zabri, S. M. (2016). Management accounting practices among small and medium enterprises. *Proceedings of the 28th International Business Information Management Association Conference*. https://www.researchgate.net/publication/311716335_Management_Accounting_Practices_Among_Small_And_Medium_Enterprises

Askary, S., Abu-Ghazaleh, N., & Tahat, Y. A. (2018). Artificial intelligence and reliability of accounting information. In *Challenges and Opportunities in the Digital Era: 17th IFIP WG 6.11 Conference on e-Business, e-Services, and e-Society, I3E 2018, Kuwait City, Kuwait, October 30–November 1, 2018, Proceedings 17* (pp. 315-324). Springer International Publishing. https://inria.hal.science/hal-02274162/file/474698_1_En_28_Chapter.pdf

Cai, C. (2022). Training Mode of Innovative Accounting Talents in Colleges Using Artificial Intelligence. *Mobile Information Systems, 2022*, 6516658. Advance online publication. doi:10.1155/2022/6516658

Cai, D., Tan, M., & Cai, J. (2011). The VAT tax burden warning model and modification based on CTAIS system data. *2011 2nd International Conference on Artificial Intelligence. Management Science and Electronic Commerce, AIMSEC 2011 - Proceedings*. 10.1109/AIMSEC.2011.6011100

Chen, H. (2021). Research on the strategies of cultivating management accounting talents in universities under the background of the development of information technology. *ACM International Conference Proceeding Series*. 10.1145/3465631.3465784

Chen, S., & Williams, A. (2022, March). Intelligent Accounting System Structure and Intelligent Accounting Algorithm Based on Computer Vision. In *The International Conference on Cyber Security Intelligence and Analytics* (pp. 97-104). Cham: Springer International Publishing. 10.1007/978-3-030-97874-7_12

Coeckelbergh, M. (2019). Artificial intelligence: some ethical issues and regulatory challenges. *Technology and Regulation, 2019*, 31-34. https://techreg.org/article/view/10999

Collins, C., Dennehy, D., Conboy, K., & Mikalef, P. (2021). Artificial intelligence in information systems research: A systematic literature review and research agenda. *International Journal of Information Management, 60*, 102383. doi:10.1016/j.ijinfomgt.2021.102383

Cong, X. (2021). Research on curriculum construction of big data and accounting under the background of big data. *Proceedings - 2021 International Conference on Big Data Engineering and Education, BDEE 2021*. 10.1109/BDEE52938.2021.00032

Dhamija, P., & Bag, S. (2020). Role of artificial intelligence in operations environment: A review and bibliometric analysis. *The TQM Journal, 32*(4), 869–896. doi:10.1108/TQM-10-2019-0243

Erwin, K. (2019). Relationship management accounting and development of information technology. *IOP Conference Series. Materials Science and Engineering, 648*(1), 012033. doi:10.1088/1757-899X/648/1/012033

Faccia, A., Al Naqbi, M. Y. K., & Lootah, S. A. (2019). Integrated cloud financial accounting cycle. How artificial intelligence, blockchain, and XBRL will change the accounting, fiscal and auditing practices. *ACM International Conference Proceeding Series*.

Fang, Y. (2021). Artificial intelligence promotes the application of "internet + education" teaching model in accounting major. *ACM International Conference Proceeding Series*. 10.1145/3465631.3465782

Fuller, T. R., & Deane, G. E. (2015). Creating complex applications via self-adapting autonomous agents in an intelligent system framework. *International Conference on Self-Adaptive and Self-Organizing Systems, SASO*. 10.1109/SASO.2015.27

Grueau, C., Antunes, A., Ferreira, B., Gonçalves, M., Gomes, J., & Carriço, N. (2019). Towards an integrated platform for decision support in water utility management. *Proceedings of the 12th IADIS International Conference Information Systems 2019, IS 2019*. 10.33965/is2019_201905C001

Han, H., Shiwakoti, R. K., Jarvis, R., Mordi, C., & Botchie, D. (2023). Accounting and auditing with blockchain technology and artificial Intelligence: A literature review. *International Journal of Accounting Information Systems*, *48*, 100598. doi:10.1016/j.accinf.2022.100598

Hasan, A. R. (2021). Artificial Intelligence (AI) in accounting & auditing: A Literature review. *Open Journal of Business and Management*, *10*(1), 440–465. doi:10.4236/ojbm.2022.101026

He, Q., & Chen, G. (2011). Research of security audit of enterprise group accounting information system under internet environment. *2011 2nd International Conference on Artificial Intelligence, Management Science and Electronic Commerce, AIMSEC 2011 - Proceedings*.

Hernes, M., Bytniewski, A., Mateńczuk, K., Rot, A., Dziuba, S., Fojcik, M., Nguyet, T. L., Golec, P., & Kozina, A. (2020). Data Quality Management in ERP Systems – Accounting Case. *Communications in Computer and Information Science*, *1287*, 353–362. doi:10.1007/978-3-030-63119-2_29

Iancu, E., & Cioban, G. L. (2016). Intangible assets, economic models, and neural network. *Proceedings of the 27th International Business Information Management Association Conference - Innovation Management and Education Excellence Vision 2020: From Regional Development Sustainability to Global Economic Growth, IBIMA 2016*.

Inghirami, I. E. (2014). Reshaping strategic management accounting systems. *Frontiers in Artificial Intelligence and Applications*.

Ionescu, L. (2020). Robotic process automation, deep learning, and natural language processing in algorithmic data-driven accounting information systems. *Analysis and Metaphysics*, *19*(0), 59–65. doi:10.22381/AM1920206

Ismailov, Z., & Kononov, D. (2018). Integrated management system for rail transport: planning of cargo turnover in conditions of uncertainty. *Proceedings of 2018 11th International Conference "Management of Large-Scale System Development", MLSD 2018*. 10.1109/MLSD.2018.8551807

Jin, S., Pan, J., Chen, Q., & Li, B. (2022). Analysis and discussion on standard cost allocation model in state grid. Lecture Notes in Computer Science (including subseries Lecture Notes in Artificial Intelligence and Lecture Notes in Bioinformatics). doi:10.1007/978-3-030-97774-0_26

Lakhanpal, V., & Samuel, R. (2018). Implementing blockchain technology in oil and gas industry: A review. *Proceedings - SPE Annual Technical Conference and Exhibition*. 10.2118/191750-MS

Lan, Y., & Tang, Y. (2020). Application of computer accounting system in internal control of enterprise accounting. *Journal of Physics: Conference Series*, *1693*(1), 012007. doi:10.1088/1742-6596/1693/1/012007

Leach, K., Zhang, F., & Weimer, W. (2017). Scotch: combining software guard extensions and system management mode to monitor cloud resource usage. Lecture Notes in ComputerScience (including subseries Lecture Notes in Artificial Intelligence and Lecture Notes in Bioinformatics).

Li, C. (2012). Research on application strategy for ERP system in enterprise accounting informationization. *Advanced Materials Research.*

Li, H., Li, Y., & Zhao, G. (2011). Demonstration the application of activity-based costing to ERP management system. *Proceedings - 2011 6th IEEE Joint International Information Technology and Artificial Intelligence Conference, ITAIC 2011.*

Li, W. (2021). Reform and innovation of higher fine arts distance education under the background of big data. *Journal of Physics: Conference Series, 1852*(3), 032026. doi:10.1088/1742-6596/1852/3/032026

Li, Y. (2011). Study on setting up lake environmental accounting account. *2011 2nd International Conference on Artificial Intelligence, Management Science and Electronic Commerce, AIMSEC 2011 - Proceedings.*

Li, Z. (2020, June). Analysis on the influence of artificial intelligence development on accounting. In *2020 International conference on big data, Artificial Intelligence and Internet of Things Engineering (ICBAIE)* (pp. 260-262). IEEE. 10.1109/ICBAIE49996.2020.00061

Lin, J., Liu, J., Zheng, C., & Chen, J. (2021). Reform on accounting teaching practice course in universities with the background of artificial intelligence. *ACM International Conference Proceeding Series.* 10.1145/3465631.3465785

Linnenluecke, M. K., Marrone, M., & Singh, A. K. (2019). Conducting systematic literature reviews and bibliometric analyses. *Australian Journal of Management, 45*(2), 175 194. doi:10.1177/0312896219877678

Liu, T. (2021). Smart financial management system based on intelligent data dimensionality reduction technology. *Proceedings of the 5th International Conference on Electronics, Communication and Aerospace Technology, ICECA 2021.* 10.1109/ICECA52323.2021.9675999

Liu, X. (2022). Research on consumers' personal information security and perception based on digital twins and Internet of Things. *Sustainable Energy Technologies and Assessments, 53*, 102706. Advance online publication. doi:10.1016/j.seta.2022.102706

Liu, Y. (2021). Research on the influence of artificial intelligence on the training of accounting talents and strategy. *ACM International Conference Proceeding Series.* 10.1145/3465631.3465786

Ma, M. (2022). Research on the development of hospital intelligent finance based on artificial intelligence. *Computational Intelligence and Neuroscience, 2022*, 6549766. Advance online publication. doi:10.1155/2022/6549766 PMID:35983131

Ma, Y. (2011). Notice of Retraction: The study of management accounting under the modern enterprise system [Retracted]. *2011 2nd International Conference on Artificial Intelligence, Management Science and Electronic Commerce, AIMSEC 2011 - Proceedings*, 5273-5275. 10.1109/AIMSEC.2011.6011299

Mahamedi, E., Wonders, M., Gerami Seresht, N., Woo, W. L., & Kassem, M. (2023). A reinforcing transfer learning approach to predict buildings energy performance. *Construction Innovation.* Advance online publication. doi:10.1108/CI-12-2022-0333

Marques, S., Gonçalves, R., da Costa, R. L., Pereira, L. F., & Dias, A. L. (2023). The Impact of Intelligent Systems on Management Accounting. *International Journal of Intelligent Information Technologies, 19*(1). doi:10.4018/IJIIT.324601

Mayer, J. H., Stritzel, O., Esswein, M., & Quick, R. (2020). Towards natural language processing: an accounting case study. In *Forty-First International Conference on Information Systems*. https://www.rcw.wi.tu-darmstadt.de/media/bwl4/forschung_9/kompetenzzentrum_1/20200927_ICIS_1383_NLP_track_23_final_version_letter_size.pdf

Medennikov, V. (2021). Management transformation with a single digital platform as exemplified by accounting. *IFAC-PapersOnLine, 54*(13), 178–182. doi:10.1016/j.ifacol.2021.10.441

Misnevs, B., & Fila, N. (2008). Analytical system for research of TTI study process trends. *MIPRO2008 - 31st International Convention Proceedings: Computers in Education.*

Nakamura, Y., Matsuda, K., & Matsuoka, M. (2016). Augmented data center infrastructure management system for minimizing energy consumption. *Proceedings - 2016 5th IEEE International Conference on Cloud Networking, CloudNet 2016*. 10.1109/CloudNet.2016.12

O'Leary, D. E. (1991). Representation of source reliability in weight of evidence. Lecture Notes in Computer Science (including subseries Lecture Notes in Artificial Intelligence and Lecture Notes in Bioinformatics). doi:10.1007/BFb0028095

Onuwabhagbe, O. P., Ngozi, O. E., & Adeboye, A. A. (2018). Teaching accounting ethics using the KPMG ethics curriculum to undergraduate accounting students at a private Christian university in Nigeria: An experimental study. *Proceedings of the 31st International Business Information Management Association Conference, IBIMA 2018: InnovationManagement and Education Excellence through Vision 2020.*

Ouchchy, L., Coin, A., & Dubljević, V. (2020). AI in the headlines: The portrayal of the ethical issues of artificial intelligence in the media. *AI & Society, 35*(4), 927–936. doi:10.1007/s00146-020-00965-5

Park, T., & Kim, H. (2013). A data warehouse-based decision support system for sewer infrastructure management. *Automation in Construction, 30*, 37–49. doi:10.1016/j.autcon.2012.11.017

Pielawa, L., Helmer, A., Brell, M., & Hein, A. (2011). Intelligent environments supporting the care of multi-morbid patients: A concept for patient-centered information management and therapy. *ACM International Conference Proceeding Series*. 10.1145/2093698.2093713

Ping, W. (2021). Data mining and XBRL integration in management accounting information based on artificial intelligence. *Journal of Intelligent & Fuzzy Systems, 40*(4), 6755–6766. doi:10.3233/JIFS-189509

Prokhorov, O., Pronchakov, Y., & Fedorovich, O. (2020). Intelligent multi-service platform for building management. *ATIT 2020 - Proceedings: 2020 2nd IEEE International Conference on Advanced Trends in Information Theory*. 10.1109/ATIT50783.2020.9349312

Purnomo, A., Aziz, A., Afia, N., Sari, A. K., & Primadani, T. I. W. (2021). E-CRM: Three decades of bibliometric networks visualizing of academic publication. *3rd International Conference on Cybernetics and Intelligent Systems, ICORIS 2021*. 10.1109/ICORIS52787.2021.9649480

Qasaimeh, G., Yousef, R., Al-Gasaymeh, A., & Alnaimi, A. (2022). The effect of artificial intelligence using neural network in estimating on an efficient accounting information system: evidence from Jordanian commercial banks. *2022 International Conference on Business Analytics for Technology and Security, ICBATS 2022*. 10.1109/ICBATS54253.2022.9759004

Qiu, J. (2021). Analysis of human interactive accounting management information systems based on artificial intelligence. *Journal of Global Information Management*, *30*(7), 1–13. doi:10.4018/JGIM.294905

Qiu, Y. L., & Xiao, G. F. (2020). Research on cost management optimization of financial sharing center based on RPA. *Procedia Computer Science*, *166*, 115–119. doi:10.1016/j.procs.2020.02.031

Raimundo, R., & Rosário, A. T. (2022). Cybersecurity in the Internet of Things in Industrial Management. *Applied Sciences (Basel, Switzerland)*, *12*(3), 1598. doi:10.3390/app12031598

Romero-Cordoba, R., Romero, F. P., Olivas, J. A., Serrano-Guerrero, J., & Peralta, A. (2016). A comparative study of soft computing software for enhancing the capabilities of business document management systems. *2016 IEEE International Conference on Fuzzy Systems, FUZZ-IEEE 2016*. 10.1109/FUZZ-IEEE.2016.7737693

Rosário, A. T., & Dias, J. C. (2023). How Industry 4.0 and Sensors Can Leverage Product Design: Opportunities and Challenges. *Sensors (Basel)*, *23*(3), 1165. doi:10.3390/s23031165 PMID:36772206

Rosário, A. T., Lopes, P. R., & Rosário, F. S. (2023). Metaverse in Marketing: Challenges and Opportunities. In A. Khang, V. Shah, & S. Rani (Eds.), *Handbook of Research on AI-Based Technologies and Applications in the Era of the Metaverse* (pp. 204–227). IGI Global. doi:10.4018/978-1-6684-8851-5.ch010

Schmidt, B., Kountanis, D., & Al-Fuqaha, A. (2015). A biologically-inspired approach to network traffic classification for resource-constrained systems. *Proceedings - 2014 InternationalSymposium on Big Data Computing, BDC 2014*.

Sharif, A. M. (2006). Advancing the state of the art in the modelling and simulation of information systems evaluation. *Proceedings of the European and Mediterranean Conference on Information Systems, EMCIS 2006*.

Sharma, S., Kataria, A., & Sandhu, J. K. (2022). Applications, tools and technologies of robotic process automation in various industries. *2022 International Conference on Decision AidSciences and Applications, DASA 2022*. 10.1109/DASA54658.2022.9765027

Shen, H., & Wang, J. (2021). Research on the application of computer technology in the optimization of department information systems. *Journal of Physics: Conference Series*, *1982*(1), 012139. doi:10.1088/1742-6596/1982/1/012139

Shetty, R., Cáceres, R., Pastrana, J., & Rabelo, L. (2012). Optical container code recognition and its impact on the maritime supply chain. *62nd IIE Annual Conference and Expo 2012*.

Shi, A., & Wu, W. (2011). Analysis on consolidated taxation in the context of headquarters economy under independent corporation accounting. *2011 2nd International Conference on Artificial Intelligence, Management Science and Electronic Commerce, AIMSEC 2011 -Proceedings*. 10.1109/AIMSEC.2011.6010251

Sun, J. (2021). Research on artificial intelligence, new retail and financial transformation. *Proceedings - 2nd International Conference on E-Commerce and Internet Technology, ECIT2021*. 10.1109/ECIT52743.2021.00031

Taghezout, N., Ascar, B., & Bessedik, I. (2012). An agent-based decision support system for spunlaced nonwovens production management: A case study of INOTIS enterprise. *Frontiers in Artificial Intelligence and Applications*.

Tweedale, J. W., Phillips-Wren, G., & Jain, L. C. (2016). *Advances in intelligent decision-making technology support*. Smart Innovation, Systems and Technologies. doi:10.1007/978-3-319-21209-8_1

Veneziano, D., Shi, X., Ballard, L., Ye, Z., & Fay, L. (2014). A benefit-cost analysis toolkit for road weather management technologies. Climatic effects on pavement and geotechnical infrastructure. *Proceedings of the International Symposium of Climatic Effects on Pavement and Geotechnical Infrastructure 2013*. 10.1061/9780784413326.022

Wang, A., Guo, S., & Li, R. (2022). Artificial intelligence technology enables the development of management accounting: The generation of Intelligent Accounting. *ACM International Conference Proceeding Series*. 10.1145/3523181.3523190

Wang, S. (2023). Research on the innovation system of computer artificial intelligence technology in museum financial management system. *2023 IEEE 3rd International Conference on Power, Electronics and Computer Applications, ICPECA 2023*. 10.1109/ICPECA56706.2023.10075850

Wang, Z., He, Y., Jiang, H., & Yu, C. (2023). *Enterprise Intelligent Accounting System Structure and Intelligent Accounting Algorithm*. Lecture Notes in Electrical Engineering. doi:10.1007/978-981-99-1428-9_140

Wang, Z., Qiong, M., & Wang, H. (2020). Risk analysis of enterprise management accounting based on big data association rule algorithm. *Journal of Physics: Conference Series*, *1631*(1), 012098. doi:10.1088/1742-6596/1631/1/012098

Wu, Y. (2021). Practical teaching of management accounting course under the background of artificial intelligence and big data. *Proceedings - 2021 International Conference on Computers, Information Processing and Advanced Education, CIPAE 2021*. 10.1109/CIPAE53742.2021.00035

Xiong, X., Wei, W., & Zhang, C. (2022). Dynamic user allocation method and artificial intelligence in the information industry financial management system application. *Proceedings - 2022 6th International Conference on Intelligent Computing and ControlSystems, ICICCS 2022*. 10.1109/ICICCS53718.2022.9788222

Xu, X., Zheng, Y., Tian, S., & Xing, M. (2021). Marketing logistics cost optimization and application research in smart living. *Proceedings - 20th IEEE/ACIS International Summer Conference on Computer and Information Science, ICIS 2021-Summer*. 10.1109/ICIS51600.2021.9516867

Xu, Y., Liu, X., Cao, X., Huang, C., Liu, E., Qian, S., Liu, X., Wu, Y., Dong, F., Qiu, C. W., Qiu, J., Hua, K., Su, W., Wu, J., Xu, H., Han, Y., Fu, C., Yin, Z., Liu, M., ... Zhang, J. (2021). Artificial intelligence: A powerful paradigm for scientific research. *Innovation (Cambridge (Mass.))*, *2*(4), 1–21. doi:10.1016/j.xinn.2021.100179 PMID:34877560

Xue, J. (2020). On the management of accounting files in public institutions based on informatization. *Journal of Physics: Conference Series*, *1533*(2), 022055. doi:10.1088/1742-6596/1533/2/022055

Yang, N. (2022). Financial big data management and control and artificial intelligence analysis method based on data mining technology. *Wireless Communications and Mobile Computing*, *2022*, 7596094. Advance online publication. doi:10.1155/2022/7596094

Yang, X. (2011). Influence of computerized accounting systems on bookkeeping conceptual framework. *2011 2nd International Conference on Artificial Intelligence, Management Science and Electronic Commerce, AIMSEC 2011 - Proceedings.*

Yang, X., & Metawa, S. (2023). *Construction of electric energy data and carbon emission management platform under computer technology*. Lecture Notes on Data Engineering and Communications Technologies. doi:10.1007/978-3-031-29097-8_20

Yang, Y., & Yin, Z. (2023). Resilient supply chains to improve the integrity of accounting data in financial institutions worldwide using blockchain technology. *International Journal of Data Warehousing and Mining*, *19*(4), 1–20. Advance online publication. doi:10.4018/ijdwm.320648

Zdravković, M., Panetto, H., & Weichhart, G. (2022). AI-enabled enterprise information systems for manufacturing. *Enterprise Information Systems*, *16*(4), 668–720. doi:10.1080/17517575.2021.1941275

Zeng, Y. (2022). Neural network technology-based optimization framework of financial and management accounting model. *Computational Intelligence and Neuroscience*, *2022*, 4991244. Advance online publication. doi:10.1155/2022/4991244 PMID:35685164

Zhang, Q., Dong, X., & Huang, R. (2011). The application of resources consumption accounting in an enterprise. *2011 2nd International Conference on Artificial Intelligence, Management Science and Electronic Commerce, AIMSEC 2011 - Proceedings.*

Zhang, X. (2021). Application of data mining and machine learning in management accounting information system. *Journal of Applied Science and Engineering (Taiwan)*, *24*(5), 813–820. doi:10.6180/jase.202110_24(5).0018

Zhao, J., & Yuan, J. (2019). An Intelligent model to reduce the energy consumption of sensor network nodes. *International Journal of Computers and Applications*. Advance online publication. doi:10.1080/1206212X.2019.1707436

Zhao, J., Zhang, L., & Zhao, Y. (2022). Informatization of accounting systems in small-and medium-sized enterprises based on artificial intelligence-enabled cloud computing. *Computational Intelligence and Neuroscience*, *2022*, 1–9. Advance online publication. doi:10.1155/2022/6089195 PMID:35990138

Zhou, K. (2023). Financial model construction of a cross-border e-commerce platform based on machine learning. *Neural Computing & Applications*, *35*(36), 25189–25199. Advance online publication. doi:10.1007/s00521-023-08456-6

ADDITIONAL READING

Arnould, E. J., & Price, L. L. (1993). River Magic: Extraordinary Experience and the Extended Service Encounter. *The Journal of Consumer Research*, *20*(June), 24–45. doi:10.1086/209331

Zhao, J. J., Zhang, L. M., & Zhao, Y. (2022). Informatization of Accounting Systems in Small- and Medium-Sized Enterprises Based on Artificial Intelligence-Enabled Cloud Computing. *Computational Intelligence and Neuroscience*, *2022*, 6089195. Advance online publication. doi:10.1155/2022/6089195 PMID:35990138

KEY TERMS AND DEFINITIONS

AI-Driven: The process that is powered by the capabilities of artificial intelligence.

Applying Natural Language Processing: Intention and simplification of understanding of human behavior by machines.

Artificial Intelligence: The multidisciplinary study that covers several areas of knowledge. Although its development has advanced further in computer science, its interdisciplinary approach involves contributions from several disciplines.

Deep Learning: Machine learning technique that teaches computers to do what comes naturally to humans.

Expert Systems: Software that simulates the reasoning of an "expert" professional in a specific area of knowledge.

Machine Learning: Computer science that focuses on using data and algorithms to mimic the way humans learn.

Optical Character Recognition: The process that converts an image of text into a machine-readable text format.

Chapter 6
Cryptocurrencies and Blockchain:
Impact on Accounting and Financial Auditing

Diogo Barbosa
Polytechnic of Cávado and Ave, Portugal

Sara Serra
https://orcid.org/0000-0003-3107-1752
Polytechnic of Cávado and Ave, Portugal

João Novais
Católica Porto Business School, Portugal

ABSTRACT

This study aims to assess the impacts that cryptocurrencies and blockchain have on financial accounting and auditing through eight interviews. The results allowed the authors to conclude that cryptocurrencies are considered cryptoassets, which can be classified in different ways, but above all, as inventories and intangible assets. Respondents believe that cryptocurrencies will have an impact on auditing, triggering a dematerialization of paper in its various stages. Therefore, the auditor will spend less time collecting and verifying information, focusing on activities with greater risk and complexity. It will also be possible to carry out an audit in real time and on the entire population. Regarding audit risk, accounting and auditing standards respond indirectly to the topic, yet the risk is considered high for most auditors, as they did not deepen their knowledge on the topic. Despite limitations, such as sample size, this study contributes to understanding the impact of cryptocurrencies on financial accounting and auditing in Portugal, being a pioneer in this field.

DOI: 10.4018/979-8-3693-0847-9.ch006

INTRODUCTION

Every day, we come across various methods for carrying out economic transactions, such as credit cards, Paysafecard, mobile applications, Paypal and, recently, cryptocurrencies. Cryptocurrencies are also associated with the blockchain network. The development of this technology is transforming traditional business models as information is kept securely, as a result of decentralization and encryption, and also allows easy access to its users (Koo & Sewell, 2023).

The rapid growth of cryptocurrencies and the incipient legislation on them have posed challenges to some sectors of activity, such as accounting and auditing. In fact, according to Vincent and Wilkins (2019), the ambiguity and lack of guidance surrounding cryptocurrency transactions impose additional audit risks.

In this study, cryptocurrencies will not be recognized as "currency", but as "cryptoassets", since this term encompasses the nomenclatures that are normally associated with them, such as tokens, coins, cryptocurrencies or virtual currencies. According to Leopold and Vollmann (2019), a cryptoactive can be characterized as a token or coin, with the criterion for differentiating it being the functionality of the asset. However, to be classified as assets, cryptoassets must meet the requirements of the asset definition and its recognition criteria.

If the definition of asset is met, there are accounting standards that can guide the accounting of this asset to 'Cash and cash equivalents'; 'Financial instruments'; 'Inventories' or 'Intangible assets'. Therefore, according to Abate (2018), the audit company must perform audit procedures to obtain knowledge of the client's intention when entering into cryptocurrency transactions.

Although cryptocurrencies can increase audit risk, the blockchain technology associated with it can bring many advantages to auditing, such as eliminating the manual collection of information (Applelbaum & Smith, 2018 and Bible et al., 2017) and allow the standardization of financial data and real-time access to them, reducing the preparatory work for the annual audit and facilitating the preparation of auditor reports (Desplebin et al., 2021).

However, a question that arises is whether registration on the blockchain constitutes sufficient proof. According to the Canadian Public Accountability Board (2019), auditors' assessment of the reliability of information obtained on the blockchain is one of the most common deficiencies in audits of the cryptoasset sector. According to Pippo (2020), the reliability of information obtained on the blockchain may depend on the source of information, as well as the adequacy of technological resources.

According to Han, Shiwakoti, Jarvis, Mordi, & Botchie (2022), blockchain can revolutionize accounting as it facilitates access to accounting information in real time. In this way, upon authorization, interested parties can see the information in more detail, thus contributing to their decision-making. It can also, for example, allow more effectively the possibility of forecasting sales, costs of sales, and taxes. Furthermore, accounting tricks motivated by a conflict of interest will be more easily detected, thus reducing the opportunistic behavior of those involved.

Within the scope of this issue, this work aims to assess the potential impacts of cryptocurrencies and blockchain on accounting and financial auditing. To this end, an empirical study was carried out through semi-structured interviews with eight individuals belonging to three groups: auditors belonging to "Big4" and "Non-Big4", as well as members of associations and companies that work directly in the area of cryptocurrencies.

In addition to this introduction, this research includes a theoretical framework of the topic and the presentation of the empirical study, namely its methodology and results. Solutions and recommendations are then presented, as well as avenues for future research, ending with the conclusion.

BACKGROUND

Cryptoasset Accounting

According to the Order of Certified Accountants (2017), there is no standard or guide to support the accounting of cryptoassets. As there is no specific accounting treatment for operations with cryptoassets, the accounting treatment principles set out in existing accounting regulations must be met.

To be classified as assets, cryptoassets must meet the requirements of the asset definition and the asset recognition criteria, namely, i) it is probable that future economic benefits will flow to the entity and ii) have a cost or value that can be measured reliably (Accounting Standardization System, 2015).

Once the definition of asset is met, there are accounting standards that classify cryptocurrencies as an asset belonging to 'Cash and cash equivalents', 'Financial instrument', 'Inventories' or 'Intangible assets'.

The 'Cash and cash equivalents' class has high liquidity, due to immediate availability and rapid conversion into cash. However, McGuire and Massoud (2018) state that, although the term "cryptocurrency" suggests that it is a currency, it does not necessarily mean money for accounting purposes. Therefore, cryptocurrencies do not fit the definition of cash equivalents because they do not have a short-term "life". Leopold and Vollmann (2019) add that, currently, cryptocurrencies do not share the properties of cash because they are not legal tender, are not issued or regulated by a Government and cannot directly influence the price of goods and services.

The concept of financial instrument is very broad, as it can include shares, bonds, bank loans, bond loans, bills, among others. However, according to the Accounting Standardization System (2015), a financial instrument is a contract that gives rise to a financial asset in one entity and a financial liability or equity instrument in another entity. Therefore, for cryptocurrencies to be recognized in accounting, the entity must be a party to the contractual provisions and the cryptocurrency holder generally does not hold any contract. Leopold and Vollmann (2019) state that possession of a cryptocurrency unit does not normally give the holder a contractual right to receive money or another financial asset, nor does the cryptocurrency come into existence as a result of a contractual relationship. According to McGuire and Massoud (2019), certain contracts for the purchase or sale of cryptocurrencies in the future, or other contracts fixed in money based on movements of a cryptocurrency, in particular, may meet the definition of a derivative and be a financial instrument in accounting.

According to the Accounting Standardization System (2015), an intangible asset is an identifiable non-monetary asset without physical substance. McGuire and Massoud (2019) state that, generally, cryptocurrencies do not meet the definition of monetary assets. Ernst & Young (2019) also states that to be identifiable, an intangible asset must be separable, that is, capable of being sold or transferred separately from the owner, or resulting from contracts or other legal rights. As most cryptoassets can be freely transferred to a buyer, they will generally be considered separable. The same applies to cryptoassets resulting from contractual rights.

Initially, intangible assets are measured at acquisition cost, however, if the acquisition of the intangible asset results from the exchange for a non-monetary asset, the cost is measured at fair value. Subsequently, cryptocurrencies can be measured using the cost model or the revaluation model.

According to Ernst and Young (2019), when there is a predictable limit to the period during which the cryptoasset is expected to generate net cash inflows for the entity, the useful life must be estimated and the cost of the cryptoasset, less any residual value, must be amortized on a systematic basis over their useful life. Therefore, we must consider, if there is, a predictable limit for the period during which the cryptoasset is expected to generate net cash inflows for the entity. If there is no predictable limit, the cryptoasset can be considered to have an indefinite useful life and, therefore, no amortization is necessary. However, according to IFRS 6 §105, an intangible asset with an indefinite life must be amortized over a maximum period of 10 years. According to McGuire and Massoud (2019), cryptocurrencies must be assessed for impairment in the same way as other intangible assets with an indefinite useful life and, second, §107 of IFRS 6 is required to test annually; or whenever there is an indication to do so.

Turning now to the revaluation model, it can be said that, as a general rule, the selected model should be applied to an entire class of intangible assets, unless there is no active market for these assets. Consequently, if no price is observable in an active market for an identical asset, the entity will need to apply the cost model to the cryptoassets in its possession (Ernst & Young, 2019).

According to McGuire and Massoud (2018), the entity must establish that there is an active market for cryptoactives, if it is its intention to use this model. An active market occurs whenever cryptocurrency transactions occur regularly, in significant quantities, thus providing consistent price information (Moosa, 2023). If such a market exists, in the revaluation model, the recognized value must reflect the fair value at the end of the period. Cross-referencing this statement with IFRS 6, the financial statement that indicates the financial position is the balance sheet and, in accordance with §73 of this standard, revaluations must be made with such regularity that on the balance sheet date the carrying amount of the asset does not differ materially from its fair value. The frequency of revaluations depends on the volatility of the fair values of the intangible assets that are being revalued (§77 of IFRS 6).

For cryptoassets to be classified as inventories, they must meet at least one of the following requirements: (1) be held for sale in the ordinary course of business activity, in the process for such sale; (2) be materials or consumables to be applied in the production process or in the provision of services. Given these conditions, for Ernst & Young (2019), cryptoactives can only be held for sale in the ordinary course of business activity, since they are not used in the production of inventories, nor are they materials or consumables used in the production process. Therefore, it is assumed that to be considered as inventory, the tangible condition is not necessary.

Still, for Leopold and Vollmann (2019), it is necessary to pay attention to the business model, to classify cryptoactives as inventories. If the intention is to hold this asset to sell in the entity's usual business model, then it will be accounted for as inventory. If the intention is to actively trade and make a profit, in the near future, through price fluctuation or on broker/dealer margin, then it falls under inventory, with the exception of broker/dealer. However, if the entity holds cryptoassets for the purpose of investment, that is, for capital appreciation, for long periods of time, then it will not meet the definition of inventory (Leopold & Vollmann, 2019).

According to Ernst & Young (2019), the cost of cryptoassets recorded as inventory may not be recoverable if those cryptoassets become totally or partially obsolete, due to a decrease in interest in cryptoassets or their applications, or if their sales prices have decreased. Likewise, the cost of cryptoasset inventories may also not be recoverable if the estimated costs to be incurred to carry out the sale have increased. Inventories are measured at the lower of cost and net realizable value. If the cost is higher than the net realizable value, we must make an adjustment to the net realizable value, recognizing an impairment. If the cost is lower than net realizable value, everything remains the same (§9 of IFRS 18).

Cryptocurrencies and Audit

The auditor's main role is to issue an opinion on the financial statements. This opinion results from carrying out an audit process, which begins with the formalization of the commitment between the auditor and the auditee. The agreed terms are defined in the commitment letter and in the contract. According to Abate (2018), when an audit client invests in cryptoassets, they are expected to know and understand how they work and what implications they will have on the financial statements, implementing controls to mitigate the risks, which is often not the case. It is essential that entities establish robust procedures and effective controls in order to properly ensure and report transactions related to cryptocurrencies. Failure to identify and understand inherent risks, without adequate implementation of internal controls, can result in financial losses and operational challenges, including possible adjustments to the financial statements. The management team must develop an appropriate business model to deal with cryptocurrencies, considering the risks inherent to this emerging technology and defining appropriate controls. Communication with the auditor can optimize the audit process (Koo & Sewell, 2023).

Another aspect to consider when carrying out an audit is the competence and capacity of those involved. Therefore, according to Abate (2018) there are aspects about cryptocurrencies that must be considered, such as: the client's competence in accounting and reporting; risk management; the implementation and maintenance of adequate internal control to mitigate risks related to cryptocurrencies; highly complex cryptography and technological information, as well as the use of experts to evaluate cryptocurrencies for financial reporting purposes. This assessment aims to mitigate the risk that the auditor accepts a commitment that he is unable to effectively execute. If the auditor accepts the engagement without gaining a full understanding of the industry and its environment, without recognizing and addressing the need for additional resources or training, it will be difficult, or may not even be possible, to perform an effective audit or comply with applicable professional standards (AICPA & CIMA, 2023). Currently, according to the Public Company Accounting Oversight Board (2023), there are practices that can contribute to increasing audit quality, such as: the creation of an internal team specialized in decentralized public records, to support teams in procedures related to cryptoassets; consultancy, in which audit teams are encouraged to consult the company's internal experts on matters related to cryptoassets, in order to guarantee the consistency of accounting policies; and the development of technological tools, with the aim of facilitating the collection and analysis of data on cryptoactive transactions, allowing detailed observation of how all these transactions are recorded in decentralized public records.

After accepting the audit, the auditor begins planning and must, for this purpose, obtain knowledge of the client's business and its internal control, in order to calculate the risk of material misstatement (ISA 315). Therefore, Abate (2018) states that the auditor must obtain knowledge of the client's purpose when entering into cryptocurrency transactions. Cryptocurrencies, despite having been on the market for some time, are a sensitive and delicate area for auditors because they carry an increased risk. In fact, the novelty, ambiguity and lack of official guidance surrounding cryptocurrency transactions impose additional audit risks (Vincent & Wilkins, 2019). According to Brender & Gauthier (2018), it is necessary to update auditing standards so that they keep up with current technology, especially blockchain. This update must focus on two aspects: firstly, they must describe how to perform an audit with blockchain and secondly, blockchain allows testing greater amounts of information and with a greater level of confidence in the data, however this is not aligned with auditing standards in place. Currently, the auditor's work is carried out using sampling, which places him in a paradoxical situation since existing auditing standards reduce the level of confidence that could be achieved with the full use of this technology.

The audit report expresses, with reasonable assurance, the auditor's opinion. The audit report is the only externally visible element, therefore the purpose of its issuance is to increase the degree of confidence of readers of the financial statements (ISA 200). According to Almeida (2019), there is a wide variety of interested parties in financial statements, who believe in the objectivity, independence and reliability of audit reports.

In 2020, Tesla invested 1.5 billion dollars in Bitcoin, so as one of the most valuable companies in the world, it could be a wake-up call for this asset class. According to the United States Securities and Exchange Commission (SEC, 2020), the company changed its investment policy, using money that was not necessary to maintain operational liquidity, in order to increase flexibility in diversification and maximize financial return. This measure was approved by the Audit Committee of the Board of Directors. The intention was to acquire and hold digital assets, sporadically or over the long term, hoping to accept bitcoin as a form of payment. The company classified digital assets as intangible assets, with an indefinite useful life. Therefore, a decrease in its fair value may lead to the recognition of an impairment loss and revisions to the market value will only be made at the time of sale. The company has been audited by PricewaterhouseCoopers and in their opinion the financial statements give a true and fair view, in all material respects, of the company's financial position and have been prepared in accordance with the applicable financial reporting framework. In fact, in the audit report, bitcoin was not mentioned in critical audit matters.

Blockchain, Accounting and Audit

Although cryptocurrencies can increase audit risk, the blockchain technology associated with it can bring many advantages to the audit. According to Applelbaum and Smith (2018) and Bible et al. (2017), blockchain will eliminate the manual collection of information and audit preparation activities that are laborious and time-consuming for management and work teams. Desplebin et al. (2021) reinforce the previous idea, mentioning that blockchain will allow the standardization of financial data and real-time access to it, reducing the preparatory work for the annual audit and facilitating the preparation of auditor reports. Furthermore, this allows the automation of all information collection, organization and processing work and also the rapid recovery of information, in the event of a catastrophe (Regelbrugge et al., 2021).

For Burns et al. (2020), blockchain will lead to a transformation in record keeping, allowing control activities and reporting to be ad hoc, automatic and on-demand. Due to all these factors, the auditor will use his professional judgment, experience, expertise and specific knowledge in higher value activities, such as risk analysis and more complex transactions (Brender & Gauthier, 2018). According to Psaila (2017), the level of security in audit work will soon see a drastic improvement, because auditors will turn to blockchain to test the entire population of transactions, within the period under analysis, thus challenging substantive tests based on samples. According to Han, Shiwakoti, Jarvis, Mordi, & Botchie (2022), the introduction of blockhain into accounting practice is transforming "traditional" processes, providing accountants and auditors with more efficient tools to focus on strategic activities and in-depth analysis. Blockchain will not completely replace these roles, as professional judgment and experience are required on topics such as fair value accounting or valuation of intangible assets, for example. Since all the manual work of collecting and validating information will disappear or be practically eliminated, this technology will open doors to new positions with the aim of guaranteeing the authenticity of documents and the value of smart-contracts. In this way, both parties will see their roles valued as they focus on more complex operations such as risk management, fraud detection, forecasting, among others, thus meeting the needs of their customers.

The assessment of an audit must be supported by relevant evidence, the question that arises is whether registration on the blockchain constitutes sufficient proof. According to the Canadian Public Accountability Board and Conseil (2019), auditors' assessment of the reliability of information obtained from blockchains is one of the five most common deficiencies in audits of the cryptoasset sector. According to the same author, the other most common deficiencies are due to the fact that the auditor does not have adequate knowledge of audit risks at the planning stage; based on information obtained from brokers and crypto custodians without evaluating the reliability of the respective information and failing to obtain sufficient proof, which proves the ownership of cryptoassets, in entities that carry out self-custody, as well as failing to obtain sufficient proof of revenue, in entities that mine cryptoassets.

Bible et al. (2017) refer to some examples of information not present in the blockchain and relevant to the auditor, stating that in a cryptocurrency transaction for a product, the auditor may not be able to understand whether the product was actually delivered. Furthermore, the transaction may be unauthorized, fraudulent or illegal; carried out between related parties; linked to a contract parallel to the network and incorrectly classified in the financial statements, with the aggravating factor being that there are transactions that use estimates.

In addition to these points, referring to the external environment of the blockchain, it is necessary to understand the extent to which blockchain information can be trusted. According to Pippo (2020), the reliability of information obtained from blockchain, to be used as audit evidence, may depend on the source of information, for example, the blockchain, as well as the adequacy of technological resources, including information technology applications used by the auditor to directly obtain information, for example, a block explorer.

The blockchain also has flaws that can be exploited for negative acts. Therefore, analyzing the source of information itself, the blockchain may suffer an attack, allowing the misappropriation of cryptoactives, or have weak protocols or algorithms, which increase the vulnerability of the "network", which may lead to forks, for example, the recording of transactions invalid on the blockchain, among others.

According to Bonsón and Bednárová, (2019), to fully integrate blockchain technology into a real accounting ecosystem, a consensus between regulators, auditors and other parties is necessary.

EMPIRICAL STUDY

Methodology and Sample

The objective of this work is to assess the impact of cryptocurrencies and blockchain on accounting and financial auditing. To this end, semi-structured interviews were carried out, the script of which was prepared from scratch based on the literature review.

In Portugal, the topic of cryptocurrencies is still recent, so a convenience sample was used, consisting of eight individuals belonging to three groups: auditors, members of associations and companies

Table 1. Sample characterization

Interviewee Number	Gender	Age	Job	Professional Experience	Big4
1 (I1)	Female	56	Auditor	30 years	Yes
2 (I2)	Male	50	President	1.5 years	-
3 (I3)	Male	40	Auditor	12 years	No
4 (I4)	Male	34	Auditor	11 years	Yes
5(I5)	Male	54	Board member	3 years	-
6 (I6)	Male	38	President	3 years	-
7 (I7)	Male	35	Founding member	3 years	-
8 (I8)	Male	43	Auditor	21 years	No

that deal with crypto assets (see Table 1). All contacts were made by email and/or mobile phone and all interviews were by telephone or video call and recorded with the participants' permission.

As can be seen in Table 1, seven of the interviewees are men and one is a woman, the age range is between thirty-four years old and fifty-six years old.

Presentation and Discussion of Results

Definition of Cryptocurrency

Initially, respondents were asked how they would define cryptocurrency. Respondents were unanimous in stating that cryptocurrency is a digital asset, without physical substance. After general agreement on these two characteristics, each person commented on different aspects in the definition of cryptocurrencies.

There were those who met the theoretical objective, saying that cryptocurrencies have both a macro and micro definition (I6). The macro definition makes disintermediation stand out and the micro definition highlights the technical aspect of cryptocurrency as it is a digital asset, based on a decentralized public record. Regarding the decentralized public record, this study addressed blockchain technology, which was also mentioned by interviewees as the technology inherent to cryptocurrencies.

Following this line of thought, I4 stated that: "cryptocurrency, in conceptual terms, is a currency that, through the validation of other pairs, or validation systems, is considered reliable or safe. In technical terms, it is a code. (…). These are validation codes that can be validated independently of any financial entity and, therefore, are not linked to any bank, any currency-issuing entity, or central entity." This point reinforces the idea of disintermediation and lack of regulation in the currency.

Based on the interviewees' responses and the ideas of Nian and Chuen (2015), Rigters (2018) and Brand (2016), it can be concluded that cryptocurrencies are digital assets independent of financial institutions, using cryptography to secure transactions in a publicly available record. This prevents a single central point of failure while facilitating transactions between participants.

Blockchain Applicability

Regarding blockchain, the majority of interviewees recognize that this technology has extensive applicability and that it is not specific to a single sector, although it is more common in the financial sector.

Table 2. Accounting classification of cryptocurrencies

Interviewees Accounting Item	I1	I2	I3	I4	I5	I6	I7	I8
Cash and Cash Equivalents		X	X		X		X	
Financial instruments		X						X
Intangible assets	X	X		X		X		
Inventories				X				

I3 states that blockchain is a mechanism for confirming a sequence of information and can be applied in several areas. I2 adds that Blockchain has immense applicability, from cryptocurrencies, cryptoassets to tokenization of physical assets and traceability of the value chain, emphasizing that this technology is relevant to all industries, not restricted to the financial sector.

E4 claims that contracts adapted to blockchain could speed up procedures such as real estate transactions, car sales and interactions with the State. Likewise, I6 mentions the application of blockchain in the public sector, such as in registry offices, notaries and intellectual and industrial property registries. Also Bible et al. (2017) refer to the possibility of applying blockchain to the public sector, allowing voting, during election periods, with greater transparency and speed, and also its use in property records.

Another aspect mentioned was the usefulness of blockchain in the energy sector. According to I7, "in the energy sector it will be immensely useful because at the beginning of the massification of renewable energies and with the liberalization of markets, companies sometimes have to create credits and debts between themselves and blockchain can be an excellent use case, in which there is an accounting blockchain so that companies can exchange credits to them among themselves." This statement corroborates the ideas of Bible et al. (2017) who states that the aim is to establish a smart grid technology that would allow surplus energy to be used as a digital asset that can be traded between consumers, through the ethereum network.

Accounting for Cryptocurrencies

Although IFRS do not directly refer to cryptocurrencies, when we asked respondents whether cryptocurrencies are assets, their agreement was complete. In the second part, the same did not occur when we asked what type of asset cryptocurrencies fall under in terms of IFRS standards (see Table 2).

As we can see, in table 2, opinions on the accounting of cryptocurrencies are divided. The most selected options were Cash and cash equivalents and Intangible assets, although some interviewees selected more than one option, because they consider the classification depends on the entity's objective regarding the asset itself.

According to those interviewed, cryptocurrencies fall into Cash and cash equivalents because they can be recognized "as money, equivalent to money, which is convertible and that is why there are exchanges" (I2). Furthermore, they fit into the same model as fiat currencies (Cash and cash equivalents). Despite not having a central bank behind them, for all intents and purposes, they are issued and tradable and have a value given by the market" (I7); and "If the objective is to use cryptocurrency as a means of payment, it is a current asset, it is almost cash or application of cash" (I3).

These arguments are contested by I4, which states that cryptocurrencies cannot be held in cash because they are not generally accepted in transactions of goods and services and are not convertible, nor guaranteed by any central issuing entity. Therefore, they are not currency, in the traditional concept of currency." These arguments are in line with those defended by Leopold and Vollmann (2019) and McGuire and Massoud (2019), who state that cryptocurrencies are not legal tender, are not issued or regulated by a government or state, nor can they directly influence the price of goods and services. Furthermore, these are difficult to immediately convert into cash, with some restrictions on conversion into traditional currency.

I5 mentions that the rules applicable to currencies must apply to cryptocurrencies, with two possibilities of classification: either as Cash and cash equivalents, which is refuted by the arguments presented above, or as financial instruments with currency derivative contracts. I8 states that cryptocurrencies are financial assets, which are similar to a share, as if it were a security traded on an exchange, which has a quote. The interviewee adds "in the same way that I can make a term deposit, I can also make an investment in cryptocurrencies." I2 also considers cryptocurrencies to be financial instruments, as they are typically a contractual right. In turn, for the same authors, it is possible to include financial instruments if this results from a contractual right, which occurs in a derivative contract.

Cryptocurrencies can also be classified as intangible assets or inventories. Respondents consider cryptocurrencies as digital/virtual assets (I1, I2 and I6), the same opinion being issued by the Bank of Portugal and the Portuguese Securities Commission CMVM) and, for this reason, would treat any digital asset as an intangible asset. In fact, cryptoassets can be accepted as intangible assets, since they are non-monetary assets (Financial Reporting & Assurance Standards Canada, 2018); are separable (Ernst & Young, 2019); have an immaterial nature; are controllable, using a distributed public record (Financial Reporting & Assurance Standards Canada, 2018) and result in a future economic benefit for the entity resulting from a sale or exchange for goods and services (Ernst & Young, 2019). In short, cryptocurrencies, although they can be traded and provide expectations of future economic benefits, are considered intangible assets due to their non-monetary nature, significant variations in value and lack of physical substance (ACCA Global).

The choice of inventories was mentioned by excluding other options, as it could not be Cash and cash equivalents, then it could be classified as Inventories or as Intangible Assets, if it met the requirements of IAS 38. According to I4, cryptocurrencies "Are not currency, in the traditional concept of currency and therefore should be treated as assets, or inventories or, if the entities have complied with all the rules underlying IAS 38, be treated as intangible assets". However, according to Leopold and Vollmann (2019), it is necessary to pay attention to the time horizon, since it can only be classified as inventories if it is sold in the entity's ordinary business model.

Cryptocurrency Audit

Since one of the objectives of this study is to assess the impact of cryptocurrencies on auditing, it is important to know whether any interviewee participated in an audit of an entity that transacts cryptocurrencies. As such, the following question was asked: Have you ever audited any entity that operates with cryptocurrencies? If so, in what year did you do your first audit of an entity that operates with cryptocurrencies?

Only one participated in an audit of entities that operate with cryptocurrencies and this was in 2014 (I6). However, I3 reported having participated in a business in which part of the payment would be made in cryptocurrencies, stating the following: "I have never audited companies that have cryptocurrencies, but I participated in the acquisition process of a business in which part of the payment was made in cryptocurrencies, not yet created. And I tried, a meeting, with a company that operates a lot in cryptocurrencies, because there were some things, that out of pure curiosity, I would like to know how they are dealing with some issues. The only thing I came closest to dealing with cryptocurrencies, in my activity, was a business in which payment, from the business itself, involved payment in cash, another part, through delivery of shares and, another part, through cryptocurrency that would be developed together, that is, it would be a cryptocurrency to be created."

In the interview, we also asked whether the interviewees considered that cryptocurrencies increase audit risk. As we will see below, audit risk is viewed differently by those interviewed.

I2 said "it depends, that is, if the auditor is equipped with all the tools that allow a correct audit, no. If the auditor is not equipped with all the tools, yes. Cryptoassets are powerful economic instruments that can be used for multiple activities, including fraud, organized crime and so on. If I don't have the tools, I can validate a set of transactions that, behind them, are not being correctly validated."

According to I4, the greater the diversity of assets, the greater the audit risk; a company that only operates with one type of asset will necessarily have less risk than a company that operates with many types of assets. Not only cryptocurrencies, but bank deposits, derivatives, inventories, customer accounts receivable, increase the audit risk, as it is an asset different from other assets. "I do not believe that it is a very significant risk for the auditor, the fact that the entity being audited has cryptocurrencies. I think it's a risk of a slightly different nature. In most, or almost all, audit opinion issues, we are talking about historical financial information and, therefore, we are able to verify the control and appreciation of that cryptocurrency in the past. There is a risk, in the future, of how much the cryptocurrency will be worth and how recoverable it will be. But similar to the risk associated with a cryptocurrency, we have the risk associated with inventories, namely biological assets, which can also quickly deteriorate. Therefore, uncertainties are already taken into account, in different audit plans, in some very traditional sectors. They increase the risk, but it is not an exponential risk, I would like the expression better, they diversify the audit risk, that is, it is a new risk that will emerge and it is not necessarily an exponentially large risk, the fact that an entity operates with cryptocurrencies. "

I1 considers that cryptocurrencies increase audit risk. This idea was corroborated by I7 and I3 when they stated, respectively, "Yes, because he has to understand technology. The big difference for an auditor who carries out traditional financial audits is the obligation to understand technology. I'll give you an example: Bitcoin is simple because you transfer from one side to the other, the end. But in the case of the ethereum blockchain, a person can be activating smart contracts, can make token transfers, etc. and if the auditor doesn't understand this, it's not accounting, it will end up being overlooked." (I7), "Yes, due to the lack of regulation. It's new, it's an unregulated reality, I'm inclined to say yes, it increases audit risk" (I3).

Audit and Auditor Preparation Stages

To assess the impact of cryptocurrencies on auditing, we asked respondents whether, in their opinion, the use of cryptocurrencies causes any changes in the audit stages and whether they consider that auditors are prepared to audit entities that operate with cryptocurrencies.

Two of the interviewees consider that cryptocurrencies do not change the audit stages because, like any other asset, they must be subject to validation tests. In this sense, I4 mentioned that cryptocurrency, like any other asset, must be subject to the same types of validation tests, as it has everything that another asset has, with a context of uncertainty. But uncertainty also exists in other assets. Therefore, cryptocurrency will not significantly change the stages of an audit process. The interviewee adds that "when we think about an asset that is not subject to registration, the auditor can also value it. You can see that it exists, I imagine, for example, a deposit of flour, you can see that the flour exists, that the flour is tradable, you can even weigh it, and the same you can do with cryptocurrency, you use it, of course, different techniques to validate. It uses different validation techniques, especially in valuation, to understand the value of that currency, on the date of issuance of accounts, but the techniques and stages will be very similar, I do not anticipate a very significant change in the audit stages, and therefore may -it will be necessary to use different techniques to confirm its validation". I7 also mentioned that, in this case, auditors, instead of looking at an invoicing program, look at the blockchain".

In line with this thought, I6 mentioned that auditors must know how to navigate the block explorer, to be able to track transactions and verify what, ultimately, the financial manager said is actually true. "In a cryptocurrency company, where the wallets are all identified and the customer identification process is well done, the famous "hammering" is not possible, that is, it is not possible for the company's numbers to become more elegant or go to the meeting the wishes of the management team. Therefore, while accounting in the traditional model can do this, if we have a blockchain process, forget it. Because in blockchain, there is no "hammering", there is no need for bank reconciliation, because the reconciliation is done in real time, the transaction does not need to be reconciled, the reconciliation itself is embedded within the blockchain. There will be dematerialization, there will be no more paperwork, everything is registered on the network."

Regarding the blockchain, I2 states that the blockchain maintains data by a single owner, which is a network, allowing full visibility of transactions with time-stamp, that is, understanding transactions unequivocally. According to Bible et al. (2017), blockchain technology could reduce the time spent verifying and confirming information, focusing efforts on more complex and high-risk transactions. Psaila (2017) states that the level of safety would have a significant improvement since it would be possible to test the entire population.

The only problem is that most work teams are not prepared to carry out this work, given that, according to I5, normally, audits are carried out based on documentary records and the entity's own documentary records can be compared with the records of third parties. "Therefore, when we are talking about bank balances or financial assets, the entity's records are compared with records from third parties, there is circularization of balances, for example, at the end of the year. And, therefore, there must be a record, a computerized assessment and a computerized comparison, not a documental one. I assume that most auditors are not prepared to do this audit." Corroborating this idea, I1 states that "the transition to this type of companies that use this type of asset, still unknown, I have certain doubts that we are prepared for it. And I have certain doubts that the standards are prepared to give instructions on how to audit this type of assets."

Interviewees also mention that dematerialization makes it difficult to carry out tests and collect evidence, meaning that an adjustment of audit teams will be necessary. As such, I1 alludes that there will be "greater difficulty in testing control over this asset, taking into account its dematerialization. Greater involvement on the part of information technology specialists. The financial team will be completely different from what it is currently. And at the level of substantive tests, the collection of audit evidence, associated with everything that is more digital, continues, at the moment, to be a problem."

However, there are interviewees who believe that auditors have the capacity to deal with this new asset because, according to I4, free access to information related to cryptocurrencies allows auditors to quickly validate their existence. The interviewee also adds that "the majority of auditors would be prepared to have this asset. There have historically been complex assets and phases of the economy in which complex assets emerged, namely when we talk about derivatives, in which auditors also needed some updating to understand, how to value them, how to disclose them in terms of financial statements, but they are all techniques, which the different teams and different profiles that I know will quickly have access to." I3 also believes that the challenges presented by cryptocurrencies do not differ substantially from other realities already existing in audits.

Following this line of thought, I8 mentions that "auditing standards indirectly respond to this question. It can take a process of adaptation and preparation before doing the work. It is not because of cryptocurrency that auditing standards will change. They are already adapted to work with this."

Despite the previous responses, I2 warns that the number of auditors currently capable of auditing cryptoassets is still small and that they are specializing in the area. "I think there are few and the few that exist are specializing in this area. It is an area of extreme potential. I think the Bar of Chartered Accountants (OROC) should have more specialization in this area. Is there know-how in this area? In my point of view, no. It is necessary to have a complete view of the potential of blockchain, as well as other technologies such as artificial intelligence and machine learning. It is necessary to have knowledge of the digital structure or a form of digital audit. It is a very recent area, in which auditors must have specialization. Unfortunately, Portugal does not have the size to have this critical mass. There is a need for subspecialization regarding transformative technologies."

Interviewees also point out the need to know the customer. Abate (2018) argues that we must have more detailed knowledge about the client, namely, knowing what motivated them to enter this type of market, whether they have skills, abilities and resources for this type of work, since anonymity and lack of regulation may be a motivating factor for carrying out illicit purposes. Some of the interviewees' opinions are in line with the study developed by Brender et al. (2019).

SOLUTIONS AND RECOMMENDATIONS

Cryptoactives are recent assets, so their number of users is still small and auditors did not feel the need to delve deeper into the topic. Some auditors are concerned about the lack of regulation, as its absence contributes to the achievement of illicit purposes, such as fraud, money laundering, terrorist financing, thus increasing the risk. Likewise, the lack of education and clarification about this ecosystem represents an increased risk. For an auditor who is equipped with all the tools to audit cryptoassets, this asset diversifies the risk, unlike an exponential increase.

According to Vincent and Wilkins (2019), risk can be measured by evaluating the skills and resources of two parties, auditor and client. If both parties have high levels of skills and resources, then the risk will be low. If skills and resources are low, the risk will be high. And it will be average if both parties have average levels of skills and resources.

Considering the above, it is recommended firstly, to create accounting and auditing standards on the use of cryptocurrency and blockchain, as well as increase training on this subject for auditors and companies that intend to transact these assets. Furthermore, the auditor must ensure that the audit procedures carried out on this matter adequately cover the risk of material misstatement and fraud, as well as require the auditee to comment on this matter in the Management Team's Declaration.

FUTURE RESEARCH DIRECTIONS

Despite the contributions of this study, the topic does not end here. Therefore, for future research, we suggest a study on the level of adoption of cryptocurrencies at an international level or just carrying out a comparative study between different countries, such as Portugal and Spain. It could also be possible to assess adoption, knowledge in the area and the impacts felt on professions such as accountants and auditors, by carrying out surveys using questionnaires or using the focus group technique.

CONCLUSION

Throughout history it is possible to see the dematerialization of currency, this evolution led to the emergence of cryptocurrencies, which are based on blockchain technology. As we can see from the number of cryptocurrencies and their market capitalization, this is a market with a lot of investment and growth. Investors saw the speed of transactions, financial freedom, low fees, as well as security and transparency, positive and attractive aspects that convinced them to invest. Still, there are aspects that make them reluctant, such as price volatility, limited use, fraud, insufficient information and the lack of regulation.

The lack of guidelines or regulations from professional bodies allows for different interpretations of cryptoassets in relation to their accounting framework. However, in recent years, we have seen greater concern and intervention from institutions such as, for example, the Bank of Portugal, which is responsible for supervising virtual assets in the prevention of money laundering and raising awareness of the risks of this asset. The Order of Certified Accountants has also issued opinions on the taxation of cryptocurrencies.

Given this reality, the present work is useful to assess the impact of cryptocurrencies and blockchain on accounting and financial auditing. In order to achieve the proposed objective, a literature review was carried out, followed by an empirical study, carried out using eight interviews with auditors, as well as companies and associations that work directly in the area of cryptocurrencies.

Validating the literature review, the results revealed that respondents consider cryptocurrencies to be cryptoactives. The audit of cryptoassets is still a recent reality, the results revealed that only one of the eight interviewees participated in an audit of an entity that operates with cryptoassets, with another auditor who participated in a business where part of the payment was made in cryptocurrencies. Although the majority of interviewees did not carry out an audit of an entity that operates with cryptoassets, they do not show a complete lack of knowledge on the matter, mentioning different regulatory standards regarding this class of assets. Still, respondents consider that there are few auditors prepared to carry out an audit of entities that operate with cryptocurrencies. The fact that the number of people and companies who deal with this type of asset is not high means that auditors still do not feel the need to deepen their knowledge in this area.

The information analyzed in the literature review and empirical study showed that cryptocurrencies have an impact on the operationalization of the audit, as they will trigger a dematerialization of paper in the various audit stages. Therefore, the auditor will spend less time verifying and validating information, focusing on activities with greater risk and complexity. It will also be possible to carry out a real-time audit and test the entire population. Regarding audit risk, as long as there are no clarifications, instructions and regulations, the risk is considered high for most auditors, as they are not prepared due to the innovation represented by this new asset.

Accounting-wise, there are several hypotheses for accounting for cryptoassets, such as Cash and cash equivalents, Financial instruments, Intangible assets and Inventories. The most selected options were Cash and cash equivalents and Intangible assets, although the literature states that of the hypotheses presented, only cash and cash equivalents are refuted because they are not issued or regulated by the government or any state, they cannot directly influence the price of goods and services and is difficult to convert into traditional currency. Regarding other hypotheses, it is necessary to check whether the requirements of the class in which they intend to fit are met.

This study has some limitations, such as the scarcity of literature that combines the areas of auditing and cryptocurrencies and the small sample size. Still, it is considered that this study contributes to the knowledge of cryptocurrencies and their impact on the operationalization of accounting and auditing. Despite being an area that has already begun to be investigated in Portugal, such as the taxation and regulation of bitcoin or IT aspects of blockchain, this is the first study in Portugal that addresses the impact that cryptocurrencies have on the operationalization of a financial audit. The interview guide used is also an innovative aspect.

REFERENCES

Abate, T. (2018). *Audit Considerations Related to Cryptocurrency Assets and Transactions*. Chartered Professional Accountants Canada.

AICPA & CIMA. (2023). *Accounting for and auditing of digital assets.* Author.

Almeida, B. (2019). *Manual de Auditoria Financeira:Uma análise integrada baseada no risco* (3rd ed.). Escolar Editora.

Applelbaum, D., & Smith, S. S. (2018). *ICYMI | Blockchain Basics and Hands-on Guidance Taking the Next Step toward Implementation and Adoption.* https://www.cpajournal.com/2019/06/27/icymi-blockchain-basics-and-hands-on-guidance/

Bonsón, E., & Bednárová, M. (2019). Blockchain and its implications for accounting and auditing. *Meditari Accountancy Research*, *27*(5), 725–740. doi:10.1108/MEDAR-11-2018-0406

Brand, W. (2016). *Bitcoin for Dummies*. John Wiley & Sons, Inc.

Brender, N., & Gauthier, M. (2018). *Impacts of Blockchain on the Auditing Profession.* ISACA. https://www.isaca.org/resources/isaca-journal/issues/2018/volume-5/impacts-of-blockchain-on-the-auditing-profession

Brender, N., Gauthier, M., Morin, J., & Salihi, A. (2019). The Potential Impact of Blockchain Technology on Audit Practice. *Journal of Strategic Innovation and Sustainability*, *14*(2), 35–59.

Burns, J., Steele, A., Cohen, E., & Ramamoorti, S. (2020). *Blockchain and Internal Control: The COSO perspective.* Academic Press.

Canadian Public Accountability Board and Conseil Canadien Sur La Reddition de Comptes. (2019). *Auditing in the Crypto-Asset Sector Inspections Insights.* Retrieved from https://www.cpab-ccrc.ca/docs/default-source/inspections-reports/2019-crypto-inspections-insights-en.pdf?sfvrsn=9aa5c0d2_20

Ernst & Young. (2019). *Accounting by holders of crypto-assets.* EY.

Han, H., Shiwakoti, R. K., Jarvis, R., Mordi, C., & Botchie, D. (2022). *Accounting and auditing with blockchain technology and artificial Intelligence: A literature review* (Vol. 48). International Journal of Accounting Information Systems. Obtido de https://www.sciencedirect.com/science/article/pii/S1467089522000501?ref=pdf_download&fr=RR-2&rr=833973d7d8ef5bea#section-cited-by

International Auditing and Assurance Standards Board. (2018). *Manual das normas internacionais de controlo de qualidade, auditoria, revisão, outros trabalhos de garantia de fiabilidade e serviços relacionados.* IAASB.

Koo, J., & Sewell, K. (2023). *Accounting for the Purchase, Sale and Receipt of Cryptocurrencies.* BDO Alliance USA. Obtido de https://www.bdo.com/insights/assurance/accounting-for-the-purchase-sale-and-receipt-of-cryptocurrencies#

Nian, L., & Chuen, D. (2015). *Handbook of Digital Currency Bitcoin, Innovation, Financial Instrument, and Big Data.* Elsevier.

PCAOB. (2023). *SPOTLIGHT: Inspection Observations Related to Public Company Audits Involving Crypto Assets.* PCAOB: Public Company Accounting Oversight Board. Obtido de https://pcaobus.org/documents/crypto-assets-spotlight.pdf

Pippo, K. (2020). *Viewpoints: Auditing Crypto-Assets: Relevance and Reliability of the Information Obtained from a Blockchain to be used as Audit Evidence.* Chartered Professional Accountants Canada.

Psaila, S. (2017). *Blockchain: A game changer for audit processes.* Deloitte.

Regelbrugge, A., Fedele, S., Mankad, M., & Connors, S. (2021). *An internal auditor's guide to blockchain - Auditing blockchain environments.* Deloitte.

Rigters, G. (2018). *Bitcoin For Beginners & Dummies - Cryptocurrency & Blockchain.* Academic Press.

SNC. (2015). Sistema de Normalização Contabilística (6ª Ediço ed.). Porto Editora.

United States Securities and Exchange Commission. (2020). *Annual report pursuant to section 13 or 15(d) of the securities exchange act of 1934 - Tesla, Inc.* Retrieved from https://sec.report/Document/0001564590-21-004599/tsla-10k_20201231.htm

Vincent, N., & Wilkins, A. (2019). *Challenges when Auditing Cryptocurrencies.* American Accounting Association. doi:10.2308/ciia-19-025

ADDITIONAL READING

Bible, W., Raphael, J., Taylor, P., & Valiente, I. O. (2017). *Blockchain Technology and Its Potential Impact on the Audit and Assurance Profession*. Chartered Professional Accountants Canada.

Pippo, K. (2020). *Viewpoints: Auditing Crypto-Assets: Relevance and Reliability of the Information Obtained from a Blockchain to be used as Audit Evidence*. Chartered Professional Accountants Canada.

PricewaterhouseCoopers. (n.d.). *Ten questions every board should ask about cryptocurrencies*. (PWC, Editor) Obtido de PWC: https://www.pwc.com/us/en/industries/financial-services/library/cryptocurrency-questions.html

Pundmann, S., Regelbrugge, A., Mankad, M., Connors, S., Bhattacharya, R., & Joshi, A. (2019). *An internal auditor's guide to blockchain: Blurring the line between physical and digital - Part one: Introduction to blockchain*. Deloitte. Obtido de https://www2.deloitte.com/content/dam/Deloitte/us/Documents/risk/us-risk-blockchain-for-internal-auditors.pdf

KEY TERMS AND DEFINITIONS

Audit Risk: Audit risk refers to the possibility that the auditor will not detect material misstatements in an entity's financial statements during the audit process. These misstatements may be caused by error or fraud and affect the integrity and accuracy of the financial information presented.

Block Explorer: Is an interface that allows blockchain data to be accessible and understandable to users, thus providing a transparent and detailed view of the activities occurring on the network.

Block Timestamps: It is the time stamp at which the block was added to the sequence. It is crucial to guarantee the integrity and trust in the network.

Cryptography: Security practice that involves the use of mathematical algorithms to protect sensitive information during data transmission or storage.

Decentralized Public Record: Is a database that stores information in a distributed way, without depending on a single centralized entity. Instead, information is shared and maintained by a network, in which all participants contribute to its validation and security.

List of Responses: No changes were requested to the submitted chapter.

Pseudoanonymity: Refers to the condition in which transactions are publicly recorded on the blockchain, but the identities of those involved in the transactions are not directly revealed. Instead of names or personal information, cryptographic addresses are used to represent the parties involved.

Reasonable Assurance: Refers to the degree of confidence that the auditor seeks to obtain when carrying out audit procedures on an entity's financial statements. When the auditor states that he or she provides "reasonable assurance," it means that he or she conducted an audit in accordance with applicable auditing standards and principles in a careful and diligent manner. This assurance does not imply absolute certainty, as the audit is based on sampling and professional judgment. Rather, it means that the auditor has performed sufficient procedures to obtain acceptable assurance that the financial statements are free from material misstatement, whether due to error or fraud. The concept of "reasonable assurance" is fundamental to understanding that the audit cannot completely eliminate risk, but seeks to provide a solid basis for users' confidence in the financial information presented by the audited entity.

Chapter 7
Machine Learning:
A Revolution in Accounting

Mohamed Ali Bejjar
https://orcid.org/0009-0004-8051-7559
Higher Business School of Sfax, Tunisia

Yosr Siala
https://orcid.org/0009-0007-4593-4586
Higher Business School of Sfax, Tunisia

ABSTRACT

This chapter provides a comprehensive analysis of the impact of machine learning on the specific domains of financial accounting and management accounting. By tracing the historical evolution, conceptually delineating key parameters, and systematizing various modalities of machine learning, the investigation highlights the notable advancements it engenders in financial management. The study underscores the central role of machine learning in automating processes, optimizing decision-making, and generating innovative analytical perspectives, while identifying ethical concerns inherent in its implementation, such as algorithmic transparency and data preservation. This research is based on a literature review approach using a descriptive analytical method. In conclusion, machine learning emerges as a significant driver of progress in the accounting domain, redefining professional standards and necessitating ethical management to fully capitalize on its benefits while minimizing potential risks.

INTRODUCTION

Over the past two decades, artificial intelligence (AI) has brought significant changes to the world, ushering in the second digital revolution (Brynjolfsson & McAfee, 2014). Cumulative evidence and changes in business practices indicate that this new digital revolution is sweeping the planet, creating a new perspective that it will profoundly and irreversibly change the way societies function (Frey & Osborne, 2017). The current wave of digitization, which includes the emergence of big data, cloud computing,

DOI: 10.4018/979-8-3693-0847-9.ch007

machine learning (ML), and autonomous algorithms, blockchain is expected to radically reshape existing business models and challenge the way work is performed in modern organizations.

This includes aspects such as strategic planning, managerial decision making, organizational control, human resource management (HRM), data analytics, and accounting, among others (Shrestha et al., 2019; Auvinen et al., 2019).

Rapidly evolving technology has led to a significant transformation in the field of accounting, and machine learning (ML) is emerging as a key driver of this revolution. The marriage of machine learning and accounting offers unique opportunities to fundamentally rethink how financial information is processed, analyzed, and interpreted. This convergence of cutting-edge technology with traditional accounting practices promises to transcend conventional boundaries and pave the way for more efficient, predictive, and strategic methods of financial data management.

This chapter aims to explore the transformative role of machine learning in accounting, highlighting its implications, potential benefits, and the challenges associated with its integration.

In this digital age, machine learning offers data analysis and processing capabilities on a scale never before imagined. In financial accounting, it is acting as a catalyst, automating complex tasks, accelerating financial statement analysis, and facilitating strategic decision-making. In auditing, ML is improving the accuracy and relevance of procedures, detecting anomalies more effectively, and contributing to greater quality assurance. Finally, in management accounting, ML is revolutionizing cost management, process optimization, and strategic planning by providing predictive models and advanced analytics (Rikhardsson & Yigitbasioglu, 2018; Moll & Yigitbasioglu, 2019; Appelbaum et al., 2017; Kashyap, 2017).

Our chapter is organized under four headings. The first provides a history of machine learning and a set of definitions. The second heading focuses on the machine learning categories of supervised learning, unsupervised learning, semi-supervised learning, and reinforcement learning. The third section describes the process of machine learning. The fourth section provides an overview of the impact of machine learning on accounting and auditing, fraud detection, and managerial accounting.

MACHINE LEARNING: HISTORY AND DEFINITIONS

Before studying any phenomenon, it's useful to know its origins. In the following, we will outline the history of machine learning, as well as the most useful definitions.

Machine Learning History

The history of machine learning is marked by revolutionary advances and key moments that changed the way machines understand and process information. The concept of machine learning has its roots in the early work of the 20th century, when pioneers such as Alan Turing laid the theoretical foundations of computation and learning. The field really took off in the 1950s and 1960s, with researchers such as Arthur Samuel introducing the term "Machine Learning" and developing algorithms capable of improving their performance through experience (Samuel, 1959).

In recent years, social science research has integrated machine learning to address complex issues beyond the capabilities of traditional econometric tools. Unlike the linear estimation approach of the OLS model, machine learning uses a training and learning method. This involves dividing the sample into three subsamples: training, validation, and test samples.

The process consists of building multiple candidate models on the training sample, then evaluating them on the validation sample to select the optimal model, followed by an unbiased evaluation on the test sample to provide an out-of-sample performance score. Designed to analyze large amounts of data, machine learning techniques have demonstrated their ability to identify complex structures and determine functional relationships with superior out-of-sample performance compared to traditional econometric tools (Mullainathan & Spiess, 2017).

Another advantage lies in the high-dimensional nature of machine learning, which overcomes the dimensionality problem often encountered by traditional econometric tools. While linear regression proves inadequate for dealing with the large number of variables that have accumulated in the literature over time, machine learning provides a powerful mechanism for testing these variables and selecting those that are robust.

Leading finance and accounting journals have already published several studies exploiting the potential of machine learning in traditionally well-researched areas. In asset pricing, for example, the use of machine learning has identified variables that are critical to stock market returns (Gu et al., 2020; Freyberger et al., 2020; Feng et al., 2020; Giglio et al., 2021). In accounting, researchers have applied machine learning to detect accounting fraud and misrepresentation (Brown et al., 2020; Bertomeu et al., 2021; Bao et al., 2020). These studies all recognize the high-dimensional challenges posed to classical regression methods and use machine learning to address these issues.

It is important to note that the intention of applying machine learning in finance and accounting studies is not to replace the classical OLS method, but rather to improve existing models by identifying robust controls and eliminating unnecessary variables (Bertomeu, 2020).

Machine Learning Categories

Machine learning is based on algorithms and models that can learn from data. Learning types are categories that describe how an algorithm learns from data. Machine learning (ML) can generally be categorized into supervised, unsupervised, semi-supervised, and reinforcement learning (e.g., Géron, 2017).

Supervised Learning

In supervised learning, the algorithm is exposed to a set of training examples consisting of input data and corresponding outputs. The model adjusts its parameters to minimize a cost function, thereby optimizing its ability to generalize and make accurate predictions on new data (Fieberg et al., 2022).

Supervised learning is widely used in tasks such as image classification, price prediction, speech recognition, and machine translation. It is particularly effective in handling complex relationships between input and output data.The main concepts of supervised learning are therefore:

- Mapping Function and Mathematical Modeling: The basis of supervised learning is the mathematical modeling of a mapping function $fX \rightarrow Y$, where X represents the feature space of the input data and Y the output space. The goal is to approximate this function with a parametric model.

The mapping function, which is learned from the training set, aims to approximate the relationship between inputs and outputs by making predictions based on input data.

- The labeled training set: The training set consists of pairs of inputs *xi* and labeled outputs *yi*. The quality of the training depends on the representativeness and diversity of this set. The training set is the collection of data used to train the model. Each example in this set consists of input data and the corresponding output.
- Objective Function and Cost Minimization: The objective function, also known as the cost function, measures the difference between the model's prediction $f(x)$ and the actual outputs y. During training, the model parameters are adjusted to minimize this function. The objective function is used to evaluate the difference between the model's predictions and the actual labels in the training set, with the goal of minimizing it to improve the model's fit to the data.
- Optimization algorithms: Supervised learning algorithms include methods such as neural networks, support vector machines (SVMs), decision trees, linear regression, and others. The choice of algorithm depends on the nature of the data and the task at hand.
- Training, Validation and Test Set: The model is trained on a set of data and evaluated on a separate set to ensure it can generalize to new data. The evaluation set is used to adjust the model's hyperparameters, while a separate test set is reserved to assess the model's performance on new data.
- Overfitting and underfitting: Overfitting occurs when the model fits the training data too well, but does not generalize well to new data. Underfitting occurs when the model is too simple to capture the complexity of the training data.
- Evaluation Metrics: The performance of a model in supervised learning is often evaluated using metrics such as precision, recall, F-measure, area under the ROC curve (AUC-ROC), etc., depending on the type of task (classification, regression, etc.).
- Generalization and model capacity: The ability of the model to generalize to new data without compromising its performance on training data is an important criterion. Model complexity must be balanced to avoid excessive overfitting.

Unsupervised Learning

Unsupervised learning is an approach to machine learning in which an algorithm is exposed to an unlabeled data set and the goal is to discover structures, patterns, or relationships inherent in that data (Gao et al., 2020). Unlike supervised learning, there are no outputs associated with the training data. Techniques such as clustering aim to group data based on intrinsic similarities, while dimensionality reduction aims to capture essential information in a lower-dimensional space.

According to Swana and Doorsamy (2021), this approach is based on several fundamental concepts:

- Clustering and Density Modeling: Clustering algorithms, such as k-means, and methods based on density modeling, such as kernel-based density estimation, are used to group data into homogeneous sets based on their characteristics.
- Dimensionality reduction and feature extraction: Dimensionality reduction techniques, such as Principal Component Analysis (PCA), condense information while preserving the data's intrinsic structure. Meanwhile, feature extraction identifies the most discriminative aspects of the data.
- Self-supervised methods: Self-supervised learning, also a subset of unsupervised learning, is based on tasks in which the data itself serves as a label. These tasks can include predicting the next word in a sequence or reconstructing a portion of the data.

- Anomaly detection and abnormal density modeling: Anomaly detection involves searching for data instances that are atypical of the rest of the ensemble. Methods based on abnormal density modeling are often used in this context.
- Validation and Evaluation: Evaluation in unsupervised learning is often more subjective and context dependent. Metrics such as silhouette for clustering or inertia can be used, but a thorough understanding of the results is often required.
- Auto-encoding neural networks: Auto-encoders, trained to reconstruct input data, are neural networks often used in unsupervised learning to learn useful representations of data.
- Self-organizing maps (SOMs): Self-organizing maps, a special type of unsupervised neural network, create a topological representation of data in two- or three-dimensional space.
- Data mining and understanding the system under study: Unsupervised learning is also used to explore and understand complex data sets, providing clues about relationships between variables and identifying latent patterns or structures.

Semi-Supervised Learning

According to Van Engelen and Hoos (2020), semi-supervised learning is an approach to machine learning that attempts to make the most of the combination of labeled and unlabeled data in the process of training a model.

Here's a closer look from a more scientific perspective:

- Statistical framework: Semi-supervised learning can be formalized in a statistical framework where the goal is to find the joint distribution of data X and labels Y while minimizing the prediction error.
- Generative models: Some semi-supervised approaches rely on generative models, such as probabilistic graphical models, which attempt to model the joint distribution of labeled and unlabeled data.
- Training Consistency: Training consistency is a key concept. It states that model predictions on similar data should be consistent, regardless of whether that data is labeled or unlabeled.
- Label propagation: Label propagation methods attempt to extend information from labeled data to unlabeled data by exploiting similarity measures or transition models.
- Self-Supervised Training: Self-supervised learning can be integrated as a component of a semi-supervised system, where self-supervised tasks, such as predicting the next word in a sequence, are used to learn useful representations.
- Mixed cost optimization: A common approach in semi-supervised learning is to define a mixed cost that combines the cost of errors on labeled data with an appropriate measure for unlabeled data.
- Co-Training and Multi-View Learning: Methods such as co-training exploit the complementarity of information between different views of the data, where each view can represent a different perspective on the problem.
- Semi-supervised cross-validation: Semi-supervised cross-validation is often used to evaluate model performance, taking into account both labeled and unlabeled data.
- Knowledge transfer: Semi-supervised learning can also involve transferring knowledge from related tasks where labeled data is more abundant to the task of interest with limited labeled data.

The goal of semi-supervised learning is to capitalize on the richness of unlabeled data while maintaining the guidance of labeled data. This improves model performance in situations where the acquisition of labeled data is costly or difficult. Semi-supervised learning research continues to explore new methods to exploit the duality of labeled and unlabeled data.

Reinforcement Learning

Reinforcement learning (RL) is a branch of machine learning that focuses on sequential decision making by an agent in a dynamic environment. The agent learns by interacting with the environment by taking actions, receiving rewards or sanctions in return, and adjusting its strategy to maximize the cumulative reward over time (Wang et al., 2020).

This is part of a formal framework based on the theory of Markov decision processes (Moerland et al., 2023).

- Markov decision process (MDP): An MDP is defined by a set of states *S*, a set of actions *A*, a probability transition function *P* describing the probability of moving from one state to another by taking an action, a reward function *R* describing the rewards associated with each state-action transition, and a discount factor γ modeling the preference for immediate over future rewards.
- Policy (π): A policy is a strategy that defines the agent's behavior. It can be represented as a probability distribution over actions conditional on the state, i.e., $\pi(a|s)$.
- Value function (*V* and *Q*): The value function $V\pi(s)$ measures the expected payoff from a state *s* under a policy π. The function $Q\pi(s,a)$ measures the expected payoff from state *s* taking action a and following policy π.
- Bellman Equation: The Bellman equation expresses a recursive relationship between the value function of a state and the values of the states attainable from that state. For the function $Q\pi$ it is defined as $Q\pi(s,a)=R(s,a)+\gamma\sum s'P(s'|s,a)V\pi(s'))$.
- Q-Learning Algorithm: The Q-Learning algorithm is an example of a reinforcement learning algorithm. It is based on the idea of iterating over the Q-function update equation to estimate optimal values. The Q-function update equation can be formulated as

Max $Q(s,a)\leftarrow(1-\alpha)$

$Q(s,a)+\alpha[R(s,a)+\gamma maxa'Q(s',a')]$ where α is the learning rate

- Exploration-Exploitation: The balance between exploration and exploitation is often formulated as a ϵ-greedy policy, where the agent explores with probability ϵ and exploits with probability $1-\epsilon$.
- Policy Optimization: Some RL algorithms, such as policy-based methods, attempt to optimize the policy directly, while others, such as value-based methods, estimate and optimize value functions.
- Optimal value functions ($V*$ and $Q*$): The optimal value functions $V*$ and $Q*$ represent the maximum rewards expected under the optimal policy for a given state or state-action pair, respectively.

Reinforcement learning is often formulated as an optimization problem aimed at finding the optimal policy or optimal value functions to maximize the cumulative reward in a given environment. Specific

Figure 1. Overview of machine learning techniques
Source: Swana et Doorsamy, 2020

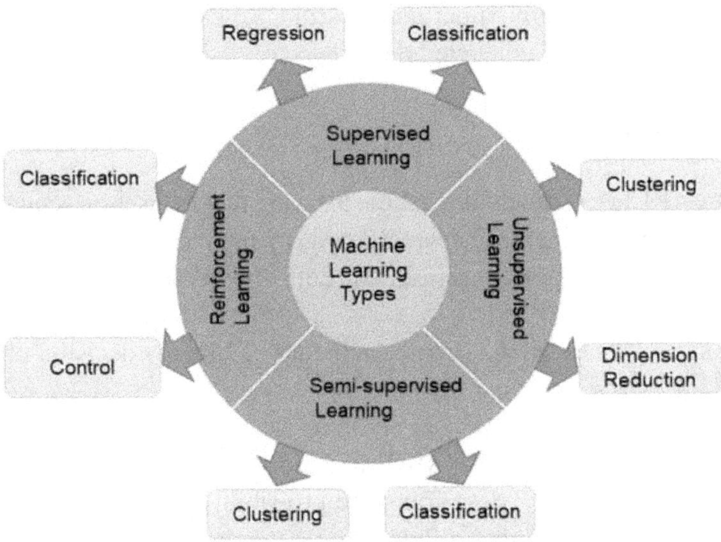

methods and algorithms vary depending on the complexity of the problem and the characteristics of the environment.

The following is a summary diagram of the machine learning categories:

THE MACHINE LEARNING PROCESS

The machine learning (ML) process is a sequence of organized steps aimed at creating, training, and deploying predictive models or intelligent systems. Although data mining (i.e., the actual application of machine learning algorithms) is only a fraction of the overall research process, finding the most appropriate machine learning algorithm and applying it correctly can be tedious and time-consuming. In particular, choosing a machine learning algorithm is not trivial. There is no generally superior machine learning algorithm, as the performance of the algorithm depends solely on the data provided (Goodfellow et al., 2016).

Here are the general steps in the machine learning process:

- Collect data from different sources: This step is summarized in the following four sub-steps:
  a) Problem Definition: Clarify the goal of the project and determine whether it's a classification, regression, clustering problem, etc.
  b) Data collection: Collect relevant data to solve the problem. Ensure the quality and relevance of the data.
- Data Cleaning and Feature Engineering: This step is divided into the following two sub-steps:
  a) Data pre-processing: consists of the following tasks

Data cleaning: removing missing values, processing outliers
Normalization: scaling data to make them comparable
Coding: converting categorical variables into numerical format.

b) Data Mining: consists of:

Statistical analysis: examine descriptive statistics to understand the distribution of data.
Statistical visualization: creating graphs to identify trends, patterns, or correlations.

- Model Building for Selecting the Right ML Algorithm: This stage is crucial for the success of the learning process. It includes the following points:

  a) Model selection: Select the most appropriate machine learning algorithm for the problem (linear regression, decision trees, neural networks, etc.)
  b) Data partitioning: dividing the data into training and test sets to evaluate model performance
  c) Model training: consists of:

Data feeding: Use the training set to teach the model to make predictions.
Parameter optimization: Adjust the parameters of the model to improve its performance.

- Evaluate the model: In this step, the test set is used to evaluate the model's ability to generalize to new data, and metrics such as precision, recall, F1 score, etc. are used to measure the model's performance. Optimization and tuning is also required. This involves fine-tuning hyperparameters to improve model performance.
- Model deployment: This involves deploying the trained model into the production system to make predictions on new data. Similarly, this phase includes the following two sub-steps:
  a) Maintenance and updating: This consists of continuous monitoring of the model's performance in production and updating to keep the model up-to-date with new data and changes in the problem.
  b) Model interpretation: Trying to understand how the model makes decisions (especially in the case of complex models such as neural networks).

The machine learning process is not linear, and some steps may need to be repeated depending on the results obtained. It requires a thorough understanding of the problem, skillful manipulation of the data, and judicious choice of algorithms to obtain powerful, generalizable models.

Below is a diagram that summarizes the steps in the machine learning process:

THE IMPACT OF MACHINE LEARNING ON ACCOUNTING

The advent of machine learning (ML) has revolutionized many fields, and accounting is no exception. This technological convergence offers innovative perspectives that are redefining the nature of accounting research and its practical applications. In exploring the implications of ML in the accounting context, we are witnessing a significant transformation in two key areas: financial accounting and auditing on

Figure 2. Steps in the machine learning process
Source: Pandian, 2020

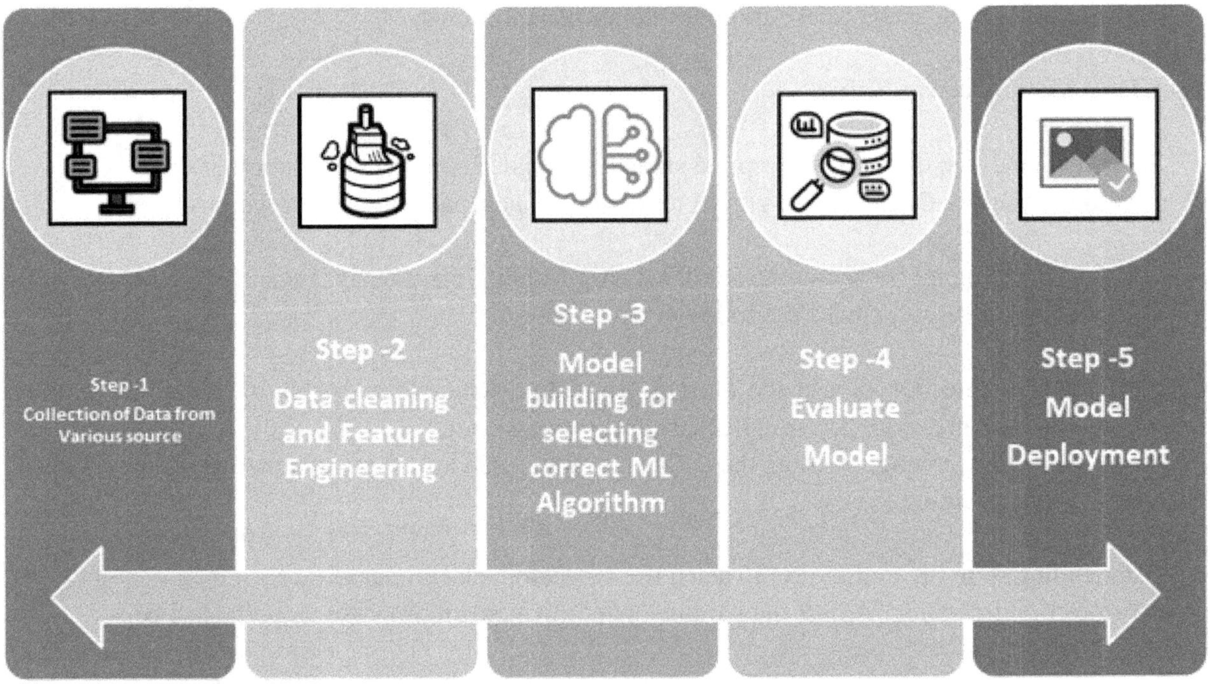

the one hand, and managerial accounting on the other. This section serves as a starting point for a closer examination of ethical considerations and the impact of ML on accounting research, highlighting new opportunities and challenges that arise at the intersection of technology and the accounting discipline.

Ethical Considerations

The integration of machine learning in accounting raises significant ethical concerns, particularly regarding algorithmic transparency and data confidentiality. Machine learning models can be opaque, making it difficult to understand decision-making mechanisms and posing challenges for accountability and trust. For example, when a model is utilized to evaluate credit risk, it may make approval or rejection decisions without transparently justifying its decision criteria. To tackle this issue, significant efforts are being made to adopt model explainability techniques. Methods such as Local Interpretable Model-Agnostic Explanations (LIME) or SHapley Additive exPlanations (SHAP) have emerged as potential solutions, providing clear and interpretable explanations of model predictions.

Safeguarding data confidentiality is paramount, especially when dealing with sensitive information such as clients' financial data. Robust protection mechanisms, such as pseudonymization, anonymization, and encryption, are crucial in reducing the risks associated with potential unauthorized disclosure of this data and ensuring data security. In addition, it is important to establish strict access management and data control policies to limit exposure to potential privacy threats.

Finally, the issue of algorithmic bias is a major concern in the development and application of machine learning models in accounting. These biases can result from biases present in training data and can lead to discriminatory or unjust decisions. To tackle this challenge, it is necessary to conduct a comprehensive evaluation of any existing biases in the data, and implement appropriate debiasing measures. These measures, which may include data balancing or the collection of additional representative data, aim to mitigate biased distortions and promote more equitable and impartial outcomes.

Integrating ethical considerations into the design and implementation of machine learning systems for accounting ensures responsible and ethical use of these technologies while preserving the rights and trust of relevant stakeholders.

Financial Accounting and Auditing

Financial accounting refers to the preparation of financial statements, while auditing refers to the examination of financial statements. The goal of an audit is to confirm with reasonable assurance that the financial statements comply with generally accepted accounting principles (GAAP). As we will see below, comparatively more machine learning (ML) research has been done on audit-related topics than on financial accounting.

Baldwin et al. (2006) discuss some key audit tasks suitable for AI, based on an earlier classification of such tasks by Abdolmohammadi (1991). They show that many of the 332 audit tasks (such as bad debts, collections, guarantees, calculation of various inventory ratios, comparative studies of sales, and returns) that Abdolmohammadi (1991) had deemed suitable for use with decision support systems are also adaptable to automation by machine learning. Specifically, Baldwin et al (2006) identify classification tasks, such as distinguishing between recoverable and doubtful receivables, or legitimate and doubtful transactions, and risk assessment tasks, such as error detection or business continuity predictions. Researchers have renewed their calls for research into the possibilities of AI in auditing (Earley, 2015; Cao et al., 2015; Gepp et al., 2018).

In addition to the studies already mentioned, many others provide insights into the application of artificial intelligence in auditing (IAASB, 2016; Sun & Vasarhelyi, 2017; Kokina & Davenport, 2017; Sun, 2019, Aitkazinov, 2023). The main conclusion is that machine learning makes auditing more efficient and effective by enabling auditors to process large amounts of structured and unstructured data that would otherwise be impossible to process.

The literature often recommends the use of machine learning (ML) for specific auditing tasks, such as business continuity prediction or error detection, rather than considering the entire auditing process as a potential application of AI. For example, No et al. (2019) suggest integrating AI into a significant part of the overall auditing process through an AI-based sampling technique. Auditors typically use sampling to examine a small percentage of the population of auditable items (e.g., assets, transactions). The next step is to extrapolate the audit findings from the sampled items to the entire population. This approach does not always provide absolute reasonable assurance for the entire set of financial statements.

First, an auditor trains the AI by filtering out the items with the highest risk of error from the total population. Then, based on these items, an AI-based outlier detection technique is used to identify other outliers. ML makes it possible to automate many of the testing and verification processes involved in an audit (Shapovalova et al., 2023). This includes anomaly detection, account verification, and other standard procedures that can significantly speed up the entire audit process.

Second, outliers are prioritized by a weighting system to reduce the auditor's test set. Similarly, auditors often deal with large amounts of data. ML can quickly process these massive amounts of data and identify trends, patterns and anomalies that would be difficult to detect using traditional methods. ML systems can help auditors plan their engagements more effectively by identifying potential risks, assessing the complexity of transactions, and recommending appropriate audit approaches (Vitali & Giuliani, 2024).

Such an approach is still rather rare in the audit research literature; in the following sections, we turn to AI-assisted audit tasks that have recently received much more attention, namely fraud detection and prediction of going concern or bankruptcy.

Fraud Detection

Accounting fraud is a global problem, as evidenced by numerous high-profile cases such as Enron in the United States, Vivendi Universal in France, Sino-Forest in China, and Wirecard in Germany. It is estimated that fraud causes global financial losses of approximately $4.5 trillion each year (Association of Certified Fraud Examiners, 2020). Auditors are responsible for ensuring that there are no material misstatements in financial statements, whether due to (unintentional) error or (intentional) fraud.

Fanning and Cogger (1998) argue that most auditors lack knowledge about the characteristics of accounting fraud and experience in detecting it. They point out that managers involved in accounting fraud attempt to mislead auditors. Fraud can be divided into financial fraud and asset misappropriation. Financial fraud involves the "manipulation, falsification or alteration of the accounting records or supporting documents from which the financial statements are prepared, or the intentional misrepresentation or omission of material events, transactions or other information from the financial statements" (SAS No. 99 Par. 6).

Asset misappropriation is characterized by "the theft of an entity's assets when the effect of the theft is to present financial statements that are not in conformity, in all material respects, with GAAP" (SAS No. 99 Par. 6). Evidence suggests that asset misappropriation is eight times more common than financial statement fraud, even though the latter results in far greater financial losses (Association of Certified Fraud Examiners, 2020).

The use of machine learning (ML) for financial statement fraud detection can be justified by the improvements associated with the ability of auditors and legislators to identify potentially fraudulent entities through more accurate fraud detection systems (Hooda et al., 2018; Kanaparthi, 2024). Fraud detection is inherently a supervised classification task. Prior to the advent of machine learning, the majority of research in this area relied on logistic regression (Dechow et al., 2011), which remains a common frame of reference in contemporary studies (Bao et al., 2021).

The related literature relies mainly on structured public financial data, such as financial statement figures (Green & Choi, 1997; Cecchini et al., 2010a; Dechow et al., 2011). However, unstructured data, especially extracted from financial reports, are also used (Cecchini et al., 2010b ; Humpherys et al., 2011 ; Purda & Skillicorn, 2015). Other sources of unstructured data include social media for textual data or financial results conference calls for auditory data (Hobson et al., 2012; Dong et al., 2018).

Methods for processing text data include counting words that predict fraudulent behavior or analyzing sentiment in social media data. This information is then used as features for the classification task. In addition to the general challenges of machine learning, such as discovering general patterns in data without overfitting, fraud detection presents its own challenges. Fraud is typically rare and adversarial in nature, with fraudsters actively attempting to prevent learning based on past events (Bao et al., 2022).

ML enables the creation of sophisticated models that can detect patterns of fraudulent behavior before they become significant. This allows for early intervention and reduction of financial losses.

Early studies linking fraud detection and machine learning (ML) used neural networks (Green & Choi, 1997; Fanning & Cogger, 1998). Green and Choi (1997) constructed a sample with an equal number of fraud and non-fraud cases. They report a fifty percent improvement using the neural network instead of random selection.

With the growing popularity of ML, many additional classification methods are being used and compared. Kotsiantis et al. (2006) use financial ratios to predict fraud in manufacturing companies listed on the Athens Stock Exchange. Instead of using individual classification methods and comparing their results, they construct a classification ensemble. Specifically, they train individual classification models and combine their predictions according to a voting scheme. They use classification models based on decision trees, neural networks, and logistic regression. With this approach, they outperform the prediction of any single ML algorithm.

Li et al. (2020) pioneered the use of raw accounting variables rather than financial or non-financial ratios (Dechow et al., 2011) in fraud detection. Although raw accounting variables form the basis of financial and non-financial ratios, the authors argue that raw accounting variables contain more information because ratios lose information during their construction. They use support vector machines (SVMs) with different kernel functions for prediction and ensemble methods. Note that they specifically use an out-of-sample (OOS) procedure rather than an in-sample (IS) approach, which is often used for causal inference (Li et al., 2020). IS leads to very optimistic predictions and is not recommended because predictions are developed using data already known to the model; thus, the more the model is overfitted, the better the predictions.

Bao et al. (2020) conduct a similar study, but extend the comparison to multiple machine learning (ML) methods, using different metrics. The predictive power of unstructured text data in combination with financial ratios is the subject of an in-depth study by Craja et al. (2020). They present a deep learning model designed to take advantage of both structured and unstructured data simultaneously. The authors report a significant improvement in prediction over commonly used ML techniques such as random forests or SVMs.

In addition, the deep learning architecture allows them to explore the "black box" of the model and identify early warning indicators at the word and sentence level. At the word level, they identify early warning indicators such as "cost" or "acquisition", and at the sentence level, statements such as "If we are unable to fully integrate acquired products, technologies or businesses, or to train, retain and motivate the employees of acquired businesses, we may not realize the intended benefits of these acquisitions, which could materially harm our business, results of operations and financial condition".

Management Accounting

Management accounting differs from financial accounting and financial reporting in that it relates to internal reporting systems. More specifically, the Institute of Management Accountants defines management accounting as "the profession that supports management decision making, develops planning and performance management systems, and provides financial reporting and control expertise to assist management in formulating and implementing an organization's strategy" (Institute of Management Accountants, 2008). Consequently, compared to financial accounting, management accounting places more emphasis on value creation, decision making, planning and forecasting, and risk management (Wang & Wang, 2016,).

Table 1. Summary table of studies on the impact of machine learning on financial accounting and auditing

Authors	Country	Method	Industry	Study
Abdolmohammadi (1991)	n/a	Qualitative	n/a	The factors that influence auditors' choice of decision support tools for different audit tasks.
Green and Choi (1997)	n/a	Quantitative	Multiple industries	The use of neural network technology to develop a model for detecting management fraud in financial statements.
Fanning and Cogger (1998)	n/a	Qualitative	n/a	Artificial Neural Networks (ANN) detects management fraud, providing valuable evidence for fraud detection.
Baldwin et al. (2006)	n/a	Qualitative	n/a	Artificial intelligence can enhance accounting and auditing.
Kotsiantis et al. (2006)	Greece	Quantitative	n/a	Machine learning techniques can detect fraudulent financial statements and identify factors associated with them.
Cecchini et al. (2010a)	n/a	Quantitative	Multiple industries	The financial kernel, along with support vector machines, serves as a useful method for distinguishing fraudulent companies.
Cecchini et al. (2010b)	n/a	Quantitative	n/a	Methodologies for automatic text analysis achieve the best prediction results in terms of bankruptcy and fraud.
Dechow et al. (2011)	n/a	Quantitative	Multiple industries	The misstatements seem to have been made to hide a decline in financial performance.
Humpherys et al. (2011)	n/a	Quantitative	n/a	Linguistic analysis could help auditors' flag questionable disclosures and assess fraud risk.
Hobson et al. (2012)	n/a	Quantitative	n/a	Vocal dissonance markers in CEO speech are positively associated with the likelihood of irregularity restatements, providing valuable evidence for detecting financial misreporting.
Cao et al. (2015)	n/a	Qualitative	n/a	Big Data analytics can improve the efficiency and effectiveness of financial statement audits.
Earley (2015)	n/a	Qualitative	n/a	Data analytics has great potential for financial statement audits.
Purda and Skillicorn (2015)	n/a	Quantitative	Finance	Our statistical method effectively predicts fraud, aiding decision-makers in choosing cost-effective fraud-detection tools.
Kokina and Davenport (2017)	n/a	Qualitative	n/a	Artificial intelligence is rapidly transforming accounting and auditing, impacting human auditors and the audit process itself.
Sun and Vasarhelyi (2017)	n/a	Qualitative	n/a	Deep learning enhances audit automation by recognizing patterns in extensive data.
Dong et al. (2018)	n/a	Quantitative	n/a	Financial social media data can enhance corporate fraud detection by providing valuable insights into firm behavior and investor confidence.
Gepp et al. (2018)	n/a	Qualitative	n/a	Big data techniques in auditing are not as widespread as in other related fields.
Hooda et al. (2018)	India	Quantitative	Multiple industries	Bayes Net and J48 algorithms highlight the potential of machine learning in improving audit quality in the future.

continued on following page

Table 1. Continued

Authors	Country	Method	Industry	Study
No et al. (2019)	n/a	Qualitative	n/a	The MADS framework enhances the effectiveness of audits by prioritizing items with higher risk of material misstatement.
Sun (2019)	n/a	Qualitative	n/a	Deep learning can enhance audit procedures by providing information identification and judgment support.
Bao et al. (2020)	US	Quantitative	n/a	The proposed frameworks offer better results than the state of the art in terms of balanced accuracy.
Craja et al. (2020)	US	Quantitative	n/a	A hierarchical attention network (HAN) is utilized to detect fraud in financial statements.
Li et al. (2020)	n/a	Quantitative	n/a	Corporate culture, encompassing innovation, integrity, quality, respect, and teamwork, positively correlates with business outcomes and performance.
Bao et al. (2021)	US	Quantitative	Multiple industries	How machine learning techniques can be used to detect accounting fraud.
Bao et al. (2022)	n/a	Qualitative	n/a	Machine learning models can effectively detect fraud.
Aitkazinov, 2023	n/a	Qualitative	n/a	Valuable insights into the integration of AI technologies in audit processes.
Shapovalova et al., 2023	Ukrania	A mixed-methods: quantitative and qualitative	n/a	Emerging technologies enable flexible, secure, and efficient processing of large data volumes, automation of processes, enhanced accuracy and transparency in accounting reporting.
Kanaparthi, 2024	n/a	Quantitative	n/a	The adoption of blockchain technology and ML promises reduced accounting expenses, heightened precision, and expeditious auditing processes.
Vitali & Giuliani, 2024	Italy	Quantitative	Accounting	Analyse the impacts of new technologies, specifically RPA and AI, on auditing firms.

In practice, management accountants' responsibilities include cost management to achieve long-term goals, management and operational control through performance measurement, and internal (cost) planning. Thus, the use of extensive corporate data provides accountants with the perfect tools to answer questions about what has happened, what is likely to happen next, and what is the optimal solution. For these tasks, they can use descriptive statistics, predictive analytics, and prescriptive analytics, respectively (Appelbaum et al., 2017). Machine learning is ideal for predictive analytics, which is likely to become more important than descriptive statistics due to increased competition from globalization and technological advances (Cokins, 2013; Chowdhury, 2023). This section examines case studies on performance management, cost management, and risk control.

Performance management can be divided into employee performance assessment and project performance assessment. In employee performance appraisal, machine learning is used to support decision making in human resource management functions related to hiring and monitoring processes (Hagemann and Klug, 2022; Ismail et al., 2024). In terms of methodology, variants of decision trees are most commonly used due to their interpretability. For example, Al-Radaideh and Al Nagi (2012) use two variants of decision trees to investigate the characteristics that are likely to affect employee performance in IT companies. The goal consists of three classes: meet, exceed, and far exceed. They report that job title and the type of university the employee graduated from have the strongest predictive power. Using the same classification techniques, Kirimi and Moturi (2016) conduct a similar study using data from the Kenyan School of Government and find that employee experience has the strongest predictive power.

Cost management follows the cycle of resource planning, cost estimation, cost budgeting, and cost control (Bhimani et al., 2019). A critical responsibility of management accountants is to accurately estimate the costs of upcoming projects in order to effectively support the organization's strategic decision makers (Lum et al., 2008). This activity takes place mainly in the pre-project planning phase, as the vast majority of costs can only be influenced at the start of the project.

Cost estimation in construction projects is a prominent area where the integration of machine learning into cost management is already remarkable (Hashemi et al., 2020). The goal of machine learning in this context is to increase the predictive power by exploiting nonlinearities, using more features, and having the ability to handle multicolinearities simultaneously. As an illustration, Son et al. (2012) develop a hybrid model that includes principal component analysis (PCA) to handle multicolinearities and support vector regression (SVR) to predict the cost performance of commercial construction projects. Their results indicate superior predictive performance compared to other techniques commonly used in data mining, such as neural networks, decision trees, and autonomous SVR. Chandanshive and Kambekar (2019) employ a more tailored neural network with various regularization techniques to improve generalization and reduce overfitting, and also report fruitful predictive capabilities.

While previous studies are often limited to using structured data as features, Williams and Gong (2014) innovate by combining structured (financial) data with unstructured textual data. Their work aims at predicting construction cost overruns and shows that certain terms and phrases in bid documents are correlated with unplanned cost increases in construction projects. Other industries where the use of machine learning for cost estimation has been documented in the scientific literature include software development and healthcare (Koh & Tan, 2011; Al Asheeri & Hammad, 2019).

In the area of risk control, the use of machine learning is aimed at detecting early warning signs of financial distress that may lead to bankruptcy. This research perspective is analogous to that of operational continuity in the auditing literature. Koyuncugil and Ozgulbas (2012) propose a system dedicated to small and medium-sized enterprises, focusing on the creation of an understandable model for managers and decision makers who lack expertise in finance or data mining. To this end, they opt for a variant of decision trees, which are known for their high interpretability. Based on financial characteristics (categorized into liquidity ratios, financial position ratios, sales ratios, and profitability ratios) and binary targets (poor versus strong financial performance), the authors identify two significant early warning signals, namely pre-tax profit to equity and return on equity.

Credit assessment is another area where machine learning contributes to the risk control function. More accurate decisions on the final acceptance of loan applicants result in reduced risk for creditors and, more importantly, lower costs (Huang et al., 2007). In their study, Huang et al. (2007) explore the combination of a genetic algorithm for feature selection and a support vector machine (SVM) for prediction, creating a hybrid model. The choice of SVM is explained by its high performance with a relatively small number of features compared to neural network or decision tree classifiers.

Since even small improvements in accuracy are effective in terms of future cost savings, the use of data mining in this area is the subject of extensive research (Kumar & Gunjan, 2020). A recent trend in the credit scoring literature is the use of deep learning (Wu et al., 2021; Dastile & Celik, 2021; Gunnarsson et al., 2021; Ranta et al., 2023). In summary, the application of machine learning in management

Table 2. Summary table of studies on the impact of machine learning on management accounting

Authors	Country	Method	Industry	Study
Huang et al. (2007)	Australia and Germany	Quantitative	Finance	SVM-based credit scoring models accurately evaluate applicants' credit scores with few input features.
Lum et al. (2008)	n/a	Qualitative	n/a	Data mining and machine learning techniques can improve software cost estimation models.
Koh and Tan (2011)	n/a	Qualitative	n/a	Data mining in healthcare can improve treatment effectiveness, and detect fraud and abuse.
Al-Radaideh and Al Nagi (2012)	n/a	Qualitative	n/a	Data mining techniques, can effectively predict employee performance using real data from various companies.
Koyuncugil and Ozgulbas (2012)	Turkey	Quantitative	Finance	The developed early warning system model using data mining detects financial risks in SMEs, and aiding in decision-making processes.
Son et al. (2012)	South Korea	Quantitative	n/a	The proposed PCA-SVR model accurately predicts cost performance of commercial building projects, providing valuable information for stakeholders.
Cokins (2013)	n/a	Qualitative	n/a	Management accounting trends include managing information technology, customer lifetime value, business analytics, and financial accounting.
Williams and Gong (2014)	California	Quantitative	Transportation	A stacking ensemble model using text mining and numerical data can accurately predict construction cost overruns, aiding in budgeting.
Kirimi and Moturi (2016)	Kenya	Quantitative	Education	A proposed model utilizes data mining classification techniques to predict employee performance.
Wang & Wang (2016)	n/a	Qualitative	n/a	Integrating data mining into managerial accounting systems can improve managerial functions and upgrade current information system
Appelbaum et al. (2017)	n/a	Qualitative	n/a	The Managerial Accounting Data Analytics (MADA) framework enables management accountants to utilize business analytics for performance measurement and decision-making.
Al Asheeri and Hammad (2019)	n/a	Quantitative	n/a	Machine learning methods can accurately predict software cost in early stages, aiding project managers and engineers in resource planning and management.
Bhimani et al. (2019)	n/a	Qualitative	n/a	Cost management follows the cycle of resource planning, cost estimation, cost budgeting, and cost control
Chandanshive and Kambekar (2019)	Mumbai, India and nearby region	Quantitative	n/a	The trained neural network model accurately predicts building construction costs at the early stage, aiding decision-making and investment management for owners and investors.
Hashemi et al. (2020)	n/a	Qualitative	n/a	Machine learning techniques are utilized for cost estimation in construction projects, identifying suitable methods to reduce time and risk assessment in decision-making

continued on following page

Table 2. Continued

Authors	Country	Method	Industry	Study
Kumar and Gunjan (2020)	n/a	Qualitative	n/a	The proposed machine learning model enhances credit scoring analysis and can potentially improve customer profile analysis in the financial sector.
Dastile and Celik (2021)	Australia and Germany	Quantitative	Finance	The proposed explainable deep learning model for credit scoring is transparent, allowing for better automated decision-making in money lending institutions.
Gunnarsson et al. (2021)	n/a	Quantitative	Finance	Deep learning algorithms are not optimal for credit scoring. XGBoost outperforms them, although it is computationally expensive, and deep neural networks fail to exceed shallower counterparts.
Wu et al. (2021)	China	Quantitative	Finance	Deep multiple kernel classifiers outperform traditional models in credit risk assessment, enhancing credit card decision-making and reducing bad debt in the Chinese credit card industry.
Hagemann and Klug (2022)	n/a	Qualitative	n/a	It provides an overview of important topics in human resource management (HRM) that are affected by digitalization and automation.
Chowdhury, 2023	n/a	Quantitative	n/a	An artificial neural network-based model predicts management information and verifies the accuracy of the model.
Ranta et al., 2023	n/a	Quantitative	Specific industries	ML methods can play a crucial role in MA research by creating, developing, and refining theories through induction and abduction.
Ismail et al., 2024	n/a	Qualitative	n/a	The reviewed articles highlight four crucial aspects of AI in the evaluation of managerial accounting processes: technological acceptance, ethical considerations, skills and competence, and decision-making processes.

accounting can shed light on hidden relationships and trends by using different types of data, such as semi-structured and unstructured data, or by using a larger volume of data overall (Wang & Wang, 2016).

In summary, the relationship between machine learning (ML) and accounting and auditing represents a powerful convergence between cutting-edge technology and traditional practices. The integration of ML into these fields offers significant benefits, redefining operational standards and improving the quality of services provided.

EMERGING TECHNOLOGIES IN THE BIG 4

This section aims to analyze the significant contributions of the BIG 4 accounting firms (PwC, Deloitte, EY, and KPMG) in adopting emerging technology within the dynamic field of financial auditing. It will delve into their innovative solutions and platforms that streamline processes, facilitate decision-making, and offer novel analytical insights by harnessing the advantages of technology.

PriceWaterhouseCoopers (PWC)

PwC has created innovative software tools that have a significant impact on business operations. One of these tools, Halo, is integrated into PwC's audit suite and streamlines cryptocurrency audits. Another platform, Aura, offers advanced features such as real-time analysis and financial forecasting to enhance strategic decision-making. Additionally, GL.ai, the first module of PwC's Audit.ai system, expedites audits by automating processes and identifying areas of genuine risk.

Deloitte

Deloitte has introduced two innovations to enhance business operations: Blockchain in a Box (BiB) and Deloitte Omnia. BiB is a self-contained platform for small-scale blockchain networks, featuring compact compute nodes, video displays, and network components. BiB is a self-contained platform for small-scale blockchain networks, featuring compact compute nodes, video displays, and network components. Deloitte Omnia is a suite of audit solutions that improves productivity, quality, and insight through automation, data analysis, and artificial intelligence.

Ernest & Young (EY)

EY has introduced two innovative solutions to address business challenges. Blockchain Analyzer enables detailed analysis of blockchain networks, providing insights into past transactions. EY Ops Chain optimizes supply chain management using smart contracts, ensuring adaptability to legal systems and secure transaction monitoring.

KPMG

KPMG has introduced two innovative platforms. KPMG Origins uses blockchain technology to provide transparency in supply chain product traceability, meeting consumer demand. KPMG Clara, powered by Microsoft Azure, is an intelligent audit platform that offers an enhanced audit methodology through a scalable, cloud-based, data-driven workflow.

CONCLUSION

This chapter provides an in-depth analysis of the impact of machine learning on financial and managerial accounting. Through a careful examination of the history, definitions, and categories of machine learning, we trace the evolution of this innovative technology from its origins to its current applications.

The study highlights machine learning's central role in automating complex processes, streamlining decision-making, and creating new analytical perspectives. These advances have significant potential to transform financial management by providing solutions that are efficient, transparent, and adaptable to today's challenges.

It is important to note, however, that the integration of machine learning into accounting is not without its challenges. Ethical considerations, including transparency of algorithms and privacy, require particular attention. The need to thoroughly understand and ethically manage the implications of this technological advance is proving to be critical to ensuring responsible adoption.

In summary, machine learning is emerging as a dominant catalyst for progress in the accounting profession, redefining the way professionals perform daily tasks and formulate strategic decisions. As we embrace these changes, it is imperative that we remain mindful of ethical issues and promote a balanced use of this technology to maximize its benefits while mitigating potential risks. By developing a deep understanding of machine learning and integrating it ethically, we will equip ourselves to successfully navigate the challenging era of digital transformation in accounting.

REFERENCES

Abdolmohammadi, M. J. (1991). Factors affecting auditors' perceptions of applicable decision aids for various audit tasks. *Contemporary Accounting Research*, *7*(2), 535–548. doi:10.1111/j.1911-3846.1991.tb00828.x

Aitkazinov, A. (2023). The role of artificial intelligence in auditing: Opportunities and challenges. *International Journal of Research in Engineering. Science and Management*, *6*(6), 117–119.

Al Asheeri, M. M., & Hammad, M. (2019, September). Machine learning models for software cost estimation. In *2019 International Conference on Innovation and Intelligence for Informatics, Computing, and Technologies (3ICT)* (pp. 1-6). IEEE. 10.1109/3ICT.2019.8910327

Al-Radaideh, Q. A., & Al Nagi, E. (2012). Using data mining techniques to build a classification model for predicting employees performance. *International Journal of Advanced Computer Science and Applications*, *3*(2).

American Institute of Certified Public Accountants. (2002). Statement on Auditing Standards: Vol. 99. American Institute of Certified Public Accountants.

Appelbaum, D., Kogan, A., Vasarhelyi, M., & Yan, Z. (2017). Impact of business analytics and enterprise systems on managerial accounting. *International Journal of Accounting Information Systems*, *25*, 29–44. doi:10.1016/j.accinf.2017.03.003

Association of Certified Fraud Examiners. (2020). *Report to the Nations: 2020 Global Study on Occupational Fraud and Abuse*. Author.

Auvinen, T., Sajasalo, P., Sintonen, T., Pekkala, K., Takala, T., & Luoma-aho, V. (2019). Evolution of strategy narration and leadership work in the digital era. *Leadership*, *15*(2), 205–225. doi:10.1177/1742715019826426

Baldwin, A. A., Brown, C. E., & Trinkle, B. S. (2006). Opportunities for artificial intelligence development in the accounting domain: The case for auditing. *Intelligent Systems in Accounting, Finance & Management. International Journal (Toronto, Ont.)*, *14*(3), 77–86.

Bao, Y., Hilary, G., & Ke, B. (2022). Artificial intelligence and fraud detection. *Innovative Technology at the Interface of Finance and Operations*, *I*, 223–247. doi:10.1007/978-3-030-75729-8_8

Bao, Y., Ke, B., Li, B., Yu, Y. J., & Zhang, J. (2020). Detecting accounting fraud in publicly traded US firms using a machine learning approach. *Journal of Accounting Research*, *58*(1), 199–235. doi:10.1111/1475-679X.12292

Bao, Y., Ke, B., Li, B., Yu, Y. J., & Zhang, J. (2021). A response to'critique of an article on machine learning in the detection of accounting fraud. *Econ Journal Watch*, *18*(1), 71–78.

Bertomeu, J. (2020). Machine learning improves accounting: Discussion, implementation and research opportunities. *Review of Accounting Studies*, *25*(3), 1135–1155. doi:10.1007/s11142-020-09554-9

Bertomeu, J., Cheynel, E., Floyd, E., & Pan, W. (2021). Using machine learning to detect misstatements. *Review of Accounting Studies*, *26*(2), 468–519. doi:10.1007/s11142-020-09563-8

Bhimani, A., Datar, S. M., Horngren, C. T., & Rajan, M. V. (2019). *Management and cost accounting* (7th ed.). Pearson Education, Limited.

Brown, N. C., Crowley, R. M., & Elliott, W. B. (2020). What are you saying? Using topic to detect financial misreporting. *Journal of Accounting Research*, *58*(1), 237–291. doi:10.1111/1475-679X.12294

Brynjolfsson, E., & McAfee, A. (2014). *The second machine age: Work, progress, and prosperity in a time of brilliant technologies*. WW Norton & Company.

Cao, M., Chychyla, R., & Stewart, T. (2015). Big data analytics in financial statement audits. *Accounting Horizons*, *29*(2), 423–429. doi:10.2308/acch-51068

Cecchini, M., Aytug, H., Koehler, G. J., & Pathak, P. (2010a). Detecting management fraud in public companies. *Management Science*, *56*(7), 1146–1160. doi:10.1287/mnsc.1100.1174

Cecchini, M., Aytug, H., Koehler, G. J., & Pathak, P. (2010b). Making words work: Using financial text as a predictor of financial events. *Decision Support Systems*, *50*(1), 164–175. doi:10.1016/j.dss.2010.07.012

Chandanshive, V., & Kambekar, A. R. (2019). Estimation of building construction cost using artificial neural networks. *Journal of Soft Computing in Civil Engineering*, *3*(1), 91–107.

Cho, S., Vasarhelyi, M. A., Sun, T., & Zhang, C. (2020). Learning from Machine Learning in Accounting and Assurance. *Journal of Emerging Technologies in Accounting*, *17*(1), 1–10. doi:10.2308/jeta-10718

Chowdhury, E. K. (2023). Integration of Artificial Intelligence Technology in Management Accounting Information System: An Empirical Study. In *Novel Financial Applications Of Machine Learning And Deep Learning: Algorithms, Product Modeling, And Applications* (pp. 35–46). Springer International Publishing. doi:10.1007/978-3-031-18552-6_3

Cokins, G. (2013). Top 7 trends in management accounting. *Strategic Finance*, *95*(6), 21–30.

Craja, P., Kim, A., & Lessmann, S. (2020). Deep learning for detecting financial statement fraud. *Decision Support Systems*, *139*, 113421. doi:10.1016/j.dss.2020.113421

Dastile, X., & Celik, T. (2021). Making deep learning-based predictions for credit scoring explainable. *IEEE Access : Practical Innovations, Open Solutions*, *9*, 50426–50440. doi:10.1109/ACCESS.2021.3068854

Dechow, P. M., Ge, W., Larson, C. R., & Sloan, R. G. (2011). Predicting material accounting misstatements. *Contemporary Accounting Research, 28*(1), 17–82. doi:10.1111/j.1911-3846.2010.01041.x

Dogan, A., & Birant, D. (2021). Machine learning and data mining in manufacturing. *Expert Systems with Applications, 166*, 1–22. doi:10.1016/j.eswa.2020.114060

Dong, W., Liao, S., & Zhang, Z. (2018). Leveraging financial social media data for corporate fraud detection. *Journal of Management Information Systems, 35*(2), 461–487. doi:10.1080/07421222.2018.1451954

Earley, C. E. (2015). Data analytics in auditing: Opportunities and challenges. *Business Horizons, 58*(5), 493–500. doi:10.1016/j.bushor.2015.05.002

Fanning, K. M., & Cogger, K. O. (1998). Neural network detection of management fraud using published financial data. *International Journal of Intelligent Systems in Accounting Finance & Management, 7*(1), 21–41. doi:10.1002/(SICI)1099-1174(199803)7:1<21::AID-ISAF138>3.0.CO;2-K

Feng, R., Mejer Hansen, T., Grana, D., & Balling, N. (2020). An unsupervised deep-learning method for porosity estimation based on poststack seismic data. *Geophysics, 85*(6), M97–M105. doi:10.1190/geo2020-0121.1

Fieberg, C., Hesse, M., Loy, T., & Metko, D. (2022). Machine learning in accounting research. In *Diginomics research perspectives: The role of digitalization in business and society* (pp. 105–124). Springer International Publishing. doi:10.1007/978-3-031-04063-4_6

Frey, C. B., & Osborne, M. A. (2017). The future of employment: How susceptible are jobs to computerisation? *Technological Forecasting and Social Change, 114*, 254–280. doi:10.1016/j.techfore.2016.08.019

Freyberger, J., Neuhierl, A., & Weber, M. (2020). Dissecting characteristics nonparametrically. *Review of Financial Studies, 33*(5), 2326–2377. doi:10.1093/rfs/hhz123

Gao, J., Zhong, C., Chen, X., Lin, H., & Zhang, Z. (2020). Unsupervised learning for passive beamforming. *IEEE Communications Letters, 24*(5), 1052–1056. doi:10.1109/LCOMM.2020.2965532

Gepp, A., Linnenluecke, M. K., O'Neill, T. J., & Smith, T. (2018). Big data techniques in auditing research and practice: Current trends and future opportunities. *Journal of Accounting Literature, 40*(1), 102–115. doi:10.1016/j.acclit.2017.05.003

Giglio, S., Kelly, B. T., & Xiu, D. (2021). Factor models, machine learning, and asset pricing. *Machine Learning, and Asset Pricing*.

Goodfellow, I., Papernot, N., McDaniel, P., Feinman, R., Faghri, F., Matyasko, A., . . . Garg, A. (2016). cleverhans v0. 1: an adversarial machine learning library. *arXiv preprint arXiv:1610.00768, 1*.

Green, B. P., & Choi, J. H. (1997). Assessing the risk of management fraud through neural network technology. *Auditing, 16*, 14–28.

Gu, R., Yang, Z., & Ji, Y. (2020). Machine learning for intelligent optical networks: A comprehensive survey. *Journal of Network and Computer Applications, 157*, 102576. doi:10.1016/j.jnca.2020.102576

Gunnarsson, B. R., Vanden Broucke, S., Baesens, B., Óskarsdóttir, M., & Lemahieu, W. (2021). Deep learning for credit scoring: Do or don't? *European Journal of Operational Research*, *295*(1), 292–305. doi:10.1016/j.ejor.2021.03.006 PMID:34955589

Hagemann, V., & Klug, K. (2022). Human resource management in a digital environment. In *Diginomics Research Perspectives: The Role of Digitalization in Business and Society* (pp. 35–64). Springer International Publishing. doi:10.1007/978-3-031-04063-4_3

Hasan, A. R. (2021). Artificial Intelligence (AI) in accounting & auditing: A Literature review. *Open Journal of Business and Management*, *10*(1), 440–465. doi:10.4236/ojbm.2022.101026

Hobson, J. L., Mayew, W. J., & Venkatachalam, M. (2012). Analyzing speech to detect financial misreporting. *Journal of Accounting Research*, *50*(2), 349–392. doi:10.1111/j.1475-679X.2011.00433.x

Hooda, N., Bawa, S., & Rana, P. S. (2018). Fraudulent firm classification: A case study of an external audit. *Applied Artificial Intelligence*, *32*(1), 48–64. doi:10.1080/08839514.2018.1451032

Huang, C. L., Chen, M. C., & Wang, C. J. (2007). Credit scoring with a data mining approach based on support vector machines. *Expert Systems with Applications*, *33*(4), 847–856. doi:10.1016/j.eswa.2006.07.007

Humpherys, S. L., Moffitt, K. C., Burns, M. B., Burgoon, J. K., & Felix, W. F. (2011). Identification of fraudulent financial statements using linguistic credibility analysis. *Decision Support Systems*, *50*(3), 585–594. doi:10.1016/j.dss.2010.08.009

Iaasb, I. A. (2016). Handbook od international quality control, auditing, review, other assurance and related services pronouncements. Academic Press.

Institute of Management Accountants. (2008). *Statements on management accounting: Definition of management accounting*. www.imanet.org

Ismail Al-Alawi, A., Almulla, D., Abbas, M., & Alkooheji, L. (2024). Process and Impact Evaluation of Artificial Intelligence in Managerial Accounting: A Systematic Literature Review. *International Journal of Computing and Digital Systems*, *15*(1), 1–26.

Kanaparthi, V. (2024). Exploring the Impact of Blockchain, AI, and ML on Financial Accounting Efficiency and Transformation. *arXiv preprint arXiv:2401.15715.*

Kashyap, P. (2017). *Machine learning for decision makers: Cognitive computing fundamentals for better decision making*. Apress.

Kirimi, J. M., & Moturi, C. A. (2016). Application of data mining classification in employee performance prediction. *International Journal of Computer Applications*, *146*(7), 28–35. doi:10.5120/ijca2016910883

Koh, H. C., & Tan, G. (2011). Data mining applications in healthcare. *Journal of Healthcare Information Management*, *19*(2), 65. PMID:15869215

Kokina, J., & Davenport, T. H. (2017). The emergence of artificial intelligence: How automation is changing auditing. *Journal of Emerging Technologies in Accounting*, *14*(1), 115–122. doi:10.2308/jeta-51730

Kotsiantis, S., Koumanakos, E., Tzelepis, D., & Tampakas, V. (2006). Forecasting fraudulent financial statements using data mining. *International Journal of Computational Intelligence, 3*(2), 104-110.

Koyuncugil, A. S., & Ozgulbas, N. (2012). Financial early warning system model and data mining application for risk detection. *Expert Systems with Applications*, *39*(6), 6238–6253. doi:10.1016/j.eswa.2011.12.021

Kumar, M. R., & Gunjan, V. K. (2020). Review of machine learning models for credit scoring analysis. *Ingeniería Solidaria, 16*(1).

Li, K., Mai, F., Shen, R., & Yan, X. (2021). Measuring corporate culture using machine learning. *Review of Financial Studies*, *34*(7), 3265–3315. doi:10.1093/rfs/hhaa079

Lum, K. T., Baker, D. R., & Hihn, J. M. (2008, June). The effects of data mining techniques on software cost estimation. In *2008 IEEE International Engineering Management Conference* (pp. 1-5). IEEE. 10.1109/IEMCE.2008.4617949

Moerland, T. M., Broekens, J., Plaat, A., & Jonker, C. M. (2023). Model-based reinforcement learning: A survey. *Foundations and Trends® in Machine Learning, 16*(1), 1-118.

Moll, J., & Yigitbasioglu, O. (2019). The role of internet-related technologies in shaping the work of accountants: New directions for accounting research. *The British Accounting Review*, *51*(6), 100833. doi:10.1016/j.bar.2019.04.002

Mullainathan, S., & Spiess, J. (2017). Machine learning: An applied econometric approach. *The Journal of Economic Perspectives*, *31*(2), 87–106. doi:10.1257/jep.31.2.87

No, W. G., Lee, K., Huang, F., & Li, Q. (2019). Multidimensional audit data selection (MADS): A framework for using data analytics in the audit data selection process. *Accounting Horizons*, *33*(3), 127–140. doi:10.2308/acch-52453

Pandian, S. (2020). *Understand machine learning and its end-to-end process.* Blog post at Analytics Vidhya. https://www. analyticsvidhya. com/blog/2020/12/understand-machine-learning-and-its-end-to-end-process

Purda, L., & Skillicorn, D. (2015). Accounting variables, deception, and a bag of words: Assessing the tools of fraud detection. *Contemporary Accounting Research*, *32*(3), 1193–1223. doi:10.1111/1911-3846.12089

Ranta, M., Ylinen, M., & Järvenpää, M. (2023). Machine learning in management accounting research: Literature review and pathways for the future. *European Accounting Review*, *32*(3), 607–636. doi:10.1080/09638180.2022.2137221

Rikhardsson, P., & Yigitbasioglu, O. (2018). Business intelligence & analytics in management accounting research: Status and future focus. *International Journal of Accounting Information Systems*, *29*, 37–58. doi:10.1016/j.accinf.2018.03.001

Samuel, A. L. (1959). Some studies in machine learning using the game of checkers. *IBM Journal of Research and Development*, *3*(3), 210–229. doi:10.1147/rd.33.0210

Shapovalova, A., Kuzmenko, O., Polishchuk, O., Larikova, T., & Myronchuk, Z. (2023). Modernization of the national accounting and auditing system using digital transformation tools. *Financial & Credit Activity: Problems of Theory & Practice*, *4*(51).

Shrestha, Y. R., Ben-Menahem, S. M., & Von Krogh, G. (2019). Organizational decision-making structures in the age of artificial intelligence. *California Management Review*, *61*(4), 66–83. doi:10.1177/0008125619862257

Son, H., Kim, C., & Kim, C. (2012). Hybrid principal component analysis and support vector machine model for predicting the cost performance of commercial building projects using pre-project planning variables. *Automation in Construction*, *27*, 60–66. doi:10.1016/j.autcon.2012.05.013

Sun, T. (2019). Applying deep learning to audit procedures: An illustrative framework. *Accounting Horizons*, *33*(3), 89–109. doi:10.2308/acch-52455

Sun, T., & Vasarhelyi, M. A. (2017). Deep Learning and the Future of Auditing: How an Evolving Technology Could Transform Analysis and Improve Judgment. *The CPA Journal*, *87*(6).

Swana, E., & Doorsamy, W. (2021). An unsupervised learning approach to condition assessment on a wound-rotor induction generator. *Energies*, *14*(3), 602. doi:10.3390/en14030602

Tayefeh Hashemi, S., Ebadati, O. M., & Kaur, H. (2020). Cost estimation and prediction in construction projects: A systematic review on machine learning techniques. *SN Applied Sciences*, *2*(10), 1–27. doi:10.1007/s42452-020-03497-1

Ucoglu, D. (2020). Current Machine Learning Applications in Accounting and Auditing. *Pressacademia*, *12*(1), 1–7. doi:10.17261/Pressacademia.2020.1337

Van Engelen, J. E., & Hoos, H. H. (2020). A survey on semi-supervised learning. *Machine Learning*, *109*(2), 373–440. doi:10.1007/s10994-019-05855-6

Vitali, S., & Giuliani, M. (2024). Emerging digital technologies and auditing firms: Opportunities and challenges. *International Journal of Accounting Information Systems*, *53*, 100676. doi:10.1016/j.accinf.2024.100676

Wang, H. N., Liu, N., Zhang, Y. Y., Feng, D. W., Huang, F., Li, D. S., & Zhang, Y. M. (2020). Deep reinforcement learning: A survey. *Frontiers of Information Technology & Electronic Engineering*, *21*(12), 1726–1744. doi:10.1631/FITEE.1900533

Wang, Y., & Wang, Z. (2016). Integrating data mining into managerial accounting system: Challenges and opportunities. *The China Business Review*, *15*(1), 33–41.

Williams, T. P., & Gong, J. (2014). Predicting construction cost overruns using text mining, numerical data and ensemble classifiers. *Automation in Construction*, *43*, 23–29. doi:10.1016/j.autcon.2014.02.014

Wu, C. F., Huang, S. C., Chiou, C. C., & Wang, Y. M. (2021). A predictive intelligence system of credit scoring based on deep multiple kernel learning. *Applied Soft Computing*, *111*, 107668. doi:10.1016/j.asoc.2021.107668

Zhang, Y., Xiong, F., Xie, Y., Fan, X., & Gu, H. (2020). The Impact of Artificial Intelligence and Blockchain on the Accounting Profession. *IEEE Access : Practical Innovations, Open Solutions*, *8*, 110461–110477. doi:10.1109/ACCESS.2020.3000505

KEY TERMS AND DEFINITIONS

Auditing: Auditing is a systematic and independent process that involves reviewing financial data, operational procedures, and systems within an organization. Its primary goal is to ensure the accuracy and reliability of the audited information. Auditing is a crucial aspect of corporate governance and risk management, as it enhances the credibility of financial statements and ensures compliance with applicable laws and regulations.

Financial Accounting: Financial accounting is a specialized field that documents, synthesizes, and discloses a company's financial transactions. Its main goal is to provide reliable information about the entity's performance and financial position to external parties, such as investors, creditors, regulators, and the general public.

Machine Learning: Machine learning, a subset of artificial intelligence, is a field devoted to the development of techniques that enable computer systems to learn from data. Unlike traditional programming, where explicit instructions are given to a computer to perform a task, machine learning involves the construction of statistical models that can be trained to recognize patterns and make decisions autonomously.

Management Accounting: Management accounting provides financial analysis and information for decision-making within an organization. It supports internal processes of planning, control, and strategy formulation, providing managers with the necessary tools for effective resource management and strategic orientation of the company.

Semi-Supervised Learning: Semi-supervised learning is a machine learning approach that combines elements of both supervised and unsupervised methods. The model is trained on a dataset where some instances are labeled, while a larger portion remains unlabeled.

Supervised Learning: Supervised learning is a fundamental approach in machine learning. It involves training a model on labeled data, where each input is associated with a known output. This allows the model to learn how to establish a precise relationship between the input data and the expected outputs.

Unsupervised Learning: Unsupervised learning is a significant approach in machine learning. It involves training a model on unlabeled data, enabling the model to recognize intrinsic patterns without explicit guidance on desired outputs, unlike supervised learning.

Chapter 8
Utilizing Big Data Technology for Online Financial Risk Management

Jayasri Kotti
https://orcid.org/0000-0001-6501-1948
GMR Institute of Technology, India

C. Naga Ganesh
G. Pullaiah College Engineering and Technology, India

R. V. Naveenan
https://orcid.org/0000-0002-4699-1458
Symbiosis Institute of Business Management, Symbiosis International University, India

Swapnil Gulabrao Gorde
https://orcid.org/0009-0000-1973-3456
MIT Art, Design, and Technology University, India

Mahabub Basha S.
https://orcid.org/0000-0002-5998-3262
International Institute of Business Studies, India

Sabyasachi Pramanik
https://orcid.org/0000-0002-9431-8751
Haldia Institute of Technology, India

Ankur Gupta
https://orcid.org/0000-0002-4651-5830
Vaish College of Engineering, India

ABSTRACT

The rise of cloud computing, internet of things, and information technology has made big data technology a common concern for many professionals and researchers. A financial risk control model, known as the MSHDS-RS model, was creatively suggested in response to the present state of inappropriate feature data design in big data risk control technology. The concept is built on multi source heterogeneous data structure (MSHDS) and random subspace (RS). This model is novel in that it uses a normalized sparse model for feature fusion optimization to create integrated features after extracting the hard and soft features from loan customer information sources. Subsequently, a base classifier is trained on the feature subset acquired via probability sampling, and its output is combined and refined by the application of evidence reasoning principles. The accuracy improvement rate of the MSHDS-RS method is approximately 3.0% and 3.6% higher than that of the current PMB-RS methods under the conditions of soft feature

DOI: 10.4018/979-8-3693-0847-9.ch008

indicators and integrated feature indicators, respectively, according to an observation of the operation results of MSHDS-RS models under various feature sets. As a result, the suggested optimization fusion approach is trustworthy and workable. This study has helped to reduce financial risks associated with the internet and may be useful in helping lenders make wise judgments.

1. OVERVIEW

As social technology advances, the Internet is gradually impacting every facet of human existence. Internet finance has discreetly infiltrated the Chinese market during the last ten years, coinciding with the increasing encroachment of online retail platforms like Taobao and JD.com into people's lives. Numerous online financial services, including P2P, credit, online banking, and third-party payment, have progressively surfaced since its inception. Due to its great speed and ease, the number of people using the Internet for financial investments is also growing daily. Internet finance is a two-edged sword that has increased dangers while also fostering the growth of China's financial sector (Lyu & Zhao, 2019). There is an information imbalance between lenders and borrowers in online credit transactions. Small and medium-sized microbusinesses will have financial challenges as a result, and borrowing costs are still high (Liu, 2021). Lenders will also be taking on more risk. For instance, the borrower's credit report is not full, making it difficult to distinguish between good and poor clients, as well as to calculate the borrowing limit and other risks associated with the payback cycle. As a result, businesses confront challenging problems that both lenders and borrowers cannot control: business risks. This significantly impedes the growth of businesses. Thus, the development of efficient technology to manage financial risks associated with the internet is imperative. Big data technology is crucial to the management of financial risk. Large-scale, dynamic change, and great processing efficiency are features of big data. The primary sources of the data are visitors, e-commerce, and social media sites. The internet finance business may assist practitioners make choices by enabling them to extract information from diverse incomplete, fuzzy, and enormous data sets that has guiding relevance for current financial behavior via the application of big data analysis technologies (Wang & Wang, 2022). Nonetheless, there are several obstacles facing the big data risk management technologies of today, chief among them being the irrational feature data design (Dutta & Saha, 2021). This study creatively mixes multi-source heterogeneous data structures and random subspaces, and it suggests a big data-based financial risk management model based on the aforementioned analytical findings. Through faster identification of new clients and a higher loan review pass rate, the initiative seeks to help lending firms more broadly.

2. CONNECTED WORK

The banking industry and Internet technology are becoming more and more integrated due to scientific and technical breakthroughs. People may find opportunities in internet finance, but there are also a lot of dangers and challenges involved. The conflict between simplicity of use and security in online finance has been the focus of several scholarly debates. Yan X et al. used the entropy weight Topsis technique and report data from four businesses to assess the risks associated with Internet insurance providers in 2019. The results showed a significant relationship between the financial risks that insurance companies confront and asset liquidity and online operating capabilities. Online insurers have to increase capital and put in place an early warning system in order to mitigate risks (Yan & Wu, 2020). Despite the many hazards involved, most publicly listed companies in today's world choose to disclose financial information via corporate Internet reports (CIR), according to Ou L and other scholars. They researched the topic, created a CIR risk communication model based on FNN, and assessed the model's efficacy via an experiment in order to further their knowledge of the CIR risk communication process (Ou & Chen, 2020). In view of the fact that today's growing network credit was vulnerable to a number of unexpected risks, Haoru W. and others proposed that a bank database system based on big data should be established quickly by the relevant professionals. Utilize big data analysis to evaluate online credit risk in order to reduce the network credit risk coefficient (Haoru et al., 2020). Regarding the development of Internet finance, Zhao N. and colleagues examined and assessed the ways in which third-party payments, peer-to-peer platforms, and crowdfunding transfer risks. Finally, this research examined the ways to mitigate the liquidity risk associated with Internet finance by fortifying network security oversight mechanisms, enhancing relevant legal frameworks, and enhancing the social credit system. This was carried out in view of China's growing Internet financial industry (Zhao & Yao, 2021). Feng R and other researchers proposed a radial basis function neural network approach based on ant colony optimization to identify the existence of Internet financial market dangers. In order to detect possible market dangers, this strategy integrated deep learning algorithms with data mining technologies, primarily via the mining of financial data from the Internet. The model performed well, as shown by the experimental results, which showed a slight error of 0.249 and a running duration of 2.212s (Feng & Qu, 2021).

Wang C. and colleagues proposed a big data-driven approach to financial risk identification that incorporates the BPNN algorithm to assess Internet financial risk from the perspective of Internet credit financing. The experiment selected financial data for analysis and validation from the Internet. The final findings showed that the recommended model could forecast risks with a high accuracy rate of 99.98% (Wang & Liu, 2021). In order to detect financial fraud on the Internet using a large public loan dataset, Fang W and colleagues created a deep neural network that combined the XGBoost algorithm and random forest approach. Experiments had shown this model to perform better, and it was able to assist small and medium-sized Internet financial firms in identifying loan fraud (Fang et al., 2021). Wen C. and colleagues took into consideration the absence of a temporal trend for Internet financial risks and developed an LSTM model based on sliding windows and attention processes. By using an attention strategy, the model was able to concentrate on important data. The correlation of loan data via the sliding window was taken into consideration by the model. The verification of accessible data sets indicated that the model performed better than ARIMA, LSTM, and GRU (Wen et al., 2021). Researchers like Wang L began by considering how to reduce supply chain finance risks in order to actively react to the national strategy of "Internet plus". The project examined blockchain technology and supply chain finance based on theoretical studies. Simultaneously, the VAR model was unveiled to assess supply chain risk. The supply chain financing partners' risks were significantly decreased by this strategy, which also improved the supply chain financing risk management system (Wang & Wang, 2022). Researchers like Al-Alwan et al. have investigated how big data technology affects the caliber of business decision-making using structured equations. To confirm, the experiment gathered information from three telecom service providers. The end result demonstrated that big data may significantly affect how well business decisions are made. In order to promptly protect themselves from any financial hazards, businesses thus required to gather precise and trustworthy data and information (Al-Alwan et al., 2022).

To sum up, a lot of scholars have worked on the research of Internet financial risk prediction. Still, the risk prediction model may be further enhanced by combining it with big data-related technologies.

Figure 1. Comparison of classification scale and classifier accuracy

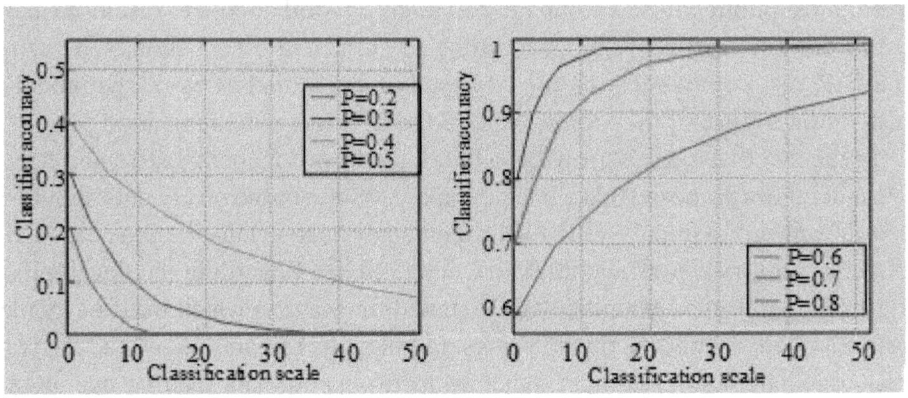

This study provides a financial risk control model based on multi-source heterogeneous data structures and random subspace, which may be useful in managing Internet financial risk and in making well-informed decisions on lending platforms.

3. COMBINED RISK MANAGEMENT AND EDUCATION

Financial risk, which relates to the uncertainty or volatility in a person's or an organization's future profits, is closely related to the volatility of financial markets. Because the financial market acts as the central center for both the consumer and commercial sectors, financial hazards are divided into two types (Namahoot & Laohavichien, 2018; Yang et al., 2018). In order to take action against risky borrowing patterns, financial risk control is the process of evaluating the relevant financial risks related to the loan topic. The most widely used machine algorithms are those for classification that are based on integrated learning, such random subspace (RS), boosting, and bagging. At the moment, the financial risk management strategy's realization depends on the ensemble learning technique. Its superiority over the standard single classification approach is evident when considering its learning stability and capability.

By meeting the needs of learner accuracy and variety, ensemble learning yields this advantage. The categorization scale and classifier accuracy are contrasted in Figure 1. The graphic shows how classification accuracy decreases as the quantity of data increases and finally drops to zero when the accuracy of the classifier is less than 0.5. The classifier's accuracy finally tends toward 1 as the data quantity increases and the accuracy surpasses 0.5. Data subsets are generated, basic classifiers are trained, and the outcomes are aggregated in ensemble learning. The synthetic output of the base classifier directly affects the quality of the integrated model. Synthesis approaches including the average method, voting method, and learning method are often used. Ensemble learning may be divided into several categories. For example, it can be categorized by data type into instance and feature ensemble learning techniques, or it can be categorized by classifier homogeneity and heterogeneity into ensemble learning methods that use both unique and the same learners. The many classifiers and secondary learning algorithms have a significant impact on the integrated model, and the training procedure for multiple classifier stacking techniques is rather complicated. The three main methods of homogenous integrated learning are RS, bagging, and boosting. The resulting training sets are randomly combined to develop an integrated process known as Bagging. It usually employs limited sample data in order to sample continuously and produce new samples that can properly reflect the original samples. This method works well for classifiers with noise effects. Of the initial noisy data samples, only 63% are from the original data set, and only one-third of the noisy samples won't be used for training. Boosting transforms weak learning algorithms into strong learning algorithms by combining n weak classifiers into higher-precision classifiers via weight voting. One popular use of this method is AdaBoost, which has the following model:

$$H(x) = \sum_{i=1}^{M} \alpha_i h_i(x) \tag{1}$$

In Equation (1), α_i represents a weight item; h_i represents the i - th classifier; M indicates the number of classifiers; x represents a sample. Through direct learning, h_1 is obtained and continuously updated to generate h_i and α_i. Assuming that ε_i is the error rate of the i - th basis classifier, the weight update expression is:

$$\alpha_i = \frac{1}{2}\ln\left(\frac{1-\varepsilon_i}{\varepsilon_i}\right) \tag{2}$$

RS is suitable for learning problems with somewhat large feature dimensions. Here is the precise procedure: To create a comparable subset of data, first randomly choose data samples according to the feature dimension; next, modify the sample data using the subspace ratio parameter; Secondly, use a subset of data to train the basic classifier; Finally, fusion rules are used to synthesize various findings. Choosing the appropriate random subspace ratio is crucial in influencing the learning impact.

4. FINANCIAL RISK CONTROL MODEL USING RANDOM SUBSPACE AND MULTI-SOURCE HETEROGENEOUS DATA STRUCTURE

4.1 Preparing Heterogeneous Data From Several Sources

Financial risk management may reduce personal default rates and company losses. Understanding how to conduct comprehensive and multifaceted studies of personal loan risks is key to developing a risk control strategy (Metawa & Metawa, 2021). The foundation of developing a risk control model is gathering and analyzing data that characterizes the risks posed to the client. Data preparation includes feature engineering screening, feature derivation, data gathering, verification, and cleaning (Shang et al., 2021). The feature derivation technique is used in the preparation stage to carry out feature extraction, integration, and screening after the data has been collected, inspected, and cleaned. Select the data features to be used in the model training. Information is gathered into two categories: soft information and hard information, in order to efficiently regulate enterprises with P2P financial concerns. The results of the information collection and study are shown in Table 1 below. The phrase "hard information" usually refers to the basic data—such as income and spending, credit ratings, past loan history, etc.—obtained from the lending platform and directly tied to customer use. This data is easily accessible, modifiable, and

Table 1. Composition of soft and hard information sources of lending customers

Information Type	Project	Classification
Hard information	Revenue and expenditure	Fixed income, variable income
	Credit rating	Whether there is a credit card, overdue records
	Loan record	Presence or absence, amount
	Overdue records	Yes or no, overdue date, overdue time, overdue repayment
Soft information	Consumption	Online mall consumption, offline physical consumption, other consumption
	Social situation	WeChat, QQ and other chat information
	Mobile phone basic information	Number of people in the address book, call records

readily available. Soft information is data that has an indirect relationship to the likelihood of a customer defaulting. Examples of this kind of data include consumer consumption, social status, and personality attributes. For example, customer consumption data from websites like as JD.com and Alipay, social media information from WeChat and QQ, etc.

Information source data particularly includes the following five types of data. The essential characteristics of loan clients may be divided into seven categories: the quantity of historical borrowings, the number of historical platforms, the degree of basic education, ethnicity, age, gender, and geography. Whether the real-name system is required, as well as the quantity and duration of calls made to friends, spouses, parents, colleagues, and classmates throughout the loan period, are among the 13 categories that comprise the characteristics of mobile phone usage. A few examples of the payment consumption features include the following: real name, payment amount, number of bound bank cards, Sesame credit score, total spending amount, total income amount, total loanable amount, and remaining loan amount. There are eight fields total. Features of consumption data from online platforms are composed of five factors: total number of purchases made online, average price per purchase, amount of the biggest single purchase, total number of orders, and average price per transaction. Social media characteristics are divided into three categories: the number of friends, fans, and followers.

In feature extraction, both soft and hard features are used. Hard feature information is mostly gathered via the public basic information platform. The 12 emotional traits plus a few textual features that were derived by using word vectors to convert qualitative and quantitative data into fields that could be learned are referred to as "soft feature information". The impact of various hard and soft information sources on financial risks varies. Therefore, before combining several information sources for risk assessment, it is essential to deal with multi-source heterogeneous characteristics. Second, based on the qualitative and quantitative data formats, the data characteristics of QQ, WeChat, and Weibo are categorized into several feature categories. First, several feature groups are created from the data gathered from different sources. In addition, the emotional traits are divided into three categories based on the emotional qualities: negative emotions, neutral emotions, and good emotions. The phrases "neutral emotional group" refers to unknown modal characteristics, "positive emotion group" refers to positive or strong modal characteristics, and "negative emotion group" refers to negative or weak modal qualities. Lastly, a heterogeneous multivariate feature set

$A = \left\{A^{(1)}, A^{(2)}, A^{(3)} \cdots A^{(i)}, \cdots A^{(s)}\right\}$ is obtained . s represents the number of information sources; The subscripts $1,2$ represent quantitative and qualitative features. The feature space after being divided into J groups is $X = (x_1^{(1)}, \cdots x_{P_1}^{(1)}, \cdots x_1^{(2)}, \cdots x_{p_2}^{(2)}, \cdots x_1^{(j)}, \cdots x_{p_j}^{(j)})$.

4.2 A financial Risk Control Model Using a Stochastic Subspace and Multi-Source Heterogeneous Data Structure

Since most existing borrower default risk control models are dependent on a single data source, the models are unstable and erroneous. After a comprehensive research, it was shown that the stochastic space sub-ensemble learning approach is more suited for the reality of financial risk management among the three ensemble learning strategies previously reported (Akinola, 2022; Ding, 2021; Hongjin, 2021). This paper proposes a risk management strategy that concurrently takes classifier diversity and accuracy into account, based on multi-source feature fusion stochastic space sub (Jakka et al., 2022; Liu et al., 2022; Park, 2022; Sahoo, 2022). The classic RS approach consists of three steps: obtaining feature subsets, creating basic classifiers, and synthesizing results. Improvements to the two phases of result fusion and feature fusion—MSHDS-RS—have been suggested by research. The detailed procedure is shown in Figure 2 down below. The adaptive fusion feature stage is the first phase. This step primarily enhances the quality of characteristics that have been retrieved and takes into account a wide range of risk indicators. As a result, the control model becomes simpler, leading to increased precision and stability. In order to identify important features and make sense of the characteristics, a feature weighting approach is initially presented. Furthermore, in light of the multi-source variability of customer risk indicators, the study introduces a sparse model (Sparse Group Lasso, SGL) to improve the outcomes. The expression for the SGL model is as follows:

$$\beta_{SGL} = \arg\min_{\beta}\{\frac{1}{2}\left\|y - \sum_{j=1}^{J} x_j \beta^{(j)}\right\|_2^2 + \lambda(1-\alpha)\sum_{j=1}^{J}\left\|\beta^{(j)}\right\|_2 + \lambda\alpha|\beta|\} \quad (3)$$

In the expression, y represents the response vector; β is regression coefficient vector; λ represents a normalization parameter; α represents a parameter; $\|\bullet\|_2$ represents the L2 norm; $\|\bullet\|_1$ represents the L1 norm. L1 norm and L2 norm respectively select intra group and inter group features. The selection parameters of both are realized through the α parameter; The normalization parameter λ adjusts the compression range of the feature.The larger the normalization parameter, the more feature weights will be compressed; The smaller the normalization parameter, the more features are retained. The feature coefficients obtained by regression of the model are used as weights, i.e. the weight vector $w^{(1)} = (w_1^{(1)}, w_2^{(1)}, \cdots w_p^{(1)}) \in R_+^p$ of feature fusion. Then, a feature subset is obtained through probability sampling.The SVM model is used to learn classification in the second stage. The fundamental concept is to use a nonlinear mapping to convert the nonlinear problem in the original space into a higher-dimensional linear problem in the space. The model uses kernel functions to reduce complexity to accomplish high-latitude linear segmentation and streamline processes. The most important component of the support vector machine is directly determined by the kernel function used.

Figure 2. MSHDS-RS technique in three phases

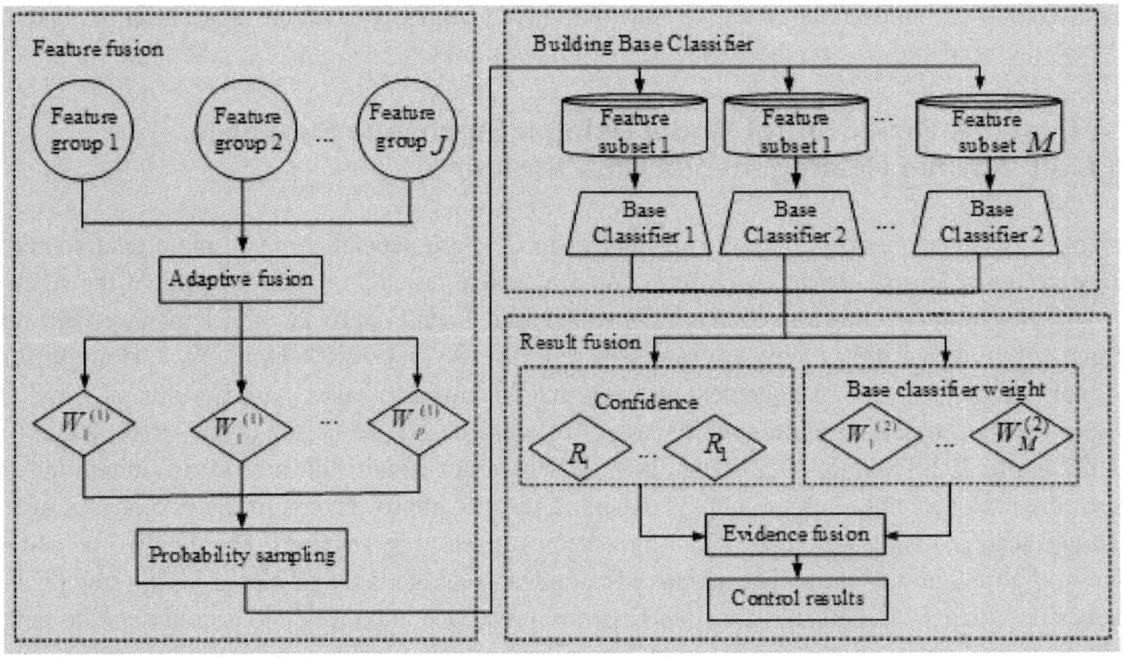

Since the base classifier in the current fusion techniques is unclear, the fusion results in the third stage lack some risk control information. The evidence is combined and the total impact is taken into consideration using the evidence inference rule (ER rule) in this study. The following is how the ER rule is stated:

$$E_i = \{(\theta, p_{\theta,i}) \forall \theta \subseteq \Theta, \sum_{\theta \subseteq \Theta} p_{\theta,i} = 1\} \tag{4}$$

In formula (4), E_i represents evidence; Θ is a set of mutually exclusive and complete hypotheses; $(\theta, p_{\theta,i})$ represents evidence elements; θ represents propositions; $p_{\theta,i}$ represents support. Combining the reliability and weight of evidence, the support degree $m_{\theta,i}$ can be expressed as:

$$\begin{gathered} m_i = \{(\theta, m_{\theta,i}) \forall \theta \subseteq \Theta, (p(\Theta), m_{p(\Theta),i}\} \\ m_{\theta,i} = \begin{cases} 0, & \theta = \varnothing \\ c_{Rw,i} m_{\theta,i}, & \theta \subseteq \Theta, \theta \neq \varnothing \\ c_{Rw,i}(1 - R_i), & \theta = p(\Theta) \end{cases} \end{gathered} \tag{5}$$

In the above formula (5), $c_{Rw,i} = \dfrac{1}{1 + w_i - R_i}$, ignoring the case of local ignorance, the total support of the proposition is expressed as:

$$m_{\theta,E(N_c)} = [(1-R_i)m_{\theta,E(i-1)} + m_{p(\Theta),E(i-1)}m_{\theta,i}], \forall\theta \subseteq \Theta \quad (6)$$

The probability of support for proposition θ in all base classifiers obtained through variable normalization is:

$$p_\theta = \frac{m_{\theta,E(L)}}{1-m_{p(\Theta),E(L)}}, \forall\theta \subseteq \Theta \quad (7)$$

Since the risk control result is an unbalanced classification situation, the AUC indicator (Area under Curve) is used to evaluate the quality of the final result. The reliability $R = (R_1, R_2, \cdots R_M)^T \in R_+^M$ is represented by the AUC index obtained from the base classifier test. Meanwhile, the reliability of the risky samples is used as the weight $w^{(2)} = (w_1^{(2)}, w_2^{(2)}, \cdots w_M^{(2)}) \in R_+^M$ of the recall base classifier.

5. FINANCIAL RISK CONTROL OUTCOMES ANALYSIS OF THE MSHDS-RS MODEL USING MULTI-SOURCE HETEROGENEOUS DATA STRUCTURE

As an experimental sample, the research included 6000 borrowers from P2P platforms with a one-year loan cycle; the default limit term was 120 days past due. In this trial, 5000 normal samples and 1000 danger samples were collected. Customer data was gathered for the experiment from five different information sources, and the AUC index, recall rate, and precision were chosen as metrics for model assessment. The normalization parameters are 0.0001, 0.001, 0.01, 0.1, and 1. The SGL adjustment parameter is set to 0.1, 0.2, 0.3, 0.4, 0.5, 0.6, 0.7, 0.8, and 0.9. The random spatial sub ratios are 0.1, 0.2, 0.3, 0.4, 0.5, 0.6, 0.7, 0.8, and 0.9. The tenfold cross validation approach was used in the experiment. Among the comparison techniques used are PBM_RS and RS algorithm, SVM, Bagging, Boosting, and Boosting. Assume that and stand for risk-free and dangerous indicators, respectively, and that the instances that arise from the classification are true negative cases, true cases, false negative cases, and false positive cases, represented by,,, and. The recall rate and accuracy calculation expressions are as follows:

$$R\_\mathrm{Re}call = \frac{TP}{TP+FN} \quad (8)$$

$$R\_\mathrm{R}recision = \frac{TP}{TP+FP} \quad (9)$$

$$NR\_\mathrm{Re}call = \frac{TN}{TN+FP} \quad (10)$$

Table 2. Comparison results of loan customer integration datasets

Method	Risky		Risk-Free	
	$R\_Rrecision$	R_Recall	$NR\_Rrecision$	NR_Recall
SVM	0.5468	0.8488	0.9543	0.8035
Bagging	0.5566	0.8694	0.9570	0.8124
Boosting	0.5689	0.8811	0.9575	0.8137
RS	0.6696	0.8783	0.9744	0.8661
ER_RS	0.6396	0.9002	0.9605	0.8356
Lasso_RS	0.6548	0.9487	0.9836	0.8454
PBM_R	0.6402	0.9472	0.9763	0.88
MSHDS-RS	0.6798	0.9554	0.9886	0.8566

$$NR\_Recall = \frac{TN}{TN + FN} \tag{11}$$

Concurrently, the experiment validated the updated algorithm of the TSAIB-RS model. The assessment and comparative results of the accuracy and recall rates of the eight classification techniques in the combined dataset are shown in Table 2. The accuracy index shows that the risk-free sample customers have a greater categorization accuracy value than the risk-distributed sample customers. Compared to the consumers in the risk category, the sample customers from the risk-free group had a lower recall rate index score. Although the misclassification is really the consequence of insufficient classifier training, the imbalance in the sample distribution may be the source of this situation. In terms of accuracy and recall, the MSHDS-RS strategy performs better for risky consumers than the other seven categorization systems. Compared to previous categorization methods, the MSHDS-RS methodology offers superior recall and accuracy for risky customers, and it still has advantages.

The results of the MSHDS-RS model using soft features, multi-source heterogeneous fusion features, and traditional basic features are shown in Figure 3. When comparing the AUC based on integrated features with the AUC based on soft features in the SVM approach, the former rises by around 5.2% and the latter by roughly 5.0%, respectively. The integrated features' AUC index value in the Bagging technique is 0.9234, up 2.4% and 2.2%, respectively, from the hard index value of 0.9034 and the soft index value of 0.9018. By 1.4% and 1.2%, respectively, above the soft index value of 0.9013 and the hard index value of 0.9035, respectively, the AUC index value of integrated features in the Boosting technique is 0.9141. The AUC index value for integrated features in the Rs method is 0.9294, up around 2.1% from the soft index value of 0.9103 and 3.0% from the hard index value of 0.9024. The AUC index value of integrated features in the ER-RS technique is 0.9324, up around 1.6% from the soft index value of 0.9181 and 3.0% from the hard index value of 0.9044. The AUC index value of integrated features in the Lasso-RS technique is 0.9385, up around 1.8% from the soft index value of 0.9217 and roughly 3.0% from the hard index value of 0.9102.

The comparison results for the eight techniques are shown in Figure 4 below. Among the three feature sets—integrated feature indicators, soft feature indicators, and hard feature indicators—the

Figure 3. Experimental outcomes using various feature sets

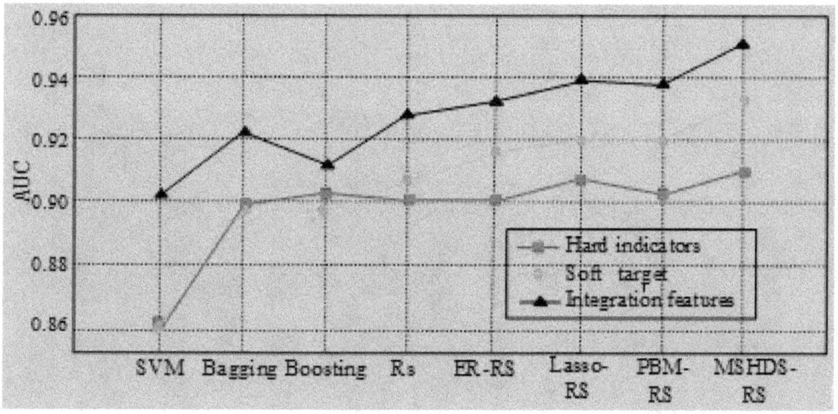

optimum risk control level has been reached. Overall, the MSHDS-RS approach's risk management is the most consistent, and its results are the most obvious. It shows the benefits of the two-stage adaptive fusion technique as well as the resilience and flexibility of the recommended approach to lower financial risk. The effect of the MSHDS-RS model on integrated feature financial risk management is much better than that of pure hard indicators and soft indicators. With more features, the MSHDS-RS model may provide better financial risk management. In comparison to the current PMB-RS approach, the MSHDS-RS approach is more practical. In terms of hard feature indicators, the accuracy of the MSHDS-RS technique is about 1.5% greater than that of the PMB-RS approach presently in use. When compared to the current PMB-RS technique, the accuracy improvement rate of the MSHDS-RS method may reach as high as 3.0% to 3.6% under the circumstances of soft feature index and integrated feature index.

The control effect of MSHDS-RS is influenced by the values of normalization parameter λ, subspace ratio γ, and adjustment parameter α. The sensitivity analysis results of the three parameters are shown in Figure 5. The subspace ratios shown in Figures (1), (2), and (3) are 0.3, 0.5, and 0.7, respectively. Under the determined integration feature conditions, the normalization parameters and adjustment parameters are analyzed. As shown in the figure, when the subspace ratio is 0.3, and λ and α are 0.01 and 0.5, respectively, the AUC of the MSHDS-RS method reaches a maximum value of 0.9492. When the subspace ratio is 0.5, and λ and α are taken as 0.001 and 0.1, respectively, the AUC of the MSHDS-RS method reaches a maximum value of 0.9481. When the subspace ratio is 0.7, and λ and α are 1 and 0.7, respectively, the AUC of the MSHDS-RS method reaches a maximum value of 0.9468. Overall, as the adjustment parameters increase, the AUC gradually decreases. This situation reflects that as α increases, the degree of sparsity within the group increases. Therefore, the control effect is more affected by changes in intragroup characteristics. Normalization λ exhibits a V-shaped pattern in the MSHDS-RS method. Therefore, when the normalization parameter is biased towards inter group or intra group features, it will have an ideal control effect. In summary, the financial risk control model based on MSHDS-RS proposed in this study has obvious feasibility and rationality.

Figure 4. Comparison results of eight classification methods

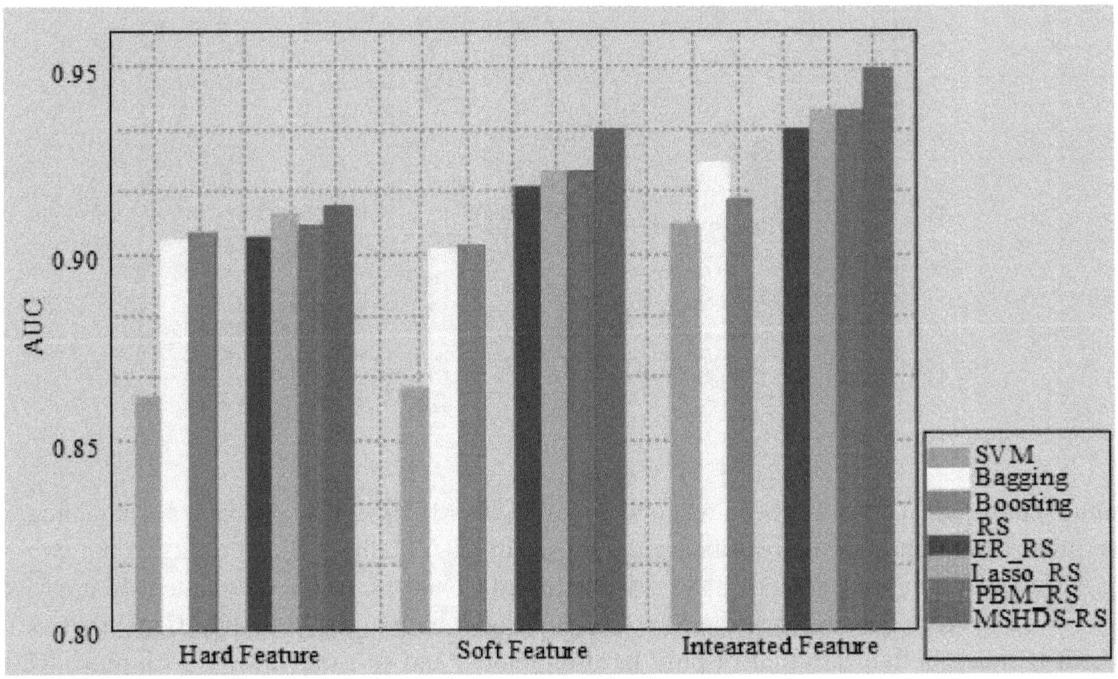

6. CONCLUSION

The rapid development of the social economy and the modernization of Internet technology have improved people's lives, but they have also created some issues. This research suggests a financial risk control model based on multi-source heterogeneous data and random subspaces, known as the MSHDS-RS model, in response to the present financial risk crises encountered by Internet finance, such as tardy payment and credit review. The experiment used a normalized sparse model for feature fusion optimization to create integrated features. It is based on the original financial risk control model, which divided feature subsets, built base classifiers, and synthesized findings. Subsequently, the experiment applies the MSHDS-RS model to various feature sets, and the results demonstrate the practicality, viability, and reliability of the

Figure 5. Sensitivity analysis results of three parameters

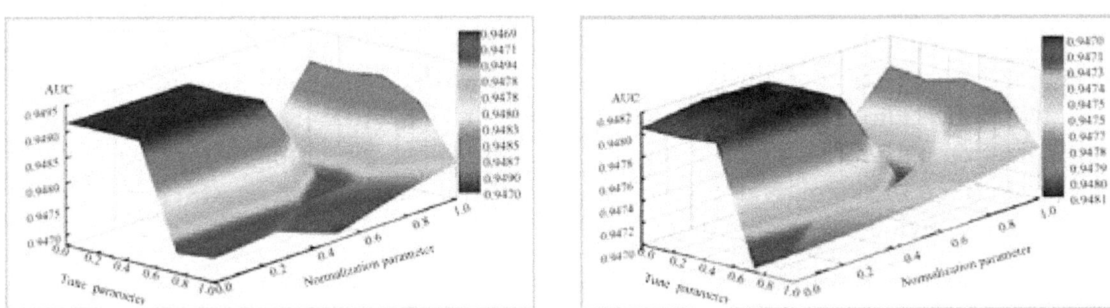

suggested optimal fusion procedure. The accuracy of the MSHDS-RS approach is around 1.5% better than the current PMB-RS methods in terms of hard feature indicators. The accuracy improvement rate of the MSHDS-RS technique is around 3.0% and 3.6% greater than that of the current PMB-RS methods under the circumstances of the soft feature index and integrated feature index, respectively. There is currently no study on the behavior of consumers following loans, which is also the next stage, because of the restricted settings of present experimental research.

REFERENCES

Akinola, A. (2022). The nexus between bank size and financial performance: Does internal control adequacy matter? *Journal of Accounting and Taxation*, *14*(1), 13–20. doi:10.5897/JAT2021.0501

Al-Alwan, M., Al-Nawafah, S., Al-Shorman, H., Khrisat, F. A., Alathamneh, F., & Al-Hawary, S. I. S. (2022). The effect of big data on decision quality: Evidence from telecommunication industry. *International Journal of Data and Network Science*, *6*(3), 693–702. doi:10.5267/j.ijdns.2022.4.003

Choi, T. M., Chan, H. K., & Yue, X. (2016). Recent development in big data analytics for business operations and risk management. *IEEE Transactions on Cybernetics*, *47*(1), 81–92. doi:10.1109/TCYB.2015.2507599 PMID:26766385

Ding, Q. (2021). Risk early warning management and intelligent real-time system of financial enterprises based on fuzzy theory. *Journal of Intelligent & Fuzzy Systems*, *40*(4), 6017–6027. doi:10.3233/JIFS-189441

Dutta, K. D., & Saha, M. (2021). Nexus of governance, macroprudential policy and financial risk: Cross-country evidence. *Economic Change and Restructuring*, *54*(4), 1253–1298. doi:10.1007/s10644-020-09301-9

Fang, W., Li, X., Zhou, P., Yan, J., Jiang, D., & Zhou, T. (2021). Deep learning anti-fraud model for internet loan: Where we are going. *IEEE Access : Practical Innovations, Open Solutions*, *9*, 9777–9784. doi:10.1109/ACCESS.2021.3051079

Feng, R., & Qu, X. (2021). Analyzing the Internet financial market risk management using data mining and deep learning methods. *Journal of Enterprise Information Management*, *35*(4/5), 1129–1147. doi:10.1108/JEIM-03-2021-0155

Haoru, W., Zhixuan, Y., & Yujia, W. (2020). Risk Assessment of Internet Credit Based on Big Data Analysis[C]//E3S Web of Conferences. *EDP Sciences*, *214*, 01012–01017.

Hongjin, S. (2021). Analysis of risk factors in financial supply chain based on machine learning and IoT technology. *Journal of Intelligent & Fuzzy Systems*, *40*(4), 6421–6431. doi:10.3233/JIFS-189482

Jakka, G., Yathiraju, N., & Ansari, M. F. (2022). Artificial intelligence in terms of spotting malware and delivering cyber risk management. *Journal of Positive School Psychology*, *6*(3), 6156–6165.

Liu, J., Jiang, Y., Gan, S., He, L., & Zhang, Q. (2022). Can digital finance promote corporate green innovation? *Environmental Science and Pollution Research International*, *29*(24), 35828–35840. doi:10.1007/s11356-022-18667-4 PMID:35061181

Liu, Y. (2021). Development and risk of internet finance based on big data. In *The International Conference on Cyber Security Intelligence and Analytics*. Springer. 10.1007/978-3-030-70042-3_75

Lyu, X., & Zhao, J. (2019). Compressed sensing and its applications in risk assessment for internet supply chain finance under big data. *IEEE Access : Practical Innovations, Open Solutions*, *7*, 53182–53187. doi:10.1109/ACCESS.2019.2909801

Metawa, N., & Metawa, S. (2021). Internet financial risk early warning based on big data analysis. *American Journal of Business and Operations Research*, *3*(1), 48–60. doi:10.54216/AJBOR.030103

Namahoot, K. S., & Laohavichien, T. (2018). Assessing the intentions to use internet banking: The role of perceived risk and trust as mediating factors. *International Journal of Bank Marketing*, *36*(2), 256–276. doi:10.1108/IJBM-11-2016-0159

Ou, L., & Chen, L. (2020). Predicting Risk Propagation of Corporate Internet Reporting Based on Fuzzy Neural Network. *Ingénierie des Systèmes d'Information*, *25*(4), 481–488. doi:10.18280/isi.250411

Park, Y. E. (2022). Developing a COVID-19 crisis management strategy using news media and social media in big data analytics. *Social Science Computer Review*, *40*(6), 1358–1375. doi:10.1177/08944393211007314

Sahoo, S. (2022). Big data analytics in manufacturing: A bibliometric analysis of research in the field of business management. *International Journal of Production Research*, *60*(22), 6793–6821. doi:10.1080/00207543.2021.1919333

Shang, H., Lu, D., & Zhou, Q. (2021). Early warning of enterprise finance risk of big data mining in internet of things based on fuzzy association rules. *Neural Computing & Applications*, *33*(9), 3901–3909. doi:10.1007/s00521-020-05510-5

Wang, C., & Liu, S. (2021). Innovative risk early warning model based on internet of things under big data technology. *IEEE Access : Practical Innovations, Open Solutions*, *9*, 100606–100614. doi:10.1109/ACCESS.2021.3095503

Wang, L., & Wang, Y. (2022). Supply chain financial service management system based on block chain IoT data sharing and edge computing. *Alexandria Engineering Journal*, *61*(1), 147–158. doi:10.1016/j.aej.2021.04.079

Wen, C., Yang, J., Gan, L., & Pan, Y. (2021). Big data driven Internet of Things for credit evaluation and early warning in finance. *Future Generation Computer Systems*, *124*, 295–307. doi:10.1016/j.future.2021.06.003

Yan, X., & Wu, Y. (2020). Financial risk assessment based on entropy weight topsis method: Take the internet insurance industry as an example. *Journal of Simulation*, *8*(6), 7–15.

Yang, D., Chen, P., Shi, F., & Wen, C. (2018). Internet finance: Its uncertain legal foundations and the role of big data in its development. *Emerging Markets Finance & Trade*, *54*(4), 721–732. doi:10.1080/1540496X.2016.1278528

Zhao, N., & Yao, F. (2021). The Transmission and Preventive Measures of Internet Financial Risk. In *International Conference on Business Intelligence and Information Technology*. Springer.

Chapter 9
Influence of Artificial Intelligence on Auditing:
Perception of Audit Professionals

Lurdes Silva
Polytechnic of Cávado and Ave, Portugal

Sara Serra
https://orcid.org/0000-0003-3107-1752
Polytechnic of Cávado and Ave, Portugal

Eva Barbosa
Polytechnic of Cávado and Ave, Portugal

ABSTRACT

The theme of artificial intelligence has sparked significant discussion and interest across all fields, and auditing is no exception. Therefore, this study aims to assess the perceptions of auditing professionals regarding the influence of artificial intelligence in auditing. For this, interviews were conducted with 14 auditing professionals. The results demonstrate that despite the current limited presence of artificial intelligence in auditing, there is a perception that its implementation will be inevitable. It is also concluded that the primary effect of using artificial intelligence in auditing is enhancing audit process efficiency. This study allows the authors to foresee the paradigm shift in auditing, constituting an essential contribution to academia, but essentially, to professional auditing bodies, in defining their change strategy.

INTRODUCTION

So far, artificial intelligence has been the most potent technological change of recent decades. The advance of artificial intelligence has changed how the world operates, including the world of business (Ali et al., 2022).

DOI: 10.4018/979-8-3693-0847-9.ch009

In 1956, John McCarthy, the Father of Artificial Intelligence, named the term "artificial intelligence" the science and engineering of creating intelligent machines. Artificial intelligence encompasses computer systems that can execute tasks that traditionally demand human intelligence. These systems can perceive their surroundings, engage in cognitive processes, acquire knowledge, and respond to their predefined objectives (McCarthy, 2007; Boucher, 2020; Taulli, 2020).

According to Hussein et al. (2016), the initial excitement surrounding artificial intelligence research was followed by the so-called "AI Winters," as the outcomes from this research were not yielding substantial results due to technological constraints. In recent times, there has been a resurgence of interest in artificial intelligence, primarily driven by increased access to vast amounts of data, advancements in the speed and accessibility of information, the introduction of new data storage and processing technologies, and, notably, the utilization of machine learning and deep learning techniques (Martha, 2018; Oliveira, 2019).

This technology is undergoing rapid evolution, and in auditing, the auditors must comprehend the capabilities of artificial intelligence and its impact on audit decision-making processes (Uglum, 2021). According to Issa et al. (2016), integrating artificial intelligence technologies into auditing work is inevitable, not only due to the perceived necessity within the profession but also because society will demand it. Confronted with the challenges posed by the transformative technologies of Industry 4.0, the field of accounting and auditing must undergo a profound transformation to ascend to the next stage (Hasan, 2022).

The futuristic vision of auditing introduces concepts that enable improving the audit process's quality, foreseeing greater transparency and accuracy in its work. Meeting the needs and demands of various stakeholders will always be a principle upheld by the auditing function because they require quick and efficient access to reliable information to support their decision-making (Deloitte, 2021).

Artificial intelligence has brought about significant enhancements in the realms of accounting and auditing, as well as other fields, improving operational processes, reporting mechanisms, and decision-making procedures (Ali et al., 2022). Artificial intelligence technologies allow for resolving problems that traditional methods may find insurmountable. Integrating these technologies into aspects of the auditing decision-making process, such as risk assessment or fraud interviews, can support auditors and enhance the overall quality of audits (Uglum, 2021). According Han et al. (2023), the increasing adoption of blockchain technology in accounting and auditing aims to enhance practices, transparency, and decision-making. Despite potential disruptions to the profession in the future, the likelihood of eliminating the need for human professionals seems relatively low (Hasan, 2022).

Ethical considerations associated with using these technologies are significant across various sectors, including the auditing profession (Uglum, 2021). This shift necessitates a discourse on the ethics of artificial intelligence, a topic that, while discussed for decades, has only recently gained broader social relevance (Stahl, 2022). This discourse becomes crucial in an era witnessing the emergence of technologies like GPT Chat, which can produce content so refined that distinguishing between human and machine authorship becomes challenging (Illia et al., 2023). Human rights concerns, particularly regarding privacy, intimacy, dignity, and the right to be forgotten, stand out as pivotal elements in the ethical considerations of artificial intelligence (Stahl, 2022; Díaz-Rodríguez et al., 2023; Lehner et al., 2022).

The broader integration of artificial intelligence into the auditing profession is anticipated to yield benefits such as enhanced efficiency, increased productivity, and improved accuracy (Hasan, 2022). In this context, this work aims to assess the perceptions of audit professionals about the influence of artificial intelligence on auditing. The methodology adopted in the investigation is part of the qualitative-interpretive paradigm, based on the systemic review of empirical studies and semi-structured interviews with a sample of 14 audit professionals.

In addition to this introduction, this study includes a literature review on auditing and artificial intelligence, highlighting the main existing empirical studies on the subject. Subsequently, the research's empirical study, conclusions, limitations, and suggestions for future research in this area are presented.

AUDITING AND ARTIFICIAL INTELLIGENCE

Study Review

The bibliographical survey on the topic is the starting point of this investigation, which will assess the state of the art and compare existing studies with the results obtained in the research we propose. Therefore, in the table below we present some empirical studies about de impact of artificial intelligence in auditing.

The literature about the application of artificial intelligence in auditing demonstrates the benefits of these tools in the auditor's work, essentially in terms of the accuracy of the audit process. Artificial intelligence tools will allow the auditor to collect and use a more significant amount of data promptly, increasing the degree of security of the auditor's opinion and reducing the audit risk.

The analysis of the impact of artificial intelligence on auditing must include two aspects: the technology aspect and the procedures aspect. There must be a complementary approach to these two aspects, allowing us to understand how artificial intelligence systems are designed and used and the impact, present and future, these systems have on users, society, and the natural environment (Mökander, 2023).

While artificial intelligence presents benefits, it also presents implementation challenges, namely the need for updating and training auditors in technological areas. This training cannot be restricted to the basic training of auditors but must be continuously updated (Omoteso, 2012; Hasan, 2022).

Training is essential for audit professionals to know the importance of artificial intelligence in business and have more profound knowledge about automatic data collection and processing. However, in Portugal, the Order of Statutory Auditors does not include any training about artificial intelligence in its 2024 training plan. Auditing firms can carry out training in this area. The Big4 are more advanced in this area and are already preparing their auditors to adopt artificial intelligence.

The other challenge that artificial intelligence poses is the need to create legal and professional standards on this topic and an ethical framework that regulates the use of these tools and the data generated by them.

Artificial Intelligence and Ethics in Auditing

The necessity to regulate artificial intelligence is unquestionable, with the complexity of the topic arising from the nature of this technology and its impacts on social standards (Almeida et al., 2021). Digital information can be misused to create inaccurate profiles, reinforce stereotypes, perpetuate biases among minorities, and maintain historical or cultural prejudices (O'neil, 2017; Díaz-Rodríguez et al., 2023). Therefore, policymakers must promote artificial intelligence that benefits people, promotes a fair society, ensures transparent and responsible disclosure, and holds developers accountable for proper functioning (Lehner et al., 2022; Munoko et al., 2022).

Table 1. Review of empirical studies

Autor/Year	Conclusions
Lombardi et al. (2014)	Traditional auditing must change to make it more relevant in the real-time economy. Auditing must be in tune with ongoing advances in the profession and society to effectively meet various stakeholders' needs.
Issa et al. (2016)	Artificial intelligence could replace auditors in several automated tasks and improve the audit process. Furthermore, these systems will be prepared to outline the entire audit plan automatically based on client knowledge and existing evidence.
Deloitte (2017)	It will not be about having more work but working better based on a virtuous circle in which platforms, solutions, resources, and, obviously, people are connected.
Meira (2019)	The implementation of artificial intelligence in auditing will be inevitable. The most significant impact will be noticed in the testing phase of controls and substantive procedures. The advantages these professionals mentioned were replacing traditional sampling tests with the total analysis of operations and the ability to guarantee greater security and reliability of financial information to stakeholders. Furthermore, most interviewees identify the role of audit assistant as the one that will suffer the most significant repercussions with adopting these technologies.
Cruz et al. (2020)	Artificial intelligence will not replace the auditor, but rather help him in more routine tasks, maintaining this professional's power of judgment. The authors also highlighted that auditors need a programming professional, specialist in artificial intelligence, incorporated into the work teams, as they will not have sufficient knowledge to deal with artificial intelligence technologies.
Couceiro et al. (2020)	The auditor will no longer perform manual work and can analyze a complete data set as an alternative to sampling techniques and the possible deviations from these techniques. Furthermore, audit efficiency will increase as professionals focus on more important tasks, such as decision-making.
Nunes et al. (2020)	Assistance in decision-making provided by these technologies, that is, in professional judgment, since analyzing a vast and complex amount of information is possible. In addition, these authors argue that all professionals who want to succeed and see their work improved will inevitably have to equip themselves with these tools.
Seethamraju and Hecimovic (2020)	Entities external to auditing firms, such as clients, audit standard bodies, professional organizations, and regulatory bodies, are reticent and are restricting the adoption and use of these technologies due to the conservative approach that still exists and the lack of technological knowledge and skills
Al-Sayyed et al. (2021)	Artificial intelligence improves audit efficiency, and quality as the collection of audit evidence improves. However, according to the authors above, the complexity of artificial intelligence technologies and the lack of experience in their use will create significant obstacles to developing and adopting these tools.
Rikhardsson et al. (2021)	The auditors see adopting artificial intelligence technologies as positive, as it will add value, leading to lower costs and increased audit quality. Younger and lower-level auditors expect artificial intelligence to have more impact on their work than older and higher-level auditors.
Rehman and Hashim (2022)	Artificial intelligence will make the auditor's role more effective shortly. However, organizations must commit to promoting the general understanding of artificial intelligence.
Fedyk et al. (2022)	Artificial intelligence improved the quality of audits and simplified the process, leading to a reduction in fees. Furthermore, it was found that people who work with artificial intelligence tend to be relatively young, predominantly male and have a bachelor's or master's degree in technical areas such as statistics, applied mathematics and computer science.
Hashid and Almaqtari (2024)	A positive relationship between artificial intelligence and perceived usefulness, implying that artificial intelligence is considered beneficial for enhancing accounting and auditing methods in Saudi Arabia. Using user-friendly artificial intelligence solutions makes accounting and auditing more efficient and effective.

In 2020, the United Nations Educational, Scientific and Cultural Organization (UNESCO) introduced the Recommendation on the Ethics of Artificial Intelligence, unanimously adopted by 193 countries. This Recommendation prioritizes human rights, transparency, and fairness in artificial intelligence, addressing its impact on data, the environment, gender equality, education, research, healthcare, and social well-being. UNESCO's initiative aligns with the organization's broader goal of promoting technology and innovation in the service of humanity (UNESCO, Recommendation on the Ethics of Artificial Intelligence, 2020).

Human rights, particularly the right to privacy, intimacy, dignity, and the right to be forgotten stand out prominently in the ethical considerations of artificial intelligence.

According to Ma et al. (2022), the trustworthiness of artificial intelligence is very broad in scope and warrants further research into ensuring the proper implementation of rules and guidelines. Trustworthiness involves legal, robust, and ethical dimensions (Díaz-Rodríguez et al., 2023).

The collaboration among experts from various communities and scientific fields is essential to achieve trustworthy artificial intelligence. Meaningful and acceptable standards can only be developed through joint efforts, ensuring the constant improvement of research (Ma et al., 2022). Standardization is identified as a strategy to build trust, with quality standards driving enhancements in artificial intelligence across various attributes (Ma et al., 2022). Developing technical standards for trustworthy artificial intelligence models is crucial for implementing reliable and responsible systems for society's present and future (Cannarsa, 2021; Díaz-Rodríguez et al., 2023; Ma et al., 2022).

In auditing, Lehner et al. (2022) identified five significant ethical challenges in artificial intelligence-based decision-making in auditing: objectivity, privacy, transparency, accountability, and trustworthiness. Uglum (2021) also mentioned that ethical considerations such as objectivity, privacy, accuracy, confidentiality, data protection, transparency, accountability, trustworthiness, and biases must be considered. So, the auditors must consider ethical implications when developing and implementing artificial intelligence to maintain public trust (Uglum, 2021). Aitkazinov (2023) added that this professional must have technical knowledge to develop and maintain artificial intelligence systems, privacy and data security concerns, potential biases in algorithms and the ethical implications associated with using artificial intelligence.

In resume, artificial intelligence is a multidisciplinary project to which professionals such as computer scientists, engineers, sociologists, philosophers, and lawyers have contributed (Mökander, 2023). This multidisciplinary approach must respond to the challenges posed by artificial intelligence, prioritizing the development of essential technical skills and providing adequate training for auditors to utilize artificial intelligence tools effectively. Additionally, establishing regulatory frameworks is crucial to guarantee the ethical use of these tools, addressing issues such as bias, privacy, and security (Aitkazinov, 2023).

These ethical challenges aim to minimize negative impacts, including automated mass manipulation, disinformation, low-quality content production, and communication barriers among stakeholders (Illia et al., 2023). Despite these ethical problems, society must persist in using artificial intelligence, ensuring the paramount focus remains on delivering value and efficiency (Hasan, 2022).

OBJECTIVE

According to Hasan (2022), the broader application of artificial intelligence in auditing is expected to provide greater efficiency, productivity, and accuracy in the audit process. However, at the same time, challenges related to the lack of standards and training and ethical issues are expected. Therefore, preparation is necessary on the part of educators, regulators, and professional bodies, addressing the paradigm shift and preparing students, policies, and future professionals for the challenges of a world entire of big data, blockchain technology, and artificial intelligence, establishing the fourth industrial revolution.

Given the importance of improving audit procedures and increasing the degree of security of the auditor's opinion, this study aims to evaluate the perception of audit professionals about the influence of artificial intelligence on auditing, specifically on financial auditing. Specifically, we will obtain the opinion of a group of Portuguese auditors on whether the use of artificial intelligence leads to greater efficiency with a smaller margin of error, allowing us to issue opinions with absolute certainty.

This research seeks to clarify the impact of artificial intelligence on auditing and the need to create a legal and ethical framework that allows the excellent use of these tools.

RESEARCH METHODOLOGY

A methodology based on two distinct approaches was adopted to achieve this objective.

The first methodological approach consisted of a literature review, using an exploratory nature through a bibliographic review, to deepen knowledge of the research topic. The second approach to the study is qualitative and involves the interview technique.

Semi-structured interviews were conducted according to a script based on the literature review. The interviews were conducted with auditing professionals of different age groups, years of experience in the profession and belonging to different auditing companies, namely Big4 and Non-Big4.

The interviews took place in September 2022 and lasted approximately 20 to 30 minutes each. When carrying out the interviews, with the due authorization of each of the interviewees, an audio recording was made so that they could later be transcribed and thus facilitate the interpretation and understanding of the information collected to obtain a better analysis of its content. When starting the interview, the interviewee was also told why the interview was being carried out, the objective of the study, and the anonymity of the data collected.

This methodology seemed to be the most appropriate for this study given the complexity and relevance of the topic and the enrichment that this methodology brings, as it was advantageous for us to collect as much information as possible.

SAMPLE CHARACTERIZATION

The target of this investigation was audit professionals, namely Statutory Auditors and Auditors. Therefore, audit professionals were sent an email about the possibility of collaborating in the interview. Of 24 contacts sent, only 14 were available to collaborate.

The sample was selected using opinion sampling and snowball sampling. The sample consists of 14 interviews with audit professionals, of which six are Statutory Auditors, and eight are Auditors.

Regarding the characterization of the sample, as shown in Table 2, it includes audit professionals aged between 24 and 65 years old, with six of the 14 interviewees aged between 24 and 29 years old, four aged between 32 and 41 years old, and the other four are in the age group of 53 to 65 years old. The strong predominance of interviewees under 41 could influence the results, given that younger auditors are generally more open to using artificial intelligence.

It was also found that half of the sample had up to four years of professional experience. However, there are five professionals with more than 20 years of experience, which also highlights the heterogeneity of the sample.

Table 2. Sample characterization

Interviewee	Age	Gender	Professional Category	Years of Experience	Type of Audit Firm
Interviewee 1 (I1)	25	Female	Auditor	4	Big4
Interviewee 2 (I2)	24	Female	Auditor	3	Big4
Interviewee 3 (I3)	41	Male	Statutory Auditor	20	Non-Big4
Interviewee 4 (I4)	54	Male	Statutory Auditor	30	Non-Big4
Interviewee 5 (I5)	36	Male	Statutory Auditor	13	Big4
Interviewee 6 (I6)	32	Female	Auditor	3	Big4
Interviewee 7 (I7)	32	Male	Statutory Auditor	9	Non-Big4
Interviewee 8 (I8)	58	Female	Statutory Auditor	32	Big4
Interviewee 9 (I9)	27	Male	Auditor	4	Non-Big4
Interviewee 10 (I10)	29	Male	Auditor	3	Non-Big4
Interviewee 11 (I11)	65	Male	Statutory Auditor	40	Non-Big4
Interviewee 12 (I12)	25	Female	Auditor	3	Big4
Interviewee 13 (I13)	24	Male	Auditor	2	Big4
Interviewee 14 (I14)	53	Female	Auditor	29	Non-Big4

Regarding gender, six audit professionals are female, and eight are male, which would be expected, given that according to the Order of Statutory Auditors Report and Accounts for 2022, 70% of Statutory Auditors are men.

The criterion of interviewing auditors and Statutory Auditors was defined given that although they work in auditing, they have slightly different skills and responsibilities, which could also influence their perception of this topic. As can be seen in Table 2, the sample includes eight auditors and six Statutory Auditors.

Regarding the type of auditing company, the sample is balanced, given that half of the interviewees belong to the Big4 and the other half to the Non-Big4.

PRESENTATION AND DISCUSSION OF RESULTS

Use of Artificial Intelligence in Auditing

To assess the use of artificial intelligence in the audit, we asked interviewees the following questions: "Do you use any tool that incorporates artificial intelligence in your professional activity? If so, which ones and in what procedures?"

We found a particular discrepancy in responses between audit professionals working in Big4 and Non-Big4. Professionals who carry out audits in the Big4 state that using technological tools is a reality in these companies. Therefore, I6 mentioned, "We use many data analytics tools, which allow us to quickly analyze patterns and operations, which makes our work much easier." In the same sense, Interviewee 13 stated that use "a tool called DataSnipper that transforms documents (text format and tables, for example), transforms the data, processes it, groups it and analyzes it and then transports it to be used in reports."

I1 also mentioned using programs for processing information and providing analysis, which help to correlate ideas between the various functions and variables to produce reports and analyses. However, I1 said he does not know whether these tools can be considered artificial intelligence ("I don't know to what extent what we use is artificial intelligence").

I5 and I8 gave a more precise answer. I5 said "I don't think so because the decisions do not all consider the model used. I use data minds and data analytics, but the model proposals and decisions are always corroborated by human analysis. There is use in some cases of exploratory data analysis. Still, in terms of decision making, I anticipate that automatic systems have never been used without human supervision having been used." Interviewee 8 stated that they do not use artificial intelligence but that use "some automated processes, but which are closer to RPA than artificial intelligence. There will be a bigger step to be smart. But programmed software is already used to perform specific tasks." In this regard, Interviewee 2 responded that they use programs that correlate data and produce reports.

Although we increasingly see technology as a work tool in auditing, artificial intelligence is still not very present in the area, especially for smaller auditing companies. The responses from audit professionals who do not work in the Big4 show this, given that they all responded that their professional activity uses some tool that incorporates artificial intelligence.

However, despite not being part of a Big4, I10 mentioned, "Our software (SIRA), when processing data and carrying out detail tests and substantive tests, the algorithms may not be very elaborate or dense, but already incorporate a degree of intelligence. In the conclusions it provides us, we can already see artificial intelligence. We still introduce the inputs, but the software itself already gives us the conclusion of the work and whether, for example, we should call into question a class of transactions or not."

This fact shows that although some auditing companies are not Big4, they already have automated procedures and technological tools are increasingly valued.

By analyzing the results obtained, we can conclude that, when applying the concept of artificial intelligence to auditing, twelve interviewees needed clarification on whether or not artificial intelligence was what they were using. This fact denotes the lack of knowledge about artificial intelligence in auditing, revealing the need for professional bodies and audit regulators to promote more training actions in this area.

The second conclusion is that artificial intelligence, even in the embryonic phase, is present in the reality of auditing, a view also proven by Meira (2019). Even so, we note that tools that incorporate a certain degree of intelligence by those working in the Big4 are natural and more noticeable than in smaller auditing companies. However, the perception of audit professionals who belong to Non-Big4 is that this trend will grow. Rodrigues (2021), who states that introducing artificial intelligence in the auditing profession will be an increasingly recurring fact, corroborate this opinion.

Continuing this theme, we asked respondents whether they consider that the auditor must develop new skills to use artificial intelligence. All interviewees responded that audit professionals would have to equip themselves with specific skills to use artificial intelligence. Reis (2019), in his study, also concluded that 90% of respondents revealed that technology training is essential for the auditor.

The interviewees' answers show a line of conformity with each other, with the distinction being that some believe that the path will involve, in the future, there being auditors-programmers. Others defend that it will not reach that point, but a specialist may first have to be incorporated into the audit work teams, as already exists in many audit companies. In its study, EY Reporting (2020), one of the Big4, mentioned that specialists in artificial intelligence technology systems in the reality of auditing companies would be necessary for professionals in this area.

The divergence in views can be traced back to the different environments in which auditors operate. Auditors from Big4 firms, which already integrate information systems specialists into their teams, have a different perspective than Non-Big4 firms. The latter group believes that creating a department solely focused on technologies may not be justified. Instead, the onus should be on the individual audit professional to acquire these skills. Interestingly, our study found no significant differences in these views based on gender or age.

Influence of Artificial Intelligence on Audit Efficiency and Margin of Error

To assess the impact of artificial intelligence on efficiency and margin of error, we asked interviewees whether they consider that using artificial intelligence will bring benefits to greater efficiency and a lower margin of error in the auditor's work.

About efficiency, we verified that all interviewees consider that artificial intelligence techniques, applied in audit work, will increase efficiency in audit processes. I3 states that using these tools, procedures will be streamlined and consequently the auditor will have more time to give importance to other issues such as planning work and analyzing risks. I4 also refer that he processes, and all work will be carried out more quickly and we will be able to analyze data in detail, so there is no doubt that it will bring efficiency to the work.

I9, I10 and I7 also reinforce the speed issue in data processing, the latter stating that efficiency is clear due to the automation of processes and the greater speed with which certain procedures can be carried out. Therefore, the auditor will focus on data interpretation and professional judgment.

However, regarding the margin of error, the interviewees' answers are not unanimous. Still, many interviewees believe that the margin of error will decrease, given that according to I8, simple automation is enough to provide greater security to the audit process. In this line of thought, I10 states, "From the outset the algorithm is created with a minimum margin of error. It is much more susceptible to error if we analyze a very dense set of data, we humans, than a machine reading and interpreting the data, [...] humans will have many more factors that lead us to error."

I4, despite not referring to the algorithm, also believes that using artificial intelligence in the audit will reduce the risk, alluding that the use of the internet or other databases will make the information more reliable. I3 adds that with the use of artificial intelligence in the audit, the auditor will have more time to analyze risks and respond to risks, consequently reducing the margin of error. I9 also states, "Once we have a tool that processes data much faster than us, I think the probability of making mistakes is much lower."

Contrary to this view, I14 alludes that some certain procedures and controls are almost impossible for artificial intelligence to achieve, because they also involve human values and reactions. The interviewee also states that certain human procedures prevent errors, such as human sensitivity and perception. Therefore, streamlining procedures could even lead to more errors. I13 also mentions that there will always be operations in companies and businesses that algorithms will not recognize.

I7 also exposes the auditor's difficulty in interpreting the data generated by artificial intelligence, stating that there will be less margin for error only if the auditor knows how to correctly interpret the data obtained from artificial intelligence, there is no doubt.

For all of this, I5 mention there is no certainty regarding what will happen with the margin of error. I11 states that this will depend on each audit process, given that in certain areas artificial intelligence will be able to analyze all the data and in terms of efficiency there is no doubt, but it could also increase the error since we also have more available information. The auditor will have to validate the veracity of the information and focus more on discrepancies that the software identifies, and this could even bring more work for the auditor.

Given the above, we found that most interviewees consider that, with artificial intelligence, efficiency increases and the margin of error decreases. This fact was also noted by several authors (Issa et al., 2016; PwC, 2019; Couceiro et al., 2020; Cruz et al., 2020; Al-Sayyed et al., 2021; Rikhardsson et al., 2021; Rodrigues, 2021; Rehman & Hashim, 2022).

It should also be noted that those interviewed who consider that artificial intelligence will not contribute to reducing the margin of error are those who are older, have professional experience, and are more accustomed to current audit procedures.

Influence of Artificial Intelligence on Timeliness

Timeliness is a characteristic that the literature argues will gain strength using artificial intelligence tools. Lombardi et al. (2014), Deloitte (2017), PwC (2019), Cruz et al. (2020) and Rodrigues (2021) highlight real-time audits as one of the new audit requirements. Therefore, we ask the following question at this point: "Do you think that timeliness is a characteristic that gains or will gain strength when using artificial intelligence techniques in auditing?"

When posed with the question, the response was overwhelmingly affirmative. Ten interviewees agreed that the introduction and evolution of artificial intelligence in audit work would bolster timeliness. They further enriched this idea by citing influencing factors such as the preparation of accounts (I5; I9; I11) and the provision of information by the client (I12; I13).

However, it is important to note that not all opinions aligned. I6, for instance, offered a contrasting viewpoint, stating that the auditor's role is not to audit in real time or monitor the institution. According to I6, the auditor's role is to issue an opinion. While artificial intelligence can facilitate understanding certain variations and the analysis of operations as they happen, it should not distort the auditor's role.

From the above, we can conclude that practically the entire sample, around 93%, creates a harmonious consensus among themselves and that the literature supports the assertions about audit reports' timeliness.

Influence of Artificial Intelligence on Professional Judgment

ISA 200 (General objectives of the independent auditor and conducting an audit by international auditing standards) requires the auditor to exercise professional judgment during the planning and execution of the audit.

Within the scope of this theme and with the aim of understanding the influence of artificial intelligence on professional judgment, we formulated the following question: "Do you consider that your professional judgment, throughout the audit work, will be enhanced with greater accuracy because artificial intelligence allows for the analysis of all data, rather than just a sample?"

Eleven of the fourteen interviewees believe that professional judgment will be executed with greater accuracy due to artificial intelligence. According to I2, I10 and I13, the increase in the accuracy of professional judgment is due to the possibility of analyzing all the data and extending the audit work. I7 also states that "If there is the possibility of a tool analyzing 100% of the data and only giving me distortions, I can say that I can go beyond the "normal" work and do more extensive work and the quality of the work could increase." Sharing the same opinion, I9 states that "If we think that we can increasingly have things computerized and the fact that we can validate more information and more areas, it means that in terms of the auditor's opinion, the auditor can have a much safer opinion than when using just one sample." In fact, one of the main causes of audit error is the use of a sample.

In the same line of thought, I4 refer that professional judgment will be executed with greater accuracy because the margin of error with these tools will be smaller.

Issa et al., (2016), PwC (2019), Cruz et al. (2020), Seethamraju and Hacomicov (2020) argue that artificial intelligence techniques can increase the quality and professional judgment of the audit, as they provide more evidence. In this way, we support the answers given in the interviews, in which we found that 50% of those interviewed responded affirmatively regarding greater accuracy in professional judgment.

Of the interviewees who did not agree that artificial intelligence contributes to improving professional judgment throughout the audit work, we were interested in the statements made by I12 and I14. Both mentioned that by applying artificial intelligence in the audit process, the auditor could lose sensitivity in their work and, consequently, this would affect their professional judgment. I14 goes further, arguing that artificial intelligence would not be able to detect certain operations or arrive at certain human procedures, giving as an example the human expressions that someone the auditor approaches transmit, and which could be useful for the work. However, it is important to note that the role of artificial intelligence is to assist and enhance the auditor's work, not to replace the human element entirely.

During the interviews, another question was raised regarding the use of samples and sampling techniques in the era of artificial intelligence. Studies by Nunes et al. (2020) and Rodrigues (2021) found that using artificial intelligence tools would no longer be necessary to apply sampling techniques. However, in this study we were unable to validate the results achieved by the authors above, since most interviewees do not believe that sampling, used in audit work, will disappear.

However, thirteen interviewees state that artificial intelligence could cause changes in the audit sampling process, which is expected. In this sense, I8 states that the concept of sample will not disappear, even analyzing all the data, deviations, anomalies, and alerts will appear and it may not be necessary to analyze all the deviations. It may not be the end of sampling, but it will be, as we know it today. Sharing the same opinion, I5 mention that sampling will not disappear, given that not all decisions can be scrutinized by automatic mechanisms. The ability of artificial intelligence to analyze multiple documents, in which each transaction was recorded in a different way and on different media, is something whose implementation cost is significant and, therefore, there are situations in which the analysis is so complex that it will not be efficient at all. Auditors configure the technology that allows them to have all the evidence.

I3 also considers that we are very far from abolishing the sample concept, given that, firstly, it depends on the assertion we intend to evaluate. For example, in the sales section, artificial intelligence can verify the existence or classification assertion. Still, it will not be able to prove the completeness assertion, that is, to verify whether all sales are registered. Computer algorithms can only run what is done, not what is not done. The interviewee adds, "From the perspective of internal audit it may be more relevant to change the sampling, but in external audit I don't believe so."

I6 also states that the impact of artificial intelligence on sampling depends on the type of procedures. As such, the sample may disappear, but not all of them. Perhaps the sample concept will be adjusted, reducing it and not being used as much.

In turn, I1 states that with access to artificial intelligence, we will analyze feedback from the entire population, but as an audit, we will not analyze all operations by themselves. Artificial intelligence will be able to read the entire population, but they will be tests that use samples are necessary to understand whether what is being analyzed in the population is correct. Sharing the same opinion, I11 refer that the concept of sample will not disappear, but it will certainly change, for example, the sample could be given in a more selective and targeted way only for the discrepancies the software identified, and the auditor will have to focus on these discrepancies.

As can be seen, artificial intelligence's impact on the audit process is undeniable, with several professional bodies discussing the possible changes that will occur within the scope of this topic.

Influence of Artificial Intelligence on the Auditor's Report

The Auditor's Report is the main audit output, as it is in this document that the auditor issues his opinion on the true and fair view of the audited entity's financial statements. This is precisely why stakeholders use the Auditor's Report to make decisions.

However, the problem that arises is that the opinion issued by the auditor in the Auditor's Report provides a reasonable degree of security, which, according to Technical Application Guide 1, is a high level of security but is not a guarantee that an audit performed by international auditing standards will always detect a material misstatement when it exists.

However, according to Nunes et al. (2020), artificial intelligence tools will revolutionize the definition of reasonable security auditors give in their reports. To test this statement, we asked the interviewees: "Do you consider that the Auditor's Report may reveal not a reasonable certainty, but an absolute certainty?"

All interviewees responded that the Auditor's Report would never provide absolute certainty, because material distortions will always exist and, consequently, the audit risk, fraud tend to evolve and the auditor will always want to exercise their professional judgment, to safeguard themselves and the audit work.

Moreover, as I5 points out, absolute assurance would necessitate a thorough examination of all management actions and representations, as well as the registration of all agreements. However, unregistered agreements that influence the accounts can legally exist. The basis for issuing an opinion is always the existing records. The auditor's greatest challenge is identifying the records that should exist but do not. While artificial intelligence can help analyze existing records, it cannot identify missing records that should have been there. This introduces uncertainty into the accounts that artificial intelligence cannot resolve. Therefore, there will always be a degree of uncertainty in the auditor's opinion.

I8 also states, "We can move towards a higher level of reasonableness, but it doesn't seem to me that a guarantee will be achieved, that is very strong. I would say that it couldn't be absolute because the management body itself would not be able to provide a guarantee that its accounts are well presented and well prepared. Also, any internal control system has its sheets, and this guarantee, if it does not come from the prepared part, I do not see how the auditor will be able to do so."

Consistent with these views, I9 asserts that while absolute assurance is unattainable, artificial intelligence can offer a more reasonable assurance and a lower likelihood of error. However, even with the aid of artificial intelligence, professional judgment will only be able to provide some assurance.

SOLUTIONS AND RECOMMENDATIONS

Various studies show that artificial intelligence can improve the efficiency and quality of the audit, facilitating the collection and analysis of data and increasing the efficiency of audit procedures, as well as the timeliness of the analyses carried out. Artificial intelligence will assist Auditors in routine tasks, allowing them to focus on more strategic activities that require human judgment.

However, there are significant challenges to consider, such as the complexity of artificial intelligence technologies and the lack of experience and expertise in their use, which can hinder the adoption of these tools.

Audit professional organizations must outline strategies for adapting traditional auditing to the new paradigm of artificial intelligence, emphasizing the importance of training in information technologies and reformulating professional standards to adjust the auditing process to this new reality. Furthermore, it is crucial to consider the new role that the Auditor may assume in the audited company.

In turn, and as reported by Noordin et al. (2022), audit firms must plan the adoption of artificial intelligence to avoid unsatisfactory results, taking care to recruit professionals capable of working with artificial intelligence technologies reducing the risk of misuse of these tools.

It is important to highlight that Seethamraju and Hecimovic (2023) mention that although artificial intelligence has the potential to improve the quality of audits and provide value-added services to audit clients, its adoption of the requirement will offset the practice of audits, taking into account the lack of control in the use of artificial intelligence.

FUTURE RESEARCH DIRECTIONS

Looking at the results obtained, we feel that the future in the panorama of artificial intelligence is still seen with fear, even though the belief that it will happen and that it will be through these technologies that auditing will evolve prevails. This work allows us to foresee the paradigm shift in the auditing profession, constituting an important contribution to academia, but essentially, to professional auditing bodies, namely, to define their strategy in this change process.

In our future research, we propose a more inclusive approach by expanding our sample to include a wider range of audit professionals, auditees, and professional bodies. To capture these stakeholders' diverse perspectives, we recommend using focus groups. This approach will foster a sense of collaboration and inclusivity in our research.

CONCLUSION

The increasingly dynamic market driven by advanced technologies has generated significant challenges for auditing, encouraging the search for more efficient, effective, and innovative tools to support the work.

There have never been such massive amounts of data and much information as today (Serman, 2016). At the same time, the market is increasingly complex and competitive. This is a promising scenario, but it also requires innovative methods and technologies to overcome limitations in data analysis (PwC, 2019; EY, Reporting 2020; Deloitte, 2021).

Although all efforts are being directed towards the control and governance of artificial intelligence, there still needs to be a significant gap between ethical principles and a functional model capable of covering all areas of knowledge required to deal with ordinary complexity (Almeida et al., 2021).

In the auditing area, Big4 was the first company to promote the application of artificial intelligence. They believe that no evolution will occur if there is no technology and training, justifying that these tools, combined with the auditor's knowledge (which will involve specific and advanced computer and technological knowledge), will be the transformative step of the audit. These two competent crusades will be the basis for the audit approach of the future. (PwC, 2019; EY Reporting, 2020; KPMG, 2020; Deloitte, 2021).

The central focus of this study, which holds significant importance for the field, was to delve into the perceptions of audit professionals regarding the influence of artificial intelligence on auditing. This was achieved through conducting semi-structured interviews with 14 seasoned audit professionals.

Our findings lead us to a compelling conclusion. Despite the current low prevalence of artificial intelligence in auditing, the perception is clear: its implementation is not just likely but inevitable. Indeed, within the Big4, tools exhibiting a degree of intelligence are already in use. In contrast, Non-Big4 firms, likely due to investment and client portfolio considerations, have yet to embrace this technological shift fully.

Our study also leads us to conclude that the primary impact of integrating artificial intelligence into auditing is a marked increase in process efficiency. Timeliness, too, is a characteristic that stands to benefit significantly from the introduction and evolution of artificial intelligence. However, it is essential to note that even with advanced techniques and artificial intelligence, legal certification of accounts can only provide some certainty. Factors such as professional judgment, material distortions, errors, and fraud ensure that a degree of reasonableness is always required.

Artificial intelligence technology will influence the future of the audit profession, allowing the audit process to be performed more effectively and efficiently (Ali et al., 2022). The literature leads us to believe that using Big Data, Cloud Computing and Deep Learning to adopt artificial intelligence in auditing practices is a reality that is here to stay (Hashid & Almaqtari, 2024). Therefore, professional bodies must redesign the professional development and training process (Hasan, 2022). However, it is essential to be aware of the most dangerous side of artificial intelligence, as it can exacerbate certain inequalities, contribute to counterfeiting and compromise privacy rights risks.

This research contributes to clarifying the impact of artificial intelligence on financial auditing and the need to create a legal and ethical framework that allows the excellent use of these tools. However, it is essential to highlight the limitations of this research, which are essentially based on the weak presence of artificial intelligence systems in auditing companies, and, therefore, the conclusions drawn are based on hypothetical facts.

ACKNOWLEDGMENT

This work is financed by national funds through FCT – Fundação para a Ciência e a Tecnologia, I.P., under the multi-annual funding UIDB/04043/2020.

REFERENCES

Aitkazinov, A. (2023). The role of artificial intelligence in auditing: Opportunities and challenges. *International Journal of Research in Engineering. Science and Management*, *6*(6), 117–119.

Al-Sayyed, S., Al-Aroud, S., & Zayed, L. (2021). The effect of artificial intelligence technologies on audit evidence. *Accounting*, *7*(2), 281–288. doi:10.5267/j.ac.2020.12.003

Ali, S. M., Hasan, Z. J., Hamdan, A., & Al-Mekhlaf, M. (2022, March). Artificial Intelligence (AI) in the Education of Accounting and Auditing Profession. In *International Conference on Business and Technology* (pp. 656-664). Cham: Springer International Publishing.

Almeida, P., Santos, C., & Farias, J. (2021). Artificial intelligence regulation: A framework for governance. *Ethics and Information Technology*, *23*(3), 505–525. doi:10.1007/s10676-021-09593-z

Boucher, P. (2020). *Artificial intelligence: How does it work, why does it matter, and what can we do about it?* EPRS | European Parliamentary Research Service. *European Parliament.*, *641*, 547.

Cannarsa, M. (2021). Ethics guidelines for trustworthy AI. The Cambridge handbook of lawyering in the digital age, 283-297.

Couceiro, B., Pedrosa, I., & Marini, A. (2020). State of the art of artificial intelligence in internal audit context. In *2020 15th Iberian Conference on Information Systems and Technologies (CISTI)*, 1-7. IEEE. 10.23919/CISTI49556.2020.9140863

Cruz, R., Bertollo, D., & Camargo, M. (2020). *O Impacto da Inteligência Artificial na Auditoria: Uma Revisão Bibliográfica. In XX Mostra de Iniciação Científica.* UCS-PPGA.

Deloitte. (2017). A auditoria do futuro começa agora. *Portal da Deloitte*. Retrieved from https://www2.deloitte.com/content/dam/Deloitte/br/Documents/audit/Deloitte-Auditoria-do-Futuro.pdf

Deloitte. (2021). O auditor do futuro é digital. *Portal da Deloitte*. Retrieved from https://mundocorporativo.deloitte.com.br/o-auditor-do-futuro-e-digital

Díaz-Rodríguez, N., Del Ser, J., Coeckelbergh, M., de Prado, M. L., Herrera-Viedma, E., & Herrera, F. (2023). Connecting the dots in trustworthy Artificial Intelligence: From AI principles, ethics, and key requirements to responsible AI systems and regulation. *Information Fusion*, *99*, 101896. doi:10.1016/j.inffus.2023.101896

Fedyk, A., Hodson, J., Khimich, N., & Fedyk, T. (2022). Is artificial intelligence improving the audit process? *Review of Accounting Studies*, *27*(3), 938–985. doi:10.1007/s11142-022-09697-x

Han, H., Shiwakoti, R., Jarvis, R., Mordi, C., & Botchie, D. (2023). Accounting and auditing with blockchain technology and artificial Intelligence: A literature review. *International Journal of Accounting Information Systems*, *48*, 100598. doi:10.1016/j.accinf.2022.100598

Hasan, A. (2022). Artificial Intelligence (AI) in accounting & auditing: A Literature review. *Open Journal of Business and Management*, *10*(1), 440–465. doi:10.4236/ojbm.2022.101026

Hashid, A., & Almaqtari, F. (2024). The Impact of Artificial Intelligence and Industry 4.0 on Transforming Accounting and Auditing Practices. *Journal of Open Innovation*, 100218.

Hussein, H., Ammar, M., & Hassan, M. (2016). Induction Motors Stator Fault Analysis based on Artificial Intelligence. *Indonesian Journal of Electrical Engineering and Computer Science*, *2*(1), 69–78. doi:10.11591/ijeecs.v2.i1.pp69-78

Illia, L., Colleoni, E., & Zyglidopoulos, S. (2023). Ethical implications of text generation in the age of artificial intelligence. *Business Ethics, the Environment & Responsibility*, *32*(1), 201–210. doi:10.1111/beer.12479

ISA 200 - *Objetivos gerais do auditor independente e condução de uma auditoria de acordo com as normas internacionais de auditoria.* Manual de Normas Internacionais de Auditoria e Controle de Qualidade. IFAC.

Issa, H., Sun, T., & Vasarhelyi, M. (2016). Research Ideas for Artificial Intelligence in Auditing: The Formalization of Audit and Workforce Supplementation. *Journal of Emerging Technologies in Accounting*, *13*(2), 1–20. doi:10.2308/jeta-10511

KPMG. (2020). *Uma necessidade urgente de mudanças para a auditoria interna. Automação inteligente.* Retrieved from https://www.auditoria-interna-automacao.pdf (assets.kpmg)

Lehner, O., Ittonen, K., Silvola, H., Ström, E., & Wührleitner, A. (2022). Artificial intelligence based decision-making in accounting and auditing: Ethical challenges and normative thinking. *Accounting, Auditing & Accountability Journal*, *35*(9), 109–135. doi:10.1108/AAAJ-09-2020-4934

Lombardi, D., Bloch, R., & Vasarhelyi, M. (2014). The future of audit. *JISTEM-Journal of Information Systems and Technology Management*, *11*, 21–32.

Ma, J., Schneider, L., Lapuschkin, S., Achtibat, R., Duchrau, M., Krois, J., Schwendicke, F., & Samek, W. (2022). Towards trustworthy ai in dentistry. *Journal of Dental Research*, *101*(11), 1263–1268. doi:10.1177/00220345221106086 PMID:35746889

Martha, G. (2018). *Você, eu e os robôs: pequeno manual do mundo digital.* Atlas.

McCarthy, J. (2007). *What is artificial intelligence?* Stanford University. http://www-formal.stanford.edu/jmc/whatisai.pdf

Meira, M. (2019). *O impacto da Inteligência Artificial na Auditoria* (Master Thesis) Faculdade de Economia da Universidade do Porto.

Mökander, J. (2023). Auditing of AI: Legal, Ethical and Technical Approaches. *Digital Society : Ethics, Socio-Legal and Governance of Digital Technology*, *2*(3), 49. doi:10.1007/s44206-023-00074-y

Munoko, I., Brown-Liburd, H., & Vasarhelyi, M. (2020). The ethical implications of using artificial intelligence in auditing. *Journal of Business Ethics*, *167*(2), 209–234. doi:10.1007/s10551-019-04407-1

Noordin, N., Hussainey, K., & Hayek, A. (2022). The use of artificial intelligence and audit quality: An analysis from the perspectives of external auditors in the UAE. *Journal of Risk and Financial Management*, *15*(8), 339. doi:10.3390/jrfm15080339

Nunes, T., Leite, J., & Pedrosa, I. (2020). Automação Inteligente de Processos: Um Olhar sobre o Futuro da AuditoriaIn *15th Iberian Conference on Information Systems and Technologies.*

O'neil, C. (2017). *Weapons of math destruction: How big data increases inequality and threatens democracy.* Crown.

Oliveira, A. (2019). *Inteligência Artificial.* Fundação Francisco Manuel dos Santos Editora.

Omoteso, K. (2012). The application of artificial intelligence in auditing: Looking back to the future. *Expert Systems with Applications, 39*(9), 8490–8495. doi:10.1016/j.eswa.2012.01.098

PwC. (2019). *The Future of Audit. Perspectives on how the audit could evolve.* Retrieved from https://www.pwc-future-of-audit-report-july-2019.pdf

Rehman, A., & Hashim, F. (2022). Can Internal Audit Function Impact Artificial Intelligence? Case of Public Listed Companies of Oman. AIP Conference Proceedings, 2472(1), 040024. doi:10.1063/5.0092755

Reis, P. (2019). *O futuro da profissão de Auditoria* (Master Thesis). ISCAP Porto.

Reporting, E. Y. (2020). *A auditoria contínua enquanto ferramenta de gestão e impulsionador tecnológico.* Retrieved from https://valoreconomico.co.ao/artigo/a-auditoria-continua-enquanto-ferramenta-de-gestao-e-impulsionador-tecnologico

Rikhardsson, P., Thórisson, K., Bergthorsson, G., & Batt, C. (2021). Artificial intelligence and auditing in small- and medium-sized firms: Expectations and applications. *AI Magazine, 43*(3), 323–336. doi:10.1002/aaai.12066

Rodrigues, L. (2021). *O impacto da inteligência artificial na área e profissão de auditoria* (Master Thesis). Instituto Politécnico do Cávado e do Ave.

Seethamraju, R., & Hecimovic, A. (2020). Impact of Artificial Intelligence on Auditing - An Exploratory Study. *Americas Conference on Information Systems (AMCIS2020) Proceedings, 8.*

Seethamraju, R., & Hecimovic, A. (2023). Adoption of artificial intelligence in auditing: An exploratory study. *Australian Journal of Management, 48*(4), 780–800. doi:10.1177/03128962221108440

Serman, D. (2016). *Auditor robô? A Inteligência Artificial como aliada da Auditoria. Plataforma do Linkedin.* Retrieved from https://pt.linkedin.com/pulse/auditor-rob%C3%B4-intelig%C3%AAncia-artificial-como-aliada-da-auditoria-serman

Stahl, B. (2022). Responsible innovation ecosystems: Ethical implications of the application of the ecosystem concept to artificial intelligence. *International Journal of Information Management, 62*, 102441. doi:10.1016/j.ijinfomgt.2021.102441

Taulli, T. (2020). *Introdução à Inteligência Artificial: Uma abordagem não técnica.* Novatec Editora.

Uglum, M. (2021). Consideration of the ethical implications of artificial intelligence in the audit profession. *Honors Program Theses.* 496.

UNESCO. (2020) *Recommendation on the ethics of artificial intelligence.* Digital Library UNESDOC. en.unesco.org

ADDITIONAL READING

Abou-El-Sood, H., Kotb, A., & Allam, A. (2019). Exploring auditors' perceptions of the usage and importance of audit information technology. *International Journal of Auditing*, *19*(3), 252–266. doi:10.1111/ijau.12039

Albawwat, I., & Frijat, Y. (2021). An analysis of auditors' perceptions towards artificial intelligence and its contribution to audit quality. *Accounting*, *7*(4), 755–762. doi:10.5267/j.ac.2021.2.009

Bizarro, P. A., & Dorian, M. (2017). Artificial intelligence: The future of auditing. *Internal Auditing*, *32*, 21–26.

Estep, C., Griffith, E., & MacKenzie, N. (2023). How do financial executives respond to the use of artificial intelligence in financial reporting and auditing? *Review of Accounting Studies*, 1–34. doi:10.1007/s11142-023-09771-y

European Commission. (2021). *Proposal for a Regulation of the European Parliament and of the Council laying down harmonized rules on artificial intelligence (Artificial Intelligence Act) and amending certain union legislative acts* (COM/2021/206 final).

Oluwagbade, O. I., Boluwaji, O. D., Azeez, O. A., & Njengo, L. M. (2024). Challenges and Opportunities of Implementing Artificial Intelligence in Auditing Practices: A Case Study of Nigerian Accounting Firms. *Asian Journal of Economics. Business and Accounting*, *24*(1), 32–45.

PwC. (2021). *Blockchain and smart contract automation: How smart contracts automate digital business*. Portal PwC.

Reporting, E. Y. (2020). *A auditoria contínua enquanto ferramenta de gestão e impulsionador tecnológico*. Retrieved from https://valoreconomico.co.ao/artigo/a-auditoria-continua-enquanto-ferramenta-de-gestao-e-impulsionador-tecnologico

Ribeiro, C. (2019). A Auditoria na era da tecnologia - Auditor 4.0. *Medium*. Retrieved from https://medium.com/@oriebir.lorak/a-auditoria-na-era-da-tecnologia-auditor-4-0-3ff9ca384acd

Stahl, B. C. (2021). *Artificial intelligence for a better future: an ecosystem perspective on the ethics of AI and emerging digital technologies*. Springer Nature. doi:10.1007/978-3-030-69978-9

Wang, Y., Gou, Y., Guo, Y., & Wang, H. H. (2020, June). Construction of Audit Internal Control Intelligent System Based on Blockchain and Cloud Storage. In *2020 4th International Conference on Trends in Electronics and Informatics (ICOEI) (48184)* (pp. 292-295). IEEE. 10.1109/ICOEI48184.2020.9143061

KEY TERMS AND DEFINITIONS

Artificial Intelligence: Multidisciplinary science that develops and applies computational techniques that resemble human behavior, potentially replacing humans in many tasks.

Audit Evidence: Set of information gathered by audit professionals that support the Auditor's opinion.

Audit Procedures: Procedures performed by the auditor (tests of controls and substantive procedures) in the auditing process to obtain audit evidence.

Auditor's Report: Report where the Auditor issues their opinion, which can be modified or unmodified.

Financial Auditing: The process performed by an auditing professional aimed at verifying whether the financial statements contain materially relevant distortions.

Non-Big4: Audit firms that are not part of the Big 4 are composed of Ernst & Young (EY), KPMG, and PwC.

Statutory Auditors: Audit professional registered in a professional auditing order, which in Portugal is the Ordem dos Revisores Oficiais de Contas (OROC).

Chapter 10
The Effect of Artificial Intelligence on the Accounting Profession

Dima Saeed Abdulhay
Beirut Arab University, Lebanon

ABSTRACT

This chapter examines how artificial intelligence (AI) is affecting the accounting sector with a particular emphasis on Lebanon. It examines the significant shifts that brought about information and communications technology (ICT)-based technologies and automation, in addition to the historical changes in accounting. The combination of AI awareness and accounting automation has resulted in a significant revolution in the industry, which has boosted AI-powered accounting education. The chapter suggests ongoing AI advancements as well as proactive cooperation between accountants and accounting companies in order to increase the effectiveness and efficiency of accounting procedures. AI can cut expenses and free up accountants' time so they may focus on making decisions using analytics and data. However, the Middle Eastern accounting sector is confronted with a number of potential risks, such as the loss of jobs, the spread of artificial intelligence in the sector, the decline in human bias, the impact on accounting education, and the recurrence of past accounting mishaps.

1. INTRODUCTION

Over the years, there has been some significant advancement in the accounting sector. Double-entry accounting, for instance, has been around for around 500 years. But the information and communications technology (ICT) revolution of the twenty-first century has ushered in a new era of change that has fundamentally altered the way that many organizations run. Specifically, automation technologies are transforming accounting practices and increasing the bar for implementing innovative solutions.

These days, accounting automation covers the entire accounting lifecycle, not just financial management departments. By simplifying processes like data recording, modification, and evaluation, this all-inclusive approach reduces the need for manual data entry and bookkeeping (Chukwuani et al., 2020).

DOI: 10.4018/979-8-3693-0847-9.ch010

The growth of robotic process automation (RPA), which automates manual, repetitive, and rule-based accounting tasks using software tools, provides more proof of this trend (Boulton, 2018).

Artificial intelligence is another revolutionary component that is transforming the accounting industry (AI). Because of its capabilities in machine learning, data mining, and semantic analysis, artificial intelligence (AI) has the potential to greatly increase the efficacy and accuracy of a number of accounting procedures, including financial reporting, fraud detection, and auditing. Businesses are starting to adopt AI and RPA technology even though it is still in its early phases, and their investments are paying off handsomely (Mohammad et al., 2020).

Artificial intelligence has an impact on practically every aspect of life, not only productivity. Accounting practices and processes are being radically changed by artificial intelligence, which is automating boring tasks and permeating daily life. The automation of accounting procedures has led to the abandonment of traditional accounting techniques (Al Hamad et al., 2022).

One of AI's primary advantages for the accounting sector is that it can speed up job processing times, freeing up accountants to focus on more crucial work. One technology development that increases efficiency is OCR software, which makes data collection procedures simpler (Lee &Tajudeen, 2020). AI additionally improves accounting data's correctness, insights, and dependability; yet, it also has disadvantages that call for the development of new talents, like job displacement and ethical conundrums (Askary et al., 2018; Chapple et al., 2020).

It's also critical to consider how AI might be used to effectively fight accounting fraud. AI offers a complete fraud protection solution with its powerful analytical powers and real-time monitoring tools. Machine learning algorithms, such those that analyze transaction data from the past to find trends that can point to fraudulent activity, enable early identification and intervention. Natural language processing algorithms can be used to search texts, such as emails and financial records, for clues about potential fraud or questionable communication patterns.AI-powered anomaly detection systems can also spot unusual financial transactions or behaviors that deviate from the norm, allowing for quicker investigations and a lower chance of fraud. Artificial intelligence and block chain technologies may also increase auditability and transparency while reducing fraud. By making full use of AI, accounting professionals can enhance their methods for spotting and preventing fraud, safeguarding financial integrity, and fostering professional trust.

Artificial intelligence (AI) based anomaly detection systems are also capable of identifying strange or unusual activity, including financial transactions, which expedites investigations and lowers the risk of fraud. Artificial intelligence and blockchain technology have the potential to reduce fraud and increase auditability and transparency. By making the most of AI, accounting professionals can enhance their methods for spotting and preventing fraud, maintaining financial integrity, and fostering professional trust.

Because it explores the relationship between AI and accounting and addresses significant issues including increasing productivity, ethical quandaries, and the evolving role of accounting professionals, this research is significant. This chapter fills a knowledge vacuum by examining the implications of artificial intelligence on the accounting sector and offering theoretical and management perspectives. This information can be useful to accounting professionals, industry stakeholders, and policymakers.

This chapter's first portion, which is divided up into several sections, provides a brief synopsis of the ways artificial intelligence is influencing the accounting sector. The theoretical foundations and earlier studies on the relationship between AI and accounting are next examined. The section that follows discusses how artificial intelligence has affected the accounting sector throughout the Middle East, with a focus on Lebanon. The chapter concludes with recommendations for future lines of inquiry.

2. THEORETICAL BACKGROUND AND LITERATURE REVIEW

2.1. Theoretical Background

This part examines the theoretical foundations of the research topic as well as the intricate relationships between artificial intelligence and the accounting sector. It also provides clarification on previous studies that examined the various impacts of AI on the accounting sector.

The evolution of artificial intelligence over the last century is proof of both human ingenuity and technology progress. Artificial intelligence (AI) has consistently pushed boundaries, transformed markets, and opened up new opportunities since its inception and continues to do so now. The first computer game, "El Ajedrecista," created in 1914 by Spanish inventor Leonardo Torres, allowed players to play chess on its own. This was a major advancement in the way algorithms and machine hardware were integrated (Mohammad et al., 2020).

Over the ensuing decades, cooperative endeavors across numerous academic and industry domains have endeavored to explore the complexities and potential of artificial intelligence. Researchers including Claude Shannon, Nathaniel Rochester, John McCarthy, Marvin Minsky, and others proposed a groundbreaking research initiative in 1956 that represented concerted efforts to explore artificial intelligence's potential for cognition. A ground-breaking study by McCarthy et al. (2006) sought to explain how computers might comprehend language, abstract ideas, tackle difficult issues that humans could only solve in the past, and even get better over time.

AI's revolutionary ramifications for society were revealed at pivotal moments in its development. Joseph Weizenbaum's 1966 innovation, ELIZA, revolutionized artificial intelligence-driven conversational interaction by providing users with contextually relevant responses. Simultaneously, the creation of "Kismet" by Cynthia Breazeal in 2000 demonstrated how artificial intelligence could detect and respond to human social cues, paving the way for the creation of emotionally intelligent robots (Best, 2017).

However, IBM's Watson in 2011 may have been one of the most significant developments in AI history. During a three-night Jeopardy contest, this cognitive computing system stunned audiences all around the world with its astounding comprehension and response to challenging natural language questions. According to IBM researchers' "DeepQA" tool, Watson sorted through enormous volumes of data faster than two of the competition's most formidable competitors thanks to its enormous processing capability. IBM's Watson was a ground-breaking technology with applications beyond game shows, including, mentioning just two, financing and healthcare. Notably, Watson's diagnostic skills transformed patient care in the medical field by enabling the identification of ailments and the discovery of cures (Mohammad et al., 2020).

Numerous industries have been impacted by IBM's Watson, and as a result, numerous AI systems have been developed in an attempt to match its cognitive powers. The fact that AI is still being used in business processes demonstrates both how revolutionary this technology can be and how swiftly artificial intelligence is taking over our society. These developments necessitate further research into the intricate relationships between artificial intelligence (AI) and the accounting industry. When artificial intelligence (AI) is used more extensively, it could drastically change accounting practices; hence accounting professionals' duties in the digital age will need to be reevaluated.

2.2 Accounting Theory in the Age of Artificial Intelligence

Reexamining long-held views is required since AI in accounting involves a paradigm change from previous methodologies. This section examines three significant accounting theories that have developed in response to the incorporation of AI: the Intelligent Mechanism Theory, the New Theory of Management Accounting, and the Value Creation Theory.

2.2.1 The New Theory of Management Accounting: Embracing Automation Without Compromising Human Intellect

The New Theory of Management Accounting emphasizes the advantages of human-robot complementarity as AI is incorporated into accounting procedures more and more. While automation technologies can expedite financial procedures and provide essential data, strategic decision-making still requires human judgment. This viewpoint holds that accountants should use AI to supplement rather than replace their current skill set, go above and beyond their regular responsibilities, and embrace a more analytical and strategic approach. This theory acknowledges the ways in which AI is transforming accounting practices. It recognizes that while financial processes are made simpler by artificial intelligence (AI), strategic decisions still require human judgment.In the backdrop of examining how AI is revolutionizing the accounting business, thus chapter highlights how accountants' roles are evolving from simple executors to strategic consultants. It emphasizes how accountants must use AI to hone their analytical abilities and provide stakeholders with access to information that is advantageous to the business. By comprehending how AI complements rather than replaces human cognition, researchers may examine how accountants adapt to the integration of AI and traverse the evolving area of management accounting (Shanmuganathan, 2020).

2.2.2 Value Creation Theory: Maximizing Enterprise Value in the Digital Era

In the era of artificial intelligence, Value Creation Theory—which highlights the relationship between financial operations and the goal of growing business value—has become even more pertinent. A few ways that AI-enabled analytics may assist firms in improving their value chains are through deeper insights into cash flow patterns, risk management strategies, and consumer value propositions. This idea suggests that accounting practices should advance to fully integrate the value-creation process, leveraging artificial intelligence to enhance financial analysis and decision-making. As companies strive to boost shareholder value and gain a competitive edge in the AI era, value creation theory is becoming more and more significant.This idea suggests that accounting practices should advance to fully integrate the value creation process and leverage AI-driven insights in order to improve financial performance.For scholars researching how AI is transforming the accounting sector, Value Creation Theory offers insights into how AI helps accountants better comprehend cash flow dynamics, risk management strategies, and client value propositions. By understanding how AI enhances value creation within businesses, researchers can assess the wider effects of AI on accounting practices and organizational performance (Horne, 2018).

2.2.3 Intelligent Mechanism Theory: Navigating Uncertainty through Adaptive Management

Intelligent Mechanism Theory offers AI-enabled adaptive management strategies in the face of erratic external events. Businesses may efficiently handle uncertainty by utilizing intelligent agents that can create goals, provide internal data, and incentivize responsible behavior. This notion highlights how important it is to have flexible frameworks for decision-making that leverage AI-driven insights to achieve strategic initiatives and meet business goals. Intelligent Mechanism Theory emphasizes the value of adaptive management strategies in reducing uncertainty and enhancing organizational performance.In this hypothesis, goal-setting, internal reporting, and rewarding moral behavior should be handled by AI-powered intelligent entities. The Intelligent Mechanism Theory looks at the impact artificial intelligence (AI) is having on the accounting industry and explains how AI helps frameworks for dynamic decision-making. Scholars should look into how accountants can use AI-driven insights to successfully lead strategic initiatives and adjust to changing external conditions. By understanding how AI increases businesses' capacity for adaptation, researchers may assess its effects on accounting practices and organizational resilience (Mohammad et al., 2020).

In conclusion, by providing theoretical frameworks that enable researchers to examine how accountants' roles are changing, how this influences the creation of organizational value, and how adaptive organizations are to technological change, each of these theories adds something worthwhile to the discussion about how artificial intelligence (AI) is affecting the accounting profession. With AI's introduction into the accounting sector, an unprecedented era of innovation and change has begun. Accounting professionals can benefit from AI's potential to create value, enhance decision-making, and handle the difficulties of the digital age if they adopt AI-enabled technology while maintaining a solid theoretical foundation.

2.3 Literature Review

Changes to our environment have begun as a result of recent advances in artificial intelligence and robotics and their practical uses. The field of accounting and the services it offers to businesses are undergoing profound transformations. There has been a meteoric rise in the popularity of AI-powered accounting solutions in the last several years. Jones made the comment in the 2020.

As the accounting profession has moved away from human data entry and toward automated computer systems, (Janaki and Clifford, 2021) observed that AI usage has increased.

While (Qiu and Lin, 2021) focused on China, other research has examined the most significant effects of AI on accounting globally. To determine whether accounting performance and AI adoption were related, they analyzed data from 235 publicly traded companies across the nation. The bottom lines of Chinese businesses saw a significant improvement after AI was used. Artificial intelligence has the potential to improve the quality of financial reports while also making them more open and accountable.

(Seda, 2021) states that research into the potential effects of AI on Saudi Arabian accounting has already taken place. The author sought the advice of renowned accountants and financial experts to achieve the goal of her qualitative investigation. Studies done in Saudi Arabia suggest that the accounting industry could benefit from artificial intelligence (AI) in terms of increased efficiency and accuracy. Accounting processes and financial reporting are expected to be enhanced with the help of AI.

In the same year (Sari and Rahardjo, 2021) academics from Indonesia looked at how AI may affect the reliability of publicly traded bank accounts. Utilizing data from 69 companies listed on the Indonesian stock market, they studied how AI affects the trustworthiness of financial reporting. The use of AI has greatly improved the speed and accuracy of accounting data, especially financial reporting. Their research shows that accounting businesses in Indonesia could gain from using AI strategies that increase efficiency and production.

According to (Al-Dalahma and Al-Amyan, 2019), the accounting business in Jordan has been impacted by AI. The study concluded that AI significantly affects the accounting industry based on interviews with Jordanian chartered accountants. Staying current with technology advances, especially those related to artificial intelligence, is crucial for accountants who wish to maintain their existing employment, according to the research.

Changes in accounting, financial analysis, and decision-making may be substantial if AI can supplant human error with more precise data. There are many more places you may get apps like this, such as:

Based on their findings, (Li and Guo, 2021) speculate that AI's capacity to process massive datasets may significantly alter fundamental accounting tasks such as financial analysis and reconciliation.

A literature study on accounting AI was carried out by (Muralidharan, 2021) as part of his bibliometric research. Increasing numbers of academics are focusing on the potential of artificial intelligence (AI) to improve the accuracy of financial evaluations, decision-making, and mistake suppression.

Artificial intelligence (AI) could transform the banking industry in ways beyond just automating routine accounting operations. Possible advantages include reduced expenditure, improved financial reporting transparency, and reduced room for human mistake in decision-making. As a conclusion, several studies have covered a wide range of subjects, and AI is already having an impact on accounting organizations, as stated by Hammad (2021). The accounting firm's AI is going to automate data entry, reconciliation, and audit trials, as planned.

In their study on the impact of AI on accounting, Shafiq and Mahmood (2020) employed bibliometrics analysis. Based on their findings, we may be able to improve accuracy, cut expenses, and provide more trustworthy financial reports if we integrate AI into accounting procedures. Artificial intelligence (AI) might drastically cut down on mistakes, which would make things more trustworthy (Li, 2020). One possible use for accountants is the generation of more accurate predictions and data inputs (Maione and Leoni, 2021). Since the amount of data is always growing, there seems to be a need for better reporting tools, and sharper predictions are also in high demand, accounting professionals have started to rely on AI technology (Tiwari and Khan, 2020).

The prospective impacts of AI on accountants were the primary topic of (Mohammad et al.'s, 2020) future-oriented research. This study aims to analyze the impact of AI on the accounting profession so that relevant governments can benefit from these advancements. Here we will examine how these technological advancements have altered the accounting industry.The findings suggest that modern accountants can relax while an automated system driven by AI takes care of all the tedious but necessary jobs.

To stay ahead of this problem, accounting companies must embrace technology and adapt to the changes. Accountants and accounting firms may be able to improve their services by keeping themselves informed of breakthroughs in artificial intelligence. If accountants can effectively transition their attention from menial, repetitive tasks to decision-making powered by data and analytics, we should see a decline in the value of the accounting business and a drop in accounting costs for firms (Stancheva-Todorova, 2018).

According to the Financial Stability Board's definition, artificial intelligence is the application of computational technology to do jobs that once needed human comprehension. Artificial intelligence's

Table 1. Summary of studies that show the impact of AI on the Accounting profession

Focus of Study	Study and Authors	Key Findings
Evolution of AI in accounting	General Trends (Janaki and Clifford, 2021)	Shift from traditional ways to digitalized ways.
AI Impact on National Practices	Chinese Accounting Practices (Qiu and Lin, 2021) &Saudi Arabian Accounting Methods (Seda, 2021)	AI positively impacts financial performance. Improves financial report quality Increases efficiency and precision Reduces resource requirements.
AI's Impact on Financial Reporting	Indonesian Stock Exchange (Sari and Rahardjo, 2021)	Positive influence on financial reporting quality.
AI Automation and Error Reduction	Automating Basic Accounting Operations (Li and Guo, 2021) &Error Reduction (Li, 2020; Maione and Leoni, 2021; Tiwari and Khan, 2020)	AI automates basic operations Improves financial analysis Reduces error rates in various accounting tasks
AI's Future Impact and Guidance	Future Implications for Accountants (Mohammad et al., 2020) &Recommendations for Accountants(Stancheva-Todorova, E. P., 2018)	Accountants should adapt to AI-driven automation for efficiency. Staying updated on AI advancements for better decision-making.
AI Definition and Characteristics	Financial Stability Board's Perspective (Financial Stability (Ali, S. et al., 2023)	AI has outstanding characteristics Enhances autonomy in accounting.
AI's Influence on the Jordanian Accounting Profession	Jordanian Accounting Profession (Al-Dalahma and Al-Amyan, 2019)	AI applications have a substantial influence on the profession in Jordan.

Source: Done by the researcher

(AI) remarkable capabilities and capacity to resolve the most intractable problems have the tech sector gushing over it. Intelligence agents, AI immunity, neural networks, and processing capacity are a few examples. Autonomy, self-tuning, self-configuration, self-monitoring, and self-healing are the most effective AI systems for accounting operations, according to (Ali et al. 2023).

The results show that accounting has the potential to change, that businesses must adopt new technologies, and that AI may boost accuracy, efficiency, and financial reporting.

Table 1 offers a more organized summary of the research topics and findings by categorizing relevant studies based on their priority and focus.

2.3.1. AI Revolutionizing Accounting in the Middle East: Implications for Lebanon and Beyond

According to studies conducted in southern Nigeria, the use of AI enhanced accounting operations (Hasan, 2022). This shows how far-reaching AI implications are for accounting firms in the Middle East and Lebanon in particular. According to (Mohammad et al. 2020), accounting will be significantly impacted by AI, especially in the long run. The arrival of AI is expected to cause a dramatic shift in the accounting industry in the next decade, according to studies (Li et al., 2022).

Despite early challenges and professional hesitation, (Vărzaru, 2022) expects that management accounting would achieve great outcomes by integrating AI. Furthermore, (Hu's, 2022) research shows that AI will have a significant impact on the accounting business, resulting in its widespread adoption and the creation of cutting-edge accounting software powered by AI. According to (Rosi and Mahyuni, 2021), the research also looked at current problems and how AI has affected the growth of the accounting sector. (Kindzeka, 2023) contends that the accounting profession will be one of many that AI will profoundly impact. This view is shared by an increasing number of scholars. Accountants in Lebanon and the Middle East will start using AI. Accounting practices, audit quality, and overall accounting operations might all be drastically changed by the advent of AI, according to the study's authors. Accounting firms in the area would do well to use AI if they want to maintain their competitive edge in the future.The rapid advancement of AI is having an impact on many sectors, accounting included. Artificial intelligence (AI) will have an impact on the Middle Eastern accounting business, namely in Lebanon. This article examines the current state of accounting in Lebanon and the surrounding Middle Eastern countries in relation to artificial intelligence (AI), as well as the potential future effects of AI on accounting positions.

The accounting industry has been profoundly impacted by the rise and development of AI, especially in the Middle East.

2.3.2. Navigating the AI Revolution: Transforming European Accounting Practices for the Digital Age

The accounting industry in Europe is increasingly under the microscope and being impacted by AI. Studies that have concentrated on the significant disruptive effects of AI on accounting staff have highlighted the necessity for firms to adapt to technological advancements. For Wael, 2023 was a watershed year. There are a lot of potential upsides to integrating AI into accounting processes, but there are also some potential downsides, such as income and wealth disparities, job loss, and an increase in the need for qualified staff (Hasan, 2022). The advent of artificial intelligence (AI) may have both beneficial and bad consequences, according to Hasan (2022), including the potential obliteration of traditional accounting and auditing professions. The use of AI has the potential to improve both precision and productivity. However, it will bring up issues related to income inequality. In light of the exponential growth of AI, it is critical for European businesses to take use of this technology's ability to transform accounting processes and encourage innovation. If accounting is to succeed in the digital era, they must also cope with difficulties.

Accounting is undergoing profound transformation as a result of advancements in artificial intelligence (AI) that are altering long-established methods and procedures. Studies have shown that AI might have significant effects on the accounting sector, thus accountants will have to learn to use new technologies and incorporate AI into their work to improve efficiency and accuracy (Azman et al., 2021). Incorporating AI into accounting is anticipated to improve business outcomes through the mitigation of errors, mitigation of risks, enhancement of efficiency, and enhancement of human resource productivity (Azman et al., 2021). Due to the widespread belief that accounting firms must incorporate AI into their operations and services going forward, a number of these companies have made substantial investments in AI technology (Azman et al., 2021). European accounting professionals need to learn to use AI, develop their skills, and embrace AI innovations if they want to foster innovation, enhance decision-making, and remain competitive in the dynamic digital market.

Artificial intelligence (AI) is changing the way accountants work by improving decision-making, automating mundane jobs, and making data analytics more powerful. The accounting sector stands to gain a great deal from artificial intelligence (AI), according to recent research. AI has the ability to revolutionize financial reporting, identify anomalies, and guarantee audit quality. Furthermore, Joh et al. Integrating AI into accounting procedures would free up accountants to focus on higher-value jobs like consulting and strategic analysis (Neumann et al., 2019). Accountants' time will be freed up, and productivity will rise as a result. Accounting AI deployments raise questions about data protection, cyber security, and the necessity of staff training to exploit AI effectively. By incorporating AI into their practice, European accounting professionals may better respond to changing client needs, encourage new ideas, and maintain a competitive edge in the modern digital marketplace.

2.3.3 From Early Notions to Contemporary Realities: Tracing the Evolution and Impact of Artificial Intelligence

Research on AI continues even if a lot of time has passed. Explore the history, development, and possible future uses of artificial intelligence to learn more about its structure and how it works (Haenlein& Kaplan, 2019). Going to big AI conferences and paying attention to the evaluations of leadership, impact, and effect is one approach to stay updated on the latest advancements in machine learning and artificial intelligence (Audibert et al., 2022). A turning point in the development of artificial intelligence, as shown in the study, happened when people hurriedly gave machines powers that were previously only available to humans (Haladjian&Montemayor, 2016). Using a global patent survey to examine the patterns of innovation in various AI disciplines is another way to measure AI progress (Liu et al., 2021). Considering AI's achievements and shortcomings can enrich our present and future knowledge of the field(Andreu-Pérez et al., 2017). When considered collectively, these sources paint a vivid picture of AI's development across time, touching on topics including turning points, groundbreaking discoveries, and the technology's far-reaching effects on other fields. Understanding artificial intelligence (AI) today and tomorrow requires an understanding of its roots. Artificial intelligence (AI), which has been around since computers were invented, could improve accounting services (Stancheva, 2018). Optimistic predictions about the field's rapid progress made by (Marvin Minsky, 1956) sparked advancements in artificial intelligence.(Issa et al. 2016) found that inadequate government financing and negative reviews prevented AI development from reaching its early potential. But in 1980, when the British government began investing in artificial intelligence technologies to compete with Japan's, there was a temporary upsurge in interest. During the years 1987–1993, interest waned because to computer manufacture and restricted government support. Once the year 1993 passed, the accounting industry's utilization of AI skyrocketed. Consider the loss of IBM's chess champion in 1997 and the fact that one of IBM's software programs won a quiz show in 2011 (Greenman, 2017).

2.3.4. AI Revolutionizing Banking: Innovations, Applications, and Future Prospects

The banking and financial industries are undergoing a dramatic transformation due to the extensive use of artificial intelligence (AI). According to (Dong, 2018), (Yildirim et al. 2023) looks into how companies are using AI tactics to increase production and enhance financial management efficiency. (Rahim et al.

2018) asserts that smart contracts and artificial intelligence will have a significant impact on Islamic banking. You might provide a prediction on the future of artificial intelligence (AI) and its applications in Islamic banking, focusing on the ways in which it could benefit Islamic finance (Tayachi et al., 2022). (Kazachenko et al. 2023) states that block chain technology is being used in ESG (environmental, social, and governance) financing as an example of how artificial intelligence is influencing the financial sector.

According to (Ahmed et al. 2022), a bibliometric analysis could help us better understand where AI and ML are at in the banking industry, provides insight into the revolutionary potential of AI in the financial sector by exploring the effects of AI and robotics on the business landscape (Dirican, 2015). The study of green investment for sustainable development is one of the numerous possible applications of artificial intelligence in the financial sector, according to research by (Duraivelu et al. 2022).

Artificial intelligence (AI) is the catchall term used by Ernst & Young (EY) to describe a variety of automation technologies that can simulate and, in some cases, surpass human intelligence. Robotic process automation solutions include rule-based automation, structured data processing, and unattended automation. Cognitive automation systems integrate RPA and AI by utilizing machine learning, human-in-the-loop operations, and data interpretation abilities.

Natural language processing, decision-making, autonomous vision and reading, and deep learning are some of the features of AI systems, which include chat bots (SEOW et al. 2019). How computers can learn new information, create opinions, and forecast future outcomes using existing data is the subject of machine learning, a subfield of AI. Due to automation, accountants now have more time to offer high-quality consulting services (Duffy, 2018).

Experts in many fields, including accounting, need a solid grounding in artificial intelligence (AI) to understand how the technology can improve client service, streamline operations, and generate new ideas, all of which have the potential to radically alter the financial services industry.

2.3.5 Navigating the Evolution of Accounting: Embracing AI, Ethical Considerations, and Workforce Dynamics

Technologies like AI and accounting automation are highly prized in today's banking sector. Artificial intelligence (AI) has improved the accuracy and efficiency of the accounting sector. Drew attention to the necessity to consider biases in the development and implementation of AI systems, and emphasize the significance of AI systems that prioritize ethics (Mehrabi et al., 2021). To understand how accounting is changing to include AI, one must look into the many responsibilities, skills, and tasks linked to AI-based accounting (Leitner-Hanetseder et al., 2021).

When auditors and accountants employ AI, it raises a lot of ethical concerns. Explain what normative thinking is and how it could be used to tackle the problems caused by auditing and accounting firms' reliance on AI for decision-making (Lehner et al., 2022). (Mansor et al. 2022) found that accounting majors, who already have a lot of experience in the industry, would gain a lot from learning about artificial intelligence. Accounting has been transformed by process automation, which has made once labor-intensive activities much easier and more exact. Perform research that highlights the pros and cons of accounting work automation in order to add to the existing literature on accounting automation (Stoica&Feleagă, 2022). Explore the effects of RPA on international accounting firms, paying special attention to the ways in which automation has boosted efficiency and adaptability (Fernandez &Aman, 2018).Accounting software, automation, AI, and other forms of communication and information technology have had a significant impact on the accounting sector. Accountants now have more options with fewer steps to complete tasks because of these technological advancements.

The job has evolved substantially due to the decreasing dependence on human systems or recordings and the automation of repetitive tasks. Accounting educators are cognizant of the potential future impact of technology on the profession and work toward simplifying the work of entry-level accountants.

2.4. Integration of Artificial Intelligence and Accounting

The relationship between artificial intelligence and accounting has been the subject of several recent studies. Human accountants may soon become obsolete, according to research on the impact of AI on accounting by (Li and Zheng, 2018). According to (Yang et al. 2019), accounting automation is a great way for SMEs to utilize AI. New roles, responsibilities, and technical competence in accounting are crucial in the era of artificial intelligence, according to (Acemoğlu & Restrepo, 2018). The current crop of accounting majors is woefully unprepared when it comes to sophisticated artificial intelligence (Ameen et al. 2021). Accounting firms and accountants' employment prospects may be affected by AI, as indicated by this study's findings.

2.4.1. Analyzing and Strategically Utilizing Automation, Not as a Replacement

Recent conversations have focused on the possible benefits of artificial intelligence (AI) in the accounting field. While AI has the potential to revolutionize accounting practices, it is more likely to augment human expertise than to supplant it. An awareness of human-robot interaction is necessary; say (Parasuraman and Riley, 1997), to assess the risks of over- or under-reliance on automated technology. In their analysis of the challenges of generating personalized writing tools, (Conijn et al. 2020) emphasize the critical importance of finding effective automated solutions. (Hu et al.2022) states that accountants can enhance their accuracy and productivity by utilizing artificial intelligence. Quick changes are occurring in the accounting industry.

2.4.2. Job Portfolio Impact and Work Efficiency

To research the relationship between job portfolio impact and work efficiency, many factors must be properly taken into account. These factors include those that affect job satisfaction, performance, and organizational outcomes. (Heimerl et al. 2020) found that there has to be more research on some aspects of the job that make hospitality workers happy in order to boost workplace health and productivity. (Tong et al. 2022) highlights the importance of competence, equilibrium, and concentration in environmental management for a portfolio of environmental activities to be as effective as feasible. The impact of integrating sustainability-related limitations into decision-making processes is examined by (Herzel et al. 2012), who also examine the cost of sustainability in perfect portfolio decisions.

2.4.3. Displacement of Jobs

Layoffs, industrial closures, and economic downturns all lead to people losing their jobs, which impact both the economy and those directly impacted. (Sullivan and Wachter, 2009) reveal that this phenomenon has long-term repercussions, drawing attention to the U-shaped influence of job migration on death rates for older workers. This demonstrates how being unemployed can have lifelong consequences. Some of the most far-reaching consequences of job displacement that (Davis &Wachter, 2011) examine include health problems, decreased educational attainment for children of relocated workers, and economic instability. What Ttunen & Kellokumpu found in their study According to (Huttunen & Kellokumpu, 2016), couples' decisions to start a family are impacted by work relocation, which is one of the numerous non-monetary impacts of displacement.

2.4.4. Navigating the AI Frontier: Exploring Efficiency, Skills, and Labor Dynamics in the Accounting Industry

Many in the accounting industry are curious about the potential effects of AI on efficiency, precision, and workflow. (Hasan, 2022) notes the potential advantages of enhanced efficiency and productivity in his study of AI's broader applicability in accounting and auditing. He also acknowledges the problems, such as wage disparity and labor changes. (Leitner-Hanetseder et al. 2021) examine the changing roles and skills required in AI-driven accounting to clarify how accounting is evolving alongside AI. Research on AI agents in this context by (Rahwan et al. 2019) suggests that, rather than displacing people, AI could enhance human decision-making. (Frey and Osborne, 2017) reveal shifts in labor dynamics and the growing long-term profitability of automation by analyzing the occupations that could be automated. (Cox, 2022) examines the potential impact of AI integration on academic libraries through the lens of competency literature, revealing how the subject could undergo a revolution.

2.4.5. Navigating the AI Transition: Implications and Adaptations in Middle Eastern Accounting Practices

In countries like Lebanon and others in the Middle East, human accountants may be displaced by AI, which may simplify operations and reduce mistakes. Some of these roles include:

a. Vacant job opportunities: In light of AI's potential to automate routine accounting operations, some are concerned that accountants as we know them may soon be obsolete. Accounting jobs may be cut in half by 2025 if current trends in technology continue (Mohammad et al. 2020).
b. Artificial Intelligence and Accounting Firms: The most reputable accounting companies have begun utilizing AI for a range of purposes, such as accounting and the detection of significant errors in financial accounts. In addition to making human accountants obsolete, this may radically alter the accounting industry on a worldwide scale, according to (Mohammad et al. 2020).
c. Prejudice Eliminated by Algorithms: AI-powered algorithms have the potential to enforce laws and regulations without bias, unlike biased humans. (Manyika et al. 2019) state that this might increase the trustworthiness of financial accounting while also decreasing the conventional necessity for human accountants.
d. Effects on Accounting Education: The high starting costs of AI in accounting could discourage recent college grads and certified public accountants in Lebanon from going into computer science or other STEM fields (Tandiono, 2023). Equally plausible is the possibility that they will opt to switch their focus to accounting.

Addressing Past Scandals: AI-based programs are seen as a way to eliminate collusion and malpractices by strictly adhering to accounting standards, providing a higher level of transparency, and reducing the potential for fraudulent activities in financial reporting.

In conclusion, while artificial intelligence technology has enormous potential for improving the efficiency and accuracy of accounting procedures, its incorporation into the accounting profession in Lebanon and the Middle East brings both possibilities and obstacles. Accounting professionals must adapt to these developments, learn new skills, and traverse an ever-changing terrain in order to prosper in the AI era.

2.5. How AI avoids the Possibility of Financial Fraud

Traditional accounting roles, which are primarily found in small and medium-sized businesses, do not really differentiate labor responsibilities within the accounting department. Because everyone in finance has access to the bookkeeping and cash flow, there is a lack of organization, which might encourage financial fraud by providing opportunities for self-serving criminals to further their own interests. But with artificial intelligence, a lot of accounting and associated work will be done by computers; accounting staff will just need to input instructions and check them. The system will automatically settle the bill and run the trial balance at the conclusion of the session. Every accounting staff member has certain rights in the accounting system (fingerprint scanner, retina scanner, etc.) and maintains distinct passwords for each account, as well as a distinct division of duties; hence, this lessens the likelihood of financial fraud to some extent. Though it's still not a perfect solution to prevent financial fraud because human staff are still needed to oversee systems, the accounting system is a wonderful place to start, especially now that artificial intelligence has made it possible to detect and monitor digital footprints (Jędrzejka, 2019).

2.6. Research Gap

This literature review examines how artificial intelligence (AI) is influencing the accounting industry globally, with a focus on Europe, the Middle East (and Lebanon in particular), and beyond. Although certain significant gaps require more research, the review successfully synthesizes the pertinent literature:

The research doesn't go into great detail on accounting in China, Saudi Arabia, Jordan, Indonesia, or Nigeria, but it does mention a few countries where accounting has been affected by artificial intelligence. Potentially fruitful avenues for further study include the cultural, legal, and economic factors that influence how various sectors employ AI in accounting. Despite a dearth of literature on accountants' specific ethical challenges, what little there is raises broad concerns regarding the use of AI in accounting, such as the potential for biased decision-making and job loss. Data protection, transparency, accountability, and honesty are some of the concerns brought up by accounting companies' AI usage. Future research could focus on these challenges.

In education and training the evaluation briefly touches on the topic of how AI will affect accounting programs, but it doesn't go into enough depth to identify what courses will be necessary to train accountants to thrive in an AI-driven profession. Possible future research directions include determining the most effective methods of teaching accounting students about AI and identifying the skills and knowledge accountants need to effectively utilize AI resources and technologies.

The long-term effects of using AI have been the subject of very little research, despite widespread speculation about the technology's possible influence on the accounting industry. To better understand the medium- to long-term effects of artificial intelligence (AI) on accounting practices, roles, and structures, longitudinal studies are needed.

The impact of AI on accounting is the only topic covered in this assessment; the review makes no mention of how AI collaborates with other emerging technologies like as block chain, RPA, or big data analytics. Possible future research directions include investigating the effects of AI integration on accounting processes and decision-making frameworks. Lastly, there are still numerous unanswered questions about the impact of AI on accountants' jobs. Research in the future should aim to fill these gaps to better understand the effects of AI-powered accounting procedures.

3. CONCLUSION

The primary objective of this study is to examine the impact of artificial intelligence (AI) on the accounting process. Previous research indicates that there are varying degrees of positive and negative correlations between AI and accounting. Artificial Intelligence (AI) holds the potential to revolutionize the Middle Eastern accounting sector, particularly in Lebanon. This technological advancement includes a broad range of instruments and methodologies, including deep learning, machine learning, robotic process automation, natural language processing, and decision-making algorithms. AI in accounting relieves accountants of laborious tasks so they can focus on offering higher-value services. However, there are advantages and disadvantages of using AI to accounting procedures. The accounting profession has been greatly impacted by automation and AI awareness, to the point where accounting curricula have been modified to incorporate AI technologies. Automation is increasing the productivity and efficiency of Lebanese accounting processes. With AI becoming more and more prevalent, it becomes more important to carefully consider the amount and timing of these developments since it raises the possibility of replacing humans in repetitive accounting tasks. The accounting sector is also being significantly impacted by AI in a variety of areas, including revenue forecasting, automation of financial accounting and reporting, deep learning-based analysis of unstructured data, and fraud prevention and detection. Alongside these advancements, the accounting industry is confronted with several significant obstacles, such as job losses, the use of AI in accounting firms, the reduction of human prejudice in judgment, the effect on accounting education, and the necessity of learning from past errors. It is suggested that accountants and accounting firms be abreast of the most recent advancements in artificial intelligence within their sector in light of the study's conclusions. Businesses may increase the efficacy and efficiency of their accounting duties by doing this, which will ultimately reduce accounting expenses and help the industry. This implies that decision-making will increasingly be data-driven and analytics-based, rather than solely focused on routine tasks. This study also highlights the need for additional empirical research to properly understand the ways that AI is influencing accounting and auditing practices. Further research should concentrate on specific aspects of AI integration in accounting environments, analyzing its implications for workforce demographics, ethical dilemmas, and accounting procedure development.

To sum up, this study shows how artificial intelligence (AI) has the power to drastically alter the accounting sector. While applying AI can improve productivity and decision-making, there are certain drawbacks that need to be properly taken into account.

REFERENCES

Acemoglu, D., & Restrepo, P. (2018). Artificial intelligence, automation, and work. In *The economics of artificial intelligence: An agenda* (pp. 197–236). University of Chicago Press.

Ahmed, S., Alshater, M. M., El Ammari, A., & Hammami, H. (2022). Artificial intelligence and machine learning in finance: A bibliometric review. *Research in International Business and Finance*, *61*, 101646. doi:10.1016/j.ribaf.2022.101646

Al Wael, H., Abdallah, W., Ghura, H., & Buallay, A. (2023). Factors influencing artificial intelligence adoption in the accounting profession: The case of public sector in kuwait. *Competitiveness Review*, *34*(1), 3–27. doi:10.1108/CR-09-2022-0137

Ameen, N., Tarhini, A., Reppel, A., & Anand, A. (2021). Customer experiences in the age of artificial intelligence. *Computers in Human Behavior*, *114*, 106548. doi:10.1016/j.chb.2020.106548 PMID:32905175

Andreu-Perez, J., Deligianni, F., Ravi, D., & Yang, G. Z. (2017). *Artificial intelligence and robotics*. UK-RAS Network. doi:10.31256/WP2017.1

Audibert, R. B., Lemos, H., Avelar, P., Tavares, A. R., & Lamb, L. C. (2022). On the Evolution of AI and Machine Learning: Towards Measuring and Understanding Impact, Influence, and Leadership at Premier AI Conferences. *arXiv preprint arXiv:*2205.13131.

Azman, N. A., Mohamed, A., & Jamil, A. M. (2021). Artificial intelligence in automated bookkeeping: A value-added function for small and medium enterprises. *JOIV: International Journal on Informatics Visualization*, *5*(3), 224. doi:10.30630/joiv.5.3.669

Conijn, R., Martinez-Maldonado, R., Knight, S., Buckingham Shum, S., Van Waes, L., & van Zaanen, M. (2022). How to provide automated feedback on the writing process? A participatory approach to design writing analytics tools. *Computer Assisted Language Learning*, *35*(8), 1838–1868. doi:10.1080/09588221.2020.1839503

Cox, A. (2023). How artificial intelligence might change academic library work: Applying the competencies literature and the theory of the professions. *Journal of the Association for Information Science and Technology*, *74*(3), 367–380. doi:10.1002/asi.24635

Davis, S. J., & Von Wachter, T. M. (2011). *Recessions and the cost of job loss (No. w17638)*. National Bureau of Economic Research. doi:10.3386/w17638

Dirican, C. (2015). The impacts of robotics, and artificial intelligence on business and economics. *Procedia: Social and Behavioral Sciences*, *195*, 564–573. doi:10.1016/j.sbspro.2015.06.134

Dong, J. (2018). *Application Research of Artificial Intelligence Technology in Enterprise Financial Management*. Academic Press.

Fernandez, D., &Aman, A. (2018). Impacts of robotic process automation on global accounting services. *Asian Journal of Accounting & Governance*.

Frey, C. B., & Osborne, M. A. (2017). The future of employment: How susceptible are jobs to computerization? *Technological Forecasting and Social Change*, *114*, 254–280. doi:10.1016/j.techfore.2016.08.019

Haenlein, M., & Kaplan, A. (2019). A brief history of artificial intelligence: On the past, present, and future of artificial intelligence. *California Management Review*, *61*(4), 5–14. doi:10.1177/0008125619864925

Haladjian, H. H., & Montemayor, C. (2016). Artificial consciousness and the consciousness-attention dissociation. *Consciousness and Cognition*, *45*, 210–225. doi:10.1016/j.concog.2016.08.011 PMID:27656787

Hasan, A. R. (2021). Artificial Intelligence (AI) in accounting & auditing: A Literature review. *Open Journal of Business and Management*, *10*(1), 440–465. doi:10.4236/ojbm.2022.101026

Heimerl, P., Haid, M., Benedikt, L., & Scholl-Grissemann, U. (2020). Factors influencing job satisfaction in hospitality industry. *SAGE Open*, *10*(4). doi:10.1177/2158244020982998

Hemanand, D., Mishra, N., Premalatha, G., Mavaluru, D., Vajpayee, A., Kushwaha, S., & Sahile, K. (2022). Applications of intelligent model to analyze the green finance for environmental development in the context of artificial intelligence. *Computational Intelligence and Neuroscience*, *2022*, 1–8. doi:10.1155/2022/2977824 PMID:35845917

Herzel, S., Nicolosi, M., & Stărică, C. (2012). The cost of sustainability in optimal portfolio decisions. *European Journal of Finance*, *18*(3-4), 333–349. doi:10.1080/1351847X.2011.587521

Hu, J. (2022). Partial differential equation-assisted accounting professional education and training artificial intelligence collaborative course system construction. *Scientific Programming*, *2022*, 1–10. doi:10.1155/2022/6357421

Hu, Z., Hu, R., Yau, O., Teng, M., Wang, P., Hu, G., & Singla, R. (2022). Tempering expectations on the medical artificial intelligence revolution: The medical trainee viewpoint. *JMIR Medical Informatics*, *10*(8), e34304. doi:10.2196/34304 PMID:35969464

Huttunen, K., & Kellokumpu, J. (2016). The effect of job displacement on couples' fertility decisions. *Journal of Labor Economics*, *34*(2), 403–442. doi:10.1086/683645

Janaki, M., & Clifford, M. M. J. (2021). *A study on the scope of artificial intelligence in accounting*. Academic Press.

Jędrzejka, D. (2019). Robotic process automation and its impact on accounting. *Zeszyty Teoretyczne Rachunkowościtom*, 137–166.

Joh, R., Hasegawa, K., Tokushige, K., Hashimoto, E., Torii, N., Yamashiro, T., & Hayashi, N. (2003). Chronic hepatitis b with flare due to co-infection of hepatitis delta virus during lamivudine therapy. *Internal Medicine (Tokyo, Japan)*, *42*(7), 581–586. doi:10.2169/internalmedicine.42.581 PMID:12879950

Kazachenok, O. P., Stankevich, G. V., Chubaeva, N. N., &Tyurina, Y. G. (2023). Economic and legal approaches to the humanization of FinTech in the economy of artificial intelligence through the integration of blockchain into ESG Finance. *Humanities and Social Sciences Communications, 10*(1), 1-9.

Kindzeka, K. A. C. (2023). Impact of Artificial Intelligence on Accounting, Auditing and Financial Reporting. *American Journal of Computing and Engineering*, *6*(1), 29–34. doi:10.47672/ajce.1433

Lehner, O. M., Ittonen, K., Silvola, H., Ström, E., & Wührleitner, A. (2022). Artificial intelligence based decision-making in accounting and auditing: Ethical challenges and normative thinking. *Accounting, Auditing & Accountability Journal, 35*(9), 109–135. doi:10.1108/AAAJ-09-2020-4934

Leitner-Hanetseder, S., Lehner, O. M., Eisl, C., & Forstenlechner, C. (2021). A profession in transition: Actors, tasks and roles in AI-based accounting. *Journal of Applied Accounting Research, 22*(3), 539–556. doi:10.1108/JAAR-10-2020-0201

Li, Z., & Zheng, L. (2018, September). The impact of artificial intelligence on accounting. In *2018 4th International Conference on Social Science and Higher Education (ICSSHE 2018).* Atlantis Press.10.2991/icsshe-18.2018.203

Liu, N., Shapira, P., Yue, X., & Guan, J. (2021). Mapping technological innovation dynamics in artificial intelligence domains: Evidence from a global patent analysis. *PLoS One, 16*(12), e0262050. doi:10.1371/journal.pone.0262050 PMID:34972173

Liu, R., Wang, Y., & Zou, J. (2022). Research on the Transformation from Financial Accounting to Management Accounting Based on Drools Rule Engine. *Computational Intelligence and Neuroscience, 2022*, 1–8. doi:10.1155/2022/9445776 PMID:35498191

Mansor, N. A., Hamid, Y., Anwar, I. S. K., Isa, N. S. M., & Abdullah, M. Q. (2022). The awareness and knowledge on artificial intelligence among accountancy students. *International Journal of Academic Research in Business & Social Sciences, 12*(11), 1629–1640. doi:10.6007/IJARBSS/v12-i11/15307

Mehrabi, N., Morstatter, F., Saxena, N., Lerman, K., & Galstyan, A. (2021). A survey on bias and fairness in machine learning. *ACM Computing Surveys, 54*(6), 1–35. doi:10.1145/3457607

Neumann, U., Whitaker, M. J., Wiegand, S., Krude, H., Porter, J. B., Digweed, D., & Blankenstein, O. (2019). *Absorption and tolerability of taste-masked hydrocortisone granules in neonates, infants and children under 6 years of age with adrenal insufficiency.* Endocrine Abstracts. doi:10.1530/endoabs.65.JA5

Parasuraman, R., & Riley, V. (1997). Humans and automation: Use, misuse, disuse, abuse. *Human Factors, 39*(2), 230–253. doi:10.1518/001872097778543886

Rahim, S. M., Mohamad, Z. Z., Bakar, J. A., Mohsin, F. H., & Isa, N. M. (2018). Artificial intelligence, smart contract and islamic finance. *Asian Social Science, 14*(2), 145. doi:10.5539/ass.v14n2p145

Rahwan, I., Cebrian, M., Obradovich, N., Bongard, J., Bonnefon, J. F., Breazeal, C., Crandall, J. W., Christakis, N. A., Couzin, I. D., Jackson, M. O., Jennings, N. R., Kamar, E., Kloumann, I. M., Larochelle, H., Lazer, D., McElreath, R., Mislove, A., Parkes, D. C., Pentland, A. S., ... Wellman, M. (2019). Machine behaviour. *Nature, 568*(7753), 477–486. doi:10.1038/s41586-019-1138-y PMID:31019318

Rosi, N. M. K., &Mahyuni, L. P. (2021). The future of accounting profession in the industrial revolution 4.0: Meta-synthesis analysis. *E-JurnalAkuntansi, 31*(4).

Sari, D. R., & Rahardjo, D. (2021). Effect of Factors Financial, Trust, Demography, and Lifestyle of Purchase Intention Property in Jabodetabek. *Budapest International Research and Critics Institute-Journal (BIRCI-Journal), 4*(4), 11408-11421.

Stoica, O. C., & Ionescu-Feleagă, L. (2021, June). Digitalization in accounting: A structured literature review. In *Proceedings of the 4th International Conference on Economics and Social Sciences: Resilience and Economic Intelligence through Digitalization and Big Data Analytics, Sciendo,* Bucharest, Romania (pp. 10-11). 10.2478/9788366675704-045

Sullivan, D., & Von Wachter, T. (2009). Job displacement and mortality: An analysis using administrative data. *The Quarterly Journal of Economics, 124*(3), 1265–1306. doi:10.1162/qjec.2009.124.3.1265

Tayachi, T., Brahimi, T., & Essafi, Y. (2022). Artificial Intelligence in the Islamic Finance: A bibliometric. *Analysis*.

Tong, X., Linderman, K., & Zhu, Q. (2023). Managing a portfolio of environmental projects: Focus, balance, and environmental management capabilities. *Journal of Operations Management, 69*(1), 127–158. doi:10.1002/joom.1201

Vărzaru, A. A. (2022). Assessing the Impact of AI Solutions' Ethical Issues on Performance in Managerial Accounting. *Electronics (Basel), 11*(14), 2221. doi:10.3390/electronics11142221

Yang, K. C., Varol, O., Davis, C. A., Ferrara, E., Flammini, A., & Menczer, F. (2019). Arming the public with artificial intelligence to counter social bots. *Human Behavior and Emerging Technologies, 1*(1), 48–61. doi:10.1002/hbe2.115

Chapter 11
New Challenges for the Accounting Profession in the Era of AI and Sustainable Development

Siriyama Kanthi Herath
Clark Atlanta University, USA

Laksitha Maheshi Herath
New York University, USA

ABSTRACT

The challenges that the accounting sector is facing in the modern era of globalization, digital technology, and artificial intelligence (AI) are addressed in this chapter. The authors achieve this by prioritizing social sustainability. One of the most important technological advancements that have drastically changed society is globalization. Additionally covered in this chapter are the significance of non-financial reporting and data quality, strategies for integrating sustainability within company operations, and management and governance ideals that promote sustainable development.

1. INTRODUCTION

The accounting profession is in a dynamic global business environment where it is facing challenges presented by the massive influence of globalization, sustainability, and fast technological changes. Accountants are compelled to respond to increasingly complex challenges and opportunities that arise, compelling the accounting movement to redefine its function and adjust to the ever-changing environment of society (Kroon et al., 2021). Accounting professionals are required to be knowledgeable regarding developments and the latest technological trends because of the competitive market. Additionally, such companies must be flexible and adaptive in adjusting appropriately to the changes in order to stay ahead while organizational change continues to accelerate, so is the increase in importance of flexible and

DOI: 10.4018/979-8-3693-0847-9.ch011

adaptive leadership among most managers and administrators (Burke & Cooper, 2004; Dess & Picken, 2000). Flexible leadership theory (Yukl & Lepsinger, 2004) stresses that the top executives have the capacity to affect key success factors like efficiency, innovative adaptation, and human capital through the implementation of pertinent behaviors and decisions regarding strategy, structure, and management programs and systems. When implanting innovations, it is essential for accountants to be committed to ethics and professional values. Accountants must also be able to recognize and adjust to changing environments and customer needs. They must also be able to communicate the goals and objectives of the organization to all stakeholders. Finally, they must be able to provide guidance and support to their employees. This can bring many challenges and difficulties to modern accountants. This chapter is aimed at defining the challenges that accounting faces as an industry of modernity, including digital technology and emerging technologies such-as AI, in times characterized by globalization.

According to Herath & Joshi (2023), globalization is one of the most significant technological advancements that has revolutionized society. Not only has globalization accelerated the diffusion of worldwide global power in corporations, but also the activities of international business have become exceedingly complicated with different problems pertaining to countries with large distances. Further, attempts towards harmonizing accounting is needed at the international level through the International Financial Reporting Standards (IFRS) to determine a common framework for financial reporting, despite the fact that there are divergent jurisdictions. The globalization of businesses continues to present accountants with sophisticated challenges in assessing the implications and intricacies that are inherent in the collection of information from countries governed by different regulatory and reporting practices. Arnold (2018) researched how technological advancements affected financial reporting, external auditing, and managerial accounting, determining whether those developments promise a more radical modification of the future of accounting and auditing research. Arnold (2018) claimed that with the emergence of several information sources, investors seek prompt information releases and hence make their decisions on the basis of unaudited information.

At the same time, the world faces a great societal change towards sustainability, which requires the accountant profession to broaden its sole focus to only financial metrics and include the three pillars of economic, social, and environmental as the core of its governance. The advent of the triple bottom line, covering both economic, social, and environmental components, has changed not only the profit-making concept but also the way businesses measure their success. Stakeholders' interest in companies sustainability management and communication has grown, resulting in increased development of how sustainability reporting evolves with a wider purpose to satisfy rising scrutiny on firm's level of impact (Hespenheide 2021). Institutional issues are also common due to the growing interest in sustainability management and the importance of an environmentally friendly company with responsibility. The Global Reporting Initiative (GRI), the Sustainability Accounting Standards Board (SASB) and the European Union Directives represent some of the main regulative frameworks, which reflect the growing demand for accurate and adequate disclosures on sustainability performance.

With the development of Industry 4.0, we have marked a revolutionary stage for industrial processes that cover various aspects of society. In contributing towards transforming society through significant breakthrough discoveries such as nanotechnology and ubiquitous artificial intelligence, it profoundly impacts society (Schwab 2016). There is a parallel development in the domain of accounting, which is the relentless evolution of automation and artificial intelligence (AI) in the processes of accounting. This is transforming the profession in general. Technologies such as robotic process automation (RPA) and machine learning simplify mundane tasks, ensuring that accountants are now able to spend their time and energy on career-defining issues, enabling them to embark on a strategic analysis and decision-making process. The adoption of intelligent virtual assistants is also quickly penetrating into applications and devices used by enterprises, including accounting (Burns & Igou, 2019). These virtual assistants are able to point out custom advice to users and turn the common processes' into actions, all while giving individualized analytics. This will enable cost reduction, customer care and enhanced production. Accountants in Industry 4.0 are also being made to advance their talents in terms of skills to correspond with the advancement of the profession, which is now associated with the increasing application of technologies (Akhter and Sultana, 2018). With the process likely to create efficiencies, a question may arise as to what the role of an accountant would be in the future, since society might question the impact of a large degree of automation. Though technology is arguably one of the major forces transforming the world-of-work, there are other forces aiding the changes, including changing individuals' expectations at the workplace, changing cultural norms and values, and new types and levels of connectivity and demographics (ACCA, 2020). Careers in the accounting profession will become more diverse, and working patterns will transform as technology blends the work divide between humans and machines.

This chapter examines the perplex challenges and promising frontiers emerging from these landscape-altering forces, not just as external advocates within the realms of the accounting profession but also as individuals who shall encounter the demands of the future explained by globalization, sustainability, and the impacts of technology. From dealing with the multiplicity of international operations and ever-changing standards of reporting to the process of shaping and handling sustainability controls and the acceptance of automated procedures, the profession of accounting faces a historical turning point; the necessity to establish adaptations is not desired but mandatory to ensure the continuity of the profession and other goals of the society affiliated with accounting.

Decision-making and communication, more effective staff training programs, and new skill development among the workforce are some of the benefits that may be realized when using AI in accounting and auditing, including quick decision-making (Omoteso, 2012). In spite of structural limitations, service orientation skills constitute one of the key retained barriers to state owned enterprises (SOEs) acquisition and implementation of the Industry 4 approach (Chamba et al., 2023). Service orientation skills are of utmost importance to SOEs that wish not only to interact adequately with stakeholders and customers, but also to maintain at least the same levels as their rivals on a global playing field. SOEs need to invest in developing these talents in order to remain competitive in the global market. The benefits of the Fourth Industrial Revolution paradoxically remain largely elusive in the African public sector, as challenges plague these countries despite its transformative measures (Chamba et al., 2023).

This chapter also focuses on non-financial reporting and qualitative data, as well as how to incorporate sustainability into organizational activities, together with management and governance views encouraging sustainable development. With their power to determine the informational and control needs of both internal and external decision-makers, accountants should be quite involved in the process of big data information governance (Coyne et al., 2018). This chapter also addresses the methods reviewed to assure ethical sustainability approaches, the application of non-financial reporting and data quality, as well as management's control mechanisms encouraging sustainable development.

There are several challenges that the accounting industry is dealing with today. They are driven by various factors, such as rapid technological development and the globalization of business. Similarly, a quite new direction—the sustainability trend—is now being adopted. One of the primary challenges facing accountants currently is the continuing growth of artificial intelligence (AI). AI has already been used to automate numerous accounting procedures and functions, and it is believed that AI will have a greater impact on the accounting industry in the future. In a decade, the accounting sector will seem very different from how it does right now. By becoming more specialized, accountants who use modern innovations like artificial intelligence will not only survive but also prosper (Shaffer et al., 2020). The increasing globalization of business presents accountants with additional difficulties. With businesses becoming more and more globally oriented, accountants need to understand how financial transactions take place across borders; hence, they should be able to address all activities along these lines. The accountants will have to be familiar with world-wide accounting laws and standards, as well as communicate effectively with clients and coworkers from different cultures.

This chapter considers the increasing involvement of accountants in advocating for sustainability, calling for accountants to comprehend environmental accounting and reporting. It focuses on the involvement of accounting and AI technology to improve corporate sustainability practices, aid in sustainable development, and pave the way for a compassionate society by addressing different industries, organizations and effects in the process, focusing on the contemporary educational evolution.

2. ACCOUNTING IN THE AI REVOLUTION: TOWARDS SUSTAINABLE DEVELOPMENT

Artificial intelligence has become a driving variable in the accounting profession with its innovative developments. Big data analytics and blockchain are among these technological innovations that could be used in the accountant's routine tasks, such as evaluating compliance measures and analyzing existing information structures dedicated to redirection (Kroon et al., 2021). The increasing significance of blockchain requires that auditors understand the consequences of this technology for their profession and see its benefits because the architecture of business becomes more complicated, necessitating auditors to use efficient and trustworthy tools to give the demanded and expected assurance (Bonyuet, 2020). The auditors need to keep abreast of all advancements in all fields of technology and trends so that they remain contemporary knowledgeable and, through their services, prepare accurate and real reliability only. Also, they have to be duly informed on the impacts of blockchain technology on the auditing process. AI driven software is automated for various accounting processes such as document entry and analysis, reporting mechanism of financial data control measures to tax regulatory standards, risk management elements that look at system support into audit quality system development for fraud detection, etc. Thus, as a result of such automation, accountants will have to deal with harder management issues. Different facets of cybersecurity and accounting, including auditing and general accounting mechanisms, should be effectively developed and incorporated with blockchain (Demirkan et al., 2020). In the future, there will be a deeper effect of AI in the accounting profession. Such software will save time for accountants and allow them to spend more time on calculations that require the knowledge of a specialist-financial analysis and recasting. This will enable the accountants to provide a broader range of value added services, although it is very possible that AI comes with so many trials for the accounting profession. One of the challenges is that technology leads to unemployment in the accounting profession. According to a study by the University of Oxford, there is a 95% risk of accountants losing their jobs as machines dominate number-crunching and data processing (Griffin, 2019). As AI software continues to grow, it is possible that accounting responsibilities will be automated. Marshall and Lambert (2018) revealed that augmented intelligence enabled better chances for accountants to execute their skills collectively, thus enabling them to focus on activities that provide the organization with higher value.

Secondly, the other issue is that there will likely be less demand for accountants with AI. Since AI can perform numerous accounting activities related to routine and non-routine tasks, businesses that employ such technologies will be less likely to demand so many accountants in the near future. As such, accountants will have to acquire some skills in order to solve this AI problem. Therefore, they will have to adopt new ones that AI cannot perfect while attending the same training on how efficiently one can use those devices driven by artificial intelligence. Davenport and Ronanki (2018) argue for a fundamental organizational perspective on AI, emphasizing that it should be used to support business capabilities instead of simply acquiring technological skills.

2.1 The Impact of AI on the Accounting Profession

Accounting became different due to the integration of artificial intelligence (AI) in various fields indirectly connected with this area but having a regular workflow. Data entry was also facilitated by artificial intelligence software, as was the analysis of related information that it provided, financial reporting and accounting made for tax compliance audits carried out before auditing. Such improvements have made it possible for the accountants to focus on more elaborate and strategic managerial responsibilities that equip them with the ability to generate values that are superior among organizations and clients.

In the field of accounting, there are several operational and feasible uses for AI. The speed, particularly in the automation that AI can provide, has also had a substantial impact on data processing and analysis, which means resources can be released as well as time freed up from tasks that were laborious. Further productivity improvement would allow the accounts to provide financial data timely as well as give strategic advice appropriately. Integration of blockchain into accounting is one of the most commonly discussed topics since it could lead to huge changes in practical work with accountants (Stafie & Grosu 2023). Blockchain could provide a better, more secure and more transparent platform for accounting records, making it easier to access and manage data. Also, it would reduce the risk of fraud and human error.

In addition, the ability of AI to recognize patterns and anomalies makes it very useful for risk management applications aimed at identifying risks and frauds. AI systems facilitate the analysis of large volumes of financial data and detection of any abnormalities or cases relevant to fraud that can also be utilized in auditing AI algorithms constantly observe transactions in real-time and after spotting unusual activity and potential risks, they prevent the escalation (Rahman, and Dekkati, 2022). Therefore, AI supports forensic accounting by increasing its accuracy and efficiency. As artificial intelligence progresses, it assumes an important role in monitoring digital transactions and tackling cybersecurity issues, boosting capabilities in digital forensics (Tuli & Thaduri, 2023). Besides, AI-supported financial forecasting and predictive analysis are having immense significance for accountants, while organizations are strategizing the budget of the future along with allocations with respect to other organizational resources. Additionally, the accounting team has managed to produce true results fast, where AI estimations have been capable of guiding organizations through financial instability without human input or direction when they need such vital guidance. For future trends, with the kind of research done nowadays, most notably by Leitner-Hanetseder et al. (2021), it shows that within such ten years, as previously mentioned, one can say I hope there are impending changes, and hence this field is just about to take a major shift in the digital world where computed based AI technology leads.

2.2 Impacts of AI on Society and Education

The emergence of the AI era has profound implications for education, sustainability and business in a large society. This part of the paper will take into account sustainability issues caused by substantial flows AI has attracted at a relatively high pace and which bring about great disbalances in diverse spheres. It reflects how heralds of human estimates and sustainable development alter social canons, programs for education and career growth. Additionally, the section highlights some potential technological improvements that could be achieved through AI and other contemporary technologies for eco-friendly communities and innovative approaches to sustainability. Developing within the AI era, these problems can be considered challenges and advantages to society in general and accountants, namely that they need deeper research on how technological changes affect societal beliefs and stereotypes related to education possibilities or career choices. Thus, such implementation will undoubtedly raise the issue of revision in accounting education as AI adoption alters responsibilities and duties for accountants (Shaffer et al., 2020).

3. GLOBALIZATION AND ITS IMPACT ON ACCOUNTING

As a result of increased globalization, one could state that accounting as an area is rather novel in regard to interdependence and complexity. Company growth requires bringing in accountants specializing in machines and also processing accounting operations at the international level when its boundaries expand. As companies currently do business across borders, multinational means accountants are expected to know about regionalities in addition to the localized systems of education they learned.

Moreover, communication thereby became an important factor in all these diverse scenarios. Accountants should be able to produce as many unambiguous signals of their goals as possible and join forces with clients and colleagues who represent completely different cultures. Thus, it can be claimed that while globalization becomes one of the most influential development trends and an integral part for many various sectors engaged in different areas, now that there is a so-called fashionable setting related to national peculiarities as well as adaptation towards working under new forms, businesses are considered valuable practical skills eventually adopted by accountants.

However, with increased globalization, there is an opinion that accounting as a field of professional activity is relatively new in terms of interest and complexity. As businesses expand into international operations, it is necessary to engage the accounting profession, which has an understanding of global workings and weight specific equipment for accounting processes. It is, therefore, a necessity for accountants to strive at refining their skills up-to this trade's modern challenges and needs in various hegemony, whereby the world of business activities evolves every day. Moreover, to work as an accountant, one must be capable of changing oneself rapidly depending on the laws of different countries. Besides, communication thereby became an important factor in all these diverse scenarios. Accountants should be able to produce as many unambiguous signals of their goals as possible and join forces with clients and colleagues who represent completely different cultures. Thus, it can be claimed that while globalization becomes one of the most influential development trends and an integral part for many various sectors engaged in different areas, now that there is a so-called fashionable setting related to national peculiarities as well as adaptation towards working under new Businesses are considered valuable practical skills eventually adopted by accountants. Figure 1 gives a vivid picture of the dynamic global forces that continue to mold the course of accounting in the future.

Figure 1. Globalization and the accounting profession

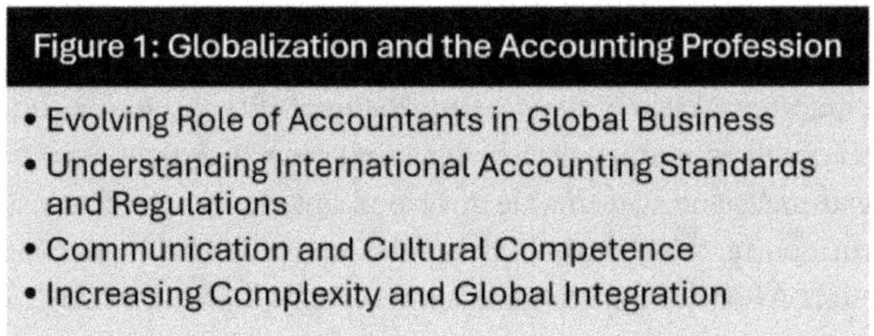

3.1 Changing Responsibilities of Accountants in the Global Business

The accountants do not work as book-keepers anymore because of globalization, and as people shift more tasks from the accountants, their jobs are becoming advisers rather than such skilled workers. Demand arises in relation to the function of an accountant as the business requires greater assistance in global strategy creation, detection of promising opportunities in foreign markets, addressing international tax law, and transfer pricing issues.

As a result, one of the major challenges facing accountants in this industry is the acquisition of new and relevant skills to be updated in the competition. As innovation like AI and information analytics is being used to give buyer's basic yet minute asset development as well as operational analysis in real time, accounting specialists should realize that it is no longer business as usual but the direction in which accounting experts need to go to remain relevant. This rather troublesome interface of AI and sustainable development is indeed associated with numerous challenges that disparate accountants have to compete with, but there is also a set of opportunities that this combination has made available for professional gain. Therefore, global accounting is overwhelming in terms of its complex nature and even more difficult because the firms work in various countries. The job of accounting professionals now requires a higher level of sophistication, with complicated global cross-border transactions that must stay in line with a wide array of international accounting rules and regulations.

In addition, stable, good cross-cultural practices and cultural competencies within the organization contribute to developing strong relationships with clients and stakeholders who belong to different cultures, which is also a significant demand. A modern account must act to address the headlong development of problems concerning international financial activities, for instance, consolidation and foreign taxation. By embracing globalization's problems and leveraging AI technology, accountants may position themselves as strategic advisers, participating in the long-term development of organizations on a global scale.

3.2 Understanding International Accounting Standards and Regulations

Since business is also carried out outside any given country, there is a recommended amount of information that an accountant should have about international standards and laws in relation to domestic rules. Since financial reporting requirements, tax measures, and disclosures could be different across countries, it is a necessity for accountants to regularly familiarize themselves with these standards that always change in order to ensure accurate statements of liquidity position and full compliance, especially with foreign transactions. Furthermore, accountants are required to be aware of the current laws and rules that may affect their clients' businesses. They must as well keep up with the new trends that are being rolled out in terms of financial reporting and accounting standards.

The financial statements should be consistent to become comparable to the relevant stakeholders, such as shareholders, creditors and investors, among others, who are supposed to finally benefit from international businesses by both national and state laws that establish continuous reporting standards, most important IFRS or GAAP. There has been a lack of an international body that controls the system and standardizes metrics and disclosures (Samans & Nelson, 2022). Due to this, numerous frameworks have emerged over time which are targeted at different scopes as well broad primary audiences. This dispersion, however, has resulted in chaos and wasted expenditure.

3.3 Communication and Cultural Competence

Globalization has led to the emergence of a varied and cross-cultural work environment in many businesses. Since the accountants have to co-operate with different culturally diversified colleagues, clients and stakeholders, they are a functional cross-cultural combination. Cultural sensitivity and multiculturalism are critical for the accountants to have good relations at work, but their importance is also in proper financial report of those representatives from other countries. The international section of the company may be served by professionals versed in cultural and multilingual issues who can tackle differences accompanied by different cultures, apart from developing financial presentations or papers relative to particular preferences depending on customers. Flexible accountants may assume interpersonal gaps.

3.4 Increasing Complexity and Global Integration

Globalization alters the economic and cultural character; therefore, complexities in monetary operations are encountered with regard to accounting. Accountants also need to be acquainted with currency conversions and international transfers, if only the thoughts of transfer pricing occur. As increased globalization between firms necessitates accounting personnel to address challenges such as those presented by consolidated financial statements in which information from multiple country subordinates and affiliates is amalgamated, accuracy in consolidation is more emphasized to provide a clear and true image of the financial undertakings an organization has, thus making easier investment decisions.

4. THE NEED FOR SUSTAINABILITY ACCOUNTING

The rise of AI and sustainable development has made sustainability accounting a forceful profession that accountants are forced to join. Emerging demand for sustainable operations has worsened some of the issues that have long existed within accounting. Today, businesses are under increasing scrutiny with regard to meeting the environmental and social dynamites caused by their activities. Therefore, accountants need to be aware that the essence of morality in their reporting and accounting procedures is essential for sustainability.

In addition to their usual knowledge of accounting, such accountants will have to be qualified in their ability to provide assistance to companies looking for help and guidance during the process of developing sustainability projects, as this helps them come up with the best plans. The accounting profession is not an exception and will also have to adjust in order to fit into the mediating role between companies that are forming new trends in green corporate life. In this chapter, there are a few subsections that can be adopted to outline the additional necessities of sustainable quantity relatively once extra principles have been accepted because environmental problems continue to rise. This part focuses on some of the channels via which a firm can benefit from its finances and acts as an accommodating accountant in their adoption of responsible transparency reporting.

The perceptions that should be gained through sustainability accounting by these accountants are also anticipated to aid in developing professional views, which have been vital for allowing this phenomenon of change from the definite systems under which organizations prepare their financial records. Indeed, accountants are excellent illustrations of strategic resources by an individual only ability that would collect social capital along with the virtues of digital capital and generic human capital (Yigitbasioglu et al., 2023). The aim of this chapter is to highlight the sustainability accounting can have in AI times and develop more accountability tasks for accounts when depicting a greener business world as well as growth.

4.1 The Evolution of Society Towards Sustainability

Sustainability accounting is also expected to have significant demand in the future. There is a high likelihood that regulatory and standard setting bodies will demand stricter reporting standards from businesses due to increasing world attention on environmental issues and social concerns. On the other hand, accounting as a discipline is likely to face challenges and opportunities related to this anticipated growth. Accountants will need to become more acquainted with the most widely used protocols for sustainability reporting, such as standards created by the Global Reporting Initiative and the Sustainability Accounting Standards Board. Secondly, they will have to keep up with prevailing and changing legislation and directives so that they do not contravene any directions set out, and the sustainability data must be timely provided and should also remain as close to what is on the ground as possible.

In addition to that, we are currently in the age of artificial intelligence and sustainable development, which makes sustainability accounting very needed. Businesses are encouraged to be more socially and environmentally accountable, requiring accounting professionals who support the objectives of businesses. In order to have transparency with regard to sustainability activities and trust among organizations, ethical reporting and accounting codes are essential.

With increasing demands for sustainability, accountants must have basic skills and knowledge of social accounting practices so they can succeed in identification, finding results, surveillance and reporting on sustainable performance needs. On the other hand, the change in emphasis on accountants as catalysts in the current development trend of sustainability accounting theory is contrary to the requirement that they should be the focal point. General professional accountants are relatively active in the practice of social accounting but act mostly as gatekeepers to sustainability managers and top management (Schaltegger & Zvezdov, 2013). While upholding sustainability accounting, responsiveness to any industry with which it happens will enable such practices, even widely thought of as teasing across various premises on a global economic stage.

4.2 Accountability for Environmental and Social Impact

As stakeholders become more aware of the negative environmental and social consequences of business operations, businesses have to be more transparent and accountable for their actions. According to Kaur and Lodhia (2018), stakeholder participation is essential for the development of strategic plans, the establishment of sustainability indicators, the evaluation of sustainability performance, and the development of sustainability reports. In such a setting, sustainability accounting is expected to play a vital role by providing a model for businesses to measure, report and monitor their environmental and social performance.

By incorporating the available sustainability measures into financial reporting, businesses can demonstrate their commitment to addressing environmental concerns, lowering carbon emissions, conserving natural resources, promoting social equality, and supporting community development initiatives. Businesses can use sustainability accounting to demonstrate their progress and contributions towards achieving UN sustainable development goals.

4.3 Ethical Reporting and Accounting

AI integration in accounting and auditing has numerous ethical considerations (Zemánková, 2019). With the widespread use of new technologies, such changes are assumed to occur in the accounting and auditing professions. The popular areas are blockchain, automation, cognitive technologies, machine learning, data analytics, and cybersecurity sustainability (Hasan, 2022). Ethics and integrity are important aspects of sustainability accounting. Accounting professionals must definitely recognize the ethical implications of their reporting and decision-making in the context of sustainable development. Accurate and fair reporting on environmental and social impacts is vital for numerous stakeholders to make informed decisions and evaluate ethical behavior. Accountants play a critical role in ensuring that sustainability data is collected and communicated in an unbiased and transparent manner, free of environmental propaganda or effort distortion.

Ethical considerations also include ensuring that sustainability efforts match with the company's fundamental principles and are not just symbolic. As innovative applications and practices evolve, so do the methods by which frauds are opened, leading to the creation of new forms of white-collar crimes (Hasan, 2022). According to Ucoglu (2020), abiding by ethical and regulatory directions is a significant consideration in accounting firms' practices. Ucoglu's (2020), call, leads one to reconsider the pivotal role of creating long-standing structures that will guarantee compliance and honesty in financial conduct.

5. CHALLENGES IN THE ACCOUNTING PROFESSION: AI AND SUSTAINABLE DEVELOPMENT ERA

In the face of new challenges that were never thought of before in the accounting industry, we are now moving to an era whereby artificial intelligence and sustainable development will be considered evident, as tucked away in these novelettes. Therefore, for these accountants and their accounting firms to even hope to survive in such a volatile scenario, there will be consequential changes in ways of doing things, skill sets and strategies. Figure 2 illustrates the diversity of challenges facing the accounting profession in the era of artificial intelligence and sustainable development, shedding light on the complexities that must be addressed for sustainable and ethical accounting practices to thrive. Furthermore, it provides useful information on accountants' new role in implementing strategies for the future that combine technological innovation with sustainable and ethical responsibility.

Figure 2. Challenges for the accounting profession in AI and sustainable development era

Figure 2: Challenges for the Accounting Profession in AI and Sustainable Development Era

- Automation and AI Integration
- Data Management and Security
- Ethical Considerations
- Skill Upgrading
- Sustainable Reporting
- Impact on Traditional Accounting Services
- Predictive Analysis and Decision Making
- Regulatory Compliance and Standards
- Interdisciplinary Collaboration
- Transparency and Accountability

5.1 Automation and AI Integration

The transformational opportunity is the function shifts designed in accounting practice using AI and automation technologies, as they provide several kinds of accounting functions that are conducted automatically, starting from data entry to financial analysis. However, accountants should embrace these technologies as well by getting the right competencies that will assist them in maintaining integrity, accuracy and confidentiality of information, besides ethical considerations. Whereas in the case of automated stimulation, automation would lead to productivity and pay millions into the accountant's purse even from minor processes since those repetitive policies are programmed through computers. However, it is important for one to advance through the stage of sustained growth since a person has not been left behind in most industries because there has been a transformation from the analog into the digital era. As such, therefore, accountants must also go ahead and make it their own personal obligation to treat the above figures as sensitive kinds of information, thus being given top priority in terms of data security or even privacy through very strict guard measures.

Additionally, they need to be careful while employing AI algorithms so that financial data accuracy and credibility are not misplaced. Collaboration is of essence in human-AI since, with the help of reasoning AI, accountants are able to comprehend what AI produces and utilize professional acceptance while drawing conclusions that affect money. Additionally, transparency can be established with the beneficiaries regarding how the integration of AI would function to their benefit to reduce fear and enhance cooperation. So, accountants' attitude is to comply with technology trends and regularly screen AI based outcomes of the process aimed at detecting possible hidden risks that might vanish along with time. Therefore, if accountants approach AI and readiness actively at every point of the interpretative process, they can comply with general principles.

5.2 Data Management and Security

One of the major concerns in this era, under the AI scare in the accounting profession, is data handling and protection; it has been a hive off performing venture for most accountants. However, in the system of accounting, using AI involves processing mind-boggling volumes of data, and thus this entire lot cannot be dealt with promptly enough provisionally for efficacy while being guaranteed safety. The accountants should have proper tools for managing data to be able to well organize financial information in vast quantities and ensure appropriate recording and monitoring. Moreover, data privacy is a big concern as accountants obtain private client's information. To avoid unauthorized entry and breach of such acts, the acts encompassing data protection laws should be followed by them Furthermore, there is a need for tight barriers to access.

Among the measures that accountants must also take is what has to be done so that there should not only be action mechanisms against such cyber threats both within and outside the system units. Therefore, more sophisticated enemies will have to secure their networks, and hence accounting firms should still invest in the actual implementation of cybersecurity safeguards. This includes emulations like encryption mechanisms, the use of different forms of authentication, and last but not least, keeping the security system aloof by making it updated according to time in order to be ready.

This necessitates the setting up of extremely stringent contractual arrangements and provisions for transmitting financial information to AI systems as well as third-party vendors. Accountants should collaborate with AI developers and technology partners in order to effectively develop trust mechanisms and transparency in data showing activity.

The impact of data breaches in the accounting sector can be enormous, involving not only financial loss associated with theft but also liability and reputational damage. As a result, the security of user personal data logs should be added to the list of issues in the contract for the provision of accounting services. So, the adoption of a culture of compliance to safeguard necessary data and some of the strict data protection standards under artificial intelligence based financial accounting can be deemed a way of building trust between the accountants and their clients, as well as other stakeholders, by a proactive nature.

5.3 Ethical Considerations

On the other hand, as time passes, the AI's power to drive the decisions made results as well, and hence some more ethical matters are coming to the limelight and are also endangering the basic portico of the accounting profession, which yet needs to be cured with the utmost precautions. Bias is a critical point that has to be dealt with since the latent backups could gain popularity since the AI system could not affirm what is right. This means that accountants should be free and ensure their financial decision-making process goes right and is transparent, so one should automatically require them to have democracy.

Secondly, the privacy of individuals when sharing their life data is assessed by the use of AI bookkeeping systems, which brings promise into disarray. Within intro-companies, accountants must be careful when dealing with sensitive personal information and comply strictly with the Data Protection Laws while making sure that AI algorithms receive consent from individuals whose data they use. Transparency is also a requisite, and thus the primary highlighting aspect that brings to light communications about customers' handling of data should be honest enough to restore faith in people's privacy rights.

Integrity benefits due to the technological introduction of the rumors actions on stakeholders as decisions have led to inspiration within which fact they need pondering further. While artificial intelligence finds the best algorithm for making decisions, due to a lack of human intervention in them, they often lead to unjustifiable results or lack humanity. Instead of giving consideration to societal or environmental factors, accountants will need to give consideration to AI-driven automation supplemented by input from humans in order for decisions to be compliant and ethical.

Nevertheless, in order for AI to be used more responsibly, the problem of accountability and responsibility should also find an appropriate solution. If the AI system is likely to attract financial decisions with unintended negative repercussions, it will be difficult to blame anyone. It is in this practice of assigning AI the role to make these decisions that businesses call for clear lines of employees' duties and responsibilities by accountants.

Moreover, the opaqueness and unsureness of AI algorithms require a mechanism for justifying to clients or stakeholders why decisions given by an algorithm are sensible. Accountants must provide information regarding the inadequacies and shortfalls of AI-result so that stakeholders will base their choices on detailed research rather than relying completely on them.

In the midst of such ethical dilemmas, therefore, what is likely to guide our accountants are professional codes of conduct as well as best practice documents that may be published by their agencies. As a result, awareness of these shifting ethical principles in all accounting meetings will give emphasis to the current set standards and thus facilitate the development of proper mechanisms necessary for determining and improving responsible artificial intelligence use while estimating finances. By ensuring algorithmic bias, privacy rights adherence, accountability and transparency measures compliance, accountants will be in a position to utilize AI capacity while maintaining the utmost ethical level in the accounting profession.

5.4 Skill Upgrading

An intensive rate of technological transformation forces major changes within accounting; one is always on the learner and adapts to everything new 24-7 As such, it ceases to be an option but a necessity because these new developments are not optional requirements for survival in the contemporary accounting world.

The phenomenon of big data and corporate reporting is perhaps one of the most recent and highly praised developments in the accounting environment. It is a significant aspect of the findings of corporate reporting with big data and dual communication flows, which provide a promising opportunity to improve prospective financial statements considerably (Al-Htaybat and Alberti-Alhtaybat, 2017). Data analytics is now the core foundation on which accountants function. The ability to harness the power of data and source useful trends as insights is an invaluable art that any account ought to learn. Through financial analysis, they can observe trends and anomalies, as well as opportunities that would otherwise be overlooked. This goes a long way in enabling accountants to have data that they can use for calculations toward projections and estimations on advice necessary for clients who shall be advised based on actual information arising from business decisions.

Moreover, now there is the highest demand among accountants to master AI tools that would facilitate all of these unnecessary tasks, automate them, minimize any possible mistakes, and thus increase overall performance. There is now a considerable scope of accounting function optimization by AI in multiple forms, from such simple automation as reconciliation to forecasting and up to auditing. Accountants need to be familiar with the use of AI algorithms, including machine learning models, in accounting. It implies not only obtaining new skills for working with AI-tools, but also providing the person with knowledge of the limitations of these instruments and how to use them responsibly.

Apart from the application of data analytics and artificial intelligence, it is also important to understand other accounting software projects that are in progress. This has been made possible by the innovation of cloud-based accounting systems and other financial management tools that have changed a lot of how accounting work is performed. Accountants will have to get used to such software tools and simultaneously work flow and access in real time, along with cooperation with clients while strengthening data security even on cloud-based platforms.

Nonetheless, upskilling in these domains is a practice that requires a consistent focus on learning and development. Some of these sessions can include workshops, webinars and industry conferences, among others, where accountants get updates on recent practice trends as well as tips with respect to practical issues regarding data analytics techniques used, such as AI tools or accounting software. Moreover, the use of these tools in practical training and application practice during the course makes one more confident and effective.

Adaptation always leads to a huge challenge, but it still has many pros. From here, accountants will move from being mere statisticians of projects to consultants used by clients' projects in order to obtain suggestions and advice. Allowing accountants to use analytics, artificial intelligence and the accounting software of the new generation makes them acquire innovation tools that guarantee success in unpredictable future work.

5.5 Sustainable Reporting

With the integration of the ESG factor, the concept of the ESG factor becomes a critical topic in reporting. As a result, accountants, in such an evolving atmosphere, need to consider questions beyond financial measures by widening the scope of concentration. Therefore, proper ESG integration is driven by an objective assessment of social and environmental ambitions along with governance frameworks in order to make the best use of the situation in which a company finds itself. Being part of the firm and industries, accountants are supposed to utilize the information associated with the stakeholders, especially the information provided by sustainability experts, to shed light on details regarding the ESG factors, which constitute a material element for the firm and the industry concerned.

In an environmental problem study of a firm, one needs to consider the issue of resource use in the company and the impact on emissions, ecological footprints, and actions that will be taken to promote sustainability. For the activity to be appropriately investigated, recognized, and made out, and the mechanisms regarding the milieu produced by the firm to be uncovered, present investigators should make up for it with the analysis of new investigation frameworks. Emphasizing the applications of renewable energy sources, decreasing greenhouse gas amounts, developing and spreading sustainable business models, and limiting the impacts on the environment from the beginning to the end of the supply chain, for instance.

The aspect of social factors would lay emphasis on that; social factors are the link between a company and its stakeholders, like employees, customers, the neighborhood community, and the rest of the stakeholders. For example, philanthropic gifts, differences and incorporation, the enlistment procedure, and the benefit of staff represent a requirement for the accountants to warn, consider the facts and make them visible. Nevertheless, admitting social elements in the financial report can allow accountants to show the transition from an entity's action to being rational with the purpose they desire and then by the effect they have.

The governance variables address whether organizational characteristics are effective and transparent systems, processes and decision – making mechanisms. The factors that accounting professionals need to address include the board's independence, CEO compensation, the rights that are vested in a shareholder, and the risk management and compliance strategy that should be followed by the company.

This means that people who are stakeholders in the organization would believe more in the integrity of the organization during the governance process, which is assumed to be fully transparent. The 2020 KPMG Sustainability Reporting Survey reported that 96% of the top global organizations report on their sustainability performance.

It is the responsibility of such tools, following the general report statements and standardized criteria, such as the GRI, the SASB, and others, to find the most appropriate approach to supporting the ESG dots to be incorporated into the financial declarations. In addition, data generated by way of technological means, data analytics and software concerning the same conveniently assure that data on the ESG has become easier and more practical to collect and release. Though different professionals may be working with financial reporting in such conditions, the primary contributor should be the accountant because it is needed to integrate an ESG component into the accounting by both corporations and stakeholders advocating for sustainable development. To assist in evaluating the health of a company operating under such conditions, accountants are required to shift their attention from traditional financial measures.

In addition to providing stakeholders with vital knowledge about a business's effectiveness and persistence, sustainability reporting requires investment, but its orientation toward measurement goal-setting performance monitoring endorsement enables enterprises to refine their deficiencies, increase production efficiency and reach growth opportunities (Hespenheide, 2021). Integration of the ESG dimension in financial accounting necessitates a more profound analysis of companies' social and environmental responsibility, including attention to quality interference indicators. Since the accountants know all the ESG factors that count to an enterprise within its sector, they should therefore team up with stakeholders and sustainable development researchers or analysts and focus on studying those components.

In environmental problem analysis, one should look not only at a company's resource consumption and discharges, but also its ecological performance footprint as well as means to get rid of such or that threat. As a result, accountants must come up with new mechanisms of accounting for activities in an objective way that will enable them to have a closer look and measure and thus indicate how much companies affect the surrounding area. The inclusion of renewable energy sources, mitigation of pollution caused by formation and again by the planet, and qualification for credible sustainable operation across the range are also details.

Social issues encompass the stakeholder boundaries between a firm and the people working for it, including consumers, residents of areas where such firms are set up, and other interested parties. Accountants are therefore required to conduct research, collect data and analyze it on such issues as charitable giving, diversity and inclusion, hiring practices and employee welfare. The social dimension so brought into the financial report would enable accountants to rationalize how a course of action pursued by a firm is in line with their pre-set objectives as far as its impact scheme.

Governance factors serve as an indicator of effectiveness and transparency popular inside the organ with regard to its internal mechanisms, policies, and structures related to decision-making. Board independence, CEO's compensation, shareholders' rights, the company's risk management, and compliance strategy, among others, are some of the factors that need to be assessed by accountants. The transparency of governance makes stakeholders in this organization consider firms with morals responsible.

It also requires an accountant to use a powerful set of measurement frameworks and reporting standards that are not simply GRI or sustainability, for example. So that ESG (Environmental, Social and Governance) will correspond adequately to the information provided in a complex report item, they have been included here. This integration therefore includes the high standards of accounting, such as those developed by ASB and various other organizations, an approach that is supposed to be consistent while reporting. Or there could be some kind of device, like analytics or reporting software, that will ensure correct generation after analysis of the efficiency of implementation if it provides stakeholders.

Consequently, the ESG issues can be included in disclosures depicting sufficient information suitable for stakeholders to make appropriate choices that align with their principles and desire towards sustainability. Additionally, it goes on to promote the use of responsible and sustainable strategies by organizations that wish to build sustainable business ideas capable of molding a somewhat sensitive international economy. This continued sense, therefore, continues to make accountants very good, for they contribute towards the souring of goodness and a better tomorrow not only in business entities but also at large.

5.6 Impact on Traditional Accounting Services

At present, AI and automation technologies may cause a revolution in the accounting industry to change market preferences when buying the usual bookkeeping process or data entry. With the slow automation of these activities, accountants have to actively change their service lines to be perceived as relevant and competitive in a fast changing environment.

It is also important to mention that AI improves the current practices of bookkeeping and data entry and therefore allows accountants to offer more value added services. Since Sap S4 takes care of the long and complicated calculations, accountants will be left with more time to provide strategic insights like data analysis or budgeting projections as accounting departments have less work. But as accountants move away from transactional acquisition to advisers and become trusted advisers and strategic partners that provide a lot of value for their clients, other new roles will arise, including job titles where you can only get the best candidate if they have worked with AI systems through effective digital technology applicability in completing tasks (Leitner-Hanetseder et al., 2021).

Furthermore, accountants can leverage the AI-driven analytics tools that enable them to convert large volumes of financial data into practical insights. Such analyses create a chance for them to establish trends, threats and areas of potential that can be identified on behalf of their client. And it is this data intensive structure that allows accountants to offer tailored personal financial advisory services, each supplemented with an elaborate description of the clients' objectives.

Given the fact that accounting services are changing, accountants need to be active learners who do not fear changes but support them by being conscious of new technologies and developing competencies in AI, data analytics and so on. This learning is an ongoing process, and it will ensure that they are always updated through various directive studies required by their customers, making them able to provide optimal solutions as new challenges emerge.

The accountant will be in a position to target the highest and the best needing digital economies by considering new services that they can possibly offer. Some of these are connected to the garnering functions that clients may need with respect to cybersecurity, ESG reporting and analysis, tax planning strategies or even implementations where AI can be used in their financial processes.

In this case, appropriate communication should be that which best suits and serves to educate the client. To prevent the mentioned misunderstanding and demonstrate that automation and integration of AI are good, accountants need to be involved in consumer work personally. First, where there is communication comes the element of trust; it tells how much accountants are cherished allies regarding one's financial triumph.

Thus, at the time of reviewing their propositions and benefiting from AI and automation-led advantages, accountants have the potential to emerge as top advisers in the digital-disruptive age. Even though adaptability technology may not deliver popularity in marketplaces faster, these accounting professionals can cause a revolution at their customers' bottom lines and last relationships with them while being competitive by providing needful enterprise performance counsel as well as help producing solutions that are transparent.

5.7 Predictive Analysis and Decision Making

AI offers exciting new opportunities because, with this capability, accountants become capable of forecasting and data-driven decision-making. This will enable accountants to acquire critical analytical intelligence regarding potential patterns, risks and opportunities that might allow them to take proactive actions based on AI algorithms or machine learning models.

Accountants should understand very well the insides of AI algorithms and models to be able to use them for predictive analysis appropriately. This calls for a thorough understanding of the application of AI technology, its approach and the compatible principles that drive it. Apart from that, there is a whole army of various concepts such as regression analysis, classification problems (clustering methods), and time-series forecasting that only give accountants several imports.

For a start, one must have an overview of AI algorithms, as this knowledge is required for several reasons. First, it can be said that this method ensures reliable and realistic data for the purpose of modeling. The reliability of the calculations is such that there will be no error imputed in any figures reported during supervision of patient care or support from a direct provider. At the same time, accountants should evaluate input quality in a scrupulous way, the appropriateness of chosen algorithms for specific tasks that need to be solved, and potential biases at all stages that impact results. This is an important review that guarantees the statistics underlying these forecasts are of good quality and accurately reflect reality.

Secondly, they can reach the level of understanding such AI models so that accountants can understand these outcomes and use them to achieve something. It is also not enough to just obtain the results presented by the AI system itself; accountants must also be able to position these findings, know their implications and communicate such analyses appropriately with relevant stakeholders.

Furthermore, the responsibility of using AI with predictive analysis requires monitoring and validation of model performance for an extended period. Accounting still works better because, in the case that new data has been received, or situational changes have been made, accountants use AI algorithms to reset them if necessity comes into play to fit forecasts for accurate prediction requirements.

Domains should also be added to the knowledge that accountants have in terms of technical aspects. Therefore, understanding the distinctive financial-economic-industry factors shaping their clients' businesses will allow accountants to apply specific modifications to these AI models in order to not only better address challenges but also seize opportunities.

Lastly, one of the issues that should be addressed by a concept in an AI course is lifelong learning owing to quick change and progressions in information technology. The AIs of the firms will need to stay on track because, due to the steady appearance of new generation sets, only others have also gotten news about the advent of new ones since the investment process was announced.

Last but not least, the potential analysis predictions and entry into a scale-preference based on data are futuristic powers that amaze an accountant by AI. However, like every other tool or methodology, its efficacy relies on AI algorithms, which harvest insights from experimentation and education obediently because one is mostly bound to rarely deal with a moving target. However, if accountants can use professional knowledge in reality and have common sense closely associated with their work due to sensory impressions, it would be feasible for trends in AI predictions to be followed by informed decision-making considering natural opportunities hiding behind every single one of these changes.

5.8 Regulatory Compliance and Standards

Nevertheless, in the dynamics of artificial intelligence and sustainable development, a change introduced an urgent requirement for new regulatory frameworks to adopt accounting standards that would be able to equally adjust at pace with advancement through technological changes. Regarding changes, it is therefore crucial for the development accountants to play a critical role, especially in developing new strategies that will ensure that this system changes not only compliance but also transparency.

This implies that a current regulatory audit should be done and others should be formulated that can suit these new trends in accounting, as is the case with automation, AI applications, etc. This must be picked up by regulators the same way algorithm accountability should also pick up data protection, and, finally, there are questions around what is regulated in terms of ethics when it comes to AI making financial decisions. In the future, such standards may be required to address a concern about how AI is introduced into the financial reporting and auditing processes in relation to bias explainability model validation as it becomes more widespread.

Similarly, since there is a middle line where the creativity of sustainable development issues gradually increases, there is a need for accounting standards to inculcate ESG elements entirely into modern business reporting tools. Reporting ESG aspects in financial based reports denotes the consideration of issues relating to data collection, measures on how it is gathered, and methodologies used when presenting. It is anticipated that these standards will provide a common ground that accountants can use in assessing and reporting on the sustainability of organizations, thus making it easier for stakeholders to compare entities' initiatives towards adopting sustainable operations.

Accountants simply have to be cautious not to fallow any new tendencies in legal or accounting standards development until they are endorsed as regulated guidance. This includes continuous professional advancement, engaging in public stakeholder discussions, and working with standard-setting bodies as well as regulators. As a result, accountants can forecast regulatory changes and adapt to them in time by changing their ways of doing things or taking advantage of evolving patterns.

Furthermore, the flexibility that comes about by embracing deviance or adherence should be more than passive conformity. The person should also take pride in the fact that by taking this step, he or she is trying to cash in on the laws when they are about to change. This type of business could, on the one hand, implement new legalization and, hence, become more transparent. It may also be able to win some credibility from its customers with an innovative approach. Moreover, these professionals may benefit at the earliest times from the adoption of repetitive reporting systems for regulatory changes in practice that really provide accountants who are quick to learn but implement trendier than others and to present innovative solutions to industry leaders specifically associated with AI-related problems or sustainable development risks.

As a conclusion, regulatory changes and adaptation within the accounting area are something inevitable with time towards an automated state of affairs developed from these powerful ai-plugins for effective development. It is also imperative that accountants appreciate the circumstances and be flexible, lest they make grave mistakes by ignoring breakthroughs in technology or incurring such convictions. This can make it possible for them to enhance the highest levels of professional conduct, foster transparency and openness, and support a transparent as well as an accountable economic environment.

5.9 Interdisciplinary Collaboration

Sustainable development is a multifaceted endeavor that demands effort and skills from various disciplines. Accountants, as financial experts, are an integral component of this collective effort. For appropriate reporting on the sustainability performance of a company, accountants have to work together with experts in environmental science, social responsibility, etc. Taha et al. (2023) state that the effectiveness of cloud auditing is enhanced by the use of external auditors who are knowledgeable about cloud, but the function is more effective in addressing strategic issues compared to organization standards and security.

Collaboration with environmental scientists is vital and essential to analyzing a company's environmental impact in detail. Environmental specialists can help accountants identify important sustainability measures, like carbon emissions, water consumption, waste generation, and resource consumption. Through associates, accountants find out how these other variables correlate with financial details. Measurement, systematization, and financial reporting accurately summarize the impact of the company's environment and reflect on the environment's KPIs in a company's financial statement. This allows for a holistic overview of the state of the environment's stakeholders.

Experts on social responsibility provide an interesting angle on the business-employee, -community, and -society interactions. By cooperating with such specialists, accountants are able to analyze phenomena concerning employee health, diversity and inclusion, community involvement initiatives, and the ethical conduct of the supply chain. Financial information can be integrated with social responsibility data to provide a more holistic picture of the company's social sustainability and ethical business practices; thus, accountants can play an important role here.

Sustainable development influence is mostly on governance principles if governance principles affect the decisions taken, responsibilities are transparent, and workers take responsibility for the actions taken by management. To measure governance efficiency, corporate governance frameworks, board independence, CEO remuneration, and risk management processes, accountants must collaborate with governance professionals. This facilitates accountants to report on the governance initiatives of the organization, and this gives confidence to stakeholders of the organization that it is morally upright.

A collaborative effort between the accountant experts and professionals from other disciplines would require good communication, respect for each other, and a high resolution to meet the sustainable development goals. More frequent meetings, workshops, and cross-disciplinary discussions lead to a better understanding of each other's perspectives, which again leads to more detailed and profound reporting.

Technology has greatly increased collaboration. By virtue of shared data platforms, collaboration tools and integrated reporting systems, information can quickly flow from one accountant to another as well as between business subject-matter experts. Such advances make the collection of data simple and, thus, allow the creation of very detailed sustainability reports.

Sustainable development is a collaborative effort that draws on the knowledge of many different stakeholders. To accurately report on a company's sustainability performance, accountants must collaborate with experts in environmental science, social responsibility, governance, and other fields. Accountants may give stakeholders in-depth knowledge of a company's environmental and social impact through successful collaboration and the promotion of transparency, accountability, and development toward a more sustainable future.

5.10 Transparency and Accountability

Transparency and accountability have become integral parts of any company or organization pursuing sustainable development, since the latter is evolving into one of the most important aspects of company operations in many countries around the world. Ethos and clinical sustainability are thus the concept that stakeholders, including regulators, clients, employees, and clients, need evidence that companies perform their activities based on ethos and sustainability, that is, clinical sustainability. In this regard, accountants play a crucial role in the fixing of financial statements, which depict commitment for the sake of sustainability, transparency and accountability.

Standards concerning sustainability were somehow incorporated into financial reporting, mainly by the accountants, as they could present a system-wide view and a clear portrayal of the company's efforts towards sustainability. Besides the financial listing, a report of analysis on the ESG performance must be presented and marked. The contribution of accountants can make sure that the financial statements are not just a mirror of the real financial results but the door to the relationships between the company and society, as the interest in people, planet and profits, along with the consequences, increases on the side of stakeholders.

Therefore, like a multitude of stakeholders are utilized to make the reporting on sustainability, the accountants should permeate sustainability reporting inspired by the aforementioned stakeholders for the sustainability of the collaboration. They enable organizations to determine their sustainability plan by defining specific objectives and procedures that help the organization achieve its sustainability mission. If a company is talking about their work concerning sustainability, then it is a kind of advertising to society that they are working transparently. Later, stakeholders' decisions can be taken as acceptable based on their beliefs.

The reliance on accountants is underpinned by assuring stakeholders that the provided data is credible and that sustainability report verification is assured. Independent accountants' pieces of evidence help stakeholders enhance their self-belief that they possess a brand and credibility, which makes them powerful champions.

In this regard, the impacts of ESG performance are seen to contribute to driving business success as investors and other stakeholders consider this factor in their decision-making practices. This function does not distinguish between different sustainability programs that the firm implements; it just enables the accountants to simplify the financial implications that these programs have on the firm and to make it a way of comparing the longer-term benefits. The book aims to convey how the function of the accountant affects the integration of insights into policy regarding financial consequences that carry implications for sustainability practices that are supported by strategic planning and thus match the financial objectives with those of sustainability.

Accountants are also vital in helping companies identify areas for improvement and efficiency gains in their sustainable practices. By analyzing financial data with ESG metrics, they can discover cost-saving opportunities and recommend sustainable investment solutions that yield long-term benefits.

Finally, an increase in the demand for sustainable development establishing firms has helped to point out the need for transparency and accountability in business. In this regard, an accountant's effort in sustainability is important because they provide information gathered on the financial accounts of a firm that usually acts as an epidemic statement of the organization's intent towards such initiatives. The integration of sustainability metrics in financial reporting efforts helps build reliability and trust by generating independent assurance by using the relevancy analysis of the non-financial information, which then encourages the decision-making process as a consequence of accountants assisting companies in providing proof that they are accountable for environmental and social sustainability.

It is this change that will truly usher the accounting profession into an epoch defined by opportunity for mile-away-from- home progress and development. At this point, where the two realms meet, accountants are empowered by the interplay of the two and can exploit opportunities to change their practices and incorporate those updates in technology and sustainable practices to be equally increased and tactical in business. With regard to this, Kommunuri (2022) highlighted the current role played by the advanced tools of AI and ML in the realm of accounting.

AI, as it offers an accountant the freedom from accounting work, empowers her to do some real-time activities and devote her time to important and critical analysis of data. Contemporary accountants, especially those using AI-derived information, can provide better advice to customers by comparing the expected books of future periods and reflecting on issues under discussion. It, therefore, unfolds as a relationship management treasure house of the professional accountants, who remain unparalleled in their praising the former's ability to further strengthen the loyalty of the client to them and the idea of them actively guiding their business.

Alongside the above, ESG assimilation has become increasingly rigid and substantive, which makes the issue of sustainable or green accounting relatively mandatory for accountants. Through such activities, they enable the ability to rationalize the much broader nature of the productivity landscape. However, it is very significant in that it helps accountants report the sustainable activities of the company, which apparently simplifies the process of promoting the relationship between it and the organization's mission and later attempts to reduce it towards long-term sustainable practices that clearly create value not only to shareholders but also to society and environmental bodies.

Therefore, achieving this sense of AI potential to ensure sustainability for development is largely determined by the fact that accountants have to justify their responses to challenges. Change is nowadays technological and hence rapid, and it is a requisite; therefore, there is constant learning and no provision for one with no knowledge of recent issues. Also, apart from the trends of emerging AI technologies, data analytics, and sustainability in the locality, the professionals should have to come up with innovation measures that will suit the requirements of the businesses and companies of their clients.

One of the other resources that qualifies for a resilient accountant is the ability to travel with any team, which includes general norms of living. Change and its acceptance and fostering are always unpleasant notions, but they are indeed necessary if we want to advance our grip on this revolutionary age. All in all, in spite of the fact that the effectiveness of accountants is indeed on indeed, any road beyond exaggeration, and for many of the reasons, the accounting practitioners in the meantime should not be on free rein against the directions of technological advance, whereas they have to guarantee interdisciplinary elements' plantation of latest burgeoning curricula and flaunt the model of service.

All the activities associated with the accounting profession are conducted with an embodiment of high morality. In this setting, rises in uptake rates of artificial intelligence (AI) and automation require ethical audits for the accountants to contend with data hacks, algorithmic bias and AI choice confusion. The emphasis on ethics is important for the support of trust relationships with clients and other stakeholders and for controlling risks arising from issues and risks engendered by AI applications.

The path that we have to say now is – the practices of AI and sustainable development have found a unique way, which is, on the one hand, very new but still curious for the accounting sector. Human accounting also provides the opportunity to take into account the concept of sustainability in accounting, as well as to move from traditional functions into a role that serves as a catalyst for the success of the client. Namely, to establish their maximum utilization, the accountants should fight against the challenges through constant learning and change of practices in response to the adopted changes, and in such a manner, they should have the highest moral integrity. Through these programs, they are able to complement their skills with the intense, escalating demand for a sound and responsible policy on financial accounting.

6. EMBRACING THE ERA OF AI AND SUSTAINABLE DEVELOPMENT

The accounting profession should also take a more proactive approach to improving their capabilities so that they remain prepared and continue reaping the benefits AI provides while adequately dealing with such challenges. Accountants should also focus on other types of knowledge, since they will apply the skills they acquire through AI. A more sophisticated form of data analysis and the skills in management using machine learning systems-strategic planning as well as coordination, including communication—may be a potential skill needed for this requirement. Additionally, the accounting profession should play a great role in supporting the achievement of sustainable development goals. Accountants possess uncommon sources of company finances and performance that can be very helpful in operationalizing the incorporation aspect associated with social or governance problems.

Notably, in this manner, accountants help with sustainable investing and contribute to the realization of a more robust global economy, as businesses will submit sustainability returns that require reporting on their activities' ESG selection.

In fact, the implementation of AI in the accounting applied sphere opens many opportunities for the modern era to improve productivity and decision-making plus services that will provide additional added value benefits to customers. On the other hand, problems must follow technological progress, such as increased risks of unemployment and responsibility or demand shifting moments caused by lower needs arising when new technologies are introduced; above all this, there is an ethical issue. In general, human intelligence will help to adapt over the years to this industry's realities and dynamics in the accounting work process, along with AI technology (Hasan, 2022).

Therefore, this dark age of the poor level of technology transfer relieves an accountant from fears that he or she is thorny with his or her aversion to decent use and makes it start not only innovative but also authoritative canon to advocate their profession more properly through virtue. In addition to this, integrated reporting is an important tool that can be used in the accomplishment of the goals of sustainable development; this approach includes considering financial objectives together with concepts based on social responsibility and environmental issues. The accounting professionals should enjoy the indicated powers of their AI technology and make moral use of them as it orients its approach to spend most on correct control over these AI tools, thus commanding them permanently but shaping them profitably tomorrow using subtle steps for creation.

7. ADDRESSING CHALLENGES AND ETHICAL CONSIDERATIONS

Based on the guide to sustainable development, it is obvious that AI did indeed render the accounting profession more competent. However, it offers accountants a particular package of problems to solve. When embracing AI's promise to ensure moral and sustainable operations, accountants must strike a balance between these potential benefits and the need for human oversight (Tan et al., 2019; Yaacoub et al., 2020). One of the greatest methods that will make accounting professionals effective in this rapidly changing era is to achieve a balance between innovations within technology and their social and environmental obligations.

While the assimilation of AI into progressive accounting brings opportunities, it comes with concerns and ethical dilemmas. Hence, when using AI algorithms in the handling of any sensitive sustainability data as a tool to work on with accountants, be very careful because some privacy and security issues surround technology. For the credibility and acceptability of sustainability reporting to be maintained, accuracy and reliability in the results generated from AI processes have to be provided. Moreover, the biased culture in the dataset that is used to develop AI may remain natural in this case. Accountants also have a professional responsibility of identifying bias if they want to make environmentally sensitive and reporting decisions.

De Villiers (2021) identified seven principles after an analysis of literature and qualitative data through focus groups, thought leader discussions, interviews, and workshops. The goal of such principles is to support the efforts of the instructors to prepare the accounting students for the machinations of automation and artificial intelligence. This research leads to the Seven Cs model, which comprises critical and conceptual thinking, an inquiry, dealing with complexity and escaping failure, creativity and innovation, conciseness, cooperation, consciousness, respectfulness, and moral fiber, curiosity, lifelong learning, and specialized generalists. This model not only helps to orient the current activity of education but also gives a base for further investigation.

All industries, including accounting, have many areas of business where they can gain by using AI together with other advanced technologies. Sustainability and benefits are countless. Let alone the elimination of labor-intensive or uninteresting ones, AI can streamline complicated workflows and perfect optimal resource employment, thereby privileging work. By using this technology, organizations will be able to have sustainable operations as algorithms, such as machine learning and AI based ones, are bound to make better decisions.

Additionally, the artificial intelligence capability of filtering information from large volumes of data to identify trends could be useful for better monitoring and management of environmental impacts. Examples of using AI involve the assessment and initialization of a carbon footprint, possible environmental impact detection, and making sure that the executive supply chain follows sustainable approaches. In agriculture, AI-focused precision farming has demonstrated developing sustainability and minimizing waste by using water and fertilizers rationally. In spite of the partial effectiveness of this technology, AI integration and application imply sustainability-related issues and ethical dilemmas. From this, some concerns arise; one of them is the potential that people may lose jobs due to automation. A fresh fear of technology is ignited in public and academic debate, with the expectation of massive job losses in the foreseeable future. (Arntz et al., 2017). The AI could replace human employees in performing some tasks, especially the repetitive ones and those that involve routine. This can result in social and economic problems, which in turn alter the way of life for people as well as society.

Decision-making through AI also brings up some ethical issues. When garbage or poor data enters the system, it can only give AI algorithms nothing but garbage when making use of sample bias. The latter may inadvertently result in inequity and prejudice when it comes to cases such as employment, investments or resource distribution.

This should be a morally and viable AI Up take to avoid the above-noted challenges. Transparency, fairness and responsibility are some of the areas that organizations must consider during design or when implementing AI systems with great caution. To some extent, the problem of algorithmic biases can be addressed by establishing diverse and inclusive AI teams. The provision of retraining for the AI's victims in addition to upskilling programs can help people fairly leverage AI as supplementary capacities rather than machines that replace them, thereby accepting adaptation towards new jobs.

Thus, because of all the drawbacks mentioned above with regard to the benefits attainable by means of AI technology applications for sustainability and decision-making while merging, it implies setting up some problems related thereto that need thorough consideration before making any decisions. A thoughtful and conscientious approach to introducing AI, coupled with specific measures aimed at overcoming the shadowing of jobs due to emerging technologies or the timely resolution of ethically significant issues, can pave the way for more sustainable development models.

8. CONCLUSION AND RECOMMENDATIONS

With the whole world busy using artificial intelligence, development and sustainability, they have seen signs of the future for the avant-garde, on which the accounting profession has a massive challenge to suitably redefine social compassion. Moral accounting is relevant to the field of preparing moral grounds for involving accountancy. Accountants play an essential role in developing moral accounting principles that preserve openness, honesty, and civic responsibility. By complying with high ethical standards and making sure that financial decisions support the well-being of both people and the environment, accountants can positively impact change both inside and outside of organizations. Faced with the challenges of disruptive technologies brought forth by Industry 4.0, the accounting and auditing discipline is required to undergo a metamorphosis in order to reach the next level (Hasan, 2022).

Focusing on one of these ESG reporting elements, the transformation approach serves. Accounting practitioners should thus understand the power of ESG regarding financial reporting because such an approach makes environmental signals as well as social impacts clear about this organization as well as its attitude towards sustainability. To encourage a more approachable culture, accountants endorse the utilization of ESG reporting that impels business forms to exercise caution by expanding their portion towards maintenance.

Accountants should know the implications of their profession in social welfare. They are completely changing the world, then making a mere number balancer. However, their right attitude and qualifications for a sustainable state help to form the total approval that human values, entire nature protection and social responsibility should be given. Accountants take part in sustainability programs actively and make efforts to push resources that are used for clean activities while defending marginalized communities.

During this period when creation principles and sustainable good advance issues dominate the debate, the accounting profession has an opportunity to shed new light on forward-coming where economic growth, social development and the protection of the earth follow in diverse ways. Recognizing their position as agents of change, accountants may help understand the inconveniences, side streams and divisions in SD, which would enable organizations to see intricacy. Living ethics and sustainability within

Table 1. Key variables

Accounting	Recording, analyzing, and reporting financial transactions of an organization.
Algorithm Transparency	Explanation and justification of AI algorithms' decisions for accountability and trustworthiness.
Artificial Intelligence (AI)	Technology simulating human intelligence in machines for tasks like learning and decision-making.
Auditing	Examining financial records to ensure accuracy, compliance, and adherence to standards.
Automation and AI integration	Adopting AI technologies in accounting processes.
Communication and cultural competence	Effective communication across cultures.
Cross-cultural practices and cultural competencies	Navigating cultural differences in global business.
Data management and security	Protecting financial data and complying with laws.
Ethical considerations	Addressing bias, privacy, and transparency in decision-making.
Ethical considerations in AI adoption	Ethical dilemmas in AI adoption, including bias and privacy.
Ethical Guidelines and Professional Codes	Standards guiding ethical practices in accounting.
Global integration and increasing complexity	Managing complexities in global operations.
Impact on Traditional Accounting Services	Changes due to AI and automation.
International accounting standards and regulations	Compliance with international financial reporting standards.
Interdisciplinary collaboration	Collaboration between accountants and experts for accurate reporting.
Predictive Analysis and Decision-Making	AI-driven analytics for forecasting trends.
Regulatory compliance and standards	Adhering to accounting standards and regulatory frameworks.
Responsibility of using AI with predictive analysis	Monitoring AI model performance for accuracy.
Skill Upgrading	Acquiring competencies in emerging technologies like AI.
Sustainability accounting	Accounting practices focusing on environmental and social impact.
Sustainable Reporting	Integrating ESG factors into financial disclosures.
Technical knowledge in accounting	Understanding financial and industry factors for AI modifications.
Transparency and accountability	Ensuring transparency and ethical conduct in financial reporting.

their daily routine might assist accountants in taking part in building up a world that is more developed and fairer, with prosperity and abundance copying as well as precedents for future generations. Other areas in which accountants can further lead in risk disclosures to business organizations include changes in climate, for instance, with respect to weather conditions like high sea levels and ocean acidity. They can also provide contributions and references to facilitate carbon offsetting in the low-carbon economy. These preventative steps support the sustainability of the environment and strengthen responsibility as corporations address climate change challenges. Some of the key concepts discussed in this chapter are shown in Table 1.

REFERENCES

Akhter, A., & Sultana, R. (2018). Sustainability of accounting profession at the age of fourth industrial revolution. *International Journal of Accounting and Financial Reporting*, *8*(4), 139. doi:10.5296/ijafr.v8i4.13689

Al-Htaybat, K., & von Alberti-Alhtaybat, L. (2017). Big Data and corporate reporting: Impacts and paradoxes. *Accounting, Auditing & Accountability Journal*, *30*(4), 850–873. doi:10.1108/AAAJ-07-2015-2139

Arnold, V. (2018). The changing technological environment and the future of behavioural research in accounting. *Accounting and Finance*, *58*(2), 315–339. doi:10.1111/acfi.12218

Arntz, M., Gregory, T., & Zierahn, U. (2017). Revisiting the risk of automation. *Economics Letters*, *159*, 157–160. doi:10.1016/j.econlet.2017.07.001

Bonyuet, D. (2020). Overview and Impact of Blockchain on Auditing. *The International Journal of Digital Accounting Research*, *20*, 31–43. doi:10.4192/1577-8517-v20_2

Burke, R. J., & Cooper, C. L. (2004). *Leading in turbulent times: Managing in the new world of work.* Blackwell Publishing.

Burns, M.B., & Igou, A. (2019). "Alexa, Write an Audit Opinion": Adopting Intelligent Virtual Assistants in Accounting Workplaces. *Journal of Emerging Technologies in Accounting, 16*(1), 81–92. https://doi.org/ doi:10.2308/jeta-52424

Chamba, L. T., Chari, F., & Zhou, H. (2023). Exploring the Potential for State-Owned Enterprises in Developing Countries to Leverage the Benefits of the Fourth Industrial Revolution for Economic Transformation. *Journal of Public Administration, 58*(2). https://doi.org/ doi:10.53973/jopa.2023.58.2.a9

Coyne, E. M., Coyne, J. G., & Walker, K. B. (2018). Big Data information governance by accountants. *International Journal of Accounting & Information Management*, *26*(1), 153–170. doi:10.1108/IJAIM-01-2017-0006

Davenport, T. H., & Ronanki, R. (2018). *Artificial Intelligence for the Real World.* Harvard Business Review (HBR). https://www.bizjournals.com/boston/news/2018/01/09/hbr-artificial-intelligence-for-the-real-world.html

De Villiers, R. (2021). Seven principles to ensure future-ready accounting graduates – a model for future research and practice. *Meditari Accountancy Research*, *29*(6), 1354–1380. doi:10.1108/MEDAR-04-2020-0867

Demirkan, S., Demirkan, I., & McKee, A. (2020). Blockchain technology in the future of business cyber security and accounting. *Journal of Management Analytics*, *7*(2), 189–208. doi:10.1080/23270012.2020.1731721

Dess, G. G., & Picken, J. C. (2000). Changing roles: Leadership in the 21st century. *Organizational Dynamics*, *28*(3), 18–33. doi:10.1016/S0090-2616(00)88447-8

Griffin, O. (2019, October 6). *How Artificial Intelligence Will Impact Accounting*. Economia. https://www.icaew.com/technical/technology/artificial-intelligence/artificial-intelligence-articles/how-artificial-intelligence-will-impact-accounting

Hasan, A. R. (2022). Artificial Intelligence (AI) in Accounting & Auditing: A Literature Review. *Open Journal of Business and Management*, *10*(1), 440–465. doi:10.4236/ojbm.2022.101026

Herath, S. K., & Joshi, P. L. (2023). Audit Data Analytics: A Game Changer for Audit Firms. *International Journal of Auditing and Accounting Studies*, *5*(1), 29–48. doi:10.47509/IJAAS.2023.v05i01.02

Hespenheide, E. (2021). *A Practical Guide to Sustainability Reporting Using GRI and SASB Standards*. Sustainability Accounting Standards Board. https://www.globalreporting.org/media/mlkjpn1i/gri-sasb-joint-publication-april-2021.pdf

Kroon, N., Alves, M. C., & Martins, I. (2021). The Impacts of Emerging Technologies on Accountants' Role and Skills: Connecting to Open Innovation—A Systematic Literature Review. *Journal of Open Innovation*, *7*(3), 163. Advance online publication. doi:10.3390/joitmc7030163

Leitner-Hanetseder, S., Lehner, O. M., Eisl, C., & Forstenlechner, C. (2021). A profession in transition: Actors, tasks and roles in AI-based accounting. *Journal of Applied Accounting Research*, *22*(3), 539–556. doi:10.1108/JAAR-10-2020-0201

Marshall, T. E., & Lambert, S. L. (2018). Cloud-Based Intelligent Accounting Applications: Accounting Task Automation Using IBM Watson Cognitive Computing. *Journal of Emerging Technologies in Accounting*, *15*(1), 199–215. doi:10.2308/jeta-52095

Omoteso, K. (2012). The application of artificial intelligence in auditing: Looking back to the future. *Expert Systems with Applications*, *39*(9), 8490–8495. doi:10.1016/j.eswa.2012.01.098

Rahman, S. S., & Dekkati, S. (2022). Revolutionizing Commerce: The Dynamics and Future of E-Commerce Web Applications. *Asian Journal of Applied Science and Engineering*, *11*(1), 65–73. doi:10.18034/ajase.v11i1.58

Rahmatian, A., Hassani, H., & Rostami-Tabar, B. (2019). Prediction and Generation of Stock Price Movements: A Data-Driven Approach. *Complexity*, *2019*, 1–18. doi:10.1155/2019/1825195

Samans, R., & Nelson, J. (2022). *Corporate reporting and accountability, Chapter in Sustainable Enterprise Value Creation*. Palgrave Macmillan. doi:10.1007/978-3-030-93560-3

Schaltegger, S., & Zvezdov, D. (2013). In control of sustainability information: Untangling the role of accountants. Accounting and Control for Sustainability, 265-296. https://doi.org/ doi:10.1108/S1479-

Stafie, G., & Grosu, V. (2023). The Impact of Artificial Intelligence on Accounting. In M. Busu (Ed.), *Digital Economy and the Green Revolution. ICBE 2022. Springer Proceedings in Business and Economics*. Springer. doi:10.1007/978-3-031-19886-1_18

Tan, B. S., & Low, K. Y. (2019). Blockchain as the database engine in the accounting system. *Australian Accounting Review*, *29*(2), 312–318. doi:10.1111/auar.12278

Tuli, F. A., & Thaduri, U. R. (2023). The Integration of Artificial Intelligence in Forensic Accounting: A Game-Changer. *Asian Accounting and Auditing Advancement*, *14*(1), 12–20.

Ucoglu, D. (2020). Current Machine Learning Applications in Accounting and Auditing. *Pressacademia*, *12*(1), 1–7. doi:10.17261/Pressacademia.2020.1337

Yakhou, M., Schulte, P., & Placzek, M. (2018). The Impact of Artificial Intelligence on Audit Procedures: The Case of Journal Entry Testing. *Journal of Emerging Technologies in Accounting*, *15*, 147–156. doi:10.2308/jeta-51915

Yigitbasioglu, O., Green, P., & Cheung, M.-Y. D. (2023). Digital transformation and accountants as advisors. *Accounting, Auditing & Accountability Journal*, *36*(1), 209–237. doi:10.1108/AAAJ-02-2019-3894

Yukl, G., & Lepsinger, R. (2005). Why integrating the leading and managing roles is essential for organizationaleffectiveness. *Organizational Dynamics*, *34*(4), 361–375. doi:10.1016/j.orgdyn.2005.08.004

Zemánková, A. (2019). Artificial Intelligence and Blockchain in Audit and Accounting: Literature Review. *WSEAS Transactions on Business and Economics, 16*, 568-581. https://www.wseas.org/multimedia/journals/economics/2019/b245107-089.pdf

Chapter 12
Harmonizing Accounting and Artificial Intelligence for the Sustainability of the Accounting Profession

I Made Laut Mertha Jaya
https://orcid.org/0000-0001-9722-7217
Universitas Mahakarya Asia, Indonesia

Mar'a Elthaf Ilahiyah
Sekolah Tinggi Ilmu Ekonomi Indonesia, Indonesia

ABSTRACT

The sustainability of the accounting profession is starting to be questioned. Will it still exist, or will it be replaced by technology? This chapter will provide a literature review on the relationship between accounting and artificial intelligence and harmonize them to maintain the sustainability of the accounting profession in Indonesia. The authors conducted this literature review process using the bibliometric analysis method and described it by embedding several assumptions from various literature opinions. In the end, according to the authors' point of view, the accountant profession will not be completely displaced by technology, but the presence of technology will actually facilitate the work of accountants, so that all processes are carried out by system and not manually. This shorter way will produce more accurate, faster, and less workforce output. Meanwhile, the presence of technology can also reduce the need for human resources (accountants). Nevertheless, the emergence of technology also opens up opportunities for the accounting profession with new technology-related expertise, such as digital forensic accounting, environmental management accounting/green accountant, and information systems-based auditing. The green accountant is an accountant who performs green accounting practices. Therefore, the scope of accounting today is no longer limited to financial matters, but also includes social and environmental matters. This integration of financial, social, and environmental accounting is called green accounting.

DOI: 10.4018/979-8-3693-0847-9.ch012

1. INTRODUCTION

Currently, globally, businesses have transformed from conventional-based to digital-based (Khalil et al., 2022). This is marked by the emergence of many technology-based companies in the fields of FinTech, E-commerce, etc (Tsai & Peng, 2017). Of course, the current developments have led to many fundamental changes in the business world, especially existing business processes. Respond to changes that are too fast, not all conventional companies are able to compete and eventually go out of business (Serrano-Cinca et al., 2019). This can be minimized if there is a professional role that can help become a value cog that can help the sustainability of a company that is constantly changing (Fleming, 2019). Many business experts refer to the era we are entering as the Industrial Revolution 4.0 era which is marked by the emergence of advanced technology such as artificial intelligence and the disruptive era, where it is feared that sophisticated technology can replace many human jobs (Ruiz-Real et al., 2021). Many people from all walks of life are worried about losing their jobs in the future because of the rise of robots (Lacurezeanu et al., 2020).

The future of the accounting profession is starting to be questioned, will it still exist or will it be replaced by technology (Stafie & Grosu, 2023). The rapid development of technology and information requires all fields of profession to continue to develop ways of working quickly and accurately so as not to be left behind by the times and to achieve goals efficiently (Malva Cakra Dewa et al., 2018). The same applies to the field of accountancy, a branch of science from economics, studying various kinds of financial analysis (Al-refiay et al., 2022). With increasingly modern technology, it demands that accounting be able to make better use of technology. This is proven by the existence of Artificial Intelligence (AI) which is widely discussed in accounting (Oprea et al., 2022). Accounting is an information system that measures business activity, processes the data into a report, and communicates the results to decision makers, which is done by accountants (Bunget & Lungu, 2023). Artificial Intelligence (AI) is a field of study regarding intelligent thoughts that can be used as a form to perform calculations (Chatterjee & Bhattacharjee, 2020). Calculations performed by AI aim to create a more controlled computerized system, make work easier for users, and analyze a problem. However, AI still raises pros and cons in implementation in accounting due to a lack of adequate information (Fleming, 2019).

Over the next few decades, intelligent systems will take on an increasing number of decision-making tasks from humans (Fleming, 2019). While accountants have been using technology for years to improve what they do and provide greater value to businesses, this is an opportunity to reimagine and radically improve the quality of business and investment decisions that is the ultimate goal of the accounting profession (JAYA & Narsa, 2022). The more the company develops, the data that is managed is also increasingly complex. Various processes of accounting are no longer done manually, considering that these processes require a long time, and require a lot of human labor, causing reduced effectiveness and time efficiency (Adamyk et al., 2023). On the other hand, accountants also often make unintentional errors (Human Error) or intentional fraud to benefit individuals and companies (Tapanjeh & Tarawneh, 2020).

When discussing the role of accountants in the digital era, we need to discuss the issue of sustainable development goals or what are known as Sustainable Development Goals (SDGs) (Marrone et al., 2020). The accounting profession has a crucial role in helping to make existing goals a reality. According to the Director of Finance of the International Federation of Accountants (IFAC), 8 of the 17 existing SDGs goals are assisted by the role of accountants in their various roles in work. Therefore, technology is here to increase company productivity by changing manual activities to technology-based ones (Chatterjee

& Bhattacharjee, 2020). With the presence of AI, within the company it can help business processes run faster, more accurately and efficiently.

Living in an era that has entered the industrial revolution 4.0, every accountant must be able to use and understand technology (Razali et al., 2022). It is undeniable that accounting and technology have become one part, so like it or not, accountants must have the ability to operate software technology. Thus, accountants as a profession that plays an important role in the business world must adapt to the changing times that are increasingly gray (Ucoglu, 2020). Accountants can be value drivers in business to achieve business sustainability. As young accountants, we should not be pessimistic about existing technological developments. We must see the development of artificial intelligence as an opportunity to make the accounting profession more efficient and useful. Accountants must continue to learn and prepare themselves by equipping and increasing their abilities so that the accounting profession continues to contribute and influence. This paper will provide a literature review on the relationship between accounting and artificial intelligence and harmonize them to maintain the sustainability of the accounting profession in Indonesia. We conducted this literature review process using the bibliometric analysis method, and described it by embedding several assumptions from various literature opinions.

2. LITERATURE REVIEW

2.1. Harmonising Accounting and Artificial Intelligence

The current generation is closely related to technological developments in the digital era (Bratina, 2019). All financial and non-financial activities have been digitized (Lee et al., 2018). The impact of this digital era has brought enormous changes to all human activities, especially the accounting profession (Malva Cakra Dewa et al., 2018). This causes an accountant to always be updated on technological developments in the digital era by looking at the opportunities that exist. The rapid development of technology and the flow of information has changed one's view of obtaining information, including in the world of accounting (Johnson et al., 2022). Technological advances mean that not too many human resources are needed within the company, including accounting staff. This makes the accounting profession not really needed because of technological advances. With the existence of technology, such as robotics and Artificial Intelligence (AI), it is only a matter of time that the control of work normally done by humans will be replaced by robots (Isnawati et al., 2021). Artificial Intelligence is artificial intelligence with simulation on machines that are programmed to imitate human intelligence processes and imitate their actions, so that the current system can think systematically and more quickly with humans, so that output can be produced instantly as well. This process includes learning (data acquisition and decisions to use data), reasoning (using situations to reach definite conclusions) and assumptions. The arrival of this technology has begun to obliterate and narrow some jobs across the industry (Fleming, 2019).

With the transformation from era 4.0 to era 5.0, we are now entering an era where humans are increasingly developing and have an impact on fundamental changes (Tee & Ong, 2016). The meaning of society 5.0 is the concept of human-centered community technology and collaboration with technology to solve social problems that are integrated in virtual and real world spaces (Hendarsyah, 2019). In this era, we will summarize several ways of working that are completed with several technologies, such as sensors, artificial intelligence, and robots that will be used to do work (Fleming, 2019). As well as changing all systems and arrangements which are also called disruptions in several fields. Disruption in the form of an analog process that becomes digital must be responded to, so that its role is not replaced by today's technological advances (Ruiz-Real et al., 2021). Digital change is currently growing rapidly among the community as a solution in carrying out daily activities in the era of society 5.0, and is increasingly replacing the role of humans in their fields (Hendarsyah, 2019). This change also introduces a 5G internet network level which has internet speed 10 times that of a 4G network. The impact of this transition, an accountant and a public accounting firm are forced to develop an application that can be accessed on mobile phones, virtual reality and the like (Isnawati et al., 2021). Auditing is also required to present real-time financial report data via mobile devices which can minimize fraud so that the presentation of reports can be accurate and transparent (Chatfield & Reddick, 2019).

Currently some accounting jobs have been replaced by Robots (Fleming, 2019). This is due to the development of Robotics and Data Analytics (Big Data) which takes over the basic work of an accountant (recording, processing and sorting types of transactions) (Kumar et al., 2021). Therefore, accounting students should start studying programming and algorithms and must improve the competencies that are important for an accountant, namely data analysis, information technology development and leadership skills.(Supra, 2017). Companies can lose their competitiveness if they do not pay attention to these changes in technological developments in their business strategy and leadership strategy (Parnell et al., 2019). So, companies really need an accountant who is aware of cloud accounting.

The continuous development and expansion of these technologies is not about taking away human involvement, but about combining human experience and machine learning models that can complement human thinking to produce outstanding results. The goal of creating new technologies is to create operating processes with high accuracy, efficient performance with the elimination of any form of error. Artificial intelligence will create a glamorous future for the accounting profession. Artificial Intelligence is an opportunity for the growth and development of today's business world. For this reason, accountant practitioners and students must get proper and adequate education and training in the development of accounting technology to gain experience, reliable skills in applying accounting and technology knowledge in combination, and become a significant value for themselves and in the business world.

2.2. Sustainability of the Accounting Profession

In the current era, accounting is in a dynamic condition of change, both in terms of knowledge, profession, and so on (Mookerjee & Rao, 2021). Especially in the current era of digital transformation, accounting knowledge is developing rapidly and it is required to continue to be able to adapt. An accountant as a professional is someone who has expertise in accounting, obtained through formal education and work experience, who demonstrates and complies with a code of ethics, maintains high professional standards and is an agent of a professional accounting organization or other legal entity. This understanding is important to know because an accountant is different from a bookkeeper.

The accounting profession has a higher role and responsibility in terms of providing interpretations and recommendations that form the basis for decision making. A competent professional accountant is an invaluable asset for a company. Based on a statement issued by IFAC (International Federation of Accountants), professional accountants have a role in helping top management develop corporate strategy, provide advice and assist businesses to reduce costs, increase the company's competitive advantage, and reduce risk. This includes analyzing, creating, and communicating information finance to create and direct the strategic direction of the business (Jackling et al., 2007).

Figure 1. Bibliometric analysis test

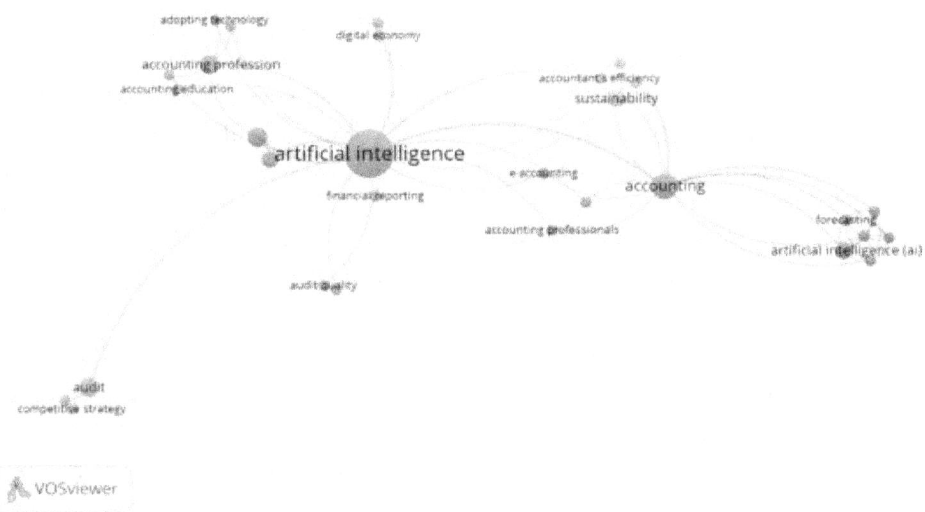

Especially, when business processes are currently shifting to digital, organizations have very large data (Yuana et al., 2021). This gap needs to be responded properly by the organization. For this reason, organizations need to carry out a strategic response consisting of two strategies, namely a digital business strategy and a digital transformation strategy (Edwards, 2021). Digital business is how an organization manages its business model, while digital transformation is a transition from the analog or traditional era to being fully digital. When changes in digital transformation occur, organizations must adapt to some of the changes. One of them is related to organizational structure, organizational culture, leadership, and the roles and abilities of employees. Companies have several barriers or challenges that limit an organization or company to transform digitally. These changes, first is the Inertia organization, a condition where the organization does not want to change because it is comfortable with the conditions that existed at that time. The second is employee resistance, where employees don't want to make changes. These two risks need to be managed for organizations to be successful in digital transformation (Edwards, 2021).

Accountants who understand technological developments must know the latest technological developments and help companies build strategic responses (Rosmida, 2019). In the area of value creation, accountants can use Big Data, Data Analytics to build a more Agile organization. In addition, accountants can also play a role in structural changes, helping organizations take advantage of the latest technology (Rosmida, 2019). Digital transformation in accounting is the processing of accounts payable and receivables, digitization in the procurement process, digitization in the audit process, and so on. Accountants can also participate in digital financial management and audit processes. Therefore, it is expected that the ability of accountants in the digital aspect must continue to develop along with the times (Isnawati et al., 2021). And to be able to survive and be successful in the era of digital onslaught, an accountant must also be able to navigate and adapt to shifts in work control that are starting to be significant. Furthermore, an accountant must also try to expand his knowledge of technology, and apply high standards that will create added value and opportunities, not only for individuals but also for entities (Mauladi et al., 2022).

We have conducted the following bibliometric analysis of 34 recent articles on the impact of AI on the sustainability of the accounting profession in several countries. The results are as follows (Figure 1).

Previous researchers have revealed their findings from several countries, such as (Ajayi & Olalekan, 2023; Al Wael et al., 2023; Fleming, 2019; Hamza et al., 2024; Johnson et al., 2022; LACUREZEANU et al., 2020; Leitner-Hanetseder et al., 2021; Loh et al., 2023; Long et al., 2020; Oprea et al., 2022; Pratiwi et al., 2023; Razali et al., 2022; Rosi & Mahyuni, 2021; Stafie & Grosu, 2023; Stancu & Duţescu, 2021; Ucoglu, 2020). The role of accountants in a company is very important. Despite experiencing many changes, the accounting profession is considered to still exist today. In order to adapt to the increasingly sophisticated era of digital transformation, an accountant needs to upgrade their quality. As a communicator of business, accountants must have technical knowledge, a positive mindset, and high adaptability. Utilization of digital technology helps the accounting profession minimize errors and reduce workload, so that accountants can take more responsibility on the advisory side. The adaption to the use of digital technology is also an urgency for the sustainability of the accounting profession in the future.

2.3. The Future of Accounting Profession

Many rumors are circulating that in the future accounting will be replaced by robots, so accountants will be threatened with losing their jobs (Worstall, 2011). According to the point of view of opinion from our group, the position of accountants will not be completely displaced by technology, but rather technology will be present in the form of accounting software that will make the work of accountants easier, so that all processes are carried out by the system and not manually and will produce more accurate, faster output, and less workforce. Of course, with the presence of this technology will reduce the need for human resources. However, the emergence of this technology also opened up new professions that required both aspects, namely technology and accounting for accountants.

The accounting profession is thought to have first appeared in England in the 15th century (Lapteş, 2020). This started when a business manager asked another party to conduct an inspection regarding fraudulent acts on the business's bookkeeping. These other parties are used as third parties by business managers to find out the truth of their business financial reports. Based on this incident, now we call someone who examines financial statements as an auditor (DeZoort & Harrison, 2018). Along with the times, the accounting profession will also always evolve following the changes that occur. The accounting profession currently consists of various fields (Abdolmohammadi & Baker, 2006).

The areas of expertise of the accounting profession consist of public accountants, corporate accountants, government accountants, and teaching accountants. To get a profession as an accountant, a person must first attend Accounting Profession Education and complete certification with satisfactory grades (Jaya et al., 2021). Based on the division of the types of accounting fields, an accountant certainly has the main task of this profession. The main task of the accountant is to provide financial information obtained through the economic activities of an agency. After that, the accountant will turn it into a financial report and will finally be communicated to the decision maker. This benefit will assist an agency in terms of planning, controlling, evaluating, and making management decisions. That is, an accountant can answer questions about the sustainability of a business and help provide strategies to improve the company's business.

There are several skills needed by an accountant in order to realize these tasks and benefits. The skills most needed by accountants are good skills and knowledge in accounting. This statement is also in line with a view which states that education and technology are based on creativity, communication skills, and critical thinking possessed by humans (Rosmida, 2019). That is, an accountant is required to always be competent in using his mind and skills to complete complex accountant work. Seeing all the efforts made by accountants in order to provide maximum service to the public, it is not surprising that the position of the accounting profession is respected in society. There are four main things that underlie the position of the accounting profession. First, the nature of the accounting profession which is closely related to honesty. Second, financial rewards are not merely an orientation for an accountant. Third, the altruism of the accounting profession focuses on providing information about financial reports that will be provided to internal and external parties in an agency. Fourth, accountants have two professional characteristics, namely personal and impersonal (Jaya et al., 2021). Professions that can be taken up by future generations of accountants, including:

a) Forensic Accountant

The definition of forensics in the accounting profession relates to the connection and application of financial facts to legal issues. Forensic accounting contains audits of accounting records to look for evidence of fraud (fraud and forgery). Forensic accounting is a specialized area of accounting. A forensic accountant investigates incidents of fraud, bribery, money laundering, and embezzlement by analyzing financial records and transactions, tracing assets, and more. In Indonesia, the role of forensic accounting focuses on uncovering corruption cases through the synergy of anti-corruption agencies, such as the Corruption Eradication Commission, the Supreme Audit Agency, and the Police. Digital forensics is a branch of forensic science for the investigation and discovery of the contents of digital devices, and is often associated with computer crime (Tuanakotta, 2010). The term digital forensics was originally synonymous with computer forensics, but has now been expanded to investigate all devices that can store digital data. Digital forensics is necessary because data on the target device is usually locked, deleted or hidden. Digital forensic accounting is a combination of theoretical concepts from forensic accounting with digital technology (Accounting information system/AIS), and its main goal is to find fraudulent financial reporting that is currently arranged using accounting information systems. The existence of artificial intelligence also makes it easier for an accountant to audit financial reports by system. Accountants can track evidence of events that violate rules/standards by including digital evidence. How to track can be done in a short time and effectively (JAYA & Narsa, 2022).

b) Green Accountant Profession

The emergence of environmental awareness due to economic activity has led to the creation of accounting methodologies designed to measure the impact of human activities on ecological systems and resources. The methodology is referred to as Environment accounting (Green Accounting) (Agustia, 2020). This methodology is categorized in three ways: 1) who is responsible (households, companies or governments); 2) the time period considered (whether past, present or future); and 3) how the impact on the environment is measured (whether in parallel with financial results, by valuing it in financial terms, or by avoiding financial measures). In Indonesia, the concept of Green Accounting is often referred to as Environmental Accounting. Green Accounting is the incorporation of principles of environmental management and nature conservation into accounting reporting practices that include cost and benefit analyses.

The stakeholders need information that is relevant, reliable, understandable and comparable, in order to evaluate, respond and make the right decisions regarding greenhouse gas emissions. This is what then encourages the accounting profession to transform into a greener one. Accountants and their conventional accounting practices are required to change in order to accommodate stakeholders' needs for information that is now more than just financial information. As a result, the green accounting profession and green accounting practices were born. Green accounting is an integrated process of recognizing, measuring, recording, summarizing, reporting, and disclosing financial, social, and environmental objects, transactions, or events in the accounting process in order to produce complete, integrated, and relevant financial, social, and environmental accounting information that is useful for users in economic and non-economic decision-making and management. The scope of accounting today is no longer limited to financial matters alone, but also includes social and environmental matters. The integration of financial, social, and environmental accounting is then named green accounting. By means of carbon accounting, green accountants calculate the carbon footprint, where various greenhouse gas emissions such as carbon dioxide, methane, and hydrofluorocarbons resulting from an event or organization over the course of a year are totaled and converted into units of carbon dioxide equivalent (CO2e). This allows a price to be paid for each greenhouse gas emitted.

Although, this topic encourages the creation of new methodologies, Green Accounting is still largely voluntary and unaudited, including in Indonesia. As a result, many business entities have not disclosed information about Environmental Accounting properly. The main challenges for the application of environmental accounting today are determining the scale of changes in human activities needed to prevent environmental degradation and incorporating several references into a measurement metric and encouraging changes in human behavior related to environmental concern. It is expected that with the existence of Environmental Accounting, accounting science and professional accountants in the future will reflect philosophical and cultural values and economic structures that govern human activities towards a Green Economy (Jaya & Padilla, 2024).

The accountant profession that focuses on maintaining company sustainability will still be needed in the future. This means that accountants do not manipulate the company's financial statements for their own purposes (earnings management). This is because they can use Artificial Intelligence wisely and precisely in calculating costs related to the welfare of stakeholders, and the surrounding environment. Accountants can work with an Information Technology expert to program computers that facilitate data processing, so that the results can be accurately predicted by accountants about how the company will continue for the next few years (Buric et al., 2022) (See Figure 2).

c) Information Systems-Based Auditing

Auditors can use Artificial Intelligence to make it easier to process Big Data in a short time. All data will be processed and analyzed using Big Data Analytics to find irregularities and fraud. With the help of technology, the auditor will verify by giving an opinion and prevent audit delay in completing the auditor's independent report (Logachev et al., 2021).

Artificial Intelligence (AI) will work to process the entire data and provide simpler results in the form of narratives and results that we need. Artificial Intelligence (AI) is designed just like humans and can even exceed humans in processing data, analyzing to provide decisions with a high level of accuracy. Artificial Intelligence is considered to be the main solution to various cases of auditor failure in detecting fraud. Admittedly, the improvement of the audit profession with the emergence of Artificial Intelligence with big data and the increasing analytical function of auditors brings new opportunities and challenges for auditors. Internal auditors and risk managers must understand how AI works and the importance of good data (not junk data) to be effective in this new environment.

Figure 2. The connection between artificial intelligence and environmental accounting under the integration of industry and finance (Liao, 2022)

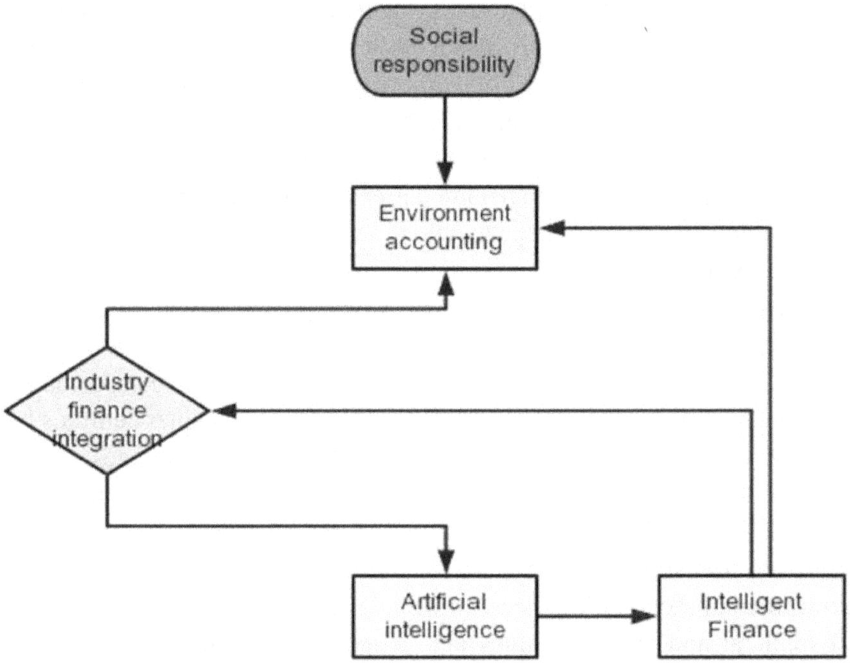

In the short term, risk managers and auditors are required to have significant skill changes. They must master data science, statistical modeling, and technology, and apply them in the context of risk. In addition, they also need encouragement to innovate to adopt Artificial Intelligence. Risk managers and internal auditors play a key role in helping organizations stay in control through the adoption of new technologies.

Artificial Intelligence can be a game changer for auditors and this can be improved through computer training on big data sources to recognize patterns and identify development trends as expected (Bizarro et al., 2019). For its application, it can be assisted by branches of Artificial Intelligence, namely Machine Learning and Natural Language Processing which function to assist auditors when searching and evaluating entire large data sets in a fast and efficient time, and produce audit information accurately and accountably. Through the application of Artificial Intelligence can also increase the flexibility of auditors to explore insights and expand brilliant innovations that can be oriented to audit plans, where at this stage auditors will never be replaced by technology, considering that human advantages are showing feelings and providing professional judgment (Bizarro et al., 2019) (See Figure 3).

3. CONCLUSION

The analysis of the literature review that has been carried out concludes that the sustainability of the accounting profession will experience many changes compared to before, due to technological developments, namely Artificial Intelligence. These changes also provide new opportunities for the sustainability of the accounting profession, such as expertise in digital forensic accounting, expertise in green accounting, and

Figure 3. Comparison of audit processes using and without the adoption of artificial intelligence (Bizarro et al., 2019)

Phase	Procedures Without AI	Procedures With AI	Types of Technology	Impact of AI on Accomplishing Phase Tasks
Planning	The auditor: • Learns industry and business environment through meetings with client management and review of BoD meeting minutes • Examines client's enterprise to estimate a level of risk	The AI computer performs the following tasks: • Produces risk assessment based on prior-year documents, business environment and industry trends for auditor's review • Records, summarizes and produces meeting minutes	• NLP • ML • Voice recognition	Moderate impact
Evaluation of internal controls	The auditor: • Reviews internal controls, policies and procedures • Interviews process owners and records details for workpapers • Performs operational test of controls by observing employees, reperforming processes and inspecting documents	The AI computer performs the following tasks: • Prepares workpaper references, including flowcharts and risk/control matrices, from recorded interview information • Analyzes screen captures of computer processes and flags those that are questionable and needing additional review • Digitally inspects documents, looking for adequate approvals	• Voice recognition • NLP • ML	High impact
Substantive procedures	The auditor: • Manually observes inventory count • Sends and manages confirmation requests • Inspects supporting documents of sales orders and cash receipts • Reviews select journal entries that fit circumstances that may reflect fraud • Analytically compares auditor's estimates and industry averages of sales and other metrics to actual enterprise performance	The auditor leverages the following technologies: • Digital/mobile applications, barcodes and QR codes, and drones assisting in inventory counts • Encrypted online platform, accessed by both auditors and customers, to manage confirmation requests The AI computer performs the following tasks: • Imports and automatically reconciles cash receipts and sales orders while comparing for discrepancies • Flags all transactions that are potential fraud cases • Creates estimation of sales and other metrics based on industry and competitor data	• NLP • Voice recognition • Drones • ML • Encryption • Internet of Things (IoT)	High impact
Closing procedures	The auditor: • Compiles audit findings and issues • Uses professional judgment to evaluate impact of findings • Forms categorical opinion • Writes audit report using the formatting provided by audit standards	The AI computer performs the following tasks: • Formulates an audit score based on client's risk, audit findings and their effects to evaluate audit risk • Forms opinion based on continuous-number grading scale • Drafts audit report based on audit score and formulated opinion	• NLP • ML	Low to moderate impact

expertise in information systems-based auditing. In achieving this, accountants need to do more learning by adding new skills that can support and are needed to adapt to current technological changes. These skills include mastery of information technology in the fields of auditing, bookkeeping/recording, and skills in analysing capital market data or other business industries. In general, an accountant also needs to develop his mindset to be able to readily solve problems through various business recommendations using technology-based big data analysis. This is done through the process of collecting accounting information and data identification, which consists of business statements, behavioural competencies, digital arguments, communication, and data interrogation, synthesis, and analysis.

From this literature review, theoretically, it also raises a hypothesis that changes or developments in current technology, such as artificial intelligence, can have a huge impact on the sustainability of the accounting profession. Thus, accountants are currently required to have additional knowledge and skills that aim to support and facilitate completing their work with the help of current technology. For example, in information system-based audit work, in addition to being able to assist auditors in preparing, authorising, distributing, collecting, managing and evaluating results. Artificial intelligence can also help in the stock-taking process that is carried out automatically using cameras and software. However, the implementation of the audit process requires a reliable auditor to be able to run it, because there are other very important processes that cannot be taken over by technology.

The limitations of this literature review research are that there are still limited references that empirically study similar themes, so the number of references used is still limited. This causes the findings obtained cannot be generalised. In addition, the theoretical findings in the form of hypotheses presented previously also need deeper empirical or experimental studies. Therefore, it is hoped that in the next empirical research to conduct empirical or experimental studies on the sustainability of the accounting profession due to artificial intelligence.

REFERENCES

Abdolmohammadi, M. J., & Baker, C. R. (2006). Accountants' value preferences and moral reasoning. *Journal of Business Ethics*, *69*(1), 11–25. doi:10.1007/s10551-006-9064-y

Adamyk, O., Benson, V., Adamyk, B., Al-Khateeb, H., & Chinnaswamy, A. (2023). Does Artificial Intelligence Help Reduce Audit Risks? *2023 13th International Conference on Advanced Computer Information Technologies, ACIT 2023 - Proceedings,* 294–298. 10.1109/ACIT58437.2023.10275661

Agustia, D. (2020). Innovation, environmental management accounting, future performance: Evidence in Indonesia. *Journal of Security and Sustainability Issues*, *9*(3), 1005–1015. doi:10.9770/jssi.2020.9.3(24)

Ajayi, F. A., & Olalekan, A. (2023). Artificial Intelligence & Internal Audit Quality Of Commercial Banks In Nigeria. *International Journal of Management and Economics Invention*, *09*(04). Advance online publication. doi:10.47191/ijmei/v9i4.05

Al-refiay, H. A. N., Abdulhussein, A. S., & Al-Shaikh, S. S. K. (2022). The Impact of Financial Accounting in Decision Making Processes in Business. *International Journal Of Professional Business Review*, *7*(4), 1–13. doi:10.26668/businessreview/2022.v7i4.e627

Al Wael, H., Abdallah, W., Ghura, H., & Buallay, A. (2023). Factors influencing artificial intelligence adoption in the accounting profession: The case of public sector in Kuwait. *Competitiveness Review*. Advance online publication. doi:10.1108/CR-09-2022-0137

Bizarro, P. A., Crum, E., & Nix, J. (2019). The Intelligent Audit. *ISACA Journal*, *6*, 23–29.

Bratina, T. (2019). Mobile Phones and Social Behavior Among Millenials – Future Teachers. *Journal Of Elementary Education*, *12*(4), 315–330.

Bunget, O.-C., & Lungu, C. (2023). A Bibliometric Analysis of the Implications of Artificial Intelligence on the Accounting Profession. *CECCAR Business Review*, *4*(4), 9–16. doi:10.37945/cbr.2023.04.02

Buric, M. N., Stojanovic, A. J., Filipovic, A. L., & Kascelan, L. (2022). Research of Attitudes toward Implementation of Green Accounting in Tourism Industry in Montenegro-Practices, and Challenges. *Sustainability (Basel)*, *14*(3), 1–26. doi:10.3390/su14031725

Chatfield, A. T., & Reddick, C. G. (2019). A framework for Internet of Things-enabled smart government: A case of IoT cybersecurity policies and use cases in U.S. federal government. *Government Information Quarterly*, *36*(2), 346–357. doi:10.1016/j.giq.2018.09.007

Chatterjee, S., & Bhattacharjee, K. K. (2020). Adoption of artificial intelligence in higher education: A quantitative analysis using structural equation modelling. *Education and Information Technologies*, *25*(January), 3443–3463. Advance online publication. doi:10.1007/s10639-020-10159-7

DeZoort, F. T., & Harrison, P. D. (2018). Understanding Auditors' Sense of Responsibility for Detecting Fraud Within Organizations. *Journal of Business Ethics*, *149*(4), 857–874. doi:10.1007/s10551-016-3064-3

Edwards, M. G. (2021). The growth paradox, sustainable development, and business strategy. *Business Strategy and the Environment*, *30*(7), 3079–3094. doi:10.1002/bse.2790

Fleming, P. (2019). Robots and Organization Studies: Why Robots Might Not Want to Steal Your Job. *Organization Studies*, *40*(1), 23–38. doi:10.1177/0170840618765568

Hamza, R. A. E. M., Alnor, N. H. A., Al-Matari, E. M., Benzerrouk, Z. S., Mohamed, A. M. E., Bennaceur, M. Y., Elhefni, A. H. M., & Elshaabany, M. M. (2024). The Impact of Artificial Intelligence (AI) on the Accounting System of Saudi Companies. *WSEAS Transactions on Business and Economics*, *21*(January), 499–511. doi:10.37394/23207.2024.21.42

Hendarsyah, D. (2019). E-Commerce Di Era Industri 4.0 Dan Society 5.0. *IQTISHADUNA: Jurnal Ilmiah Ekonomi Kita*, *8*(2), 171–184. doi:10.46367/iqtishaduna.v8i2.170

Isnawati, E. L., & Indriani, E. (2021). Profesi Akuntan : Akahkah Hilang di Era Digital 4.0? *Jurnal Penelitian Akuntansi*, *2*(1), 29–41.

Jackling, B., Cooper, B. J., Leung, P., & Dellaportas, S. (2007). Professional accounting bodies' perceptions of ethical issues, causes of ethical failure and ethics education. *Managerial Auditing Journal*, *22*(9), 928–944. doi:10.1108/02686900710829426

Jaya, I. M. L. M., & Narsa, I. M. (2022). The Nexus Between Forensic Tax and Accounting Knowledge After Pandemic COVID-19 in Indonesia. In A. Pego (Ed.), Handbook of Research on Global Networking Post COVID-19 (pp. 480–494). IGI Global Publishing. doi:10.4018/978-1-7998-8856-7.ch026

Jaya, I. M. L. M., & Padilla, M. A. E. (2024). Tax Carbon Policy: Momentum to Accelerate Indonesia's Sustainable Economic Growth Towards Green Economy. In Green Economy and Renewable Energy Transitions for Sustainable Development (pp. 171–183). IGI Global Publishing.

Jaya, I. M. L. M., Sawarjuwono, T., Sungkono, S., & Ilahiyah, M. E. (2021). Ethics, behaviors, and characters of memayu hayuning bawono, ambrasto dur hangkoro accountant in java. *Jurnal Kajian Akuntansi*, *5*(2), 142–155. doi:10.33603/jka.v5i2.5110

Johnson, P. C., Laurell, C., Ots, M., & Sandström, C. (2022). Digital innovation and the effects of artificial intelligence on firms' research and development – Automation or augmentation, exploration or exploitation? *Technological Forecasting and Social Change*, *179*(March), 121636. Advance online publication. doi:10.1016/j.techfore.2022.121636

Khalil, A., Abdelli, M. E. A., & Mogaji, E. (2022). Do Digital Technologies Influence the Relationship between the COVID-19 Crisis and SMEs' Resilience in Developing Countries? *Journal of Open Innovation*, *8*(2), 100. doi:10.3390/joitmc8020100

Kumar, S., Sureka, R., Lim, W. M., Kumar Mangla, S., & Goyal, N. (2021). What do we know about business strategy and environmental research? Insights from Business Strategy and the Environment. *Business Strategy and the Environment*, *30*(8), 3454–3469. doi:10.1002/bse.2813

Lacurezeanu, R., Tiron-Tudor, A., & Bresfelean, V. P. (2020). Robotic Process Automation in Audit and Accounting. *Audit Financiar*, *18*(160), 752–770. doi:10.20869/AUDITF/2020/160/024

Lapteş, R. (2020). Ethics and Integrity of the Professional Accountant. *Series V - Economic Sciences*, *12*(2), 87–92. doi:10.31926/but.es.2019.12.61.2.11

Lee, Y. Y., Falahat, M., & Porter, M. (2018). *The Impact of Digitalization and Resources on Gaining Competitive Advantage in International Markets : The Mediating Role of Marketing*. Innovation and Learning Capabilities.

Leitner-Hanetseder, S., Lehner, O. M., Eisl, C., & Forstenlechner, C. (2021). A profession in transition: Actors, tasks and roles in AI-based accounting. *Journal of Applied Accounting Research*, *22*(3), 539–556. doi:10.1108/JAAR-10-2020-0201

Liao, P. (2022). *Proceedings of the 2022 6th International Seminar on Education, Management and Social Sciences (ISEMSS 2022)*. Atlantis Press SARL. 10.2991/978-2-494069-31-2

Logachev, M. S., Orekhovskaya, N. A., Seregina, T. N., Shishov, S., & Volvak, S. F. (2021). Information system for monitoring and managing the quality of educational programs. *Journal of Open Innovation*, *7*(1), 93. Advance online publication. doi:10.3390/joitmc7010093

Loh, C.-T., Ng, Y.-H., Lee, A.-S., Chin, Y.-M., & Foo, P.-Y. (2023). *Challenges Faced by Accounting Professionals in Artificial Intelligence-Based Technology Environment and Determinants of Acceptance* (Issue Bafe). Atlantis Press International BV. doi:10.2991/978-94-6463-342-9_5

Long, G. J., Lin, B. H., Cai, H. X., & Nong, G. Z. (2020). Developing an artificial intelligence (AI) management system to improve product quality and production efficiency in furniture manufacture. *Procedia Computer Science*, *166*, 486–490. doi:10.1016/j.procs.2020.02.060

Malva Cakra Dewa, M., Widya Yunia Kharisyami, P., Diva Navael, L., & Maulana, A. (2018). *Peran Akuntan Dalam Menghadapi Digitalisasi Ekonomi Menjelang Era Society 5.0*. doi:10.29407/jae.v7i3.18492

Marrone, M., Linnenluecke, M. K., Richardson, G., & Smith, T. (2020). Trends in environmental accounting research within and outside of the accounting discipline. *Accounting, Auditing & Accountability Journal*, *33*(8), 2167–2193. doi:10.1108/AAAJ-03-2020-4457

Mauladi, K. F., Jaya, I. M. L. M., & Esquivias, M. A. (2022). Exploring the Link Between Cashless Society and Cybercrime in Indonesia. *Journal of Telecommunications and the Digital Economy*, *10*(3), 58–76. doi:10.18080/jtde.v10n3.533

Mookerjee, J., & Rao, O. R. S. (2021). A Review of the Robotic Process Automation's Impact as a Disruptive Innovation in Accounting and Audit. *Turkish Journal of Computer and Mathematics Education*, *12*(12), 3675–3682.

Oprea, O., Hoinaru, R., Păcuraru-Ionescu, C.-P., & Neamţu, D. (2022). Accounting for the future: practice, Artificial Intelligence and regulation. *Proceedings of the International Conference on Business Excellence*, *16*(1), 817–826. 10.2478/picbe-2022-0076

Parnell, J., & Brady, M. (2019). Capabilities, strategies and firm performance in the United Kingdom. *Journal of Strategy and Management*, *12*(1), 153–172. doi:10.1108/JSMA-10-2018-0107

Pratiwi, Y. E., Desi Lastianti, S., Wijayanto, I., Hidayat, U. S., & Susanto, I. W. (2023). Artificial Intelligence Auditing: Embracing the Disruption. Are You Prepared? *Proceeding International Conference on Economic Business Management, and Accounting (ICOEMA), August.*

Razali, F. A., Jusoh, M. A., Abu Talib, S. L., & Awang, N. (2022). The Impact of Industry 4.0 Towards Accounting Profession and Graduate's Career Readiness: A Review of Literature. *Malaysian Journal of Social Sciences and Humanities*, *7*(7), e001624. doi:10.47405/mjssh.v7i7.1624

Rosi, N. M. K., & Mahyuni, L. P. (2021). The Future Of Accounting Profession In The Industrial Revolution 4.0: Meta-Synthesis Analysis. *E-Jurnal Akuntansi*, *31*(4). Advance online publication. doi:10.24843/EJA.2021.v31.i04.p17

Rosmida. (2019). Transformasi Peran Akuntan dalam Era Revolusi Industri 4.0 dan Tantangan Era Society 5.0. *Inovbiz:Jurnal Inovasi Bisnis, 7*, 206–212. www.ejournal.polbeng.ac.id/index.php/IBP

Ruiz-Real, J. L., Uribe-Toril, J., Torres, J. A., & Pablo, J. D. E. (2021). Artificial intelligence in business and economics research: Trends and future. *Journal of Business Economics and Management*, *22*(1), 98–117. doi:10.3846/jbem.2020.13641

Serrano-Cinca, C., Gutiérrez-Nieto, B., & Bernate-Valbuena, M. (2019). The use of accounting anomalies indicators to predict business failure. *European Management Journal*, *37*(3), 353–375. doi:10.1016/j.emj.2018.10.006

Stafie, G., & Grosu, V. (2023). The Impact of Artificial Intelligence on Accounting. *Springer Proceedings in Business and Economics*, 247–265. doi:10.1007/978-3-031-19886-1_18

Stancu, M. S., & Duţescu, A. (2021). The impact of the Artificial Intelligence on the accounting profession, a literature's assessment. *Proceedings of the International Conference on Business Excellence*, *15*(1), 749–758. 10.2478/picbe-2021-0070

Supra, D. (2017). Kecerdasan Intelektual, Kecerdasan Emosional, Dan Kecerdasan Spiritual Berpengaruh Terhadap Pemahaman Akuntansi Pada Mahasiswa. *Jemasi: Jurnal Ekonomi Manajemen Dan Akuntansi*, *13*(1), 1–18. doi:10.35449/jemasi.v13i1.1

Tapanjeh, A. M. A., & Al Tarawneh, A. R. (2020). Applicability of forensic accounting to reduce fraud and its effects on financial statement of jordanian shareholding companies from the perspective of judiciary and certified public accountant. *International Journal of Financial Research*, *11*(2), 436. Advance online publication. doi:10.5430/ijfr.v11n2p436

Tee, H. H., & Ong, H. B. (2016). Cashless payment and economic growth. *Financial Innovation*, *2*(1), 1–9. doi:10.1186/s40854-016-0023-z

Tsai, C. H., & Peng, K. J. (2017). The FinTech Revolution and Financial Regulation: The Case of Online Supply-Chain Financing. *Asian Journal of Law and Society*, *4*(1), 109–132. doi:10.1017/als.2016.65

Tuanakotta, T. M. (2010). Akuntansi Forensik dan AuditorInvestigatif (Indonesia). Lembaga Penerbit Fakultas Ekonomi Universitas Indonesia (LPFE UI). Edisi ke 2: Jakarta.

Ucoglu, D. (2020). Effects of artificial intelligence technology on accounting profession and education. *Pressacademia*, *11*(1), 16–21. doi:10.17261/Pressacademia.2020.1232

Worstall, T. (2011). Will Robots Take Our Jobs? Who cares? *Forbes*, 1–3. http://www.forbes.com/sites/timworstall/2011/11/06/will-robots-take-out-jobs-who-cares/#6279428b538e

Yuana, R., Prasetio, E. A., Syarief, R., Arkeman, Y., & Suroso, A. I. (2021). System dynamic and simulation of business model innovation in digital companies: An open innovation approach. *Journal of Open Innovation*, *7*(4), 219. Advance online publication. doi:10.3390/joitmc7040219

Chapter 13
Artificial Intelligence Technologies:
Benefits, Risks, and Challenges for Sustainable Business Models

Ana Isabel Torres
https://orcid.org/0000-0002-0621-956X
University of Aveiro, Portugal & INESC TEC, Porto, Portugal

Gabriela Beirão
https://orcid.org/0000-0001-7259-1709
INESC TEC, Faculty of Engineering, University of Porto, Portugal

ABSTRACT

This chapter aims to contribute to the understanding of how artificial intelligence (AI) technologies can promote increased business revenues, cost reductions, and enhanced customer experience, as well as society´s well-being in a sustainable way. However, these AI benefits also come with risks and challenges concerning organizations, the environment, customers, and society, which need further investigation. This chapter also examines and discusses how AI can either enable or inhibit the delivery of the goals recognized in the UN 2030 Agenda for Sustainable Business Models Development. In this chapter, the authors conduct a bibliometric review of the emerging literature on artificial intelligence (AI) technologies implications on sustainable business models (SBM), in the perspective of Sustainable Development Goals (SDGs) and investigate research spanning the areas of AI, and SDGs within the economic group. The authors examine an effective sample of 69 publications from 49 different journals, 225 different institutions, and 47 different countries. On the basis of the bibliometric analysis, this study selected the most significant published sources and examined the changes that have occurred in the conceptual framework of AI and SBM in light of SDGs research. This chapter makes some significant contributions to the literature by presenting a detailed bibliometric analysis of the research on the impacts of AI on SBM, enhancing the understanding of the knowledge structure of this research topic and helping to identify key knowledge gaps and future challenges.

DOI: 10.4018/979-8-3693-0847-9.ch013

1. INTRODUCTION

The Digital Era we live in is creating an entirely new and challenging environment, more recently driven by Artificial Intelligence (AI). AI is shaping an increasing range of sectors, affecting, for example, global productivity, equality and inclusion, and environmental outcomes.

For businesses, AI is expected to improve operations management in the supply chain, smart manufacturing, and the performance of product design to be more economically, environmentally, and socially sustainable (Kusiak, 2018).

Remarkably, small retail firms have managed to increase their visibility and expand their business globally by capitalizing on AI subdomains - e.g., Machine Learning and Deep Learning - technologies and other digital platform features (Meltzer, 2018). Regardless of the cost-driven savings by AI technologies, there are several benefits of AI in business, enabled by the general purpose of machine learning (ML) algorithms to manage massive and various data (video, audio, text) and to improve the accuracy of product demand forecasting, by analyzing customer behavior. However, there are also risks and challenges concerning organizations' equity, environmental resources and customers, which might impact the Sustainable Development Goals (SDGs) of the United Nations (UN) 2030 Agenda.

AI contributes to achieving SDGs goals in several ways. Documented connections between AI and the SDGs across the three pillars of sustainable development, namely Society, Economy, and Environment, provide relevant evidence that AI may act as an enabler of sustainability.

Vinuesa and colleagues (2020) systematically assessed the extent to which AI might impact all aspects of sustainable development of the 17 Sustainable Development Goals (SDGs). The study shows relevant evidence that AI may act as an enabler in the three pillars of sustainable development, namely Society (82%), Economy (70%), and Environment (93%). However, the three general areas of influence of AI, also across all SDG, may experience a negative impact from the development of AI, respectively, Society (38%), Economy (33%), and Environment (30%) (Vinuesa et al., 2020).

Moreover, the articles considering social sustainability and environmental sustainability were mostly rooted in economic sustainability. This claim emphasizes the central role of the Economy pillar, especially concerning sustainable business models (SBM), in achieving SDGs.

However, after reviewing recent studies, DiVaio and colleagues (2020) noted that the role of AI in the development of SBM, from the perspective of SDGs, is under-explored in academic literature.

Despite the importance of the topic, comprehensive reviews of AI and SBM literature in the context of the Economic pillar of SDGs are scarce, especially addressing SDGs: 8, "aims promoting inclusive and sustainable economic growth, employment and decent work for all"; 9, "seeks to build resilient infrastructure, promote sustainable and inclusive industrialization and foster innovation"; 10, "Reduced inequalities within-and between- countries, requires equitable resource distribution, investing in education and skills development, combating discrimination, supporting marginalized groups and fostering international cooperation for fair trade and financial systems"; 12, "Ensure sustainable consumption and production patterns which is key to sustain the livelihoods of current and future generations", and 17, "Aims to strength and revitalize global partnerships to achieve sustainable development".

Therefore, incorporating AI-based technologies to enable sustainable business development is critical. Failure to do so could result in gaps in transparency, safety, and ethical standards. Although AI-enabled technology can act as a catalyst to achieve the 2030 Agenda, it may also trigger inequalities that may act as inhibitors of SDGs.

Nevertheless, there is limited research connecting AI with the sustainability of business models, particularly in the context of economic impacts that can serve as either enablers or inhibitors, especially concerning SDGs 8, 9, 10, 12, and 17.

To address this gap in academic literature, this chapter aims to examine the scientific research on the topic to enhance its understanding and identify future challenges. Specifically, we intend to achieve the following goals: (i) to analyze the evolution of the research on the link between AI, sustainable BM, and SDGs of the economy pillar, (ii) to identify the most productive journals and authors, (iii) to identify the most impactful articles in the research topic, (iv) to identify and to synthesize the predominant research themes, and (v) to suggest future research challenges.

This chapter makes some significant contributions to the literature. First, it presents a broad analysis of the research on the impacts of AI on sustainable BM through a bibliometric analysis, which contributes to the understanding of the knowledge structure of the research topic and helps to recognize key knowledge gaps and future challenges.

Second, this chapter offers an in-depth understanding of the linkage between AI and BM sustainability from the perspective of the impacts on SDGs in its Economy dimension. In this study, we adopt the concept of sustainability from the 17 Sustainable Development Goals (SDGs) internationally agreed in the United Nations 2030 Agenda[1], framed on its Economy pillar, which includes SDGs 8, 9, 10, 12, and 17.

Finally, we suggest potential directions for further research by proposing a research agenda.

The remainder of this chapter is organized as follows. Section 2 introduces the theoretical background of the topic. Section 3 describes the methodology used in the study. Section 4 provides a discussion of the results. Finally, section 5 reports the main conclusions, theoretical and practical implications, limitations and proposes a future research agenda.

2. THEORETICAL FRAMEWORK

2.1 Artificial Intelligence and Sustainable Business Models

Artificial Intelligence (AI) has been defined as "a machine-based system that can, for a given set of human-defined objectives, make predictions, recommendations, or decisions influencing real or virtual environments. AI systems are designed to operate with varying levels of autonomy" (OECD, 2016), and "Intelligent systems can faithfully reproduce human behaviours which have cognitive, emotional and social intelligence" (Haenlein and Kaplan, 2019, p. 6).

Remarkable advances in AI are driven by machine learning (ML), a subset of AI (Jordan and Mitchell, 2015) which can be defined as a "machine's ability to keep improving its performance without humans having to explain exactly how to accomplish all the tasks it's given" (Brynjolfsson and Mcafee, 2017). The advances in Machine Learning and Deep Learning – a specialized class of machine learning built on artificial neural networks (LeCun *et al.*, 2015) – are exponentially improved by the shift from rule-based to algorithmic, increasing their power and functionality. These machine-based systems aim to provide and manage intelligent products, services, and experiences by sharing information for cooperation or creating optimal and sustainable value (Gretzel, Sigala, Xiang and Koo, 2015).

According to OECD[2] (2019), AI boosts productivity by automating tasks traditionally done by humans and enabling systems to operate and adapt to changing conditions with minimal or no human intervention. As a result, the use of these AI technologies allows benefits for both companies and customers.

In the last decade, data shared on the internet has exceeded those of the entire history of mankind. As such, the company that owns, analyses, and links this data properly will gain a competitive advantage. AI plays a pivotal role in understanding and predicting consumer demand across interconnected supply chains and tailoring their shopping experiences (Anica-Popa *et al.*, 2021).

For customers, there are two main categories of emerging AI technologies that help to improve the customer experience: (1) technologies facilitating direct interactions with customers and (2) technologies allowing for a better treatment of customer demands and expectations (BearingPoint, 2019). For example, semantic recognition technologies (i.e. chatbots) improve customer experience by offering round-the-clock service, significantly reducing the volume of low-added value contacts that require human intervention; voice recognition technologies using virtual assistants able to perform various tasks (taking phone orders, searching for information, sending recommendations to customers); visual recognition technologies, integrated with virtual assistants capable of identifying shapes or individuals, empower retailers to recognize frequent shoppers or loyalty card holders as soon as they enter the store; when facial recognition is combined with digital signage and Big Data analysis, it can directly target a specific customer based on his or her previous buying behavior; technologies that use autonomous robots that help customers find products in a store; and predictive analytics technologies enable large companies to anticipate future customer behavior by analyzing past and current behavioral patterns, thus supporting their strategic decision-making. Predictive analytics could also reduce the customer churn rate (by identifying dissatisfied customers) and detect risk situations, helping companies effectively segment their customers (Faria *et al.*, 2023).

Next, a detailed assessment of AI's positive and negative impacts on the development of SBMs from the perspective of the SDGs related to the pillar of Economy, together with illustrative examples, is discussed.

2.2 Artificial Intelligence and Sustainable Development Goals of Economy Pillar

AI-SDG Positive Impact

Besides the two business drivers, customer experience improvement and revenue increase, there are significant AI-driven cost savings for organizations. Cost reduction should be carefully reflected when considering the impact of emerging AI technologies on companies' sustainability.

Previous researchers pointed out some generators for AI-driven cost savings: reaching the target consumers more effectively (Grewal et al., 2017), human workforce reduction (Inman and Nikolova, 2017; van Doorn et al., 2017), and inventory optimization. First, reaching targeted consumers with lower costs is crucial for retail survival. According to Bradlow and colleagues (2017), AI tools generate significant cost savings: processing ever-increasing volume of data with fewer technical requirements, incomparably less time and money than humans or pre-existing computer systems, while running without errors or interruption. These AI tolls may have a positive impact on SDG 8, acting as an enabler of decent work and economic growth.

Secondly, human workforce saving using sensors, smart shelves, mobile, and AI technologies provide new possibilities for cutting down on in-store staff accomplishing "algorithmic" task execution (Olsen and Tomlin, 2020). This trend also demonstrates the industry's crucial role in the new educational era in replacing low-wage tasks with higher-wage jobs. This may positively impact SDG 8 and affect social cohesion with consequences in the context of SDG 10 on reduced inequalities.

Thirdly, inventory optimization emerges as a key application for AI adoption by retail companies, which enables the minimization of inventory costs, encompassing both direct expenses such as storage costs, and indirect costs stemming from lost sales. Addressing these challenges represents one of the most critical optimization endeavors for the retail sector, ultimately leading to profit maximization (Anica-Popa et al., 2021).

Fourthly, AI is expected to foster smart manufacturing and consequently ensure sustainability as one of the six pillars of smart manufacturing (Kusiak, 2018).

For instance, the sustainable design of a smart vehicle results in autonomous, personal, shared, and sustainable transportation and may improve economic, environmental, and social sustainability. In particular, maintenance of economic sustainability by supporting meeting demand preferences and reducing manufacturing costs when designing a product can be achieved using a product-configuration tool based on artificial intelligence. Therefore, AI tolls may have a positive impact on promoting sustainable industrialization and fostering innovation (SDG 9), which, in turn, impact economic growth (SDG 8), social development (SDG 10), sustainable production and consumption (SDG 12), and climate action (SDG 13), given their heavy reliance on investments in infrastructure, sustainable industrial development, and technological advancements.

In sum, AI-enabled technologies are expected to increase productivity and labor efficiency, provide intelligent products and services, and enhance customer experiences through sharing information for cooperation or creating optimal and sustainable value (Gretzel *et al.*, 2015).

Vinuesa and colleagues (2020) argue that the technological advantages provided by AI may positively impact the achievement of several SDGs within the Economy group. The authors identified benefits from AI on 42 targets (70%) from SDGs 08, 09,10, 12, and 17, whereas negative impacts are reported in 20 targets (33%).

Similarly, from a systematic literature review, Di Vaio and colleagues (2020) analyzed a great body of research that reports a net positive impact of AI-enabled technologies associated with increased productivity, efficiency, and sustainable business models.

Together, these trends demonstrate the potential of AI as an enabler of SDGs 08, 09, 10, and 12.

Despite the benefits for companies' revenues and customer experience, AI technology implementation has several challenges and risks that might act as inhibitors of sustainability. Even though their capacity for autonomous functioning benefits businesses and society, it also creates risks, challenges, and uncertainties not inherent in traditional technologies (Dwivedi *et al.*, 2021), as discussed next.

AI-SDG Negative Impact

There are negative economic implications between AI and SBM. Thus, it is essential to prioritize not only the maximization of market share and business profitability but also the mitigation of undesirable organizational conflicts and inequity driven by the implementation of AI technologies (Balakrishnan et al., 2004).

Dirican (2015) highlights and conceptualizes the future of future of robots and artificial intelligence from a business perspective. This study concluded that rapidly changing technologies would have severe impacts on the business world as well as on countries and world economics—for example, Banking System, training, coaching, accounting, taxes, etc.

AI and Robotics may have a negative impact on businesses and economies and, therefore, on sustainability. For instance, advanced machine-based systems (e.g., LLM) using massive data and computational resources consume a lot of energy having a very high carbon footprint. For instance, cryptocurrency applications, such as Bitcoin, are globally using as much electricity as some nations' electrical demand (Truby, 2018) compromising outcomes in the SDGs 07 and 13 (Vinuesa *et al.* 2020). Jones (2018) estimates suggest that the total electricity demand for information and communications technologies (ICTs) could require up to 20% of the global electricity demand by 2030, which calls for the Green growth of ICT technology in the years to come.

AI implementation may also raise inequalities and generate an economic bias. There is strong evidence that citizens living in developed industrialized countries enjoy far more prosperous and healthy lives than those who reside in the least developed countries (LDCs) (UNIDO, 2020). The former benefit from high levels of education, better social security and health services, sophisticated transport and communication networks, and access to information, knowledge, technology, and financial resources essential for business operations.

However, some aspects of AI can also be negative and, if not addressed, can jeopardize the achievement of different objectives. First of all, the vast wealth that AI can generate could go mainly to those who are already well-off and educated, leaving all others behind. This could also lead to disparities due to unevenly distributed education and resources around the world. Therefore, AI investments will generate an economic bias, which can also exacerbate inequality within nations (Brynjolfsson and McAfee, 2014), as resources are not equally available in low- and middle-income countries. Hence, the introduction of these inequalities could increase the existing economic gap, thereby negatively affecting SDGs 08 (decent work and economic growth), 09 (industry, innovation, and infrastructure), and 10 (reduced inequalities) in multiple ways:

For example, the automation of tasks redistributes corporate income from labor to capital, favoring company owners over employees. This shift from workers to investors could result in reduced salaries and job displacement because of AI implementation (Vinuesa et al., 2020). Also, the application of computerized techniques leveraging AI holds significant promise for professionals seeking effective methods to analyze datasets and enhance the marketing function within an organization (Orriols-Puig *et al.*, 2013). Nevertheless, primary concerns relate to job displacement for lower-skilled workers and the shift in income distribution from labor to capital (Sachs et al., 2019).

In addition, AI recommendation systems are an effective marketing tool but also a powerful manipulation tool. Despite the benefits for companies' sales revenues and customer experience, there are several risks of AI-enabled aggressive strategies. For instance, AI recommendation systems may lead to sales driven by consumers not feeling in control of the automated systems of retail processes and worrying about opportunities they could lose. Therefore, AI recommendation systems are creating consumption patterns decided by machines, stressing consumer decision-making and, consequently, affecting sustainable consumption (Faria *et al.*, 2023). This trend may negatively impact SDG 12 and several other SDGs.

SDG Challenges

The United Nations Industrial Development Organization (UNIDO, 20203) report is fully committed to contributing to achieving the SDGs while delivering on its mandate to support Member States in achieving inclusive and sustainable industrial development (ISID). Specifically, focusing on SDG 9 which "calls for building resilient infrastructure, promoting sustainable industrialization, and fostering innovation." This report provides statistical evidence demonstrating the intricate connection between industrial development and the living conditions and overall quality of life for people. It considers the significance of well-being for sustainable development, providing guidelines on establishing well-designed measurement frameworks (OECD Framework for Measuring Well-Being and Progress). This framework builds upon three distinct major components, each with its own relevant dimensions, namely: 1) material conditions, 2) quality of life, and 3) sustainability, each with their relevant dimensions.

Furthermore, research pointed out a gap in understanding the implications of AI for SDG 12 (Di Vaio et al. 2020). Therefore, these objectives urge enterprises, especially large corporations, to embrace sustainable practices and assist developing nations in enhancing their scientific and technological capacities to devise and implement more sustainable frameworks. This includes the development and deployment of production and consumption tools aimed at monitoring the effects of sustainable development. This may be boosted by developing partnerships for the SDG 17 goal.

Despite the overlaps of AI on SDG impacts on the interlinked pillars– society, environment, and economy – (with benefits across SDGs 07, 11, and 13 on climate action), there have been recent updates to the UN 2030 Agenda for SD, especially to SDG12 that discusses AI in current and future trends in business. The relevance of SDG12 might be because companies are increasingly required to face the challenge of sustainability by trying to improve the scope of innovations to preserve the integrity of the ecosystem and improve the use of natural resources (Di Vaio *et al.*, 2020). Indeed, most companies consider the development of sustainable products as a competitive opportunity (Kuo and Smith, 2018). However, to achieve sustainable development, it is essential to harmonize three fundamental elements: profit, social protection, and environmental respect. These elements are interdependent and reliant on each other to guarantee the well-being of individuals and societies (Di Vaio *et al.* 2020, p. 284).

Therefore, the SDG12 specifically targets businesses, advocating for sustainable production and consumption models that promote efficient and responsible use of natural resources, to "do more and better with less" (Di Vaio *et al.* 2020).

The use of AI in SBMs can support managers' choices in decision-making and management processes to improve the company's sustainable performance and problem-solving skills (Haseeb, Hussain, Ślusarczyk, & Jermsittiparsert, 2019). Moreover, to be competitive in contemporary turbulent environments, firms must be capable of processing huge amounts of information and effectively converting it into actionable knowledge. Using genetic algorithms to operate unsupervised is particularly helpful in the marketing context, where problems are also usually highly complex, unstructured, and ill-defined (Orriols-Puig *et al.*, 2013) remains a challenge for business sustainable performance and problem-solving.

The next section describes the methodology used in this study.

3. METHODOLOGY

This study uses a bibliometric analysis focusing on articles relating AI and the SDGs. Bibliometric analysis is based on statistical tools to systematically map and decipher large amounts of scientific data, enabling a rigorous understanding of the contribution and impact of publications in a determined research area (Donthu et al., 2021).

Data Collection

The sample articles were collected on the ISI Web on Knowledge (WoS) database. WoS and Scopus are the most used databases. However, WoS has considerably greater coverage of Social Sciences than

Scopus (Gusenbauer, 2022). Thus, only the WoS database was used for this study. The research process was conducted in three steps: (1) extraction of articles, (2) sample refinement to exclude non-relevant articles, and (3) bibliometric analysis of the final sample.

The WoS search was performed using the keywords: "Artificial Intelligence" OR AI AND "Sustainable development goal* OR SDG*. The search was performed on the title, abstract, and keywords to obtain all relevant publications. The publications were extracted on December 20, 2023. The initial search yielded 452 publications. The sample was refined using the following inclusion criteria: the language of publication (English) and the type of publication (article, proceeding paper, review article, and early access). This resulted in 446 publications. Then, since the purpose is to limit the publications addressing the SDGs related to the economic pillar, the sample was further refined using WoS classification of publications according to the SDGs 8, 9, 10, and 12. WoS compares the Sustainable Development Goals to Micro Citation Topics and assigns each publication to one or more of the 1 to 16 SDGs. It should be noted that WoS does not classify publications on the 17 SDG. The screening process resulted in a sample of 69 publications (59 articles, 14 review papers, and 2 proceeding papers). The first publication is from 2019. The United Nations adopted the 2030 Agenda and its goals in 2015, but the first publication connecting AI and the 8, 9, 10, and 12 SDGs only appeared in 2019.

Data Analysis

The bibliometric analysis was done using two freely available software:

1. VOSviewer software (van Eck & Waltman, 2010); and
2. Bibliometrics R-tool (Aria & Cuccurullo, 2017).

VOSviewer (Visualization of similarities viewer) identifies the interlinkages between the keywords, enabling understanding of the key research areas and linkages between publications. This co-word analysis is based on "the idea that the co-occurrence of keywords describes the contents of the documents" (Callon et al., 1991). Also, the interlinkage between keywords is shown by the co-occurrence of keywords in a particular cluster (van Eck & Waltman, 2010). Vosviewer displays clusters of frequently co-occurring keywords in maps.

To conduct the co-occurrence analysis, the bibliographic information was inserted in VOSviewer, which used the keywords appearing most frequently in authors' keywords and keywords plus. A thesaurus file was inserted to eliminate keyword inconsistency (e.g., singular vs. plural keywords). The network was generated by including keywords that occur at least three times in the publications sample, which resulted in the filtering of 470 keywords to 63 that met the threshold. The keywords that were not relevant to this study (i.e., keywords related to methodology) were deleted, resulting in 40 keywords.

The selected articles were also analyzed on Bibliometrics, which enables to perform a "comprehensive science mapping analysis" (Aria & Cuccurullo, 2017). This software enables reporting bibliometric descriptive statistics such as the top authors, affiliations, contributing sources, most productive countries, top-cited papers, and evolving keywords in the underlying study field by subject area.

Table 1. Number of publications by SDGs

		SDGs Combination								
SDGs	**# Articles**	**1**	**2**	**3**	**8**	**9**	**10**	**11**	**12**	**13**
09 Industry Innovation And Infrastructure	47	11			1				23	1
12 Responsible Consumption And Production	41		1			23		3		2
08 Decent Work And Economic Growth	4	1		2		1	1			
10 Reduced Inequality	2		2				1			

4. FINDINGS

This section presents the bibliometric analysis of the selected publications (using Bibliometrics and VOSviewer). The following analyses were undertaken: classification by SDGs, most preferred and productive sources, productive author, journal and country, most cited documents, and keyword co-occurrence analysis. The detailed results are as follows.

Sample Descriptive Statistics

The sample of 69 publications is assigned to one or more of the 1 to 16 SDGs by WoS. Thus, one paper can belong to more than one SDGs, making difficult to separate the analysis by each SDG. Table 1 shows the papers by SDG and the combination of publications classified in more than one SDG. Results show that SDG 9 and 12 have been researched more intensively and together.

The publications are from 49 different journals, 225 different institutions, and 47 different countries. Also, the number of papers is scarce, and the first focusing on the economic pillar is from 2019, indicating that this field is in its initial stage and needs further research. Further, there are 285 authors, and no author with more than three papers. Thus, there are no dominant authors yet. The number of co-authors per publication is 4.22, and international co-authorship is 44.93%. Also, results showed that researchers from different backgrounds have contributed to the field.

Figure 1 displays the number of publications and citations from 2019 to 2023, showing that this number has increased considerably over time. Figure 2 shows the number of citations per country.

The top publications with more than 25 citations contributing to the area of AI and SDG economic pillar are shown in Table 2. The most influential article to date is from Dwivedi et al. (2022), which has 149 citations. This paper is an editorial reflection by several authors on the role of technology and its challenges in achieving a more climate friendly society.

Figure 3 displays an overview of the sample displaying a three-field plot. The plot shows the result using the top twelve countries (AU_CO) with the highest number of publications on the left, the twelve most frequent author's keywords (DE) in the center, and the most cited sources (SO) on the right. India, China, USA, and the UK have the maximum contributions. Interestingly, most of the research on the topic under study was done in countries outside of the EU. The most frequently occurring keywords are sustainable development goals, artificial intelligence, sustainability, industry 4.0, circular economy, and internet of things. Finally, regarding the sources, Sustainability is the major producer, with 13 publications. The plot shows the links between countries, the most frequent keywords being worked on, and the top journals where the research is published.

Figure 1. Number of publications and times cited over time

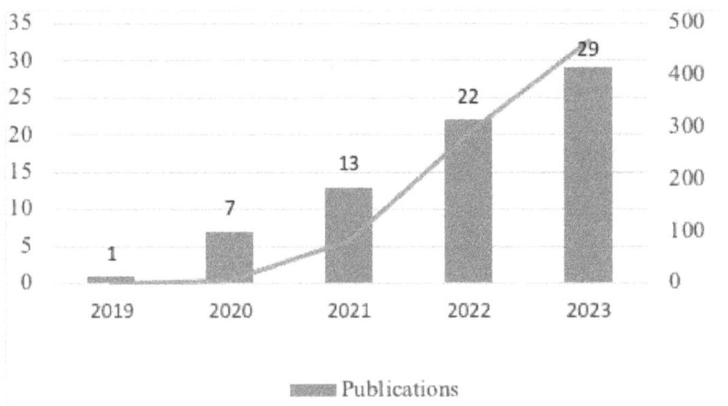

Figure 2. Citations by country

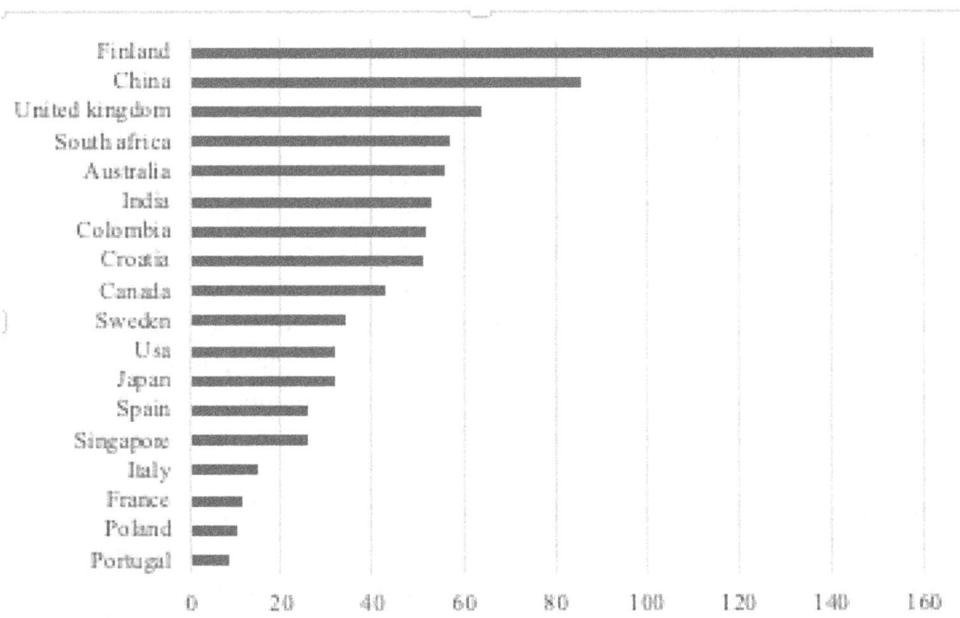

Analysis by Subject Area

Figure 4 categorizes the publications across fields of study. Most research is conducted in the fields of environmental sciences and studies and green sustainable science technology.

Keywords Co-Occurrence Analysis

This section shows the most prominent topics in current research on AI and SDGs. The co-occurrence analysis of keywords formed five distinct clusters (Figure 5). These clusters are grouped as follows.

Table 2. Most cited publications

Authors	Publication Title	Average Citations per Year	Total Citations
(Dwivedi et al., 2022)	Climate change and COP26: Are digital technologies and information management part of the problem or the solution? An editorial reflection and call to action	74,5	149
(Ajwani-Ramchandani et al., 2021)	Towards a circular economy for packaging waste by using new technologies: The case of large multinationals in emerging economies	18,7	56
(Zhou & Liu, 2022)	The geography of poverty: Review and research prospects	27,0	54
(Rojas et al., 2021)	Society 5.0: A Japanese Concept for a Superintelligent Society	17,3	52
(Jambrak et al., 2021)	Internet of Nonthermal Food Processing Technologies (IoNTP): Food Industry 4.0 and Sustainability	17,0	51
(Hoosain et al., 2020)	The Impact of 4IR Digital Technologies and Circular Thinking on the United Nations Sustainable Development Goals	12,3	49
(Shahsavar et al., 2021)	Constructing a smart framework for supplying the biogas energy in green buildings using an integration of response surface methodology, artificial intelligence and petri net modelling	14,3	43
(Nayal et al., 2022)	Supply chain firm performance in circular economy and digital era to achieve sustainable development goals	13,0	39
(Lillford & Hermansson, 2021)	Global missions and the critical needs of food science and technology	10,3	31
(Tang, 2022)	Innovative Technology and Operations for Alleviating Poverty through Women's Economic Empowerment	9,3	28
(Tsui et al., 2023)	Machine learning and circular bioeconomy: Building new resource efficiency from diverse waste streams	13,0	26

The red cluster represents industry, technology, and big data usage. It includes keywords such as big data, industry 4.0, supply chain, internet, augmented reality, esgs, and technology. It. The yellow color cluster represents AI and includes keywords such as AI, internet of things, systems, policy, and education. The green color cluster represents sustainability. It covers keywords such as sustainability, SDGs, sustainable development, optimization, design, cost, food waste, life cycle, and machine learning. The blue cluster represents digitalization and challenges. It includes keywords like circular economy, challenges, digitalization, digital technologies, future, opportunities, and strategies. The purple cluster represents business and management. It covers keywords related to business, industry, management, and innovation.

Next, to display a broad picture highlighting the most common words in the abstracts of the publication, we used a "WordCloud". Figure 6 displays the "WordCloud," highlighting the most common words in the abstracts of the publications. The size of the words depends on their frequency. The most frequent relevant words are sustainable (126 times), development (119 times), digital (81 times), technologies (72 times), goals (68 times), AI (67 times), industry (54 times), sustainability (52 times), data (48 times), food (40 times), waste (38 times), energy (35 times), and management (35 times).

Figure 3. Three-field plots, Country versus authors' keywords versus sources

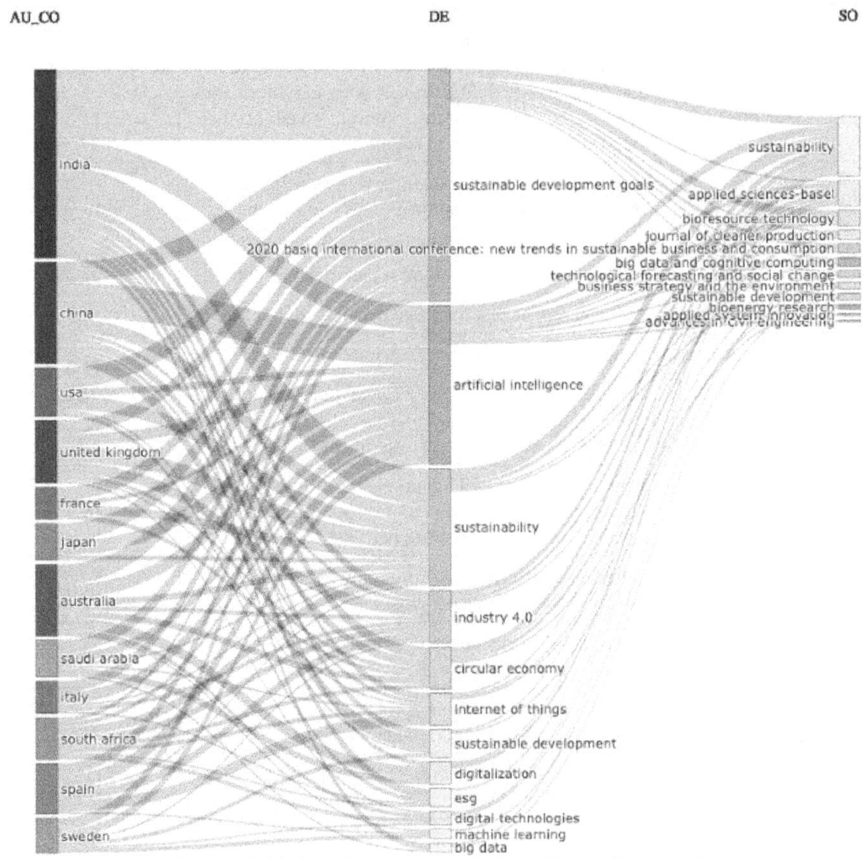

Figure 4. Publications by subject area

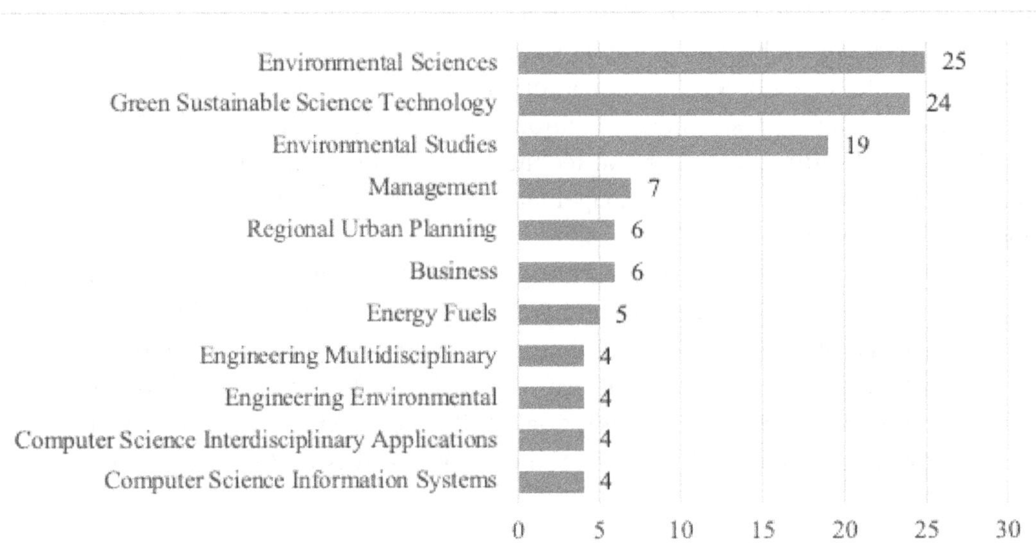

Figure 5. Keywords co-occurrence analysis

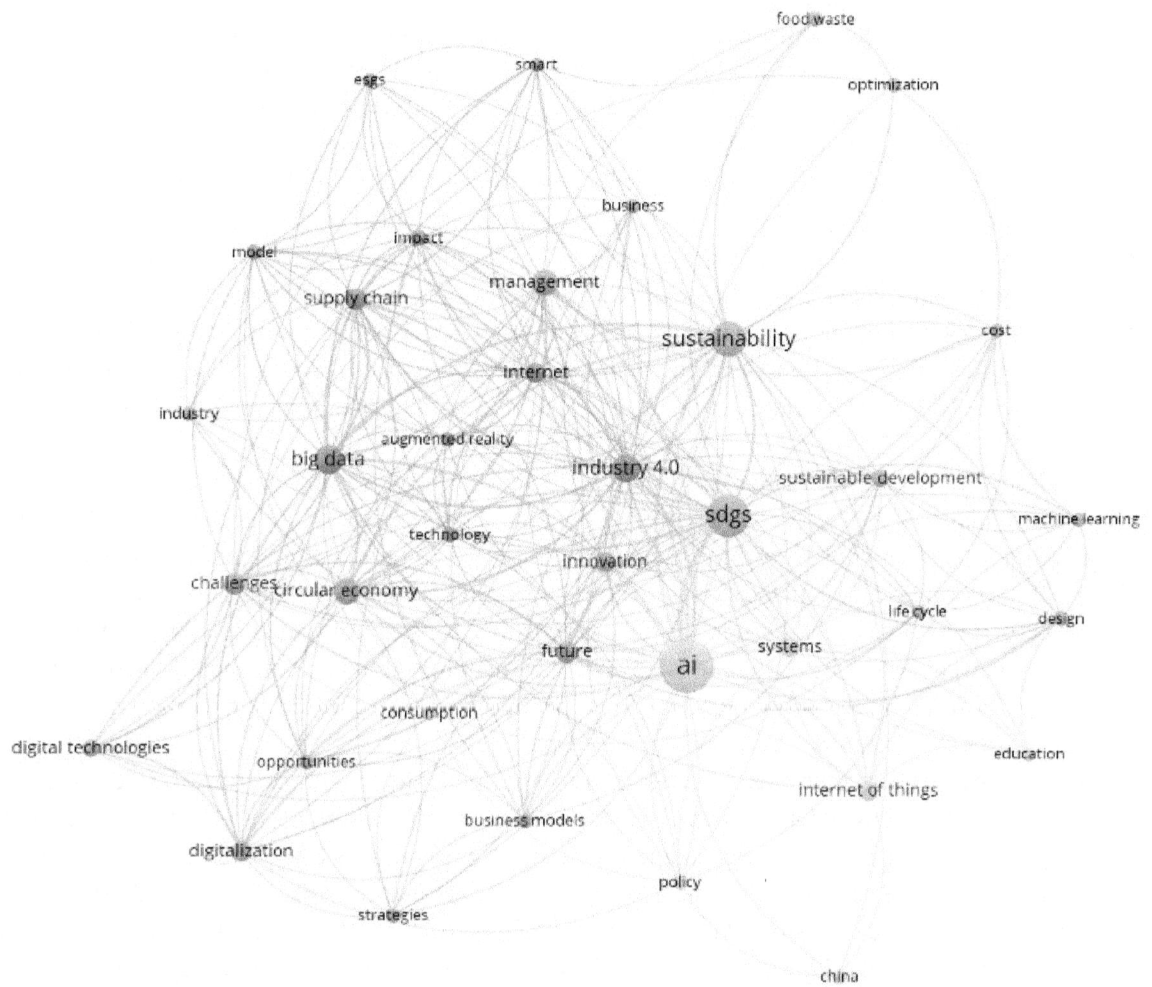

Figure 6. WordCloud with the most frequent words in the publications' abstracts

5. CONCLUSION

This book chapter contributes to the understanding of how new AI technologies can promote increased business revenues/returns, cost reductions, and enhanced customer experience, as well as society´s well-being, in a sustainable way. Furthermore, these AI benefits also come with risks and challenges concerning organizations, environment, customers, and society, as investigated. Additionally, this chapter examines and discusses the implications of how AI can either enable or inhibit the delivery of the goals recognized in the UN 2030 Agenda for Sustainable Business Models Development.

To address the research goals, this book chapter adopts a literature review using bibliometric methods, which aims to analyze and map the literature on business associated benefits, risks, and challenges generated by implementing artificial intelligence technologies, connecting with SDGs within the Economic group. The bibliometric analysis draws on statistical tools to systematically map and decipher large amounts of scientific data and rigorously assess the contribution and impact of publications in the research field.

Using bibliometric methodologies, this study selected the most significant published sources and examined the changes that have occurred in the conceptual framework of AI and SBM in the light of SDGs research. The screening process resulted in a sample of 69 publications, the first publication being from 2019. From 2015 to 2019, there were no major publications in the field; however, since 2019, there has been an increase in the number of publications in terms of volume. The UN 2030 agenda for sustainability was published in 2015, and since 2019, as technology advances, the SDGs on economic outcomes have become increasingly important, and academia is now focusing on this issue as the digitalization of services continues to increase.

However, scarce research relates AI with business models sustainability from the perspective of Economic impacts that may act as enablers or inhibitors, especially for SDGs 8, 9, 10, 12, and 17. The number of papers is rare, and the first focusing on the economic pillar is from 2019, indicating that this field is in its initial stage and needs further research. From our main results, we conclude that there is a research gap in the field regarding AI´s impacts on SDGs 08, 09, 10, and 12. This finding is in line with Di Vaio and colleagues (2020), which have shown that there is still a research gap concerning AI's implications for SDG12, and the role of AI in the development of SBMs from the perspective of SDGs is currently not addressed in academic literature.

Furthermore, there is also a research gap concerning the combination of SDGs, especially 08 and 10, with the other goals regarding the impacts of AI technologies. However, due to the SDG's interlinked nature, it is undeniable that the achievement of SDG 09 is linked to meeting the other Goals and targets of the 2030 Agenda. Unarguably, inclusive and sustainable industrialization drives sustained economic growth and the creation of decent jobs and income (SDG 8); it helps reduce poverty (SDG 01), hunger (SDG 02), and inequalities (SDGs 05 and 10) while improving health and well-being (SDG 03), increasing resource and energy efficiency (SDGs 06, 07, 11, 12) and reducing greenhouse gas and other polluting emissions, including from chemicals (SDGs 13, 14, 15) (UNIDO, 2020).

Another conclusion concerns the overlaps of SDG 12 (responsible consumption and production – ensure sustainable consumption and production patterns), with other goals being central to the UN 2030 agenda, in particular SDG 09 (industry, innovation, and infrastructure). These goals are intrinsically connected because innovation is the engine of business, and through innovative technologies, it is possible to implement sustainable models of production and consumption, perfectly in line with the goals of the UN 2030 Agenda, in particular with SDG 12. This goal lies at the "heart" of the other SDGs because responsible and sustainable consumption and production will ensure new social and environmental needs, protection of the ecosystem and people, and ensuring social equity. Moreover, several authors have stressed this will disseminate sustainable business models in which sustainability consists of balancing all three dimensions (economic, environmental, and social) that are "indissolubly connected and interdependent," showing that SDG outcomes depend on the interaction between human, technical and natural systems (Di Vaio, 2020 p. 284).

Hence, this finding entails several managerial implications. This goal (SDG12) should encourage enterprises, particularly large businesses and multinationals, to adopt sustainable practices and to provide support to developing countries in improving their scientific and technological capabilities to create and implement more sustainable models, as well as production and consumption tools to monitor the impacts of sustainable development. This may be boosted with the development of partnerships for the goals SDG17.

To achieve these goals, as Bocken and colleagues (2014) point out, stakeholders of companies are essential for implementing corporate innovation with an impact on greater sustainability. This will help organisations to create a competitive advantage based on sustainable business model archetypes. The involvement of stakeholders in decision-making concerning AI implementations towards sustainability is vital.

The technological advantages provided by AI might have greater positive impacts on the achievement of several SDGs within the Economy group.

Nevertheless, self-interest can be expected to bias the AI research community and industry toward publishing positive results towards SDGs, as researchers caution (Vinuesa et al., 2023). This is true concerning the frequently positive impacts of SDG 8 on the environment, especially on SDG 13.

Nonetheless, despite the several benefits for businesses, customers, and society in general, AI entails several risks and challenges on SDGs outcomes for companies and political policies to tackle.

For instance, AI implementations have managerial implications concerning the technical realm of learning algorithms and big data processing. The potential increase in retail revenues due to AI implementation is intrinsically dependent on the quality and quantity of personal data that companies collect from their customers. Knowing and forecasting consumers' demand across interconnected supply chains and then customizing their shopping experience are central AI drivers (Anica-Popa *et al.*, 2021). However, this leads to ethical considerations relative to the right balance between personalization benefits and privacy risks, and these concerns are growing in AI contexts, as consumer data is being extracted and processed by machines and biased algorithms, which may increase inequalities. As such, many actors might attempt to define principles for the responsible use of AI, and common themes include transparency, auditability, robustness, safety, fairness, and ethics (Faria *et al.*, 2023).

Building upon these challenges, we propose a research agenda for both academics and managers in the following section.

5.1. Future Research Directions

Future research initiatives can help to address the shortcomings of this study. The fact that the bibliometric data was generated only from the Web of Science is a research constraint. Hence, different data sources, such as Scopus or SpringerLink, should be used in the next investigations. The study, which is based on 69 documents, provides an overview of a variety of factors, such as published document categories, publication sources, and VOSviewer-referenced research. Furthermore, a more detailed oriented analysis can be performed to understand the impact of each SDG research area found in this current study, as shown in the results section (table 1.) regarding SDG's combinations across publications. This study also focused solely on SDGs of the economic pillar – SDGs 08, 09, 10, and 12. However, academics can further research the SDGs of the interconnected dimensions (e.g., environment, economy and society) and interrelate them.

Such themes have so far not been sufficiently documented. These aspects are further discussed below, where gaps in AI research are identified.

To understand what remains to be discovered regarding these themes and the challenges associated with the field, we uncover some future research issues that may help guide academics research agenda. Following, we address several research gaps in the AI field, as well as the implications of sustainable business models, which are identified below.

- The long-term benefits of AI on the economy are perhaps not so extensively characterized by currently available methods. Discovering detrimental aspects of AI may require longer-term studies. As a result, the impact of new technologies should be assessed from the points of view of efficiency, ethics, and sustainability prior to launching large-scale AI deployments. This also entails key challenges for the 4.0 Industrial Revolution. Therefore, this is a relevant area for future research.
- Self-interest can be expected to bias the AI research community and industry towards publishing positive results towards SDGs. We acknowledge that conducting controlled experimental trials for evaluating real-world impacts of AI, instead of conducting these studies in controlled laboratory environments to evaluate the real-world effects, often remains a challenge.
- A recent World Economic Forum (2018) report raises concerns due to the integration of AI in the financial sector. Therefore, assessing the long-term impact of such algorithms on equity, security, and fairness is critical.
- Other issues involving enterprises are related to the lack of robust research methods to assess the long-term impact of AI, covering ethical and privacy issues associated with the intensity of AI applications to sensitive personal data. For instance, in the health sector, which represents one of the main drivers of the economy of each country, the most considerable difficulties lie in the patients' big data and hospital and laboratory information systems. This remains a critical research area.
- The underlying risk when using AI to evaluate and predict human behavior is the inherent bias in the data, which may increase inequalities and security risks among individuals. AI concerns with ethical implications involving ML algorithms, which are prone to incorporate the biases that could lead to consequences such as discriminatory algorithms - racist or sexist – remains a critical research area. Therefore, responsible development and training of AI algorithms is mandatory to avoid costly errors.

REFERENCES

Ajwani-Ramchandani, R., Figueira, S., de Oliveira, R. T., Jha, S., Ramchandani, A., & Schuricht, L. (2021). Towards a circular economy for packaging waste by using new technologies: The case of large multinationals in emerging economies. *Journal of Cleaner Production*, *281*(16), 125139. Advance online publication. doi:10.1016/j.jclepro.2020.125139

Anica-Popa, I., Anica-Popa, L., Rădulescu, C., & Vrîncianu, M. (2021). The Integration of Artificial Intelligence in Retail: Benefits. *Amfiteatru Economic*, *23*(56), 120. Advance online publication. doi:10.24818/EA/2021/56/120

Aria, M., & Cuccurullo, C. (2017). bibliometrix: An R-tool for comprehensive science mapping analysis. *Journal of Informetrics*, *11*(4), 959–975. doi:10.1016/j.joi.2017.08.007

Balakrishnan, P., Gupta, R., & Jacob, V. S. (2004). Development of Hybrid Genetic Algorithms for Product Line Designs. *IEEE Trans. Syst. Man Cybern. Part B*, *34*, 468–483.

BearingPoint. (2019). *L'expérience client à l'ère de l'intelligence artificielle*. Available at: https://www.bearingpoint.com/files/L_exp%C3%A9rience_client_%C3%A01_%C3%A8re_de_l_intelligence_artificielle.pdf? download=0&itemId=571534

Bocken, N. M., Short, S. W., Rana, P., & Evans, S. (2014). A literature and practice review to develop sustainable business model archetypes. *Journal of Cleaner Production*, *65*, 42–56. doi:10.1016/j.jclepro.2013.11.039

Bradlow, E. T., Gangwar, M., Kopalle, P., & Voleti, S. (2017). The role of Big Data and predictive analytics in retailing. *Journal of Retailing*, *93*(1), 79–95. doi:10.1016/j.jretai.2016.12.004

Brynjolfsson, E., & McAfee, A. (2014). *The Second Machine Age: Work, Progress, and Prosperity in a Time of Brilliant Technologies*. W. W. Norton & Company.

Brynjolfsson, E., & McAfee, A. (2017, July). The business of artificial intelligence. *Harvard Business Review*, 1–20.

Callon, M., Courtial, J. P., & Laville, F. (1991). Co-word analysis as a tool for describing the network of interactions between basic and technological research: The case of polymer chemsitry. *Scientometrics*, *22*(1), 155–205. doi:10.1007/BF02019280

Di Vaio, A., Palladinoa, R., Hassanb, R., & Escobar, O. (2020). Artificial intelligence and business models in the sustainable development goals perspective: A systematic literature review. *Journal of Business Research*, *121*, 283–314. doi:10.1016/j.jbusres.2020.08.019

Donthu, N., Kumar, S., Mukherjee, D., Pandey, N., & Lim, W. M. (2021). How to conduct a bibliometric analysis: An overview and guidelines. *Journal of Business Research*, *133*, 285–296. doi:10.1016/j.jbusres.2021.04.070

Dwivedi, Y. K., Hughes, L., Ismagilova, E., Aarts, G., Coombs, C., Crick, T., Duan, Y., Dwivedi, R., Edwards, J., Eirug, A., Galanos, V., Ilavarasan, P. V., Janssen, M., Jones, P., Kar, A. K., Kizgin, H., Kronemann, B., Lal, B., Lucini, B., ... Williams, M. D. (2021). Artificial Intelligence (AI): Multidisciplinary perspectives on emerging challenges, opportunities, and agenda for research, practice and policy. *International Journal of Information Management*, *57*, 101994. Advance online publication. doi:10.1016/j.ijinfomgt.2019.08.002

Dwivedi, Y. K., Hughes, L., Kar, A. K., Baabdullah, A. M., Grover, P., Abbas, R., Andreini, D., Abumoghli, I., Barlette, Y., Bunker, D., Kruse, L. C., Constantiou, I., Davison, R. M., De, R., Dubey, R., Fenby-Taylor, H., Gupta, B., He, W., Kodama, M., ... Wade, M. (2022). Climate change and COP26: Are digital technologies and information management part of the problem or the solution? An editorial reflection and call to action. *International Journal of Information Management*, *63*(39), 102456. Advance online publication. doi:10.1016/j.ijinfomgt.2021.102456

Faria, R., Torres, A., & Beirão, G. (2023). Trustworthy Artificial Intelligence and Machine Learning: Implications on Users' Security and Privacy Perceptions. In Confronting Security and Privacy Challenges in Digital Marketing. doi:10.4018/978-1-6684-8958-1

Gretzel, U., Sigala, M., Xiang, Z., & Koo, C. (2015). Smart tourism: Foundations and developments. *Electronic Markets*, *25*(3), 179–188. doi:10.1007/s12525-015-0196-8

Grewal, D., Roggeveen, A.L. and Nordfält, J. (2017). The Future of Retailing. *Journal of Retailing*, *93*(1), 1-6. . doi:10.1016/j.jretai.2016.12.008

Gusenbauer, M. (2022). Search where you will find most: Comparing the disciplinary coverage of 56 bibliographic databases. *Scientometrics*, *127*(5), 2683–2745. doi:10.1007/s11192-022-04289-7 PMID:35571007

Haenlein, M., & Kaplan, A. (2019). A brief history of artificial intelligence: On the past, present, and future of artificial intelligence. *California Management Review*, *61*(4), 5–14. doi:10.1177/0008125619864925

Haseeb, M., Hussain, H. I., Ślusarczyk, B., & Jermsittiparsert, K. (2019). Industry 4.0: A solution towards technology challenges of sustainable business performance. *Social Sciences (Basel, Switzerland)*, *8*(5), 154. doi:10.3390/socsci8050154

Hoosain, M. S., Paul, B. S., & Ramakrishna, S. (2020). The Impact of 4IR Digital Technologies and Circular Thinking on the United Nations Sustainable Development Goals. *Sustainability, 12*(23), 16. doi:10.3390/su122310143

Inman, J. J., & Nikolova, H. (2017). Shopper-Facing Retail Technology: A Retailer Adoption Decision Framework Incorporating Shopper Attitudes and Privacy Concerns. *Journal of Retailing*, *93*(1), 7–28. doi:10.1016/j.jretai.2016.12.006

Jambrak, A. R., Nutrizio, M., Djekic, I., Pleslic, S., & Chemat, F. (2021). Internet of Nonthermal Food Processing Technologies (IoNTP): Food Industry 4.0 and Sustainability. *Applied Sciences-Basel, 11*(2), Article 686. https://doi.org/ doi:10.3390/app11020686

Jones, N. (2018). How to stop data centres from gobbling up the world's electricity. *Nature*, *561*(7722), 163–166. doi:10.1038/d41586-018-06610-y PMID:30209383

Jordan, M. I., & Mitchell, T. M. (2015). Machine learning:Trends, perspectives, and prospects. *Science*, *349*(6245), 255–260. doi:10.1126/science.aaa8415 PMID:26185243

Kuo, T. C., & Smith, S. (2018). A systematic review of technologies involving eco-innovation for enterprises moving towards sustainability. *Journal of Cleaner Production*, *192*, 207–220. doi:10.1016/j.jclepro.2018.04.212

Kusiak, A. (2017). Smart manufacturing. *International Journal of Production Research, 56*(1-2), 508–517. doi:10.1080/00207543.2017.1351644 PMID:28383012

LeCun, Y., Bengio, Y., & Hinton, G. (2015). Deep learning. *Nature, 521*(7553), 436–444. doi:10.1038/nature14539 PMID:26017442

Lillford, P., & Hermansson, A. M. (2021). Global missions and the critical needs of food science and technology. *Trends in Food Science & Technology, 111*, 800–811. doi:10.1016/j.tifs.2020.04.009

Meltzer, J. (2018). *The impact of artificial intelligence on international trade*. Brookings Institution. Available at: https://www.brookings.edu/research/the-impact-of-artificial-intelligence-on-international-trade/

Nayal, K., Kumar, S., Raut, R. D., Queiroz, M. M., Priyadarshinee, P., & Narkhede, B. E. (2022). Supply chain firm performance in circular economy and digital era to achieve sustainable development goals. *Business Strategy and the Environment, 31*(3), 1058–1073. doi:10.1002/bse.2935

OECD. (2016). *Artificial Intelligence on Society*. OECD Publishing. Retrieved from https://www.oecd-ilibrary.org/.ors

Olsen, T. L., & Tomlin, B. (2020). Industry 4.0: Opportunities and Challenges for Operations Management. *Manufacturing & Service Operations Management, 22*(1), 113–122. doi:10.1287/msom.2019.0796

Orriols-Puig, A., Martínez-López, F. J., Casillas, J., & Lee, N. (2013). Unsupervised KDD to creatively support managers' decision making with fuzzy association rules: A distribution channel application. *Industrial Marketing Management, 42*(4), 532–543. doi:10.1016/j.indmarman.2013.03.005

Rojas, C. N., Penafiel, G. A. A., Buitrago, D. F. L., & Romero, C. A. T. (2021). Society 5.0: A Japanese Concept for a Superintelligent Society. *Sustainability, 13*(12), 16. doi:10.3390/su13126567

Shahsavar, M. M., Akrami, M., Gheibi, M., Kavianpour, B., Fathollahi-Fard, A. M., & Behzadian, K. (2021). Constructing a smart framework for supplying the biogas energy in green buildings using an integration of response surface methodology, artificial intelligence and petri net modelling. *Energy Conversion and Management, 248*(17), 114794. Advance online publication. doi:10.1016/j.enconman.2021.114794

Tang, C. S. S. (2022). Innovative Technology and Operations for Alleviating Poverty through Women's Economic Empowerment. *Production and Operations Management, 31*(1), 32–45. doi:10.1111/poms.13349

Truby, J. (2018). Decarbonizing Bitcoin: Law and policy choices for reducing the energy consumption of Blockchain technologies and digital currencies. *Energy Research & Social Science, 44*, 399–410. doi:10.1016/j.erss.2018.06.009

Tsui, T. H., van Loosdrecht, M. C. M., Dai, Y. J., & Tong, Y. W. (2023). Machine learning and circular bioeconomy: Building new resource efficiency from diverse waste streams. *Bioresource Technology, 369*(10), 128445. Advance online publication. doi:10.1016/j.biortech.2022.128445 PMID:36473583

UN General Assembly (UNGA). (2015). A/RES/70/1Transforming our world: The 2030 Agenda for Sustainable Development. *Resolut, 25*, 1–35.

United Nations Industrial Development Organization (UNIDO). (2020). *How industrial development matters to the well-being of the population: Some Statistical Evidence.* https://www.unido.org/sites/default/files/files/2020-02/HOW%20INDUSTRIAL%20DEVELOPMENT%20MATTERS%20TO%20THE%20WELL-BEING%20OF%20THE%20POPULATION%20FIN.pdf

van Doorn, J., Mende, M., Noble, S. M., Hulland, J., Ostrom, A. L., Grewal, D., & Petersen, A. J. (2017). Domo Arigato Mr. Roboto: The Emergence of Automated Social Presence in Customers' Service Experiences. *Journal of Service Research, 20*(1), 43–58. doi:10.1177/1094670516679272

van Eck, N. J., & Waltman, L. (2010). Software survey: VOSviewer, a computer program for bibliometric mapping. *Scientometrics, 84*(2), 523–538. doi:10.1007/s11192-009-0146-3 PMID:20585380

Vinuesa, R., Azizpour, H., Leite, I., Balaam, M., Dignum, V., Domisch, S., Felländer, A., Langhans, S. D., Tegmark, M., & Fuso Nerini, F. (2020). The role of artificial intelligence in achieving the Sustainable Development Goals. *Nature Communications, 11*(1), 233. doi:10.1038/s41467-019-14108-y PMID:31932590

World Economic Forum (WEF). (2018). *The New Physics of Financial Services – How Artificial Intelligence is Transforming the Financial Ecosystem.* World Economic Forum.

Zhou, Y., & Liu, Y. S. (2022). The geography of poverty: Review and research prospects. *Journal of Rural Studies, 93*, 408–416. doi:10.1016/j.jrurstud.2019.01.008

ENDNOTES

1 United Nations, 2015 (https://www.un.org/sustainabledevelopment/)

2 OECD, 2019: Artificial Intelligence in Society.

3 https://www.unido.org/sites/default/files/files/2020-02

Chapter 14
Effects of Taxation on Innovation and Implications for the Sustainable Development Goals:
Literature Review

Vera Godinho
University of Aveiro, Portugal

Carla Monteiro
Banco de Portugal, Portugal

Graça Azevedo
https://orcid.org/0000-0002-6346-4035
University of Aveiro, Portugal

ABSTRACT

Innovation plays a crucial role in the realisation of Sustainable Development Goals (SDGs) because it makes it possible to find creative and sustainable solutions that meet global challenges. However, the relationship between taxation and innovation is not linear and much less simple, as it can depend on various factors, such as the structure of the tax system, government policies, and how tax resources are used. This study aims to review the literature on the effects of taxation on innovation and its implications for achieving the SDGs. In this sense, a literature review was carried out that showed that taxation can have both positive and negative effects on innovation and that high tax rates and complex tax systems can discourage innovation because they reduce companies' financial capacity. The implications for Sustainable Development Goals are significant. Innovation and taxation are determinant factors in achieving the SDGs, as they drive technological advances and enable the development of sustainable solutions to tackle global challenges.

DOI: 10.4018/979-8-3693-0847-9.ch014

INTRODUCTION

The Sustainable Development Goals (SDGs) provide a holistic framework to address global challenges, considering three main dimensions: economic growth, social inclusion, and environmental protection. Several studies emphasize the need for integrated approaches to sustainable development, emphasising the interconnectedness between the goals. For instance, Vandenbergh and Gilligan (2017) argue that actions taken to achieve one goal could have spillovers effects on others. This interconnectedness highlights the importance of a comprehensive and coordinated approach in achieving the goals collectively.

So, innovation plays a crucial role in achieving SDGs because it enables creative and sustainable solutions to be found that are suited to global challenges. According to Kouam and Asongu (2022), innovation enables the creation and implementation of innovative solutions and technologies and the introduction of practices whose aim is to strike a balance between economic development environmental protection, and social welfare.

Nevertheless, the effects of taxation extend beyond financial implications, significantly impacting various aspects of the economy. One such crucial area where taxation can have far-reaching consequences is innovation, a critical driver of sustainable development. Taxation plays a vital role in contributing to the achievement of SDGs (Rahman, 2023).

There is a significant relationship between taxation and the SDGs. The SDGs are a set of global goals adopted by the United Nations in 2015 to create a more sustainable future for all. Overall, taxation is a critical tool for governments to generate funds and redistribute resources necessary for sustainable development. It contributes to several SDGs by mobilizing resources, reducing inequality, financing social services, promoting sustainable consumption, combating illicit financial flows, fostering good governance, and contributing financially to innovation (Giri & Chaparro, 2023).

According to scientific evidence, innovation depends above all on an entrepreneurial environment and tax rules that encourage companies to invest in innovation projects (Weckel, 1983). This study aims to carry out a literature review on the effects of taxation on innovation and its implications for achieving the SDGs.

Several studies emphasise the need for integrated approaches to sustainable development, emphasising the interconnectedness between the goals. For instance, Vandenbergh and Gilligan (2017) argue that actions taken to achieve one goal could have spill over effects on others. This interconnectedness highlights the importance of a comprehensive and coordinated approach to achieving the goals collectively.

The relationship between taxation and innovation is not linear and much less simple, bearing in mind that it may depend on several factors, such as the structure of the tax system, government policies, and how tax resources are used. Thus, taxation can have positive and negative effects on innovation, however, it is a crucial tool used by governments around the world to generate revenue and promote economic stability and sustainable development.

Initially, we will analyse the relationship between taxation and business innovation. Next, we will analyse the effects of taxation on innovation capacity. Finally, we will reflect on the implications of taxation for achieving the SDGs.

The Relationship Between Taxation and Business Innovation

In recent years, the study of the influence of innovation on economic development and growth has aroused much interest among researchers and policymakers (Bamel et al., 2022; Parra-Requena et al.,

2022). This contribution began to be emphasised because innovation began to take on a leading role in the stimulus framework, from the moment it began to be used as an incentive for a country's economic and social development and growth (Kouam & Asongu, 2022). Innovation is often an object of study in economics and management (Kochetkov, 2023).

Innovation has been identified as a key element in meeting the challenges of sustainable development, as it can drive new business models to be more socially and environmentally responsible (Azmat et. al., 2023). However, the outcome of innovation depends on the context in which it is found, with the business context being the most favourable due to the constant search for competitive advantage. The industrial sector is where innovation takes place (Malerba, 2004; Klepper, 1997).

Sustainable development and innovation are two intrinsically linked concepts, because that innovation promotes more sustainable solutions, while sustainable development provides an opportunity and direction for innovation, and they aim to boost a society's economic, social, and environmental progress (Zhang & Vigne, 2021). Thus, by promoting sustainable innovation, we can create a more prosperous, just, and sustainable future for all (Azmat et al., 2023).

Although innovation is vital to ensuring a country's long-term economic growth and competitive advantage, motivating and stimulating innovation is no easy task (Hsu et al., 2014). Innovation management is as important as the development of innovation itself (Bamel et al., 2022). The innovation process is long and unpredictable, affects firm performance, and have with a very high probability of failure (Saunila, 2022). Decision-making regarding the implementation of innovation processes affects the present and the future and requires a careful and strategic approach because it involves significant risks, including short- and long-term financial impact, technological uncertainties, and possible internal resistance (Tavassoli, 2015).

Most financial decisions are increasingly complex and demanding, requiring more than intuition to make the right choices. In an increasingly globalised context, where financial decisions are particularly important for the sustainability of companies, innovation plays an increasingly prominent role in defining the competitive advantages of companies and the economies of the countries where it all happens (d`Andria & Savin, 2018).

As a process, business innovation involves the creation, development, and implementation of new ideas, products, services, processes, or methods, which take place in various sectors, accompanied by various financial constraints and the interactive effect of innovation capability, which provide improvement and value creation in organisations and society (Hurtado-Palomino et al., 2022). Therefore, tackling the challenges of innovation through the ability to co-create with partners from different sectors, allows access to different perspectives, the sharing of knowledge and resources, the reduction of costs and risks, and an increase in the speed of innovation projects (Zhang & Guo, 2019).

Therefore, by implementing a sequence of phases aimed at achieving a specific result, companies use various management tools and techniques combined with various economic and financial resources to ensure that processes run efficiently and effectively (Hsu et al., 2014). Creating an organisational culture that encourages creativity and innovation is crucial, as it allows companies to thrive in today's competitive and rapidly changing environment (Martins & Terblanche, 2003).

Unsurprisingly, the financial resources that will support the realisation of the innovation process are not always available or easily accessible (Kaushik, 2023). Looking at their substance, they can come from different sources, as they depend on the nature of the project and the stage the company is at (Tavassoli, 2015). Although they are crucial to driving and sustaining innovation, insufficiency will be seen as a challenge and a limitation, situations that can reduce the ability to innovate, since most innovation projects require significant investments (Kouam & Asongu, 2022).

Although the decision comes from an individual initiative, the literature states that the path does not have to be travelled alone, companies need to have support, and this requires the inclusion of other actors to enable the exchange of synergies (Zhang & Guo, 2019). When innovation is seen as a continuous process that is implemented with the collaboration of various players, it is easy to understand that integration and cooperation between partners, the exchange of knowledge, experiences, and resources, is enriching and essential for finding innovative and sustainable solutions (Panda & Ramanathan, 1996).

As a rule, companies incur various costs in carrying out their activities, which are categorised according to their nature. According to Jacob (2022), taxes represent an important cost factor for companies, which are included in the expenses component, thus playing a comprehensive role in investment and financing decisions in companies. However, according to the doctrinal definition, tax is not seen as an expense, it is a financial obligation that companies have to pay according to their ability to pay, the purpose of which is to finance public spending, such as health, education, security, among others. Although the approach is not consensual, because there are different perspectives, the financial impact is the same, in fact implying an outflow of resources. So what is taxation?

Taxation, on the other hand, is the process, act, or effect of taxing. From a conceptual point of view, it is broader, encompassing the various methods, rules, and regulations relating to the collection, and administration of taxes. Taxation includes the entire system of levying and collecting taxes, as well as the procedures for determining tax amounts, filing tax returns and enforcing tax legislation. As such, this little background is crucial, as we are dealing with different expressions.

In addition to this distinction, innovation is also characterised by being a complex and multifaceted process, stimulated by various factors, with taxation being identified as a possible determinant. We are faced with the realisation of a common point, not because of the complexity involved, but because of the incentive that taxation can give to innovation. The starting point!

Although the answer is unclear (Zheng & Zhang, 2021), the evidence shows that taxation can make a positive contribution through its influence on the achievement of results (Chen et al., 2021; Fang et al., 2023). Therefore, as scientific evidence recognises the positive effect of taxation through reductions in the tax rate on profits and investments, as well as tax incentive policies, it is fair to say that innovation depends on a tax environment that is conducive to business development (Atanassov & Liu, 2020; Akcigit et al., 2022).

In this specific context, the state, all of us, now plays a leading role in promoting and encouraging business innovation (Weckel, 1983). Given the extreme importance of the state in stimulating a country's economic and social development, a collaboration between the state, private companies, academia, and civil society is fundamental to promoting an environment that is favourable to innovation, so that the benefits can be widely disseminated (Kouam & Asongu, 2022).

Therefore, given the role that companies play as economic agents that encourage innovation and contribute to economic growth, it is interesting to reflect on the influence of taxation on innovation in the business context (Zheng & Zhang, 2021). Although the effects of taxation on the growth of companies is a very important topic, it still lacks depth (Shahroodi, 2010). According to Akanbi (2020), the debate on the effectiveness of taxation as a tool for promoting economic growth remains inconclusive, as several studies indicate mixed effects of taxation on economic growth.

The predominant policy instrument used to promote investment in innovative activities in companies is tax incentives (Labeaga et al., 2021). Precisely, tax incentives have proved to be an important tool for combining policies to support business innovation. Therefore, with innovation as a priority in policy preferences, governments have been encouraged to intervene by designing tax incentives, with the advantages and disadvantages that characterise policy instruments (Kaushik, 2023).

Tax incentives are usually granted generically to companies, without a more in-depth assessment of their capacity for innovation and their economic impact. This ends up favouring established companies with greater financial power, to the detriment of small innovative companies, which often have great growth potential but face difficulties in accessing financial resources (Zhang & Guo, 2019).

Although tax schemes offer additional and indispensable tax incentives for research and innovation, most of the time access is conditional on meeting conditions, thus making it difficult to operationalise the programs (Dai & Chapman, 2022).

Fiscal support from the government through an efficient and appropriate tax framework, favourable to companies that want to innovate, influences and facilitates decision-making regarding the implementation of innovation processes in companies, thus contributing to increasing a country's sustainable prosperity. Therefore, successful program interventions related to tax incentives depend on efficient and effective design (Howlett, 2018). So what are the effects of taxation on companies' capacity for innovation?

Effects of Taxation on Companies' Capacity for Innovation

Taxation is one of the mechanisms that the government uses to achieve its financial objectives and is seen by many as a brake on long-term economic growth (Kouam & Asongu, 2022; Zheng & Zhang, 2021). However, taxation is not only a means that is used to fulfil the state's financial needs, it is also an instrument for distributing income and wealth (Halim & Rahman, 2022).

Although tax policy is an important determinant of innovative behaviour, in reality, it is only one of many factors that influence the level of innovation (Obschonka et al., 2023). Therefore, analysing the issue of taxation is not straightforward, in the sense that innovative activity in companies is influenced by other factors, such as compliance costs, the complexity of tax systems, the uncertainty of tax legislation, and the various levels of taxation (Shahroodi, 2010).

Therefore, we will focus our study on the effects that corporate profit taxation may have on innovation, disregarding the influence of compliance costs because innovation is not directly taxed, but only tax implications. Given that taxes are seen as an important and effective policy instrument that is increasingly being used by governments to induce innovation, assessing the effects of taxation is no easy task (OECD, 2010).

However, as taxation can occur in two different ways, one involving the direct application of a tax rate on the taxable event and the other through the use of other tax advantages based on tax mitigation mechanisms, its effects are difficult to measure and unclear (Zheng & Zhang, 2021).

According to Akcigit et al. (2022), as tax reduces profits and financial return as a rule, it is understandable that it has a negative connotation with innovation, as it discourages the dynamisation of projects. But if innovation is the result of an intentional endeavour, which implies a proactive approach, reducing the expected net return seems contradictory, given that innovation is expected to make a positive contribution to society. Hence the government's efforts to provide preferential tax treatment to the economic results of innovation activities using mitigation mechanisms (Appelt et al., 2023).

Although higher taxes have been found to negatively affect the quantity and location of innovation, the average quality of innovation tends to remain unchanged (Akcigit et al., 2022). However, the idea that lower tax rates positively affect business development is not new, naturally because of the impact they have on the value of the tax, and their ability to modify behaviour and stimulate economic growth (Laffer, 2004).

Reducing the tax burden is an indispensable component of a company's overall strategy. (Mukherjee et al., 2017) point out that high tax rates on corporate profits reduce companies' capacity for innovation. A reduction in the amount of tax does not only have to be achieved through a reduction in nominal rates but can also occur through deductions, specific rules for deducting tax losses, exemptions, tax incentives, and tax benefits. In this way, the relief takes place and the effective tax rate is lower than it would be under standard taxation (Steinmüller et al., 2019; Uemura, 2022).

To promote and incentivise innovation, it is important to bear in mind that tax systems must be equipped with specific measures that are implemented through tax incentives so that companies invest in innovative activities (Zhang & Song, 2022). Furthermore, in many cases, although innovation incentive programs exist, their implementation and management fail because they do not respond effectively to the needs of innovative companies. They also fail because companies are simply unaware of their existence or are not eligible (Zheng & Zhang, 2021).

Tax incentives make it possible to realise the transfer of public resources by reducing tax liability compared to the standard taxation system, which reflects a country's political priorities. This policy instrument makes it possible to reduce the effective tax rate compared to that which would result from standard taxation and to balance the public funding needed to stimulate innovation with the tax burden on companies that want to innovate (Jacob, 2022).

Corporate taxes directly affect the incentive to accumulate capital and carry out research and investment. Exemptions or reductions in tax rates allow companies to make a return on their investments and strengthen their cash flow, to create an equitable and stable business environment capable of driving sustainable growth (Federici & Parisi, 2015).

According to Chen et al. (2021), high tax rates can create a less competitive business environment, as companies have less incentive to invest in new technologies and innovative processes, thus jeopardising economic growth. High taxes can also discourage entrepreneurs from starting new businesses, as the tax burden presents itself as an obstacle, hindering the success and growth of these companies.

However, there are also arguments to the contrary. Some believe that taxes are necessary to fund research and development programs, education, and infrastructure, and are fundamental to promoting innovation in a society (Abdul, 2015). In addition, taxes can be used to discourage certain environmentally damaging activities, such as green taxation. Green taxation refers to a set of tax measures that aim to incentivise more environmentally friendly practices and reduce pollution and environmental impacts caused by economic activity. A crossroads?

In their genesis, tax incentives have the necessary characteristics to play the role of promoting innovation, and are recognised by scientific evidence as being mechanisms that are used by governments to encourage companies to invest in research and development (R&D) and innovative activities (Zhang & Song, 2022). However, another question arises: do tax incentives promote real innovation or do them contribute to the relocation of innovation activities and therefore the operationalisation of profit shifting (Haufler & Schindler, 2023). This question arises because there is no harmonisation of corporate taxation, which is used by states to attract foreign direct investment.

As the tax rates that tax company profits vary between countries, considering that each country designs its tax policy, this can be a motivating factor for projects to move to jurisdictions with lower taxation (Bauman & Schadewald, 2001). However, more recently, the nominal tax rate has taken on a less important role, that of signaling, to give relevance to the effective tax rate. Effective tax rates are commonly used in policy proposals, both to evaluate them and to institute them in tax systems, because they take into account, for example, the effects of tax incentives (Janský, 2023).

There is an indirect and complex relationship between tax incentives for innovation and profit shifting. However, the existence of specific and different tax rules, which vary from country to country, can incentivise companies to look for ways to transfer profits to lower tax jurisdictions to reduce their overall tax burden. However, it is important to emphasise that transferring profits for purely tax purposes, unrelated to actual innovation activities, can be considered tax evasion or aggressive tax planning (Kempkes & Stähler, 2022).

Innovation plays a crucial role in achieving the SDGs because it enables creative and sustainable solutions to be found that are appropriate to global challenges. So what are the implications of taxation for achieving the SDGs?

Implications of Taxation for Achieving the SDGs

The Sustainable Development Goals (SDGs) provide a holistic framework to address global challenges, considering three main dimensions: economic growth, social inclusion, and environmental protection. Several studies emphasize the need for integrated approaches to sustainable development, emphasizing the interconnectedness between the goals. For instance, Vandenbergh and Gilligan (2017) argue that actions taken to achieve one goal could have spill overs effects on others. This interconnectedness highlights the importance of a comprehensive and coordinated approach to achieving the goals collectively.

Taxation is a crucial tool employed by governments worldwide to generate revenue and promote economic stability and development. Nevertheless, the effects of taxation extend beyond financial implications, significantly impacting various aspects of the economy. In this sense, some of the implications of taxation for achieving the SDGs include: financing the SDGs, reducing income inequality, promoting sustainable consumption and production, mobilizing domestic resources, enhancing transparency and accountability, strengthening governance and institutions, and promoting international cooperation (Giri & Chaparro, 2023; Rahman, 2023).

Still in this segment, these scientific articles provide valuable insights into the use of taxes as policy tools for promoting sustainable consumption and production. They discuss various aspects, including the effectiveness of taxation, consumer behaviour, and policy implications (Athanassoglou & Xepapadeas, 2011; Chai & Mueller, 2018; Grilli et al., 2018; Hey & Moreno-Ternero, 2015; Paru & Lennqvist;).

So, in relation to financing the SDGs, taxation is a primary source of public revenue, which can be used to finance projects and programs related to the SDGs. It helps governments allocate funds to priority areas such as education, healthcare, clean energy, and infrastructure development. In addition to the above, it makes it possible to reduce income inequality, since progressive taxation can help reduce income inequality by redistributing wealth from the rich to the less privileged. Addressing inequality is crucial to achieving the SDGs, since poverty reduction, and access to quality education and healthcare are among the goals linked to reducing inequality.

About sustainable consumption and production, taxes can be used as policy tools to incentivise sustainable practices and discourage harmful activities. For instance, imposing taxes on carbon emissions can encourage the shift towards cleaner energy alternatives, contributing to SDG 7 (Affordable and Clean Energy) and SDG 13 (Climate Action). Taxation can help mobilize domestic resources so that countries reduce their dependence on external financing and encourage self-sufficiency. The mobilization of domestic resources through effective tax systems allows governments to have greater control over their development agenda, aligned with the SDGs.

Therefore, taxation fosters transparency and accountability in public finances. When citizens pay taxes, they become more invested in holding governments accountable for how those revenues are spent. Transparent and accountable use of tax revenue contributes to achieving the SDGs by ensuring efficient resource allocation. Tax systems require effective governance and well-functioning institutions to ensure compliance, fairness, and efficiency. By strengthening tax administration and governance, countries can improve their global institutional capacity, which is crucial for the effective implementation of the SDGs.

Finally, taxation can also foster international cooperation in achieving the SDGs. Collaborative efforts to address tax evasion, aggressive tax planning, and illicit financial flows can help prevent revenue loss and promote fair taxation globally. Increased tax cooperation contributes to SDG 17 (Partnerships for the Goals). Overall, taxation plays a pivotal role in providing the necessary resources, reducing inequality, promoting sustainable practices, and strengthening governance and accountability, all of which are essential for achieving the SDGs.

Although taxes are often used to raise revenue to finance public spending, they can also be used for other purposes (Kalkuhl et al., 2018). The absence or low investments in education, one of the most important areas in the economy, implies less innovation and, as a consequence, stagnation in teaching. More and more, financial education plays a significant role in supporting the achievement of several SDGs (Bardhan et al., 2019, Mensah et al., 2021; Prado, 2020; Zaman et al., 2020, Zikmundova et al., 2021; Eskelinen & Eskelinen, 2019).

Firstly, it contributes to achieving SDG 1 (No Poverty) by empowering individuals with knowledge and skills to manage their finances effectively and break the cycle of poverty. This area can teach people how to save, budget, and last but not least, make informed financial decisions, ultimately enabling them to improve their economic well-being.

In addition, financial education is instrumental in advancing SDG 4 (Quality Education) by integrating financial literacy into the education system, individuals can learn important financial concepts from an early age. This area in schools has great importance for the following reasons: (i) Provide students with practical and relevant life skills that they will need to navigate the complex financial landscape of the modern world; (ii) Can provide opportunities for students to learn from real-life scenarios and case studies, which can help them to develop critical thinking and problem-solving skills; (iii) Can help reduce the risk of financial mistakes, such as overspending or accumulating debt, which can significantly impact their financial well-being; (iv) Help individuals make better financial decisions, which can lead to greater financial stability. By understanding how to manage their money effectively, they can avoid debt, save money, and invest wisely; (v) With fiscal literacy, individuals learn how to create and stick to budgets, save for rainy days, and avoid financial pitfalls. These positive financial behaviours promote financial well-being across the lifespan; (vi) With knowledge of personal finances, individuals are less vulnerable to fraud and scams targeting their money. This helps protect their money and their financial security; (vii) Empower individuals to take greater control over their financial situation. With a strong financial knowledge foundation, they can ask better financial questions, negotiate effectively, and take charge of their financial future and (viii) When more citizens are financially literate, they are better equipped to participate in the economy as consumers, investors, and entrepreneurs. This can lead to greater economic growth and prosperity for both the individual and the community.

Financial literacy has become a prominent issue on the financial and economic agenda worldwide (Williams & Satchell, 2011; Postmus et al., 2013). Financial literacy is treated as having the proper knowledge of making the right decision in choosing financial products and services (Fernandes et al., 2014). Worthington (2016) highlighted financial literacy as the ability to decision-making in all aspects of people's budgeting, saving, and spending matters. Huston (2010) specified financial knowledge as an input to model the need for financial education and explain variation in financial outcomes. Understanding financial language is crucial to improve financial education.

Zaman et al. (2020) found a positive relationship between financial development and the achievement of SDGs, indicating that a well-developed financial system can contribute to sustainable development, i.e., financial development influences positively economic growth, poverty, and environmental sustainability. Their study reveals that financial literacy and institutional quality are important factors that mediate the relationship between financial development and SDGs. It suggests that countries should focus on enhancing financial literacy and improving institutional quality to maximize the positive impact of financial development on sustainable development. This way, institutions can play a crucial role in mobilizing funds and allocating resources towards sustainable projects.

Lastly, financial education supports SDG 17 (Partnerships for the Goals). It fosters collaboration between governments, civil society organizations and financial institutions to promote financial literacy, and ensure the achievement of the SDG. Working together and sharing resources, stakeholders can create comprehensive financial education programs that reach a wide audience.

Second Zikmundova et al. (2021) refers that financial literacy is positively associated with a greater understanding of the SDGs and a higher level of engagement with sustainable practices. Besides that, their study also highlight the importance of educational initiatives to enhance financial literacy and promote sustainable development.

In turn, Mensah et al. (2021) highlights the importance of financial literacy in shaping savings behaviour and its potential for promoting sustainable development in Ghana. The results suggest that financial literacy has a positive impact on sustainable development, as individuals with higher levels of financial literacy are more likely to engage in sustainable behaviour.

Eskelinen and Eskelinen (2019), in their article, proposed an integrated approach to address the SDGs, financial education, and entrepreneurship education. The authors argue that financial education is crucial for individuals to make informed financial decisions, while entrepreneurship education promotes creative problem-solving and innovation. Moreover, the article suggests that by integrating these two forms of education, individuals can better understand the financial implications of their entrepreneurial ventures. That integrated approach has the potential to enhance economic growth, reduce poverty, and promote sustainable consumption and production. Lastly, the authors argue that policymakers, educational institutions, and stakeholders should collaborate to develop inclusive and multifaceted programs that foster financial and entrepreneurship education, thus contributing to the achievement of the SDGs.

Inside financial literacy, there's digital financial literacy, being its importance highlighted by Prado (2020). This area is becoming increasingly important in today's digital age. With the rise of online banking, digital payments, and financial apps, having a solid understanding of how to navigate these tools is crucial for financial success and security. Digital financial literacy enables individuals to manage their finances effectively, make informed decisions about investments and savings, and protect themselves from scams and fraud. It empowers people to take control of their financial well-being, giving them access to various financial tools and resources that can help them achieve their financial goals. Additionally, as technology continues to advance and shape the future of finance, digital financial literacy will only become more critical to thrive in the digital economy. Prado (2020) is one of the authors who highlights the importance of financial literacy in today's complex world and its relevance to sustainable development. Other authors with the same vison are Davis and Hasler (2021), OCDE (2017, 2018), Lyons and Kass-Hanna (2021).

Digital financial literacy is important for several reasons: (i) Empowerment: Digital financial literacy allows individuals to take control of their financial lives. It helps them understand and make informed decisions about various digital financial services, such as online banking, mobile payments, cryptocurrencies, and investment platforms. With this knowledge, individuals are better equipped to navigate the digital financial landscape and make the most of the opportunities available to them; (ii) Security: Digital financial literacy teaches individuals about the importance of online security and how to protect their personal and financial information. This includes knowledge about safe browsing practices, using secure payment methods, recognizing phishing attempts, and choosing strong passwords. By being digitally literate, individuals can safeguard themselves against financial fraud and digital scams; (iii) Financial Inclusion: As technology advances, digital financial services are becoming more prevalent. Digital financial literacy ensures that individuals, especially those from underserved or marginalized communities, have the knowledge and skills to access and utilize these services. It promotes financial inclusion by providing individuals with the tools they need to actively participate in the digital economy and take advantage of financial opportunities; (iv) Economic Growth: Digital financial literacy contributes to economic growth at both individual and societal levels. By understanding digital financial tools and services, individuals can make wise financial decisions, manage their money effectively, and engage in investments or entrepreneurial activities. This leads to improved financial well-being, increased savings, and investment in the economy, ultimately driving economic growth and stability; (v) Future Readiness: Digital financial literacy is crucial for preparing individuals for the future of work and entrepreneurship. As technology continues to disrupt traditional industries, individuals must be equipped with digital skills and financial knowledge. This includes understanding digital payment systems, managing digital assets, and adapting to emerging financial technologies. Digital financial literacy ensures individuals can adapt and thrive in an increasingly digital and financially driven world. The presented reasons are supported by authors as Nichols-Barrer et al. (2017), Cocco et al. (2005), Demir et al. (2020), Demirguc-Kunt et al. (2018), Shen et al. (2020), Disney and Gathergood (2013), Guisoand (2014), Kezar and Yang (2010), Lusardi and Mitchell (2014), Maturana and Nickerson (2019), Paiella (2016), Rashidin et al. (2020a), Berry et al. (2018), Hogagarth (2006) and Pompei and Selezneva (2019).

CONCLUSION

This study carried out a literature review to verify the state of the art on the effects of taxation on innovation and the implications for achieving the SDGs. The literature review carried out on the effects of taxation on innovation found a positive relationship, so it can be said that a decrease in the effective tax rate on company profits leads to an increase in innovative activity. Consequently, the higher the nominal tax rate in a given country, the more likely it is not to implement innovation processes.

So, the relationship between taxation and innovation is not linear and much less simple, given that it can depend on various factors, such as the structure of the tax system, government policies, and how tax resources are used. Thus, taxation can have both positive and negative effects on innovation. The way taxes are structured and used by the government, along with other factors such as the regulation of activities, education, and investments in infrastructure, will determine the impact of taxation on a country's ability to foster business innovation, economic growth, and sustainable development.

Taxation is a determining factor in innovation. The effects of taxation on innovation can vary depending on the specific circumstances and the nature of the taxation measures implemented. However, there are some potential effects that taxation can have on innovation, such as reduced financial resources, and high taxes that can reduce the available resources for businesses to invest in R&D activities. This can limit their ability to innovate and develop new products or technologies.

Other conclusion, high taxes can drive talented individuals and innovative companies away to lower-tax jurisdictions. This can result in a loss of innovative potential and hinder technological progress within a country. High taxation can lead businesses to shift their focus from R&D and innovation to cost-cutting measures and tax avoidance strategies. This can stifle innovation as resources are diverted away from productive activities.

In addition to the aforementioned tax incentives are a powerful incentive for innovation. Governments may provide tax credits or deductions for businesses that invest in R&D, which can encourage companies to allocate more resources toward innovation. Funding for public, tax revenues can be used to fund public research and development initiatives. By allocating a portion of taxes towards innovation-focused programs, governments can support the creation of new knowledge and technologies that benefit society as a whole.

It is important to note that the effects of taxation on innovation are complex and depend on various factors, such as the level of taxation, the structure of the tax system, and the overall economic environment.

The relationship between financial literacy and the effects of taxation on innovation is an important and complex topic, particularly in the context of sustainable development goals. Financial literacy, which refers to the ability to understand and effectively use various financial skills, such as personal financial management, budgeting, and investing, is increasingly recognized as a crucial factor in economic development and individual financial well-being.

When examining the effects of taxation on innovation, it is essential to consider how tax policies can either incentivize or hinder innovation. Tax policies can have a significant impact on the incentives for individuals and businesses to engage in activities that lead to technological advancements, new products, processes, and market expansion. Therefore, understanding the relationship between financial literacy and the effects of taxation on innovation is imperative for policymakers, businesses, and individuals seeking to drive sustainable economic growth and development.

Financial literacy can play a vital role in shaping attitudes and behaviors regarding innovation and taxation. For individuals and entrepreneurs, financial literacy can impact their ability to understand the potential tax implications of their innovative activities, including the ability to take advantage of tax credits and incentives designed to promote innovation. Furthermore, financially literate individuals and businesses may be better equipped to navigate the complexities of tax laws and regulations, enabling them to make informed decisions about to innovation and investment.

Moreover, financial literacy can also influence the effectiveness of government-led initiatives aimed at promoting innovation through tax policies. Financially literate citizens are more likely to engage with and take advantage of government incentives for innovation, thereby enhancing the overall impact of such policies on economic growth and sustainable development.

The link between financial literacy, taxation, and innovation has significant implications for achieving sustainable development goals. Sustainable development goals encompass a broad range of objectives, including economic growth, innovation, poverty reduction, and environmental sustainability. Each of these goals can be influenced by the interplay between financial literacy and taxation on innovation.

i. Economic Growth: financial literacy can empower individuals and businesses to make sound financial decisions, leading to increased investment in innovative activities. When coupled with well-designed tax policies that encourage innovation, financial literacy can contribute to sustained economic growth, job creation, and overall prosperity.
ii. Innovation: Taxation policies can either support or impede innovation. Financially literate individuals and businesses are better positioned to understand and respond to the tax implications of their innovation-related activities. This awareness can affect their willingness to invest in research and development, adopt new technologies, and bring innovative products and services to market.
iii. Poverty Reduction: Sustainable economic development is crucial for poverty reduction. By promoting financial literacy and implementing tax policies that incentivize innovation, governments and organizations can foster an environment conducive to entrepreneurship, job creation, and income generation, thereby contributing to poverty alleviation.
iv. Environmental Sustainability: Innovative technologies and business practices are essential for achieving environmental sustainability. Tax policies can influence the adoption of green technologies and sustainable business practices. Financially literate individuals and businesses are better equipped to assess the financial implications of adopting such practices and leveraging tax incentives to support their implementation.

Given the complex interactions between financial literacy, taxation, and innovation, several policy implications emerge:

i. Financial Education: Governments and organizations should prioritize financial education and literacy programs to equip individuals and businesses with the knowledge and skills needed to navigate the financial implications of innovation and taxation. Such programs could include workshops, online resources, and educational initiatives in schools and workplaces.
ii. Tax Incentives: Policymakers should carefully design and implement tax incentives aimed at promoting innovation. These incentives should be communicated effectively to the public, ensuring that financially literate individuals and businesses are aware of and can take advantage of them.
iii. Regulatory Clarity: Clarity and transparency in tax regulations are essential for promoting innovation. Governments should strive to create clear and stable tax frameworks that provide predictability for innovators and businesses, thus fostering an environment conducive to long-term investment in innovation.
iv. Cross-Sector Collaboration: Collaboration between government agencies, financial institutions, educational institutions, and businesses can facilitate the integration of financial literacy and taxation into broader innovation strategies. Such collaboration can lead to the development of holistic approaches to promoting innovation and sustainable development.
v. By recognizing the interconnected nature of financial literacy, taxation, and innovation, policymakers can develop more effective strategies to drive sustainable economic growth and development. Furthermore, businesses and individuals can leverage their financial literacy to make informed decisions regarding innovation and taxation, ultimately contributing to the achievement of sustainable development goals.

There are several avenues for future research that can be gauged from this study. For example, we can analyse whether, in practice, financial literacy contributes to sustained economic growth, job creation and general prosperity. We can also analyse whether, for example, companies and individuals take advantage of their financial literacy to make informed decisions.

REFERENCES

Abdul, I. (2015). Ibn Khaldun's theory of taxation and its relevance today. *Turkish Journal of Islamic Economics, 2*(10.15238), 2-1.

Akanbi, A. (2020). The Impact of Tax Collection and Incentives on Economic Growth: Evidence from Nigeria. *International Journal of Business and Economics Research, 9*(4), 170–175. doi:10.11648/j.ijber.20200904.12

Akcigit, U., Grigsby, J., Nicholas, T., & Stantcheva, S. (2022). Taxation and Innovation in the Twentieth Century. *The Quarterly Journal of Economics, 1*(137), 329–385. doi:10.1093/qje/qjab022

Appelt, S., Cabral, A. C. G., Hanappi, T., Galindo-Rueda, F., & O'Reilly, P. (2023). Cost and uptake of income-based tax incentives for R&D and innovation. *OECD Science, Technology and Industry Working Papers, No. 2023/03*, OECD Publishing. doi:10.1787/18151965

Atanassov, J., & Liu, X. (2020). Can Corporate Income Tax Cuts Stimulate Innovation? *Journal of Financial and Quantitative Analysis, 55*(5), 1415–1465. doi:10.1017/S0022109019000152

Azmat, F., Lim, W. M., Moyeen, A., Voola, R., & Gupta, G. (2023). Convergence of business, innovation, and sustainability at the tipping point of the sustainable development goals. *Journal of Business Research, 167*, 114170. Advance online publication. doi:10.1016/j.jbusres.2023.114170

Bamel, N., Kumar, S., Bamel, U., Lim, W. M., & Sureka, R. (2022). The state of the art of innovation management: Insights from a retrospective review. *European Journal of Innovation Management*. Advance online publication. doi:10.1108/EJIM-07-2022-0361

Bardhan, A., López, J. A., & Sayeed, L. (2019). Financial Literacy and Household Savings in Developing Economies - Evidence from Bangladesh. *Journal of Sustainable Finance & Investment, 9*(2), 118–146.

Bauman, C., & Schadewald, M. (2001). Impact of foreign operations on reported effective tax rates: interplay of foreign taxes, U.S. taxes and U.S. *Journal of International Accounting, Auditing and Taxation, 10*(2), 177-196. https://doi.org/ (01)00043-X. doi:10.1016/S1061-9518

Berry, J., Karlan, D., & Pradhan, M. (2018). The impact of financial education for youth in Ghana. *World Development, 102*, 71–89. doi:10.1016/j.worlddev.2017.09.011

Chen, Z., Liu, Z., Serrato, J. C. S., & Xu, D. Y. (2021). Notching R&D Investment with Corporate Income Tax Cuts in China. *The American Economic Review, 111*(7), 2065–2100. doi:10.1257/aer.20191758

Cocco, J. F., Gomes, F. J., & Maenhout, P. J. (2005). Consumption and portfolio choice over the life cycle. *Review of Financial Studies, 18*(2), 491–533. doi:10.1093/rfs/hhi017

d'Andria, D., & Savin, I. (2018). A Win-Win-Win? Motivating innovation in a knowledge economy with tax incentives. *Technological Forecasting and Social Change, 127*, 38–56. doi:10.1016/j.techfore.2017.05.030

Dai, X., & Chapman, G. (2022). R&D tax incentives and innovation: Examining the role of programme design in China. *Technovation, 113*, 102419. Advance online publication. doi:10.1016/j.technovation.2021.102419

Davis, H., & Hasler, A. (2021) *Testing the Use of the Mint App in an Interactive Personal Finance Module*. www.gflec.org

Demir, A., Pesqué-Cela, V., Altunbas, Y., & Murinde, V. (2020). Fintech, financial inclusion and income inequality: A quantile regression approach. *European Journal of Finance*, *1*(28), 86–107.

Demirguc-Kunt, A., Klapper, L., Singer, D., Ansar, S., & Hess, J. (2018). Global FinTech Database 2017: Measuring financial inclusion and the FinTech revolution. World Bank.

Disney, R., & Gathergood, J. (2013). Financial literacy and consumer credit portfolios. *Journal of Banking & Finance*, *37*(7), 2246–2254. doi:10.1016/j.jbankfin.2013.01.013

Fang, H., Droga, D., Fu, N., & Hu, W. (2023). Enterprise income tax and corporate innovation: Evidence from China. *Applied Economics*, *44*(55), 5230–5249. doi:10.1080/00036846.2023.2211335

Federici, D., & Parisi, V. (2015). Do corporate taxes reduce investments? Evidence from Italian firm-level panel data. *Cogent Economics & Finance*, *1*(3), 1012435. doi:10.1080/23322039.2015.1012435

Fernandes, D., Lynch, J. G. Jr, & Netemeyer, R. G. (2014). Financial literacy, financial education, and downstream financial behaviors. *Management Science*, *60*(8), 1861–1883. doi:10.1287/mnsc.2013.1849

Giri, F. S., & Chaparro, T. S. (2023). Measuring business impacts on the SDGs: a systematic literature review, *Sustainable Technology and Entrepreneurship, 2*(3). . doi:10.1016/j.stae.2023.100044

Guiso, L., & Viviano, E. (2014). How much can financial literacy help? *1 Rev. Financ.*, *19*(4), 1347–1382.

Halim, A., & Rahman, M. (2022). The effect of taxation on sustainable development goals: Evidence from emerging countries. *Heliyon*, *9*(8), e10512. doi:10.1016/j.heliyon.2022.e10512 PMID:36590560

Haufler, A., & Schindler, D. (2023). Attracting profit shifting or fostering innovation? On patent boxes and R&D subsidies. *European Economic Review*, *155*, 104446. Advance online publication. doi:10.1016/j.euroecorev.2023.104446

Hogarth, J. M. (2006). Financial education and economic development. In: International conference hosted. *Russian G8 Presidency in cooperation with the OECD*, 72–94.

Howlett, M. (2018). The criteria for effective policy design: Character and context in policy instrument choice. *Journal of Asian Public Policy*, *3*(11), 245–266. doi:10.1080/17516234.2017.1412284

Hsu, P., Tian, X., & Xu, Y. (2014). Financial development and innovation: Cross-country evidence. *Journal of Financial Economics*, *1*(112), 116–135. doi:10.1016/j.jfineco.2013.12.002

Hurtado-Palomino, A., Gala-Velásquez, B., & Ccorisapra-Quintana, J. (2022). The interactive effect of innovation capability and potential absorptive capacity on innovation performance. *Journal of Innovation & Knowledge*, *7*(4), 100259. Advance online publication. doi:10.1016/j.jik.2022.100259

Huston, S. (2010). Measuring Financial Literacy. *The Journal of Consumer Affairs*, *44*(2), 296–316. doi:10.1111/j.1745-6606.2010.01170.x

Jacob, M. (2022). Real Effects of Corporate Taxation: A Review. *European Accounting Review*, *1*(31), 269–296. doi:10.1080/09638180.2021.1934055

Janský, P. (2023). Corporate Effective Tax Rates for Research and Policy. *Public Finance Review*, *51*(2), 171–205. doi:10.1177/10911421221137203

Kaushik, A. (2023). The effectiveness of research and development tax incentives in India: A quasi-experimental approach. *Int J Syst Assur Eng Manag*, *14*(6), 2329–2336. doi:10.1007/s13198-023-02077-x

Kempkes, G., & Stähler, N. (2022). Re-allocating taxing rights and minimum tax rates in international profit taxation. *Journal of Government and Economics*, *7*, 100048. Advance online publication. doi:10.1016/j.jge.2022.100048

Kezar, A., & Yang, H. (2010). The importance of financial literacy. *About Campus: Enriching the Student Learning Experience*, *14*(6), 15–21. doi:10.1002/abc.20004

Klepper, S. (1997). Industry Life Cycles. *Industrial and Corporate Change*, *1*(6), 145–182. doi:10.1093/icc/6.1.145

Kochetkov, D. M. (2023). Innovation: A state-of-the-art review and typology. *International Journal of Innovation Studies*, *4*(7), 263–272. doi:10.1016/j.ijis.2023.05.004

Kouam, J. C., & Asongu, S. A. (2022). Effects of taxation on social innovation and implications for achieving sustainable development goals in developing countries: *A literature review. International Journal of Innovation Studies*, *6*(4), 259–275. doi:10.1016/j.ijis.2022.08.002

Labeaga, J., Martínez-Ros, E., Sanchis, A., & Sanchis, J. A. (2021). Does persistence in using R&D tax credits help to achieve product innovations? *Technological Forecasting and Social Change*, *173*, 121065. Advance online publication. doi:10.1016/j.techfore.2021.121065

Laffer, A. B. (2004). The Laffer Curve: Past, Present, and Future. *The Heritage Foundation Backgrounder*, *1765*(1), 1–16.

Lusardi, A., & Mitchell, O. S. (2014). The economic importance of financial literacy: Theory and evidence. *Journal of Economic Literature*, *32*(1), 7–11. doi:10.1257/jel.52.1.5 PMID:28579637

Lyons, A. C., & Kass-Hanna, J. (2021). A methodological overview to defining and measuring "digital" financial literacy. *Financial Planning Review*, *4*(2), 1–19. doi:10.1002/cfp2.1113

Malerba, F. (2004). *Sectoral systems of innovation: how and why innovation differs across sectors. Handbook of innovation.* doi:10.1017/CBO9780511493270

Martins, E. C., & Terblanche, F. (2003). Building organisational culture that stimulates creativity and innovation. *European Journal of Innovation Management*, *1*(6), 64–74. doi:10.1108/14601060310456337

Maturana, G., & Nickerson, J. (2019). Teachers teaching teachers: The role of workplace peer effects in financial decisions. *Review of Financial Studies*, *32*(10), 3920–3957. doi:10.1093/rfs/hhy136

Mensah, S. I., & Ewur, G. K. (2021). Financial Literacy, Savings Behavior, and Sustainable Development: Evidence from Ghana. *The Journal of Consumer Affairs*, *55*(1), 135–160.

Mukherjee, A., Singh, M., & Žaldokas, A. (2017). Do corporate taxes hinder innovation? *Journal of Financial Economics*, *1*(124), 195–221. doi:10.1016/j.jfineco.2017.01.004

Nichols-Barrer, C., Lewis, C. T. L., & Cook, T. D. (2017). *Digital Financial Services: Challenges and Opportunities for Emerging Markets*. The World Bank.

Obschonka, M., Tavassoli, S., Rentfrow, P. J., Potter, J., & Gosling, S. D. (2023). Innovation and inter-city knowledge spillovers: Social, geographical, and technological connectedness and psychological openness. *Research Policy*, *52*(8), 104849. Advance online publication. doi:10.1016/j.respol.2023.104849

OECD. (2010). *Taxation*. Innovation and the Environment.

OECD. (2017). *G20/OECD INFE REPORT - Ensuring financial education and consumer protection for all in the digital age*. Academic Press.

OECD. (2018). *G20/OECD INFE policy guidance on digitalisation and financial literacy'*. Academic Press.

Oliver, W., & Satchell, S. (2011). Social welfare issues of financial literacy and their implications for regulation. *Journal of Regulatory Economics*, *1*(40), 1–40. doi:10.1007/s11149-011-9151-6

Paiella, M. (2016). Financial literacy and subjective expectations questions: A validation exercise. *Research in Economics*, *70*(2), 360–374. doi:10.1016/j.rie.2015.11.004

Panda, H., & Ramanathan, K. (1996). Technological capability assessment of a firm in the electricity sector. *Technovation*, *10*(16), 561–588. doi:10.1016/S0166-4972(97)82896-9

Parra-Requena, G., Ruiz-Ortega, M. J., Garcia-Villaverde, P. M., & Ramírez, F. J. (2022). Innovativeness and performance: The joint effect of relational trust and combinative capability. *European Journal of Innovation Management*, *25*(1), 191–213. doi:10.1108/EJIM-04-2020-0117

Pompei, F., & Selezneva, E. (2019). Unemployment and education mismatch in the EU before and after the financial crisis. *Journal of Policy Modeling*. Advance online publication. doi:10.1016/j.jpolmod.2019.09.009

Prado, L. A. (2020). Promoting Financial Literacy for Sustainable Development Goals: Exploring the Role of Digital Technologies. *International Journal of Innovation and Sustainable Development*, *14*(3), 253–270.

Rahman, M. (2023). Impact of taxes on the 2030 agenda for sustainable development: Evidence from Organization for Economic Co-operation and Development (OECD) countries. *Regional Sustainability*, *3*(4), 235–248. doi:10.1016/j.regsus.2023.07.001

Rashidin, M. S., Javed, S., Chen, L., & Jian, W. (2020a). Assessing the competitiveness of Chinese multinational enterprises development: Evidence from electronics sector. *SAGE Open*, *10*(1). Advance online publication. doi:10.1177/2158244019898214

Saunila, M. (2020). Innovation capability in SMEs: A systematic review of the literature. *Journal of Innovation & Knowledge*, *4*(5), 260–265. doi:10.1016/j.jik.2019.11.002

Shahroodi, S. (2010). Investigation of the effective factors in the efficiency of tax system. *Journal of Accounting and Taxation*, *2*(3), 42-45. http://www.academicjournals.org/JAT

Shen, Y., Hueng, C. J., & Hu, W. (2020). Using digital technology to improve financial inclusion in China. *Applied Economics Letters*, *27*(1), 30–34. doi:10.1080/13504851.2019.1606401

Steinmüller, E., Thunecke, G., & Wamser, G. (2019). Corporate income taxes around the world: A survey on forward-looking tax measures and two applications. *International Tax and Public Finance*, *26*(2), 418–456. doi:10.1007/s10797-018-9511-6

Tavassoli, S. (2015). Innovation determinants over industry life cycle. *Technological Forecasting and Social Change*, *91*, 18–32. doi:10.1016/j.techfore.2013.12.027

Uemura, T. (2022). Evaluating Japan's corporate income tax reform using firm-specific effective tax rates. *Japan and the World Economy*, *61*, 101115. Advance online publication. doi:10.1016/j.japwor.2022.101115

Vandenbergh, M. P., & Gilligan, J. M. (2017). Beyond politics. *Science*, *356*(6345), 492–493.

Weckel, P. (1983). *La fiscalité et la stimulation de l'innovation industrielle dans la Communauté: Sept propositions pour encourager l'innovation.* Office des publications officielles des Communautés européennes.

Worthington, A. C. (2016). Financial literacy and financial literacy programmes in Australia. *Financ Lit Limits Financ Decis-Mak*, *6*(18), 281–301. doi:10.1007/978-3-319-30886-9_14

Zaman, S., Shahbaz, M., & Loganathan, N. (2020). Financial Development and Sustainable Development Goals: Evidence from Asia-Pacific Region. *Journal of Cleaner Production*, *244*, 118706.

Zhang, D., & Guo, Y. (2019). Financing R&D in Chinese private firms: Business associations or political connection? *Economic Modelling*, *79*, 247–261. doi:10.1016/j.econmod.2018.12.010

Zhang, D., & Vigne, S. A. (2021). How does innovation efficiency contribute to green productivity? A financial constraint perspective. *Journal of Cleaner Production*, *280*, 124000. Advance online publication. doi:10.1016/j.jclepro.2020.124000

Zhang, Y., & Song, Y. (2022). Tax rebates, technological innovation and sustainable development: Evidence from Chinese micro-level data. *Technological Forecasting and Social Change*, *176*, 121481. Advance online publication. doi:10.1016/j.techfore.2022.121481

Zheng, W., & Zhang, J. (2021). Does tax reduction spur innovation? Firm-level evidence from China. *Finance Research Letters*, *39*, 101575. Advance online publication. doi:10.1016/j.frl.2020.101575

Zikmundova, M., Hronek, J., Stastna, L., & Sperkova, M. (2021). Financial Literacy and Sustainable Development Goals: A Case Study of Czech Republic. *Sustainability*, *13*(3), 1017.

Compilation of References

AA.VV. (2006). *The History of Artificial Intelligence*. University of Washington.

Abate, T. (2018). *Audit Considerations Related to Cryptocurrency Assets and Transactions*. Chartered Professional Accountants Canada.

Abdel-Hamid, O., Mohamed, A. R., Jiang, H., Deng, L., Penn, G., & Yu, D. (2014). Convolutional neural networks for speech recognition. *IEEE/ACM Transactions on Audio, Speech, and Language Processing*, *22*(10), 1533–1545. doi:10.1109/TASLP.2014.2339736

Abdi, M. R., Labib, A., Edalat, F. D., & Abdi, A. (2018). *Integrated reconfigurable manufacturing systems and smart value chain: Sustainable infrastructure for the factory of the future*. Springer International Pu. doi:10.1007/978-3-319-76846-5

Abdolmohammadi, M. J. (1991). Factors affecting auditors' perceptions of applicable decision aids for various audit tasks. *Contemporary Accounting Research*, *7*(2), 535–548. doi:10.1111/j.1911-3846.1991.tb00828.x

Abdolmohammadi, M. J., & Baker, C. R. (2006). Accountants' value preferences and moral reasoning. *Journal of Business Ethics*, *69*(1), 11–25. doi:10.1007/s10551-006-9064-y

Abdul, I. (2015). Ibn Khaldun's theory of taxation and its relevance today. *Turkish Journal of Islamic Economics, 2*(10.15238), 2-1.

Acemoglu, D., & Restrepo, P. (2018). Artificial intelligence, automation, and work. In *The economics of artificial intelligence: An agenda* (pp. 197–236). University of Chicago Press.

Adamyk, O., Benson, V., Adamyk, B., Al-Khateeb, H., & Chinnaswamy, A. (2023). Does Artificial Intelligence Help Reduce Audit Risks? *2023 13th International Conference on Advanced Computer Information Technologies, ACIT 2023 - Proceedings,* 294–298. 10.1109/ACIT58437.2023.10275661

Agustia, D. (2020). Innovation, environmental management accounting, future performance: Evidence in Indonesia. *Journal of Security and Sustainability Issues*, *9*(3), 1005–1015. doi:10.9770/jssi.2020.9.3(24)

Agustí, M. A., & Orta-Pérez, M. (2023). Big data and artificial intelligence in the fields of accounting and auditing: A bibliometric analysis. *Spanish Journal of Finance and Accounting. Revista Española de Financiación y Contabilidad, 52*(3), 412–438. doi:10.1080/02102412.2022.2099675

Ahmad, K., & Zabri, S. M. (2016). Management accounting practices among small and medium enterprises. *Proceedings of the 28th International Business Information Management Association Conference - Vision 2020: Innovation Management, Development Sustainability, and Competitive Economic Growth.* 10.4018/979-8-3693-0044-2.ch024

Ahmad, K., & Zabri, S. M. (2016). Management accounting practices among small and medium enterprises. *Proceedings of the 28th International Business Information Management Association Conference*. https://www.researchgate.net/publication/311716335_Management_Accounting_Practices_Among_Small_And_Medium_Enterprises

Ahmed, S., Alshater, M. M., El Ammari, A., & Hammami, H. (2022). Artificial intelligence and machine learning in finance: A bibliometric review. *Research in International Business and Finance*, *61*, 101646. doi:10.1016/j.ribaf.2022.101646

AICPA & CIMA. (2023). *Accounting for and auditing of digital assets.* Author.

Aitkazinov, A. (2023). The role of artificial intelligence in auditing: Opportunities and challenges. *International Journal of Research in Engineering. Science and Management*, *6*(6), 117–119.

Ajayi, F. A., & Olalekan, A. (2023). Artificial Intelligence & Internal Audit Quality Of Commercial Banks In Nigeria. *International Journal of Management and Economics Invention*, *09*(04). Advance online publication. doi:10.47191/ijmei/v9i4.05

Ajwani-Ramchandani, R., Figueira, S., de Oliveira, R. T., Jha, S., Ramchandani, A., & Schuricht, L. (2021). Towards a circular economy for packaging waste by using new technologies: The case of large multinationals in emerging economies. *Journal of Cleaner Production*, *281*(16), 125139. Advance online publication. doi:10.1016/j.jclepro.2020.125139

Akanbi, A. (2020). The Impact of Tax Collection and Incentives on Economic Growth: Evidence from Nigeria. *International Journal of Business and Economics Research*, *9*(4), 170–175. doi:10.11648/j.ijber.20200904.12

Akcigit, U., Grigsby, J., Nicholas, T., & Stantcheva, S. (2022). Taxation and Innovation in the Twentieth Century. *The Quarterly Journal of Economics*, *1*(137), 329–385. doi:10.1093/qje/qjab022

Akhter, A., & Sultana, R. (2018). Sustainability of accounting profession at the age of fourth industrial revolution. *International Journal of Accounting and Financial Reporting*, *8*(4), 139. doi:10.5296/ijafr.v8i4.13689

Akinola, A. (2022). The nexus between bank size and financial performance: Does internal control adequacy matter? *Journal of Accounting and Taxation*, *14*(1), 13–20. doi:10.5897/JAT2021.0501

Al Asheeri, M. M., & Hammad, M. (2019, September). Machine learning models for software cost estimation. In *2019 International Conference on Innovation and Intelligence for Informatics, Computing, and Technologies (3ICT)* (pp. 1-6). IEEE. 10.1109/3ICT.2019.8910327

Al Wael, H., Abdallah, W., Ghura, H., & Buallay, A. (2023). Factors influencing artificial intelligence adoption in the accounting profession: The case of public sector in kuwait. *Competitiveness Review*, *34*(1), 3–27. doi:10.1108/CR-09-2022-0137

Al-Alwan, M., Al-Nawafah, S., Al-Shorman, H., Khrisat, F. A., Alathamneh, F., & Al-Hawary, S. I. S. (2022). The effect of big data on decision quality: Evidence from telecommunication industry. *International Journal of Data and Network Science*, *6*(3), 693–702. doi:10.5267/j.ijdns.2022.4.003

Al-Htaybat, K., & von Alberti-Alhtaybat, L. (2017). Big Data and corporate reporting: Impacts and paradoxes. *Accounting, Auditing & Accountability Journal*, *30*(4), 850–873. doi:10.1108/AAAJ-07-2015-2139

Ali, Y. A. (1980). *Explanation of the General Principles of the Penal Code, Part 1.* Dar Al-Nahda Al-Arabiya.

Ali, S. M., Hasan, Z. J., Hamdan, A., & Al-Mekhlaf, M. (2022, March). Artificial Intelligence (AI) in the Education of Accounting and Auditing Profession. In *International Conference on Business and Technology* (pp. 656-664). Cham: Springer International Publishing.

Aliusta, H. (2023). Bibliometric Analysis of Research on The Relationship of Accounting and Information Systems/ Technologies. *İşletme Araştırmaları Dergisi*, *15*(2), 797-815.

Almeida, B. (2019). *Manual de Auditoria Financeira: Uma análise integrada baseada no risco* (3rd ed.). Escolar Editora.

Almeida, P., Santos, C., & Farias, J. (2021). Artificial intelligence regulation: A framework for governance. *Ethics and Information Technology*, *23*(3), 505–525. doi:10.1007/s10676-021-09593-z

Al-Qusi, H. (2018). The Problem of the Person Responsible for Operating the Robot - A Prospective Analytical Study in the European Civil Law Rules for Robots. Generation Journal of In-Depth Legal Research, 89-93.

Al-Radaideh, Q. A., & Al Nagi, E. (2012). Using data mining techniques to build a classification model for predicting employees performance. *International Journal of Advanced Computer Science and Applications*, *3*(2).

Al-refiay, H. A. N., Abdulhussein, A. S., & Al-Shaikh, S. S. K. (2022). The Impact of Financial Accounting in Decision Making Processes in Business. *International Journal Of Professional Business Review*, *7*(4), 1–13. doi:10.26668/businessreview/2022.v7i4.e627

Al-Sayyed, S., Al-Aroud, S., & Zayed, L. (2021). The effect of artificial intelligence technologies on audit evidence. *Accounting*, *7*(2), 281–288. doi:10.5267/j.ac.2020.12.003

Amaral. (2002). Reflexão sobre alguns aspectos jurídicos do 11 de Setembro e suas séquelas. In Estudos em Homenagem à Professora Doutora Isabel de Magalhães Collaço (vol. 2). Almedina.

Ameen, N., Tarhini, A., Reppel, A., & Anand, A. (2021). Customer experiences in the age of artificial intelligence. *Computers in Human Behavior*, *114*, 106548. doi:10.1016/j.chb.2020.106548 PMID:32905175

American Institute of Certified Public Accountants. (2002). Statement on Auditing Standards: Vol. 99. American Institute of Certified Public Accountants.

Andreu-Perez, J., Deligianni, F., Ravi, D., & Yang, G. Z. (2017). *Artificial intelligence and robotics*. UK-RAS Network. doi:10.31256/WP2017.1

Anica-Popa, I., Anica-Popa, L., Rădulescu, C., & Vrîncianu, M. (2021). The Integration of Artificial Intelligence in Retail: Benefits. *Amfiteatru Economic*, *23*(56), 120. Advance online publication. doi:10.24818/EA/2021/56/120

Anvari, S., & Turkay, M. (2017). The facility location problem from the perspective of triple bottom line accounting of sustainability. *International Journal of Production Research*, *55*(21), 6266–6287. doi:10.1080/00207543.2017.1341064

Appelbaum, D., Kogan, A., Vasarhelyi, M., & Yan, Z. (2017). Impact of business analytics and enterprise systems on managerial accounting. *International Journal of Accounting Information Systems*, *25*, 29–44. doi:10.1016/j.accinf.2017.03.003

Appelt, S., Cabral, A. C. G., Hanappi, T., Galindo-Rueda, F., & O'Reilly, P. (2023). Cost and uptake of income-based tax incentives for R&D and innovation. *OECD Science, Technology and Industry Working Papers, No. 2023/03*, OECD Publishing. doi:10.1787/18151965

Applelbaum, D., & Smith, S. S. (2018). *ICYMI | Blockchain Basics and Hands-on Guidance Taking the Next Step toward Implementation and Adoption*. https://www.cpajournal.com/2019/06/27/icymi-blockchain-basics-and-hands-on-guidance/

Aria, M., & Cuccurullo, C. (2017). bibliometrix: An R-tool for comprehensive science mapping analysis. *Journal of Informetrics*, *11*(4), 959–975. doi:10.1016/j.joi.2017.08.007

Arnold, V. (2018). The changing technological environment and the future of behavioural research in accounting. *Accounting and Finance*, *58*(2), 315–339. doi:10.1111/acfi.12218

Arntz, M., Gregory, T., & Zierahn, U. (2017). Revisiting the risk of automation. *Economics Letters*, *159*, 157–160. doi:10.1016/j.econlet.2017.07.001

Ashley. (2017). Artificial Intelligence and Legal Analytics, new tools for law practice in the digital age, University of Pittsburgh School of Law. Cambridge University Press.

Askary, S., Abu-Ghazaleh, N., & Tahat, Y. A. (2018). Artificial intelligence and reliability of accounting information. In *Challenges and Opportunities in the Digital Era: 17th IFIP WG 6.11 Conference on e-Business, e-Services, and e-Society, I3E 2018, Kuwait City, Kuwait, October 30–November 1, 2018, Proceedings 17* (pp. 315-324). Springer International Publishing. https://inria.hal.science/hal-02274162/file/474698_1_En_28_Chapter.pdf

Association of Certified Fraud Examiners. (2020). *Report to the Nations: 2020 Global Study on Occupational Fraud and Abuse*. Author.

Atanassov, J., & Liu, X. (2020). Can Corporate Income Tax Cuts Stimulate Innovation? *Journal of Financial and Quantitative Analysis*, *55*(5), 1415–1465. doi:10.1017/S0022109019000152

Atif, M., Hassan, M. K., Rabbani, M. R., & Khan, S. (2021). Islamic FinTech: The digital transformation bringing sustainability to islamic finance. In COVID-19 and Islamic Social Finance (pp. 91-103). doi:10.4324/9781003121718-9

Audibert, R. B., Lemos, H., Avelar, P., Tavares, A. R., & Lamb, L. C. (2022). On the Evolution of AI and Machine Learning: Towards Measuring and Understanding Impact, Influence, and Leadership at Premier AI Conferences. *arXiv preprint arXiv:*2205.13131.

Auvinen, T., Sajasalo, P., Sintonen, T., Pekkala, K., Takala, T., & Luoma-aho, V. (2019). Evolution of strategy narration and leadership work in the digital era. *Leadership*, *15*(2), 205–225. doi:10.1177/1742715019826426

Azman, N. A., Mohamed, A., & Jamil, A. M. (2021). Artificial intelligence in automated bookkeeping: A value-added function for small and medium enterprises. *JOIV: International Journal on Informatics Visualization*, *5*(3), 224. doi:10.30630/joiv.5.3.669

Azmat, F., Lim, W. M., Moyeen, A., Voola, R., & Gupta, G. (2023). Convergence of business, innovation, and sustainability at the tipping point of the sustainable development goals. *Journal of Business Research*, *167*, 114170. Advance online publication. doi:10.1016/j.jbusres.2023.114170

Baker, H. K., Pandey, N., Kumar, S., & Haldar, A. (2020). A bibliometric analysis of board diversity: Current status, development, and future research directions. *Journal of Business Research*, *108*, 232–246. doi:10.1016/j.jbusres.2019.11.025

Balakrishnan, P., Gupta, R., & Jacob, V. S. (2004). Development of Hybrid Genetic Algorithms for Product Line Designs. *IEEE Trans. Syst. Man Cybern. Part B*, *34*, 468–483.

Baldwin, A. A., Brown, C. E., & Trinkle, B. S. (2006). Opportunities for artificial intelligence development in the accounting domain: The case for auditing. *Intelligent Systems in Accounting, Finance & Management. International Journal (Toronto, Ont.)*, *14*(3), 77–86.

Bamel, N., Kumar, S., Bamel, U., Lim, W. M., & Sureka, R. (2022). The state of the art of innovation management: Insights from a retrospective review. *European Journal of Innovation Management*. Advance online publication. doi:10.1108/EJIM-07-2022-0361

Bansal, A., Sharma, R., Sharma, V., & Jain, A. K. 2023. A Deep Learning Approach to Detect and Classify Wheat Leaf Spot Using Faster R-CNN and Support Vector Machine. *IEEE 8th International Conference for Convergence in Technology (I2CT)*. 10.1109/I2CT57861.2023.10126124

Bao, Y., Hilary, G., & Ke, B. (2022). Artificial intelligence and fraud detection. *Innovative Technology at the Interface of Finance and Operations*, *I*, 223–247. doi:10.1007/978-3-030-75729-8_8

Bao, Y., Ke, B., Li, B., Yu, Y. J., & Zhang, J. (2020). Detecting accounting fraud in publicly traded US firms using a machine learning approach. *Journal of Accounting Research*, *58*(1), 199–235. doi:10.1111/1475-679X.12292

Bao, Y., Ke, B., Li, B., Yu, Y. J., & Zhang, J. (2021). A response to'critique of an article on machine learning in the detection of accounting fraud. *Econ Journal Watch*, *18*(1), 71–78.

Bardhan, A., López, J. A., & Sayeed, L. (2019). Financial Literacy and Household Savings in Developing Economies - Evidence from Bangladesh. *Journal of Sustainable Finance & Investment*, *9*(2), 118–146.

Bauman, C., & Schadewald, M. (2001). Impact of foreign operations on reported effective tax rates: interplay of foreign taxes, U.S. taxes and U.S. *Journal of International Accounting, Auditing and Taxation, 10*(2), 177-196. https://doi.org/(01)00043-X. doi:10.1016/S1061-9518

BearingPoint. (2019). *L'expérience client à l'ère de l'intelligence artificielle.* Available at: https://www.bearingpoint.com/files/L_exp%C3%A9rience_client_ %C3%A0 1_%C3%A8re _de_ 1_intelligence_artificielle.pdf?download=0&itemId=571534

Beck, S. (2019). *Autonomous Systems and Criminal Law – new impulses for the concept of responsibility?* https://www.inf.uni-hamburg.de/en/inst/ab/eit/about/newsfeed/2019/ 20190703-beck.html

Berberich & Diepold. (2018). The virtuous machine - Old ethics for new technology? Cornell University.

Berry, J., Karlan, D., & Pradhan, M. (2018). The impact of financial education for youth in Ghana. *World Development*, *102*, 71–89. doi:10.1016/j.worlddev.2017.09.011

Bertomeu, J. (2020). Machine learning improves accounting: Discussion, implementation and research opportunities. *Review of Accounting Studies*, *25*(3), 1135–1155. doi:10.1007/s11142-020-09554-9

Bertomeu, J., Cheynel, E., Floyd, E., & Pan, W. (2021). Using machine learning to detect misstatements. *Review of Accounting Studies*, *26*(2), 468–519. doi:10.1007/s11142-020-09563-8

Bhimani, A., Datar, S. M., Horngren, C. T., & Rajan, M. V. (2019). *Management and cost accounting* (7th ed.). Pearson Education, Limited.

Bilal, A. A. (2010). *Principles of the Egyptian Penal Code - General Section.* Dar Al-Nahda Al-Arabiya.

Bizarro, P. A., Crum, E., & Nix, J. (2019). The Intelligent Audit. *ISACA Journal*, *6*, 23–29.

Bocken, N. M., Short, S. W., Rana, P., & Evans, S. (2014). A literature and practice review to develop sustainable business model archetypes. *Journal of Cleaner Production*, *65*, 42–56. doi:10.1016/j.jclepro.2013.11.039

Bonsón, E., & Bednárová, M. (2019). Blockchain and its implications for accounting and auditing. *Meditari Accountancy Research*, *27*(5), 725–740. doi:10.1108/MEDAR-11-2018-0406

Bonyuet, D. (2020). Overview and Impact of Blockchain on Auditing. *The International Journal of Digital Accounting Research*, *20*, 31–43. doi:10.4192/1577-8517-v20_2

Boucher, P. (2020). Artificial intelligence: How does it work, why does it macer, and what can we do about it? EPRS, European Parliamentary Research Service, Scienfic Foresight Unit (STOA).

Boucher, P. (2020). *Artificial intelligence: How does it work, why does it matter, and what can we do about it?* EPRS | European Parliamentary Research Service. *European Parliament.*, *641*, 547.

Bradlow, E. T., Gangwar, M., Kopalle, P., & Voleti, S. (2017). The role of Big Data and predictive analytics in retailing. *Journal of Retailing*, *93*(1), 79–95. doi:10.1016/j.jretai.2016.12.004

Brand, W. (2016). *Bitcoin for Dummies*. John Wiley & Sons, Inc.

Bratina, T. (2019). Mobile Phones and Social Behavior Among Millenials – Future Teachers. *Journal Of Elementary Education*, *12*(4), 315–330.

Brender, N., & Gauthier, M. (2018). *Impacts of Blockchain on the Auditing Profession.* ISACA. https://www.isaca.org/resources/isaca-journal/issues/2018/volume-5/impacts-of-blockchain-on-the-auditing-profession

Brender, N., Gauthier, M., Morin, J., & Salihi, A. (2019). The Potential Impact of Blockchain Technology on Audit Practice. *Journal of Strategic Innovation and Sustainability*, *14*(2), 35–59.

Brown, N. C., Crowley, R. M., & Elliott, W. B. (2020). What are you saying? Using topic to detect financial misreporting. *Journal of Accounting Research*, *58*(1), 237–291. doi:10.1111/1475-679X.12294

Brynjolfsson, E., & McAfee, A. (2014). *The Second Machine Age: Work, Progress, and Prosperity in a Time of Brilliant Technologies*. W. W. Norton & Company.

Brynjolfsson, E., & McAfee, A. (2014). *The second machine age: Work, progress, and prosperity in a time of brilliant technologies*. WW Norton & Company.

Brynjolfsson, E., & McAfee, A. (2017, July). The business of artificial intelligence. *Harvard Business Review*, 1–20.

Buchert, T., Ko, N., Graf, R., Vollmer, T., Alkhayat, M., Brandenburg, E., Stark, R., Klocke, F., Leistner, P., & Schleifenbaum, J. H. (2019). Increasing resource efficiency with an engineering decision support system for comparison of product design variants. *Journal of Cleaner Production*, *210*, 1051–1062. doi:10.1016/j.jclepro.2018.11.104

Bunget, O.-C., & Lungu, C. (2023). A Bibliometric Analysis of the Implications of Artificial Intelligence on the Accounting Profession. *CECCAR Business Review*, *4*(4), 9–16. doi:10.37945/cbr.2023.04.02

Buric, M. N., Stojanovic, A. J., Filipovic, A. L., & Kascelan, L. (2022). Research of Attitudes toward Implementation of Green Accounting in Tourism Industry in Montenegro-Practices, and Challenges. *Sustainability (Basel)*, *14*(3), 1–26. doi:10.3390/su14031725

Burke, R. J., & Cooper, C. L. (2004). *Leading in turbulent times: Managing in the new world of work.* Blackwell Publishing.

Burns, J., Steele, A., Cohen, E., & Ramamoorti, S. (2020). *Blockchain and Internal Control: The COSO perspective.* Academic Press.

Burns, M.B., & Igou, A. (2019). "Alexa, Write an Audit Opinion": Adopting Intelligent Virtual Assistants in Accounting Workplaces. *Journal of Emerging Technologies in Accounting, 16*(1), 81–92. https://doi.org/ doi:10.2308/jeta-52424

Burritt, R. L., Schaltegger, S., & Christ, K. L. (2023). Environmental Management Accounting – Developments Over the Last 20 years from a Framework Perspective. *Australian Accounting Review*, *33*(4), 336–351. doi:10.1111/auar.12407

Cai, D., Tan, M., & Cai, J. (2011). The VAT tax burden warning model and modification based on CTAIS system data. *2011 2nd International Conference on Artificial Intelligence. Management Science and Electronic Commerce, AIMSEC 2011 - Proceedings.* 10.1109/AIMSEC.2011.6011100

Cai, C. (2022). Training Mode of Innovative Accounting Talents in Colleges Using Artificial Intelligence. *Mobile Information Systems*, *2022*, 6516658. Advance online publication. doi:10.1155/2022/6516658

Callon, M., Courtial, J. P., & Laville, F. (1991). Co-word analysis as a tool for describing the network of interactions between basic and technological research: The case of polymer chemsitry. *Scientometrics*, *22*(1), 155–205. doi:10.1007/BF02019280

Calo, R., Froomkin, A. M., & Kerr, I. (2016). *Robot Law*. Edward Elgar Publishing Limited. doi:10.4337/9781783476732

Canadian Public Accountability Board and Conseil Canadien Sur La Reddition de Comptes. (2019). *Auditing in the Crypto-Asset Sector Inspections Insights*. Retrieved from https://www.cpab-ccrc.ca/docs/default-source/inspections-reports/2019-crypto-inspections-insights-en.pdf?sfvrsn=9aa5c0d2_20

Cannarsa, M. (2021). Ethics guidelines for trustworthy AI. The Cambridge handbook of lawyering in the digital age, 283-297.

Cao, M., Chychyla, R., & Stewart, T. (2015). Big data analytics in financial statement audits. *Accounting Horizons*, *29*(2), 423–429. doi:10.2308/acch-51068

Cecchini, M., Aytug, H., Koehler, G. J., & Pathak, P. (2010a). Detecting management fraud in public companies. *Management Science*, *56*(7), 1146–1160. doi:10.1287/mnsc.1100.1174

Cecchini, M., Aytug, H., Koehler, G. J., & Pathak, P. (2010b). Making words work: Using financial text as a predictor of financial events. *Decision Support Systems*, *50*(1), 164–175. doi:10.1016/j.dss.2010.07.012

Chamba, L. T., Chari, F., & Zhou, H. (2023). Exploring the Potential for State-Owned Enterprises in Developing Countries to Leverage the Benefits of the Fourth Industrial Revolution for Economic Transformation. *Journal of Public Administration, 58*(2). https://doi.org/ doi:10.53973/jopa.2023.58.2.a9

Chandanshive, V., & Kambekar, A. R. (2019). Estimation of building construction cost using artificial neural networks. *Journal of Soft Computing in Civil Engineering*, *3*(1), 91–107.

Chatfield, A. T., & Reddick, C. G. (2019). A framework for Internet of Things-enabled smart government: A case of IoT cybersecurity policies and use cases in U.S. federal government. *Government Information Quarterly*, *36*(2), 346–357. doi:10.1016/j.giq.2018.09.007

Chatterjee, S., & Bhattacharjee, K. K. (2020). Adoption of artificial intelligence in higher education: A quantitative analysis using structural equation modelling. *Education and Information Technologies*, *25*(January), 3443–3463. Advance online publication. doi:10.1007/s10639-020-10159-7

Cheng, H. D., Jiang, X. H., Sun, Y., & Wang, J. (2001). Color image segmentation: Advances and prospects. *Pattern Recognition*, *34*(12), 2259–2281. doi:10.1016/S0031-3203(00)00149-7

Chen, H. (2021). Research on the strategies of cultivating management accounting talents in universities under the background of the development of information technology. *ACM International Conference Proceeding Series*. 10.1145/3465631.3465784

Chen, S., & Williams, A. (2022, March). Intelligent Accounting System Structure and Intelligent Accounting Algorithm Based on Computer Vision. In *The International Conference on Cyber Security Intelligence and Analytics* (pp. 97-104). Cham: Springer International Publishing. 10.1007/978-3-030-97874-7_12

Chen, Z., Liu, Z., Serrato, J. C. S., & Xu, D. Y. (2021). Notching R&D Investment with Corporate Income Tax Cuts in China. *The American Economic Review*, *111*(7), 2065–2100. doi:10.1257/aer.20191758

Chernov, V. A. (2020). Implementation of digital technologies in financial management. *Economy of Regions*, *16*(1), 283–297. doi:10.17059/2020-1-21

Choi, T. M., Chan, H. K., & Yue, X. (2016). Recent development in big data analytics for business operations and risk management. *IEEE Transactions on Cybernetics*, *47*(1), 81–92. doi:10.1109/TCYB.2015.2507599 PMID:26766385

Cho, S., Vasarhelyi, M. A., Sun, T., & Zhang, C. (2020). Learning from Machine Learning in Accounting and Assurance. *Journal of Emerging Technologies in Accounting*, *17*(1), 1–10. doi:10.2308/jeta-10718

Chowdhury, E. K. (2023). Integration of Artificial Intelligence Technology in Management Accounting Information System: An Empirical Study. In *Novel Financial Applications Of Machine Learning And Deep Learning: Algorithms, Product Modeling, And Applications* (pp. 35–46). Springer International Publishing. doi:10.1007/978-3-031-18552-6_3

Chowdhury, R. R., Arko, P. S., Ali, M. E., Khan, M. A. I., & Apon, S. H. (2020). Nowrin, F. and Wasif, A. "Identification and recognition of rice diseases and pests using convolutional neural networks". *Biosystems Engineering*, *194*, 112–120. doi:10.1016/j.biosystemseng.2020.03.020

Chung, J., & Tsay, M. Y. (2017). A bibliometric analysis of the literature on open access in Scopus. *Qualitative and Quantitative Methods in Libraries*, *4*(4), 821–841.

Chuy. (2018). *Operação Hastag, A primeira condenação de terroristas islâmicos na América La.na.* Novo Século.

Cocco, J. F., Gomes, F. J., & Maenhout, P. J. (2005). Consumption and portfolio choice over the life cycle. *Review of Financial Studies*, *18*(2), 491–533. doi:10.1093/rfs/hhi017

Coeckelbergh, M. (2019). Artificial intelligence: some ethical issues and regulatory challenges. *Technology and Regulation, 2019*, 31-34. https://techreg.org/article/view/10999

Cokins, G. (2013). Top 7 trends in management accounting. *Strategic Finance*, *95*(6), 21–30.

Collins, C., Dennehy, D., Conboy, K., & Mikalef, P. (2021). Artificial intelligence in information systems research: A systematic literature review and research agenda. *International Journal of Information Management*, *60*, 102383. doi:10.1016/j.ijinfomgt.2021.102383

Cong, X. (2021). Research on curriculum construction of big data and accounting under the background of big data. *Proceedings - 2021 International Conference on Big Data Engineering and Education, BDEE 2021*. 10.1109/BDEE52938.2021.00032

Conijn, R., Martinez-Maldonado, R., Knight, S., Buckingham Shum, S., Van Waes, L., & van Zaanen, M. (2022). How to provide automated feedback on the writing process? A participatory approach to design writing analytics tools. *Computer Assisted Language Learning*, *35*(8), 1838–1868. doi:10.1080/09588221.2020.1839503

Corrales, M., Fenwick, M., & Forgó, N. (2018). *Robotics, AI and the Future of Law, Perspectives in Law, Business, and Innovation*. Kyushu University, Springer International Publishing AG.

Couceiro, B., Pedrosa, I., & Marini, A. (2020). State of the art of artificial intelligence in internal audit context. In *2020 15th Iberian Conference on Information Systems and Technologies (CISTI)*, 1-7. IEEE. 10.23919/CISTI49556.2020.9140863

Cox, A. (2023). How artificial intelligence might change academic library work: Applying the competencies literature and the theory of the professions. *Journal of the Association for Information Science and Technology*, *74*(3), 367–380. doi:10.1002/asi.24635

Coyne, E. M., Coyne, J. G., & Walker, K. B. (2018). Big Data information governance by accountants. *International Journal of Accounting & Information Management*, *26*(1), 153–170. doi:10.1108/IJAIM-01-2017-0006

Craja, P., Kim, A., & Lessmann, S. (2020). Deep learning for detecting financial statement fraud. *Decision Support Systems*, *139*, 113421. doi:10.1016/j.dss.2020.113421

Cristiano Almonte vs. Averna Vision & Robotics, Inc.; United States District Court, W.D. New York. No. 11-CV-1088 EAW, 128 F.Supp.3d 729 (2015), Signed August 31, 2015.

Cruz, R., Bertollo, D., & Camargo, M. (2020). *O Impacto da Inteligência Artificial na Auditoria: Uma Revisão Bibliográfica. In XX Mostra de Iniciação Científica.* UCS-PPGA.

d'Andria, D., & Savin, I. (2018). A Win-Win-Win? Motivating innovation in a knowledge economy with tax incentives. *Technological Forecasting and Social Change, 127*, 38–56. doi:10.1016/j.techfore.2017.05.030

Dahshan, Y. I. (2020). *Criminal Responsibility for Artificial Intelligence Crimes. Sharia and Law Journal, (82).*

Dai, X., & Chapman, G. (2022). R&D tax incentives and innovation: Examining the role of programme design in China. *Technovation, 113*, 102419. Advance online publication. doi:10.1016/j.technovation.2021.102419

Dastile, X., & Celik, T. (2021). Making deep learning-based predictions for credit scoring explainable. *IEEE Access : Practical Innovations, Open Solutions, 9*, 50426–50440. doi:10.1109/ACCESS.2021.3068854

Davenport, T. H., & Ronanki, R. (2018). *Artificial Intelligence for the Real World.* Harvard Business Review (HBR). https://www.bizjournals.com/boston/news/2018/01/09/hbr-artificial-intelligence-for-the-real-world.html

Davis, H., & Hasler, A. (2021) *Testing the Use of the Mint App in an Interactive Personal Finance Module.* www.gflec.org

Davis, S. J., & Von Wachter, T. M. (2011). *Recessions and the cost of job loss (No. w17638).* National Bureau of Economic Research. doi:10.3386/w17638

de Villiers, C., Dimes, R., & Molinari, M. (2024). How will AI text generation and processing impact sustainability reporting? Critical analysis, a conceptual framework and avenues for future research. *Sustainability Accounting. Management and Policy Journal, 15*(1), 96–118. doi:10.1108/SAMPJ-02-2023-0097

De Villiers, R. (2021). Seven principles to ensure future-ready accounting graduates – a model for future research and practice. *Meditari Accountancy Research, 29*(6), 1354–1380. doi:10.1108/MEDAR-04-2020-0867

Dechow, P. M., Ge, W., Larson, C. R., & Sloan, R. G. (2011). Predicting material accounting misstatements. *Contemporary Accounting Research, 28*(1), 17–82. doi:10.1111/j.1911-3846.2010.01041.x

Deloitte. (2017). A auditoria do futuro começa agora. *Portal da Deloitte.* Retrieved from https://www2.deloitte.com/content/dam/Deloitte/br/Documents/audit/Deloitte-Auditoria-do-Futuro.pdf

Deloitte. (2021). O auditor do futuro é digital. *Portal da Deloitte.* Retrieved from https://mundocorporativo.deloitte.com.br/o-auditor-do-futuro-e-digital

Demir, A., Pesqué-Cela, V., Altunbas, Y., & Murinde, V. (2020). Fintech, financial inclusion and income inequality: A quantile regression approach. *European Journal of Finance, 1*(28), 86–107.

Demirguc-Kunt, A., Klapper, L., Singer, D., Ansar, S., & Hess, J. (2018). Global FinTech Database 2017: Measuring financial inclusion and the FinTech revolution. World Bank.

Demirkan, S., Demirkan, I., & McKee, A. (2020). Blockchain technology in the future of business cyber security and accounting. *Journal of Management Analytics, 7*(2), 189–208. doi:10.1080/23270012.2020.1731721

Dess, G. G., & Picken, J. C. (2000). Changing roles: Leadership in the 21st century. *Organizational Dynamics, 28*(3), 18–33. doi:10.1016/S0090-2616(00)88447-8

DeZoort, F. T., & Harrison, P. D. (2018). Understanding Auditors' Sense of Responsibility for Detecting Fraud Within Organizations. *Journal of Business Ethics, 149*(4), 857–874. doi:10.1007/s10551-016-3064-3

Dhamija, P., & Bag, S. (2020). Role of artificial intelligence in operations environment: A review and bibliometric analysis. *The TQM Journal*, *32*(4), 869–896. doi:10.1108/TQM-10-2019-0243

Di Vaio, A., Palladinoa, R., Hassanb, R., & Escobar, O. (2020). Artificial intelligence and business models in the sustainable development goals perspective: A systematic literature review. *Journal of Business Research*, *121*, 283–314. doi:10.1016/j.jbusres.2020.08.019

Díaz-Rodríguez, N., Del Ser, J., Coeckelbergh, M., de Prado, M. L., Herrera-Viedma, E., & Herrera, F. (2023). Connecting the dots in trustworthy Artificial Intelligence: From AI principles, ethics, and key requirements to responsible AI systems and regulation. *Information Fusion*, *99*, 101896. doi:10.1016/j.inffus.2023.101896

Ding, Q. (2021). Risk early warning management and intelligent real-time system of financial enterprises based on fuzzy theory. *Journal of Intelligent & Fuzzy Systems*, *40*(4), 6017–6027. doi:10.3233/JIFS-189441

Dirican, C. (2015). The impacts of robotics, and artificial intelligence on business and economics. *Procedia: Social and Behavioral Sciences*, *195*, 564–573. doi:10.1016/j.sbspro.2015.06.134

Disney, R., & Gathergood, J. (2013). Financial literacy and consumer credit portfolios. *Journal of Banking & Finance*, *37*(7), 2246–2254. doi:10.1016/j.jbankfin.2013.01.013

Dogan, A., & Birant, D. (2021). Machine learning and data mining in manufacturing. *Expert Systems with Applications*, *166*, 1–22. doi:10.1016/j.eswa.2020.114060

Dong, J. (2018). *Application Research of Artificial Intelligence Technology in Enterprise Financial Management*. Academic Press.

Dong, W., Liao, S., & Zhang, Z. (2018). Leveraging financial social media data for corporate fraud detection. *Journal of Management Information Systems*, *35*(2), 461–487. doi:10.1080/07421222.2018.1451954

Donthu, N., Kumar, S., Mukherjee, D., Pandey, N., & Lim, W. M. (2021). How to conduct a bibliometric analysis: An overview and guidelines. *Journal of Business Research*, *133*, 285–296. doi:10.1016/j.jbusres.2021.04.070

Dutta, K. D., & Saha, M. (2021). Nexus of governance, macroprudential policy and financial risk: Cross-country evidence. *Economic Change and Restructuring*, *54*(4), 1253–1298. doi:10.1007/s10644-020-09301-9

Dwivedi, Y. K., Hughes, L., Ismagilova, E., Aarts, G., Coombs, C., Crick, T., Duan, Y., Dwivedi, R., Edwards, J., Eirug, A., Galanos, V., Ilavarasan, P. V., Janssen, M., Jones, P., Kar, A. K., Kizgin, H., Kronemann, B., Lal, B., Lucini, B., ... Williams, M. D. (2021). Artificial Intelligence (AI): Multidisciplinary perspectives on emerging challenges, opportunities, and agenda for research, practice and policy. *International Journal of Information Management*, *57*, 101994. Advance online publication. doi:10.1016/j.ijinfomgt.2019.08.002

Dwivedi, Y. K., Hughes, L., Kar, A. K., Baabdullah, A. M., Grover, P., Abbas, R., Andreini, D., Abumoghli, I., Barlette, Y., Bunker, D., Kruse, L. C., Constantiou, I., Davison, R. M., De, R., Dubey, R., Fenby-Taylor, H., Gupta, B., He, W., Kodama, M., ... Wade, M. (2022). Climate change and COP26: Are digital technologies and information management part of the problem or the solution? An editorial reflection and call to action. *International Journal of Information Management*, *63*(39), 102456. Advance online publication. doi:10.1016/j.ijinfomgt.2021.102456

Dwivedi, Y. K., Sharma, A., Rana, N. P., Giannakis, M., Goel, P., & Dutot, V. (2023). Evolution of artificial intelligence research in Technological Forecasting and Social Change: Research topics, trends, and future directions. *Technological Forecasting and Social Change*, *192*, 122579. Advance online publication. doi:10.1016/j.techfore.2023.122579

Earley, C. E. (2015). Data analytics in auditing: Opportunities and challenges. *Business Horizons*, *58*(5), 493–500. doi:10.1016/j.bushor.2015.05.002

Edwards, M. G. (2021). The growth paradox, sustainable development, and business strategy. *Business Strategy and the Environment, 30*(7), 3079–3094. doi:10.1002/bse.2790

El-Behairy, A. S. G. (2019). *The Impact of Artificial Intelligence Applications on Raising the Efficiency of Security Performance by Application to Road Securing* [Doctoral dissertation]. Police Academy.

Eli-Chukwu, N. C. (2019). Applications of Artificial Intelligence in Agriculture: A Review. *Engineering, Technology & Applied Science Research, 9*(4), 4377-4383. https://orcid.org/0000-0002-3995-9118

El-Kady, R. (2022). Criminal confrontation of encrypted digital currencies and artificial intelligence crimes Analytical study in Egyptian and comparative legislation. *Journal Sharia and Law*, (89). Available at: https://scholarworks.uaeu.ac.ae/sharia_and_law/vol2022/iss89/6

El-Kady, R. (2021). Towards approving rules for criminal liability and punishment for misuse of artificial intelligence applications. *Journal of Legal and Economic Research (Mansoura), 11*(1), 875–924. doi:10.21608/mjle.2022.217213

Ernst & Young. (2019). *Accounting by holders of crypto-assets.* EY.

Erwin, K. (2019). Relationship management accounting and development of information technology. *IOP Conference Series. Materials Science and Engineering, 648*(1), 012033. doi:10.1088/1757-899X/648/1/012033

European Police & Darktrace. (2019). *How Technology Will Shape the Future of Cybercrime?* https://www.emarataly-oum.com/

Faccia, A., Al Naqbi, M. Y. K., & Lootah, S. A. (2019). Integrated cloud financial accounting cycle. How artificial intelligence, blockchain, and XBRL will change the accounting, fiscal and auditing practices. *ACM International Conference Proceeding Series.*

Fang, H., Droga, D., Fu, N., & Hu, W. (2023). Enterprise income tax and corporate innovation: Evidence from China. *Applied Economics, 44*(55), 5230–5249. doi:10.1080/00036846.2023.2211335

Fang, W., Li, X., Zhou, P., Yan, J., Jiang, D., & Zhou, T. (2021). Deep learning anti-fraud model for internet loan: Where we are going. *IEEE Access : Practical Innovations, Open Solutions, 9*, 9777–9784. doi:10.1109/ACCESS.2021.3051079

Fang, Y. (2021). Artificial intelligence promotes the application of "internet + education" teaching model in accounting major. *ACM International Conference Proceeding Series.* 10.1145/3465631.3465782

Fanning, K. M., & Cogger, K. O. (1998). Neural network detection of management fraud using published financial data. *International Journal of Intelligent Systems in Accounting Finance & Management, 7*(1), 21–41. doi:10.1002/(SICI)1099-1174(199803)7:1<21::AID-ISAF138>3.0.CO;2-K

Faria, R., Torres, A., & Beirão, G. (2023). Trustworthy Artificial Intelligence and Machine Learning: Implications on Users' Security and Privacy Perceptions. In Confronting Security and Privacy Challenges in Digital Marketing. doi:10.4018/978-1-6684-8958-1

Federici, D., & Parisi, V. (2015). Do corporate taxes reduce investments? Evidence from Italian firm-level panel data. *Cogent Economics & Finance, 1*(3), 1012435. doi:10.1080/23322039.2015.1012435

Fedyk, A., Hodson, J., Khimich, N., & Fedyk, T. (2022). Is artificial intelligence improving the audit process? *Review of Accounting Studies, 27*(3), 938–985. doi:10.1007/s11142-022-09697-x

Feng, R., Mejer Hansen, T., Grana, D., & Balling, N. (2020). An unsupervised deep-learning method for porosity estimation based on poststack seismic data. *Geophysics, 85*(6), M97–M105. doi:10.1190/geo2020-0121.1

Feng, R., & Qu, X. (2021). Analyzing the Internet financial market risk management using data mining and deep learning methods. *Journal of Enterprise Information Management*, *35*(4/5), 1129–1147. doi:10.1108/JEIM-03-2021-0155

Fernandes, D., Lynch, J. G. Jr, & Netemeyer, R. G. (2014). Financial literacy, financial education, and downstream financial behaviors. *Management Science*, *60*(8), 1861–1883. doi:10.1287/mnsc.2013.1849

Fernandez, D., &Aman, A. (2018). Impacts of robotic process automation on global accounting services. *Asian Journal of Accounting & Governance*.

Fieberg, C., Hesse, M., Loy, T., & Metko, D. (2022). Machine learning in accounting research. In *Diginomics research perspectives: The role of digitalization in business and society* (pp. 105–124). Springer International Publishing. doi:10.1007/978-3-031-04063-4_6

Fleming, P. (2019). Robots and Organization Studies: Why Robots Might Not Want to Steal Your Job. *Organization Studies*, *40*(1), 23–38. doi:10.1177/0170840618765568

Freyberger, J., Neuhierl, A., & Weber, M. (2020). Dissecting characteristics nonparametrically. *Review of Financial Studies*, *33*(5), 2326–2377. doi:10.1093/rfs/hhz123

Frey, C. B., & Osborne, M. A. (2017). The future of employment: How susceptible are jobs to computerisation? *Technological Forecasting and Social Change*, *114*, 254–280. doi:10.1016/j.techfore.2016.08.019

Fuller, T. R., & Deane, G. E. (2015). Creating complex applications via self-adapting autonomous agents in an intelligent system framework. *International Conference on Self-Adaptive and Self-Organizing Systems, SASO*. 10.1109/SASO.2015.27

Ganatra, N., & Patel, A. (2018). A Survey on Diseases Detection and Classification of Agriculture Products using Image Processing and Machine Learning. *International Journal of Computer Applications*, *180*(13), 7–12. doi:10.5120/ijca2018916249

Gao, J., Zhong, C., Chen, X., Lin, H., & Zhang, Z. (2020). Unsupervised learning for passive beamforming. *IEEE Communications Letters*, *24*(5), 1052–1056. doi:10.1109/LCOMM.2020.2965532

Gepp, A., Linnenluecke, M. K., O'Neill, T. J., & Smith, T. (2018). Big data techniques in auditing research and practice: Current trends and future opportunities. *Journal of Accounting Literature*, *40*(1), 102–115. doi:10.1016/j.acclit.2017.05.003

Ghaitas, G. M. (2017). Internet and Digital Transformation Department. International Policy Journal, (180).

Ghobakhloo, M., Asadi, S., Iranmanesh, M., Foroughi, B., Mubarak, M. F., & Yadegaridehkordi, E. (2023). Intelligent automation implementation and corporate sustainability performance: The enabling role of corporate social responsibility strategy. *Technology in Society*, *102301*, 102301. Advance online publication. doi:10.1016/j.techsoc.2023.102301

Giglio, S., Kelly, B. T., & Xiu, D. (2021). Factor models, machine learning, and asset pricing. *Machine Learning, and Asset Pricing*.

Giri, F. S., & Chaparro, T. S. (2023). Measuring business impacts on the SDGs: a systematic literature review, *Sustainable Technology and Entrepreneurship, 2*(3). . doi:10.1016/j.stae.2023.100044

Gless, Silverman, & Weigend. (2016). If Robots Cause Harm, who is to Blame? Self-Driving Cars and Criminal Liability. *New Criminal Law Review*, 1-12.

Goeldner. (2015, March). The emergence of care robotics – A patent and publication analysis. *Technological Forecasting and Social Change*, *92*.

Goodfellow, I., Papernot, N., McDaniel, P., Feinman, R., Faghri, F., Matyasko, A., . . . Garg, A. (2016). cleverhans v0. 1: an adversarial machine learning library. *arXiv preprint arXiv:1610.00768, 1*.

Green, B. P., & Choi, J. H. (1997). Assessing the risk of management fraud through neural network technology. *Auditing*, *16*, 14–28.

Greenleaf, G., Mowbray, A., & Chung, P. (2018). Building sustainable free legal advisory systems: Experiences from the history of AI & law. *Computer Law & Security Report*, *34*(2), 314–326. doi:10.1016/j.clsr.2018.02.007

Gretzel, U., Sigala, M., Xiang, Z., & Koo, C. (2015). Smart tourism: Foundations and developments. *Electronic Markets*, *25*(3), 179–188. doi:10.1007/s12525-015-0196-8

Grewal, D., Roggeveen, A.L. and Nordfält, J. (2017). The Future of Retailing. *Journal of Retailing*, *93*(1), 1-6. . doi:10.1016/j.jretai.2016.12.008

Griffin, O. (2019, October 6). *How Artificial Intelligence Will Impact Accounting*. Economia. https://www.icaew.com/technical/technology/artificial-intelligence/artificial-intelligence-articles/how-artificial-intelligence-will-impact-accounting

Grueau, C., Antunes, A., Ferreira, B., Gonçalves, M., Gomes, J., & Carriço, N. (2019). Towards an integrated platform for decision support in water utility management. *Proceedings of the 12th IADIS International Conference Information Systems 2019, IS 2019*. 10.33965/is2019_201905C001

Guiso, L., & Viviano, E. (2014). How much can financial literacy help? *1 Rev. Financ.*, *19*(4), 1347–1382.

Gunnarsson, B. R., Vanden Broucke, S., Baesens, B., Óskarsdóttir, M., & Lemahieu, W. (2021). Deep learning for credit scoring: Do or don't? *European Journal of Operational Research*, *295*(1), 292–305. doi:10.1016/j.ejor.2021.03.006 PMID:34955589

Gu, R., Yang, Z., & Ji, Y. (2020). Machine learning for intelligent optical networks: A comprehensive survey. *Journal of Network and Computer Applications*, *157*, 102576. doi:10.1016/j.jnca.2020.102576

Gusenbauer, M. (2022). Search where you will find most: Comparing the disciplinary coverage of 56 bibliographic databases. *Scientometrics*, *127*(5), 2683–2745. doi:10.1007/s11192-022-04289-7 PMID:35571007

Haenlein, M., & Kaplan, A. (2019). A brief history of artificial intelligence: On the past, present, and future of artificial intelligence. *California Management Review*, *61*(4), 5–14. doi:10.1177/0008125619864925

Haftor, D. M., Costa Climent, R., & Lundström, J. E. (2021). How machine learning activates data network effects in business models: Theory advancement through an industrial case of promoting ecological sustainability. *Journal of Business Research*, *131*, 196–205. doi:10.1016/j.jbusres.2021.04.015

Hagemann, V., & Klug, K. (2022). Human resource management in a digital environment. In *Diginomics Research Perspectives: The Role of Digitalization in Business and Society* (pp. 35–64). Springer International Publishing. doi:10.1007/978-3-031-04063-4_3

Haladjian, H. H., & Montemayor, C. (2016). Artificial consciousness and the consciousness-attention dissociation. *Consciousness and Cognition*, *45*, 210–225. doi:10.1016/j.concog.2016.08.011 PMID:27656787

Halder, M., Sarkar, A., & Bahar, H. (2019). Plant Disease Detection By Image Processing: A Literature Review. *SDRP Journal of Food Science & Technology*, *3*(6), 534–538. doi:10.25177/JFST.3.6.6

Halim, A., & Rahman, M. (2022). The effect of taxation on sustainable development goals: Evidence from emerging countries. *Heliyon*, *9*(8), e10512. doi:10.1016/j.heliyon.2022.e10512 PMID:36590560

Hallevy, G. (2010). The Criminal Liability of Artificial Intelligence Entities – from Science Fictions to Legal Social Control. Akron Law Journal, 4(2), 132.

Hallevy, G. (2013). *When robots kill: Artificial intelligence under criminal law*. Northeastern University Press.

Hallioui, A., Herrou, B., Santos, R. S., Katina, P. F., & Egbue, O. (2022). Systems-based approach to contemporary business management: An enabler of business sustainability in a context of industry 4.0, circular economy, competitiveness and diverse stakeholders. *Journal of Cleaner Production*, *373*, 133819. Advance online publication. doi:10.1016/j.jclepro.2022.133819

Hamza, R. A. E. M., Alnor, N. H. A., Al-Matari, E. M., Benzerrouk, Z. S., Mohamed, A. M. E., Bennaceur, M. Y., Elhefni, A. H. M., & Elshaabany, M. M. (2024). The Impact of Artificial Intelligence (AI) on the Accounting System of Saudi Companies. *WSEAS Transactions on Business and Economics*, *21*(January), 499–511. doi:10.37394/23207.2024.21.42

Han, H., Shiwakoti, R. K., Jarvis, R., Mordi, C., & Botchie, D. (2022). *Accounting and auditing with blockchain technology and artificial Intelligence: A literature review* (Vol. 48). International Journal of Accounting Information Systems. Obtido de https://www.sciencedirect.com/science/article/pii/S1467089522000501?ref=pdf_download&fr=RR-2&rr=833973d7d8ef5bea#section-cited-by

Han, H., Shiwakoti, R. K., Jarvis, R., Mordi, C., & Botchie, D. (2023). Accounting and auditing with blockchain technology and artificial Intelligence: A literature review. *International Journal of Accounting Information Systems*, *48*, 100598. doi:10.1016/j.accinf.2022.100598

Haoru, W., Zhixuan, Y., & Yujia, W. (2020). Risk Assessment of Internet Credit Based on Big Data Analysis[C]//E3S Web of Conferences. *EDP Sciences*, *214*, 01012–01017.

Hasan, A. R. (2021). Artificial Intelligence (AI) in accounting & auditing: A Literature review. *Open Journal of Business and Management*, *10*(1), 440–465. doi:10.4236/ojbm.2022.101026

Haseeb, M., Hussain, H. I., Ślusarczyk, B., & Jermsittiparsert, K. (2019). Industry 4.0: A solution towards technology challenges of sustainable business performance. *Social Sciences (Basel, Switzerland)*, *8*(5), 154. doi:10.3390/socsci8050154

Hashid, A., & Almaqtari, F. (2024). The Impact of Artificial Intelligence and Industry 4.0 on Transforming Accounting and Auditing Practices. *Journal of Open Innovation*, 100218.

Haufler, A., & Schindler, D. (2023). Attracting profit shifting or fostering innovation? On patent boxes and R&D subsidies. *European Economic Review*, *155*, 104446. Advance online publication. doi:10.1016/j.euroecorev.2023.104446

He, Q., & Chen, G. (2011). Research of security audit of enterprise group accounting information system under internet environment. *2011 2nd International Conference on Artificial Intelligence, Management Science and Electronic Commerce, AIMSEC 2011 - Proceedings*.

Heimerl, P., Haid, M., Benedikt, L., & Scholl-Grissemann, U. (2020). Factors influencing job satisfaction in hospitality industry. *SAGE Open*, *10*(4). doi:10.1177/2158244020982998

Hemanand, D., Mishra, N., Premalatha, G., Mavaluru, D., Vajpayee, A., Kushwaha, S., & Sahile, K. (2022). Applications of intelligent model to analyze the green finance for environmental development in the context of artificial intelligence. *Computational Intelligence and Neuroscience*, *2022*, 1–8. doi:10.1155/2022/2977824 PMID:35845917

Hendarsyah, D. (2019). E-Commerce Di Era Industri 4.0 Dan Society 5.0. *IQTISHADUNA: Jurnal Ilmiah Ekonomi Kita*, *8*(2), 171–184. doi:10.46367/iqtishaduna.v8i2.170

Herath, S. K., & Joshi, P. L. (2023). Audit Data Analytics: A Game Changer for Audit Firms. *International Journal of Auditing and Accounting Studies*, *5*(1), 29–48. doi:10.47509/IJAAS.2023.v05i01.02

Hermann, E., Hermann, G., & Tremblay, J. C. (2021). Ethical Artificial Intelligence in Chemical Research and Development: A Dual Advantage for Sustainability. *Science and Engineering Ethics*, *27*(4), 45. Advance online publication. doi:10.1007/s11948-021-00325-6 PMID:34231042

Hernes, M., Bytniewski, A., Mateńczuk, K., Rot, A., Dziuba, S., Fojcik, M., Nguyet, T. L., Golec, P., & Kozina, A. (2020). Data Quality Management in ERP Systems – Accounting Case. *Communications in Computer and Information Science, 1287*, 353–362. doi:10.1007/978-3-030-63119-2_29

Herzel, S., Nicolosi, M., & Stărică, C. (2012). The cost of sustainability in optimal portfolio decisions. *European Journal of Finance*, *18*(3-4), 333–349. doi:10.1080/1351847X.2011.587521

Hespenheide, E. (2021). *A Practical Guide to Sustainability Reporting Using GRI and SASB Standards.* Sustainability Accounting Standards Board. https://www.globalreporting.org/media/mlkjpn1i/gri-sasb-joint-publication-april-2021.pdf

Hobson, J. L., Mayew, W. J., & Venkatachalam, M. (2012). Analyzing speech to detect financial misreporting. *Journal of Accounting Research*, *50*(2), 349–392. doi:10.1111/j.1475-679X.2011.00433.x

Hogarth, J. M. (2006). Financial education and economic development. In: International conference hosted. *Russian G8 Presidency in cooperation with the OECD*, 72–94.

Hongjin, S. (2021). Analysis of risk factors in financial supply chain based on machine learning and IoT technology. *Journal of Intelligent & Fuzzy Systems*, *40*(4), 6421–6431. doi:10.3233/JIFS-189482

Hooda, N., Bawa, S., & Rana, P. S. (2018). Fraudulent firm classification: A case study of an external audit. *Applied Artificial Intelligence*, *32*(1), 48–64. doi:10.1080/08839514.2018.1451032

Hoosain, M. S., Paul, B. S., & Ramakrishna, S. (2020). The Impact of 4IR Digital Technologies and Circular Thinking on the United Nations Sustainable Development Goals. *Sustainability, 12*(23), 16. doi:10.3390/su122310143

Hosni, M. N. (1992). *Criminal Contribution to Arab Legislation*. Dar Al-Nahda Al-Arabi.

Howlett, M. (2018). The criteria for effective policy design: Character and context in policy instrument choice. *Journal of Asian Public Policy*, *3*(11), 245–266. doi:10.1080/17516234.2017.1412284

Hsu, P., Tian, X., & Xu, Y. (2014). Financial development and innovation: Cross-country evidence. *Journal of Financial Economics*, *1*(112), 116–135. doi:10.1016/j.jfineco.2013.12.002

Hu, X., Zou, Y., Xue, Z., & Wang, W. (2020). Plant Disease Identification Based on Deep Learning Algorithm in Smart Farming. Hindawi Discrete Dynamics in Nature and Society. doi:10.1155/2020/2479172

Huang, C. L., Chen, M. C., & Wang, C. J. (2007). Credit scoring with a data mining approach based on support vector machines. *Expert Systems with Applications*, *33*(4), 847–856. doi:10.1016/j.eswa.2006.07.007

Hu, J. (2022). Partial differential equation-assisted accounting professional education and training artificial intelligence collaborative course system construction. *Scientific Programming*, *2022*, 1–10. doi:10.1155/2022/6357421

Humpherys, S. L., Moffitt, K. C., Burns, M. B., Burgoon, J. K., & Felix, W. F. (2011). Identification of fraudulent financial statements using linguistic credibility analysis. *Decision Support Systems*, *50*(3), 585–594. doi:10.1016/j.dss.2010.08.009

Hurtado-Palomino, A., Gala-Velásquez, B., & Ccorisapra-Quintana, J. (2022). The interactive effect of innovation capability and potential absorptive capacity on innovation performance. *Journal of Innovation & Knowledge*, *7*(4), 100259. Advance online publication. doi:10.1016/j.jik.2022.100259

Hussein, H., Ammar, M., & Hassan, M. (2016). Induction Motors Stator Fault Analysis based on Artificial Intelligence. *Indonesian Journal of Electrical Engineering and Computer Science*, *2*(1), 69–78. doi:10.11591/ijeecs.v2.i1.pp69-78

Huston, S. (2010). Measuring Financial Literacy. *The Journal of Consumer Affairs*, *44*(2), 296–316. doi:10.1111/j.1745-6606.2010.01170.x

Huttunen, K., & Kellokumpu, J. (2016). The effect of job displacement on couples' fertility decisions. *Journal of Labor Economics*, *34*(2), 403–442. doi:10.1086/683645

Hu, Z., Hu, R., Yau, O., Teng, M., Wang, P., Hu, G., & Singla, R. (2022). Tempering expectations on the medical artificial intelligence revolution: The medical trainee viewpoint. *JMIR Medical Informatics*, *10*(8), e34304. doi:10.2196/34304 PMID:35969464

Iaasb, I. A. (2016). Handbook od international quality control, auditing, review, other assurance and related services pronouncements. Academic Press.

Iancu, E., & Cioban, G. L. (2016). Intangible assets, economic models, and neural network. *Proceedings of the 27th International Business Information Management Association Conference - Innovation Management and Education Excellence Vision 2020: From Regional Development Sustainability to Global Economic Growth, IBIMA 2016.*

Ibrahim, A. I. M. (2020). *Criminal Liability Resulting from Artificial Intelligence Errors in UAE Legislation - A Comparative Study* [Doctoral dissertation]. Ain Shams University.

Illia, L., Colleoni, E., & Zyglidopoulos, S. (2023). Ethical implications of text generation in the age of artificial intelligence. *Business Ethics, the Environment & Responsibility*, *32*(1), 201–210. doi:10.1111/beer.12479

Information and Decision Support Center of the Egyptian Cabinet (IDSC). (2020). Artificial intelligence is the most essential element of the Fourth Industrial Revolution. *Bulletin of Future Directions, 1*(1).

Inghirami, I. E. (2014). Reshaping strategic management accounting systems. *Frontiers in Artificial Intelligence and Applications.*

Inman, J. J., & Nikolova, H. (2017). Shopper-Facing Retail Technology: A Retailer Adoption Decision Framework Incorporating Shopper Attitudes and Privacy Concerns. *Journal of Retailing*, *93*(1), 7–28. doi:10.1016/j.jretai.2016.12.006

Institute of Management Accountants. (2008). *Statements on management accounting: Definition of management accounting*. www.imanet.org

International Auditing and Assurance Standards Board. (2018). *Manual das normas internacionais de controlo de qualidade, auditoria, revisão, outros trabalhos de garantia de fiabilidade e serviços relacionados.* IAASB.

Ionescu, L. (2020). Robotic process automation, deep learning, and natural language processing in algorithmic data-driven accounting information systems. *Analysis and Metaphysics*, *19*(0), 59–65. doi:10.22381/AM1920206

ISA 200 - *Objetivos gerais do auditor independente e condução de uma auditoria de acordo com as normas internacionais de auditoria.* Manual de Normas Internacionais de Auditoria e Controle de Qualidade. IFAC.

Ismail Al-Alawi, A., Almulla, D., Abbas, M., & Alkooheji, L. (2024). Process and Impact Evaluation of Artificial Intelligence in Managerial Accounting: A Systematic Literature Review. *International Journal of Computing and Digital Systems*, *15*(1), 1–26.

Ismailov, Z., & Kononov, D. (2018). Integrated management system for rail transport: planning of cargo turnover in conditions of uncertainty. *Proceedings of 2018 11th International Conference "Management of Large-Scale System Development", MLSD 2018.* 10.1109/MLSD.2018.8551807

Isnawati, E. L., & Indriani, E. (2021). Profesi Akuntan : Akahkah Hilang di Era Digital 4.0? *Jurnal Penelitian Akuntansi*, *2*(1), 29–41.

Issa, H., Sun, T., & Vasarhelyi, M. (2016). Research Ideas for Artificial Intelligence in Auditing: The Formalization of Audit and Workforce Supplementation. *Journal of Emerging Technologies in Accounting*, *13*(2), 1–20. doi:10.2308/jeta-10511

Jackling, B., Cooper, B. J., Leung, P., & Dellaportas, S. (2007). Professional accounting bodies' perceptions of ethical issues, causes of ethical failure and ethics education. *Managerial Auditing Journal*, *22*(9), 928–944. doi:10.1108/02686900710829426

Jacob, M. (2022). Real Effects of Corporate Taxation: A Review. *European Accounting Review*, *1*(31), 269–296. doi:10.1080/09638180.2021.1934055

Jakka, G., Yathiraju, N., & Ansari, M. F. (2022). Artificial intelligence in terms of spotting malware and delivering cyber risk management. *Journal of Positive School Psychology*, *6*(3), 6156–6165.

Jambrak, A. R., Nutrizio, M., Djekic, I., Pleslic, S., & Chemat, F. (2021). Internet of Nonthermal Food Processing Technologies (IoNTP): Food Industry 4.0 and Sustainability. *Applied Sciences-Basel*, *11*(2), Article 686. https://doi.org/ doi:10.3390/app11020686

Janaki, M., & Clifford, M. M. J. (2021). *A study on the scope of artificial intelligence in accounting*. Academic Press.

Jannah, R., Sari, M. P., Utaminingsih, N. S., Halimah, W. N., Pradana, P. T., & Rahmawati, D. A. (2023). Environmental Accounting System Model in the Era Artificial Intelligence and Blockchain Technology: A Bibliometric Analysis. *Economic Education Analysis Journal*, *1*(1), 182–197.

Janský, P. (2023). Corporate Effective Tax Rates for Research and Policy. *Public Finance Review*, *51*(2), 171–205. doi:10.1177/10911421221137203

Jaya, I. M. L. M., & Narsa, I. M. (2022). The Nexus Between Forensic Tax and Accounting Knowledge After Pandemic COVID-19 in Indonesia. In A. Pego (Ed.), Handbook of Research on Global Networking Post COVID-19 (pp. 480–494). IGI Global Publishing. doi:10.4018/978-1-7998-8856-7.ch026

Jaya, I. M. L. M., & Padilla, M. A. E. (2024). Tax Carbon Policy: Momentum to Accelerate Indonesia's Sustainable Economic Growth Towards Green Economy. In Green Economy and Renewable Energy Transitions for Sustainable Development (pp. 171–183). IGI Global Publishing.

Jaya, I. M. L. M., Sawarjuwono, T., Sungkono, S., & Ilahiyah, M. E. (2021). Ethics, behaviors, and characters of memayu hayuning bawono, ambrasto dur hangkoro accountant in java. *Jurnal Kajian Akuntansi*, *5*(2), 142–155. doi:10.33603/jka.v5i2.5110

Jędrzejka, D. (2019). Robotic process automation and its impact on accounting. *Zeszyty Teoretyczne Rachunkowościtom*, 137–166.

Jesse, F. F., Antonini, C., & Luque-Vilchez, M. (2023). A circularity accounting network: CO2 measurement along supply chains using machine learning. *Revista de Contabilidad*, *26*(Special Issue), 21–33. doi:10.6018/rcsar.564901

Jiang, N. (2011). Economic analysis of the energy saving and emission reduction. *2011 2nd International Conference on Artificial Intelligence, Management Science and Electronic Commerce, AIMSEC 2011 – Proceedings*.

Jin, S., Pan, J., Chen, Q., & Li, B. (2022). Analysis and discussion on standard cost allocation model in state grid. Lecture Notes in Computer Science (including subseries Lecture Notes in Artificial Intelligence and Lecture Notes in Bioinformatics). doi:10.1007/978-3-030-97774-0_26

Johnson, P. C., Laurell, C., Ots, M., & Sandström, C. (2022). Digital innovation and the effects of artificial intelligence on firms' research and development – Automation or augmentation, exploration or exploitation? *Technological Forecasting and Social Change*, *179*(March), 121636. Advance online publication. doi:10.1016/j.techfore.2022.121636

Joh, R., Hasegawa, K., Tokushige, K., Hashimoto, E., Torii, N., Yamashiro, T., & Hayashi, N. (2003). Chronic hepatitis b with flare due to co-infection of hepatitis delta virus during lamivudine therapy. *Internal Medicine (Tokyo, Japan)*, *42*(7), 581–586. doi:10.2169/internalmedicine.42.581 PMID:12879950

Jones, N. (2018). How to stop data centres from gobbling up the world's electricity. *Nature*, *561*(7722), 163–166. doi:10.1038/d41586-018-06610-y PMID:30209383

Jordan, M. I., & Mitchell, T. M. (2015). Machine learning:Trends, perspectives, and prospects. *Science*, *349*(6245), 255–260. doi:10.1126/science.aaa8415 PMID:26185243

Joshua Drexler vs. Tel Nexx, Inc., etc.; United States District Court, D. Massachusetts, Civil Action No. 13-cv-13009-DPW, 125 F.Supp.3d 361 (2015), Signed August 28, 2015.

Kalbouneh, A., Aburisheh, K., Shaheen, L., & Aldabbas, Q. (2023). The intellectual structure of sustainability accounting in the corporate environment: A literature review. *Cogent Business and Management*, *10*(2), 2211370. Advance online publication. doi:10.1080/23311975.2023.2211370

Kamble, P. L., & Pise, A. C. (2016). Review on Agricultural Plant Disease Detection by using Image Processing. *International Journal of Latest Trends in Engineering & Technology*, *7*(1), 335–339. doi:10.21172/1.71.048

Kamilaris, A., & Prenafeta-Boldú, F. X. (2018). A review of the use of convolutional neural networks in agriculture. *Journal of Agricultural Science*, *156*(3), 312–322. doi:10.1017/S0021859618000436

Kanaparthi, V. (2024). Exploring the Impact of Blockchain, AI, and ML on Financial Accounting Efficiency and Transformation. *arXiv preprint arXiv:2401.15715*.

Karakaya, E., Nuur, C., & Assbring, L. (2018). Potential transitions in the iron and steel industry in Sweden: Towards a hydrogen-based future? *Journal of Cleaner Production*, *195*, 651–663. doi:10.1016/j.jclepro.2018.05.142

Kashyap, P. (2017). *Machine learning for decision makers: Cognitive computing fundamentals for better decision making*. Apress.

Kaushik, A. (2023). The effectiveness of research and development tax incentives in India: A quasi-experimental approach. *Int J Syst Assur Eng Manag*, *14*(6), 2329–2336. doi:10.1007/s13198-023-02077-x

Kazachenok, O. P., Stankevich, G. V., Chubaeva, N. N., &Tyurina, Y. G. (2023). Economic and legal approaches to the humanization of FinTech in the economy of artificial intelligence through the integration of blockchain into ESG Finance. *Humanities and Social Sciences Communications, 10*(1), 1-9.

Kempkes, G., & Stähler, N. (2022). Re-allocating taxing rights and minimum tax rates in international profit taxation. *Journal of Government and Economics*, *7*, 100048. Advance online publication. doi:10.1016/j.jge.2022.100048

Kezar, A., & Yang, H. (2010). The importance of financial literacy. *About Campus: Enriching the Student Learning Experience*, *14*(6), 15–21. doi:10.1002/abc.20004

Khalifa, M. M. T. (2018). *Artificial Intelligence in the Balance of Legislation*. Academic Press.

Khalifa, M. M. T. (2018). Artificial Intelligence in the Balance of Legislation. Dubai Legal Journal, (28).

Khalil, A., Abdelli, M. E. A., & Mogaji, E. (2022). Do Digital Technologies Influence the Relationship between the COVID-19 Crisis and SMEs' Resilience in Developing Countries? *Journal of Open Innovation*, *8*(2), 100. doi:10.3390/joitmc8020100

Khandelwal, P. M., & Chavhan, H. (2019). Artificial Intelligence in Agriculture: An Emerging Era of Research. *Journal of Green Engineering*, *10*(11), 1–12.

Khan, H. M. R., Ahmad, S., Javed, R., & Nasir, N. (2023). The Significance of Artificial Intelligence in Business and Accounting: A Bibliometric Analysis. *Pakistan Journal of Humanities and Social Sciences*, *11*(2), 1088–1110. doi:10.52131/pjhss.2023.1102.0417

Kindzeka, K. A. C. (2023). Impact of Artificial Intelligence on Accounting, Auditing and Financial Reporting. *American Journal of Computing and Engineering*, *6*(1), 29–34. doi:10.47672/ajce.1433

Kingston, J. (2016). Artificial Intelligence and Legal Liability. *International Conference on Innovative Techniques and Applications of Artificial Intelligence.*

Kirimi, J. M., & Moturi, C. A. (2016). Application of data mining classification in employee performance prediction. *International Journal of Computer Applications*, *146*(7), 28–35. doi:10.5120/ijca2016910883

Klarin, A., Ali Abadi, H., & Sharmelly, R. (2024). Professionalism in artificial intelligence: The link between technology and ethics. *Systems Research and Behavioral Science*, sres.2994. Advance online publication. doi:10.1002/sres.2994

Klepper, S. (1997). Industry Life Cycles. *Industrial and Corporate Change*, *1*(6), 145–182. doi:10.1093/icc/6.1.145

Kochetkov, D. M. (2023). Innovation: A state-of-the-art review and typology. *International Journal of Innovation Studies*, *4*(7), 263–272. doi:10.1016/j.ijis.2023.05.004

Koh, H. C., & Tan, G. (2011). Data mining applications in healthcare. *Journal of Healthcare Information Management*, *19*(2), 65. PMID:15869215

Kokina, J., & Davenport, T. H. (2017). The emergence of artificial intelligence: How automation is changing auditing. *Journal of Emerging Technologies in Accounting*, *14*(1), 115–122. doi:10.2308/jeta-51730

Koo, J., & Sewell, K. (2023). *Accounting for the Purchase, Sale and Receipt of Cryptocurrencies.* BDO Alliance USA. Obtido de https://www.bdo.com/insights/assurance/accounting-for-the-purchase-sale-and-receipt-of-cryptocurrencies#

Kothari, J. D. (2018). Plant Disease Identification using Artificial Intelligence: Machine Learning Approach. *International Journal of Innovative Research in Computer and Communication Engineering*, *7*(11), 11082–11085.

Kotsiantis, S., Koumanakos, E., Tzelepis, D., & Tampakas, V. (2006). Forecasting fraudulent financial statements using data mining. *International Journal of Computational Intelligence, 3*(2), 104-110.

Kouam, J. C., & Asongu, S. A. (2022). Effects of taxation on social innovation and implications for achieving sustainable development goals in developing countries: *A literature review. International Journal of Innovation Studies*, *6*(4), 259–275. doi:10.1016/j.ijis.2022.08.002

Koyuncugil, A. S., & Ozgulbas, N. (2012). Financial early warning system model and data mining application for risk detection. *Expert Systems with Applications*, *39*(6), 6238–6253. doi:10.1016/j.eswa.2011.12.021

KPMG. (2020). *Uma necessidade urgente de mudanças para a auditoria interna. Automação inteligente*. Retrieved from https://www.auditoria-interna-automacao.pdf (assets.kpmg)

Kroon, N., Alves, M. C., & Martins, I. (2021). The Impacts of Emerging Technologies on Accountants' Role and Skills: Connecting to Open Innovation—A Systematic Literature Review. *Journal of Open Innovation, 7*(3), 163. Advance online publication. doi:10.3390/joitmc7030163

Kumar, M. R., & Gunjan, V. K. (2020). Review of machine learning models for credit scoring analysis. *Ingeniería Solidaria, 16*(1).

Kumar, S., Sureka, R., Lim, W. M., Kumar Mangla, S., & Goyal, N. (2021). What do we know about business strategy and environmental research? Insights from Business Strategy and the Environment. *Business Strategy and the Environment, 30*(8), 3454–3469. doi:10.1002/bse.2813

Kumar, V., & Vani, K. (2018). Agricultural Robot: Leaf Disease Detection and Monitoring the Field Condition Using Machine Learning and Image Processing. *International Journal of Computational Intelligence Research, 14*(7), 551–561.

Kuo, T. C., & Smith, S. (2018). A systematic review of technologies involving eco-innovation for enterprises moving towards sustainability. *Journal of Cleaner Production, 192*, 207–220. doi:10.1016/j.jclepro.2018.04.212

Kurki, V. A. J., & Pietrzykowski, T. (2017). *Legal Personhood: Animals, Artificial Intelligence and the Unborn*. Springer International Publishing AG. doi:10.1007/978-3-319-53462-6

Kusiak, A. (2017). Smart manufacturing. *International Journal of Production Research, 56*(1-2), 508–517. doi:10.1080/00207543.2017.1351644 PMID:28383012

Labeaga, J., Martínez-Ros, E., Sanchis, A., & Sanchis, J. A. (2021). Does persistence in using R&D tax credits help to achieve product innovations? *Technological Forecasting and Social Change, 173*, 121065. Advance online publication. doi:10.1016/j.techfore.2021.121065

Lacurezeanu, R., Tiron-Tudor, A., & Bresfelean, V. P. (2020). Robotic Process Automation in Audit and Accounting. *Audit Financiar, 18*(160), 752–770. doi:10.20869/AUDITF/2020/160/024

Laffer, A. B. (2004). The Laffer Curve: Past, Present, and Future. *The Heritage Foundation Backgrounder, 1765*(1), 1–16.

Lakhanpal, V., & Samuel, R. (2018). Implementing blockchain technology in oil and gas industry: A review. *Proceedings - SPE Annual Technical Conference and Exhibition*. 10.2118/191750-MS

Lan, Y., & Tang, Y. (2020). Application of computer accounting system in internal control of enterprise accounting. *Journal of Physics: Conference Series, 1693*(1), 012007. doi:10.1088/1742-6596/1693/1/012007

Lapteş, R. (2020). Ethics and Integrity of the Professional Accountant. *Series V - Economic Sciences, 12*(2), 87–92. doi:10.31926/but.es.2019.12.61.2.11

Le Cun, Y., & Bengio, Y. (1995). Convolutional networks for images, speech, and time series. In M. A. Arbib (Ed.), *The Handbook of Brain Theory and Neural Networks* (pp. 255–258). MIT Press.

Leach, K., Zhang, F., & Weimer, W. (2017). Scotch: combining software guard extensions and system management mode to monitor cloud resource usage. Lecture Notes in ComputerScience (including subseries Lecture Notes in Artificial Intelligence and Lecture Notes in Bioinformatics).

LeCun, Y., Bengio, Y., & Hinton, G. (2015). Deep learning. *Nature, 521*(7553), 436–444. doi:10.1038/nature14539 PMID:26017442

Leemans, T. & Jacquemin, H. (2017). *La Responsabilité Extracontractuelle de l'Intelligence Artificielle*. Master en droit, Faculté de droit et de criminologie (DRT), Université Catholique de Louvain.

Lee, Y. Y., Falahat, M., & Porter, M. (2018). *The Impact of Digitalization and Resources on Gaining Competitive Advantage in International Markets : The Mediating Role of Marketing*. Innovation and Learning Capabilities.

Lehner, O., Ittonen, K., Silvola, H., Ström, E., & Wührleitner, A. (2022). Artificial intelligence based decision-making in accounting and auditing: Ethical challenges and normative thinking. *Accounting, Auditing & Accountability Journal, 35*(9), 109–135. doi:10.1108/AAAJ-09-2020-4934

Leitner-Hanetseder, S., Lehner, O. M., Eisl, C., & Forstenlechner, C. (2021). A profession in transition: Actors, tasks and roles in AI-based accounting. *Journal of Applied Accounting Research, 22*(3), 539–556. doi:10.1108/JAAR-10-2020-0201

Lester, A. (2021). *Project Management, Planning and Control: Managing Engineering*. Construction and Manufacturing Projects to PMI, APM and BSI Standards. doi:10.1016/B978-0-12-824339-8.01001-4

Li, H., Li, Y., & Zhao, G. (2011). Demonstration the application of activity-based costing to ERP management system. *Proceedings - 2011 6th IEEE Joint International Information Technology and Artificial Intelligence Conference, ITAIC 2011.*

Li, Y. (2011). Study on setting up lake environmental accounting account. *2011 2nd International Conference on Artificial Intelligence, Management Science and Electronic Commerce, AIMSEC 2011 - Proceedings.*

Li, Z. (2020, June). Analysis on the influence of artificial intelligence development on accounting. In *2020 International conference on big data, Artificial Intelligence and Internet of Things Engineering (ICBAIE)* (pp. 260-262). IEEE. 10.1109/ICBAIE49996.2020.00061

Li, Z., & Zheng, L. (2018, September). The impact of artificial intelligence on accounting. In *2018 4th International Conference on Social Science and Higher Education (ICSSHE 2018).* Atlantis Press. 10.2991/icsshe-18.2018.203

Liao, P. (2022). *Proceedings of the 2022 6th International Seminar on Education, Management and Social Sciences (ISEMSS 2022).* Atlantis Press SARL. 10.2991/978-2-494069-31-2

Li, C. (2012). Research on application strategy for ERP system in enterprise accounting informationization. *Advanced Materials Research.*

Liciotti, Zingaretti, & Placidi. (2014). An automa`c analysis of shoppers behaviour using a distributed rgb-d cameras system. *Mechatronic and Embedded Systems and Applica.ons (MESA), 2014 IEEE/ASME 10th International Conference.*

Lievrouw, L. A. (1989). The invisible college reconsidered: Bibliometrics and the development of scientific communication theory. *Communication Research, 16*(5), 615–628. doi:10.1177/009365089016005004

Li, K., Mai, F., Shen, R., & Yan, X. (2021). Measuring corporate culture using machine learning. *Review of Financial Studies, 34*(7), 3265–3315. doi:10.1093/rfs/hhaa079

Lillford, P., & Hermansson, A. M. (2021). Global missions and the critical needs of food science and technology. *Trends in Food Science & Technology, 111*, 800–811. doi:10.1016/j.tifs.2020.04.009

Lin, J., Liu, J., Zheng, C., & Chen, J. (2021). Reform on accounting teaching practice course in universities with the background of artificial intelligence. *ACM International Conference Proceeding Series.* 10.1145/3465631.3465785

Linnenluecke, M. K., Marrone, M., & Singh, A. K. (2019). Conducting systematic literature reviews and bibliometric analyses. *Australian Journal of Management, 45*(2), 175–194. doi:10.1177/0312896219877678

Liu, L., & Zhou, G. (2009). Extraction of the Rice Leaf Disease Image Based on BP Neural Network. *International Conference on Computational Intelligence and Software Engineering 2009.* 10.1109/CISE.2009.5363225

Liu, H., & Chahl, J. S. (2021). Proximal detecting invertebrate pestson crops using a deep residual convolutional neural network trained by virtual images. *Artificial Intelligence in Agriculture*, *5*, 13–23. doi:10.1016/j.aiia.2021.01.003

Liu, J., Jiang, Y., Gan, S., He, L., & Zhang, Q. (2022). Can digital finance promote corporate green innovation? *Environmental Science and Pollution Research International*, *29*(24), 35828–35840. doi:10.1007/s11356-022-18667-4 PMID:35061181

Liu, N., Shapira, P., Yue, X., & Guan, J. (2021). Mapping technological innovation dynamics in artificial intelligence domains: Evidence from a global patent analysis. *PLoS One*, *16*(12), e0262050. doi:10.1371/journal.pone.0262050 PMID:34972173

Liu, R., Wang, Y., & Zou, J. (2022). Research on the Transformation from Financial Accounting to Management Accounting Based on Drools Rule Engine. *Computational Intelligence and Neuroscience*, *2022*, 1–8. doi:10.1155/2022/9445776 PMID:35498191

Liu, T. (2021). Smart financial management system based on intelligent data dimensionality reduction technology. *Proceedings of the 5th International Conference on Electronics, Communication and Aerospace Technology, ICECA 2021*. 10.1109/ICECA52323.2021.9675999

Liu, X. (2022). Research on consumers' personal information security and perception based on digital twins and Internet of Things. *Sustainable Energy Technologies and Assessments*, *53*, 102706. Advance online publication. doi:10.1016/j.seta.2022.102706

Liu, Y. (2021). Development and risk of internet finance based on big data. In *The International Conference on Cyber Security Intelligence and Analytics*. Springer. 10.1007/978-3-030-70042-3_75

Liu, Y. (2021). Research on the influence of artificial intelligence on the training of accounting talents and strategy. *ACM International Conference Proceeding Series*. 10.1145/3465631.3465786

Li, W. (2021). Reform and innovation of higher fine arts distance education under the background of big data. *Journal of Physics: Conference Series*, *1852*(3), 032026. doi:10.1088/1742-6596/1852/3/032026

Llanos-Herrera, G., & Merigo, J. M. (2018). Overview of brand personality research with bibliometric indicators. *Kybernetes*, *48*(3), 546–569. doi:10.1108/K-02-2018-0051

Logachev, M. S., Orekhovskaya, N. A., Seregina, T. N., Shishov, S., & Volvak, S. F. (2021). Information system for monitoring and managing the quality of educational programs. *Journal of Open Innovation*, *7*(1), 93. Advance online publication. doi:10.3390/joitmc7010093

Loh, C.-T., Ng, Y.-H., Lee, A.-S., Chin, Y.-M., & Foo, P.-Y. (2023). *Challenges Faced by Accounting Professionals in Artificial Intelligence-Based Technology Environment and Determinants of Acceptance* (Issue Bafe). Atlantis Press International BV. doi:10.2991/978-94-6463-342-9_5

Lombardi, D., Bloch, R., & Vasarhelyi, M. (2014). The future of audit. *JISTEM-Journal of Information Systems and Technology Management*, *11*, 21–32.

Long, G. J., Lin, B. H., Cai, H. X., & Nong, G. Z. (2020). Developing an artificial intelligence (AI) management system to improve product quality and production efficiency in furniture manufacture. *Procedia Computer Science*, *166*, 486–490. doi:10.1016/j.procs.2020.02.060

Lum, K. T., Baker, D. R., & Hihn, J. M. (2008, June). The effects of data mining techniques on software cost estimation. In *2008 IEEE International Engineering Management Conference* (pp. 1-5). IEEE. 10.1109/IEMCE.2008.4617949

Lusardi, A., & Mitchell, O. S. (2014). The economic importance of financial literacy: Theory and evidence. *Journal of Economic Literature, 32*(1), 7–11. doi:10.1257/jel.52.1.5 PMID:28579637

Lyons, A. C., & Kass-Hanna, J. (2021). A methodological overview to defining and measuring "digital" financial literacy. *Financial Planning Review, 4*(2), 1–19. doi:10.1002/cfp2.1113

Lyu, X., & Zhao, J. (2019). Compressed sensing and its applications in risk assessment for internet supply chain finance under big data. *IEEE Access : Practical Innovations, Open Solutions, 7*, 53182–53187. doi:10.1109/ACCESS.2019.2909801

Ma, Y. (2011). Notice of Retraction: The study of management accounting under the modern enterprise system [Retracted]. *2011 2nd International Conference on Artificial Intelligence, Management Science and Electronic Commerce, AIMSEC 2011 - Proceedings*, 5273-5275. 10.1109/AIMSEC.2011.6011299

Magas, M., & Kiritsis, D. (2022). Industry Commons: An ecosystem approach to horizontal enablers for sustainable cross-domain industrial innovation (a positioning paper). *International Journal of Production Research, 60*(2), 479–492. doi:10.1080/00207543.2021.1989514

Mahamedi, E., Wonders, M., Gerami Seresht, N., Woo, W. L., & Kassem, M. (2023). A reinforcing transfer learning approach to predict buildings energy performance. *Construction Innovation*. Advance online publication. doi:10.1108/CI-12-2022-0333

Ma, J., Schneider, L., Lapuschkin, S., Achtibat, R., Duchrau, M., Krois, J., Schwendicke, F., & Samek, W. (2022). Towards trustworthy ai in dentistry. *Journal of Dental Research, 101*(11), 1263–1268. doi:10.1177/00220345221106086 PMID:35746889

Malerba, F. (2004). *Sectoral systems of innovation: how and why innovation differs across sectors. Handbook of innovation.* doi:10.1017/CBO9780511493270

Malva Cakra Dewa, M., Widya Yunia Kharisyami, P., Diva Navael, L., & Maulana, A. (2018). *Peran Akuntan Dalam Menghadapi Digitalisasi Ekonomi Menjelang Era Society 5.0.* doi:10.29407/jae.v7i3.18492

Ma, M. (2022). Research on the development of hospital intelligent finance based on artificial intelligence. *Computational Intelligence and Neuroscience, 2022*, 6549766. Advance online publication. doi:10.1155/2022/6549766 PMID:35983131

Mansor, N. A., Hamid, Y., Anwar, I. S. K., Isa, N. S. M., & Abdullah, M. Q. (2022). The awareness and knowledge on artificial intelligence among accountancy students. *International Journal of Academic Research in Business & Social Sciences, 12*(11), 1629–1640. doi:10.6007/IJARBSS/v12-i11/15307

Marques, S., Gonçalves, R., da Costa, R. L., Pereira, L. F., & Dias, A. L. (2023). The Impact of Intelligent Systems on Management Accounting. *International Journal of Intelligent Information Technologies, 19*(1). doi:10.4018/IJIIT.324601

Marrone, M., Linnenluecke, M. K., Richardson, G., & Smith, T. (2020). Trends in environmental accounting research within and outside of the accounting discipline. *Accounting, Auditing & Accountability Journal, 33*(8), 2167–2193. doi:10.1108/AAAJ-03-2020-4457

Marshall, T. E., & Lambert, S. L. (2018). Cloud-Based Intelligent Accounting Applications: Accounting Task Automation Using IBM Watson Cognitive Computing. *Journal of Emerging Technologies in Accounting, 15*(1), 199–215. doi:10.2308/jeta-52095

Martha, G. (2018). *Você, eu e os robôs: pequeno manual do mundo digital.* Atlas.

Martins, E. C., & Terblanche, F. (2003). Building organisational culture that stimulates creativity and innovation. *European Journal of Innovation Management, 1*(6), 64–74. doi:10.1108/14601060310456337

Maturana, G., & Nickerson, J. (2019). Teachers teaching teachers: The role of workplace peer effects in financial decisions. *Review of Financial Studies*, *32*(10), 3920–3957. doi:10.1093/rfs/hhy136

Mauladi, K. F., Jaya, I. M. L. M., & Esquivias, M. A. (2022). Exploring the Link Between Cashless Society and Cybercrime in Indonesia. *Journal of Telecommunications and the Digital Economy*, *10*(3), 58–76. doi:10.18080/jtde.v10n3.533

Mayer, J. H., Stritzel, O., Esswein, M., & Quick, R. (2020). Towards natural language processing: an accounting case study. In *Forty-First International Conference on Information Systems*. https://www.rcw.wi.tu-darmstadt.de/media/bwl4/forschung_9/kompetenzzentrum_1/20200927_ICIS_1383_NLP_track_23_final_version_letter_size.pdf

Mayer-Schönberger, V., & Cukier, K. (2013). *Big Data: A Revolution that Will Transform How We Live, Work and Think*. John Murray.

McCarthy, J. (2007). *What is artificial intelligence?* Stanford University. http://www-formal.stanford.edu/jmc/whatisai.pdf

McCarthy, J., Minsky, M. L., Rochester, N., & Shannon, C. E. (2006). A proposal for the dartmouth summer research project on artificial intelligence, 31 August, 1955. *AI Magazine*, *27*(4), 12–12.

Medennikov, V. (2021). Management transformation with a single digital platform as exemplified by accounting. *IFAC-PapersOnLine*, *54*(13), 178–182. doi:10.1016/j.ifacol.2021.10.441

Mehrabi, N., Morstatter, F., Saxena, N., Lerman, K., & Galstyan, A. (2021). A survey on bias and fairness in machine learning. *ACM Computing Surveys*, *54*(6), 1–35. doi:10.1145/3457607

Meira, M. (2019). *O impacto da Inteligência Artificial na Auditoria* (Master Thesis) Faculdade de Economia da Universidade do Porto.

Meitei, A. J., Rai, P., & Rajkishan, S. S. (2023). Application of AI/ML techniques in achieving SDGs: A bibliometric study. *Environment, Development and Sustainability*, 1–37. doi:10.1007/s10668-023-03935-1

Meltzer, J. (2018). *The impact of artificial intelligence on international trade*. Brookings Institution. Available at: https://www.brookings.edu/research/the-impact-of-artificial-intelligence-on-international-trade/

Mensah, S. I., & Ewur, G. K. (2021). Financial Literacy, Savings Behavior, and Sustainable Development: Evidence from Ghana. *The Journal of Consumer Affairs*, *55*(1), 135–160.

Merigó, J. M., & Yang, J. B. (2017). Accounting research: A bibliometric analysis. *Australian Accounting Review*, *27*(1), 71–100. doi:10.1111/auar.12109

Metawa, N., & Metawa, S. (2021). Internet financial risk early warning based on big data analysis. *American Journal of Business and Operations Research*, *3*(1), 48–60. doi:10.54216/AJBOR.030103

Mishra, M., Desul, S., Santos, C. A. G., Mishra, S. K., Kamal, A. H. M., Goswami, S., Kalumba, A. M., Biswal, R., da Silva, R. M., dos Santos, C. A. C., & Baral, K. (2023). A bibliometric analysis of sustainable development goals (SDGs): A review of progress, challenges, and opportunities. *Environment, Development and Sustainability*, 1–43. doi:10.1007/s10668-023-03225-w PMID:37362966

Misnevs, B., & Fila, N. (2008). Analytical system for research of TTI study process trends. *MIPRO2008 - 31st International Convention Proceedings: Computers in Education.*

Moerland, T. M., Broekens, J., Plaat, A., & Jonker, C. M. (2023). Model-based reinforcement learning: A survey. *Foundations and Trends® in Machine Learning, 16*(1), 1-118.

Mohamed, S. T. (2020). *Legal Aspects of Artificial Intelligence and Robotics*. https://democraticac.de/?p=64965

Mökander, J. (2023). Auditing of AI: Legal, Ethical and Technical Approaches. *Digital Society : Ethics, Socio-Legal and Governance of Digital Technology*, *2*(3), 49. doi:10.1007/s44206-023-00074-y

Moll, J., & Yigitbasioglu, O. (2019). The role of internet-related technologies in shaping the work of accountants: New directions for accounting research. *The British Accounting Review*, *51*(6), 100833. doi:10.1016/j.bar.2019.04.002

Mookerjee, J., & Rao, O. R. S. (2021). A Review of the Robotic Process Automation's Impact as a Disruptive Innovation in Accounting and Audit. *Turkish Journal of Computer and Mathematics Education*, *12*(12), 3675–3682.

Moses & Chan. (2014). Using Big Data for legal and law enforcement decisions: Tes`ng the new tools. *UNSW Law Journal, 37*(2).

Mowbray, A., Chung, P., & Greenleaf, G. (2023). Explainable AI (XAI) in Rules as Code (RaC): The DataLex approach. *Computer Law & Security Report*, *48*, 105771. Advance online publication. doi:10.1016/j.clsr.2022.105771

Mukherjee, A., Singh, M., & Žaldokas, A. (2017). Do corporate taxes hinder innovation? *Journal of Financial Economics*, *1*(124), 195–221. doi:10.1016/j.jfineco.2017.01.004

Mullainathan, S., & Spiess, J. (2017). Machine learning: An applied econometric approach. *The Journal of Economic Perspectives*, *31*(2), 87–106. doi:10.1257/jep.31.2.87

Munoko, I., Brown-Liburd, H., & Vasarhelyi, M. (2020). The ethical implications of using artificial intelligence in auditing. *Journal of Business Ethics*, *167*(2), 209–234. doi:10.1007/s10551-019-04407-1

Murugesan, R., Sudarsanam, S.K., & Malathi, G.V., Vijayakumar, Neelanarayanan, V., Venugopal, R., Rekha, D., Saha, S., Baja' R., Miral, A., & Malolan, V. (2019). Artificial Intelligence and Agriculture 5. 0. *International Journal of Recent Technology and Engineering*, *8*(2), 2277–3878.

Nakamura, Y., Matsuda, K., & Matsuoka, M. (2016). Augmented data center infrastructure management system for minimizing energy consumption. *Proceedings - 2016 5th IEEE International Conference on Cloud Networking, CloudNet 2016*. 10.1109/CloudNet.2016.12

Namahoot, K. S., & Laohavichien, T. (2018). Assessing the intentions to use internet banking: The role of perceived risk and trust as mediating factors. *International Journal of Bank Marketing*, *36*(2), 256–276. doi:10.1108/IJBM-11-2016-0159

Nayal, K., Kumar, S., Raut, R. D., Queiroz, M. M., Priyadarshinee, P., & Narkhede, B. E. (2022). Supply chain firm performance in circular economy and digital era to achieve sustainable development goals. *Business Strategy and the Environment*, *31*(3), 1058–1073. doi:10.1002/bse.2935

Nedbálek, K. (2018). *The Future Inclusion of Criminal Liability of the Robots and Artificial Intelligence in the Czech Republic*. Paradigm of Law and Public Administration, Interregional Academy for Personnel Management. Available at https://maup.com.ua/assets/files/expert/1/the-future-inclusion-of-criminal.pdf

Neumann, U., Whitaker, M. J., Wiegand, S., Krude, H., Porter, J. B., Digweed, D., & Blankenstein, O. (2019). *Absorption and tolerability of taste-masked hydrocortisone granules in neonates, infants and children under 6 years of age with adrenal insufficiency*. Endocrine Abstracts. doi:10.1530/endoabs.65.JA5

Nevejans, N. (2016). Directorate-General for Internal Policies, Policy Department C: Citizens' Rights and Constitutional Affairs, Legal Affairs. *European Civil Law Rules in Robotics*, No. EA n° 2471.

Nian, L., & Chuen, D. (2015). *Handbook of Digital Currency Bitcoin, Innovation, Financial Instrument, and Big Data*. Elsevier.

Nichols-Barrer, C., Lewis, C. T. L., & Cook, T. D. (2017). *Digital Financial Services: Challenges and Opportunities for Emerging Markets*. The World Bank.

Nilsson. (2009). The Quest for artificial intelligence, A History of ideias and Achievements. Cambridge University Press.

Noordin, N., Hussainey, K., & Hayek, A. (2022). The use of artificial intelligence and audit quality: An analysis from the perspectives of external auditors in the UAE. *Journal of Risk and Financial Management*, *15*(8), 339. doi:10.3390/jrfm15080339

No, W. G., Lee, K., Huang, F., & Li, Q. (2019). Multidimensional audit data selection (MADS): A framework for using data analytics in the audit data selection process. *Accounting Horizons*, *33*(3), 127–140. doi:10.2308/acch-52453

Nuhu, S. K., Manan, Z. A., Wan Alwi, S. R., & Md Reba, M. N. (2021). Roles of geospatial technology in eco-industrial park site selection: State–of–the-art review. *Journal of Cleaner Production*, *309*, 127361. Advance online publication. doi:10.1016/j.jclepro.2021.127361

Nunes, T., Leite, J., & Pedrosa, I. (2020). Automação Inteligente de Processos: Um Olhar sobre o Futuro da AuditoriaIn *15th Iberian Conference on Information Systems and Technologies*.

O'Leary, D. E. (1991). Representation of source reliability in weight of evidence. Lecture Notes in Computer Science (including subseries Lecture Notes in Artificial Intelligence and Lecture Notes in Bioinformatics). doi:10.1007/BFb0028095

O'neil, C. (2017). *Weapons of math destruction: How big data increases inequality and threatens democracy*. Crown.

Obschonka, M., Tavassoli, S., Rentfrow, P. J., Potter, J., & Gosling, S. D. (2023). Innovation and inter-city knowledge spillovers: Social, geographical, and technological connectedness and psychological openness. *Research Policy*, *52*(8), 104849. Advance online publication. doi:10.1016/j.respol.2023.104849

OECD. (2010). *Taxation*. Innovation and the Environment.

OECD. (2016). *Artificial Intelligence on Society*. OECD Publishing. Retrieved from https://www.oecd-ilibrary.org/.ors

OECD. (2017). *G20/OECD INFE REPORT - Ensuring financial education and consumer protection for all in the digital age*. Academic Press.

OECD. (2018). *G20/OECD INFE policy guidance on digitalisation and financial literacy'*. Academic Press.

Oliveira, A. (2019). *Inteligência Artificial*. Fundação Francisco Manuel dos Santos Editora.

Oliveira. (2019). Inteligência Artificial. Fundação Francisco Manuel dos Santos.

Oliver, W., & Satchell, S. (2011). Social welfare issues of financial literacy and their implications for regulation. *Journal of Regulatory Economics*, *1*(40), 1–40. doi:10.1007/s11149-011-9151-6

Olsen, T. L., & Tomlin, B. (2020). Industry 4.0: Opportunities and Challenges for Operations Management. *Manufacturing & Service Operations Management*, *22*(1), 113–122. doi:10.1287/msom.2019.0796

Omoteso, K. (2012). The application of artificial intelligence in auditing: Looking back to the future. *Expert Systems with Applications*, *39*(9), 8490–8495. doi:10.1016/j.eswa.2012.01.098

Onuwabhagbe, O. P., Ngozi, O. E., & Adeboye, A. A. (2018). Teaching accounting ethics using the KPMG ethics curriculum to undergraduate accounting students at a private Christian university in Nigeria: An experimental study. *Proceedings of the 31st International Business Information Management Association Conference, IBIMA 2018: InnovationManagement and Education Excellence through Vision 2020.*

Oprea, O., Hoinaru, R., Păcuraru-Ionescu, C.-P., & Neamţu, D. (2022). Accounting for the future: practice, Artificial Intelligence and regulation. *Proceedings of the International Conference on Business Excellence, 16*(1), 817–826. 10.2478/picbe-2022-0076

Orriols-Puig, A., Martínez-López, F. J., Casillas, J., & Lee, N. (2013). Unsupervised KDD to creatively support managers' decision making with fuzzy association rules: A distribution channel application. *Industrial Marketing Management, 42*(4), 532–543. doi:10.1016/j.indmarman.2013.03.005

Ouchchy, L., Coin, A., & Dubljević, V. (2020). AI in the headlines: The portrayal of the ethical issues of artificial intelligence in the media. *AI & Society, 35*(4), 927–936. doi:10.1007/s00146-020-00965-5

Ou, L., & Chen, L. (2020). Predicting Risk Propagation of Corporate Internet Reporting Based on Fuzzy Neural Network. *Ingénierie des Systèmes d'Information, 25*(4), 481–488. doi:10.18280/isi.250411

Paiella, M. (2016). Financial literacy and subjective expectations questions: A validation exercise. *Research in Economics, 70*(2), 360–374. doi:10.1016/j.rie.2015.11.004

Pan, C. L., Chen, H. E., Ou, Z. Q., & Chen, Y. (2022). ESG Report Intelligent Writing Assistant - Assist Chinese Enterprises in ESG Information Disclosure. *2022 IEEE Technology and Engineering Management Society Conference - Asia Pacific, TEMSCON-ASPAC.*

Panda, H., & Ramanathan, K. (1996). Technological capability assessment of a firm in the electricity sector. *Technovation, 10*(16), 561–588. doi:10.1016/S0166-4972(97)82896-9

Pandian, S. (2020). *Understand machine learning and its end-to-end process.* Blog post at Analytics Vidhya. https:// www. analyticsvidhya. com/blog/2020/12/understand-machine-learning-and-its-end-to-end-process

Parasuraman, R., & Riley, V. (1997). Humans and automation: Use, misuse, disuse, abuse. *Human Factors, 39*(2), 230–253. doi:10.1518/001872097778543886

Park, T., & Kim, H. (2013). A data warehouse-based decision support system for sewer infrastructure management. *Automation in Construction, 30*, 37–49. doi:10.1016/j.autcon.2012.11.017

Park, Y. E. (2022). Developing a COVID-19 crisis management strategy using news media and social media in big data analytics. *Social Science Computer Review, 40*(6), 1358–1375. doi:10.1177/08944393211007314

Parliament, UK. (2016). *Robotics and artificial intelligence.* Report of the Committee on Science and Technology.

Parnell, J., & Brady, M. (2019). Capabilities, strategies and firm performance in the United Kingdom. *Journal of Strategy and Management, 12*(1), 153–172. doi:10.1108/JSMA-10-2018-0107

Parra-Requena, G., Ruiz-Ortega, M. J., Garcia-Villaverde, P. M., & Ramírez, F. J. (2022). Innovativeness and performance: The joint effect of relational trust and combinative capability. *European Journal of Innovation Management, 25*(1), 191–213. doi:10.1108/EJIM-04-2020-0117

Patil, S. B., & Bodhe, S. K. (2011). Leaf disease severity measurement using image processing. *IACSIT International Journal of Engineering and Technology, 3*(5), 297–301.

Pawar, A., Pawaskar, M., & Ghodke, S. (2020). Review of Plant Disease Detection and Diagnosis Using Deep Learning Model. *IJFGCN, 13*(2), 456–460.

PCAOB. (2023). *SPOTLIGHT: Inspection Observations Related to Public Company Audits Involving Crypto Assets.* PCAOB: Public Company Accounting Oversight Board. Obtido de https://pcaobus.org/documents/crypto-assets-spotlight.pdf

Pellicer, E., Sierra, L. A., & Yepes, V. (2016). Appraisal of infrastructure sustainability by graduate students using an active-learning method. *Journal of Cleaner Production*, *113*, 884–896. doi:10.1016/j.jclepro.2015.11.010

Pham, Q. V., Nguyen, D. C., Hwang, W. J., & Pathirana, P. N. (2020). *Artificial Intelligence (AI) and Big Data for Coronavirus (COVID-19) Pandemic: A Survey on the State-of-the-Arts*. Academic Press.

Pielawa, L., Helmer, A., Brell, M., & Hein, A. (2011). Intelligent environments supporting the care of multi-morbid patients: A concept for patient-centered information management and therapy. *ACM International Conference Proceeding Series*. 10.1145/2093698.2093713

Ping, W. (2021). Data mining and XBRL integration in management accounting information based on artificial intelligence. *Journal of Intelligent & Fuzzy Systems*, *40*(4), 6755–6766. doi:10.3233/JIFS-189509

Pippo, K. (2020). *Viewpoints: Auditing Crypto-Assets: Relevance and Reliability of the Information Obtained from a Blockchain to be used as Audit Evidence*. Chartered Professional Accountants Canada.

Poirot-Mazeresdu. (2015). Robotique et médecine: Quelle(s) responsabilité(s)? *Journal International de Bioéthique*, *24*(4).

Pompei, F., & Selezneva, E. (2019). Unemployment and education mismatch in the EU before and after the financial crisis. *Journal of Policy Modeling*. Advance online publication. doi:10.1016/j.jpolmod.2019.09.009

Prado, L. A. (2020). Promoting Financial Literacy for Sustainable Development Goals: Exploring the Role of Digital Technologies. *International Journal of Innovation and Sustainable Development*, *14*(3), 253–270.

Pratiwi, Y. E., Desi Lastianti, S., Wijayanto, I., Hidayat, U. S., & Susanto, I. W. (2023). Artificial Intelligence Auditing: Embracing the Disruption. Are You Prepared? *Proceeding International Conference on Economic Business Management, and Accounting (ICOEMA), August*.

Prokhorov, O., Pronchakov, Y., & Fedorovich, O. (2020). Intelligent multi-service platform for building management. *ATIT 2020 - Proceedings: 2020 2nd IEEE International Conference on Advanced Trends in Information Theory*. 10.1109/ATIT50783.2020.9349312

Psaila, S. (2017). *Blockchain: A game changer for audit processes*. Deloitte.

Pugliese, R., Regondi, S., & Marini, R. (2021). Machine learning-based approach: Global trends, research directions, and regulatory standpoints. *Data Science and Management*, *4*, 19–29. doi:10.1016/j.dsm.2021.12.002

Pulselli, R. M., Marchi, M., Neri, E., Marchettini, N., & Bastianoni, S. (2019). Carbon accounting framework for decarbonisation of European city neighbourhoods. *Journal of Cleaner Production*, *208*, 850–868. doi:10.1016/j.jclepro.2018.10.102

Purda, L., & Skillicorn, D. (2015). Accounting variables, deception, and a bag of words: Assessing the tools of fraud detection. *Contemporary Accounting Research*, *32*(3), 1193–1223. doi:10.1111/1911-3846.12089

Purnomo, A., Aziz, A., Afia, N., Sari, A. K., & Primadani, T. I. W. (2021). E-CRM: Three decades of bibliometric networks visualizing of academic publication. *3rd International Conference on Cybernetics and Intelligent Systems, ICORIS 2021*. 10.1109/ICORIS52787.2021.9649480

PwC. (2019). *The Future of Audit. Perspectives on how the audit could evolve*. Retrieved from https://www.pwc-future-of-audit-report-july-2019.pdf

Qasaimeh, G., Yousef, R., Al-Gasaymeh, A., & Alnaimi, A. (2022). The effect of artificial intelligence using neural network in estimating on an efficient accounting information system: evidence from Jordanian commercial banks. *2022 International Conference on Business Analytics for Technology and Security, ICBATS 2022*. 10.1109/ICBATS54253.2022.9759004

Qiu, J. (2021). Analysis of human interactive accounting management information systems based on artificial intelligence. *Journal of Global Information Management*, *30*(7), 1–13. doi:10.4018/JGIM.294905

Qiu, Y. L., & Xiao, G. F. (2020). Research on cost management optimization of financial sharing center based on RPA. *Procedia Computer Science*, *166*, 115–119. doi:10.1016/j.procs.2020.02.031

Rahim, S. M., Mohamad, Z. Z., Bakar, J. A., Mohsin, F. H., & Isa, N. M. (2018). Artificial intelligence, smart contract and islamic finance. *Asian Social Science*, *14*(2), 145. doi:10.5539/ass.v14n2p145

Rahman, M. (2023). Impact of taxes on the 2030 agenda for sustainable development: Evidence from Organization for Economic Co-operation and Development (OECD) countries. *Regional Sustainability*, *3*(4), 235–248. doi:10.1016/j.regsus.2023.07.001

Rahman, S. S., & Dekkati, S. (2022). Revolutionizing Commerce: The Dynamics and Future of E-Commerce Web Applications. *Asian Journal of Applied Science and Engineering*, *11*(1), 65–73. doi:10.18034/ajase.v11i1.58

Rahmatian, A., Hassani, H., & Rostami-Tabar, B. (2019). Prediction and Generation of Stock Price Movements: A Data-Driven Approach. *Complexity*, *2019*, 1–18. doi:10.1155/2019/1825195

Rahwan, I., Cebrian, M., Obradovich, N., Bongard, J., Bonnefon, J. F., Breazeal, C., Crandall, J. W., Christakis, N. A., Couzin, I. D., Jackson, M. O., Jennings, N. R., Kamar, E., Kloumann, I. M., Larochelle, H., Lazer, D., McElreath, R., Mislove, A., Parkes, D. C., Pentland, A. S., ... Wellman, M. (2019). Machine behaviour. *Nature*, *568*(7753), 477–486. doi:10.1038/s41586-019-1138-y PMID:31019318

Raimundo, R., & Rosário, A. T. (2022). Cybersecurity in the Internet of Things in Industrial Management. *Applied Sciences (Basel, Switzerland)*, *12*(3), 1598. doi:10.3390/app12031598

Rajan, R., Dhir, S., & Sushil. (2020). Alliance termination research: A bibliometric review and research agenda. *Journal of Strategy and Management*, *13*(3), 351–375. doi:10.1108/JSMA-10-2019-0184

Ramesh, S., Hebber, R., Niveditha, M., Pooja, R., Prasad, B. N., Shashank, N., & Vinod, P. V. (2018). Plant Disease Detection Using Machine Learning. *International Conference on Design Innovations for 3Cs Compute Communicate Control (ICDI3C)*, 41-45. 10.1109/ICDI3C.2018.00017

Ramos. (2015). A prova digital na inves`gação do (ciber)terrorismo. In *Inves.gação Criminal*. ASFIC.

Ranta, M., Ylinen, M., & Järvenpää, M. (2023). Machine learning in management accounting research: Literature review and pathways for the future. *European Accounting Review*, *32*(3), 607–636. doi:10.1080/09638180.2022.2137221

Rashidin, M. S., Javed, S., Chen, L., & Jian, W. (2020a). Assessing the competitiveness of Chinese multinational enterprises development: Evidence from electronics sector. *SAGE Open*, *10*(1). Advance online publication. doi:10.1177/2158244019898214

Razali, F. A., Jusoh, M. A., Abu Talib, S. L., & Awang, N. (2022). The Impact of Industry 4.0 Towards Accounting Profession and Graduate's Career Readiness: A Review of Literature. *Malaysian Journal of Social Sciences and Humanities*, *7*(7), e001624. doi:10.47405/mjssh.v7i7.1624

Reddy, V., & Rekha, S. K. (2022). Plant Disease Detection using Advanced Convolutional Neural Networks with Region of Interest Awareness. *Journal of Immunology Research & Reports*, *2*(4), 1–7.

Regelbrugge, A., Fedele, S., Mankad, M., & Connors, S. (2021). *An internal auditor's guide to blockchain - Auditing blockchain environments*. Deloitte.

Rehman, A., & Hashim, F. (2022). Can Internal Audit Function Impact Artificial Intelligence? Case of Public Listed Companies of Oman. AIP Conference Proceedings, 2472(1), 040024. doi:10.1063/5.0092755

Reis, P. (2019). *O futuro da profissão de Auditoria* (Master Thesis). ISCAP Porto.

Reporting, E. Y. (2020). *A auditoria contínua enquanto ferramenta de gestão e impulsionador tecnológico*. Retrieved from https://valoreconomico.co.ao/artigo/a-auditoria-continua-enquanto-ferramenta-de-gestao-e-impulsionador-tecnologico

Revathi, P., & Hemlatha, M. (2012). Classification of cotton leaf spot diseases using image processing edge detection technique. *International Conference on Emerging Trends in Science, Engineering and Technology (INCOSET)*. 10.1109/INCOSET.2012.6513900

Ricther. (2019). A Review of Fundamentals and Influencial Factors of Artificial Intelligence. *International Journal of Computer and Informa.on Technology, 8*, 145.

Rigters, G. (2018). *Bitcoin For Beginners & Dummies - Cryptocurrency & Blockchain*. Academic Press.

Rikhardsson, P., Thórisson, K., Bergthorsson, G., & Batt, C. (2021). Artificial intelligence and auditing in small- and medium-sized firms: Expectations and applications. *AI Magazine, 43*(3), 323–336. doi:10.1002/aaai.12066

Rikhardsson, P., & Yigitbasioglu, O. (2018). Business intelligence & analytics in management accounting research: Status and future focus. *International Journal of Accounting Information Systems, 29*, 37–58. doi:10.1016/j.accinf.2018.03.001

Rodrigues, L. (2021). *O impacto da inteligência artificial na área e profissão de auditoria* (Master Thesis). Instituto Politécnico do Cávado e do Ave.

Rogeiro. (2004). O Novo terrorismo internacional como desafio emergente de segurança, Novas e velhas dimensões de um conceito problemá`co. In Terrorismo – coordenação de Adriano Moreira (2nd ed.). Almedina.

Rojas, C. N., Penafiel, G. A. A., Buitrago, D. F. L., & Romero, C. A. T. (2021). Society 5.0: A Japanese Concept for a Superintelligent Society. *Sustainability, 13*(12), 16. doi:10.3390/su13126567

Romero-Cordoba, R., Romero, F. P., Olivas, J. A., Serrano-Guerrero, J., & Peralta, A. (2016). A comparative study of soft computing software for enhancing the capabilities of business document management systems. *2016 IEEE International Conference on Fuzzy Systems, FUZZ-IEEE 2016*. 10.1109/FUZZ-IEEE.2016.7737693

Rosário, A. T., & Dias, J. C. (2023). How Industry 4.0 and Sensors Can Leverage Product Design: Opportunities and Challenges. *Sensors (Basel), 23*(3), 1165. doi:10.3390/s23031165 PMID:36772206

Rosário, A. T., Lopes, P. R., & Rosário, F. S. (2023). Metaverse in Marketing: Challenges and Opportunities. In A. Khang, V. Shah, & S. Rani (Eds.), *Handbook of Research on AI-Based Technologies and Applications in the Era of the Metaverse* (pp. 204–227). IGI Global. doi:10.4018/978-1-6684-8851-5.ch010

Rosi, N. M. K., &Mahyuni, L. P. (2021). The future of accounting profession in the industrial revolution 4.0: Meta-synthesis analysis. *E-JurnalAkuntansi, 31*(4).

Rosi, N. M. K., & Mahyuni, L. P. (2021). The Future Of Accounting Profession in The Industrial Revolution 4.0: Meta-Synthesis Analysis. *E-Jurnal Akuntansi, 31*(4). Advance online publication. doi:10.24843/EJA.2021.v31.i04.p17

Rosmida. (2019). Transformasi Peran Akuntan dalam Era Revolusi Industri 4.0 dan Tantangan Era Society 5.0. *Inovbiz:Jurnal Inovasi Bisnis, 7*, 206–212. www.ejournal.polbeng.ac.id/index.php/IBP

Ruiz-Real, J. L., Uribe-Toril, J., Torres, J. A., & Pablo, J. D. E. (2021). Artificial intelligence in business and economics research: Trends and future. *Journal of Business Economics and Management, 22*(1), 98–117. doi:10.3846/jbem.2020.13641

Russell, S., & Norving, P. (2009). *Artificial Intelligence - A Modern Approach* (3rd ed.). Prentice-Hall.

Sahoo, S. (2022). Big data analytics in manufacturing: A bibliometric analysis of research in the field of business management. *International Journal of Production Research, 60*(22), 6793–6821. doi:10.1080/00207543.2021.1919333

Samans, R., & Nelson, J. (2022). *Corporate reporting and accountability, Chapter in Sustainable Enterprise Value Creation*. Palgrave Macmillan. doi:10.1007/978-3-030-93560-3

Sambasivam, G., & Opiyo, G. D. (2021). A predictive machine learning application in agriculture: Cassava disease detection and classification with imbalanced dataset using convolutional neural networks. *Egyptian Informatics Journal, 22*(1), 27–34. doi:10.1016/j.eij.2020.02.007

Samuel, A. L. (1959). Some studies in machine learning using the game of checkers. *IBM Journal of Research and Development, 3*(3), 210–229. doi:10.1147/rd.33.0210

Santos, J., Ferreira, A., & Flintsch, G. (2017). A multi-objective optimisation-based pavement management decision-support system for enhancing pavement sustainability. *Journal of Cleaner Production, 164*, 1380–1393. doi:10.1016/j.jclepro.2017.07.027

Sari, D. R., & Rahardjo, D. (2021). Effect of Factors Financial, Trust, Demography, and Lifestyle of Purchase Intention Property in Jabodetabek. *Budapest International Research and Critics Institute-Journal (BIRCI-Journal), 4*(4), 11408-11421.

Saunila, M. (2020). Innovation capability in SMEs: A systematic review of the literature. *Journal of Innovation & Knowledge, 4*(5), 260–265. doi:10.1016/j.jik.2019.11.002

Saxena, A., Suna, T., & Regi, D. S. (2020). Application of Artificial Intelligence in Indian Agriculture. In *Souvenir: 19 National Convention*. RCA Alumni Association.

Scarpellini, S. (2022). Social impacts of a circular business model: An approach from a sustainability accounting and reporting perspective. *Corporate Social Responsibility and Environmental Management, 29*(3), 646–656. doi:10.1002/csr.2226

Schaltegger, S., & Zvezdov, D. (2013). In control of sustainability information: Untangling the role of accountants. Accounting and Control for Sustainability, 265-296. https://doi.org/ doi:10.1108/S1479-

Schmidt, B., Kountanis, D., & Al-Fuqaha, A. (2015). A biologically-inspired approach to network traffic classification for resource-constrained systems. *Proceedings - 2014 InternationalSymposium on Big Data Computing, BDC 2014.*

Schwab, K. (2017). The Fourth Industrial Revolution - A Book in Minutes. In Summaries of international books. Mohammed bin Zayed Knowledge Foundation.

Schwab. (2016). A quarta revolução industrial. Edipro.

Seethamraju, R., & Hecimovic, A. (2020). Impact of Artificial Intelligence on Auditing - An Exploratory Study. *Americas Conference on Information Systems (AMCIS2020) Proceedings, 8.*

Seethamraju, R., & Hecimovic, A. (2023). Adoption of artificial intelligence in auditing: An exploratory study. *Australian Journal of Management, 48*(4), 780–800. doi:10.1177/03128962221108440

Serman, D. (2016). *Auditor robô? A Inteligência Artificial como aliada da Auditoria. Plataforma do Linkedin.* Retrieved from https://pt.linkedin.com/pulse/auditor-rob%C3%B4-intelig%C3%AAncia-artificial-como-aliada-da-auditoria-serman

Serrano-Cinca, C., Gutiérrez-Nieto, B., & Bernate-Valbuena, M. (2019). The use of accounting anomalies indicators to predict business failure. *European Management Journal, 37*(3), 353–375. doi:10.1016/j.emj.2018.10.006

Shahroodi, S. (2010). Investigation of the effective factors in the efficiency of tax system. *Journal of Accounting and Taxation, 2*(3), 42-45. http://www.academicjournals.org/JAT

Shahsavar, M. M., Akrami, M., Gheibi, M., Kavianpour, B., Fathollahi-Fard, A. M., & Behzadian, K. (2021). Constructing a smart framework for supplying the biogas energy in green buildings using an integration of response surface methodology, artificial intelligence and petri net modelling. *Energy Conversion and Management*, *248*(17), 114794. Advance online publication. doi:10.1016/j.enconman.2021.114794

Shang, H., Lu, D., & Zhou, Q. (2021). Early warning of enterprise finance risk of big data mining in internet of things based on fuzzy association rules. *Neural Computing & Applications*, *33*(9), 3901–3909. doi:10.1007/s00521-020-05510-5

Shapovalova, A., Kuzmenko, O., Polishchuk, O., Larikova, T., & Myronchuk, Z. (2023). Modernization of the national accounting and auditing system using digital transformation tools. *Financial & Credit Activity: Problems of Theory & Practice*, *4*(51).

Sharif, A. M. (2006). Advancing the state of the art in the modelling and simulation of information systems evaluation. *Proceedings of the European and Mediterranean Conference on Information Systems, EMCIS 2006*.

Sharma, S., Kataria, A., & Sandhu, J. K. (2022). Applications, tools and technologies of robotic process automation in various industries. *2022 International Conference on Decision AidSciences and Applications, DASA 2022*. 10.1109/DASA54658.2022.9765027

Shen, H., & Wang, J. (2021). Research on the application of computer technology in the optimization of department information systems. *Journal of Physics: Conference Series*, *1982*(1), 012139. doi:10.1088/1742-6596/1982/1/012139

Shen, Y., Hueng, C. J., & Hu, W. (2020). Using digital technology to improve financial inclusion in China. *Applied Economics Letters*, *27*(1), 30–34. doi:10.1080/13504851.2019.1606401

Shetty, R., Cáceres, R., Pastrana, J., & Rabelo, L. (2012). Optical container code recognition and its impact on the maritime supply chain. *62nd IIE Annual Conference and Expo 2012*.

Shi, A., & Wu, W. (2011). Analysis on consolidated taxation in the context of headquarters economy under independent corporation accounting. *2011 2nd International Conference on Artificial Intelligence, Management Science and Electronic Commerce, AIMSEC 2011 -Proceedings*. 10.1109/AIMSEC.2011.6010251

Shrestha, Y. R., Ben-Menahem, S. M., & Von Krogh, G. (2019). Organizational decision-making structures in the age of artificial intelligence. *California Management Review*, *61*(4), 66–83. doi:10.1177/0008125619862257

Singh, G. S., & Chouhanb, J.S. (n.d.). Application of Artificial Intelligence in detection of diseases in plants:. A Survey. *Turkish Journal of Computer and Mathematics Education, 12*(3), 3301-3330.

SNC. (2015). Sistema de Normalização Contabilística (6ª Ediço ed.). Porto Editora.

Solanki, U., Jaliya, U. K., & Thakore, D. G. (2015). A survey on detection of disease and fruit grading. *International Journal of Innovative and Emerging Research in Engineering, 2*(2), 109-114.

Son, H., Kim, C., & Kim, C. (2012). Hybrid principal component analysis and support vector machine model for predicting the cost performance of commercial building projects using pre-project planning variables. *Automation in Construction*, *27*, 60–66. doi:10.1016/j.autcon.2012.05.013

Sood, K., Dhanaraj, R. K., Balamurugan, B., Grima, S., & Uma Maheshwari, R. (2022). *Big data: A game changer for insurance industry*. https://doi.org/ doi:10.1108/978-1-80262-605-62022100

Sorour, A. F. (2003). *Constitutional Criminal Law*. Dar Al Shorouk.

Stafie, G., & Grosu, V. (2023). The Impact of Artificial Intelligence on Accounting. In M. Busu (Ed.), *Digital Economy and the Green Revolution. ICBE 2022. Springer Proceedings in Business and Economics*. Springer. doi:10.1007/978-3-031-19886-1_18

Stahl, B. (2022). Responsible innovation ecosystems: Ethical implications of the application of the ecosystem concept to artificial intelligence. *International Journal of Information Management, 62*, 102441. doi:10.1016/j.ijinfomgt.2021.102441

Stancu, M. S., & Duţescu, A. (2021). The impact of the Artificial Intelligence on the accounting profession, a literature's assessment. *Proceedings of the International Conference on Business Excellence, 15*(1), 749–758. 10.2478/picbe-2021-0070

Steinmüller, E., Thunecke, G., & Wamser, G. (2019). Corporate income taxes around the world: A survey on forward-looking tax measures and two applications. *International Tax and Public Finance, 26*(2), 418–456. doi:10.1007/s10797-018-9511-6

Stoica, O. C., & Ionescu-Feleagă, L. (2021, June). Digitalization in accounting: A structured literature review. In *Proceedings of the 4th International Conference on Economics and Social Sciences: Resilience and Economic Intelligence through Digitalization and Big Data Analytics, Sciendo,* Bucharest, Romania (pp. 10-11). 10.2478/9788366675704-045

Sujawata, G. S., & Chouhan, J. S. (2021). Application of Artificial Intelligence in detection of diseases in plants: A Survey. *Turkish Journal of Computer and Mathematics Education, 12*(3), 3301–3305.

Sullivan, D., & Von Wachter, T. (2009). Job displacement and mortality: An analysis using administrative data. *The Quarterly Journal of Economics, 124*(3), 1265–1306. doi:10.1162/qjec.2009.124.3.1265

Sun, J. (2021). Research on artificial intelligence, new retail and financial transformation. *Proceedings - 2nd International Conference on E-Commerce and Internet Technology, ECIT2021*. 10.1109/ECIT52743.2021.00031

Sungkur, R. K., Baichoo, S., & Poligadu, A. (2013). An Automated System to Recognise Fungi caused Diseases on Sugarcane Leaves. *Proceedings of Global Engineering, Science and Technology Conference Singapore.*

Sun, T. (2019). Applying deep learning to audit procedures: An illustrative framework. *Accounting Horizons, 33*(3), 89–109. doi:10.2308/acch-52455

Sun, T., & Vasarhelyi, M. A. (2017). Deep Learning and the Future of Auditing: How an Evolving Technology Could Transform Analysis and Improve Judgment. *The CPA Journal, 87*(6).

Supra, D. (2017). Kecerdasan Intelektual, Kecerdasan Emosional, Dan Kecerdasan Spiritual Berpengaruh Terhadap Pemahaman Akuntansi Pada Mahasiswa. *Jemasi: Jurnal Ekonomi Manajemen Dan Akuntansi, 13*(1), 1–18. doi:10.35449/jemasi.v13i1.1

Swana, E., & Doorsamy, W. (2021). An unsupervised learning approach to condition assessment on a wound-rotor induction generator. *Energies, 14*(3), 602. doi:10.3390/en14030602

Taghezout, N., Ascar, B., & Bessedik, I. (2012). An agent-based decision support system for spunlaced nonwovens production management: A case study of INOTIS enterprise. *Frontiers in Artificial Intelligence and Applications.*

Talaviya, T., Shah, D., Patel, N., & Shah, M. (2020). Implementation of artificial intelligence in agriculture for optimization of irrigation and application of pesticides and herbicides. *Artificial Intelligence in Agriculture, 4*, 58–73. doi:10.1016/j.aiia.2020.04.002

Tan, B. S., & Low, K. Y. (2019). Blockchain as the database engine in the accounting system. *Australian Accounting Review, 29*(2), 312–318. doi:10.1111/auar.12278

Tang, C. S. S. (2022). Innovative Technology and Operations for Alleviating Poverty through Women's Economic Empowerment. *Production and Operations Management*, *31*(1), 32–45. doi:10.1111/poms.13349

Tapanjeh, A. M. A., & Al Tarawneh, A. R. (2020). Applicability of forensic accounting to reduce fraud and its effects on financial statement of jordanian shareholding companies from the perspective of judiciary and certified public accountant. *International Journal of Financial Research*, *11*(2), 436. Advance online publication. doi:10.5430/ijfr.v11n2p436

Taulli, T. (2020). *Introdução à Inteligência Artificial: Uma abordagem não técnica*. Novatec Editora.

Tavares, M. C., Azevedo, G., Marques, R. P., & Bastos, M. A. (2023). Challenges of education in the accounting profession in the Era 5.0: A systematic review. *Cogent Business and Management*, *10*(2), 2220198. Advance online publication. doi:10.1080/23311975.2023.2220198

Tavassoli, S. (2015). Innovation determinants over industry life cycle. *Technological Forecasting and Social Change*, *91*, 18–32. doi:10.1016/j.techfore.2013.12.027

Tayachi, T., Brahimi, T., & Essafi, Y. (2022). Artificial Intelligence in the Islamic Finance: A bibliometric. *Analysis*.

Tayefeh Hashemi, S., Ebadati, O. M., & Kaur, H. (2020). Cost estimation and prediction in construction projects: A systematic review on machine learning techniques. *SN Applied Sciences*, *2*(10), 1–27. doi:10.1007/s42452-020-03497-1

Tee, H. H., & Ong, H. B. (2016). Cashless payment and economic growth. *Financial Innovation*, *2*(1), 1–9. doi:10.1186/s40854-016-0023-z

Teh, D., & Rana, T. (2023). The Use of Internet of Things, Big Data Analytics and Artificial Intelligence for Attaining UN's SDGs. In Handbook of Big Data and Analytics in Accounting and Auditing (pp. 235-253). doi:10.1007/978-981-19-4460-4_11

Tian, Y., Zhao, C., Lu, S., & Guo, X. (2011). Multiple Classifier Combination For Recognition Of Wheat Leaf Diseases. *Intelligent Automation & Soft Computing, 17*(5). 10.1109/ICCUBEA.2016.7860043

Tigabu, A. D., Berkhout, F., & van Beukering, P. (2015). Technology innovation systems and technology diffusion: Adoption of bio-digestion in an emerging innovation system in Rwanda. *Technological Forecasting and Social Change, 90*(PA), 318-330. doi:10.1016/j.techfore.2013.10.011

Tiwari, K., & Khan, M. S. (2020). Sustainability accounting and reporting in the industry 4.0. *Journal of Cleaner Production*, *258*, 120783. Advance online publication. doi:10.1016/j.jclepro.2020.120783

Tong, X., Linderman, K., & Zhu, Q. (2023). Managing a portfolio of environmental projects: Focus, balance, and environmental management capabilities. *Journal of Operations Management*, *69*(1), 127–158. doi:10.1002/joom.1201

Torabi Moghadam, S., Delmastro, C., Corgnati, S. P., & Lombardi, P. (2017). Urban energy planning procedure for sustainable development in the built environment: A review of available spatial approaches. *Journal of Cleaner Production*, *165*, 811–827. doi:10.1016/j.jclepro.2017.07.142

Truby, J. (2018). Decarbonizing Bitcoin: Law and policy choices for reducing the energy consumption of Blockchain technologies and digital currencies. *Energy Research & Social Science*, *44*, 399–410. doi:10.1016/j.erss.2018.06.009

Tsai, C. H., & Peng, K. J. (2017). The FinTech Revolution and Financial Regulation: The Case of Online Supply-Chain Financing. *Asian Journal of Law and Society*, *4*(1), 109–132. doi:10.1017/als.2016.65

Tsui, T. H., van Loosdrecht, M. C. M., Dai, Y. J., & Tong, Y. W. (2023). Machine learning and circular bioeconomy: Building new resource efficiency from diverse waste streams. *Bioresource Technology*, *369*(10), 128445. Advance online publication. doi:10.1016/j.biortech.2022.128445 PMID:36473583

Tuanakotta, T. M. (2010). Akuntansi Forensik dan AuditorInvestigatif (Indonesia). Lembaga Penerbit Fakultas Ekonomi Universitas Indonesia (LPFE UI). Edisi ke 2: Jakarta.

Tuli, F. A., & Thaduri, U. R. (2023). The Integration of Artificial Intelligence in Forensic Accounting: A Game-Changer. *Asian Accounting and Auditing Advancement*, *14*(1), 12–20.

Tweedale, J. W., Phillips-Wren, G., & Jain, L. C. (2016). *Advances in intelligent decision-making technology support*. Smart Innovation, Systems and Technologies. doi:10.1007/978-3-319-21209-8_1

Ucoglu, D. (2020). Current Machine Learning Applications in Accounting and Auditing. *Pressacademia*, *12*(1), 1–7. doi:10.17261/Pressacademia.2020.1337

Ucoglu, D. (2020). Effects of artificial intelligence technology on accounting profession and education. *Pressacademia*, *11*(1), 16–21. doi:10.17261/Pressacademia.2020.1232

Uemura, T. (2022). Evaluating Japan's corporate income tax reform using firm-specific effective tax rates. *Japan and the World Economy*, *61*, 101115. Advance online publication. doi:10.1016/j.japwor.2022.101115

Uglum, M. (2021). Consideration of the ethical implications of artificial intelligence in the audit profession. *Honors Program Theses*. 496.

UN General Assembly (UNGA). (2015). A/RES/70/1Transforming our world: The 2030 Agenda for Sustainable Development. *Resolut*, *25*, 1–35.

UNESCO. (2020) *Recommendation on the ethics of artificial intelligence*. Digital Library UNESDOC. en.unesco.org

United Nations Congress on Crime Prevention and Criminal Justice. (2020). *Current Crime Trends, Recent Developments, and Emerging Solutions, especially New Technologies as Means of Committing Crime and Tools for Combating Crime*. Workshop at the Fourteenth Congress held in Kyoto, Japan.

United Nations Industrial Development Organization (UNIDO). (2020). *How industrial development matters to the well-being of the population: Some Statistical Evidence*. https://www.unido.org/sites/default/files/files/2020-02/HOW%20INDUSTRIAL%20DEVELOPMENT%20MATTERS%20TO%20THE%20WELL-BEING%20OF%20THE%20POPULATION%20FIN.pdf

United States Securities and Exchange Commission. (2020). *Annual report pursuant to section 13 or 15(d) of the securities exchange act of 1934 - Tesla, Inc*. Retrieved from https://sec.report/Document/0001564590-21-004599/tsla-10k_20201231.htm

van Doorn, J., Mende, M., Noble, S. M., Hulland, J., Ostrom, A. L., Grewal, D., & Petersen, A. J. (2017). Domo Arigato Mr. Roboto: The Emergence of Automated Social Presence in Customers' Service Experiences. *Journal of Service Research*, *20*(1), 43–58. doi:10.1177/1094670516679272

van Eck, N. J., & Waltman, L. (2010). Software survey: VOSviewer, a computer program for bibliometric mapping. *Scientometrics*, *84*(2), 523–538. doi:10.1007/s11192-009-0146-3 PMID:20585380

Van Engelen, J. E., & Hoos, H. H. (2020). A survey on semi-supervised learning. *Machine Learning*, *109*(2), 373–440. doi:10.1007/s10994-019-05855-6

van Schalkwyk, M. A., & Grobbelaar, S. S. (2020). A decision support system (DSS) framework for leveraging idle resources as a sustainable socio-economic enterprise: The case of a house in Velddrif. *26th International Association for Management of Technology Conference, IAMOT 2017*. 10.1007/978-3-030-72624-9_10

Vandenbergh, M. P., & Gilligan, J. M. (2017). Beyond politics. *Science*, *356*(6345), 492–493.

Vărzaru, A. A. (2022). Assessing the Impact of AI Solutions' Ethical Issues on Performance in Managerial Accounting. *Electronics (Basel)*, *11*(14), 2221. doi:10.3390/electronics11142221

Veneziano, D., Shi, X., Ballard, L., Ye, Z., & Fay, L. (2014). A benefit-cost analysis toolkit for road weather management technologies. Climatic effects on pavement and geotechnical infrastructure. *Proceedings of the International Symposium of Climatic Effects on Pavement and Geotechnical Infrastructure 2013.* 10.1061/9780784413326.022

Ventura & Carvalho. (2020). *Da Radicalização ideológica ao terrorismo: uma digressão.* Diário de Bordo.

Ventura. (2023). *Os "lobos solitários".* Terrorismo e (in)Sanidade Mental, Diário de Bordo.

Viana. (2010). Acerca de "Terrorismo" e de "Terrorismos." *Nação e Defesa.*

Vincent, N., & Wilkins, A. (2019). *Challenges when Auditing Cryptocurrencies.* American Accounting Association. doi:10.2308/ciia-19-025

Vinuesa, R., Azizpour, H., Leite, I., Balaam, M., Dignum, V., Domisch, S., Felländer, A., Langhans, S. D., Tegmark, M., & Fuso Nerini, F. (2020). The role of artificial intelligence in achieving the Sustainable Development Goals. *Nature Communications*, *11*(1), 233. doi:10.1038/s41467-019-14108-y PMID:31932590

Vitali, S., & Giuliani, M. (2024). Emerging digital technologies and auditing firms: Opportunities and challenges. *International Journal of Accounting Information Systems*, *53*, 100676. doi:10.1016/j.accinf.2024.100676

Wang, J., Sun, W., Zhang, Y., Ma, W., & Wang, L. (2011). Notice of Retraction: Case study: Rainwater utilisation and water saving design of a village [Retracted]. *2011 2nd International Conference on Artificial Intelligence, Management Science and Electronic Commerce, AIMSEC 2011 - Proceedings*, 6172-6175. 10.1109/AIMSEC.2011.6009626

Wang, S. (2023). Research on the innovation system of computer artificial intelligence technology in museum financial management system. *2023 IEEE 3rd International Conference on Power, Electronics and Computer Applications, ICPECA 2023.* 10.1109/ICPECA56706.2023.10075850

Wang, A., Guo, S., & Li, R. (2022). Artificial intelligence technology enables the development of management accounting: The generation of Intelligent Accounting. *ACM International Conference Proceeding Series.* 10.1145/3523181.3523190

Wang, C., & Liu, S. (2021). Innovative risk early warning model based on internet of things under big data technology. *IEEE Access : Practical Innovations, Open Solutions*, *9*, 100606–100614. doi:10.1109/ACCESS.2021.3095503

Wang, H. N., Liu, N., Zhang, Y. Y., Feng, D. W., Huang, F., Li, D. S., & Zhang, Y. M. (2020). Deep reinforcement learning: A survey. *Frontiers of Information Technology & Electronic Engineering*, *21*(12), 1726–1744. doi:10.1631/FITEE.1900533

Wang, L., & Wang, Y. (2022). Supply chain financial service management system based on block chain IoT data sharing and edge computing. *Alexandria Engineering Journal*, *61*(1), 147–158. doi:10.1016/j.aej.2021.04.079

Wang, X., Wang, H., Bhandari, B., & Cheng, L. (2023). *AI-Empowered Methods for Smart Energy Consumption: A Review of Load Forecasting, Anomaly Detection and Demand Response.* International Journal of Precision Engineering and Manufacturing - Green Technology., doi:10.1007/s40684-023-00537-0

Wang, Y., & Wang, Z. (2016). Integrating data mining into managerial accounting system: Challenges and opportunities. *The China Business Review*, *15*(1), 33–41.

Wang, Z., He, Y., Jiang, H., & Yu, C. (2023). *Enterprise Intelligent Accounting System Structure and Intelligent Accounting Algorithm.* Lecture Notes in Electrical Engineering. doi:10.1007/978-981-99-1428-9_140

Wang, Z., Qiong, M., & Wang, H. (2020). Risk analysis of enterprise management accounting based on big data association rule algorithm. *Journal of Physics: Conference Series*, *1631*(1), 012098. doi:10.1088/1742-6596/1631/1/012098

Wazir, A. M. (2008). *Explanation of the Penal Code - General Section, The General Theory of Crime*. Dar Al-Nahda Al-Arabiya.

Weckel, P. (1983). *La fiscalité et la stimulation de l'innovation industrielle dans la Communauté: Sept propositions pour encourager l'innovation.* Office des publications officielles des Communautés européennes.

Wen, C., Yang, J., Gan, L., & Pan, Y. (2021). Big data driven Internet of Things for credit evaluation and early warning in finance. *Future Generation Computer Systems*, *124*, 295–307. doi:10.1016/j.future.2021.06.003

Weng. (2015, February). Intersection of "Tokku" Special Zone, Robots, and the Law: A Case Study on Legal Impacts to Humanoid Robots. *International Journal of Social Robotics*.

Williams, T. P., & Gong, J. (2014). Predicting construction cost overruns using text mining, numerical data and ensemble classifiers. *Automation in Construction*, *43*, 23–29. doi:10.1016/j.autcon.2014.02.014

Wilson, C., & van der Velden, M. (2022). Sustainable AI: An integrated model to guide public sector decision-making. *Technology in Society*, *68*, 101926. Advance online publication. doi:10.1016/j.techsoc.2022.101926

Windston. (2014). *The Genesis Story Understanding and Story Telling System A 21st Century Step toward Artificial Intelligence*. Center of Brains, Minds & Machines (CBMM).

World Economic Forum (WEF). (2018). *The New Physics of Financial Services – How Artificial Intelligence is Transforming the Financial Ecosystem*. World Economic Forum.

Worstall, T. (2011). Will Robots Take Our Jobs? Who cares? *Forbes*, 1–3. http://www.forbes.com/sites/timworstall/2011/11/06/will-robots-take-out-jobs-who-cares/#6279428b538e

Worthington, A. C. (2016). Financial literacy and financial literacy programmes in Australia. *Financ Lit Limits Financ Decis-Mak*, *6*(18), 281–301. doi:10.1007/978-3-319-30886-9_14

Wu, Y. (2021). Practical teaching of management accounting course under the background of artificial intelligence and big data. *Proceedings - 2021 International Conference on Computers, Information Processing and Advanced Education, CIPAE 2021*. 10.1109/CIPAE53742.2021.00035

Wu, C. F., Huang, S. C., Chiou, C. C., & Wang, Y. M. (2021). A predictive intelligence system of credit scoring based on deep multiple kernel learning. *Applied Soft Computing*, *111*, 107668. doi:10.1016/j.asoc.2021.107668

Xiong, X., Wei, W., & Zhang, C. (2022). Dynamic user allocation method and artificial intelligence in the information industry financial management system application. *Proceedings - 2022 6th International Conference on Intelligent Computing and ControlSystems, ICICCS 2022*. 10.1109/ICICCS53718.2022.9788222

Xu, X., Zheng, Y., Tian, S., & Xing, M. (2021). Marketing logistics cost optimization and application research in smart living. *Proceedings - 20th IEEE/ACIS International Summer Conference on Computer and Information Science, ICIS 2021-Summer*. 10.1109/ICIS51600.2021.9516867

Xue, J. (2020). On the management of accounting files in public institutions based on informatization. *Journal of Physics: Conference Series*, *1533*(2), 022055. doi:10.1088/1742-6596/1533/2/022055

Xu, Y., Liu, X., Cao, X., Huang, C., Liu, E., Qian, S., Liu, X., Wu, Y., Dong, F., Qiu, C. W., Qiu, J., Hua, K., Su, W., Wu, J., Xu, H., Han, Y., Fu, C., Yin, Z., Liu, M., ... Zhang, J. (2021). Artificial intelligence: A powerful paradigm for scientific research. *Innovation (Cambridge (Mass.))*, *2*(4), 1–21. doi:10.1016/j.xinn.2021.100179 PMID:34877560

Yakhou, M., Schulte, P., & Placzek, M. (2018). The Impact of Artificial Intelligence on Audit Procedures: The Case of Journal Entry Testing. *Journal of Emerging Technologies in Accounting*, *15*, 147–156. doi:10.2308/jeta-51915

Yang, X. (2011). Influence of computerized accounting systems on bookkeeping conceptual framework. *2011 2nd International Conference on Artificial Intelligence, Management Science and Electronic Commerce, AIMSEC 2011 - Proceedings.*

Yang, D., Chen, P., Shi, F., & Wen, C. (2018). Internet finance: Its uncertain legal foundations and the role of big data in its development. *Emerging Markets Finance & Trade*, *54*(4), 721–732. doi:10.1080/1540496X.2016.1278528

Yang, K. C., Varol, O., Davis, C. A., Ferrara, E., Flammini, A., & Menczer, F. (2019). Arming the public with artificial intelligence to counter social bots. *Human Behavior and Emerging Technologies*, *1*(1), 48–61. doi:10.1002/hbe2.115

Yang, N. (2022). Financial big data management and control and artificial intelligence analysis method based on data mining technology. *Wireless Communications and Mobile Computing*, *2022*, 7596094. Advance online publication. doi:10.1155/2022/7596094

Yang, X., & Metawa, S. (2023). *Construction of electric energy data and carbon emission management platform under computer technology*. Lecture Notes on Data Engineering and Communications Technologies. doi:10.1007/978-3-031-29097-8_20

Yang, Y., & Yin, Z. (2023). Resilient supply chains to improve the integrity of accounting data in financial institutions worldwide using blockchain technology. *International Journal of Data Warehousing and Mining*, *19*(4), 1–20. Advance online publication. doi:10.4018/ijdwm.320648

Yan, X., & Wu, Y. (2020). Financial risk assessment based on entropy weight topsis method: Take the internet insurance industry as an example. *Journal of Simulation*, *8*(6), 7–15.

Yıgıtbasioglu, O., Green, P., & Cheung, M.-Y. D. (2023). Digital transformation and accountants as advisors. *Accounting, Auditing & Accountability Journal*, *36*(1), 209–237. doi:10.1108/AAAJ-02-2019-3894

Yoon, S., Naderpajouh, N., & Hastak, M. (2019). Decision model to integrate community preferences and nudges into the selection of alternatives in infrastructure development. *Journal of Cleaner Production*, *228*, 1413–1424. doi:10.1016/j.jclepro.2019.04.243

Yuana, R., Prasetio, E. A., Syarief, R., Arkeman, Y., & Suroso, A. I. (2021). System dynamic and simulation of business model innovation in digital companies: An open innovation approach. *Journal of Open Innovation*, *7*(4), 219. Advance online publication. doi:10.3390/joitmc7040219

Yukl, G., & Lepsinger, R. (2005). Why integrating the leading and managing roles is essential for organizationaleffectiveness. *Organizational Dynamics*, *34*(4), 361–375. doi:10.1016/j.orgdyn.2005.08.004

Zaman, S., Shahbaz, M., & Loganathan, N. (2020). Financial Development and Sustainable Development Goals: Evidence from Asia-Pacific Region. *Journal of Cleaner Production*, *244*, 118706.

Zdravković, M., Panetto, H., & Weichhart, G. (2022). AI-enabled enterprise information systems for manufacturing. *Enterprise Information Systems*, *16*(4), 668–720. doi:10.1080/17517575.2021.1941275

Zemánková, A. (2019). Artificial Intelligence and Blockchain in Audit and Accounting: Literature Review. *WSEAS Transactions on Business and Economics, 16*, 568-581. https://www.wseas.org/multimedia/journals/economics/2019/b245107-089.pdf

Zeng, Y. (2022). Neural network technology-based optimization framework of financial and management accounting model. *Computational Intelligence and Neuroscience*, *2022*, 4991244. Advance online publication. doi:10.1155/2022/4991244 PMID:35685164

Zhang, F., & Han, Y. (2011). Notice of Retraction: Climate change on forestry development in Heilongjiang Province and countermeasures [Retracted]. *2011 2nd International Conference on Artificial Intelligence, Management Science and Electronic Commerce, AIMSEC 2011 - Proceedings*, 7001-7003. 10.1109/AIMSEC.2011.6011455

Zhang, Q., Dong, X., & Huang, R. (2011). The application of resources consumption accounting in an enterprise. *2011 2nd International Conference on Artificial Intelligence, Management Science and Electronic Commerce, AIMSEC 2011 - Proceedings.*

Zhang, D., & Guo, Y. (2019). Financing R&D in Chinese private firms: Business associations or political connection? *Economic Modelling*, *79*, 247–261. doi:10.1016/j.econmod.2018.12.010

Zhang, D., & Vigne, S. A. (2021). How does innovation efficiency contribute to green productivity? A financial constraint perspective. *Journal of Cleaner Production*, *280*, 124000. Advance online publication. doi:10.1016/j.jclepro.2020.124000

Zhang, X. (2021). Application of data mining and machine learning in management accounting information system. *Journal of Applied Science and Engineering (Taiwan)*, *24*(5), 813–820. doi:10.6180/jase.202110_24(5).0018

Zhang, Y. C., Mao, H. P., Hu, B., & Li, M. X. (2007). Features selection of cotton disease leaves image based on fuzzy feature selection techniques. *International conference on Wavelet Analysis and Pattern Recognition.* 10.1109/ICWAPR.2007.4420649

Zhang, Y., & Song, Y. (2022). Tax rebates, technological innovation and sustainable development: Evidence from Chinese micro-level data. *Technological Forecasting and Social Change*, *176*, 121481. Advance online publication. doi:10.1016/j.techfore.2022.121481

Zhang, Y., Xiong, F., Xie, Y., Fan, X., & Gu, H. (2020). The Impact of Artificial Intelligence and Blockchain on the Accounting Profession. *IEEE Access : Practical Innovations, Open Solutions*, *8*, 110461–110477. doi:10.1109/ACCESS.2020.3000505

Zhao, N., & Yao, F. (2021). The Transmission and Preventive Measures of Internet Financial Risk. In *International Conference on Business Intelligence and Information Technology*. Springer.

Zhao, J., & Gómez Fariñas, B. (2023). Artificial intelligence and sustainable decisions. *European Business Organization Law Review*, *24*(1), 1–39. doi:10.1007/s40804-022-00262-2

Zhao, J., & Yuan, J. (2019). An Intelligent model to reduce the energy consumption of sensor network nodes. *International Journal of Computers and Applications.* Advance online publication. doi:10.1080/1206212X.2019.1707436

Zhao, J., Zhang, L., & Zhao, Y. (2022). Informatization of accounting systems in small-and medium-sized enterprises based on artificial intelligence-enabled cloud computing. *Computational Intelligence and Neuroscience*, *2022*, 1–9. Advance online publication. doi:10.1155/2022/6089195 PMID:35990138

Zheng, W., & Zhang, J. (2021). Does tax reduction spur innovation? Firm-level evidence from China. *Finance Research Letters*, *39*, 101575. Advance online publication. doi:10.1016/j.frl.2020.101575

Zhou, K. (2023). Financial model construction of a cross-border e-commerce platform based on machine learning. *Neural Computing & Applications*, *35*(36), 25189–25199. Advance online publication. doi:10.1007/s00521-023-08456-6

Zhou, Y., & Liu, Y. S. (2022). The geography of poverty: Review and research prospects. *Journal of Rural Studies*, *93*, 408–416. doi:10.1016/j.jrurstud.2019.01.008

Zikmundova, M., Hronek, J., Stastna, L., & Sperkova, M. (2021). Financial Literacy and Sustainable Development Goals: A Case Study of Czech Republic. *Sustainability*, *13*(3), 1017.

About the Contributors

Maria C Tavares holds a PhD in Business Science from the University of Minho, an Advanced Training Course ("PhD Course") in Accounting, a Master's degree in Management, branch Marketing and International Business, and a degree in Accounting and Business Administration, from the University of Aveiro. She also holds a Professional Qualification in Teaching Accounting and Administration; and a Course of Specialized Higher Studies in Business Administration. She has published several scientific articles, namely in international journals, and has participated in several international and national conferences and congresses, being a member of several Scientific and organisational Committees. Her main research interests are the following: Social Responsibility; Accounting in the Public Sector; Non-financial Reporting; Sustainability and Integrated Reporting; Intellectual Capital and Human Resources; Teaching, Education and Training in the Business Sciences; Accountability, Sustainability and Sustainable Development; Research Theories in the Business Sciences; Accounting in the Digital Era.

Graça Azevedo has a PhD in Management (scientific field: Accounting) at the Institute of Higher Labor and Enterprise – ISCTE. She has published and presented several articles in national and international journals and conferences as well. She is a member of the Editorial Board of international journal "Accounting and Finance Research". She currently teaches courses in scientific field of Financial Accounting at the Institute of Higher Learning in Accounting and Administration of the University of Aveiro. Her research interests are related to financial reporting, impression management strategies and international accounting standards.

José Vale holds a PhD in Management - Accounting and Management Control - from the Faculty of Economics of the University of Porto, a Master's degree in Business Administration and Management from the Portuguese Catholic University (UCP) and a degree in Accounting and Administration from ISCAP. He also has an MBA in Business Operations Management from UCP. He is an associate professor at ISCAP.PP in the Accounting area. He has published several scientific articles, namely in international journals, and has also participated in different international and national conferences and congresses, being a member of several Scientific Committees. His main research interests focus on accounting and management control, intellectual capital, knowledge management, non-financial disclosure and sustainability. He coordinates the "accountability and reporting" line at CEOS.PP and is a member of the Portuguese Certified Accountants Association.

Rui Pedro Figueiredo Marques received the PhD degree in Computer Science in 2014 from the universities of Minho, Aveiro and Porto, three of the top universities in the north of Portugal. In 2008 he concluded his Masters degree in Electronics and Telecommunications Engineering, at the University of

Aveiro, and in 2005 he graduated in the same area, also from the University of Aveiro. His main research interests are related to the integration of Information Systems into organizational topics, contributing with solutions to improve the risk management and the organizational efficiency. He is Professor of Information Systems and Technology since 2007 at the Higher Institute of Accounting and Administration, University of Aveiro, Portugal.

Maria Anunciação Bastos holds a PhD Accounting from the joint doctoral program between the University of Aveiro and the University of Minho. She holds a Master Degree in Accounting and Auditing from the University of Aveiro and a Degree in Accounting and Administration, with a major in Accounting and Auditing, from the University of Aveiro - Institute of Accounting and Administration (ISCA-UA). She is an Adjunct Professor at ISCA-UA. She teaches several courses in the area of Accounting Sciences, such as Introduction to Accounting and Financial Accounting. She is member of the research unit on Governance, Competitiveness and Public Policies (GOVCOPP), participating in the research group of Decision Support Systems as a PhD student. She is also a member of the Portuguese Certified Accountants Order and the Portuguese Network of Accounting Research (grudis). Her main research interests include: Financial Accounting, Financial Reporting and Accounting Regulation.

* * *

Gabriela Beirão (B.S. from University of Aveiro, Master and PhD from University of Porto) is Assistant Professor at Faculty of Engineering, University of Porto. Her research focuses on services, particularly on service ecosystems, value co-creation, innovation and sustainability. She has been involved in several research projects. Her research has been published in Journal of Service Management, Transport Policy, and others.

Mohamed Ali Bejjar, Prof at Higher business school of Sfax. PhD thesis, University of Sfax in Financial methods and Accounting. Holder of Master in "Strategy and Information System" from the Faculty of Economics and Management of Sfax. Holder of Master in "Accounting and Information System" from the Higher Institute of Management of Tunis. "Member of the Research Unit of URECA FSEG Sfax.

Ramy El-Kady is a Full Professor of Criminal Law at the Police Academy and holds the position of Head of the Criminal Law Department. He was rewarded with the State Encouragement Award in Legal and Economic Sciences, Citizenship and Human Rights Branch, on the topic of "Right to protection for persons cooperating with justice in international conventions and national legislation.". He graduated from the Police College in 1999. He obtained a postgraduate diploma in criminal sciences and public law, which is equivalent to a master's degree in criminal law, in 2003. He obtained a PhD in criminal law from the Faculty of Law, Cairo University, on the topic of (Mediation as an Alternative to a Criminal Case: A Comparative Study. He currently teaches criminal law subjects to college students. He supervised numerous studies submitted for doctoral degrees and higher diplomas and authored a host of research in the criminal law field. He has previously judged numerous research papers in a number of refereed regional scientific journals. He published a host of research in refereed and indexed periodicals and took part in a number of international and local conferences and symposia.

Ankur Gupta has received the B.Tech and M.Tech in Computer Science and Engineering from Ganga Institute of Technology and Management, Kablana affiliated with Maharshi Dayanand University, Rohtak in 2015 and 2017. He is an Assistant Professor in the Department of Computer Science and Engineering at Vaish College of Engineering, Rohtak, and has been working there since January 2019. He has many publications in various reputed national/ international conferences, journals, and online book chapter contributions (Indexed by SCIE, Scopus, ESCI, ACM, DBLP, etc). He is doing research in the field of cloud computing, data security & machine learning. His research work in M.Tech was based on biometric security in cloud computing.

Laksitha M. Herath earned her Master of Science in Accounting degree at New York University's Stern School of Business and works at Pricewaterhouse Coopers (PwC). Prior to her current endeavor, she gained valuable experience as a program accountant at Enstar Group Limited, a well-known global insurance company, and at Deloitte, a Big Four accounting firm, in Atlanta and New York. Laksitha holds a Bachelor of Arts degree in Accounting from Clark Atlanta University, where she held executive positions in its Toastmasters Club and she and a team of selected classmates won the Deloitte Regional Case Study Competition. She also published two book chapters and an article in a reputable journal. In her leisure time, she enjoys photography, cooking, and quality time with her family and friends.

Siriyama Kanthi Herath is an Associate Professor of Accounting at Clark Atlanta University's School of Business (CAU) and was a Renwick Faculty Fellow at New York University's Stern School of Business in 2022. She earned a Bachelor of Commerce Honors and an MBA from the University of Colombo in Sri Lanka, as well as a Ph.D. and a Master of Commerce Honors in Accounting from the University of Wollongong in Australia. She worked at the University of Lynchburg, Georgia State University and Georgia Institute of Technology before joining CAU. Prior to relocating to the United States, Dr. Herath worked in Australia at the University of Wollongong and Western Sydney University and in Sri Lanka at the University of Ruhuna and the University of Colombo. She holds positions on the editorial boards of multiple academic journals and has contributed over 70 publications to a diverse range of journals. Her research areas include Accounting Education, Management Control and Outsourcing, Cost Management, Corporate Governance, Data Analytics, and Sustainability Accounting. She is a Distinguished Toastmaster and served as the President and Treasurer of the Georgia Institute of Technology Toastmasters International Club from 2019 to 2020, the Treasurer of the Emory University Toastmasters International Club from 2019 to 2020, and as an Area Director from 2020 to 2021 in Georgia, United States. Additionally, she possesses the TESOL Professional Certificate from Arizona State University and the Professional Certificate in Google Data Analytics. In her leisure time, she enjoys traveling and gardening.

Jayasri Kotti is working as Associate Professor, in the Department of Information Technology, GMR Institute of Technology, Rajam- 532127, Andhra Pradesh. She obtained her M.Tech in Information Technology from Andhra University College of Engineering, Visakhapatnam. She received her Ph.D. Degree from Andhra University. And received Gold Medal for her best thesis. She is having around 35 publications in various journals and conferences. She is having 16 years of teaching & Research experience. Her research interests are Safety Critical Computer Systems, Software Engineering, Machine Learning, and Data Science.

R.V. Naveenan is working with Symbiosis International University, Bengaluru, India as Assistant Professor. He has two postgraduation to his credit, which includes MBA in Finance and MA in Economics. He has obtained his Ph.D. in Management (Finance) from Manonmaniam Sundaranar University, Tamil Nadu, India. He has thirteen years of experience in academics and research. He is a passionate teacher and enthusiastic researcher. He has presented his research ideas in various national and international conferences. He has published around 15 research papers in Journals. His area of research is Green Banking, Sustainable Finance, Financial Inclusion and Fintech.

João Novais is a Guest Lecturer in Católica Porto. PhD student in EEG of University of Minho.

Sabyasachi Pramanik is a professional IEEE member. He obtained a PhD in Computer Science and Engineering from Sri Satya Sai University of Technology and Medical Sciences, Bhopal, India. Presently, he is an Associate Professor, Department of Computer Science and Engineering, Haldia Institute of Technology, India. He has many publications in various reputed international conferences, journals, and book chapters (Indexed by SCIE, Scopus, ESCI, etc). He is doing research in the fields of Artificial Intelligence, Data Privacy, Cybersecurity, Network Security, and Machine Learning. He also serves on the editorial boards of several international journals. He is a reviewer of journal articles from IEEE, Springer, Elsevier, Inderscience, IET and IGI Global. He has reviewed many conference papers, has been a keynote speaker, session chair, and technical program committee member at many international conferences. He has authored a book on Wireless Sensor Network. He has edited 8 books from IGI Global, CRC Press, Springer and Wiley Publications.

Albérico Travassos Rosário is a Ph.D. Marketing and Strategy of the Universities of Aveiro (UA), Minho (UM) and Beira Interior (UBI). With affiliation to the GOVCOPP research center of the University of Aveiro. Master in Marketing and Degree in Marketing, Advertising and Public Relations, degree from ISLA Campus Lisbon-European University I Laureate International Universities. Has the title of Marketing Specialist and teaches with the category of Assistant Professor at IADE-Faculty of Design, Technology and Communication of the European University and as a visiting Associate Professor at the Santarém Higher School of Management and Technology (ESGTS) of the Polytechnic Institute of Santarém. He taught at IPAM-School of Marketing I Laureate International Universities, ISLA- Higher Institute of Management and Administration of Santarém (ISLA-Santarém), was Director of the Commercial Management Course, Director of the Professional Technical Course (TeSP) of Sales and Commercial Management, Chairman of the Pedagogical Council and Member of the Technical Council and ISLA-Santarém Scientific Researcher. He is also a marketing and strategy consultant for SMEs.

Mahabub Basha S. is presently working as Assistant Professor, Department of Commerce and Management in International Institute of Business Studies, Bangalore. He holds Master's degree in Management from JNTU Hyderabad and M.Phill from SCSVMV University, Kanchipuram. He has more than 8 years of teaching and 6 years of Industry experience, under-graduate and post-graduate students in Commerce and Management departments. He has published research articles in National and International Journals apart from presenting research papers at conferences. Three books published in his Credit. His areas of expertise are: Supply Chain Management, Portfolio Management, Consumer Behavior, Investment Management, Management Accounting, Financial Accounting, Financial Management, and Business Research Methods. In his credit he crossed 1000 google scholar citations.

Sara Serra is a PhD in Accounting from the University of Minho. Adjunct Professor at the Polytechnic of Cávado and Ave in the Audit area. Member of the Center for Research in Accounting and Taxation (CICF). Author of papers in national and international journals and reviewer at conferences and journals. The research area is Financial Auditing.

Yosr Siala is a research master's student in accounting at Higher Business School of Sfax.

Lurdes Silva is a PhD in Business Sciences (Accounting) at the University of Vigo since November 2012. She is an Adjunct Professor in the Accounting and Taxation department of the School of Management of the Polytechnic Institute of Cávado and Ave. The predominant research area is Financial Accounting and Intellectual Capita. Author of articles in national and international journals.Member of the Center for Research in Accounting and Taxation (CICF).

Ana Isabel Torres holds a PhD in Management Science and MSc in Marketing and Strategy, both from University of Porto, Faculty of Economics. She is a Coordinating Professor at the Accounting and Business Administration Institute, University of Aveiro and a researcher at the Laboratory of Artificial Intelligence and Decision Support, Institute for Systems and Computer Engineering, Technology and Science - INESC TEC. Her teaching areas include Marketing Strategy, Digital Economy, Services Management and Digital Consumer Behaviour. She engages in multidisciplinary research that bridges managerial and design-related fields such as digital services management with technology-oriented fields. Her academic work has been published in several leading international scientific publications, such as the British Journal of Educational Technology, Journal of Intellectual Capital, Journal of Revenue and Pricing Management, Management Research, IGI Global, Exploring Service Science, and in proceedings of international conferences. She has business experience in Marketing Management consultancy across different industries and service sectors, for several years.

Index

www.ingramcontent.com/pod-product-compliance
Lightning Source LLC
LaVergne TN
LVHW080641011026
849160LV00014B/1280